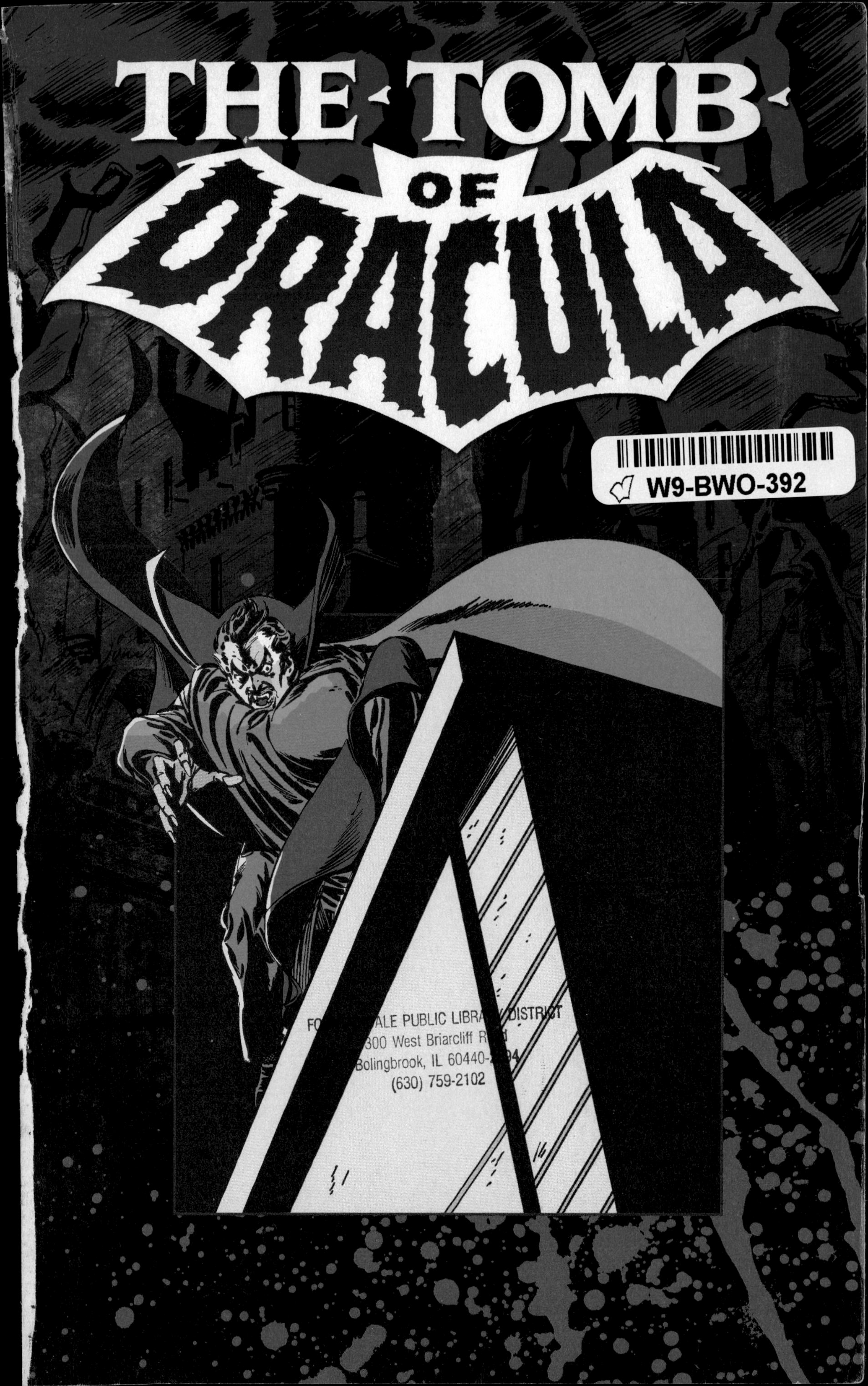
THE TOMB
OF
DRACULA

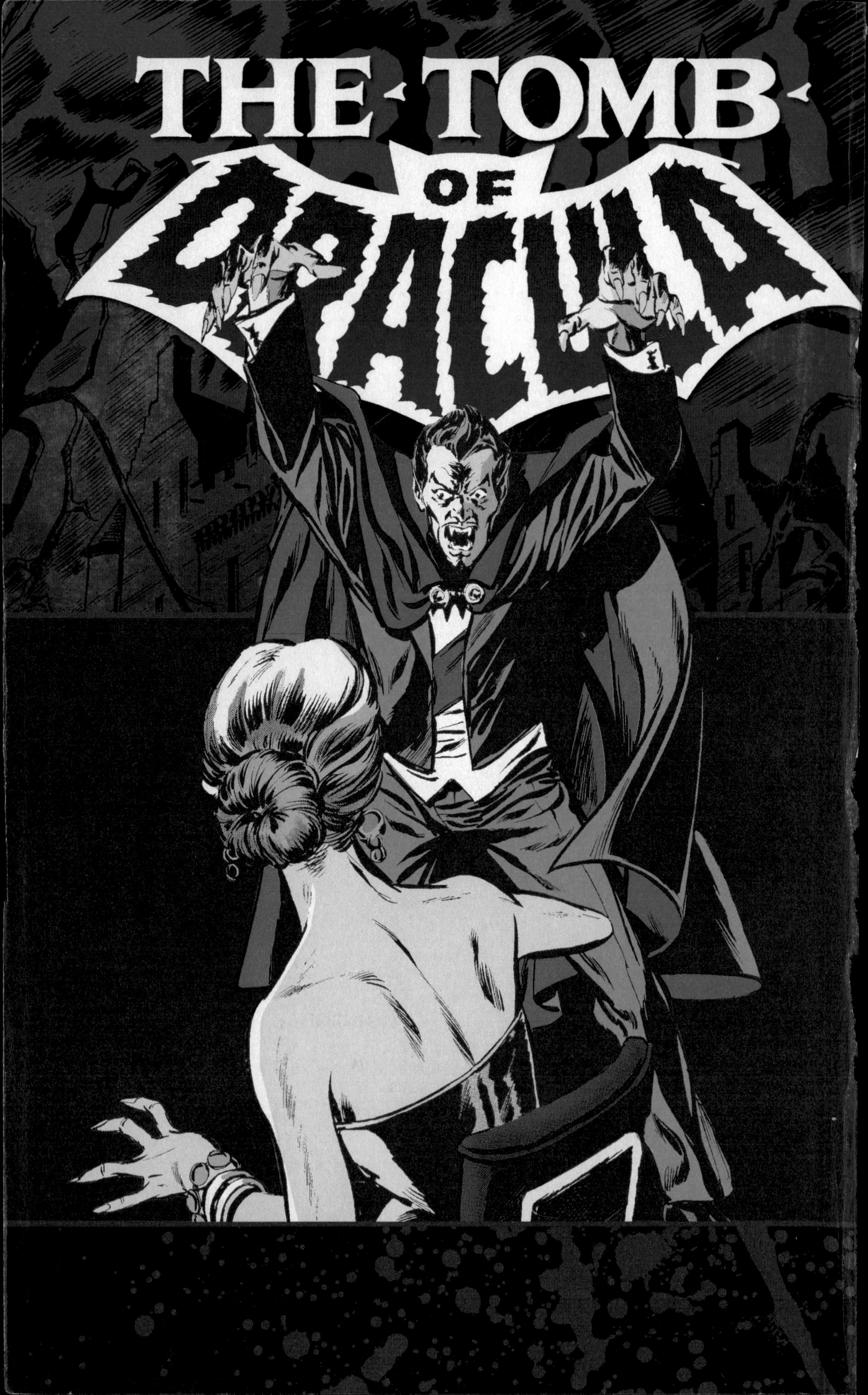
THE TOMB
OF
DRACULA

writers: MARV WOLFMAN
WITH CHRIS CLAREMONT & DAVID ANTHONY KRAFT
pencilers: GENE COLAN & DON HECK
inkers: TOM PALMER, FRANK McLAUGHLIN &
FRANK SPRINGER
colorists: TOM PALMER, LINDA LESSMAN &
PETRA GOLDBERG
letterers: CHARLOTTE JETTER, JOHN COSTANZA,
RAY HOLLOWAY & ART SIMEK
editors: ROY THOMAS & LEN WEIN

cover artists: GIL KANE & TOM PALMER
front cover colorist: THOMAS MASON
back cover colorist: AVALON STUDIOS

collection editor: MARK D. BEAZLEY
editorial assistants: JOE HOCHSTEIN
& JAMES EMMETT
assistant editors: NELSON RIBEIRO &
ALEX STARBUCK
editor, special projects: JENNIFER GRÜNWALD
senior editor, special projects: JEFF YOUNGQUIST
production: JERRON QUALITY COLOR
color reconstruction: COLORTEK & TOM SMITH
select art reconstruction: TOM ZIUKO & DIGIKORE
senior vice president of sales: DAVID GABRIEL

editor in chief: JOE QUESADA
publisher: DAN BUCKLEY
executive producer: ALAN FINE

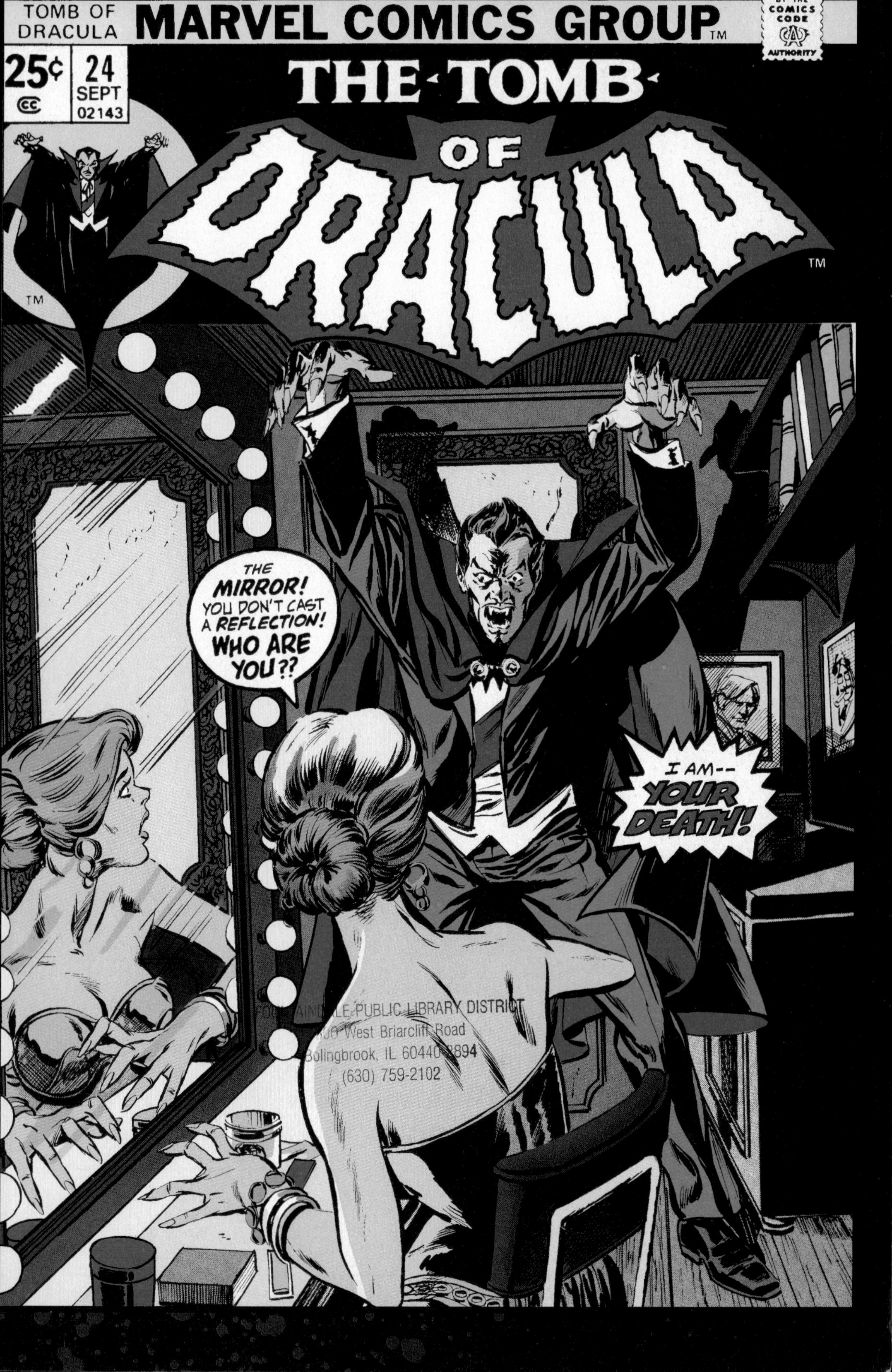
TOMB OF DRACULA
MARVEL COMICS GROUP
APPROVED BY THE COMICS CODE AUTHORITY
25¢
24 SEPT
02143
THE TOMB OF DRACULA
THE MIRROR! YOU DON'T CAST A REFLECTION! WHO ARE YOU??
I AM-- YOUR DEATH!

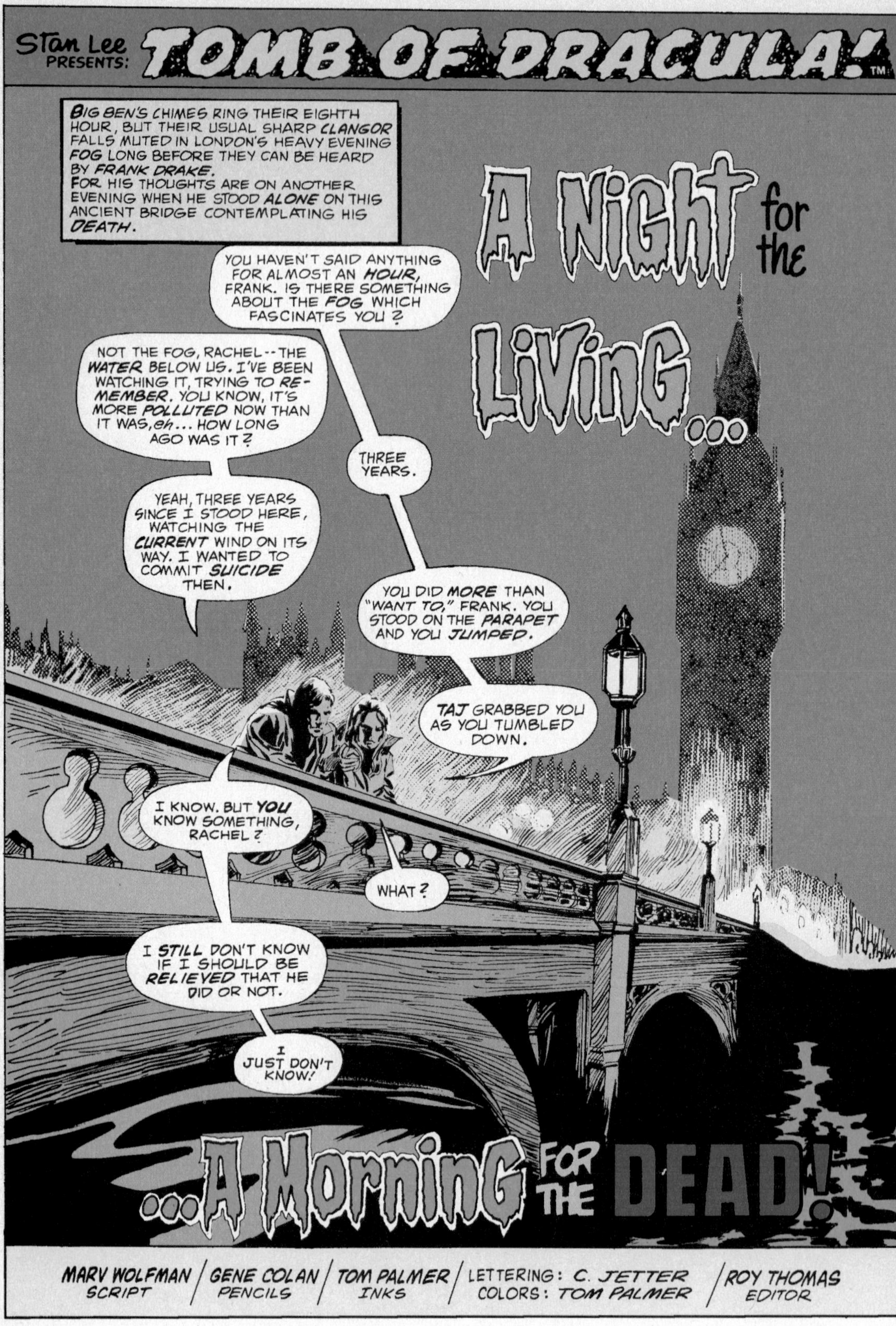
Stan Lee PRESENTS: TOMB OF DRACULA! ™
BIG BEN'S CHIMES RING THEIR EIGHTH HOUR, BUT THEIR USUAL SHARP CLANGOR FALLS MUTED IN LONDON'S HEAVY EVENING FOG LONG BEFORE THEY CAN BE HEARD BY FRANK DRAKE. FOR HIS THOUGHTS ARE ON ANOTHER EVENING WHEN HE STOOD ALONE ON THIS ANCIENT BRIDGE CONTEMPLATING HIS DEATH.
A NIGHT for the LIVING...
YOU HAVEN'T SAID ANYTHING FOR ALMOST AN HOUR, FRANK. IS THERE SOMETHING ABOUT THE FOG WHICH FASCINATES YOU?
NOT THE FOG, RACHEL--THE WATER BELOW US. I'VE BEEN WATCHING IT, TRYING TO RE-MEMBER. YOU KNOW, IT'S MORE POLLUTED NOW THAN IT WAS, eh... HOW LONG AGO WAS IT?
THREE YEARS.
YEAH, THREE YEARS SINCE I STOOD HERE, WATCHING THE CURRENT WIND ON ITS WAY. I WANTED TO COMMIT SUICIDE THEN.
YOU DID MORE THAN "WANT TO," FRANK. YOU STOOD ON THE PARAPET AND YOU JUMPED.
TAJ GRABBED YOU AS YOU TUMBLED DOWN.
I KNOW. BUT YOU KNOW SOMETHING, RACHEL?
WHAT?
I STILL DON'T KNOW IF I SHOULD BE RELIEVED THAT HE DID OR NOT.
I JUST DON'T KNOW!
...A MORNING FOR THE DEAD!
MARV WOLFMAN SCRIPT / GENE COLAN PENCILS / TOM PALMER INKS / LETTERING: C. JETTER COLORS: TOM PALMER / ROY THOMAS EDITOR

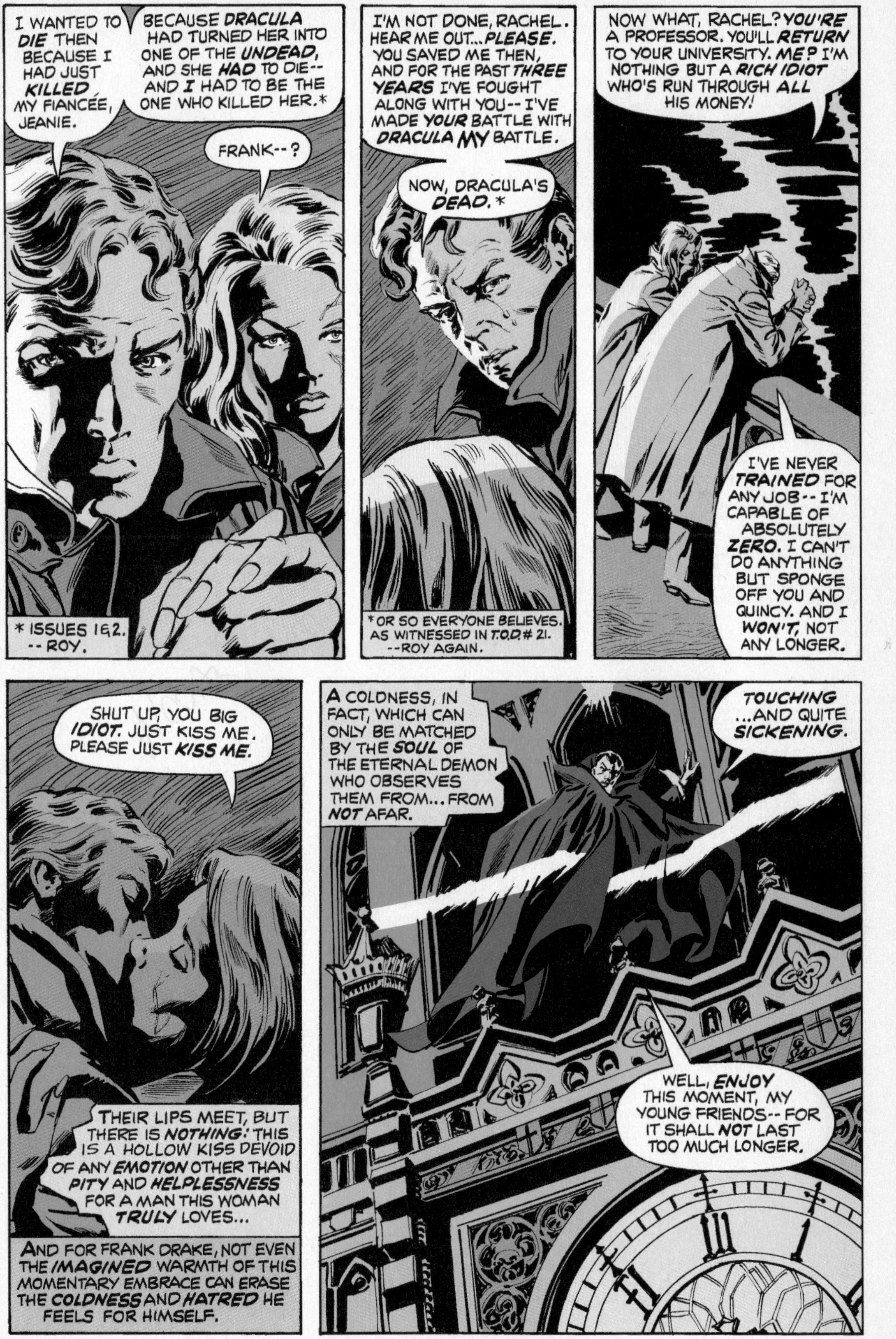
I WANTED TO DIE THEN BECAUSE I HAD JUST KILLED MY FIANCÉE, JEANIE.
BECAUSE DRACULA HAD TURNED HER INTO ONE OF THE UNDEAD, AND SHE HAD TO DIE-- AND I HAD TO BE THE ONE WHO KILLED HER.*
FRANK--?
* ISSUES 1&2. -- ROY.
I'M NOT DONE, RACHEL. HEAR ME OUT... PLEASE. YOU SAVED ME THEN, AND FOR THE PAST THREE YEARS I'VE FOUGHT ALONG WITH YOU-- I'VE MADE YOUR BATTLE WITH DRACULA MY BATTLE.
NOW, DRACULA'S DEAD.*
*OR SO EVERYONE BELIEVES. AS WITNESSED IN T.O.D. # 21. --ROY AGAIN.
NOW WHAT, RACHEL? YOU'RE A PROFESSOR. YOU'LL RETURN TO YOUR UNIVERSITY. ME? I'M NOTHING BUT A RICH IDIOT WHO'S RUN THROUGH ALL HIS MONEY!
I'VE NEVER TRAINED FOR ANY JOB -- I'M CAPABLE OF ABSOLUTELY ZERO. I CAN'T DO ANYTHING BUT SPONGE OFF YOU AND QUINCY. AND I WON'T, NOT ANY LONGER.
SHUT UP, YOU BIG IDIOT. JUST KISS ME. PLEASE JUST KISS ME.
THEIR LIPS MEET, BUT THERE IS NOTHING: THIS IS A HOLLOW KISS DEVOID OF ANY EMOTION OTHER THAN PITY AND HELPLESSNESS FOR A MAN THIS WOMAN TRULY LOVES...
AND FOR FRANK DRAKE, NOT EVEN THE IMAGINED WARMTH OF THIS MOMENTARY EMBRACE CAN ERASE THE COLDNESS AND HATRED HE FEELS FOR HIMSELF.
A COLDNESS, IN FACT, WHICH CAN ONLY BE MATCHED BY THE SOUL OF THE ETERNAL DEMON WHO OBSERVES THEM FROM... FROM NOT AFAR.
TOUCHING ...AND QUITE SICKENING.
WELL, ENJOY THIS MOMENT, MY YOUNG FRIENDS-- FOR IT SHALL NOT LAST TOO MUCH LONGER.

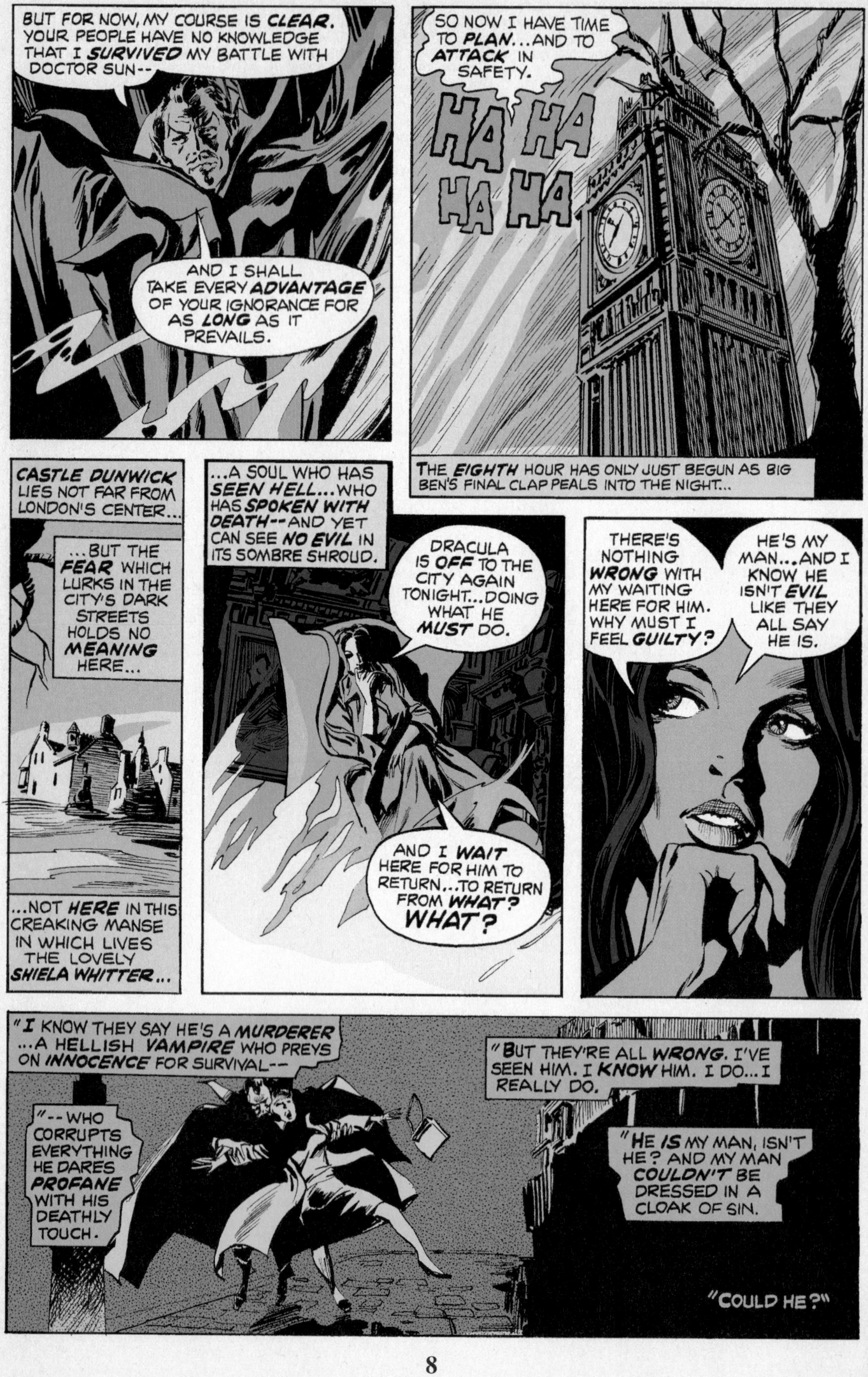
BUT FOR NOW, MY COURSE IS CLEAR. YOUR PEOPLE HAVE NO KNOWLEDGE THAT I SURVIVED MY BATTLE WITH DOCTOR SUN--
AND I SHALL TAKE EVERY ADVANTAGE OF YOUR IGNORANCE FOR AS LONG AS IT PREVAILS.
SO NOW I HAVE TIME TO PLAN...AND TO ATTACK IN SAFETY.
HA HA HA HA
THE EIGHTH HOUR HAS ONLY JUST BEGUN AS BIG BEN'S FINAL CLAP PEALS INTO THE NIGHT...
CASTLE DUNWICK LIES NOT FAR FROM LONDON'S CENTER...
...BUT THE FEAR WHICH LURKS IN THE CITY'S DARK STREETS HOLDS NO MEANING HERE...
...NOT HERE IN THIS CREAKING MANSE IN WHICH LIVES THE LOVELY SHIELA WHITTER...
...A SOUL WHO HAS SEEN HELL...WHO HAS SPOKEN WITH DEATH--AND YET CAN SEE NO EVIL IN ITS SOMBRE SHROUD.
DRACULA IS OFF TO THE CITY AGAIN TONIGHT...DOING WHAT HE MUST DO.
AND I WAIT HERE FOR HIM TO RETURN...TO RETURN FROM WHAT? WHAT?
THERE'S NOTHING WRONG WITH MY WAITING HERE FOR HIM. WHY MUST I FEEL GUILTY?
HE'S MY MAN...AND I KNOW HE ISN'T EVIL LIKE THEY ALL SAY HE IS.
"I KNOW THEY SAY HE'S A MURDERER ...A HELLISH VAMPIRE WHO PREYS ON INNOCENCE FOR SURVIVAL--
"--WHO CORRUPTS EVERYTHING HE DARES PROFANE WITH HIS DEATHLY TOUCH.
"BUT THEY'RE ALL WRONG. I'VE SEEN HIM. I KNOW HIM. I DO...I REALLY DO.
"HE IS MY MAN, ISN'T HE? AND MY MAN COULDN'T BE DRESSED IN A CLOAK OF SIN.
"COULD HE?"

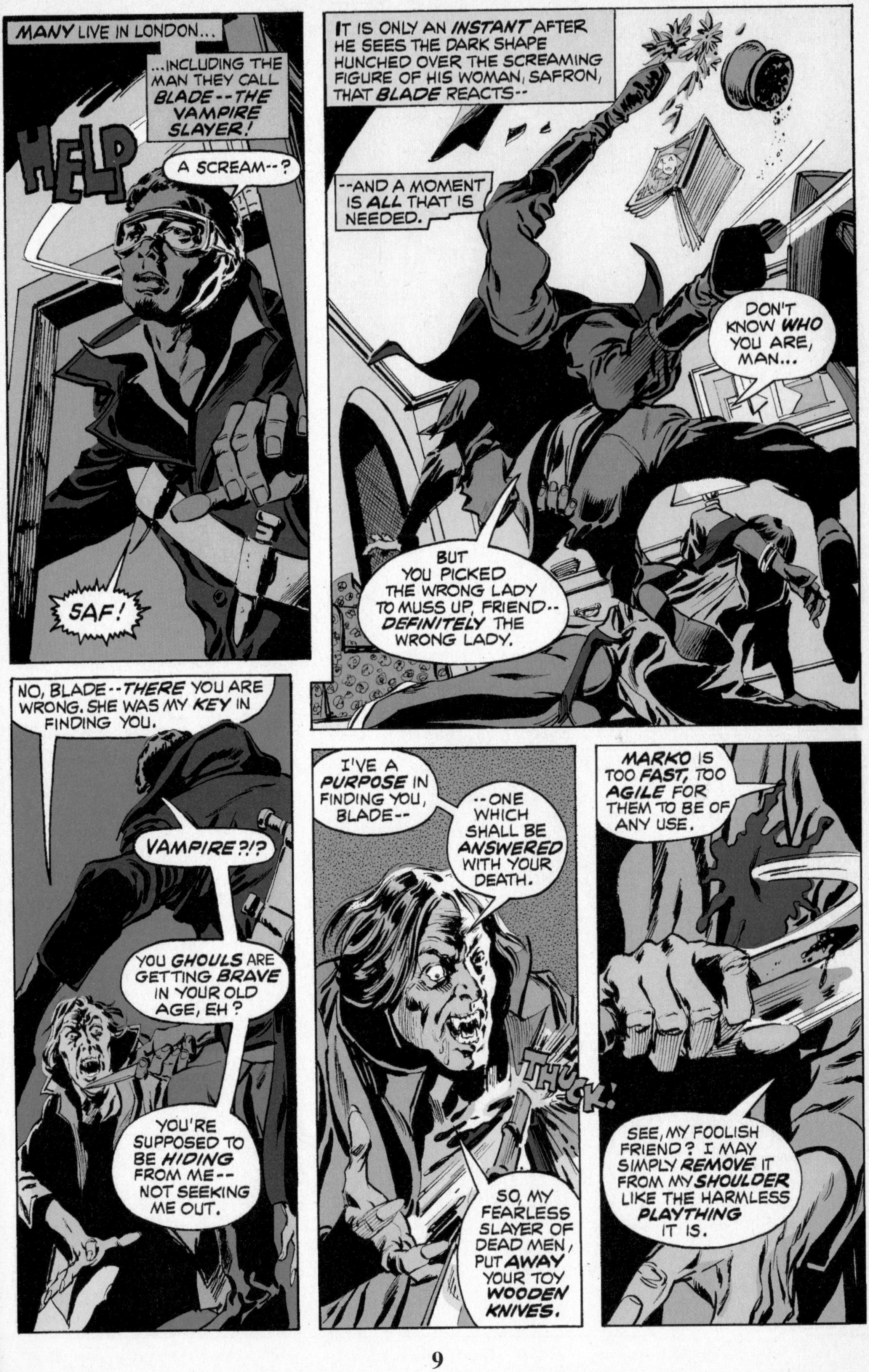
MANY LIVE IN LONDON...
...INCLUDING THE MAN THEY CALL BLADE--THE VAMPIRE SLAYER!
HELP
A SCREAM--?
SAF!
IT IS ONLY AN INSTANT AFTER HE SEES THE DARK SHAPE HUNCHED OVER THE SCREAMING FIGURE OF HIS WOMAN, SAFRON, THAT BLADE REACTS--
--AND A MOMENT IS ALL THAT IS NEEDED.
DON'T KNOW WHO YOU ARE, MAN...
BUT YOU PICKED THE WRONG LADY TO MUSS UP, FRIEND--DEFINITELY THE WRONG LADY.
NO, BLADE--THERE YOU ARE WRONG. SHE WAS MY KEY IN FINDING YOU.
VAMPIRE?!?
YOU GHOULS ARE GETTING BRAVE IN YOUR OLD AGE, EH?
YOU'RE SUPPOSED TO BE HIDING FROM ME--NOT SEEKING ME OUT.
I'VE A PURPOSE IN FINDING YOU, BLADE--
--ONE WHICH SHALL BE ANSWERED WITH YOUR DEATH.
THUCK!
SO, MY FEARLESS SLAYER OF DEAD MEN, PUT AWAY YOUR TOY WOODEN KNIVES.
MARKO IS TOO FAST, TOO AGILE FOR THEM TO BE OF ANY USE.
SEE, MY FOOLISH FRIEND? I MAY SIMPLY REMOVE IT FROM MY SHOULDER LIKE THE HARMLESS PLAYTHING IT IS.

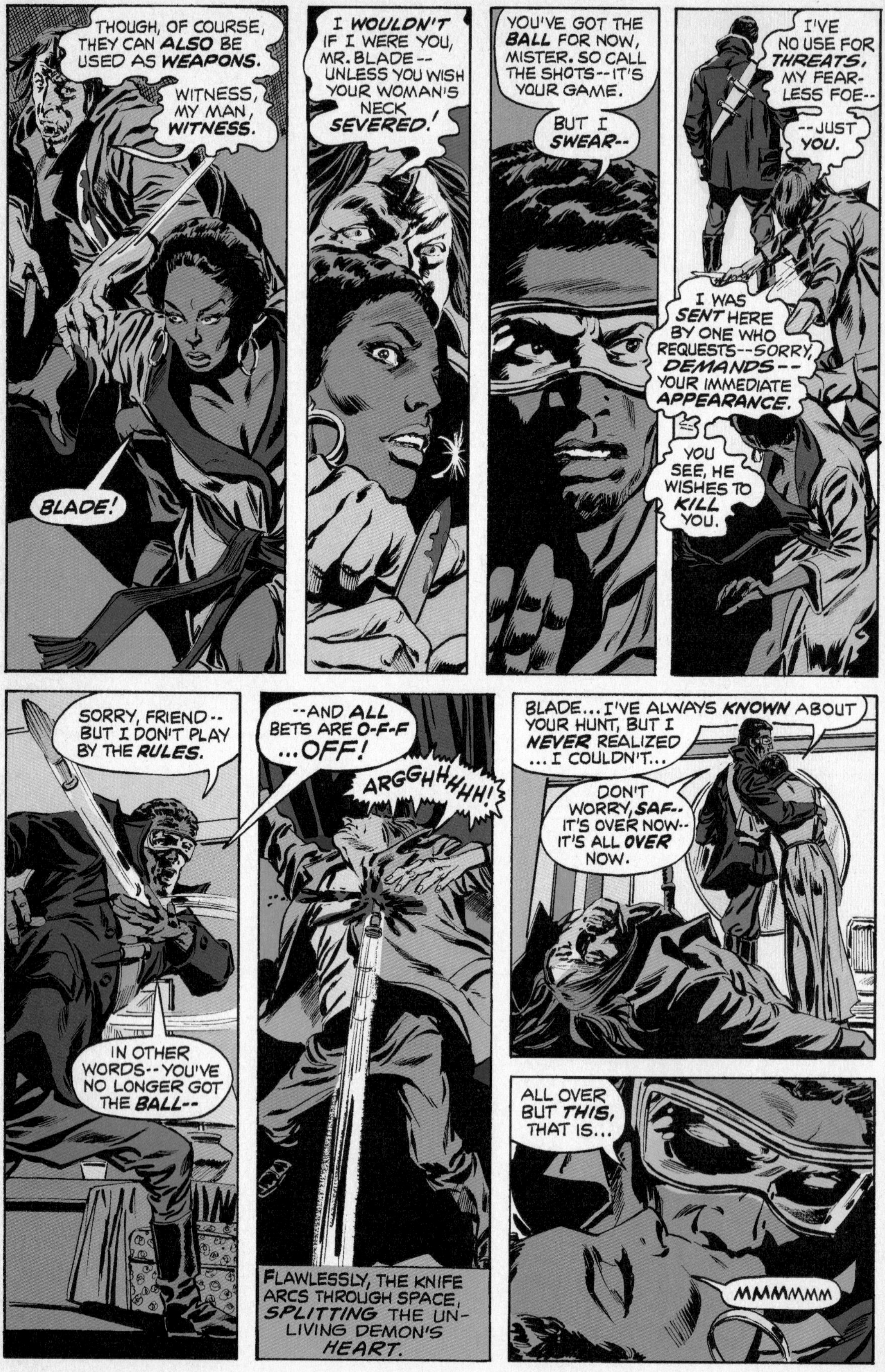
THOUGH, OF COURSE, THEY CAN ALSO BE USED AS WEAPONS.
WITNESS, MY MAN, WITNESS.
BLADE!
I WOULDN'T IF I WERE YOU, MR. BLADE-- UNLESS YOU WISH YOUR WOMAN'S NECK SEVERED!
YOU'VE GOT THE BALL FOR NOW, MISTER. SO CALL THE SHOTS--IT'S YOUR GAME.
BUT I SWEAR--
I'VE NO USE FOR THREATS, MY FEARLESS FOE--
--JUST YOU.
I WAS SENT HERE BY ONE WHO REQUESTS--SORRY, DEMANDS-- YOUR IMMEDIATE APPEARANCE.
YOU SEE, HE WISHES TO KILL YOU.
SORRY, FRIEND-- BUT I DON'T PLAY BY THE RULES.
IN OTHER WORDS--YOU'VE NO LONGER GOT THE BALL--
--AND ALL BETS ARE O-F-F ...OFF!
ARGGHHHHH!
FLAWLESSLY, THE KNIFE ARCS THROUGH SPACE, SPLITTING THE UNLIVING DEMON'S HEART.
BLADE... I'VE ALWAYS KNOWN ABOUT YOUR HUNT, BUT I NEVER REALIZED ... I COULDN'T...
DON'T WORRY, SAF-- IT'S OVER NOW-- IT'S ALL OVER NOW.
ALL OVER BUT THIS, THAT IS...
MMMMMM

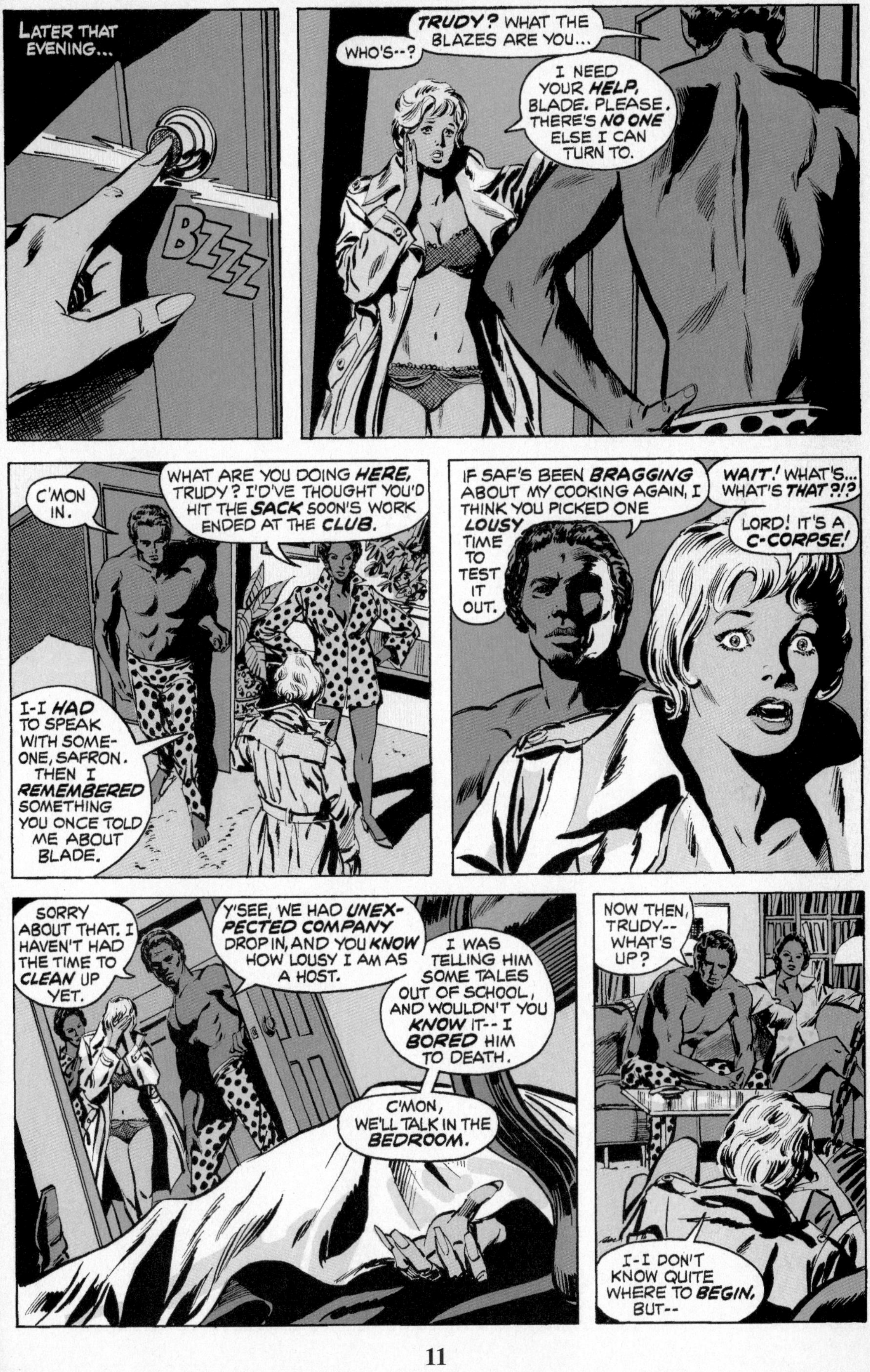
LATER THAT EVENING...
BZZZ
WHO'S--?
TRUDY? WHAT THE BLAZES ARE YOU...
I NEED YOUR HELP, BLADE. PLEASE. THERE'S NO ONE ELSE I CAN TURN TO.
C'MON IN.
WHAT ARE YOU DOING HERE, TRUDY? I'D'VE THOUGHT YOU'D HIT THE SACK SOON'S WORK ENDED AT THE CLUB.
I-I HAD TO SPEAK WITH SOME-ONE, SAFRON. THEN I REMEMBERED SOMETHING YOU ONCE TOLD ME ABOUT BLADE.
IF SAF'S BEEN BRAGGING ABOUT MY COOKING AGAIN, I THINK YOU PICKED ONE LOUSY TIME TO TEST IT OUT.
WAIT! WHAT'S... WHAT'S THAT?!?
LORD! IT'S A C-CORPSE!
SORRY ABOUT THAT. I HAVEN'T HAD THE TIME TO CLEAN UP YET.
Y'SEE, WE HAD UNEXPECTED COMPANY DROP IN, AND YOU KNOW HOW LOUSY I AM AS A HOST.
I WAS TELLING HIM SOME TALES OUT OF SCHOOL, AND WOULDN'T YOU KNOW IT-- I BORED HIM TO DEATH.
C'MON, WE'LL TALK IN THE BEDROOM.
NOW THEN, TRUDY-- WHAT'S UP?
I-I DON'T KNOW QUITE WHERE TO BEGIN, BUT--

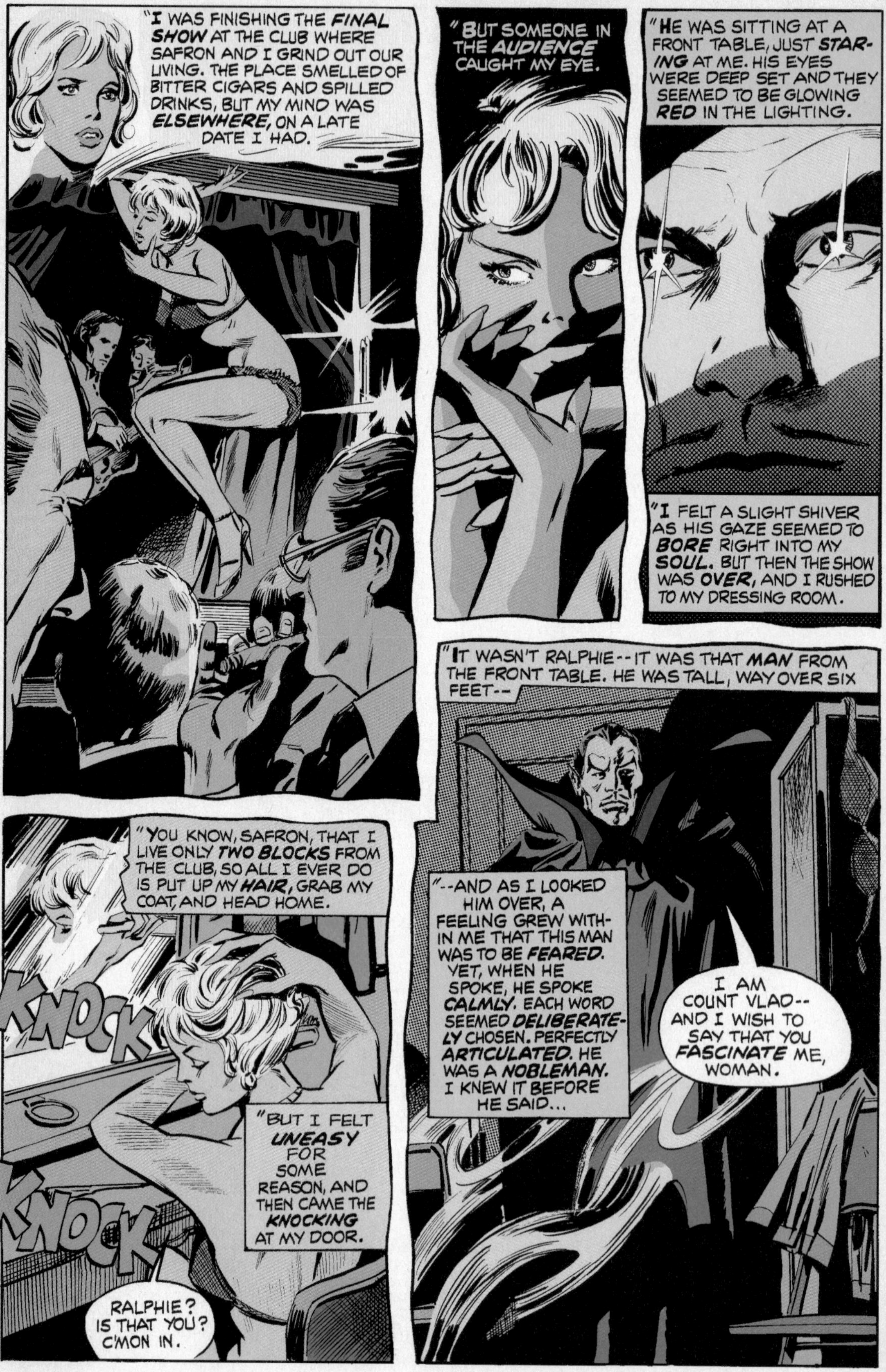
"I WAS FINISHING THE FINAL SHOW AT THE CLUB WHERE SAFRON AND I GRIND OUT OUR LIVING. THE PLACE SMELLED OF BITTER CIGARS AND SPILLED DRINKS, BUT MY MIND WAS ELSEWHERE, ON A LATE DATE I HAD.
"BUT SOMEONE IN THE AUDIENCE CAUGHT MY EYE.
"HE WAS SITTING AT A FRONT TABLE, JUST STARING AT ME. HIS EYES WERE DEEP SET AND THEY SEEMED TO BE GLOWING RED IN THE LIGHTING.
"I FELT A SLIGHT SHIVER AS HIS GAZE SEEMED TO BORE RIGHT INTO MY SOUL. BUT THEN THE SHOW WAS OVER, AND I RUSHED TO MY DRESSING ROOM.
"YOU KNOW, SAFRON, THAT I LIVE ONLY TWO BLOCKS FROM THE CLUB, SO ALL I EVER DO IS PUT UP MY HAIR, GRAB MY COAT, AND HEAD HOME.
KNOCK
KNOCK
"BUT I FELT UNEASY FOR SOME REASON, AND THEN CAME THE KNOCKING AT MY DOOR.
RALPHIE? IS THAT YOU? C'MON IN.
"IT WASN'T RALPHIE--IT WAS THAT MAN FROM THE FRONT TABLE. HE WAS TALL, WAY OVER SIX FEET--
"--AND AS I LOOKED HIM OVER, A FEELING GREW WITHIN ME THAT THIS MAN WAS TO BE FEARED. YET, WHEN HE SPOKE, HE SPOKE CALMLY. EACH WORD SEEMED DELIBERATELY CHOSEN. PERFECTLY ARTICULATED. HE WAS A NOBLEMAN. I KNEW IT BEFORE HE SAID...
I AM COUNT VLAD--AND I WISH TO SAY THAT YOU FASCINATE ME, WOMAN.

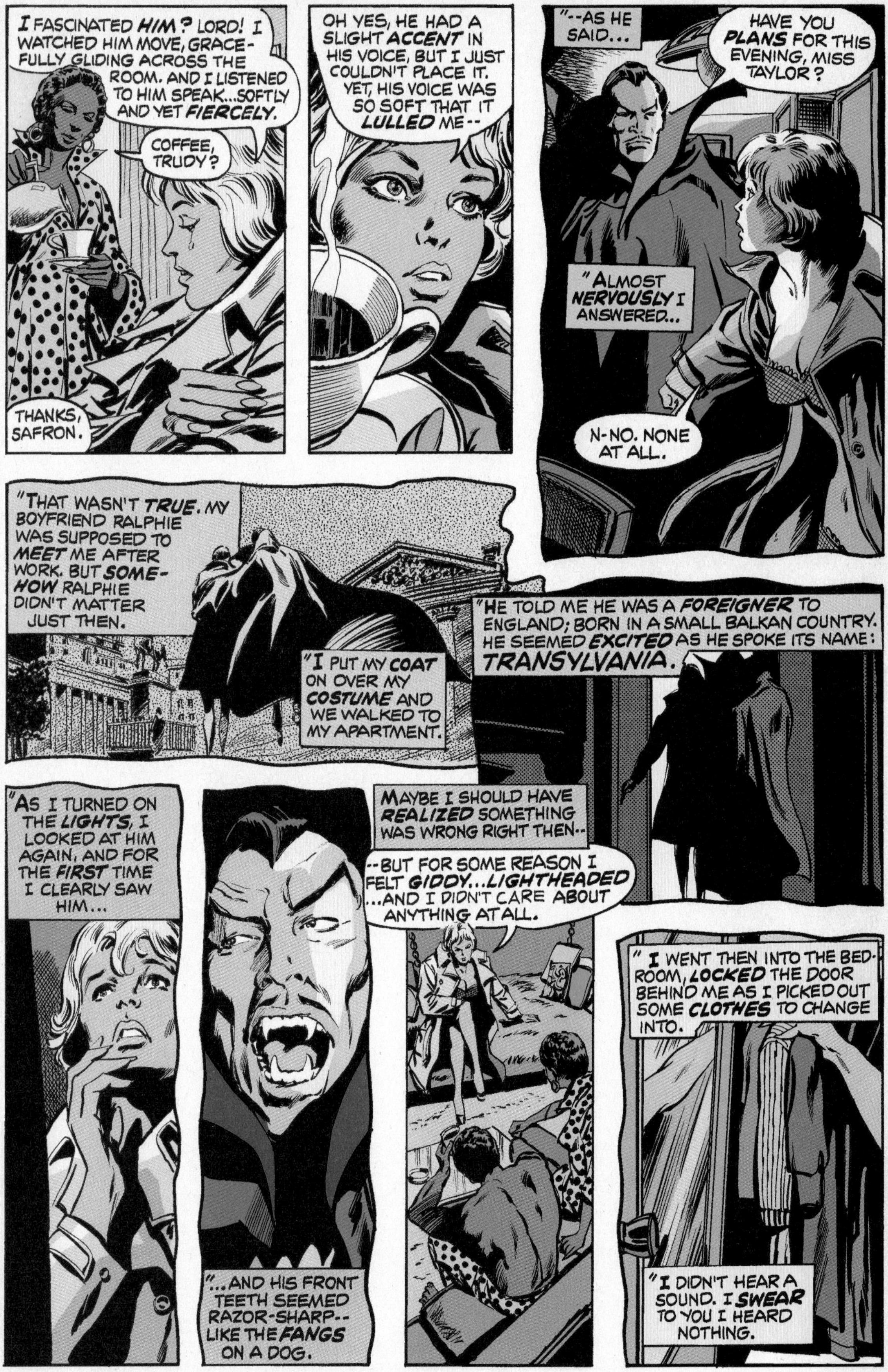
I FASCINATED HIM? LORD! I WATCHED HIM MOVE, GRACEFULLY GLIDING ACROSS THE ROOM. AND I LISTENED TO HIM SPEAK...SOFTLY AND YET FIERCELY.
COFFEE, TRUDY?
THANKS, SAFRON.
OH YES, HE HAD A SLIGHT ACCENT IN HIS VOICE, BUT I JUST COULDN'T PLACE IT. YET, HIS VOICE WAS SO SOFT THAT IT LULLED ME--
"--AS HE SAID...
HAVE YOU PLANS FOR THIS EVENING, MISS TAYLOR?
"ALMOST NERVOUSLY I ANSWERED...
N-NO. NONE AT ALL.
"THAT WASN'T TRUE. MY BOYFRIEND RALPHIE WAS SUPPOSED TO MEET ME AFTER WORK. BUT SOMEHOW RALPHIE DIDN'T MATTER JUST THEN.
"I PUT MY COAT ON OVER MY COSTUME AND WE WALKED TO MY APARTMENT.
"HE TOLD ME HE WAS A FOREIGNER TO ENGLAND; BORN IN A SMALL BALKAN COUNTRY. HE SEEMED EXCITED AS HE SPOKE ITS NAME: TRANSYLVANIA.
"AS I TURNED ON THE LIGHTS, I LOOKED AT HIM AGAIN, AND FOR THE FIRST TIME I CLEARLY SAW HIM...
"...AND HIS FRONT TEETH SEEMED RAZOR-SHARP--LIKE THE FANGS ON A DOG.
MAYBE I SHOULD HAVE REALIZED SOMETHING WAS WRONG RIGHT THEN--
--BUT FOR SOME REASON I FELT GIDDY...LIGHTHEADED ...AND I DIDN'T CARE ABOUT ANYTHING AT ALL.
"I WENT THEN INTO THE BEDROOM, LOCKED THE DOOR BEHIND ME AS I PICKED OUT SOME CLOTHES TO CHANGE INTO.
"I DIDN'T HEAR A SOUND. I SWEAR TO YOU I HEARD NOTHING.

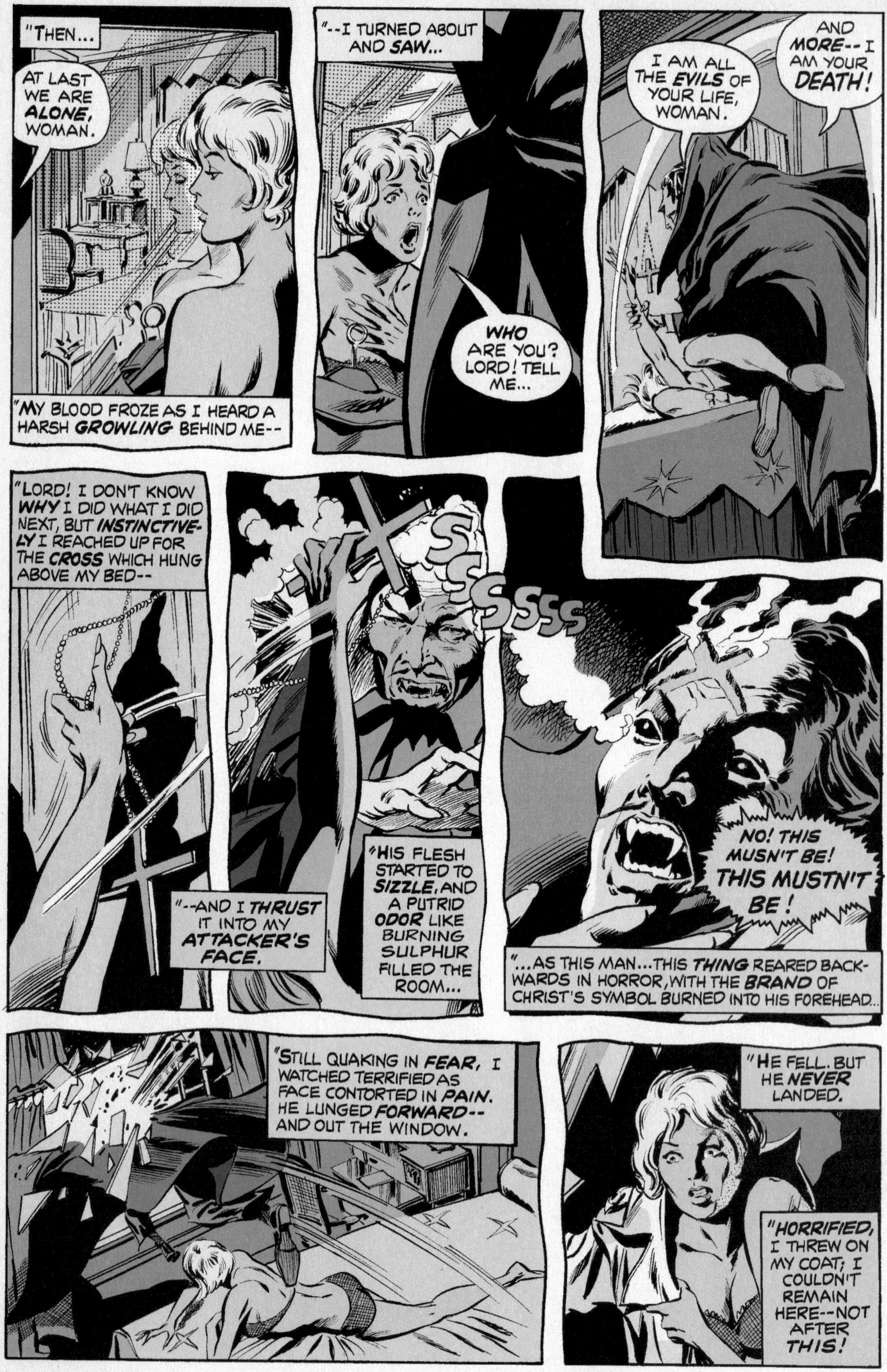
"THEN...
AT LAST WE ARE ALONE, WOMAN.
"MY BLOOD FROZE AS I HEARD A HARSH GROWLING BEHIND ME--
"--I TURNED ABOUT AND SAW...
WHO ARE YOU? LORD! TELL ME...
I AM ALL THE EVILS OF YOUR LIFE, WOMAN.
AND MORE--I AM YOUR DEATH!
"LORD! I DON'T KNOW WHY I DID WHAT I DID NEXT, BUT INSTINCTIVE-LY I REACHED UP FOR THE CROSS WHICH HUNG ABOVE MY BED--
"--AND I THRUST IT INTO MY ATTACKER'S FACE.
SSSSSSS
"HIS FLESH STARTED TO SIZZLE, AND A PUTRID ODOR LIKE BURNING SULPHUR FILLED THE ROOM...
NO! THIS MUSN'T BE! THIS MUSTN'T BE!
"...AS THIS MAN...THIS THING REARED BACK-WARDS IN HORROR, WITH THE BRAND OF CHRIST'S SYMBOL BURNED INTO HIS FOREHEAD...
"STILL QUAKING IN FEAR, I WATCHED TERRIFIED AS FACE CONTORTED IN PAIN. HE LUNGED FORWARD--AND OUT THE WINDOW.
"HE FELL. BUT HE NEVER LANDED.
"HORRIFIED, I THREW ON MY COAT; I COULDN'T REMAIN HERE--NOT AFTER THIS!

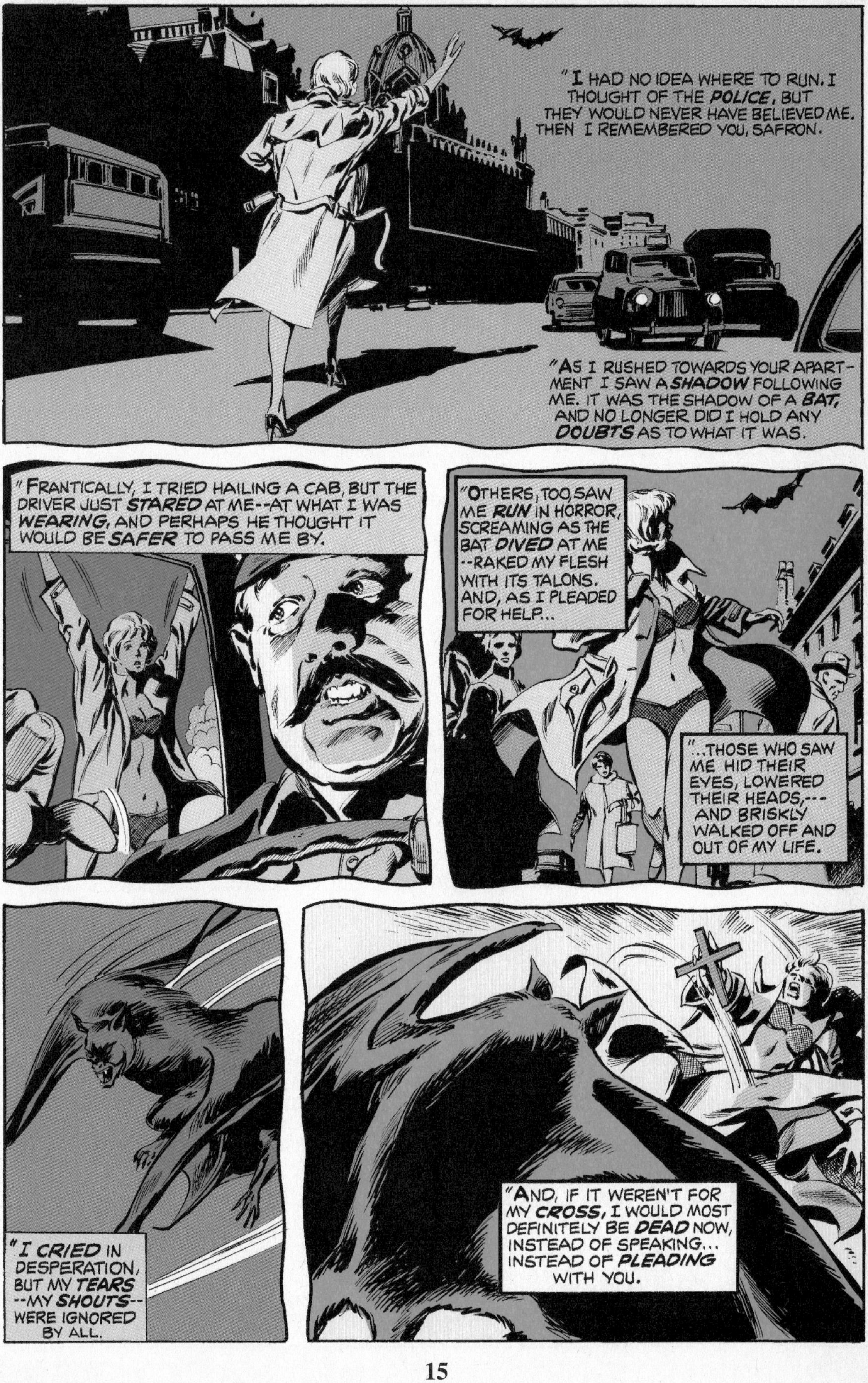
"I HAD NO IDEA WHERE TO RUN. I THOUGHT OF THE POLICE, BUT THEY WOULD NEVER HAVE BELIEVED ME. THEN I REMEMBERED YOU, SAFRON.
"AS I RUSHED TOWARDS YOUR APARTMENT I SAW A SHADOW FOLLOWING ME. IT WAS THE SHADOW OF A BAT, AND NO LONGER DID I HOLD ANY DOUBTS AS TO WHAT IT WAS.
"FRANTICALLY, I TRIED HAILING A CAB, BUT THE DRIVER JUST STARED AT ME--AT WHAT I WAS WEARING, AND PERHAPS HE THOUGHT IT WOULD BE SAFER TO PASS ME BY.
"OTHERS, TOO, SAW ME RUN IN HORROR, SCREAMING AS THE BAT DIVED AT ME --RAKED MY FLESH WITH ITS TALONS. AND, AS I PLEADED FOR HELP...
"...THOSE WHO SAW ME HID THEIR EYES, LOWERED THEIR HEADS,--- AND BRISKLY WALKED OFF AND OUT OF MY LIFE.
"I CRIED IN DESPERATION, BUT MY TEARS --MY SHOUTS-- WERE IGNORED BY ALL.
"AND, IF IT WEREN'T FOR MY CROSS, I WOULD MOST DEFINITELY BE DEAD NOW, INSTEAD OF SPEAKING... INSTEAD OF PLEADING WITH YOU.

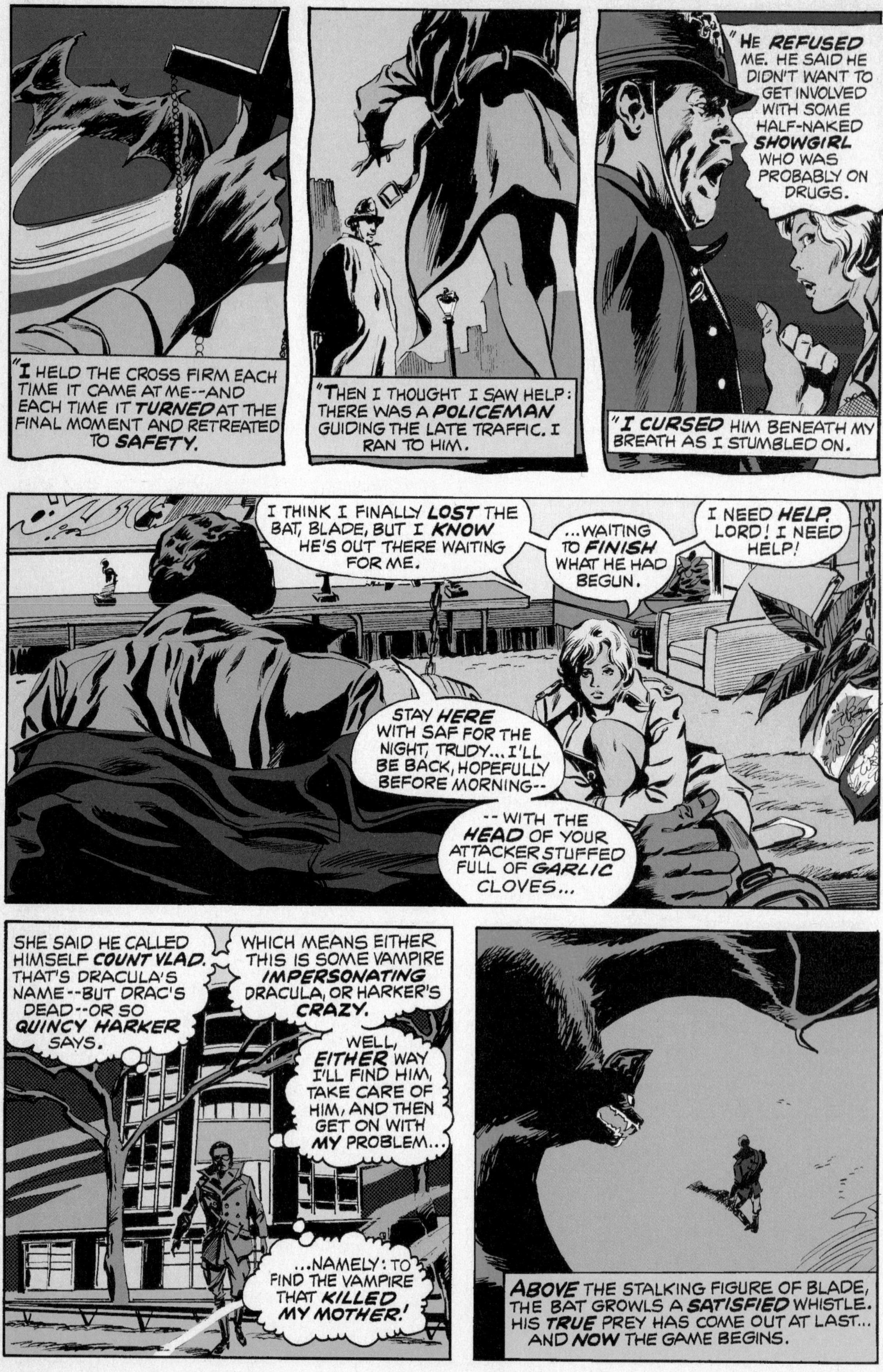
"I HELD THE CROSS FIRM EACH TIME IT CAME AT ME--AND EACH TIME IT TURNED AT THE FINAL MOMENT AND RETREATED TO SAFETY.
"THEN I THOUGHT I SAW HELP: THERE WAS A POLICEMAN GUIDING THE LATE TRAFFIC. I RAN TO HIM.
"HE REFUSED ME. HE SAID HE DIDN'T WANT TO GET INVOLVED WITH SOME HALF-NAKED SHOWGIRL WHO WAS PROBABLY ON DRUGS.
"I CURSED HIM BENEATH MY BREATH AS I STUMBLED ON.
I THINK I FINALLY LOST THE BAT, BLADE, BUT I KNOW HE'S OUT THERE WAITING FOR ME.
...WAITING TO FINISH WHAT HE HAD BEGUN.
I NEED HELP. LORD! I NEED HELP!
STAY HERE WITH SAF FOR THE NIGHT, TRUDY... I'LL BE BACK, HOPEFULLY BEFORE MORNING--
-- WITH THE HEAD OF YOUR ATTACKER STUFFED FULL OF GARLIC CLOVES...
SHE SAID HE CALLED HIMSELF COUNT VLAD. THAT'S DRACULA'S NAME--BUT DRAC'S DEAD--OR SO QUINCY HARKER SAYS.
WHICH MEANS EITHER THIS IS SOME VAMPIRE IMPERSONATING DRACULA, OR HARKER'S CRAZY.
WELL, EITHER WAY I'LL FIND HIM, TAKE CARE OF HIM, AND THEN GET ON WITH MY PROBLEM...
...NAMELY: TO FIND THE VAMPIRE THAT KILLED MY MOTHER!
ABOVE THE STALKING FIGURE OF BLADE, THE BAT GROWLS A SATISFIED WHISTLE. HIS TRUE PREY HAS COME OUT AT LAST... AND NOW THE GAME BEGINS.

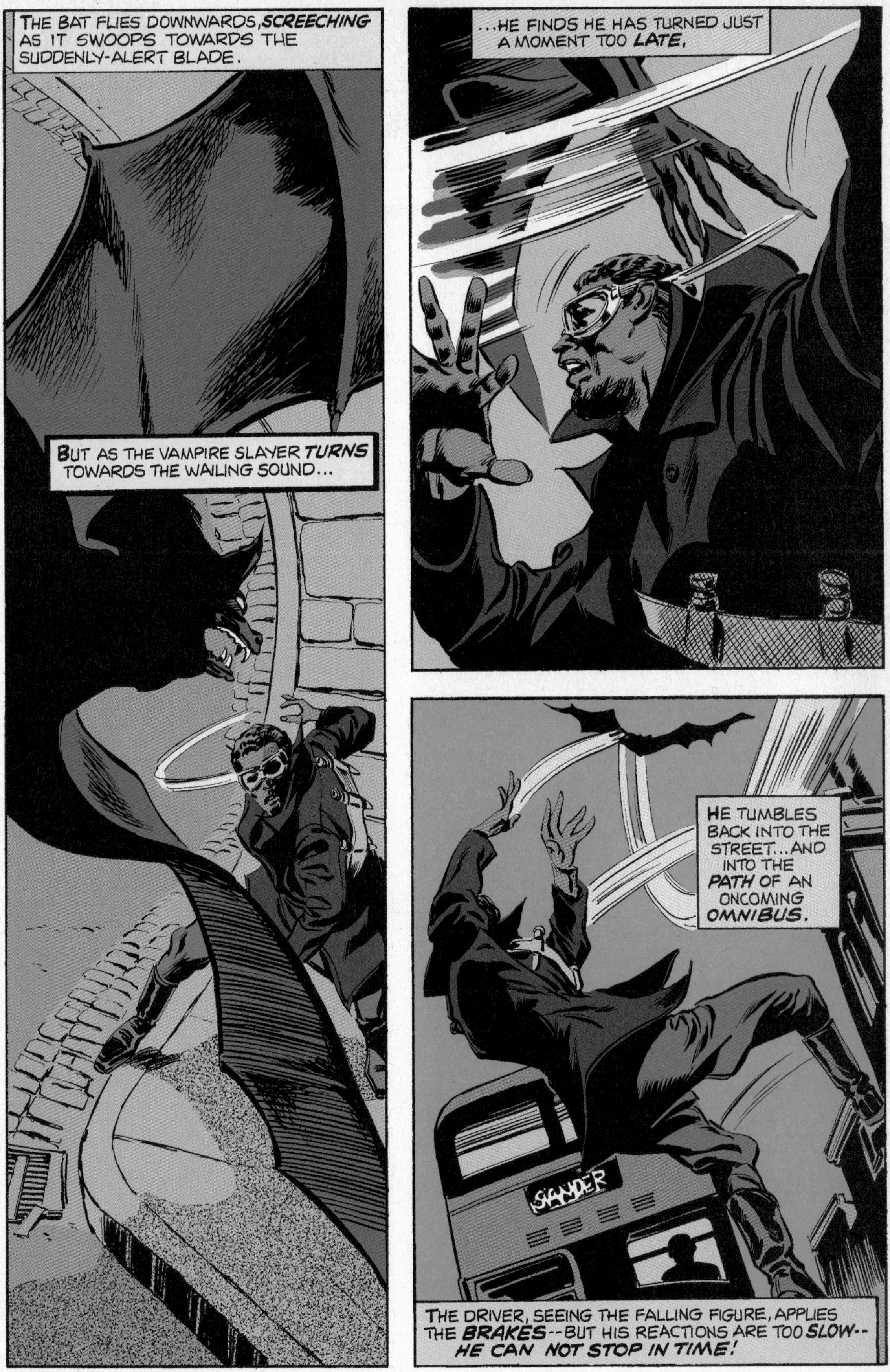
THE BAT FLIES DOWNWARDS, SCREECHING AS IT SWOOPS TOWARDS THE SUDDENLY-ALERT BLADE.
BUT AS THE VAMPIRE SLAYER TURNS TOWARDS THE WAILING SOUND...
...HE FINDS HE HAS TURNED JUST A MOMENT TOO LATE.
HE TUMBLES BACK INTO THE STREET...AND INTO THE PATH OF AN ONCOMING OMNIBUS.
THE DRIVER, SEEING THE FALLING FIGURE, APPLIES THE BRAKES--BUT HIS REACTIONS ARE TOO SLOW--HE CAN NOT STOP IN TIME!

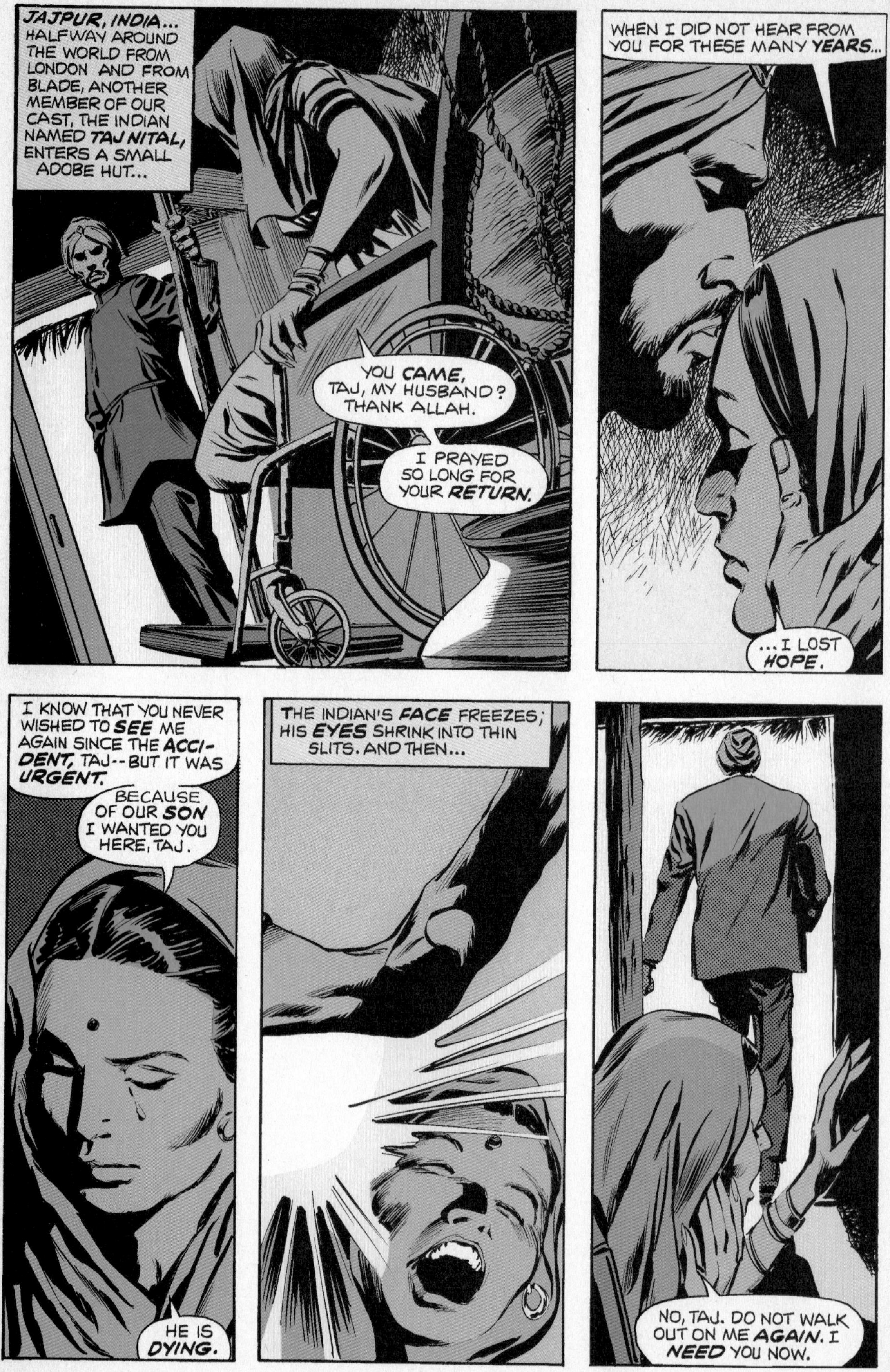
JAJPUR, INDIA... HALFWAY AROUND THE WORLD FROM LONDON AND FROM BLADE, ANOTHER MEMBER OF OUR CAST, THE INDIAN NAMED TAJ NITAL, ENTERS A SMALL ADOBE HUT...
YOU CAME, TAJ, MY HUSBAND? THANK ALLAH.
I PRAYED SO LONG FOR YOUR RETURN.
WHEN I DID NOT HEAR FROM YOU FOR THESE MANY YEARS...
...I LOST HOPE.
I KNOW THAT YOU NEVER WISHED TO SEE ME AGAIN SINCE THE ACCI-DENT, TAJ--BUT IT WAS URGENT.
BECAUSE OF OUR SON I WANTED YOU HERE, TAJ.
HE IS DYING.
THE INDIAN'S FACE FREEZES; HIS EYES SHRINK INTO THIN SLITS. AND THEN...
NO, TAJ. DO NOT WALK OUT ON ME AGAIN. I NEED YOU NOW.

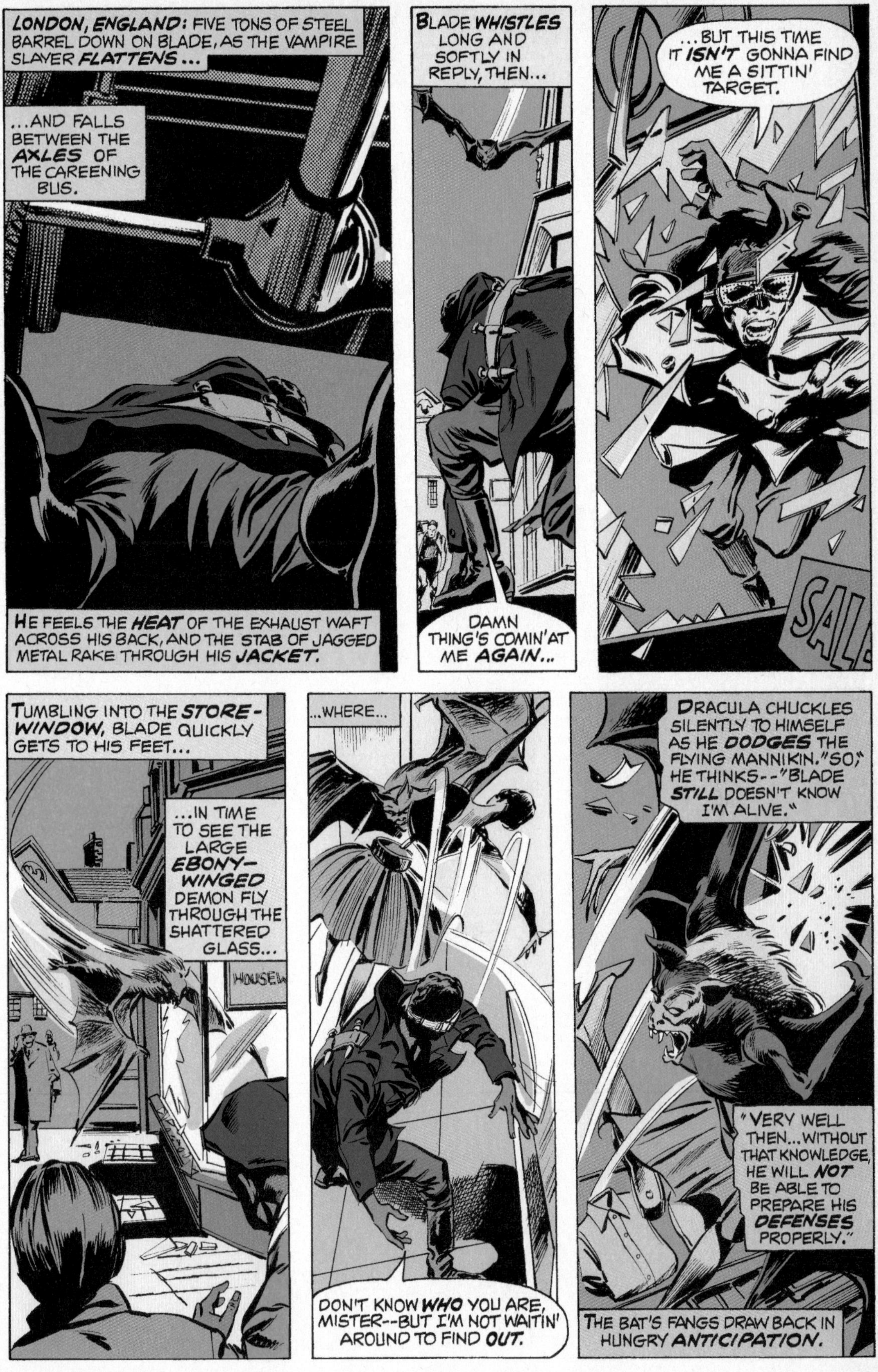
LONDON, ENGLAND: FIVE TONS OF STEEL BARREL DOWN ON BLADE, AS THE VAMPIRE SLAYER FLATTENS...
...AND FALLS BETWEEN THE AXLES OF THE CAREENING BUS.
HE FEELS THE HEAT OF THE EXHAUST WAFT ACROSS HIS BACK, AND THE STAB OF JAGGED METAL RAKE THROUGH HIS JACKET.
BLADE WHISTLES LONG AND SOFTLY IN REPLY, THEN...
DAMN THING'S COMIN' AT ME AGAIN...
...BUT THIS TIME IT ISN'T GONNA FIND ME A SITTIN' TARGET.
TUMBLING INTO THE STORE-WINDOW, BLADE QUICKLY GETS TO HIS FEET...
...IN TIME TO SEE THE LARGE EBONY-WINGED DEMON FLY THROUGH THE SHATTERED GLASS...
...WHERE...
DON'T KNOW WHO YOU ARE, MISTER--BUT I'M NOT WAITIN' AROUND TO FIND OUT.
DRACULA CHUCKLES SILENTLY TO HIMSELF AS HE DODGES THE FLYING MANNIKIN. "SO," HE THINKS--"BLADE STILL DOESN'T KNOW I'M ALIVE."
"VERY WELL THEN...WITHOUT THAT KNOWLEDGE, HE WILL NOT BE ABLE TO PREPARE HIS DEFENSES PROPERLY."
THE BAT'S FANGS DRAW BACK IN HUNGRY ANTICIPATION.

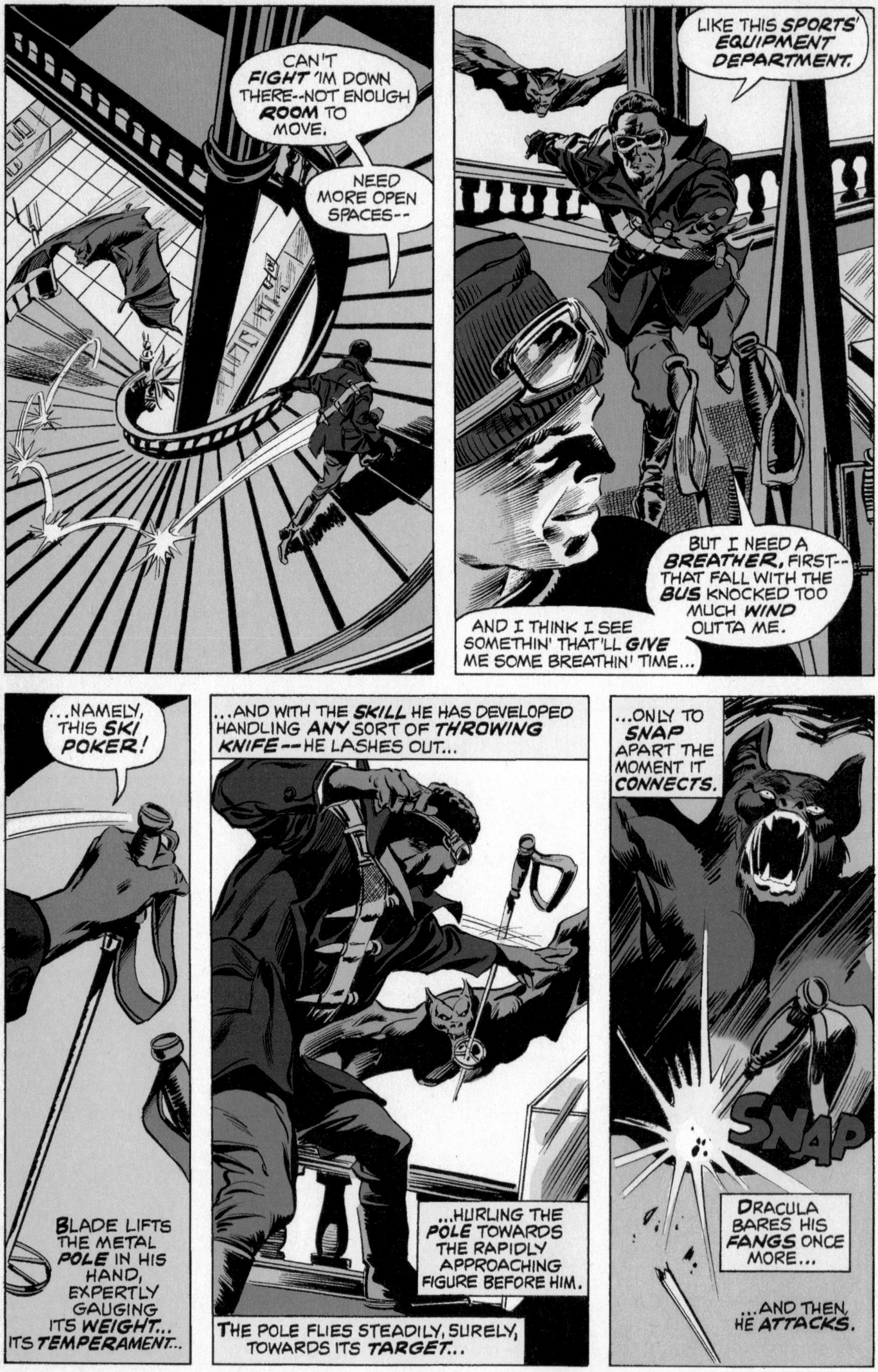
CAN'T FIGHT 'IM DOWN THERE--NOT ENOUGH ROOM TO MOVE.
NEED MORE OPEN SPACES--
LIKE THIS SPORTS' EQUIPMENT DEPARTMENT.
BUT I NEED A BREATHER, FIRST-- THAT FALL WITH THE BUS KNOCKED TOO MUCH WIND OUTTA ME.
AND I THINK I SEE SOMETHIN' THAT'LL GIVE ME SOME BREATHIN' TIME...
...NAMELY, THIS SKI POKER!
BLADE LIFTS THE METAL POLE IN HIS HAND, EXPERTLY GAUGING ITS WEIGHT... ITS TEMPERAMENT...
...AND WITH THE SKILL HE HAS DEVELOPED HANDLING ANY SORT OF THROWING KNIFE--HE LASHES OUT...
...HURLING THE POLE TOWARDS THE RAPIDLY APPROACHING FIGURE BEFORE HIM.
THE POLE FLIES STEADILY, SURELY, TOWARDS ITS TARGET...
...ONLY TO SNAP APART THE MOMENT IT CONNECTS.
SNAP
DRACULA BARES HIS FANGS ONCE MORE...
...AND THEN, HE ATTACKS.

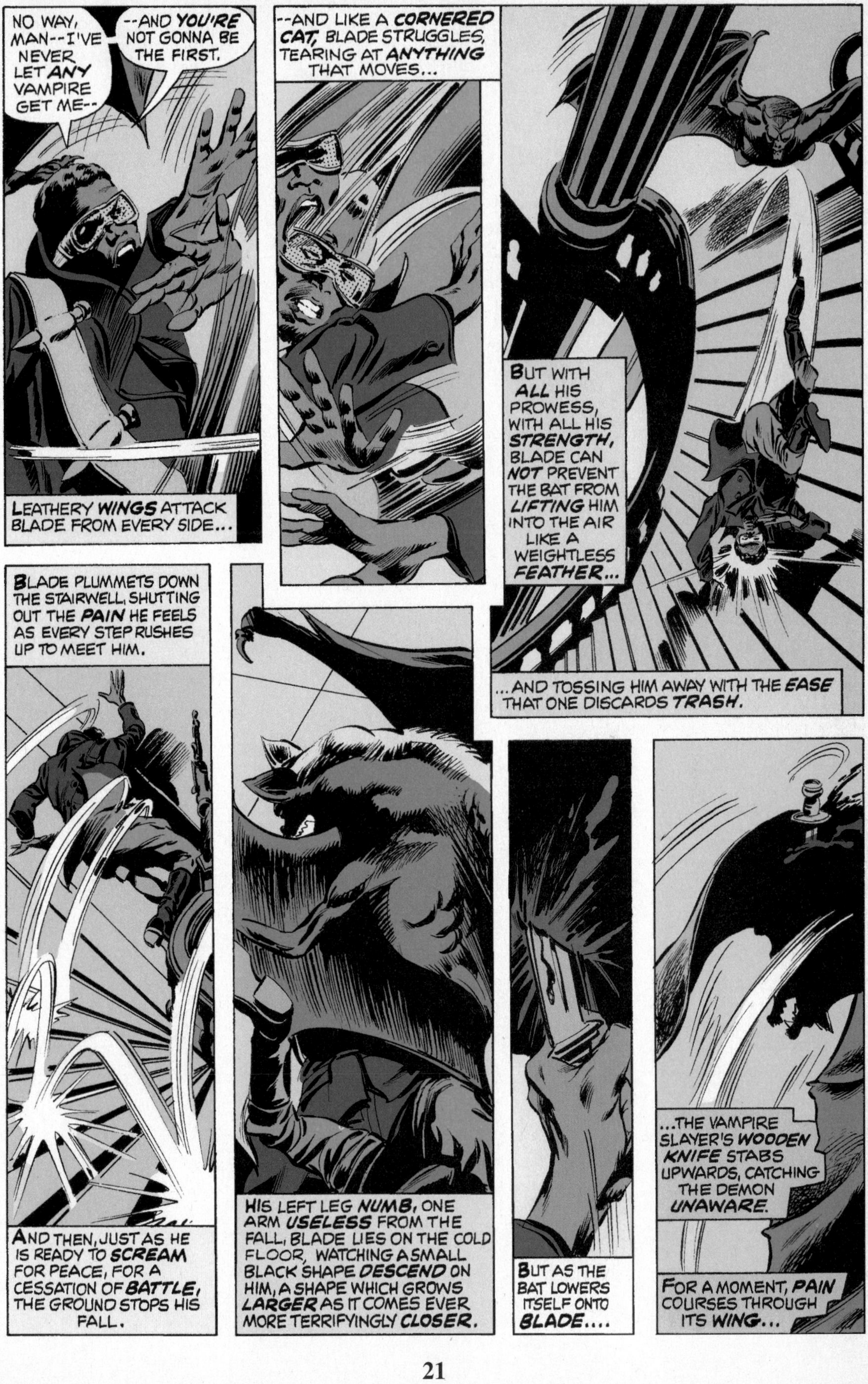

NO WAY, MAN--I'VE NEVER LET ANY VAMPIRE GET ME--
--AND YOU'RE NOT GONNA BE THE FIRST.
LEATHERY WINGS ATTACK BLADE FROM EVERY SIDE...
--AND LIKE A CORNERED CAT, BLADE STRUGGLES, TEARING AT ANYTHING THAT MOVES...
BUT WITH ALL HIS PROWESS, WITH ALL HIS STRENGTH, BLADE CAN NOT PREVENT THE BAT FROM LIFTING HIM INTO THE AIR LIKE A WEIGHTLESS FEATHER...
...AND TOSSING HIM AWAY WITH THE EASE THAT ONE DISCARDS TRASH.
BLADE PLUMMETS DOWN THE STAIRWELL, SHUTTING OUT THE PAIN HE FEELS AS EVERY STEP RUSHES UP TO MEET HIM.
AND THEN, JUST AS HE IS READY TO SCREAM FOR PEACE, FOR A CESSATION OF BATTLE, THE GROUND STOPS HIS FALL.
HIS LEFT LEG NUMB, ONE ARM USELESS FROM THE FALL, BLADE LIES ON THE COLD FLOOR, WATCHING A SMALL BLACK SHAPE DESCEND ON HIM, A SHAPE WHICH GROWS LARGER AS IT COMES EVER MORE TERRIFYINGLY CLOSER.
BUT AS THE BAT LOWERS ITSELF ONTO BLADE....
...THE VAMPIRE SLAYER'S WOODEN KNIFE STABS UPWARDS, CATCHING THE DEMON UNAWARE.
FOR A MOMENT, PAIN COURSES THROUGH ITS WING...

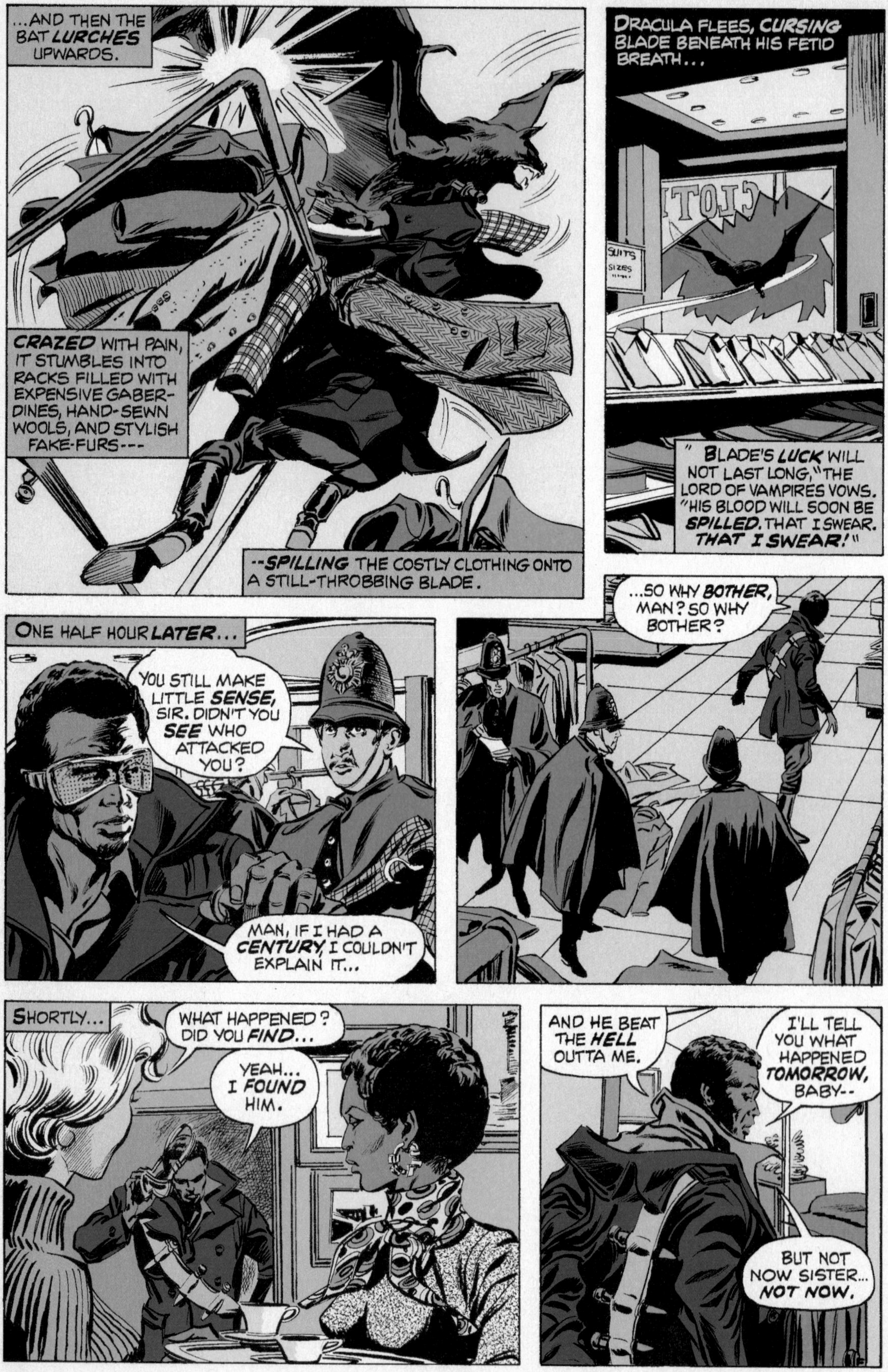
...AND THEN THE BAT LURCHES UPWARDS.
CRAZED WITH PAIN, IT STUMBLES INTO RACKS FILLED WITH EXPENSIVE GABER-DINES, HAND-SEWN WOOLS, AND STYLISH FAKE-FURS---
--SPILLING THE COSTLY CLOTHING ONTO A STILL-THROBBING BLADE.
DRACULA FLEES, CURSING BLADE BENEATH HIS FETID BREATH...
SUITS
SIZES
"BLADE'S LUCK WILL NOT LAST LONG," THE LORD OF VAMPIRES VOWS. "HIS BLOOD WILL SOON BE SPILLED. THAT I SWEAR. THAT I SWEAR!"
ONE HALF HOUR LATER...
YOU STILL MAKE LITTLE SENSE, SIR. DIDN'T YOU SEE WHO ATTACKED YOU?
MAN, IF I HAD A CENTURY, I COULDN'T EXPLAIN IT...
...SO WHY BOTHER, MAN? SO WHY BOTHER?
SHORTLY...
WHAT HAPPENED? DID YOU FIND...
YEAH... I FOUND HIM.
AND HE BEAT THE HELL OUTTA ME.
I'LL TELL YOU WHAT HAPPENED TOMORROW, BABY--
BUT NOT NOW SISTER... NOT NOW.

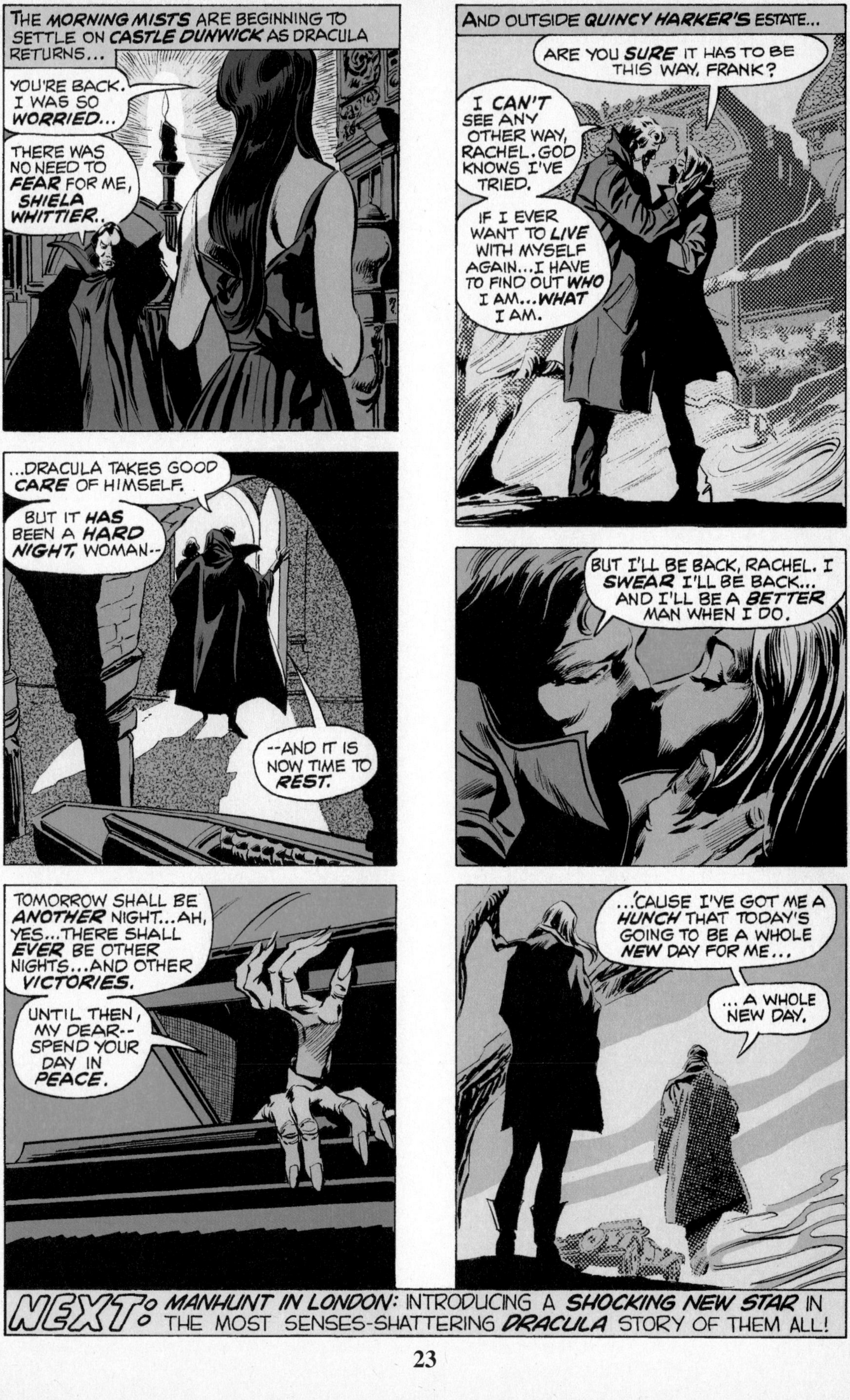
THE MORNING MISTS ARE BEGINNING TO SETTLE ON CASTLE DUNWICK AS DRACULA RETURNS...
YOU'RE BACK. I WAS SO WORRIED...
THERE WAS NO NEED TO FEAR FOR ME, SHIELA WHITTIER...
...DRACULA TAKES GOOD CARE OF HIMSELF.
BUT IT HAS BEEN A HARD NIGHT, WOMAN--
--AND IT IS NOW TIME TO REST.
TOMORROW SHALL BE ANOTHER NIGHT...AH, YES...THERE SHALL EVER BE OTHER NIGHTS...AND OTHER VICTORIES.
UNTIL THEN, MY DEAR--SPEND YOUR DAY IN PEACE.
AND OUTSIDE QUINCY HARKER'S ESTATE...
ARE YOU SURE IT HAS TO BE THIS WAY, FRANK?
I CAN'T SEE ANY OTHER WAY, RACHEL. GOD KNOWS I'VE TRIED.
IF I EVER WANT TO LIVE WITH MYSELF AGAIN...I HAVE TO FIND OUT WHO I AM...WHAT I AM.
BUT I'LL BE BACK, RACHEL. I SWEAR I'LL BE BACK... AND I'LL BE A BETTER MAN WHEN I DO.
...'CAUSE I'VE GOT ME A HUNCH THAT TODAY'S GOING TO BE A WHOLE NEW DAY FOR ME...
... A WHOLE NEW DAY.
NEXT: MANHUNT IN LONDON: INTRODUCING A SHOCKING NEW STAR IN THE MOST SENSES-SHATTERING DRACULA STORY OF THEM ALL!

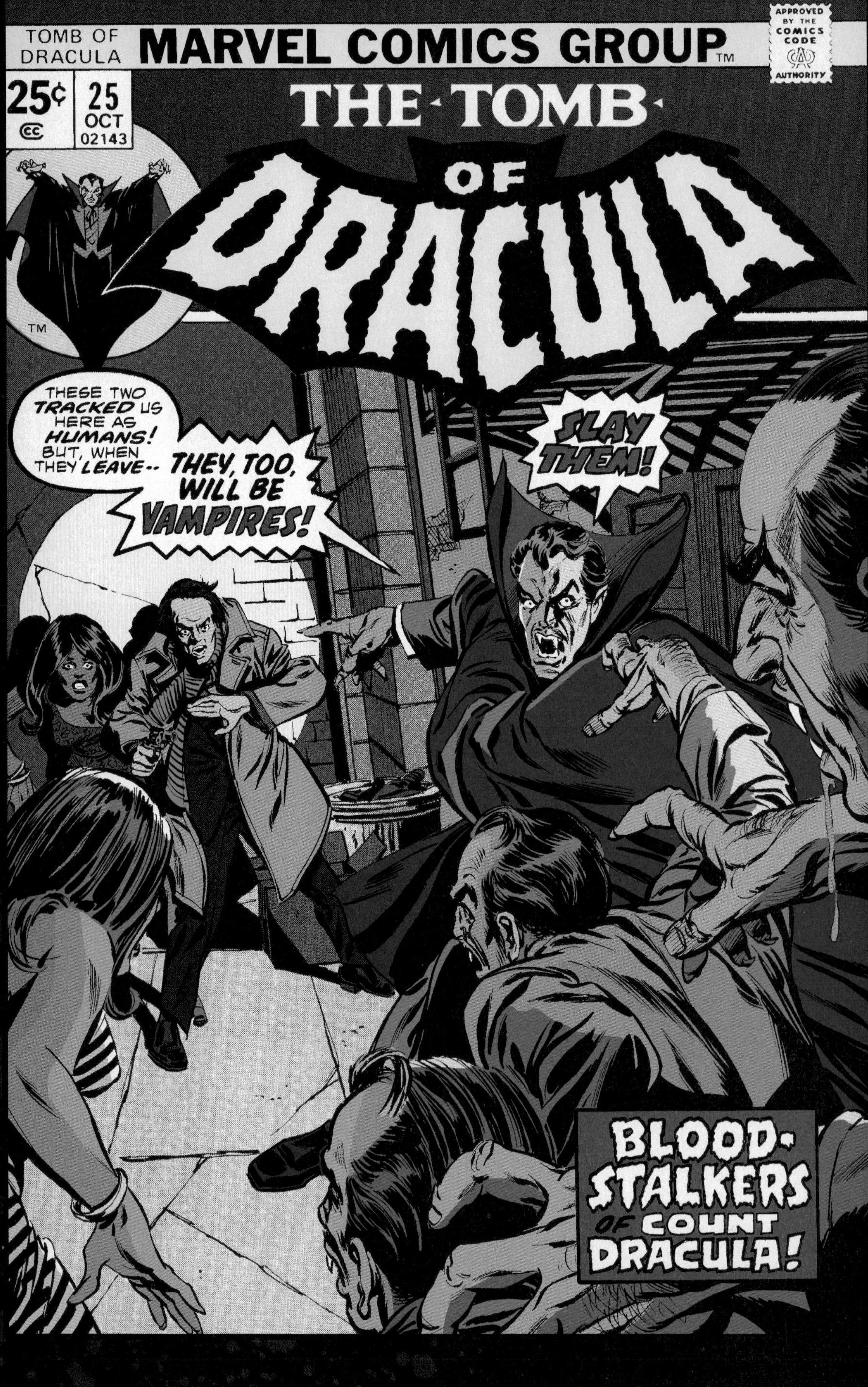

TOMB OF DRACULA
MARVEL COMICS GROUP
APPROVED BY THE COMICS CODE AUTHORITY
25¢
25 OCT 02143
THE TOMB OF DRACULA
THESE TWO TRACKED US HERE AS HUMANS! BUT, WHEN THEY LEAVE-- THEY, TOO, WILL BE VAMPIRES!
SLAY THEM!
BLOOD-STALKERS OF COUNT DRACULA!

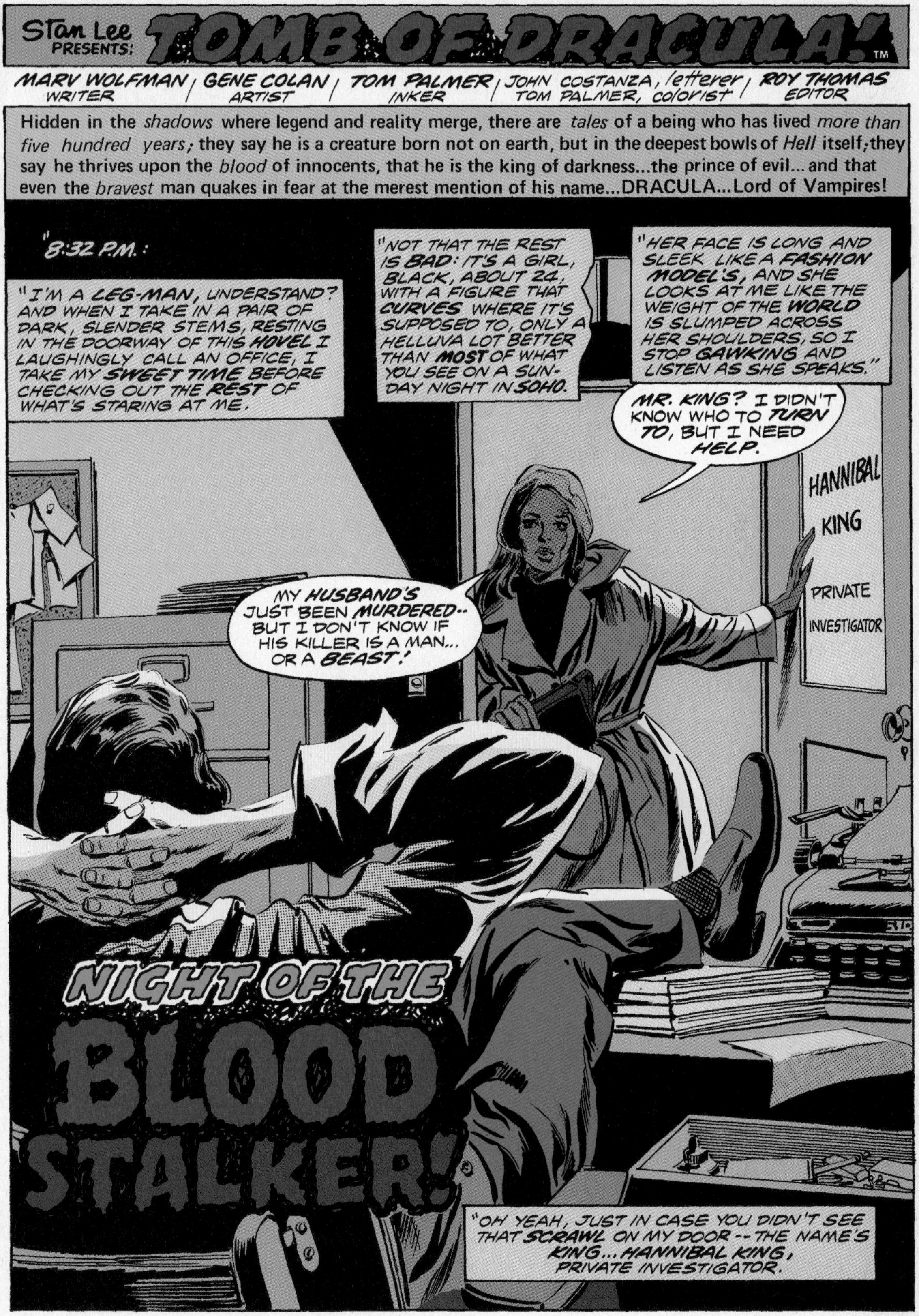
Stan Lee PRESENTS: TOMB OF DRACULA! TM
MARV WOLFMAN WRITER / GENE COLAN ARTIST / TOM PALMER INKER / JOHN COSTANZA, letterer TOM PALMER, colorist / ROY THOMAS EDITOR
Hidden in the shadows where legend and reality merge, there are tales of a being who has lived more than five hundred years; they say he is a creature born not on earth, but in the deepest bowls of Hell itself; they say he thrives upon the blood of innocents, that he is the king of darkness...the prince of evil... and that even the bravest man quakes in fear at the merest mention of his name...DRACULA...Lord of Vampires!
"8:32 P.M.:
"I'M A LEG-MAN, UNDERSTAND? AND WHEN I TAKE IN A PAIR OF DARK, SLENDER STEMS, RESTING IN THE DOORWAY OF THIS HOVEL I LAUGHINGLY CALL AN OFFICE, I TAKE MY SWEET TIME BEFORE CHECKING OUT THE REST OF WHAT'S STARING AT ME.
"NOT THAT THE REST IS BAD: IT'S A GIRL, BLACK, ABOUT 24, WITH A FIGURE THAT CURVES WHERE IT'S SUPPOSED TO, ONLY A HELLUVA LOT BETTER THAN MOST OF WHAT YOU SEE ON A SUN-DAY NIGHT IN SOHO.
"HER FACE IS LONG AND SLEEK LIKE A FASHION MODEL'S, AND SHE LOOKS AT ME LIKE THE WEIGHT OF THE WORLD IS SLUMPED ACROSS HER SHOULDERS, SO I STOP GAWKING AND LISTEN AS SHE SPEAKS."
MR. KING? I DIDN'T KNOW WHO TO TURN TO, BUT I NEED HELP.
HANNIBAL KING PRIVATE INVESTIGATOR
MY HUSBAND'S JUST BEEN MURDERED-- BUT I DON'T KNOW IF HIS KILLER IS A MAN... OR A BEAST!
NIGHT OF THE BLOOD STALKER!
"OH YEAH, JUST IN CASE YOU DIDN'T SEE THAT SCRAWL ON MY DOOR -- THE NAME'S KING... HANNIBAL KING, PRIVATE INVESTIGATOR.

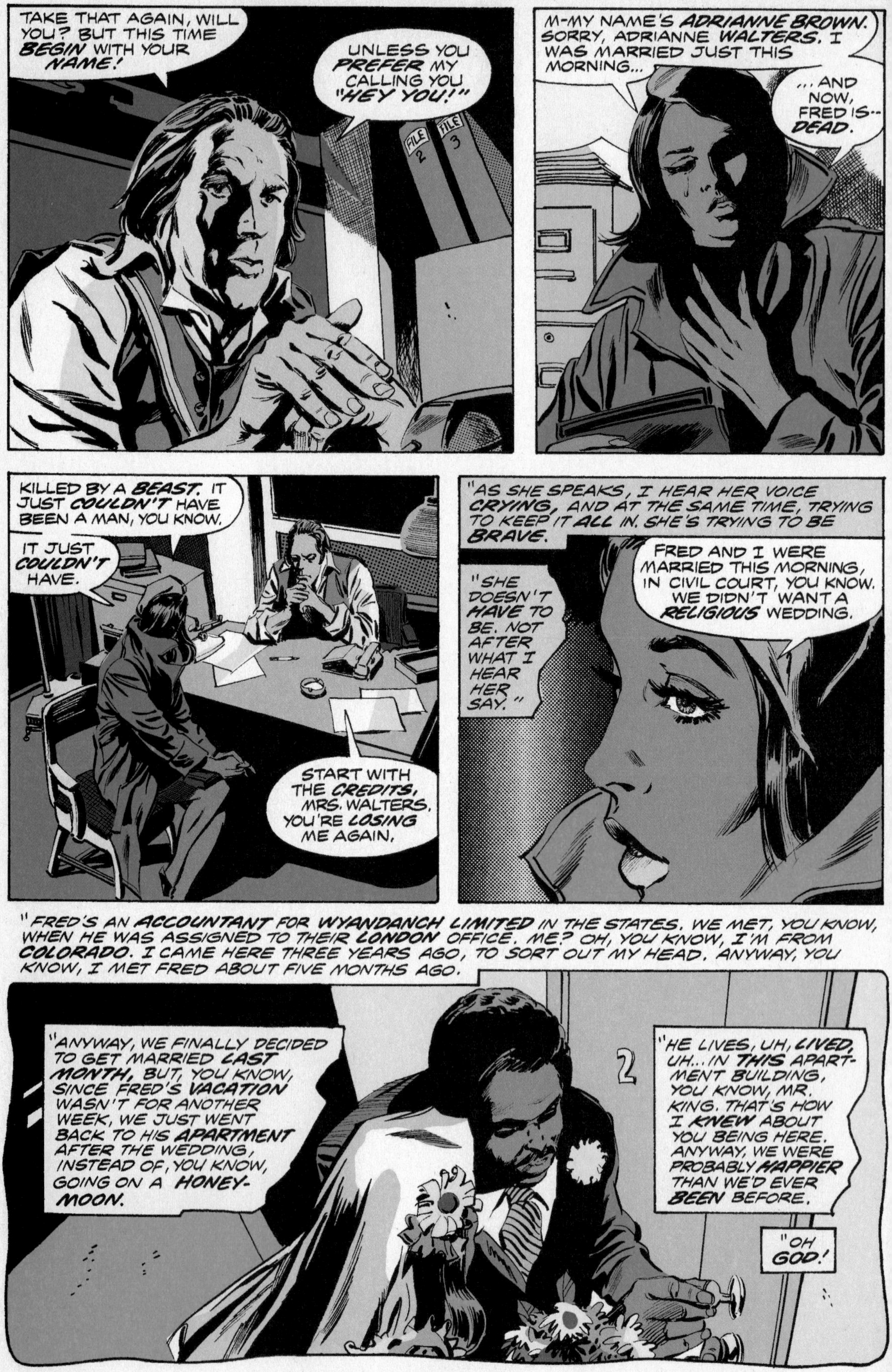
TAKE THAT AGAIN, WILL YOU? BUT THIS TIME BEGIN WITH YOUR NAME!
UNLESS YOU PREFER MY CALLING YOU "HEY YOU!"
FILE 2
FILE 3
M-MY NAME'S ADRIANNE BROWN. SORRY, ADRIANNE WALTERS. I WAS MARRIED JUST THIS MORNING...
...AND NOW, FRED IS-- DEAD.
KILLED BY A BEAST. IT JUST COULDN'T HAVE BEEN A MAN, YOU KNOW.
IT JUST COULDN'T HAVE.
START WITH THE CREDITS, MRS. WALTERS. YOU'RE LOSING ME AGAIN.
"AS SHE SPEAKS, I HEAR HER VOICE CRYING, AND AT THE SAME TIME, TRYING TO KEEP IT ALL IN. SHE'S TRYING TO BE BRAVE.
"SHE DOESN'T HAVE TO BE. NOT AFTER WHAT I HEAR HER SAY."
FRED AND I WERE MARRIED THIS MORNING, IN CIVIL COURT, YOU KNOW. WE DIDN'T WANT A RELIGIOUS WEDDING.
"FRED'S AN ACCOUNTANT FOR WYANDANCH LIMITED IN THE STATES. WE MET, YOU KNOW, WHEN HE WAS ASSIGNED TO THEIR LONDON OFFICE. ME? OH, YOU KNOW, I'M FROM COLORADO. I CAME HERE THREE YEARS AGO, TO SORT OUT MY HEAD. ANYWAY, YOU KNOW, I MET FRED ABOUT FIVE MONTHS AGO.
"ANYWAY, WE FINALLY DECIDED TO GET MARRIED LAST MONTH, BUT, YOU KNOW, SINCE FRED'S VACATION WASN'T FOR ANOTHER WEEK, WE JUST WENT BACK TO HIS APARTMENT AFTER THE WEDDING, INSTEAD OF, YOU KNOW, GOING ON A HONEY-MOON.
2
"HE LIVES, UH, LIVED, UH...IN THIS APART-MENT BUILDING, YOU KNOW, MR. KING. THAT'S HOW I KNEW ABOUT YOU BEING HERE. ANYWAY, WE WERE PROBABLY HAPPIER THAN WE'D EVER BEEN BEFORE.
"OH GOD!

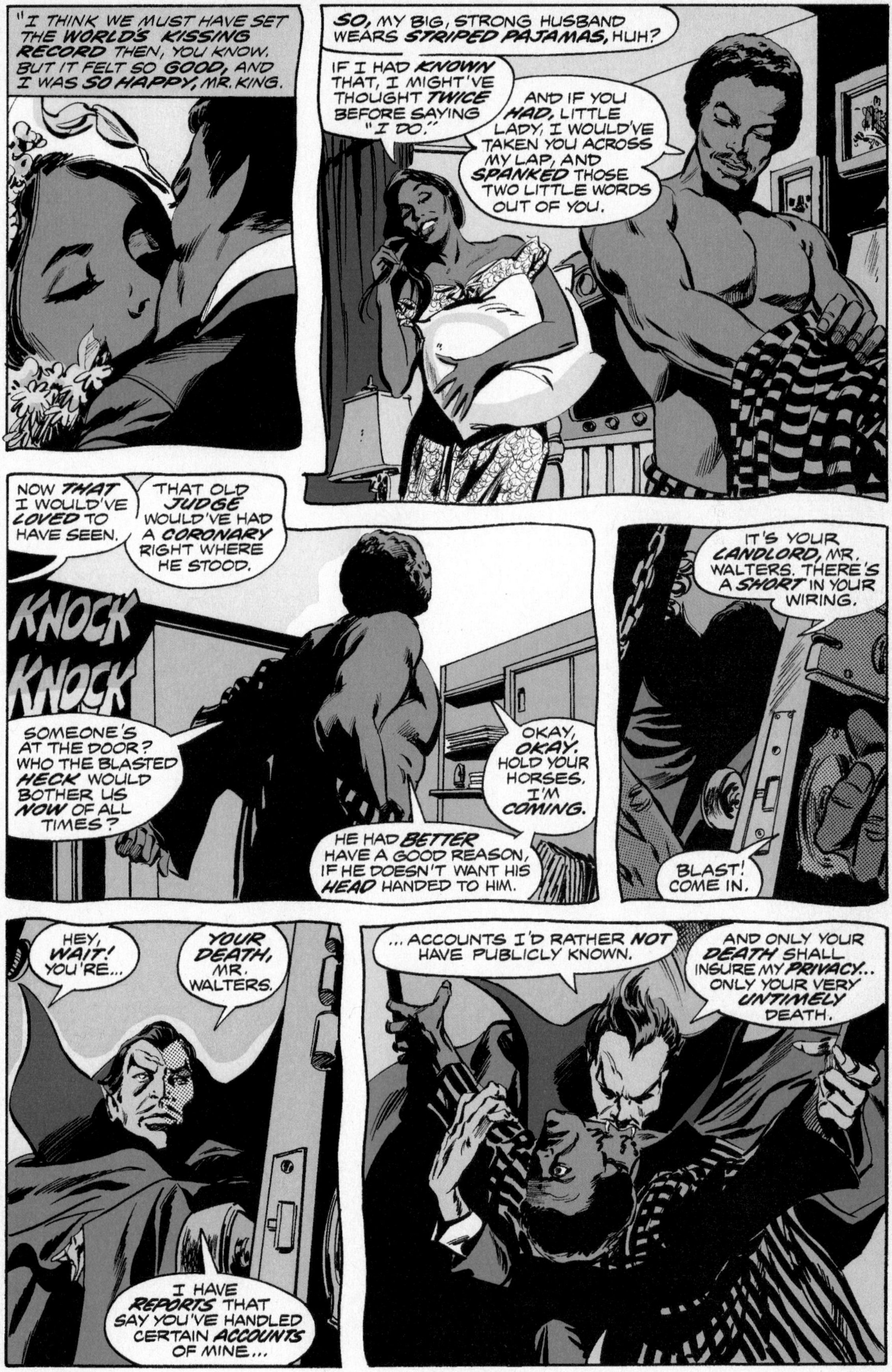
"I THINK WE MUST HAVE SET THE WORLD'S KISSING RECORD THEN, YOU KNOW. BUT IT FELT SO GOOD, AND I WAS SO HAPPY, MR. KING.
SO, MY BIG, STRONG HUSBAND WEARS STRIPED PAJAMAS, HUH?
IF I HAD KNOWN THAT, I MIGHT'VE THOUGHT TWICE BEFORE SAYING "I DO."
AND IF YOU HAD, LITTLE LADY, I WOULD'VE TAKEN YOU ACROSS MY LAP, AND SPANKED THOSE TWO LITTLE WORDS OUT OF YOU.
NOW THAT I WOULD'VE LOVED TO HAVE SEEN.
THAT OLD JUDGE WOULD'VE HAD A CORONARY RIGHT WHERE HE STOOD.
KNOCK
KNOCK
SOMEONE'S AT THE DOOR? WHO THE BLASTED HECK WOULD BOTHER US NOW OF ALL TIMES?
OKAY, OKAY. HOLD YOUR HORSES. I'M COMING.
HE HAD BETTER HAVE A GOOD REASON, IF HE DOESN'T WANT HIS HEAD HANDED TO HIM.
IT'S YOUR LANDLORD, MR. WALTERS. THERE'S A SHORT IN YOUR WIRING.
BLAST! COME IN.
HEY, WAIT! YOU'RE...
YOUR DEATH, MR. WALTERS.
I HAVE REPORTS THAT SAY YOU'VE HANDLED CERTAIN ACCOUNTS OF MINE...
... ACCOUNTS I'D RATHER NOT HAVE PUBLICLY KNOWN.
AND ONLY YOUR DEATH SHALL INSURE MY PRIVACY... ONLY YOUR VERY UNTIMELY DEATH.

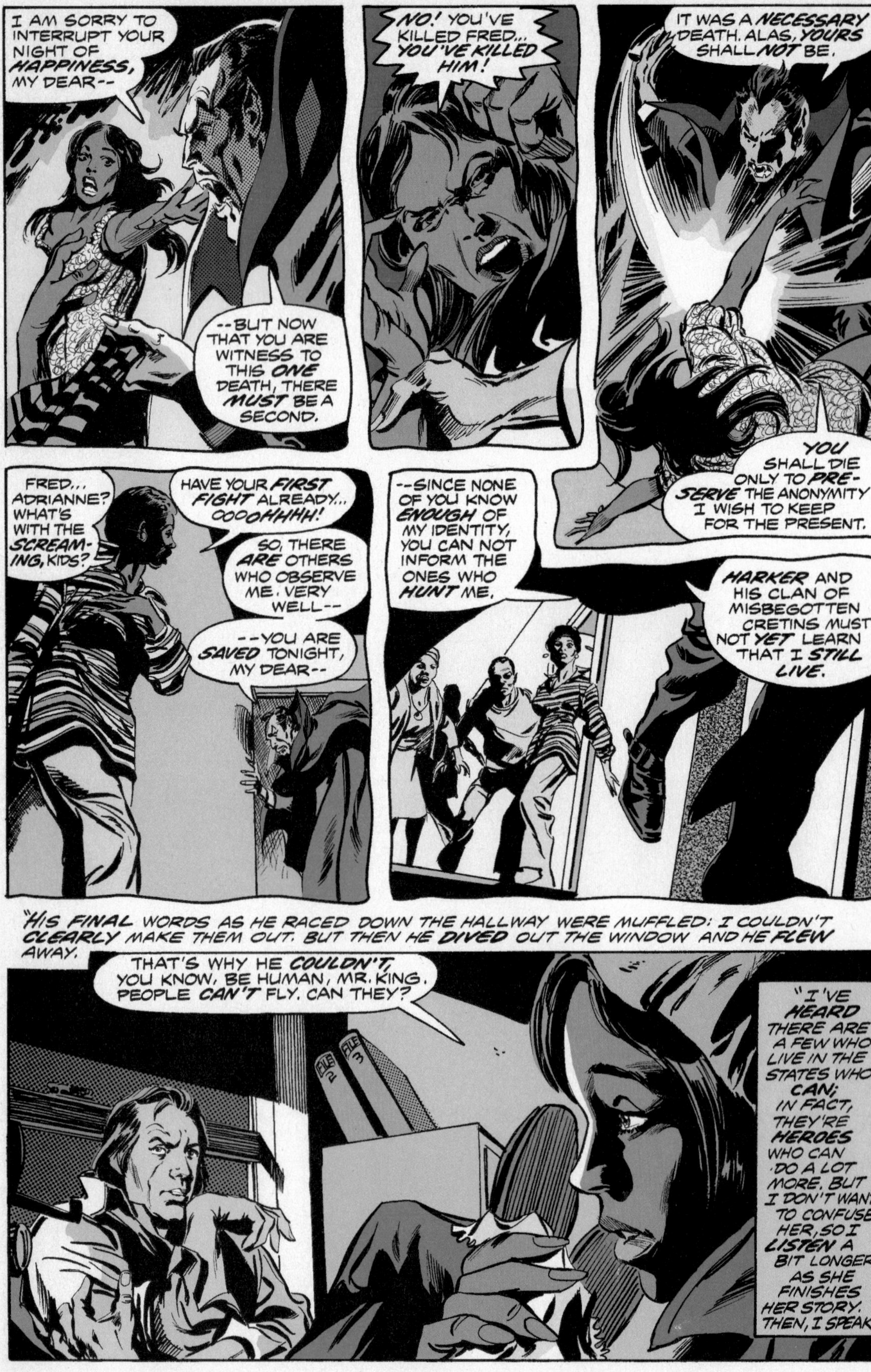

I AM SORRY TO INTERRUPT YOUR NIGHT OF HAPPINESS, MY DEAR--
--BUT NOW THAT YOU ARE WITNESS TO THIS ONE DEATH, THERE MUST BE A SECOND.
NO! YOU'VE KILLED FRED... YOU'VE KILLED HIM!
IT WAS A NECESSARY DEATH. ALAS, YOURS SHALL NOT BE.
YOU SHALL DIE ONLY TO PRESERVE THE ANONYMITY I WISH TO KEEP FOR THE PRESENT.
FRED... ADRIANNE? WHAT'S WITH THE SCREAMING, KIDS?
HAVE YOUR FIRST FIGHT ALREADY... OOOOHHHH!
SO, THERE ARE OTHERS WHO OBSERVE ME. VERY WELL--
--YOU ARE SAVED TONIGHT, MY DEAR--
--SINCE NONE OF YOU KNOW ENOUGH OF MY IDENTITY, YOU CAN NOT INFORM THE ONES WHO HUNT ME.
HARKER AND HIS CLAN OF MISBEGOTTEN CRETINS MUST NOT YET LEARN THAT I STILL LIVE.
"HIS FINAL WORDS AS HE RACED DOWN THE HALLWAY WERE MUFFLED: I COULDN'T CLEARLY MAKE THEM OUT. BUT THEN HE DIVED OUT THE WINDOW AND HE FLEW AWAY.
THAT'S WHY HE COULDN'T, YOU KNOW, BE HUMAN, MR. KING. PEOPLE CAN'T FLY. CAN THEY?
"I'VE HEARD THERE ARE A FEW WHO LIVE IN THE STATES WHO CAN; IN FACT, THEY'RE HEROES WHO CAN DO A LOT MORE. BUT I DON'T WANT TO CONFUSE HER, SO I LISTEN A BIT LONGER AS SHE FINISHES HER STORY. THEN, I SPEAK.
FILE 2
FILE 3

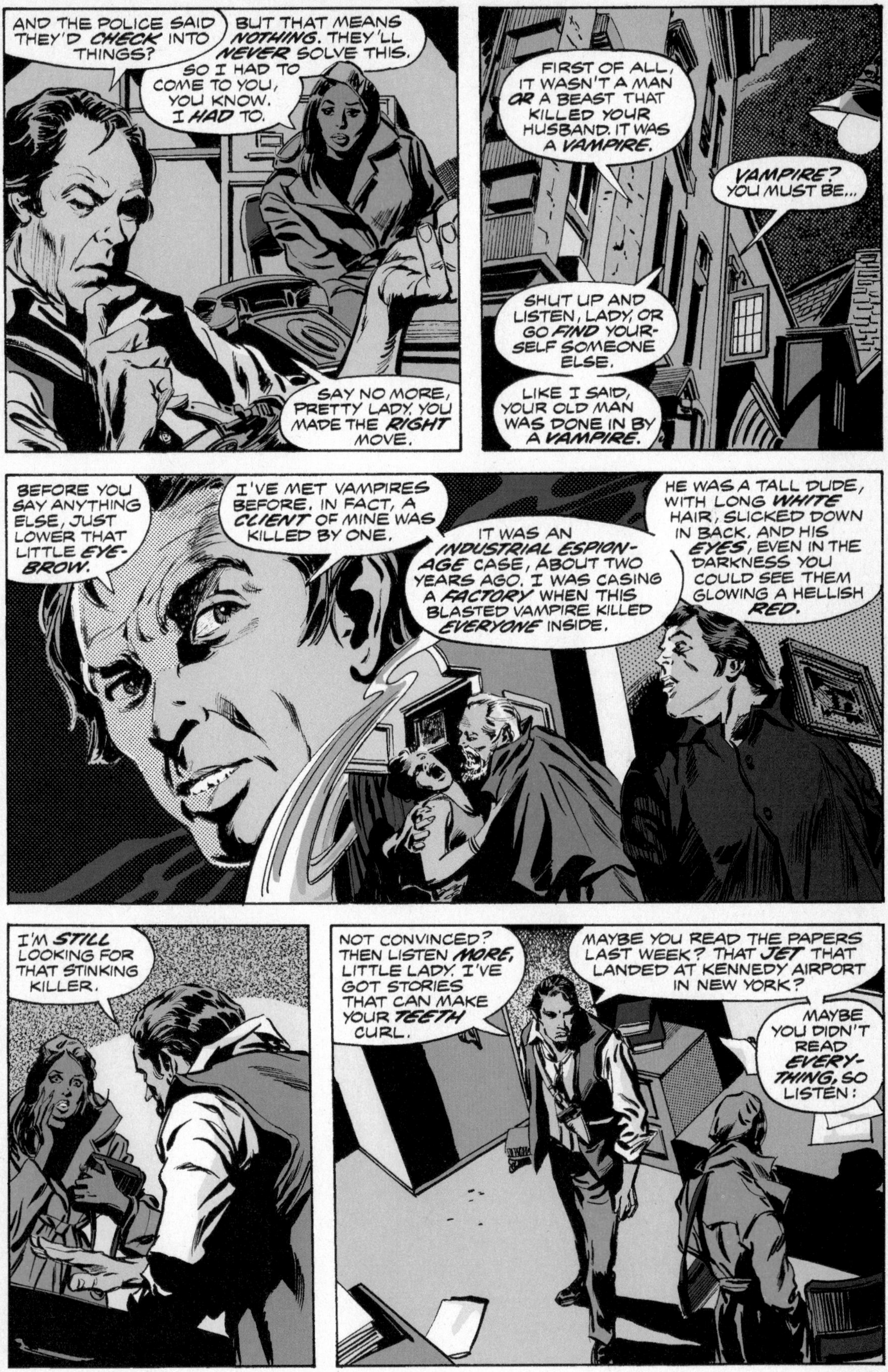
AND THE POLICE SAID THEY'D CHECK INTO THINGS?
BUT THAT MEANS NOTHING. THEY'LL NEVER SOLVE THIS.
SO I HAD TO COME TO YOU, YOU KNOW. I HAD TO.
SAY NO MORE, PRETTY LADY. YOU MADE THE RIGHT MOVE.
FIRST OF ALL, IT WASN'T A MAN OR A BEAST THAT KILLED YOUR HUSBAND. IT WAS A VAMPIRE.
VAMPIRE? YOU MUST BE...
SHUT UP AND LISTEN, LADY, OR GO FIND YOURSELF SOMEONE ELSE.
LIKE I SAID, YOUR OLD MAN WAS DONE IN BY A VAMPIRE.
BEFORE YOU SAY ANYTHING ELSE, JUST LOWER THAT LITTLE EYE-BROW.
I'VE MET VAMPIRES BEFORE. IN FACT, A CLIENT OF MINE WAS KILLED BY ONE.
IT WAS AN INDUSTRIAL ESPIONAGE CASE, ABOUT TWO YEARS AGO. I WAS CASING A FACTORY WHEN THIS BLASTED VAMPIRE KILLED EVERYONE INSIDE.
HE WAS A TALL DUDE, WITH LONG WHITE HAIR, SLICKED DOWN IN BACK. AND HIS EYES, EVEN IN THE DARKNESS YOU COULD SEE THEM GLOWING A HELLISH RED.
I'M STILL LOOKING FOR THAT STINKING KILLER.
NOT CONVINCED? THEN LISTEN MORE, LITTLE LADY. I'VE GOT STORIES THAT CAN MAKE YOUR TEETH CURL.
MAYBE YOU READ THE PAPERS LAST WEEK? THAT JET THAT LANDED AT KENNEDY AIRPORT IN NEW YORK?
MAYBE YOU DIDN'T READ EVERYTHING, SO LISTEN:

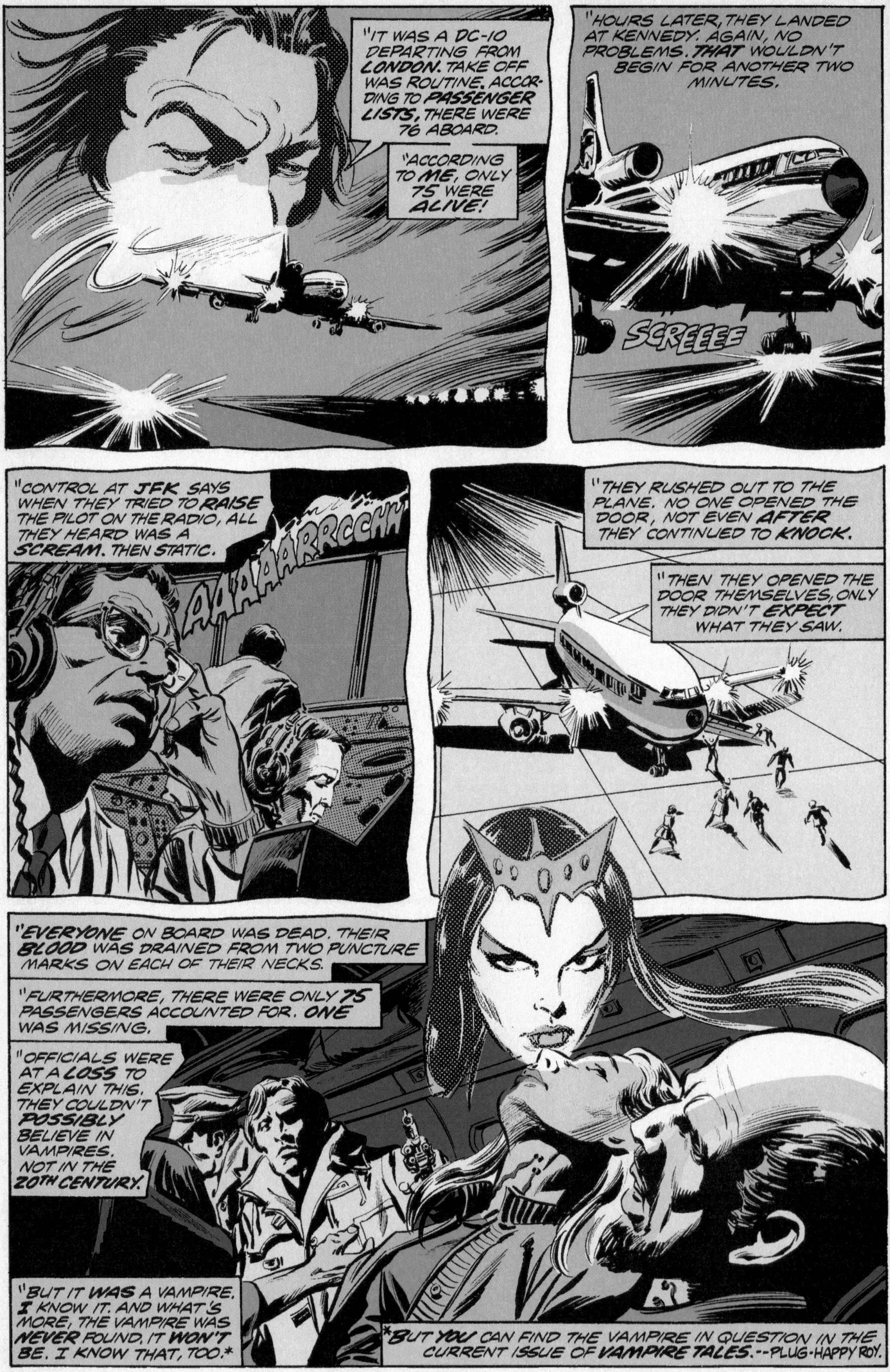
"IT WAS A DC-10 DEPARTING FROM LONDON. TAKE OFF WAS ROUTINE. ACCORDING TO PASSENGER LISTS, THERE WERE 76 ABOARD.
"ACCORDING TO ME, ONLY 75 WERE ALIVE!
"HOURS LATER, THEY LANDED AT KENNEDY. AGAIN, NO PROBLEMS. THAT WOULDN'T BEGIN FOR ANOTHER TWO MINUTES.
SCREEEEE
"CONTROL AT JFK SAYS WHEN THEY TRIED TO RAISE THE PILOT ON THE RADIO, ALL THEY HEARD WAS A SCREAM. THEN STATIC.
AAAAARRCCHH
"THEY RUSHED OUT TO THE PLANE. NO ONE OPENED THE DOOR, NOT EVEN AFTER THEY CONTINUED TO KNOCK.
"THEN THEY OPENED THE DOOR THEMSELVES, ONLY THEY DIDN'T EXPECT WHAT THEY SAW.
"EVERYONE ON BOARD WAS DEAD. THEIR BLOOD WAS DRAINED FROM TWO PUNCTURE MARKS ON EACH OF THEIR NECKS.
"FURTHERMORE, THERE WERE ONLY 75 PASSENGERS ACCOUNTED FOR. ONE WAS MISSING.
"OFFICIALS WERE AT A LOSS TO EXPLAIN THIS. THEY COULDN'T POSSIBLY BELIEVE IN VAMPIRES. NOT IN THE 20TH CENTURY.
"BUT IT WAS A VAMPIRE. I KNOW IT. AND WHAT'S MORE, THE VAMPIRE WAS NEVER FOUND. IT WON'T BE. I KNOW THAT, TOO.*
*BUT YOU CAN FIND THE VAMPIRE IN QUESTION IN THE CURRENT ISSUE OF VAMPIRE TALES.--PLUG-HAPPY ROY.

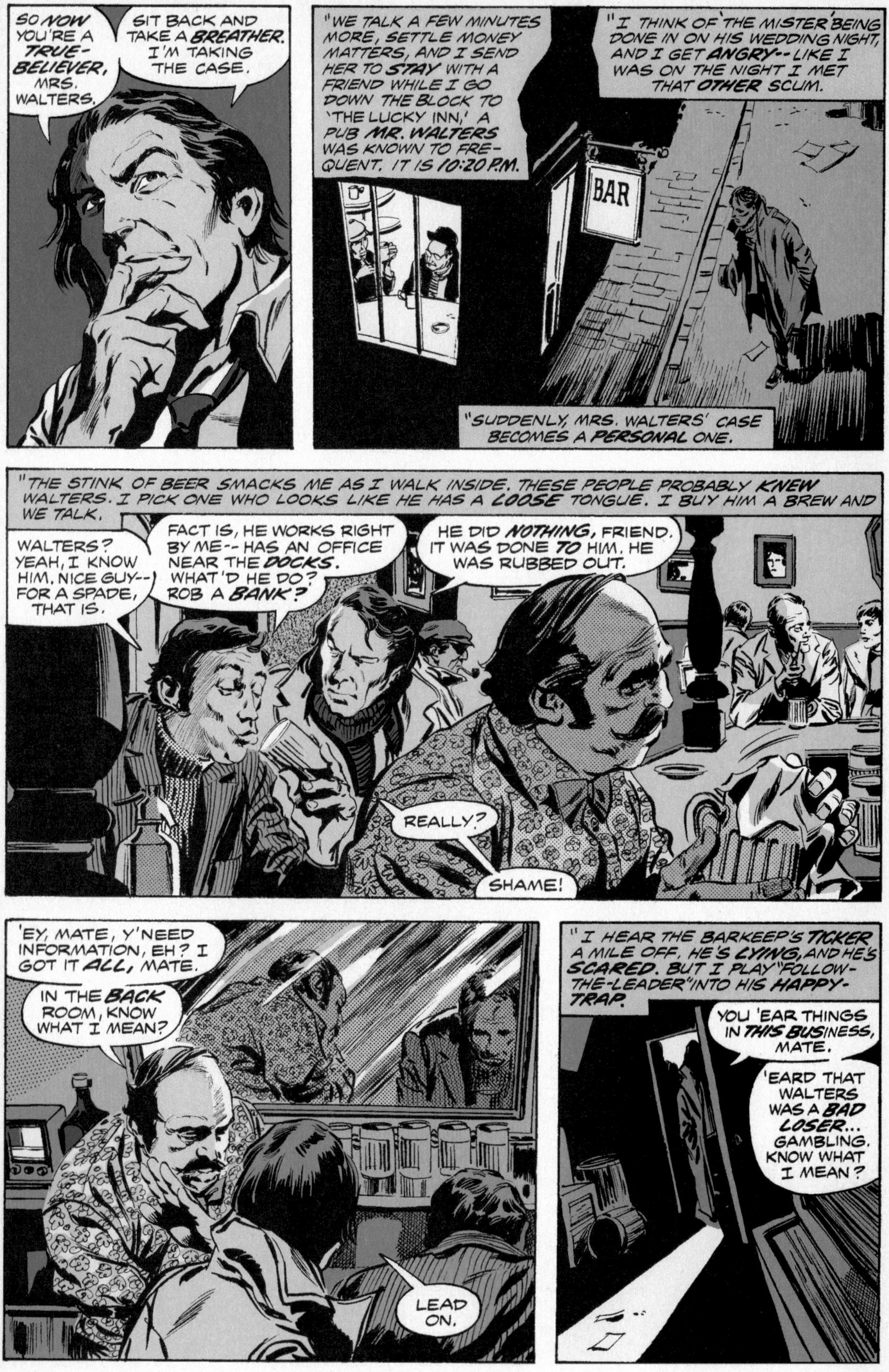
SO NOW YOU'RE A TRUE-BELIEVER, MRS. WALTERS.
SIT BACK AND TAKE A BREATHER. I'M TAKING THE CASE.
"WE TALK A FEW MINUTES MORE, SETTLE MONEY MATTERS, AND I SEND HER TO STAY WITH A FRIEND WHILE I GO DOWN THE BLOCK TO 'THE LUCKY INN,' A PUB MR. WALTERS WAS KNOWN TO FREQUENT. IT IS 10:20 P.M.
BAR
"I THINK OF THE MISTER BEING DONE IN ON HIS WEDDING NIGHT, AND I GET ANGRY-- LIKE I WAS ON THE NIGHT I MET THAT OTHER SCUM.
"SUDDENLY, MRS. WALTERS' CASE BECOMES A PERSONAL ONE.
"THE STINK OF BEER SMACKS ME AS I WALK INSIDE. THESE PEOPLE PROBABLY KNEW WALTERS. I PICK ONE WHO LOOKS LIKE HE HAS A LOOSE TONGUE. I BUY HIM A BREW AND WE TALK.
WALTERS? YEAH, I KNOW HIM. NICE GUY-- FOR A SPADE, THAT IS.
FACT IS, HE WORKS RIGHT BY ME-- HAS AN OFFICE NEAR THE DOCKS. WHAT'D HE DO? ROB A BANK?
HE DID NOTHING, FRIEND. IT WAS DONE TO HIM. HE WAS RUBBED OUT.
REALLY?
SHAME!
'EY, MATE, Y'NEED INFORMATION, EH? I GOT IT ALL, MATE.
IN THE BACK ROOM, KNOW WHAT I MEAN?
LEAD ON.
"I HEAR THE BARKEEP'S TICKER A MILE OFF. HE'S LYING, AND HE'S SCARED. BUT I PLAY "FOLLOW-THE-LEADER" INTO HIS HAPPY-TRAP.
YOU 'EAR THINGS IN THIS BUSINESS, MATE.
'EARD THAT WALTERS WAS A BAD LOSER... GAMBLING. KNOW WHAT I MEAN?

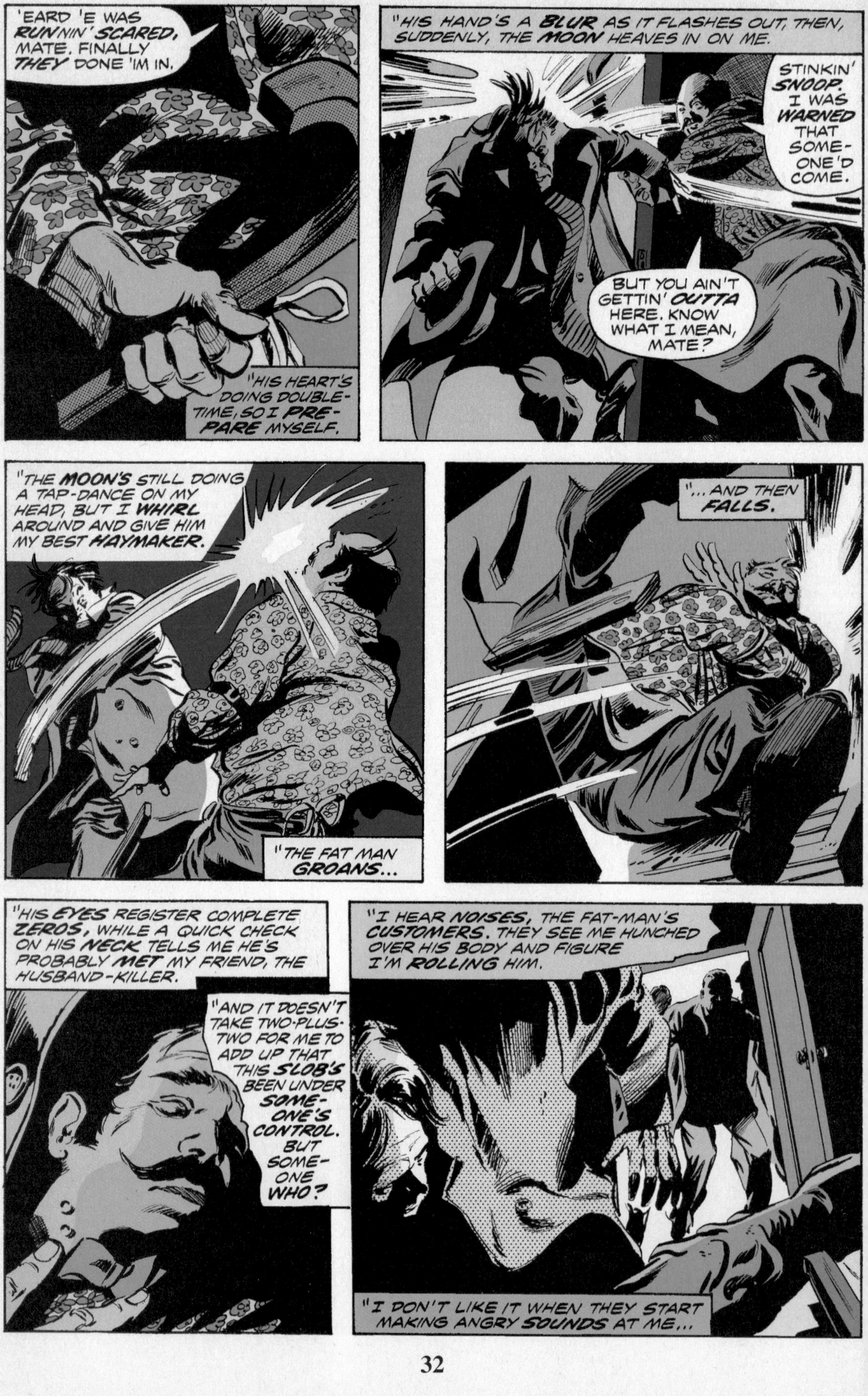
'EARD 'E WAS RUNNIN' SCARED, MATE. FINALLY THEY DONE 'IM IN.
"HIS HEART'S DOING DOUBLE-TIME, SO I PRE-PARE MYSELF.
"HIS HAND'S A BLUR AS IT FLASHES OUT, THEN, SUDDENLY, THE MOON HEAVES IN ON ME.
STINKIN' SNOOP. I WAS WARNED THAT SOME-ONE'D COME.
BUT YOU AIN'T GETTIN' OUTTA HERE. KNOW WHAT I MEAN, MATE?
"THE MOON'S STILL DOING A TAP-DANCE ON MY HEAD, BUT I WHIRL AROUND AND GIVE HIM MY BEST HAYMAKER.
"THE FAT MAN GROANS...
"...AND THEN FALLS.
"HIS EYES REGISTER COMPLETE ZEROS, WHILE A QUICK CHECK ON HIS NECK TELLS ME HE'S PROBABLY MET MY FRIEND, THE HUSBAND-KILLER.
"AND IT DOESN'T TAKE TWO-PLUS-TWO FOR ME TO ADD UP THAT THIS SLOB'S BEEN UNDER SOME-ONE'S CONTROL. BUT SOME-ONE WHO?
"I HEAR NOISES, THE FAT-MAN'S CUSTOMERS. THEY SEE ME HUNCHED OVER HIS BODY AND FIGURE I'M ROLLING HIM.
"I DON'T LIKE IT WHEN THEY START MAKING ANGRY SOUNDS AT ME...

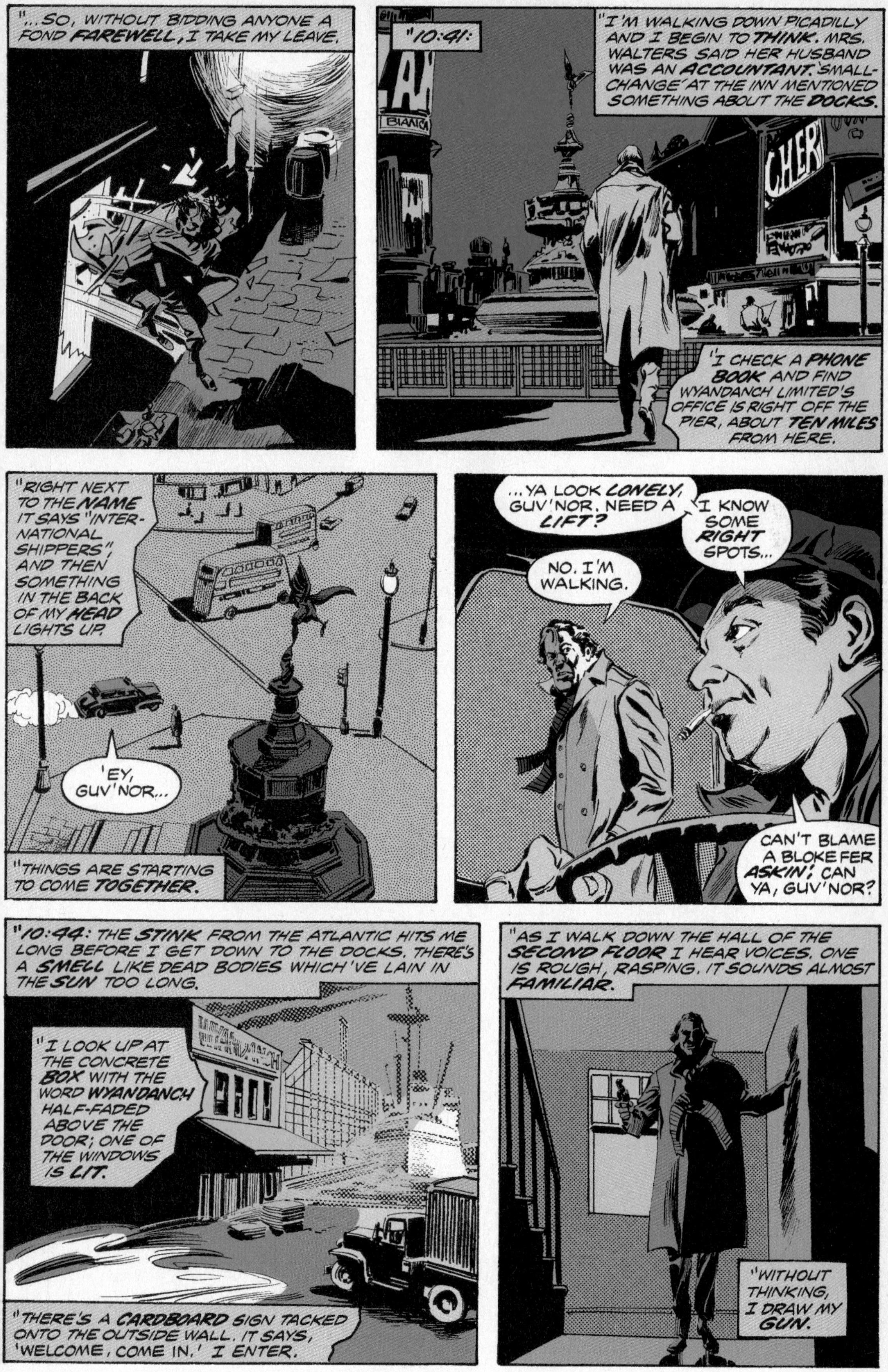
"...SO, WITHOUT BIDDING ANYONE A FOND FAREWELL, I TAKE MY LEAVE.
"10:41:
"I'M WALKING DOWN PICADILLY AND I BEGIN TO THINK. MRS. WALTERS SAID HER HUSBAND WAS AN ACCOUNTANT. 'SMALL-CHANGE' AT THE INN MENTIONED SOMETHING ABOUT THE DOCKS.
"I CHECK A PHONE BOOK AND FIND WYANDANCH LIMITED'S OFFICE IS RIGHT OFF THE PIER, ABOUT TEN MILES FROM HERE.
"RIGHT NEXT TO THE NAME IT SAYS "INTERNATIONAL SHIPPERS", AND THEN SOMETHING IN THE BACK OF MY HEAD LIGHTS UP.
'EY, GUV'NOR...
"THINGS ARE STARTING TO COME TOGETHER.
...YA LOOK LONELY, GUV'NOR. NEED A LIFT?
I KNOW SOME RIGHT SPOTS...
NO. I'M WALKING.
CAN'T BLAME A BLOKE FER ASKIN'! CAN YA, GUV'NOR?
"10:44: THE STINK FROM THE ATLANTIC HITS ME LONG BEFORE I GET DOWN TO THE DOCKS. THERE'S A SMELL LIKE DEAD BODIES WHICH'VE LAIN IN THE SUN TOO LONG.
"I LOOK UP AT THE CONCRETE BOX WITH THE WORD WYANDANCH HALF-FADED ABOVE THE DOOR; ONE OF THE WINDOWS IS LIT.
"THERE'S A CARDBOARD SIGN TACKED ONTO THE OUTSIDE WALL. IT SAYS, 'WELCOME, COME IN.' I ENTER.
"AS I WALK DOWN THE HALL OF THE SECOND FLOOR I HEAR VOICES. ONE IS ROUGH, RASPING. IT SOUNDS ALMOST FAMILIAR.
"WITHOUT THINKING, I DRAW MY GUN.

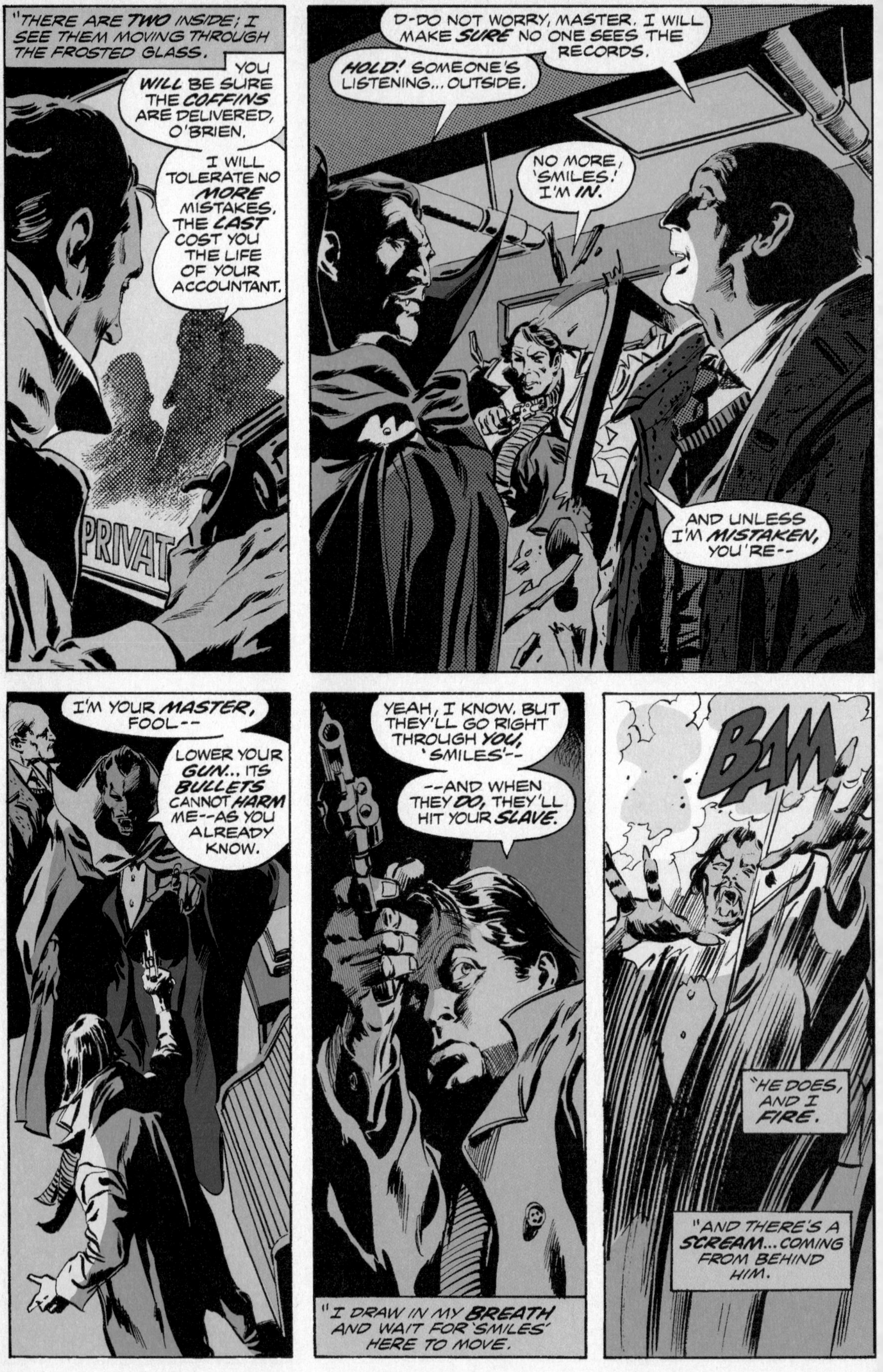
"THERE ARE TWO INSIDE; I SEE THEM MOVING THROUGH THE FROSTED GLASS.
YOU WILL BE SURE THE COFFINS ARE DELIVERED, O'BRIEN.
I WILL TOLERATE NO MORE MISTAKES. THE LAST COST YOU THE LIFE OF YOUR ACCOUNTANT.
PRIVAT
D-DO NOT WORRY, MASTER. I WILL MAKE SURE NO ONE SEES THE RECORDS.
HOLD! SOMEONE'S LISTENING... OUTSIDE.
NO MORE, 'SMILES.' I'M IN.
AND UNLESS I'M MISTAKEN, YOU'RE--
I'M YOUR MASTER, FOOL--
LOWER YOUR GUN... ITS BULLETS CANNOT HARM ME--AS YOU ALREADY KNOW.
YEAH, I KNOW. BUT THEY'LL GO RIGHT THROUGH YOU, 'SMILES'--
--AND WHEN THEY DO, THEY'LL HIT YOUR SLAVE.
"I DRAW IN MY BREATH AND WAIT FOR 'SMILES' HERE TO MOVE.
BAM
"HE DOES, AND I FIRE.
"AND THERE'S A SCREAM... COMING FROM BEHIND HIM.

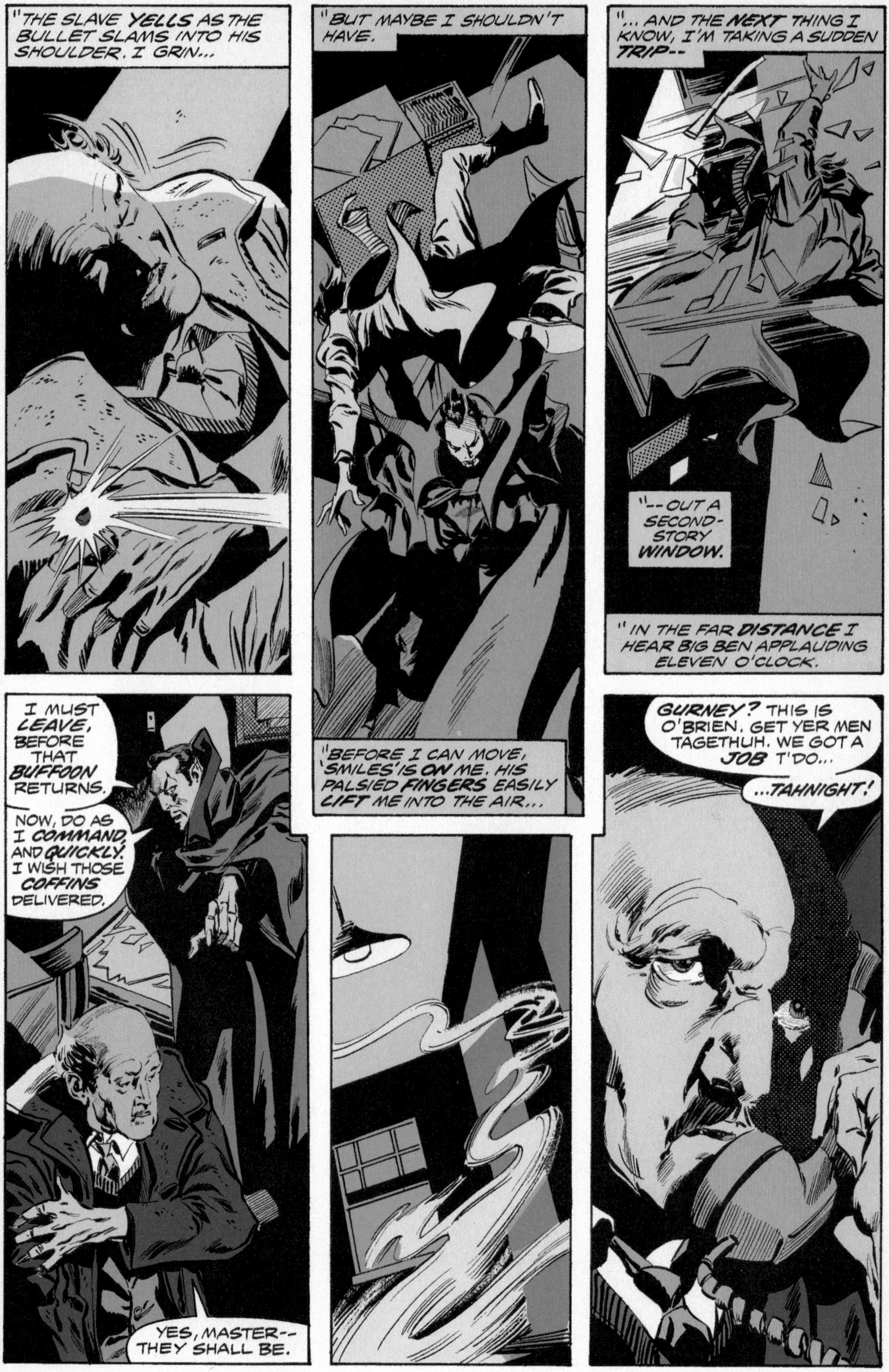
"THE SLAVE YELLS AS THE BULLET SLAMS INTO HIS SHOULDER. I GRIN...
"BUT MAYBE I SHOULDN'T HAVE.
"BEFORE I CAN MOVE, 'SMILES' IS ON ME. HIS PALSIED FINGERS EASILY LIFT ME INTO THE AIR...
"... AND THE NEXT THING I KNOW, I'M TAKING A SUDDEN TRIP--
"--OUT A SECOND-STORY WINDOW.
"IN THE FAR DISTANCE I HEAR BIG BEN APPLAUDING ELEVEN O'CLOCK.
I MUST LEAVE, BEFORE THAT BUFFOON RETURNS.
NOW, DO AS I COMMAND, AND QUICKLY. I WISH THOSE COFFINS DELIVERED.
YES, MASTER-- THEY SHALL BE.
GURNEY? THIS IS O'BRIEN. GET YER MEN TAGETHUH. WE GOT A JOB T'DO...
...TAHNIGHT!

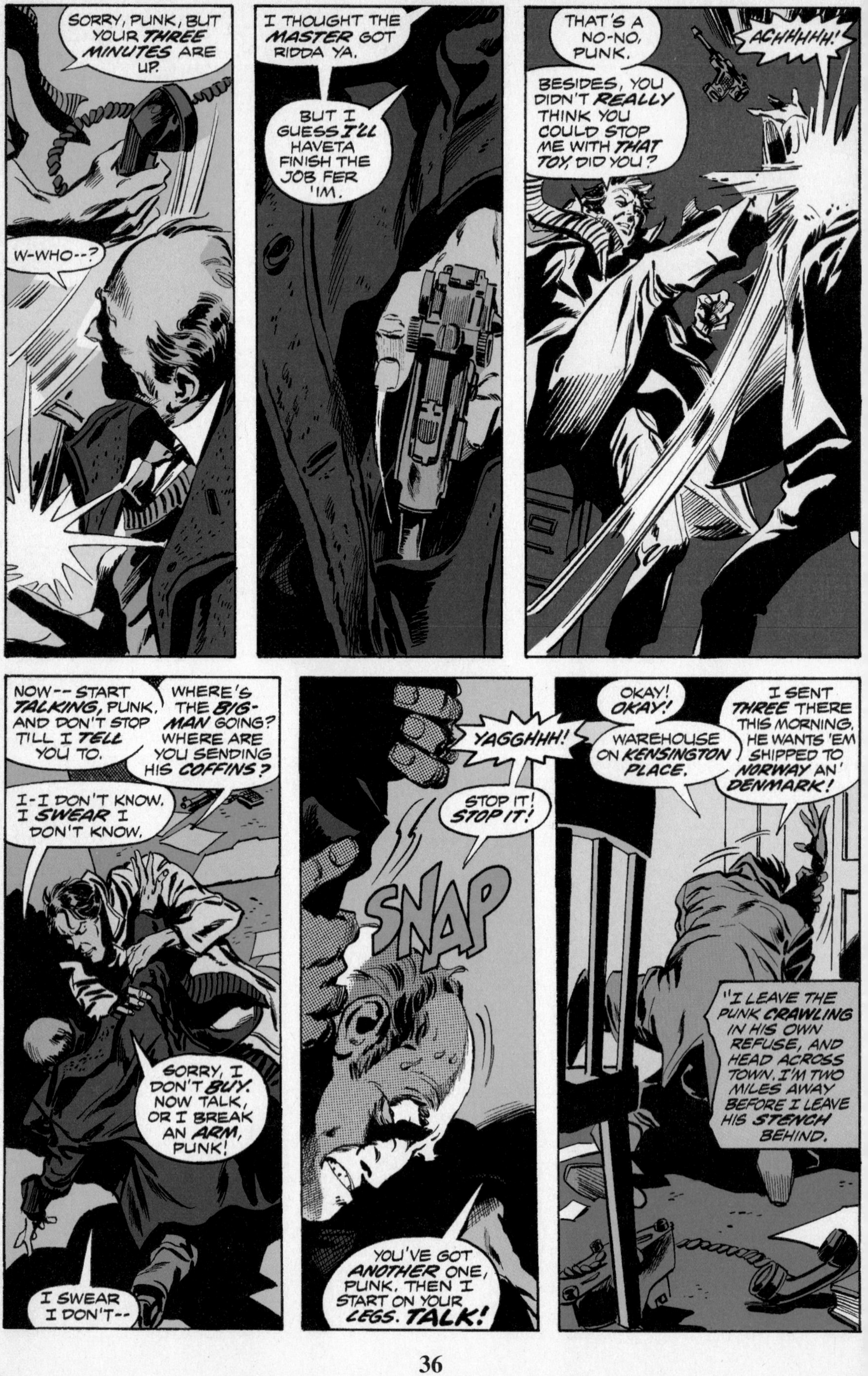
SORRY, PUNK, BUT YOUR THREE MINUTES ARE UP.
W-WHO--?
I THOUGHT THE MASTER GOT RIDDA YA.
BUT I GUESS I'LL HAVETA FINISH THE JOB FER 'IM.
THAT'S A NO-NO, PUNK.
BESIDES, YOU DIDN'T REALLY THINK YOU COULD STOP ME WITH THAT TOY, DID YOU?
ACHHHHH!
NOW-- START TALKING, PUNK. AND DON'T STOP TILL I TELL YOU TO.
WHERE'S THE BIG-MAN GOING? WHERE ARE YOU SENDING HIS COFFINS?
I-I DON'T KNOW. I SWEAR I DON'T KNOW.
SORRY, I DON'T BUY. NOW TALK, OR I BREAK AN ARM, PUNK!
I SWEAR I DON'T--
YAGGHHH!
STOP IT! STOP IT!
SNAP
YOU'VE GOT ANOTHER ONE, PUNK. THEN I START ON YOUR LEGS. TALK!
OKAY! OKAY!
WAREHOUSE ON KENSINGTON PLACE.
I SENT THREE THERE THIS MORNING. HE WANTS 'EM SHIPPED TO NORWAY AN' DENMARK!
"I LEAVE THE PUNK CRAWLING IN HIS OWN REFUSE, AND HEAD ACROSS TOWN. I'M TWO MILES AWAY BEFORE I LEAVE HIS STENCH BEHIND.

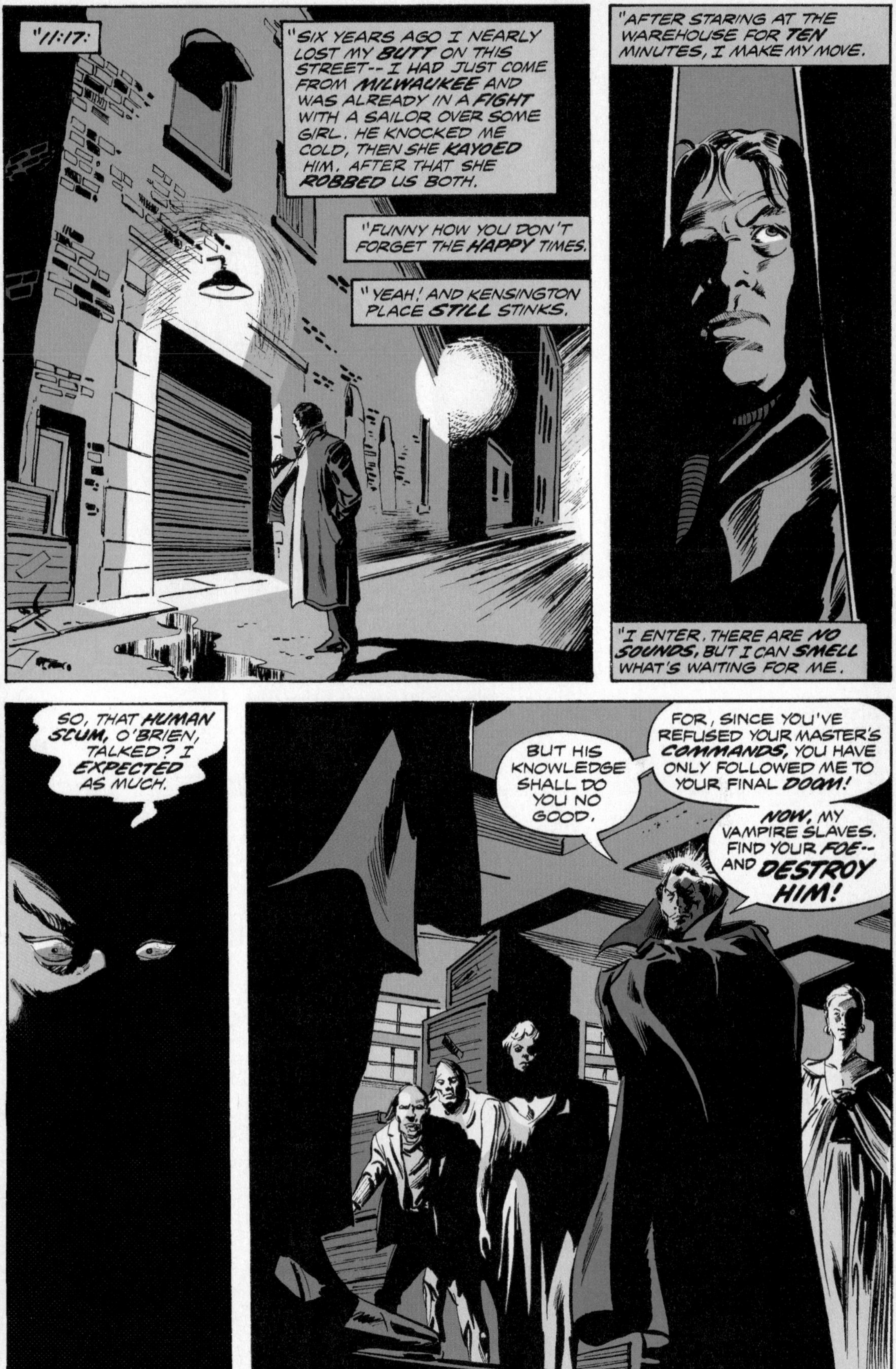
"11:17:
"SIX YEARS AGO I NEARLY LOST MY BUTT ON THIS STREET-- I HAD JUST COME FROM MILWAUKEE AND WAS ALREADY IN A FIGHT WITH A SAILOR OVER SOME GIRL. HE KNOCKED ME COLD, THEN SHE KAYOED HIM. AFTER THAT SHE ROBBED US BOTH.
"FUNNY HOW YOU DON'T FORGET THE HAPPY TIMES.
"YEAH! AND KENSINGTON PLACE STILL STINKS.
"AFTER STARING AT THE WAREHOUSE FOR TEN MINUTES, I MAKE MY MOVE.
"I ENTER. THERE ARE NO SOUNDS, BUT I CAN SMELL WHAT'S WAITING FOR ME.
SO, THAT HUMAN SCUM, O'BRIEN, TALKED? I EXPECTED AS MUCH.
BUT HIS KNOWLEDGE SHALL DO YOU NO GOOD.
FOR, SINCE YOU'VE REFUSED YOUR MASTER'S COMMANDS, YOU HAVE ONLY FOLLOWED ME TO YOUR FINAL DOOM!
NOW, MY VAMPIRE SLAVES. FIND YOUR FOE-- AND DESTROY HIM!

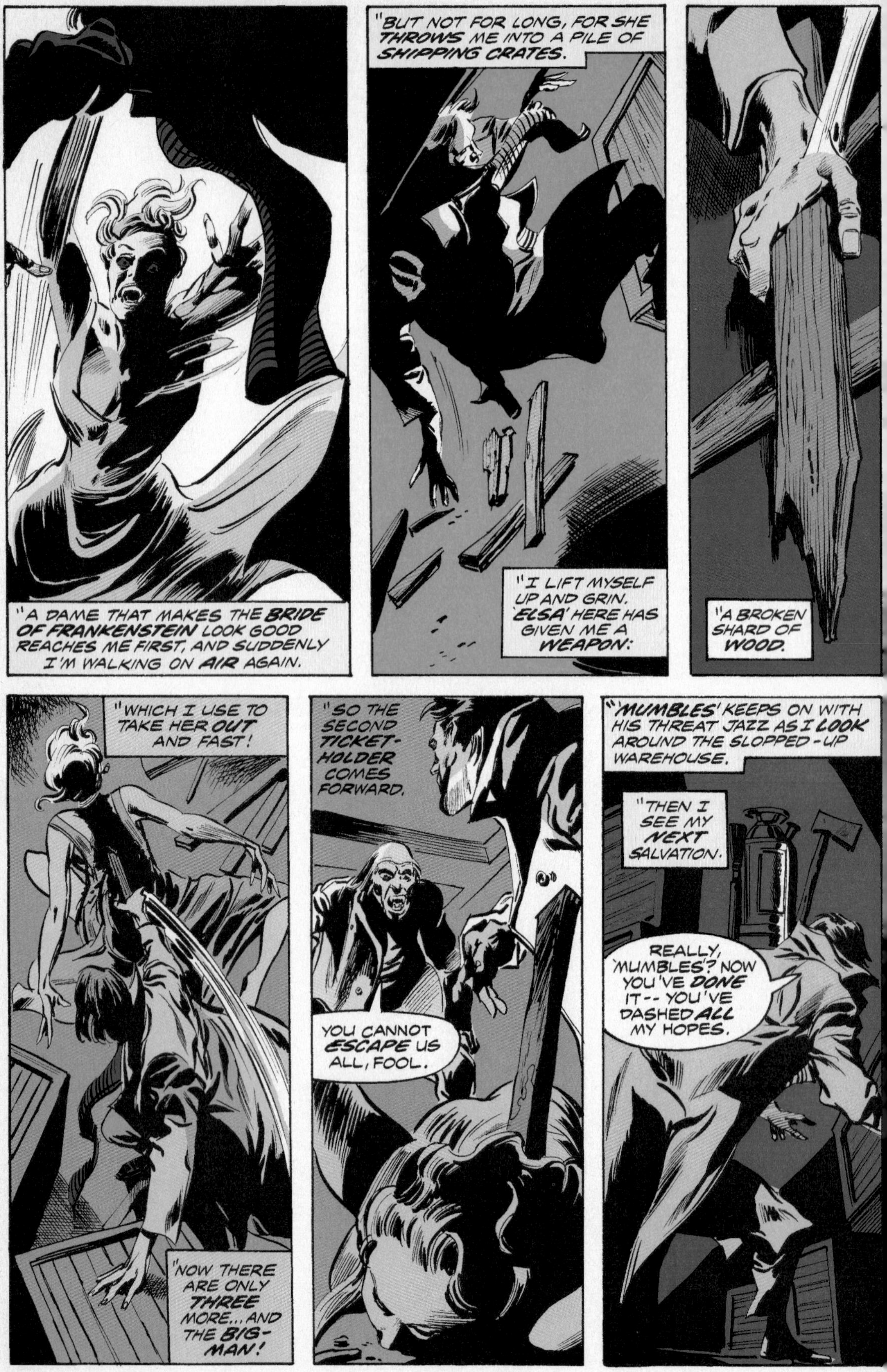
"A DAME THAT MAKES THE BRIDE OF FRANKENSTEIN LOOK GOOD REACHES ME FIRST, AND SUDDENLY I'M WALKING ON AIR AGAIN.
"BUT NOT FOR LONG, FOR SHE THROWS ME INTO A PILE OF SHIPPING CRATES.
"I LIFT MYSELF UP AND GRIN. 'ELSA' HERE HAS GIVEN ME A WEAPON:
"A BROKEN SHARD OF WOOD.
"WHICH I USE TO TAKE HER OUT AND FAST!
"NOW THERE ARE ONLY THREE MORE... AND THE BIG-MAN!
"SO THE SECOND TICKET-HOLDER COMES FORWARD.
YOU CANNOT ESCAPE US ALL, FOOL.
"'MUMBLES' KEEPS ON WITH HIS THREAT JAZZ AS I LOOK AROUND THE SLOPPED-UP WAREHOUSE.
"THEN I SEE MY NEXT SALVATION.
REALLY, 'MUMBLES'? NOW YOU'VE DONE IT-- YOU'VE DASHED ALL MY HOPES.

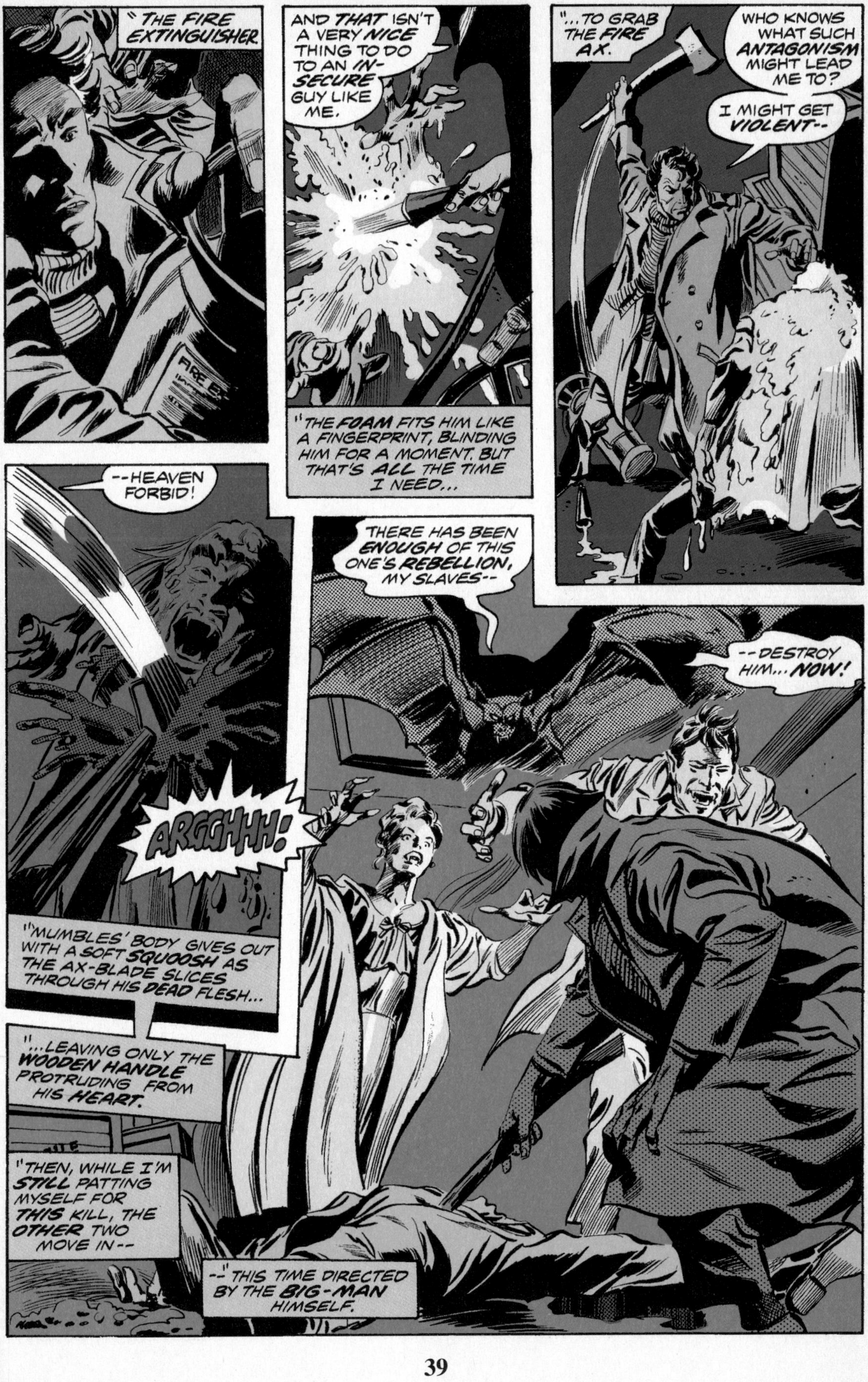
"THE FIRE EXTINGUISHER.
AND THAT ISN'T A VERY NICE THING TO DO TO AN IN-SECURE GUY LIKE ME.
"THE FOAM FITS HIM LIKE A FINGERPRINT, BLINDING HIM FOR A MOMENT. BUT THAT'S ALL THE TIME I NEED...
"...TO GRAB THE FIRE AX.
WHO KNOWS WHAT SUCH ANTAGONISM MIGHT LEAD ME TO?
I MIGHT GET VIOLENT--
--HEAVEN FORBID!
ARGGHHH!
"MUMBLES' BODY GIVES OUT WITH A SOFT SQUOOSH AS THE AX-BLADE SLICES THROUGH HIS DEAD FLESH...
"...LEAVING ONLY THE WOODEN HANDLE PROTRUDING FROM HIS HEART.
THERE HAS BEEN ENOUGH OF THIS ONE'S REBELLION, MY SLAVES--
--DESTROY HIM... NOW!
"THEN, WHILE I'M STILL PATTING MYSELF FOR THIS KILL, THE OTHER TWO MOVE IN--
--" THIS TIME DIRECTED BY THE BIG-MAN HIMSELF.

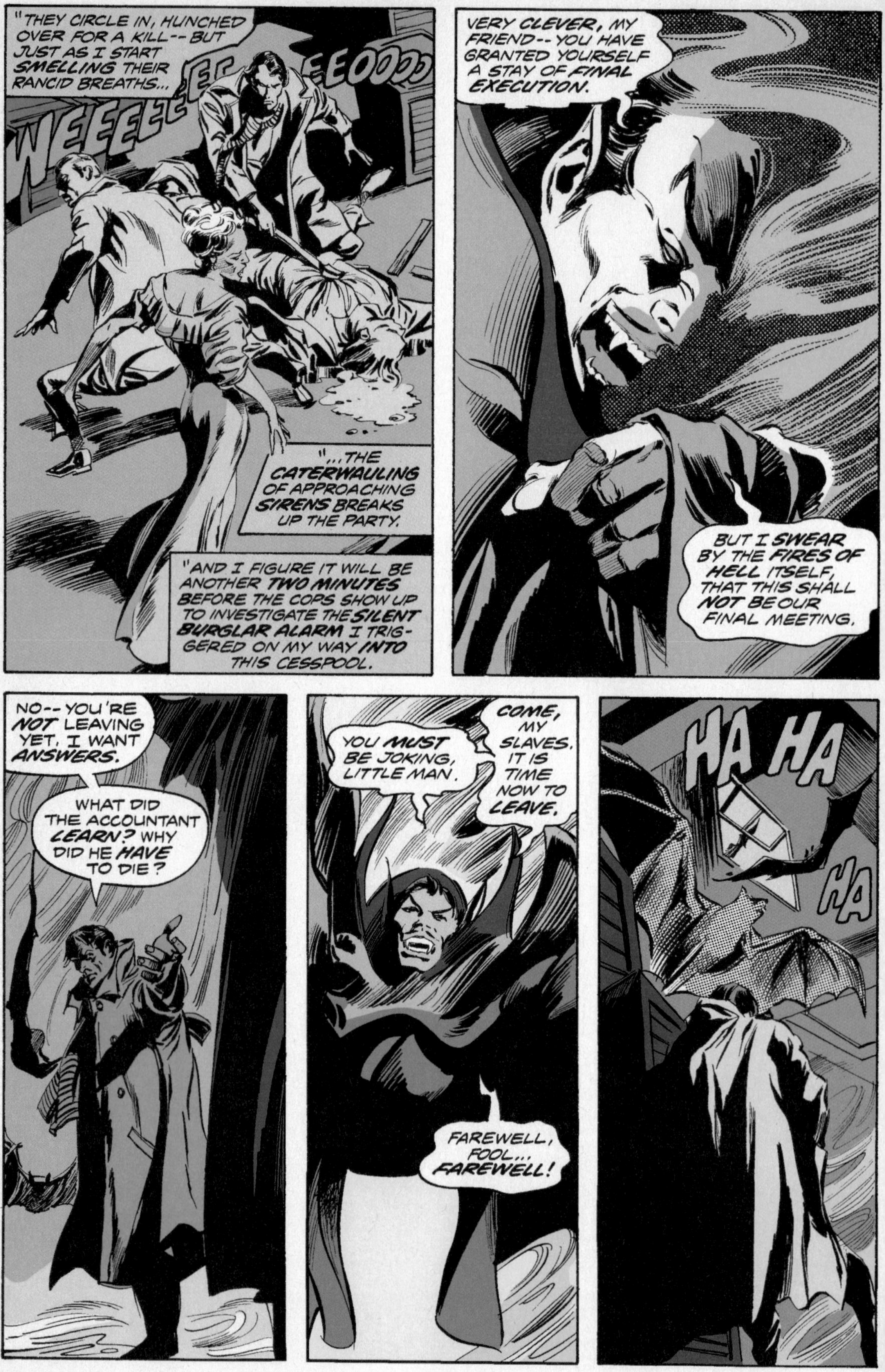
"THEY CIRCLE IN, HUNCHED OVER FOR A KILL-- BUT JUST AS I START SMELLING THEIR RANCID BREATHS...
"...THE CATERWAULING OF APPROACHING SIRENS BREAKS UP THE PARTY.
"AND I FIGURE IT WILL BE ANOTHER TWO MINUTES BEFORE THE COPS SHOW UP TO INVESTIGATE THE SILENT BURGLAR ALARM I TRIGGERED ON MY WAY INTO THIS CESSPOOL.
VERY CLEVER, MY FRIEND-- YOU HAVE GRANTED YOURSELF A STAY OF FINAL EXECUTION.
BUT I SWEAR BY THE FIRES OF HELL ITSELF, THAT THIS SHALL NOT BE OUR FINAL MEETING.
NO-- YOU'RE NOT LEAVING YET, I WANT ANSWERS.
WHAT DID THE ACCOUNTANT LEARN? WHY DID HE HAVE TO DIE?
YOU MUST BE JOKING, LITTLE MAN.
COME, MY SLAVES. IT IS TIME NOW TO LEAVE.
FAREWELL, FOOL... FAREWELL!
HA HA
HA

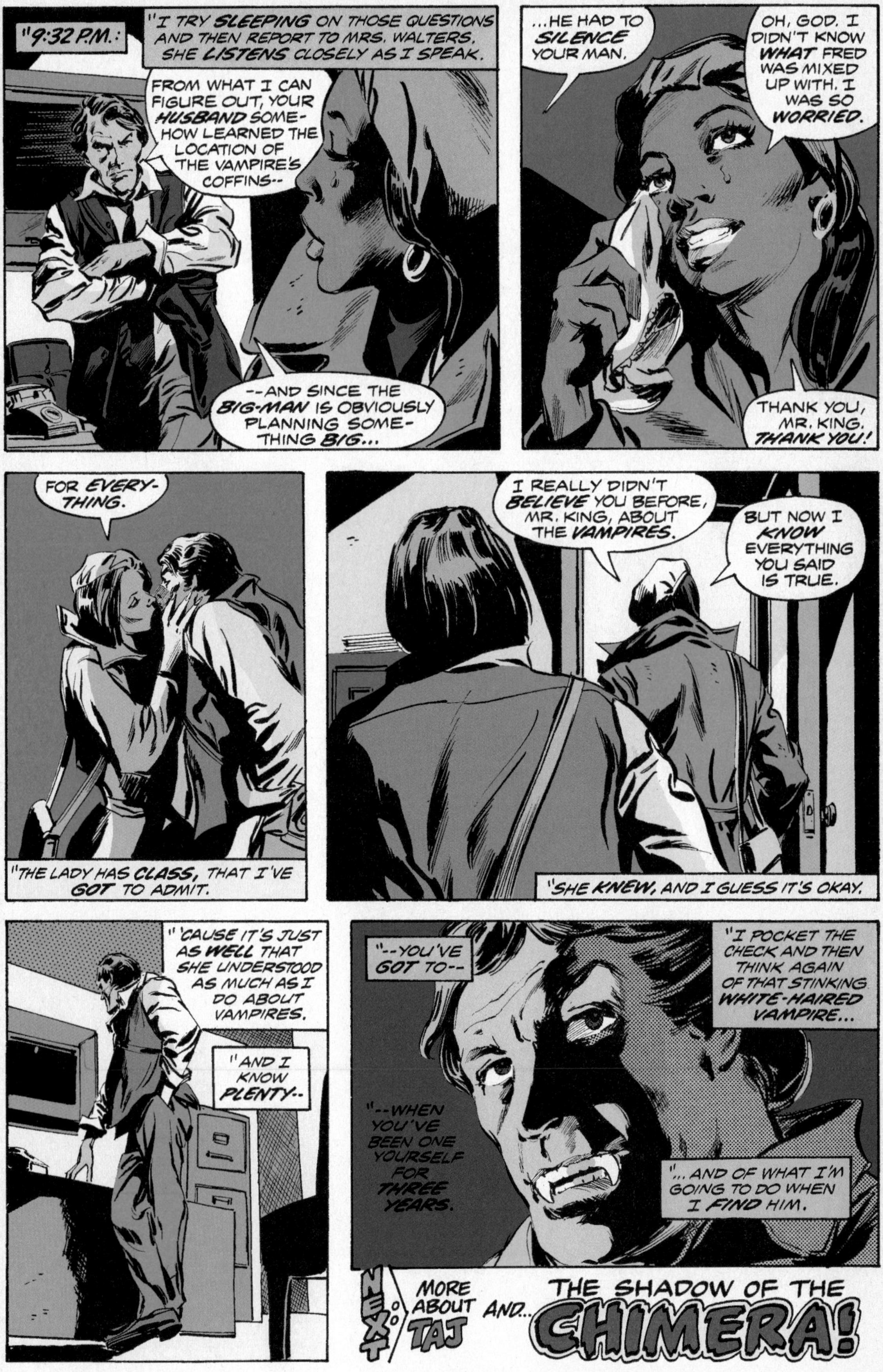
"9:32 P.M.:
"I TRY SLEEPING ON THOSE QUESTIONS AND THEN REPORT TO MRS. WALTERS. SHE LISTENS CLOSELY AS I SPEAK.
FROM WHAT I CAN FIGURE OUT, YOUR HUSBAND SOMEHOW LEARNED THE LOCATION OF THE VAMPIRE'S COFFINS--
--AND SINCE THE BIG-MAN IS OBVIOUSLY PLANNING SOMETHING BIG...
...HE HAD TO SILENCE YOUR MAN.
OH, GOD. I DIDN'T KNOW WHAT FRED WAS MIXED UP WITH. I WAS SO WORRIED.
THANK YOU, MR. KING. THANK YOU!
FOR EVERYTHING.
"THE LADY HAS CLASS, THAT I'VE GOT TO ADMIT.
I REALLY DIDN'T BELIEVE YOU BEFORE, MR. KING, ABOUT THE VAMPIRES.
BUT NOW I KNOW EVERYTHING YOU SAID IS TRUE.
"SHE KNEW, AND I GUESS IT'S OKAY.
"'CAUSE IT'S JUST AS WELL THAT SHE UNDERSTOOD AS MUCH AS I DO ABOUT VAMPIRES.
"AND I KNOW PLENTY--
"--YOU'VE GOT TO--
"--WHEN YOU'VE BEEN ONE YOURSELF FOR THREE YEARS.
"I POCKET THE CHECK AND THEN THINK AGAIN OF THAT STINKING WHITE-HAIRED VAMPIRE...
"...AND OF WHAT I'M GOING TO DO WHEN I FIND HIM.
NEXT: MORE ABOUT TAJ AND... THE SHADOW OF THE CHIMERA!

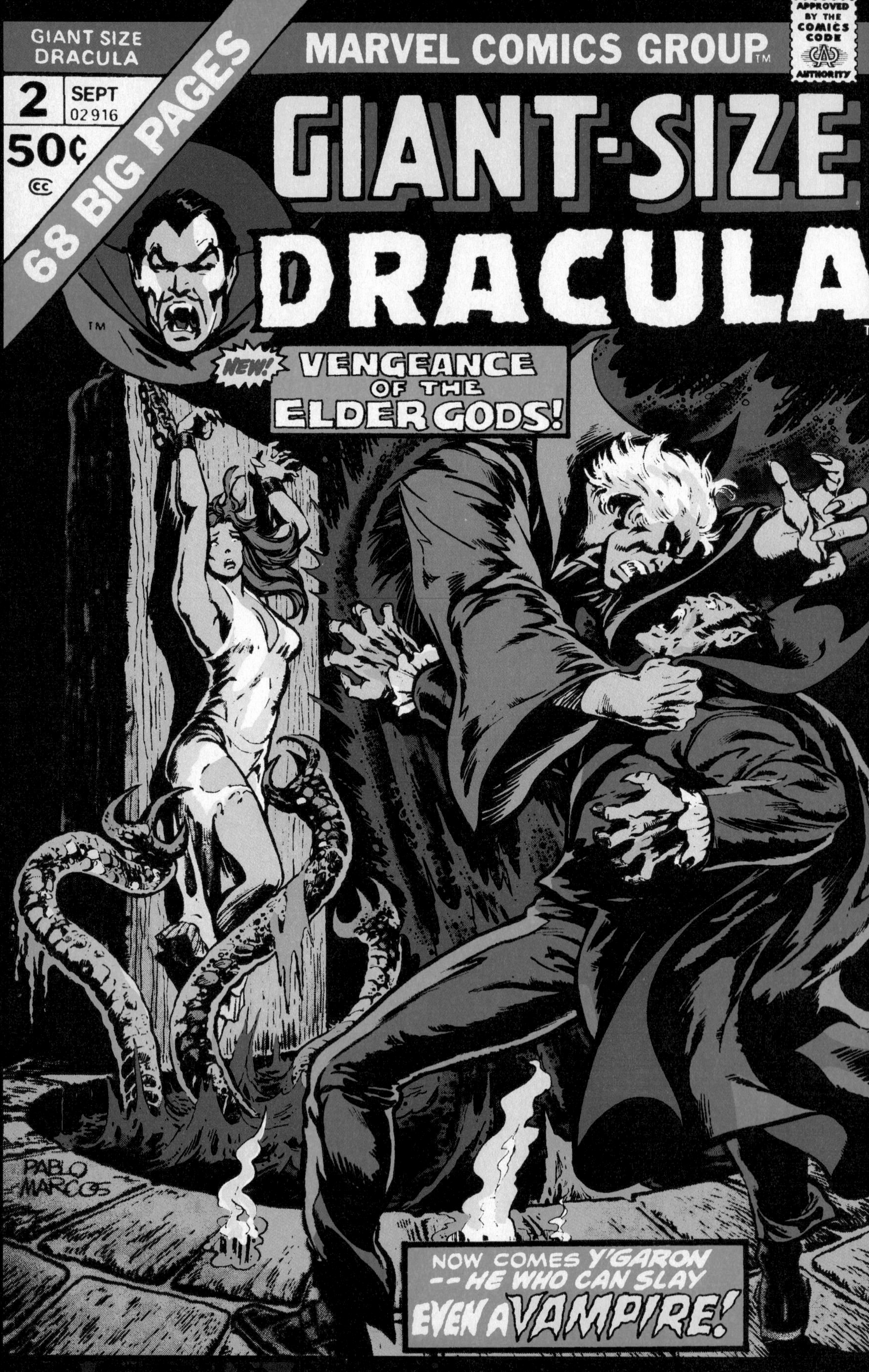
GIANT SIZE DRACULA
68 BIG PAGES
MARVEL COMICS GROUP
APPROVED BY THE COMICS CODE AUTHORITY
2 SEPT 02916
50¢
GIANT-SIZE DRACULA
NEW! VENGEANCE OF THE ELDER GODS!
PABLO MARCOS
NOW COMES Y'GARON -- HE WHO CAN SLAY EVEN A VAMPIRE!

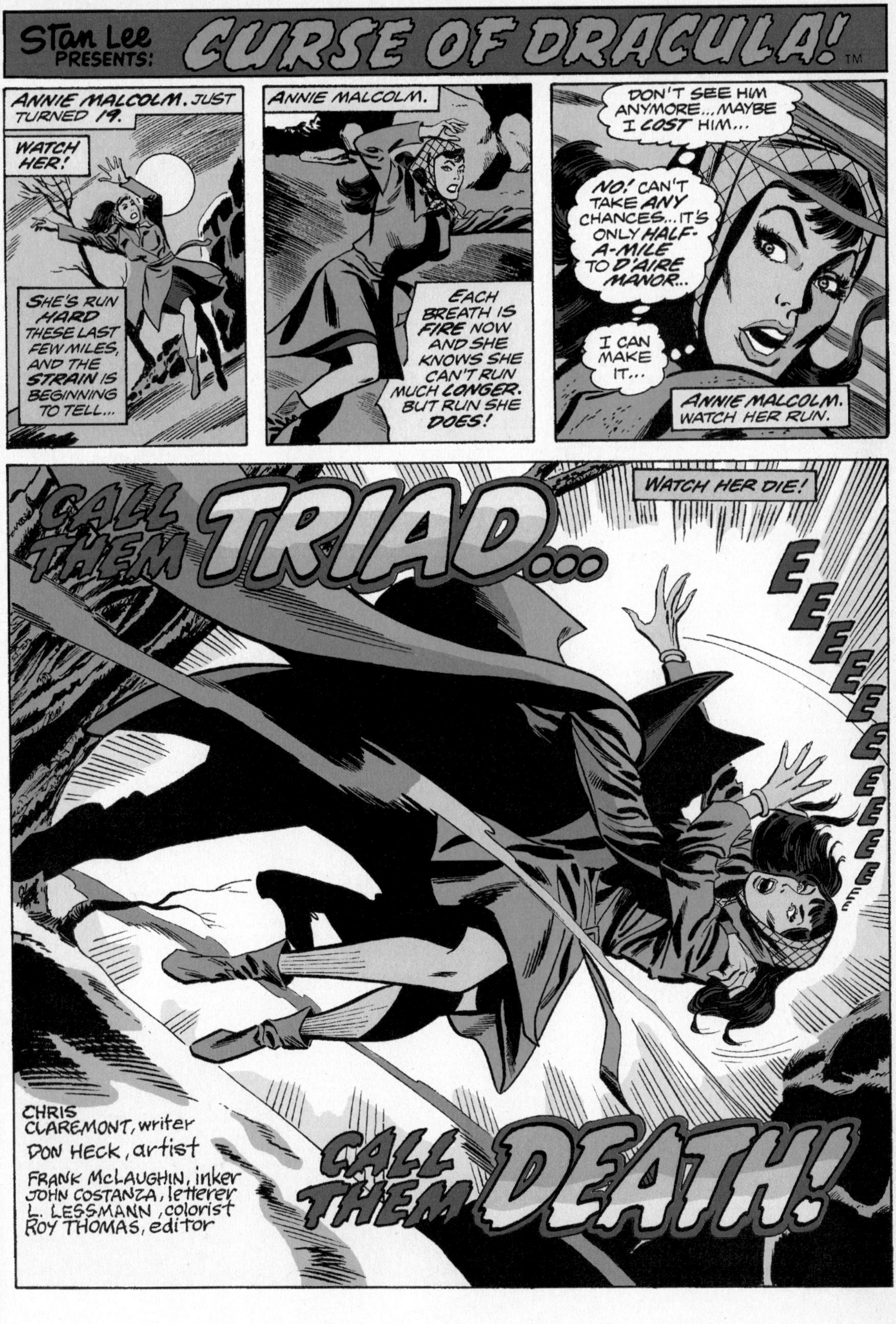
Stan Lee PRESENTS:
CURSE OF DRACULA!
ANNIE MALCOLM. JUST TURNED 19.
WATCH HER!
SHE'S RUN HARD THESE LAST FEW MILES, AND THE STRAIN IS BEGINNING TO TELL...
ANNIE MALCOLM.
EACH BREATH IS FIRE NOW AND SHE KNOWS SHE CAN'T RUN MUCH LONGER. BUT RUN SHE DOES!
DON'T SEE HIM ANYMORE... MAYBE I LOST HIM...
NO! CAN'T TAKE ANY CHANCES... IT'S ONLY HALF-A-MILE TO D'AIRE MANOR...
I CAN MAKE IT...
ANNIE MALCOLM. WATCH HER RUN.
WATCH HER DIE!
CALL THEM TRIAD...
EEEEEEEEEEEEE
CALL THEM DEATH!
CHRIS CLAREMONT, writer
DON HECK, artist
FRANK McLAUGHLIN, inker
JOHN COSTANZA, letterer
L. LESSMANN, colorist
ROY THOMAS, editor

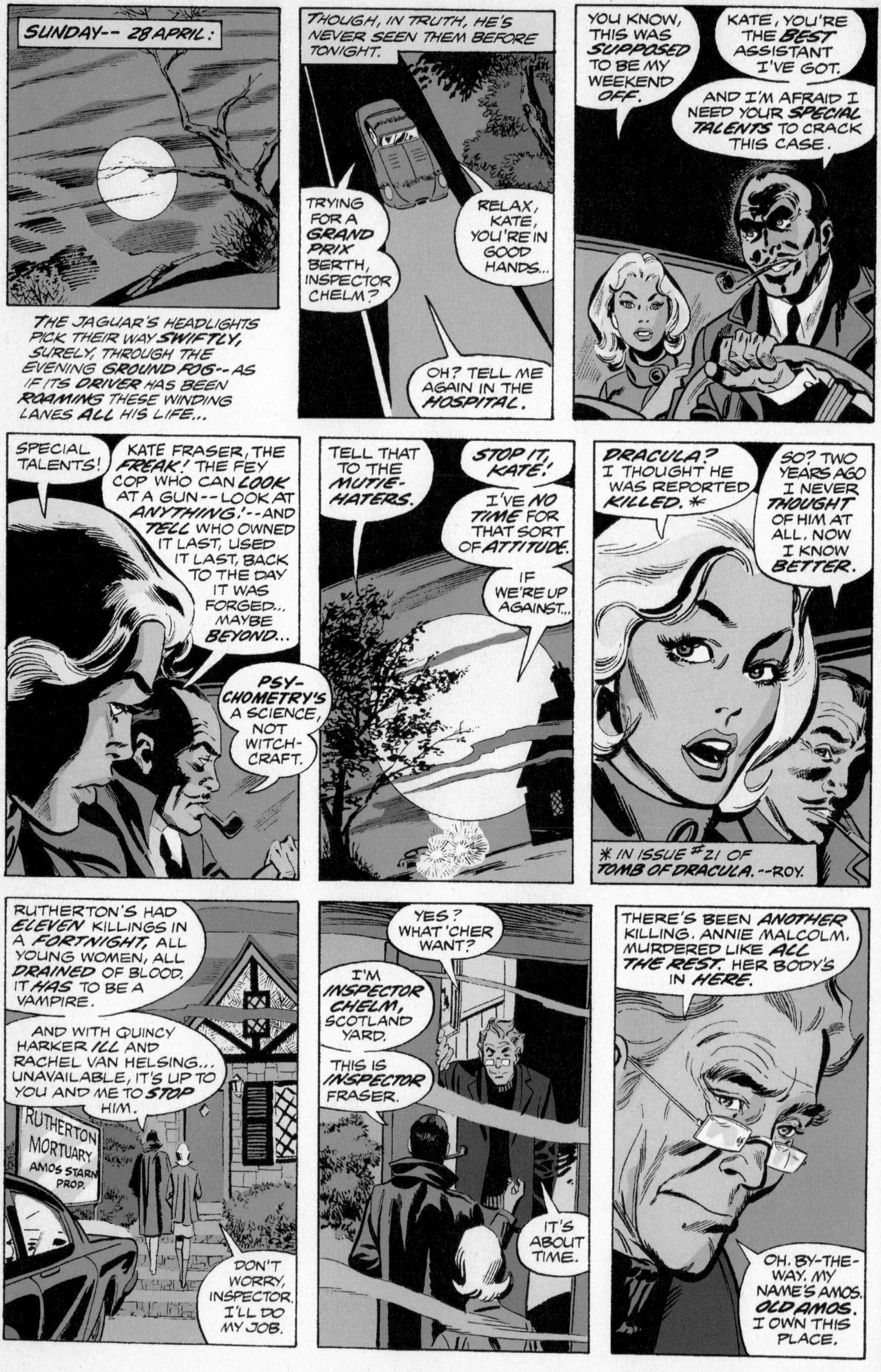
SUNDAY-- 28 APRIL:
THE JAGUAR'S HEADLIGHTS PICK THEIR WAY SWIFTLY, SURELY, THROUGH THE EVENING GROUND FOG-- AS IF ITS DRIVER HAS BEEN ROAMING THESE WINDING LANES ALL HIS LIFE...
THOUGH, IN TRUTH, HE'S NEVER SEEN THEM BEFORE TONIGHT.
TRYING FOR A GRAND PRIX BERTH, INSPECTOR CHELM?
RELAX, KATE, YOU'RE IN GOOD HANDS...
OH? TELL ME AGAIN IN THE HOSPITAL.
YOU KNOW, THIS WAS SUPPOSED TO BE MY WEEKEND OFF.
KATE, YOU'RE THE BEST ASSISTANT I'VE GOT.
AND I'M AFRAID I NEED YOUR SPECIAL TALENTS TO CRACK THIS CASE.
SPECIAL TALENTS!
KATE FRASER, THE FREAK! THE FEY COP WHO CAN LOOK AT A GUN--LOOK AT ANYTHING!--AND TELL WHO OWNED IT LAST, USED IT LAST, BACK TO THE DAY IT WAS FORGED... MAYBE BEYOND...
PSYCHOMETRY'S A SCIENCE, NOT WITCHCRAFT.
TELL THAT TO THE MUTIE-HATERS.
STOP IT, KATE!
I'VE NO TIME FOR THAT SORT OF ATTITUDE.
IF WE'RE UP AGAINST...
DRACULA? I THOUGHT HE WAS REPORTED KILLED.*
SO? TWO YEARS AGO I NEVER THOUGHT OF HIM AT ALL. NOW I KNOW BETTER.
* IN ISSUE #21 OF TOMB OF DRACULA.--ROY.
RUTHERTON'S HAD ELEVEN KILLINGS IN A FORTNIGHT, ALL YOUNG WOMEN, ALL DRAINED OF BLOOD. IT HAS TO BE A VAMPIRE.
AND WITH QUINCY HARKER ILL AND RACHEL VAN HELSING... UNAVAILABLE, IT'S UP TO YOU AND ME TO STOP HIM.
RUTHERTON MORTUARY AMOS STARN PROP.
DON'T WORRY, INSPECTOR. I'LL DO MY JOB.
YES? WHAT'CHER WANT?
I'M INSPECTOR CHELM, SCOTLAND YARD.
THIS IS INSPECTOR FRASER.
IT'S ABOUT TIME.
THERE'S BEEN ANOTHER KILLING. ANNIE MALCOLM. MURDERED LIKE ALL THE REST. HER BODY'S IN HERE.
OH. BY-THE-WAY. MY NAME'S AMOS. OLD AMOS. I OWN THIS PLACE.

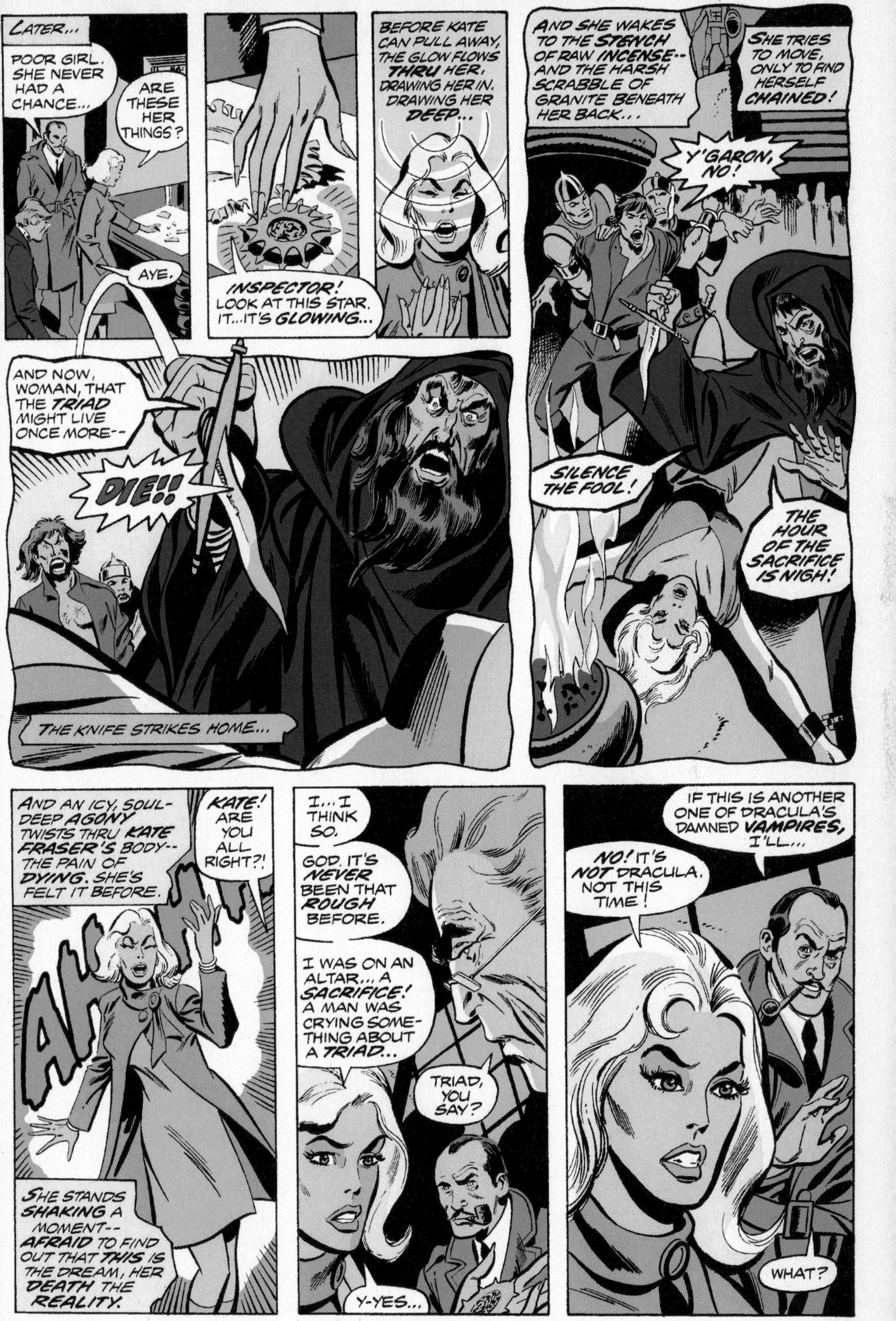

LATER...
POOR GIRL. SHE NEVER HAD A CHANCE...
ARE THESE HER THINGS?
AYE.
INSPECTOR! LOOK AT THIS STAR. IT... IT'S GLOWING...
BEFORE KATE CAN PULL AWAY, THE GLOW FLOWS THRU HER, DRAWING HER IN. DRAWING HER DEEP...
AND SHE WAKES TO THE STENCH OF RAW INCENSE-- AND THE HARSH SCRABBLE OF GRANITE BENEATH HER BACK...
SHE TRIES TO MOVE, ONLY TO FIND HERSELF CHAINED!
Y'GARON, NO!
SILENCE THE FOOL!
THE HOUR OF THE SACRIFICE IS NIGH!
AND NOW, WOMAN, THAT THE TRIAD MIGHT LIVE ONCE MORE--
DIE!!
THE KNIFE STRIKES HOME...
AND AN ICY, SOUL-DEEP AGONY TWISTS THRU KATE FRASER'S BODY-- THE PAIN OF DYING. SHE'S FELT IT BEFORE.
KATE! ARE YOU ALL RIGHT?!
SHE STANDS SHAKING A MOMENT-- AFRAID TO FIND OUT THAT THIS IS THE DREAM, HER DEATH THE REALITY.
I... I THINK SO.
GOD. IT'S NEVER BEEN THAT ROUGH BEFORE.
I WAS ON AN ALTAR... A SACRIFICE! A MAN WAS CRYING SOMETHING ABOUT A TRIAD...
TRIAD, YOU SAY?
Y-YES...
IF THIS IS ANOTHER ONE OF DRACULA'S DAMNED VAMPIRES, I'LL...
NO! IT'S NOT DRACULA. NOT THIS TIME!
WHAT?

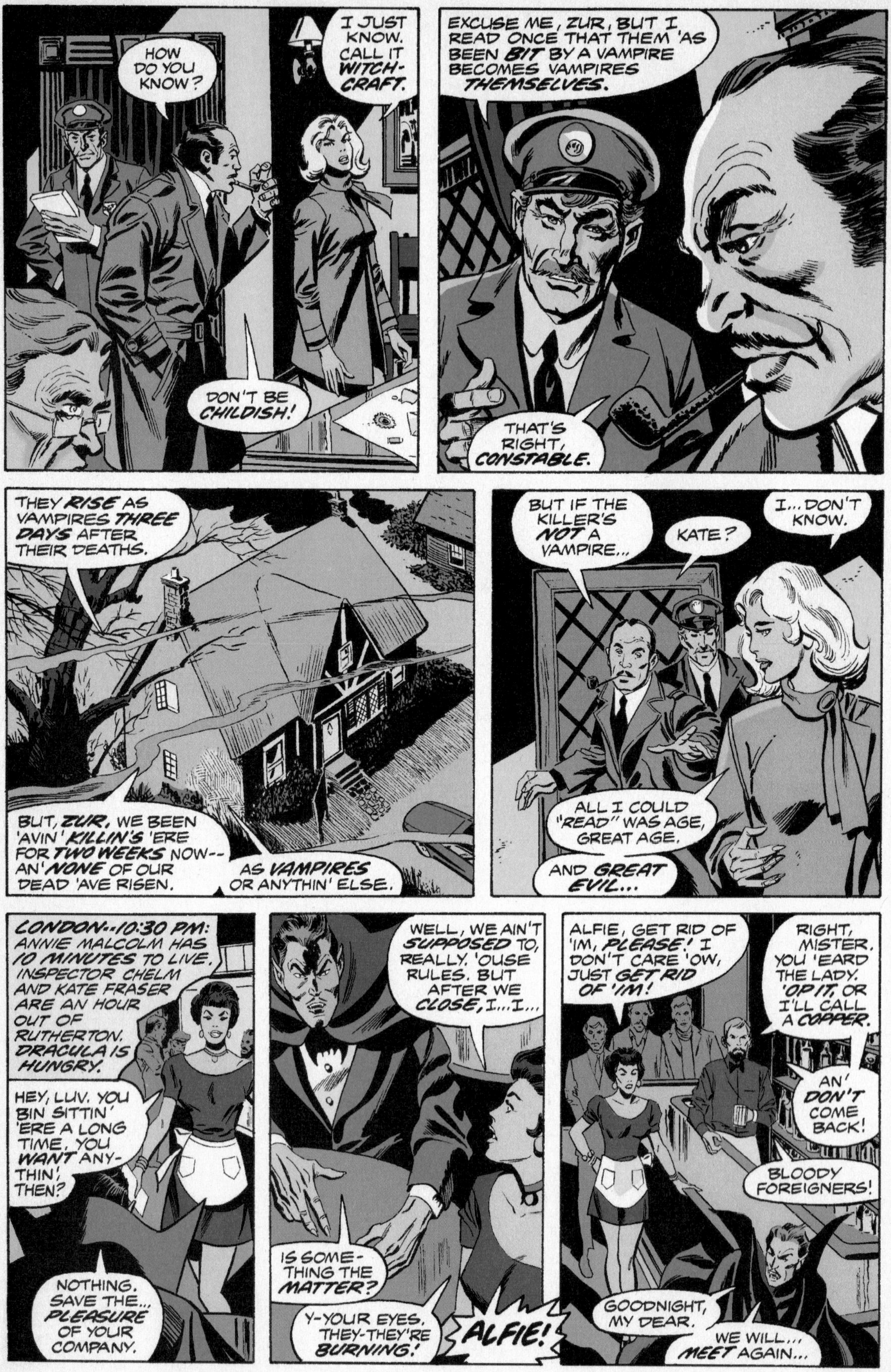
HOW DO YOU KNOW?
I JUST KNOW. CALL IT WITCH-CRAFT.
DON'T BE CHILDISH!
EXCUSE ME, ZUR, BUT I READ ONCE THAT THEM 'AS BEEN BIT BY A VAMPIRE BECOMES VAMPIRES THEMSELVES.
THAT'S RIGHT, CONSTABLE.
THEY RISE AS VAMPIRES THREE DAYS AFTER THEIR DEATHS.
BUT, ZUR, WE BEEN 'AVIN' KILLIN'S 'ERE FOR TWO WEEKS NOW-- AN' NONE OF OUR DEAD 'AVE RISEN.
AS VAMPIRES OR ANYTHIN' ELSE.
BUT IF THE KILLER'S NOT A VAMPIRE...
KATE?
I... DON'T KNOW.
ALL I COULD "READ" WAS AGE, GREAT AGE.
AND GREAT EVIL...
LONDON--10:30 PM: ANNIE MALCOLM HAS 10 MINUTES TO LIVE. INSPECTOR CHELM AND KATE FRASER ARE AN HOUR OUT OF RUTHERTON. DRACULA IS HUNGRY.
HEY, LUV. YOU BIN SITTIN' 'ERE A LONG TIME. YOU WANT ANY-THIN', THEN?
NOTHING. SAVE THE... PLEASURE OF YOUR COMPANY.
WELL, WE AIN'T SUPPOSED TO, REALLY. 'OUSE RULES. BUT AFTER WE CLOSE, I...I...
IS SOME-THING THE MATTER?
Y-YOUR EYES. THEY-THEY'RE BURNING!
ALFIE!
ALFIE, GET RID OF 'IM, PLEASE! I DON'T CARE 'OW, JUST GET RID OF 'IM!
RIGHT, MISTER. YOU 'EARD THE LADY. 'OP IT, OR I'LL CALL A COPPER.
AN' DON'T COME BACK!
BLOODY FOREIGNERS!
GOODNIGHT, MY DEAR.
WE WILL... MEET AGAIN...

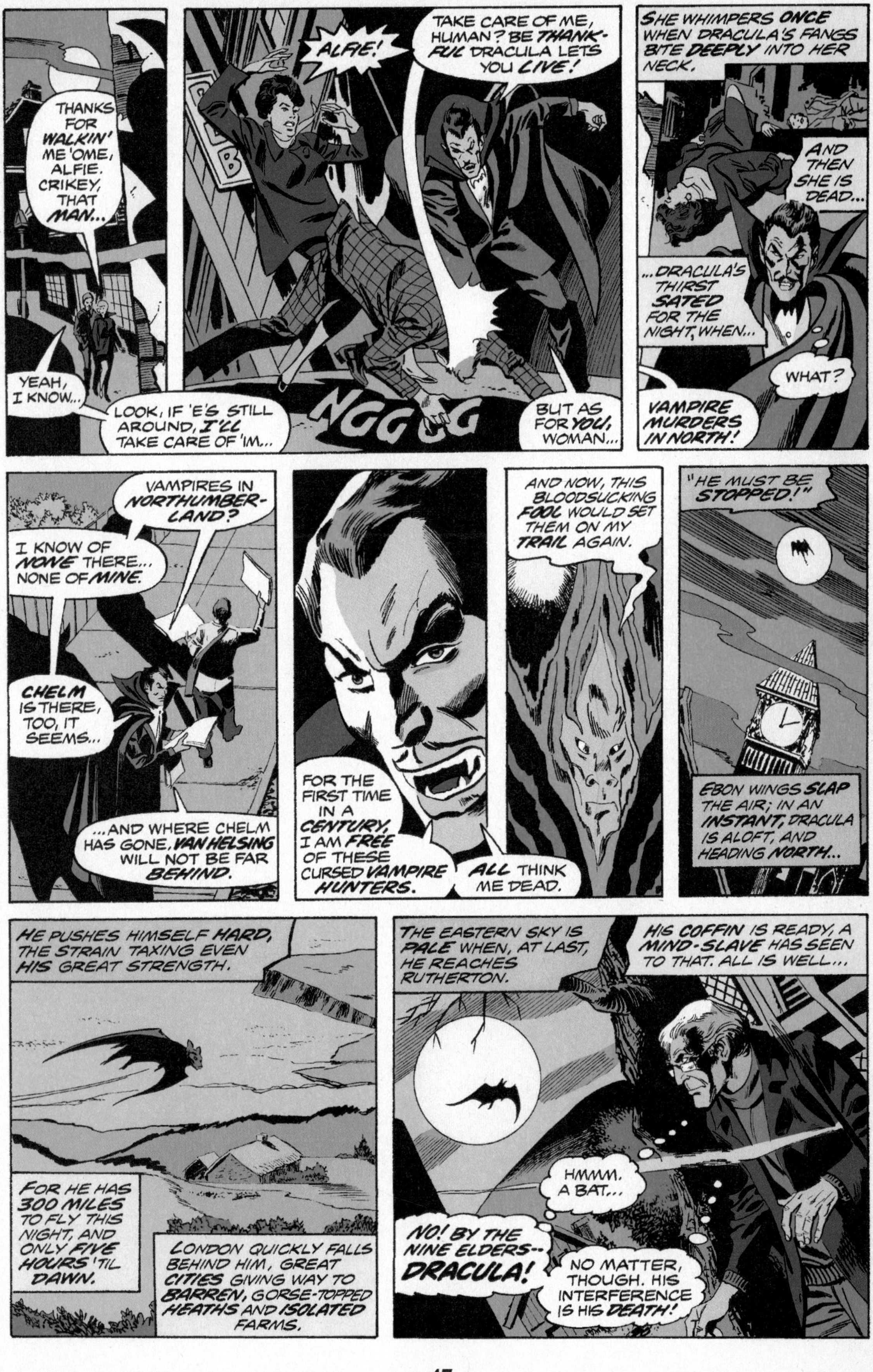
THANKS FOR WALKIN' ME 'OME, ALFIE. CRIKEY, THAT MAN...
YEAH, I KNOW...
LOOK, IF 'E'S STILL AROUND, I'LL TAKE CARE OF 'IM...
ALFIE!
TAKE CARE OF ME, HUMAN? BE THANKFUL DRACULA LETS YOU LIVE!
NGGGG
BUT AS FOR YOU, WOMAN...
SHE WHIMPERS ONCE WHEN DRACULA'S FANGS BITE DEEPLY INTO HER NECK.
AND THEN SHE IS DEAD...
...DRACULA'S THIRST SATED FOR THE NIGHT, WHEN...
WHAT?
VAMPIRE MURDERS IN NORTH!
VAMPIRES IN NORTHUMBERLAND?
I KNOW OF NONE THERE... NONE OF MINE.
CHELM IS THERE, TOO, IT SEEMS...
...AND WHERE CHELM HAS GONE, VAN HELSING WILL NOT BE FAR BEHIND.
FOR THE FIRST TIME IN A CENTURY, I AM FREE OF THESE CURSED VAMPIRE HUNTERS.
ALL THINK ME DEAD.
AND NOW, THIS BLOODSUCKING FOOL WOULD SET THEM ON MY TRAIL AGAIN.
"HE MUST BE STOPPED!"
EBON WINGS SLAP THE AIR; IN AN INSTANT, DRACULA IS ALOFT, AND HEADING NORTH...
HE PUSHES HIMSELF HARD, THE STRAIN TAXING EVEN HIS GREAT STRENGTH.
FOR HE HAS 300 MILES TO FLY THIS NIGHT, AND ONLY FIVE HOURS 'TIL DAWN.
LONDON QUICKLY FALLS BEHIND HIM, GREAT CITIES GIVING WAY TO BARREN, GORSE-TOPPED HEATHS AND ISOLATED FARMS.
THE EASTERN SKY IS PALE WHEN, AT LAST, HE REACHES RUTHERTON.
HIS COFFIN IS READY, A MIND-SLAVE HAS SEEN TO THAT. ALL IS WELL...
HMMM. A BAT...
NO! BY THE NINE ELDERS-- DRACULA!
NO MATTER, THOUGH. HIS INTERFERENCE IS HIS DEATH!

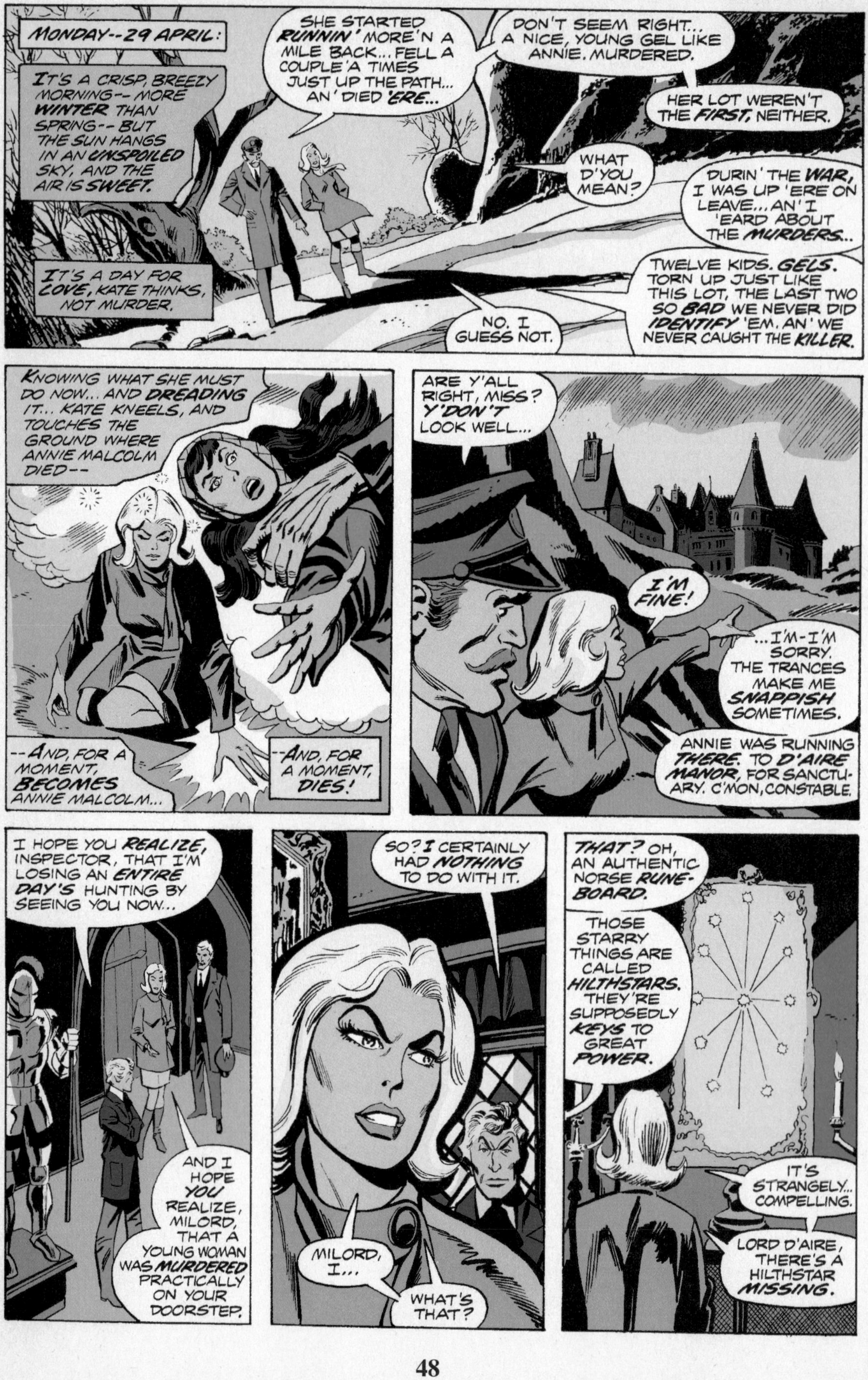
MONDAY--29 APRIL:
IT'S A CRISP, BREEZY MORNING-- MORE WINTER THAN SPRING-- BUT THE SUN HANGS IN AN UNSPOILED SKY, AND THE AIR IS SWEET.
SHE STARTED RUNNIN' MORE'N A MILE BACK... FELL A COUPLE'A TIMES JUST UP THE PATH... AN' DIED 'ERE...
DON'T SEEM RIGHT... A NICE, YOUNG GEL LIKE ANNIE. MURDERED.
HER LOT WEREN'T THE FIRST, NEITHER.
WHAT D'YOU MEAN?
DURIN' THE WAR, I WAS UP 'ERE ON LEAVE... AN' I 'EARD ABOUT THE MURDERS...
TWELVE KIDS. GELS. TORN UP JUST LIKE THIS LOT, THE LAST TWO SO BAD WE NEVER DID IDENTIFY 'EM. AN' WE NEVER CAUGHT THE KILLER.
IT'S A DAY FOR LOVE, KATE THINKS, NOT MURDER.
NO. I GUESS NOT.
KNOWING WHAT SHE MUST DO NOW... AND DREADING IT... KATE KNEELS, AND TOUCHES THE GROUND WHERE ANNIE MALCOLM DIED--
--AND, FOR A MOMENT, BECOMES ANNIE MALCOLM...
--AND, FOR A MOMENT, DIES!
ARE Y'ALL RIGHT, MISS? Y'DON'T LOOK WELL...
I'M FINE!
...I'M-I'M SORRY. THE TRANCES MAKE ME SNAPPISH SOMETIMES.
ANNIE WAS RUNNING THERE. TO D'AIRE MANOR, FOR SANCTUARY. C'MON, CONSTABLE.
I HOPE YOU REALIZE, INSPECTOR, THAT I'M LOSING AN ENTIRE DAY'S HUNTING BY SEEING YOU NOW...
AND I HOPE YOU REALIZE, MILORD, THAT A YOUNG WOMAN WAS MURDERED PRACTICALLY ON YOUR DOORSTEP.
SO? I CERTAINLY HAD NOTHING TO DO WITH IT.
MILORD, I...
WHAT'S THAT?
THAT? OH, AN AUTHENTIC NORSE RUNE-BOARD.
THOSE STARRY THINGS ARE CALLED HILTHSTARS. THEY'RE SUPPOSEDLY KEYS TO GREAT POWER.
IT'S STRANGELY... COMPELLING.
LORD D'AIRE, THERE'S A HILTHSTAR MISSING.

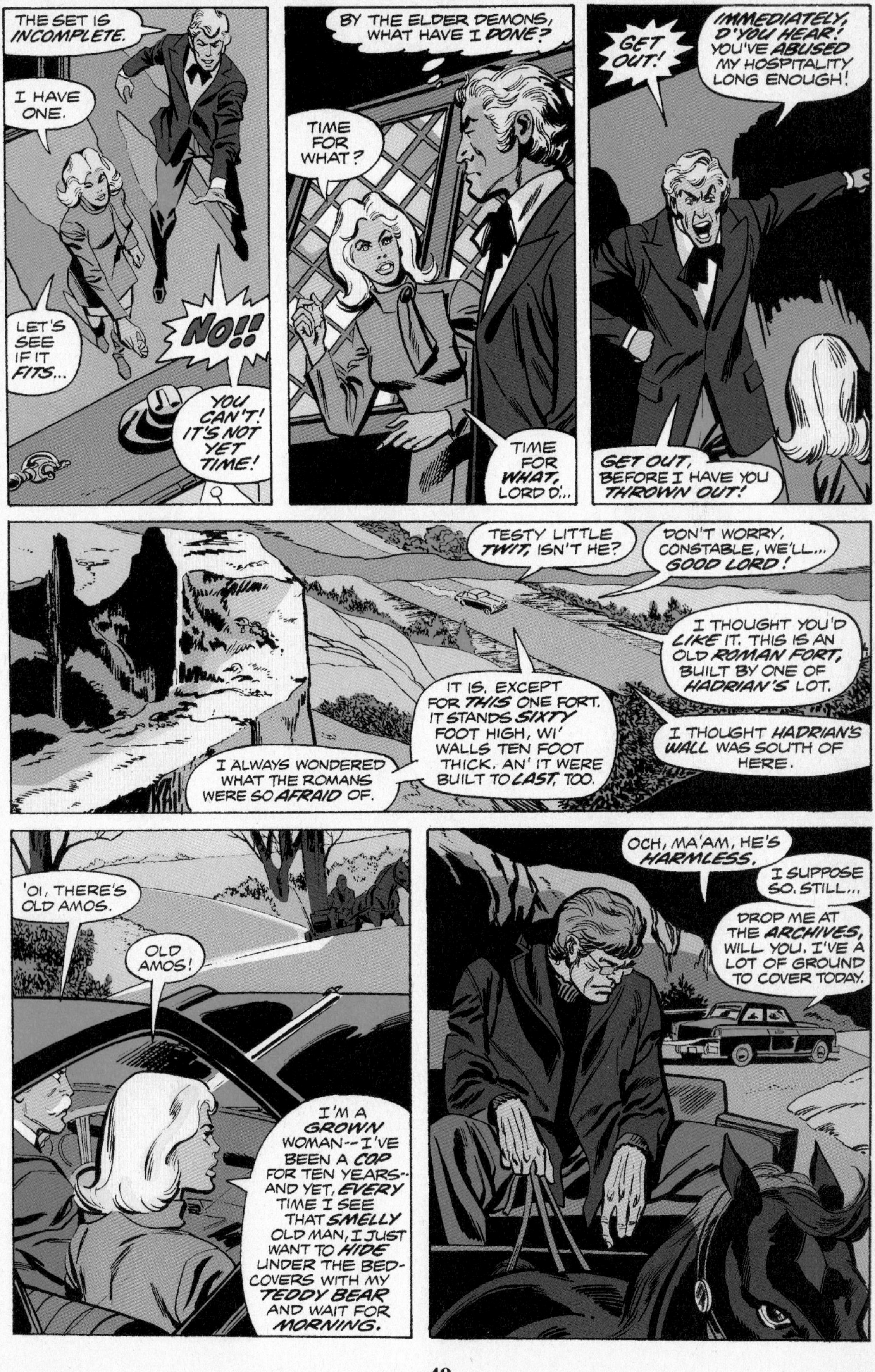

THE SET IS INCOMPLETE.
I HAVE ONE.
LET'S SEE IF IT FITS...
NO!!
YOU CAN'T! IT'S NOT YET TIME!
BY THE ELDER DEMONS, WHAT HAVE I DONE?
TIME FOR WHAT?
TIME FOR WHAT, LORD D'...
GET OUT!
IMMEDIATELY, D'YOU HEAR! YOU'VE ABUSED MY HOSPITALITY LONG ENOUGH!
GET OUT, BEFORE I HAVE YOU THROWN OUT!
TESTY LITTLE TWIT, ISN'T HE?
DON'T WORRY, CONSTABLE, WE'LL... GOOD LORD!
I THOUGHT YOU'D LIKE IT. THIS IS AN OLD ROMAN FORT, BUILT BY ONE OF HADRIAN'S LOT.
I THOUGHT HADRIAN'S WALL WAS SOUTH OF HERE.
IT IS. EXCEPT FOR THIS ONE FORT. IT STANDS SIXTY FOOT HIGH, WI' WALLS TEN FOOT THICK. AN' IT WERE BUILT TO LAST, TOO.
I ALWAYS WONDERED WHAT THE ROMANS WERE SO AFRAID OF.
'OI, THERE'S OLD AMOS.
OLD AMOS!
I'M A GROWN WOMAN--I'VE BEEN A COP FOR TEN YEARS--AND YET, EVERY TIME I SEE THAT SMELLY OLD MAN, I JUST WANT TO HIDE UNDER THE BED-COVERS WITH MY TEDDY BEAR AND WAIT FOR MORNING.
OCH, MA'AM, HE'S HARMLESS.
I SUPPOSE SO. STILL...
DROP ME AT THE ARCHIVES, WILL YOU. I'VE A LOT OF GROUND TO COVER TODAY.

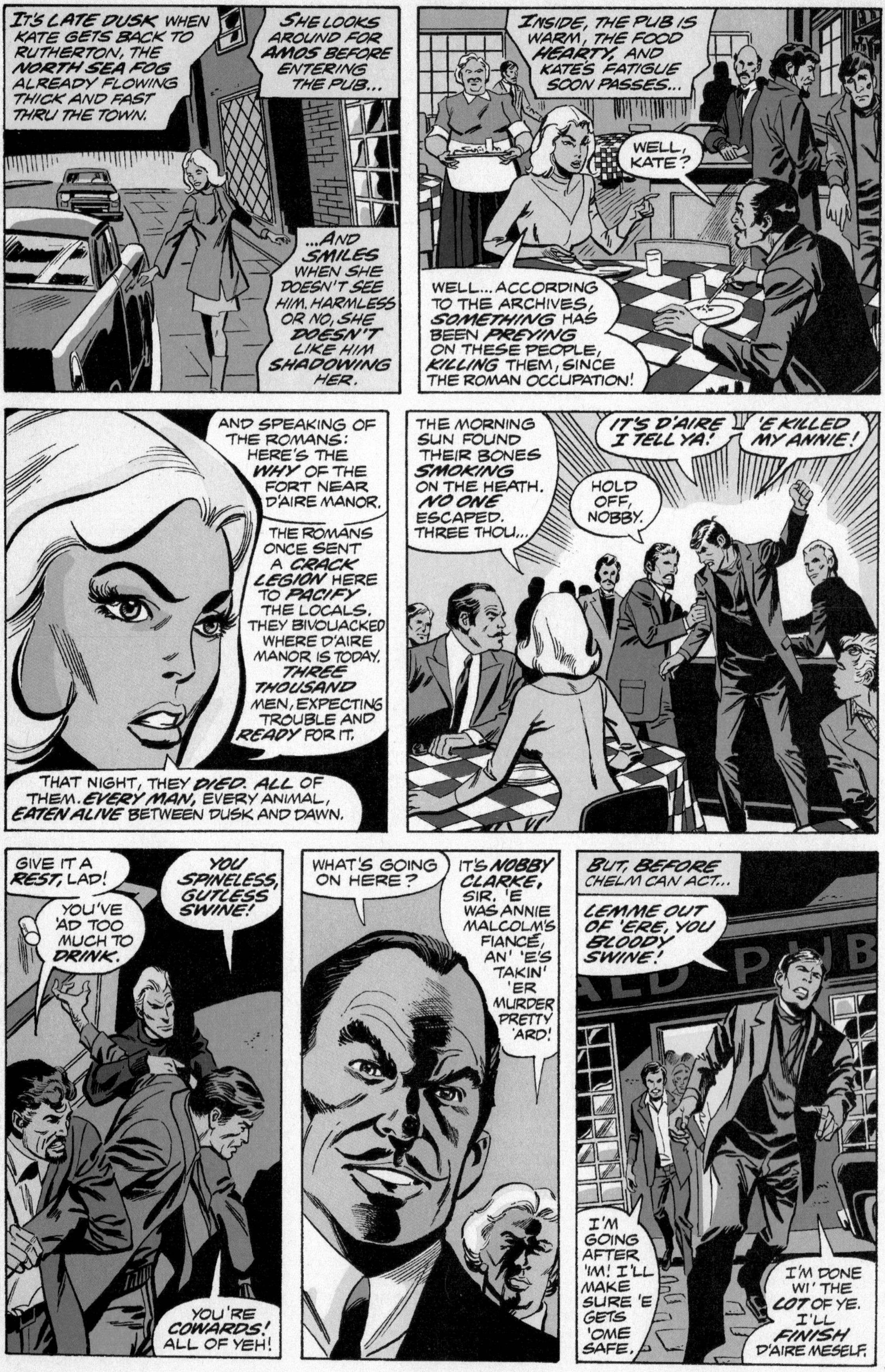
IT'S LATE DUSK WHEN KATE GETS BACK TO RUTHERTON, THE NORTH SEA FOG ALREADY FLOWING THICK AND FAST THRU THE TOWN.
SHE LOOKS AROUND FOR AMOS BEFORE ENTERING THE PUB...
...AND SMILES WHEN SHE DOESN'T SEE HIM. HARMLESS OR NO, SHE DOESN'T LIKE HIM SHADOWING HER.
INSIDE, THE PUB IS WARM, THE FOOD HEARTY, AND KATE'S FATIGUE SOON PASSES...
WELL, KATE?
WELL... ACCORDING TO THE ARCHIVES, SOMETHING HAS BEEN PREYING ON THESE PEOPLE, KILLING THEM, SINCE THE ROMAN OCCUPATION!
AND SPEAKING OF THE ROMANS: HERE'S THE WHY OF THE FORT NEAR D'AIRE MANOR.
THE ROMANS ONCE SENT A CRACK LEGION HERE TO PACIFY THE LOCALS. THEY BIVOUACKED WHERE D'AIRE MANOR IS TODAY. THREE THOUSAND MEN, EXPECTING TROUBLE AND READY FOR IT.
THAT NIGHT, THEY DIED. ALL OF THEM. EVERY MAN, EVERY ANIMAL, EATEN ALIVE BETWEEN DUSK AND DAWN.
THE MORNING SUN FOUND THEIR BONES SMOKING ON THE HEATH. NO ONE ESCAPED. THREE THOU...
IT'S D'AIRE I TELL YA!
'E KILLED MY ANNIE!
HOLD OFF, NOBBY.
GIVE IT A REST, LAD!
YOU'VE 'AD TOO MUCH TO DRINK.
YOU SPINELESS, GUTLESS SWINE!
YOU'RE COWARDS! ALL OF YEH!
WHAT'S GOING ON HERE?
IT'S NOBBY CLARKE, SIR. 'E WAS ANNIE MALCOLM'S FIANCÉ, AN' 'E'S TAKIN' 'ER MURDER PRETTY 'ARD!
BUT, BEFORE CHELM CAN ACT...
LEMME OUT OF 'ERE, YOU BLOODY SWINE!
I'M GOING AFTER 'IM! I'LL MAKE SURE 'E GETS 'OME SAFE.
I'M DONE WI' THE LOT OF YE. I'LL FINISH D'AIRE MESELF.

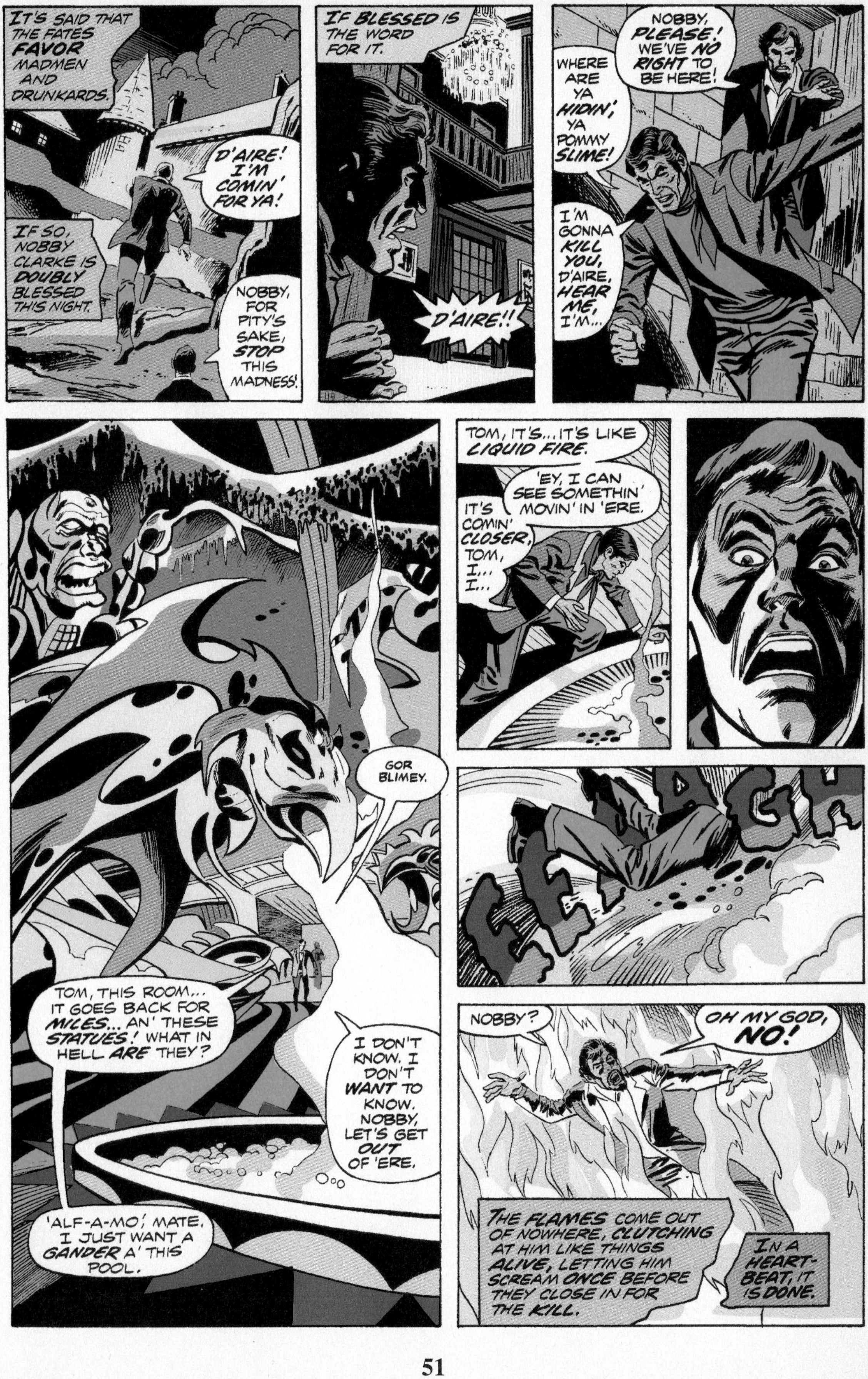

IT'S SAID THAT THE FATES FAVOR MADMEN AND DRUNKARDS.
D'AIRE! I'M COMIN' FOR YA!
IF SO, NOBBY CLARKE IS DOUBLY BLESSED THIS NIGHT.
NOBBY, FOR PITY'S SAKE, STOP THIS MADNESS!
IF BLESSED IS THE WORD FOR IT.
D'AIRE!!
NOBBY, PLEASE! WE'VE NO RIGHT TO BE HERE!
WHERE ARE YA HIDIN', YA POMMY SLIME!
I'M GONNA KILL YOU, D'AIRE, HEAR ME, I'M...
GOR BLIMEY.
TOM, THIS ROOM... IT GOES BACK FOR MILES... AN' THESE STATUES! WHAT IN HELL ARE THEY?
I DON'T KNOW. I DON'T WANT TO KNOW. NOBBY, LET'S GET OUT OF 'ERE.
'ALF-A-MO', MATE. I JUST WANT A GANDER A' THIS POOL.
TOM, IT'S... IT'S LIKE LIQUID FIRE.
'EY, I CAN SEE SOMETHIN' MOVIN' IN 'ERE.
IT'S COMIN' CLOSER, TOM, I... I...
EEAAGH
NOBBY?
OH MY GOD, NO!
THE FLAMES COME OUT OF NOWHERE, CLUTCHING AT HIM LIKE THINGS ALIVE, LETTING HIM SCREAM ONCE BEFORE THEY CLOSE IN FOR THE KILL.
IN A HEART-BEAT, IT IS DONE.

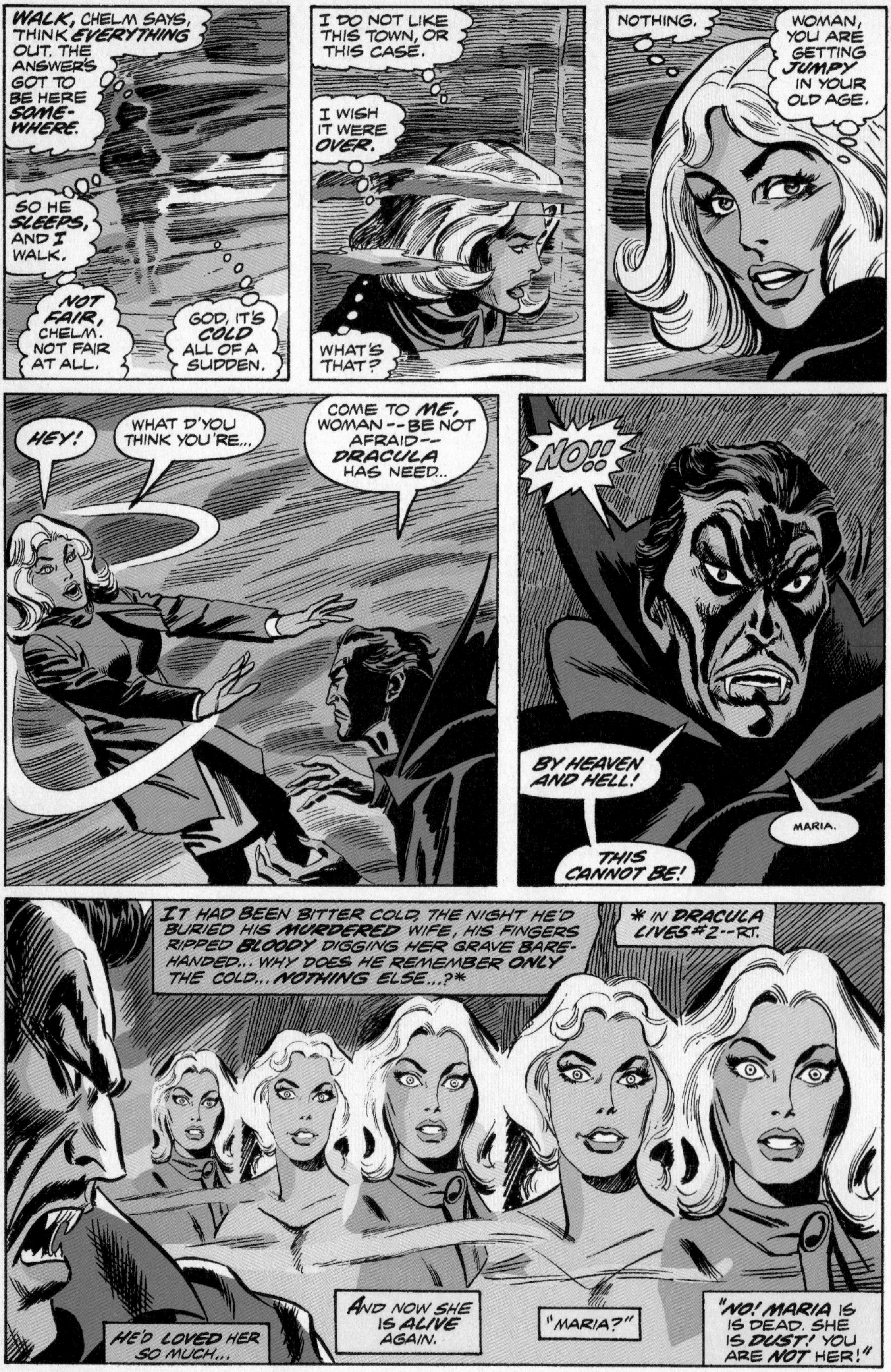

WALK, CHELM SAYS, THINK EVERYTHING OUT. THE ANSWER'S GOT TO BE HERE SOME-WHERE.
SO HE SLEEPS, AND I WALK.
NOT FAIR, CHELM. NOT FAIR AT ALL.
GOD, IT'S COLD ALL OF A SUDDEN.
I DO NOT LIKE THIS TOWN, OR THIS CASE.
I WISH IT WERE OVER.
WHAT'S THAT?
NOTHING.
WOMAN, YOU ARE GETTING JUMPY IN YOUR OLD AGE.
HEY!
WHAT D'YOU THINK YOU'RE...
COME TO ME, WOMAN--BE NOT AFRAID--DRACULA HAS NEED...
NO!!
BY HEAVEN AND HELL!
THIS CANNOT BE!
MARIA.
IT HAD BEEN BITTER COLD, THE NIGHT HE'D BURIED HIS MURDERED WIFE, HIS FINGERS RIPPED BLOODY DIGGING HER GRAVE BARE-HANDED... WHY DOES HE REMEMBER ONLY THE COLD... NOTHING ELSE...?*
* IN DRACULA LIVES #2--RT.
HE'D LOVED HER SO MUCH...
AND NOW SHE IS ALIVE AGAIN.
"MARIA?"
"NO! MARIA IS IS DEAD. SHE IS DUST! YOU ARE NOT HER!"

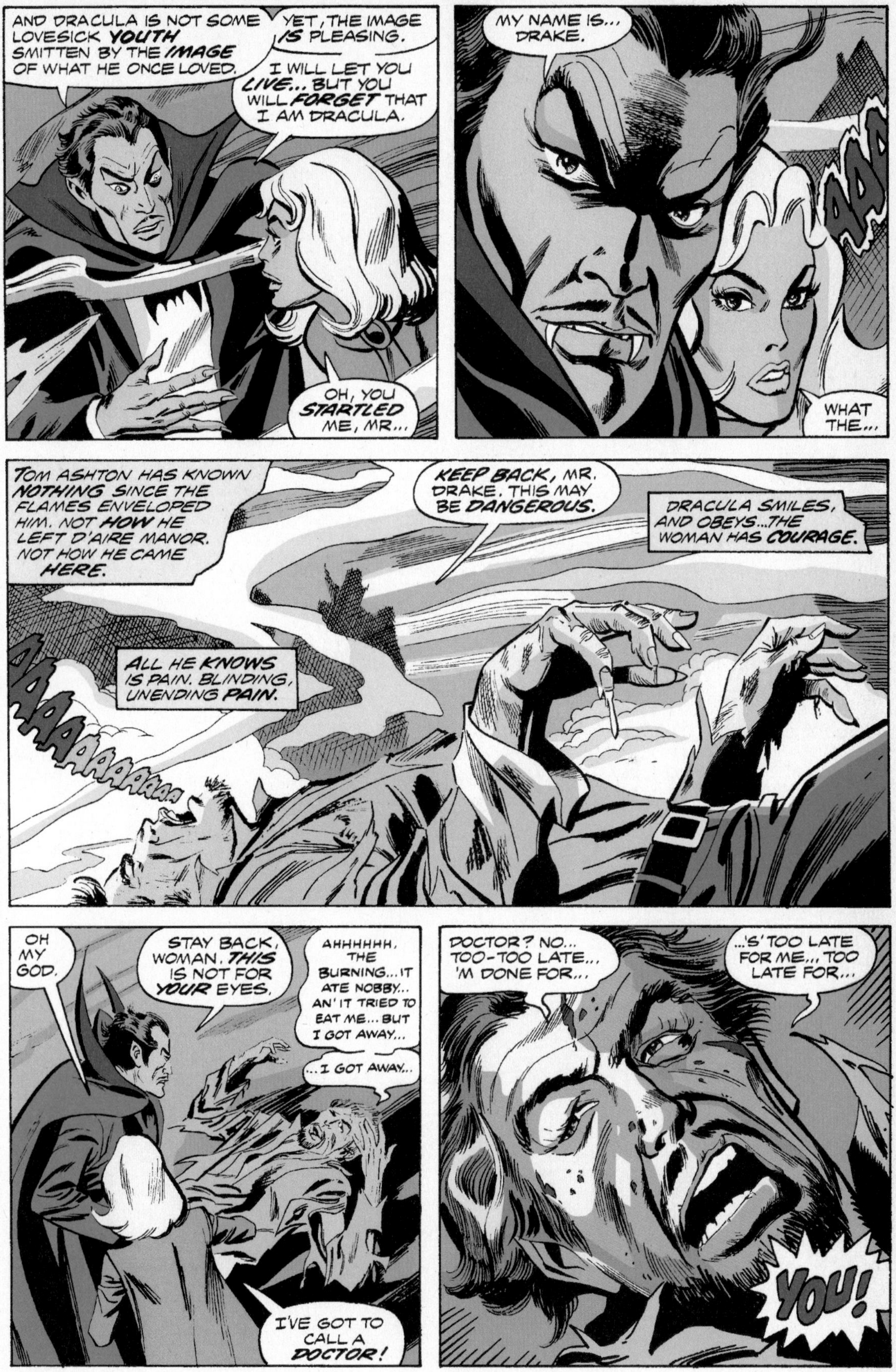

AND DRACULA IS NOT SOME LOVESICK YOUTH SMITTEN BY THE IMAGE OF WHAT HE ONCE LOVED.
YET, THE IMAGE IS PLEASING.
I WILL LET YOU LIVE... BUT YOU WILL FORGET THAT I AM DRACULA.
OH, YOU STARTLED ME, MR...
MY NAME IS... DRAKE.
WHAT THE...
TOM ASHTON HAS KNOWN NOTHING SINCE THE FLAMES ENVELOPED HIM. NOT HOW HE LEFT D'AIRE MANOR. NOT HOW HE CAME HERE.
KEEP BACK, MR. DRAKE. THIS MAY BE DANGEROUS.
DRACULA SMILES, AND OBEYS...THE WOMAN HAS COURAGE.
ALL HE KNOWS IS PAIN. BLINDING, UNENDING PAIN.
AAAAAAAAAAAAaaa
OH MY GOD.
STAY BACK, WOMAN. THIS IS NOT FOR YOUR EYES.
AHHHHHH, THE BURNING... IT ATE NOBBY... AN' IT TRIED TO EAT ME... BUT I GOT AWAY...
...I GOT AWAY...
I'VE GOT TO CALL A DOCTOR!
DOCTOR? NO... TOO-TOO LATE... 'M DONE FOR...
...'S' TOO LATE FOR ME... TOO LATE FOR...
YOU!

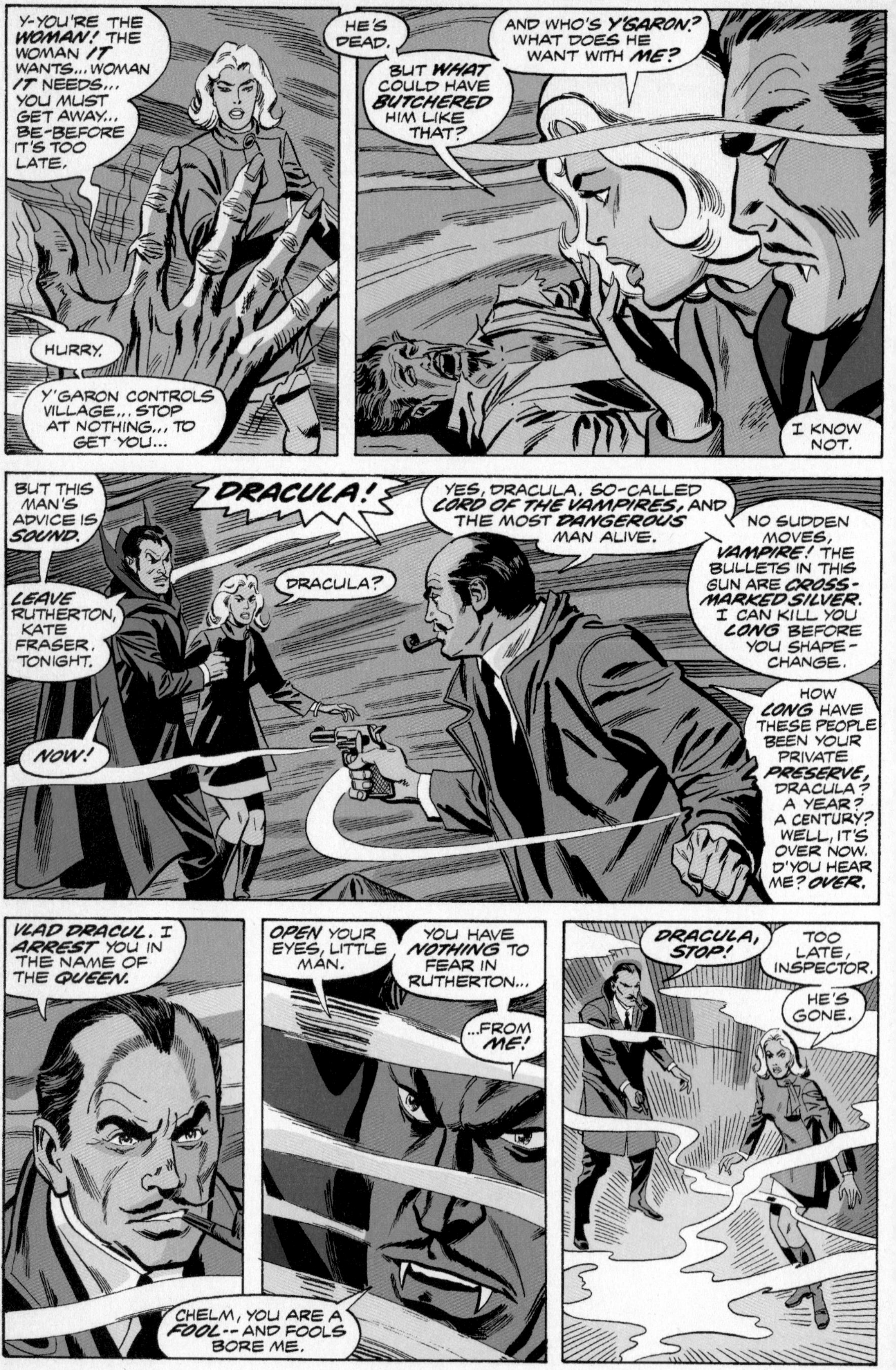
Y-YOU'RE THE WOMAN! THE WOMAN IT WANTS... WOMAN IT NEEDS... YOU MUST GET AWAY... BE-BEFORE IT'S TOO LATE.
HURRY.
Y'GARON CONTROLS VILLAGE... STOP AT NOTHING... TO GET YOU...
HE'S DEAD.
BUT WHAT COULD HAVE BUTCHERED HIM LIKE THAT?
AND WHO'S Y'GARON? WHAT DOES HE WANT WITH ME?
I KNOW NOT.
BUT THIS MAN'S ADVICE IS SOUND.
LEAVE RUTHERTON, KATE FRASER. TONIGHT.
NOW!
DRACULA!
DRACULA?
YES, DRACULA. SO-CALLED LORD OF THE VAMPIRES, AND THE MOST DANGEROUS MAN ALIVE.
NO SUDDEN MOVES, VAMPIRE! THE BULLETS IN THIS GUN ARE CROSS-MARKED SILVER. I CAN KILL YOU LONG BEFORE YOU SHAPE-CHANGE.
HOW LONG HAVE THESE PEOPLE BEEN YOUR PRIVATE PRESERVE, DRACULA? A YEAR? A CENTURY? WELL, IT'S OVER NOW. D'YOU HEAR ME? OVER.
VLAD DRACUL. I ARREST YOU IN THE NAME OF THE QUEEN.
CHELM, YOU ARE A FOOL-- AND FOOLS BORE ME.
OPEN YOUR EYES, LITTLE MAN.
YOU HAVE NOTHING TO FEAR IN RUTHERTON...
...FROM ME!
DRACULA, STOP!
TOO LATE, INSPECTOR.
HE'S GONE.

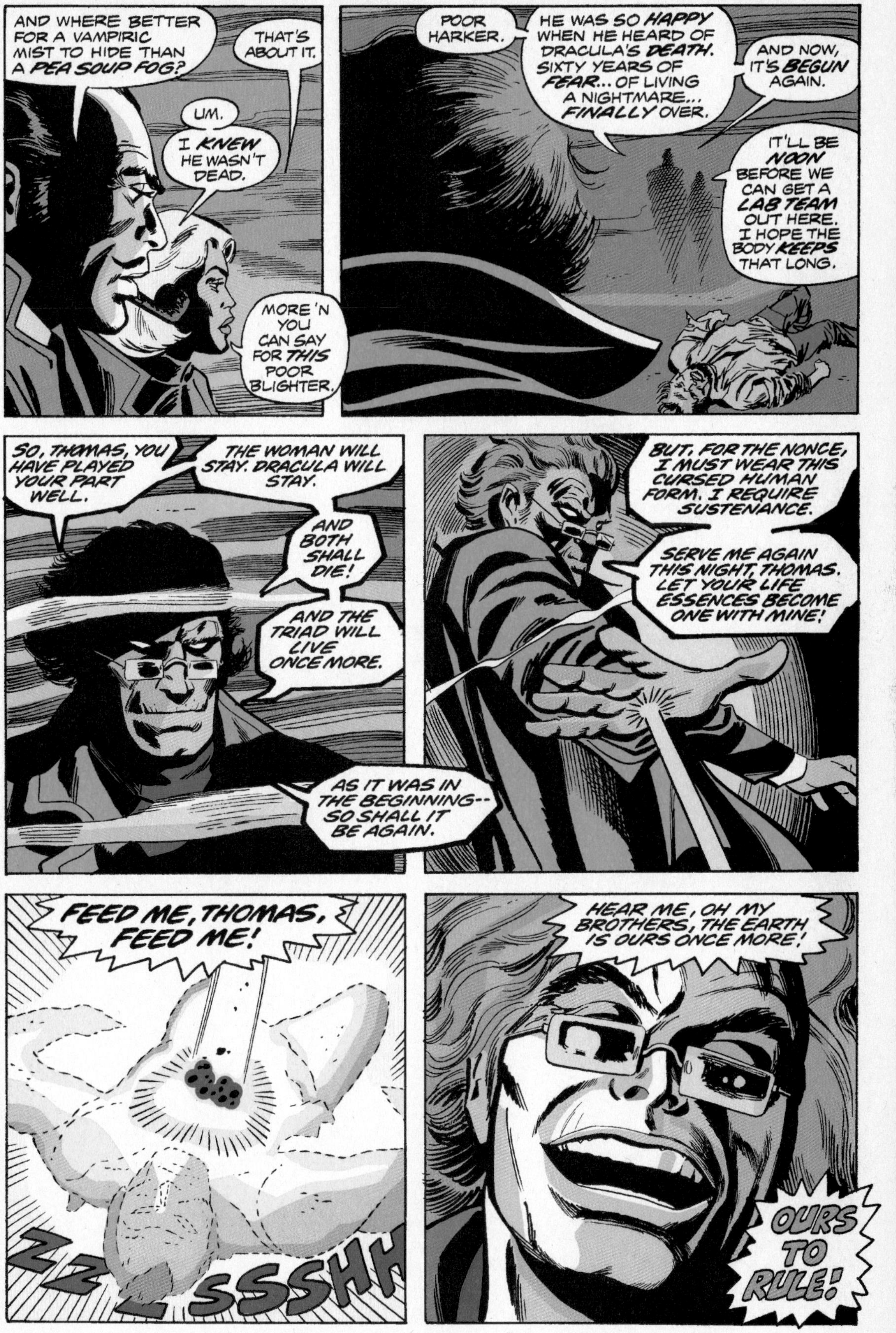
AND WHERE BETTER FOR A VAMPIRIC MIST TO HIDE THAN A PEA SOUP FOG?
THAT'S ABOUT IT.
UM.
I KNEW HE WASN'T DEAD.
MORE 'N YOU CAN SAY FOR THIS POOR BLIGHTER.
POOR HARKER.
HE WAS SO HAPPY WHEN HE HEARD OF DRACULA'S DEATH. SIXTY YEARS OF FEAR... OF LIVING A NIGHTMARE... FINALLY OVER.
AND NOW, IT'S BEGUN AGAIN.
IT'LL BE NOON BEFORE WE CAN GET A LAB TEAM OUT HERE. I HOPE THE BODY KEEPS THAT LONG.
SO, THOMAS, YOU HAVE PLAYED YOUR PART WELL.
THE WOMAN WILL STAY. DRACULA WILL STAY.
AND BOTH SHALL DIE!
AND THE TRIAD WILL LIVE ONCE MORE.
AS IT WAS IN THE BEGINNING-- SO SHALL IT BE AGAIN.
BUT, FOR THE NONCE, I MUST WEAR THIS CURSED HUMAN FORM. I REQUIRE SUSTENANCE.
SERVE ME AGAIN THIS NIGHT, THOMAS. LET YOUR LIFE ESSENCES BECOME ONE WITH MINE!
FEED ME, THOMAS, FEED ME!
ZZZSSSSHH
HEAR ME, OH MY BROTHERS, THE EARTH IS OURS ONCE MORE!
OURS TO RULE!

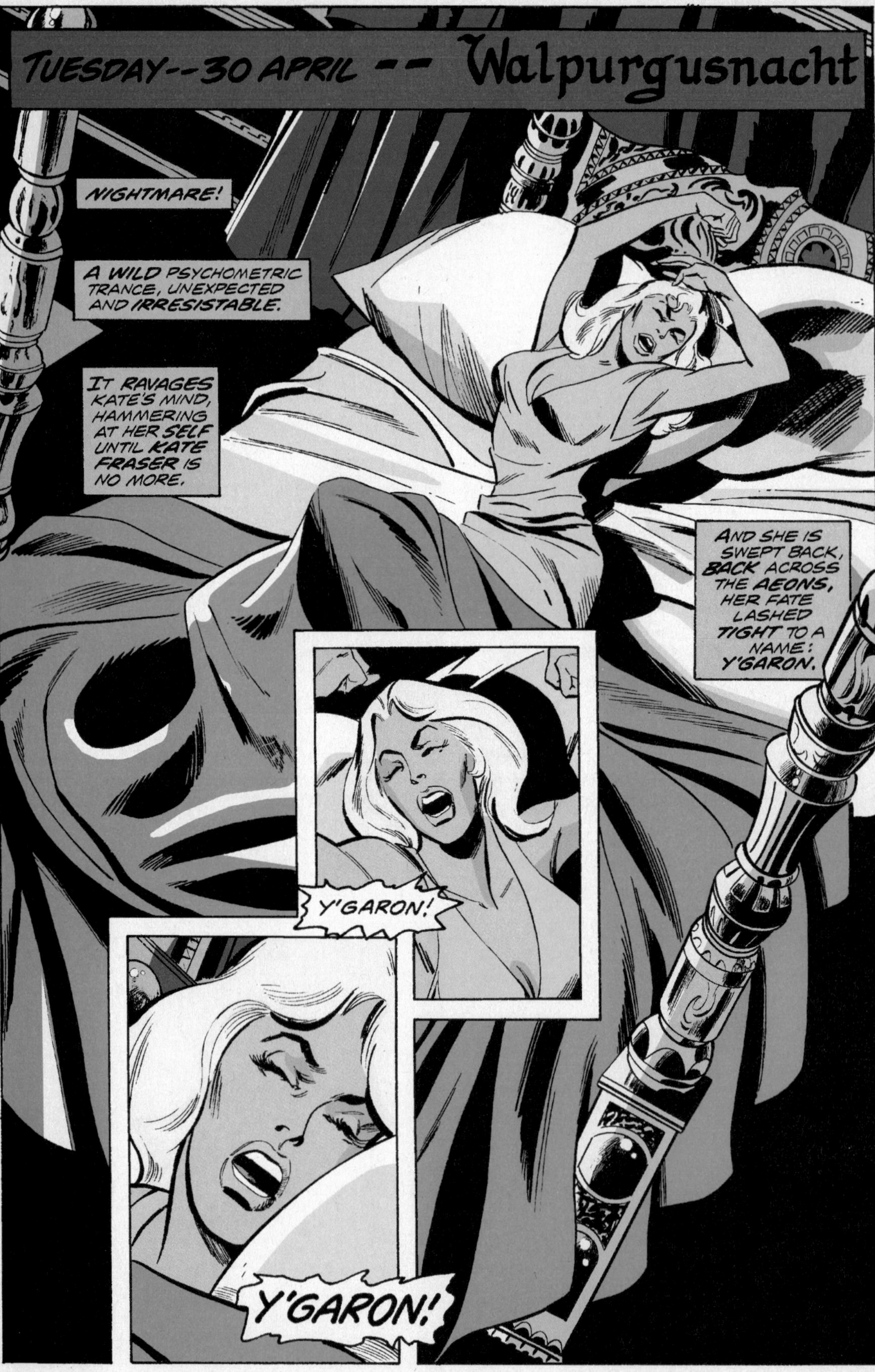
TUESDAY--30 APRIL -- Walpurgusnacht
NIGHTMARE!
A WILD PSYCHOMETRIC TRANCE, UNEXPECTED AND IRRESISTABLE.
IT RAVAGES KATE'S MIND, HAMMERING AT HER SELF UNTIL KATE FRASER IS NO MORE.
AND SHE IS SWEPT BACK, BACK ACROSS THE AEONS, HER FATE LASHED TIGHT TO A NAME: Y'GARON.
Y'GARON!
Y'GARON!

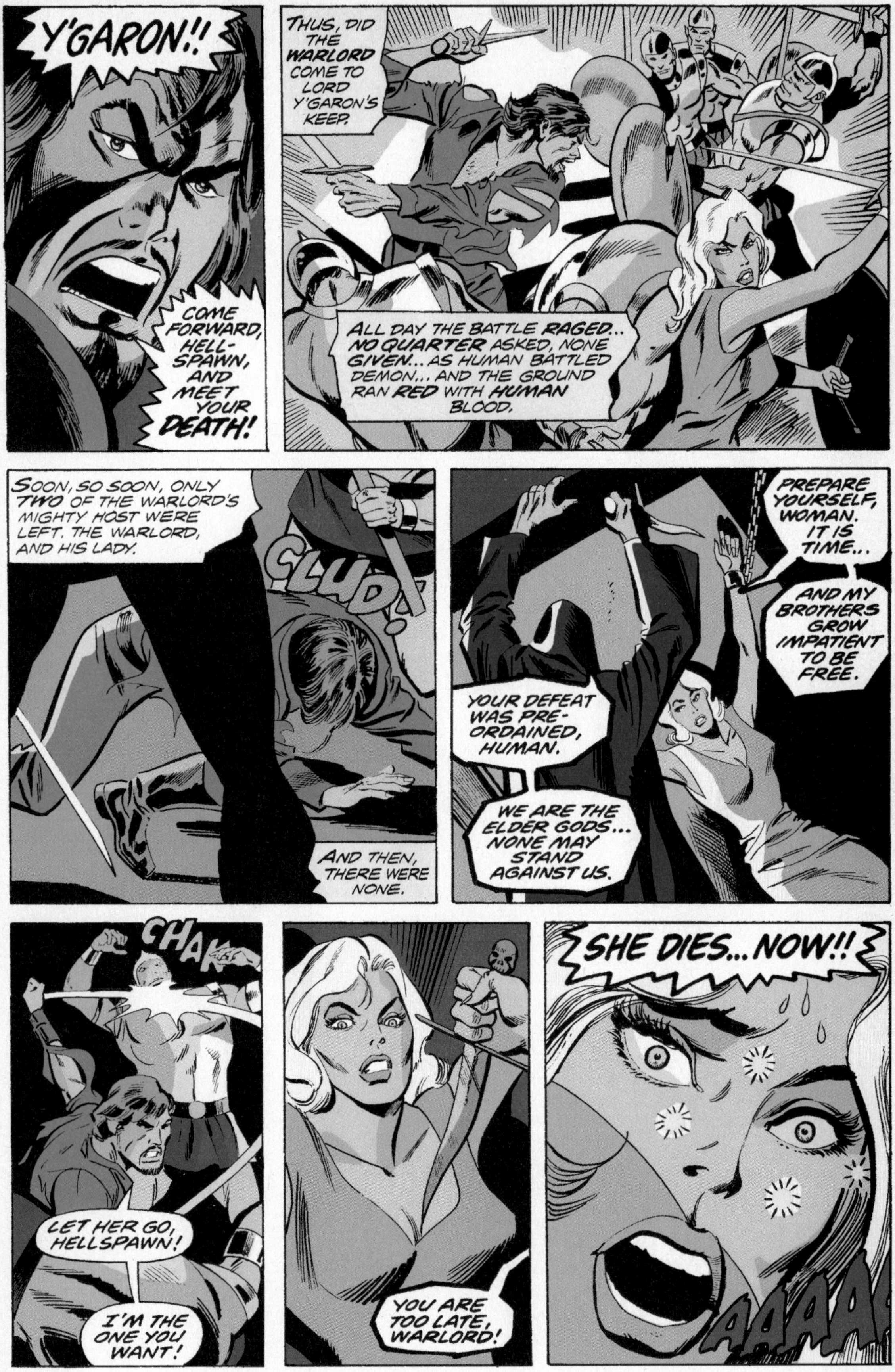
Y'GARON!!
COME FORWARD, HELL-SPAWN, AND MEET YOUR DEATH!
THUS, DID THE WARLORD COME TO LORD Y'GARON'S KEEP.
ALL DAY THE BATTLE RAGED... NO QUARTER ASKED, NONE GIVEN... AS HUMAN BATTLED DEMON... AND THE GROUND RAN RED WITH HUMAN BLOOD.
SOON, SO SOON, ONLY TWO OF THE WARLORD'S MIGHTY HOST WERE LEFT. THE WARLORD, AND HIS LADY.
CLUD!
AND THEN, THERE WERE NONE.
PREPARE YOURSELF, WOMAN. IT IS TIME...
AND MY BROTHERS GROW IMPATIENT TO BE FREE.
YOUR DEFEAT WAS PRE-ORDAINED, HUMAN.
WE ARE THE ELDER GODS... NONE MAY STAND AGAINST US.
CHAK
LET HER GO, HELLSPAWN!
I'M THE ONE YOU WANT!
YOU ARE TOO LATE, WARLORD!
SHE DIES...NOW!!
AAAA

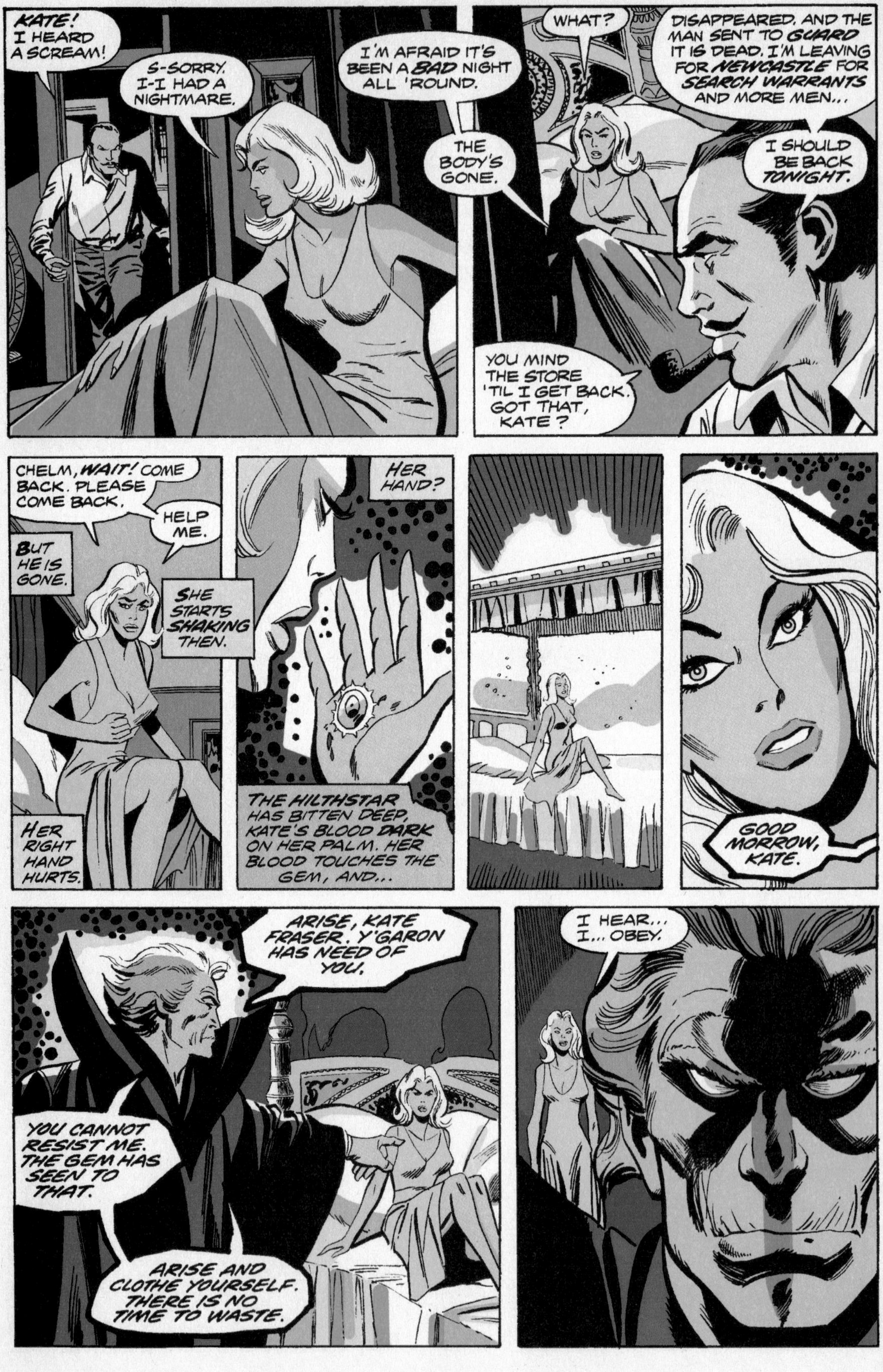

KATE! I HEARD A SCREAM!
S-SORRY. I-I HAD A NIGHTMARE.
I'M AFRAID IT'S BEEN A BAD NIGHT ALL 'ROUND.
THE BODY'S GONE.
WHAT?
DISAPPEARED. AND THE MAN SENT TO GUARD IT IS DEAD. I'M LEAVING FOR NEWCASTLE FOR SEARCH WARRANTS AND MORE MEN...
I SHOULD BE BACK TONIGHT.
YOU MIND THE STORE 'TIL I GET BACK. GOT THAT, KATE?
CHELM, WAIT! COME BACK. PLEASE COME BACK.
HELP ME.
BUT HE IS GONE.
SHE STARTS SHAKING THEN.
HER RIGHT HAND HURTS.
HER HAND?
THE HILTHSTAR HAS BITTEN DEEP, KATE'S BLOOD DARK ON HER PALM. HER BLOOD TOUCHES THE GEM, AND...
GOOD MORROW, KATE.
ARISE, KATE FRASER. Y'GARON HAS NEED OF YOU.
YOU CANNOT RESIST ME. THE GEM HAS SEEN TO THAT.
ARISE AND CLOTHE YOURSELF. THERE IS NO TIME TO WASTE.
I HEAR... I... OBEY.

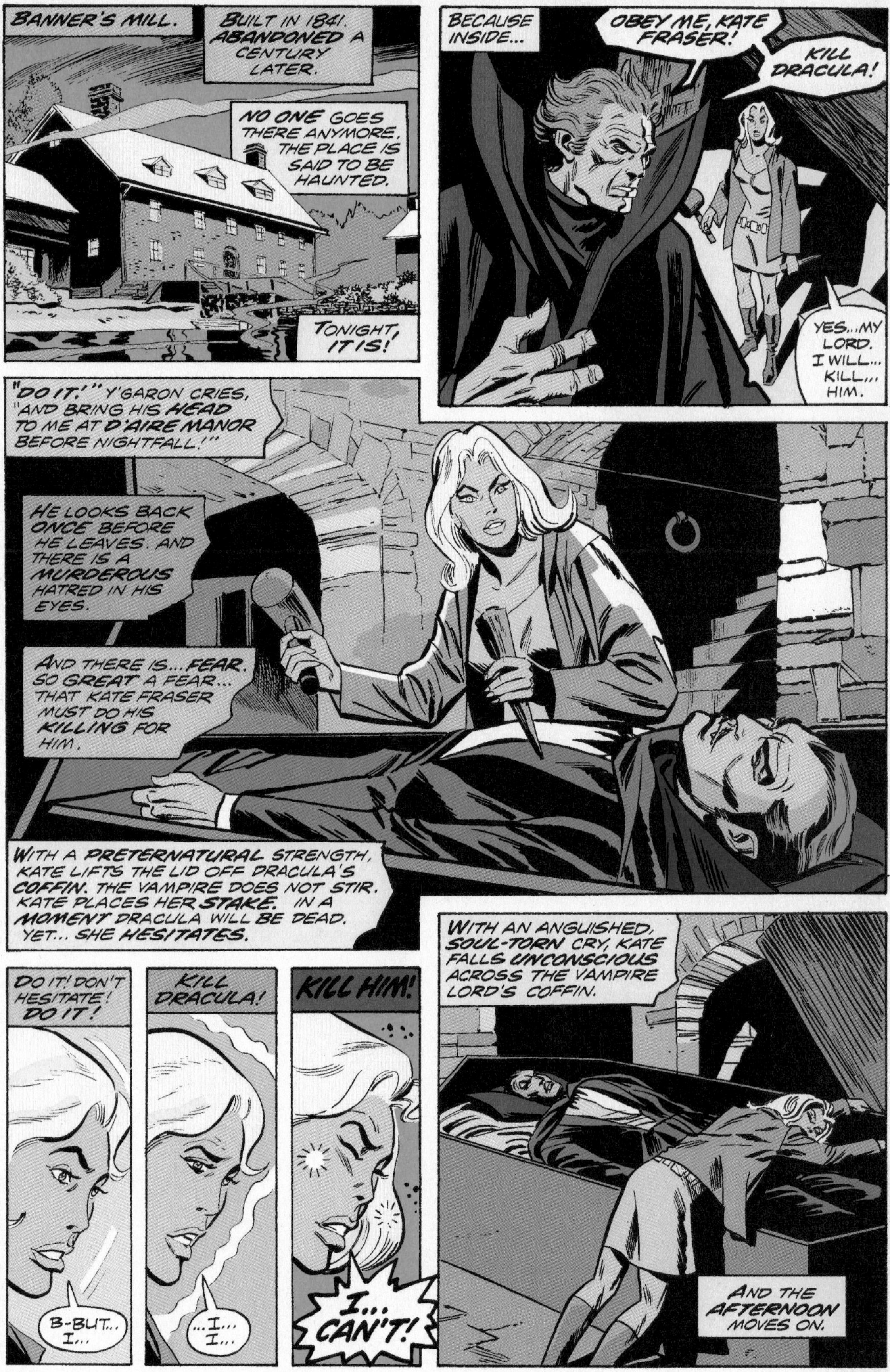
BANNER'S MILL.
BUILT IN 1841. ABANDONED A CENTURY LATER.
NO ONE GOES THERE ANYMORE. THE PLACE IS SAID TO BE HAUNTED.
TONIGHT, IT IS!
BECAUSE INSIDE...
OBEY ME, KATE FRASER!
KILL DRACULA!
YES...MY LORD. I WILL... KILL... HIM.
"DO IT!" Y'GARON CRIES, "AND BRING HIS HEAD TO ME AT D'AIRE MANOR BEFORE NIGHTFALL!"
HE LOOKS BACK ONCE BEFORE HE LEAVES. AND THERE IS A MURDEROUS HATRED IN HIS EYES.
AND THERE IS...FEAR. SO GREAT A FEAR... THAT KATE FRASER MUST DO HIS KILLING FOR HIM.
WITH A PRETERNATURAL STRENGTH, KATE LIFTS THE LID OFF DRACULA'S COFFIN. THE VAMPIRE DOES NOT STIR. KATE PLACES HER STAKE. IN A MOMENT DRACULA WILL BE DEAD. YET... SHE HESITATES.
DO IT! DON'T HESITATE! DO IT!
B-BUT... I...
KILL DRACULA!
...I... I...
KILL HIM!
I... CAN'T!
WITH AN ANGUISHED, SOUL-TORN CRY, KATE FALLS UNCONSCIOUS ACROSS THE VAMPIRE LORD'S COFFIN.
AND THE AFTERNOON MOVES ON.

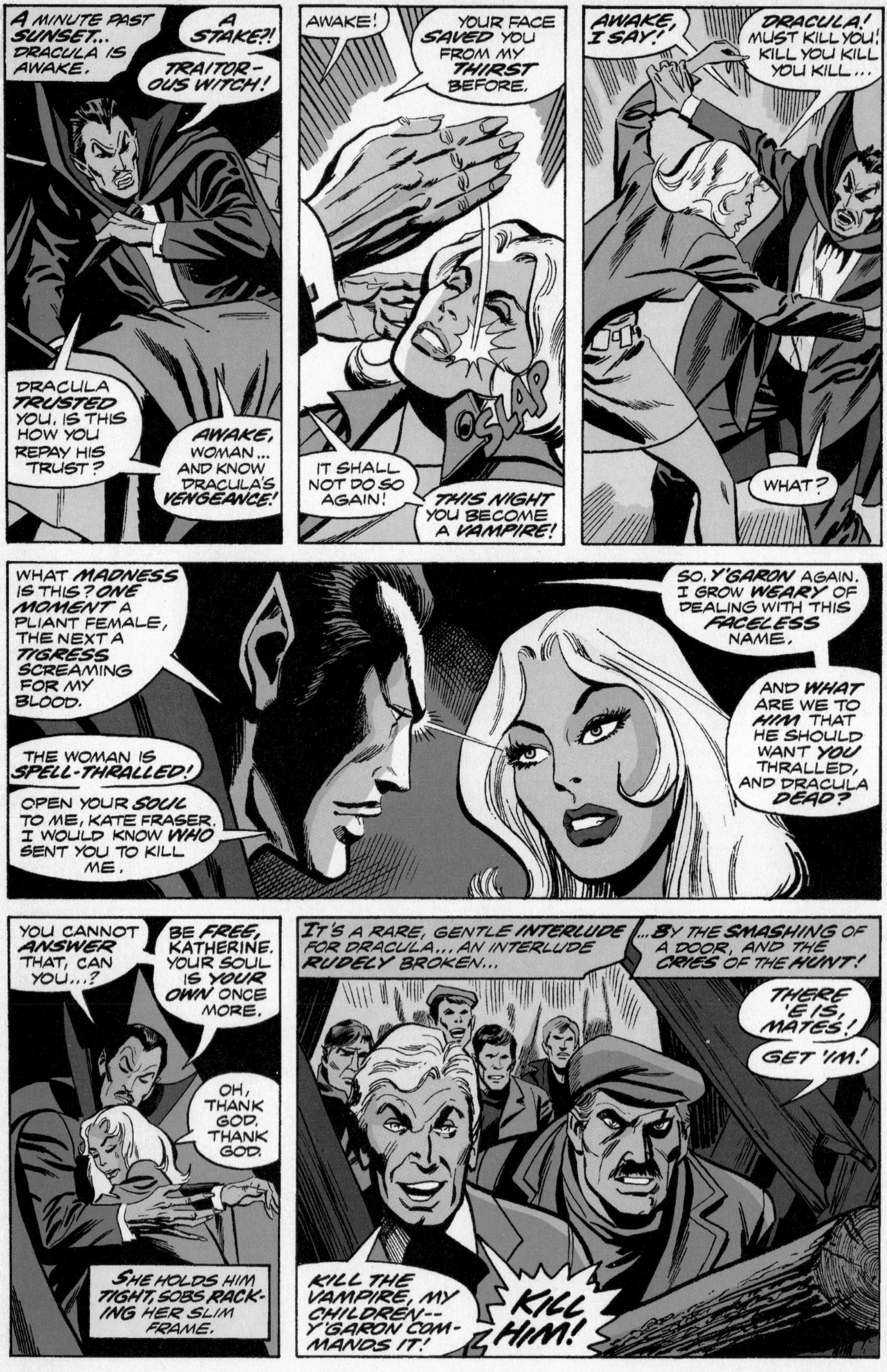
A MINUTE PAST SUNSET... DRACULA IS AWAKE.
A STAKE?!
TRAITOROUS WITCH!
DRACULA TRUSTED YOU. IS THIS HOW YOU REPAY HIS TRUST?
AWAKE, WOMAN... AND KNOW DRACULA'S VENGEANCE!
AWAKE!
YOUR FACE SAVED YOU FROM MY THIRST BEFORE.
SLAP
IT SHALL NOT DO SO AGAIN!
THIS NIGHT YOU BECOME A VAMPIRE!
AWAKE, I SAY!
DRACULA! MUST KILL YOU! KILL YOU KILL YOU KILL...
WHAT?
WHAT MADNESS IS THIS? ONE MOMENT A PLIANT FEMALE, THE NEXT A TIGRESS SCREAMING FOR MY BLOOD.
THE WOMAN IS SPELL-THRALLED!
OPEN YOUR SOUL TO ME, KATE FRASER. I WOULD KNOW WHO SENT YOU TO KILL ME.
SO, Y'GARON AGAIN. I GROW WEARY OF DEALING WITH THIS FACELESS NAME.
AND WHAT ARE WE TO HIM THAT HE SHOULD WANT YOU THRALLED, AND DRACULA DEAD?
YOU CANNOT ANSWER THAT, CAN YOU...?
BE FREE, KATHERINE. YOUR SOUL IS YOUR OWN ONCE MORE.
OH, THANK GOD, THANK GOD.
SHE HOLDS HIM TIGHT, SOBS RACKING HER SLIM FRAME.
IT'S A RARE, GENTLE INTERLUDE FOR DRACULA... AN INTERLUDE RUDELY BROKEN...
...BY THE SMASHING OF A DOOR, AND THE CRIES OF THE HUNT!
THERE 'E IS, MATES!
GET 'IM!
KILL THE VAMPIRE, MY CHILDREN-- Y'GARON COMMANDS IT!
KILL HIM!

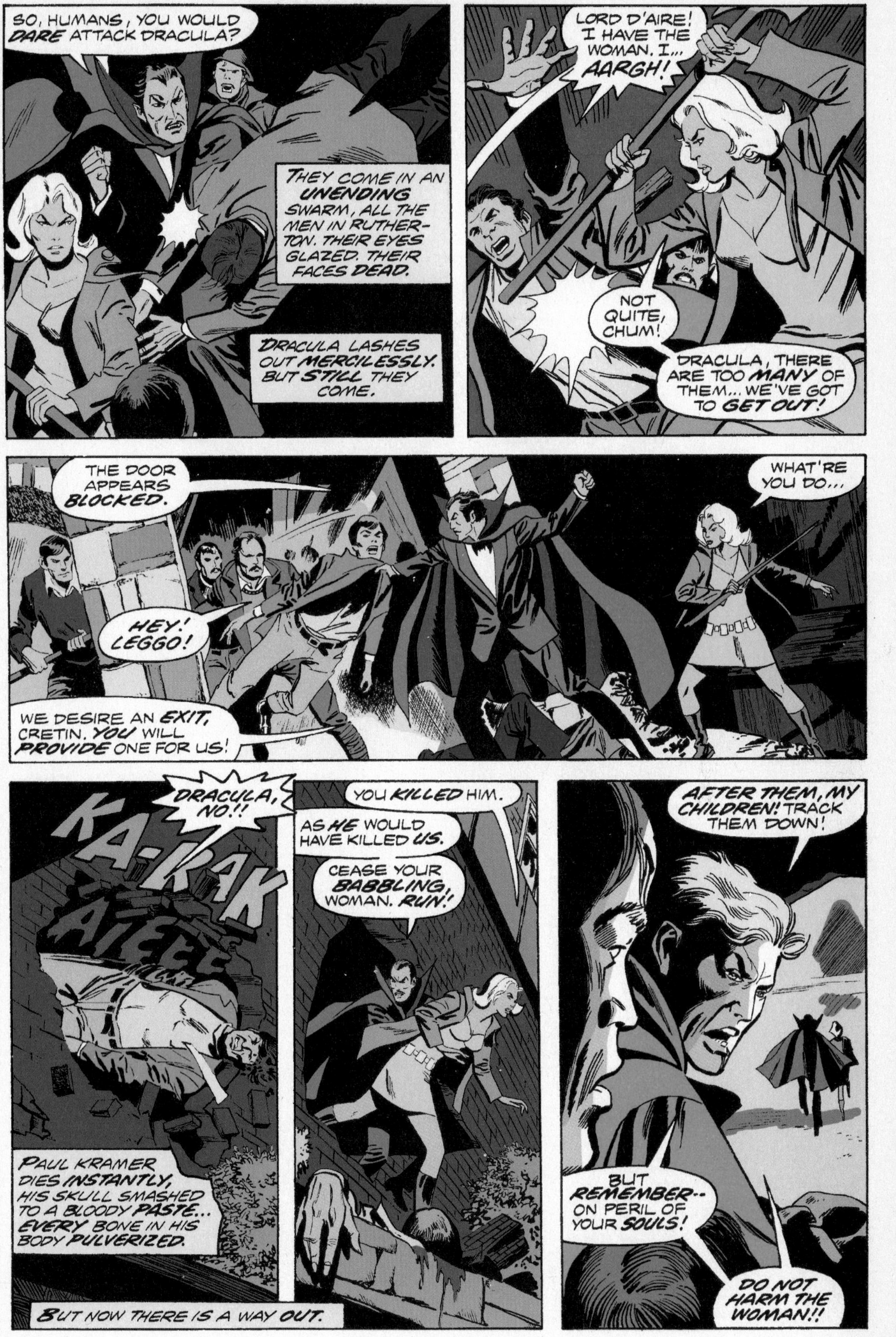
SO, HUMANS, YOU WOULD DARE ATTACK DRACULA?
THEY COME IN AN UNENDING SWARM, ALL THE MEN IN RUTHERTON. THEIR EYES GLAZED. THEIR FACES DEAD.
DRACULA LASHES OUT MERCILESSLY. BUT STILL THEY COME.
LORD D'AIRE! I HAVE THE WOMAN. I... AARGH!
NOT QUITE, CHUM!
DRACULA, THERE ARE TOO MANY OF THEM... WE'VE GOT TO GET OUT!
THE DOOR APPEARS BLOCKED.
HEY! LEGGO!
WE DESIRE AN EXIT, CRETIN. YOU WILL PROVIDE ONE FOR US!
WHAT'RE YOU DO...
KA-RAK
AIEEE
DRACULA, NO!!
PAUL KRAMER DIES INSTANTLY, HIS SKULL SMASHED TO A BLOODY PASTE... EVERY BONE IN HIS BODY PULVERIZED.
BUT NOW THERE IS A WAY OUT.
YOU KILLED HIM.
AS HE WOULD HAVE KILLED US.
CEASE YOUR BABBLING, WOMAN. RUN!
AFTER THEM, MY CHILDREN! TRACK THEM DOWN!
BUT REMEMBER-- ON PERIL OF YOUR SOULS!
DO NOT HARM THE WOMAN!!

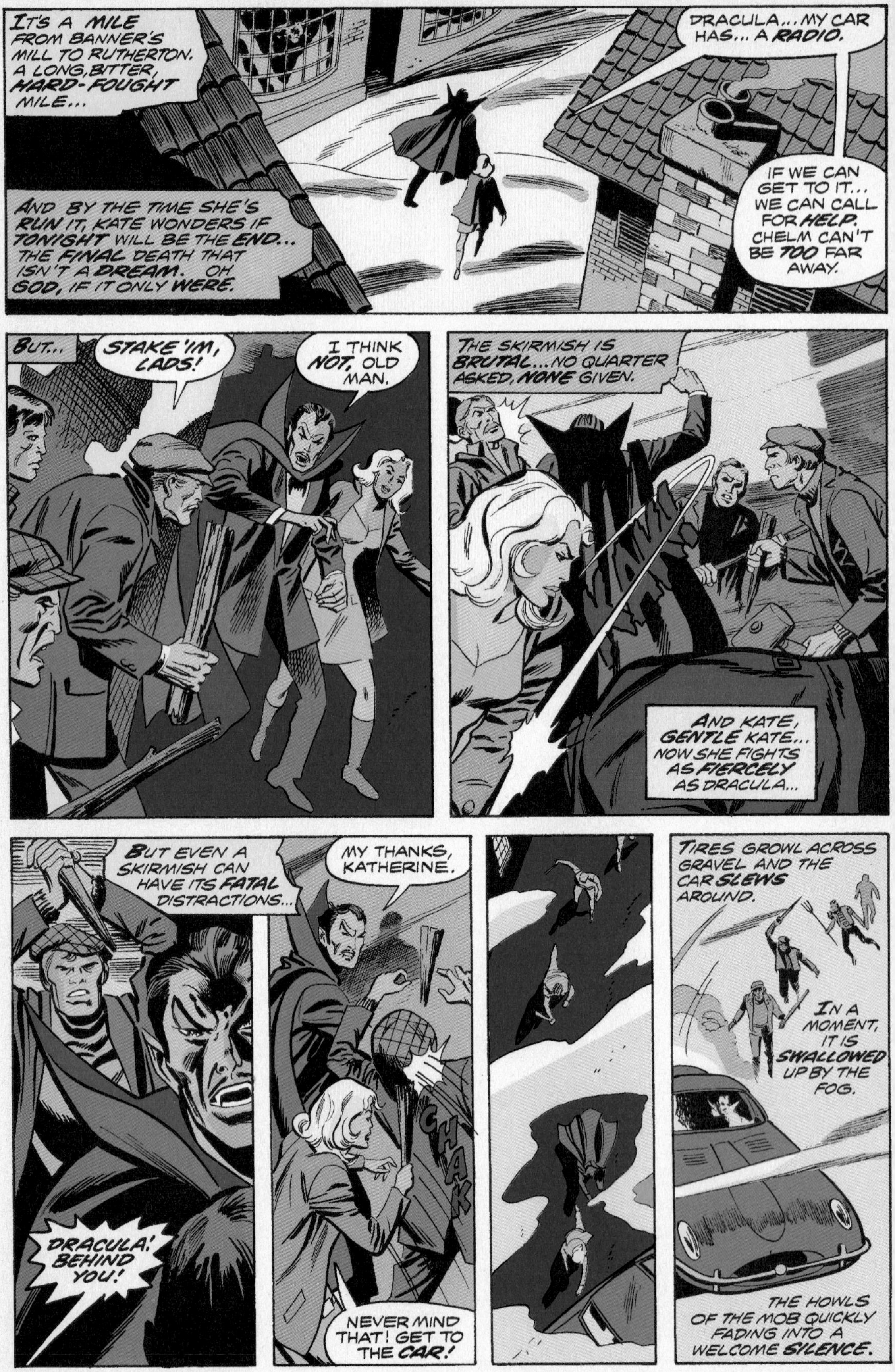
IT'S A MILE FROM BANNER'S MILL TO RUTHERTON. A LONG, BITTER, HARD-FOUGHT MILE...
AND BY THE TIME SHE'S RUN IT, KATE WONDERS IF TONIGHT WILL BE THE END... THE FINAL DEATH THAT ISN'T A DREAM. OH GOD, IF IT ONLY WERE.
DRACULA... MY CAR HAS... A RADIO.
IF WE CAN GET TO IT... WE CAN CALL FOR HELP. CHELM CAN'T BE TOO FAR AWAY.
BUT...
STAKE 'IM, LADS!
I THINK NOT, OLD MAN.
THE SKIRMISH IS BRUTAL... NO QUARTER ASKED, NONE GIVEN.
AND KATE, GENTLE KATE... NOW SHE FIGHTS AS FIERCELY AS DRACULA...
BUT EVEN A SKIRMISH CAN HAVE ITS FATAL DISTRACTIONS...
DRACULA! BEHIND YOU!
MY THANKS, KATHERINE.
CHAK
NEVER MIND THAT! GET TO THE CAR!
TIRES GROWL ACROSS GRAVEL AND THE CAR SLEWS AROUND.
IN A MOMENT, IT IS SWALLOWED UP BY THE FOG.
THE HOWLS OF THE MOB QUICKLY FADING INTO A WELCOME SILENCE.

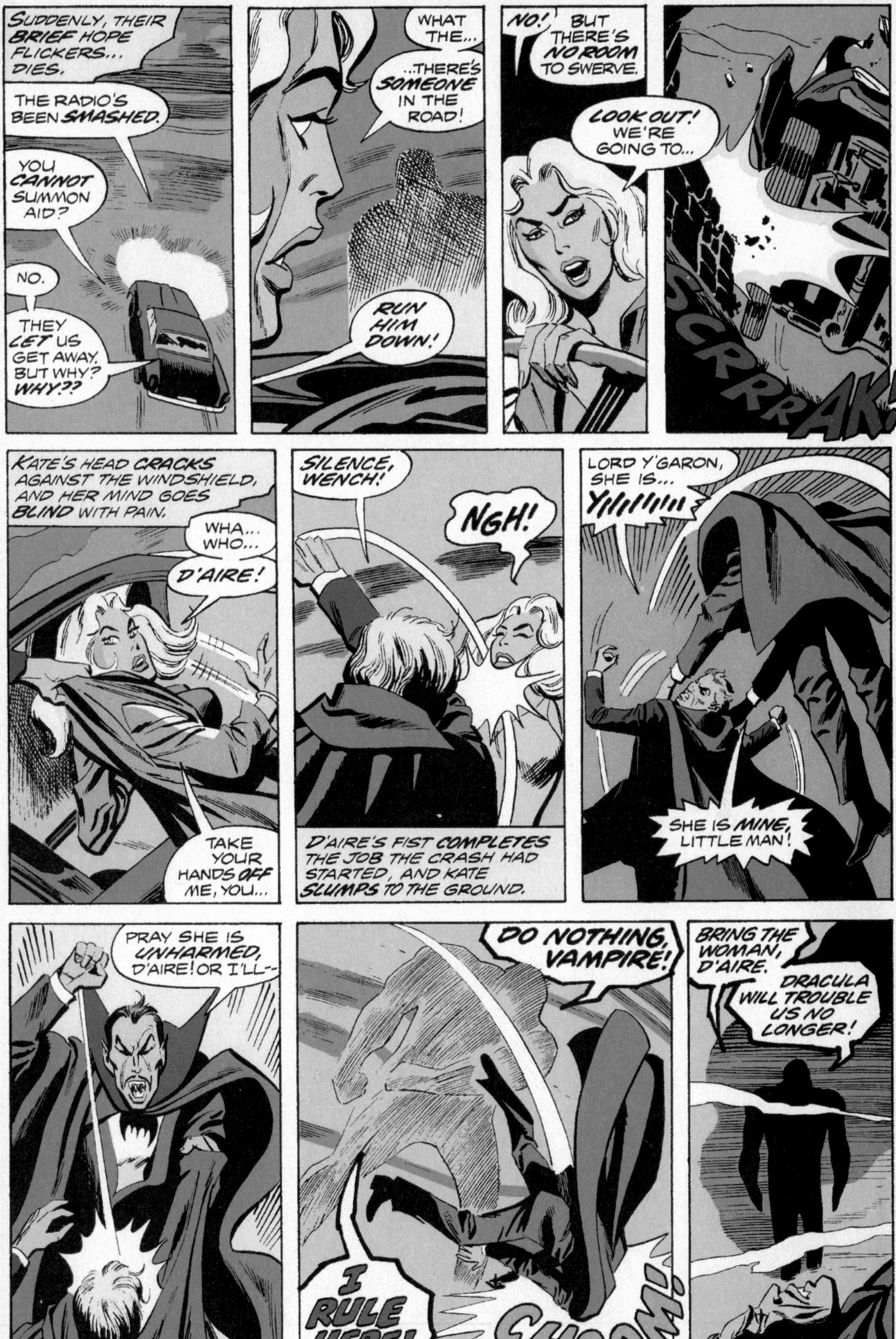
SUDDENLY, THEIR BRIEF HOPE FLICKERS... DIES.
THE RADIO'S BEEN SMASHED.
YOU CANNOT SUMMON AID?
NO.
THEY LET US GET AWAY. BUT WHY? WHY??
WHAT THE...
...THERE'S SOMEONE IN THE ROAD!
RUN HIM DOWN!
NO! BUT THERE'S NO ROOM TO SWERVE.
LOOK OUT! WE'RE GOING TO...
SCRRRAK!
KATE'S HEAD CRACKS AGAINST THE WINDSHIELD, AND HER MIND GOES BLIND WITH PAIN.
WHA... WHO...
D'AIRE!
TAKE YOUR HANDS OFF ME, YOU...
SILENCE, WENCH!
NGH!
D'AIRE'S FIST COMPLETES THE JOB THE CRASH HAD STARTED, AND KATE SLUMPS TO THE GROUND.
LORD Y'GARON, SHE IS...
YIIIIIIII
SHE IS MINE, LITTLE MAN!
PRAY SHE IS UNHARMED, D'AIRE! OR I'LL--
DO NOTHING, VAMPIRE!
I RULE HERE!
CHOOM!
BRING THE WOMAN, D'AIRE.
DRACULA WILL TROUBLE US NO LONGER!

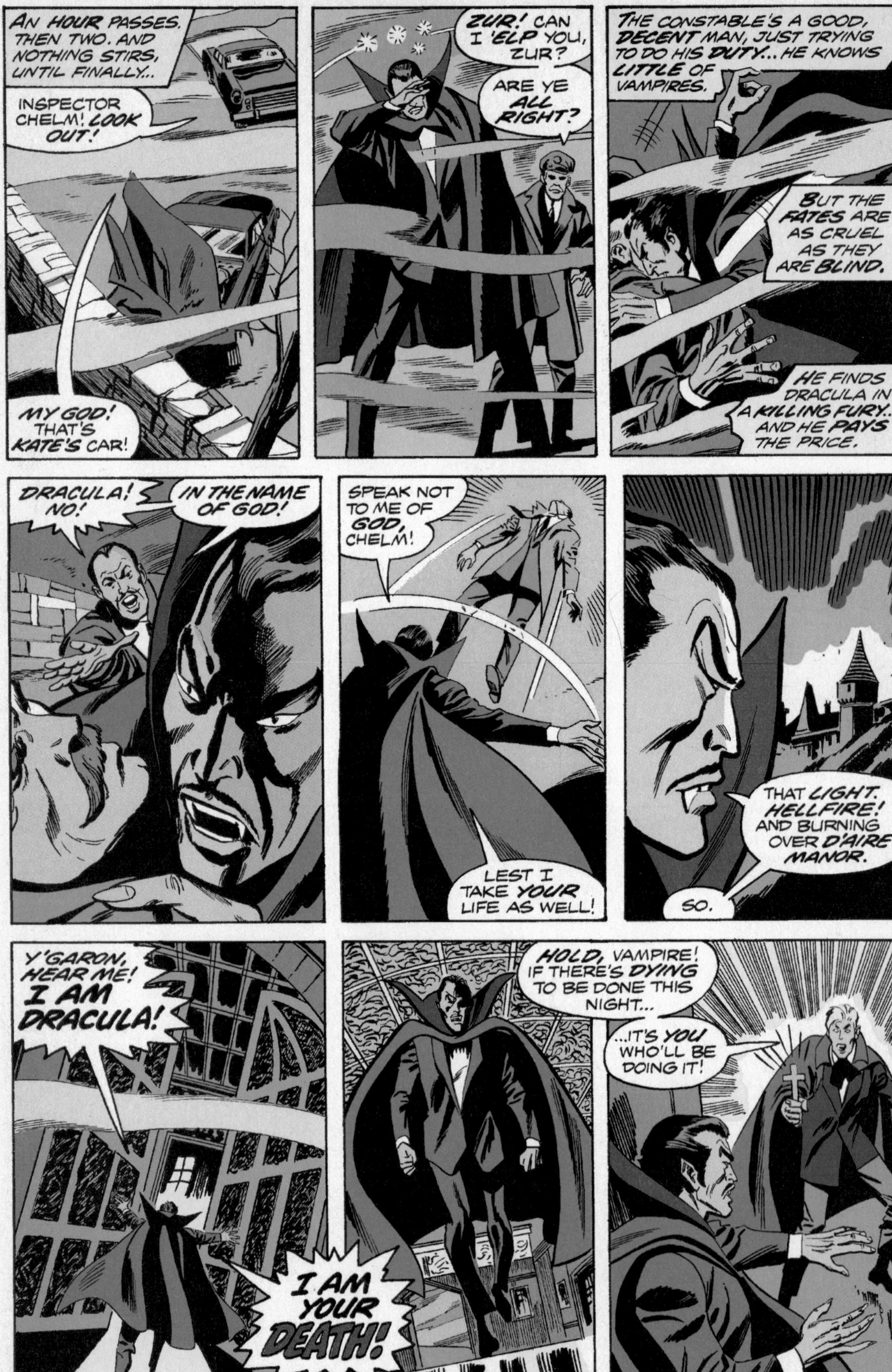
AN HOUR PASSES. THEN TWO. AND NOTHING STIRS, UNTIL FINALLY...
INSPECTOR CHELM! LOOK OUT!
MY GOD! THAT'S KATE'S CAR!
ZUR! CAN I 'ELP YOU, ZUR?
ARE YE ALL RIGHT?
THE CONSTABLE'S A GOOD, DECENT MAN, JUST TRYING TO DO HIS DUTY... HE KNOWS LITTLE OF VAMPIRES.
BUT THE FATES ARE AS CRUEL AS THEY ARE BLIND.
HE FINDS DRACULA IN A KILLING FURY... AND HE PAYS THE PRICE.
DRACULA! NO!
IN THE NAME OF GOD!
SPEAK NOT TO ME OF GOD, CHELM!
LEST I TAKE YOUR LIFE AS WELL!
THAT LIGHT. HELLFIRE! AND BURNING OVER D'AIRE MANOR.
SO.
Y'GARON, HEAR ME! I AM DRACULA!
I AM YOUR DEATH!
HOLD, VAMPIRE! IF THERE'S DYING TO BE DONE THIS NIGHT...
...IT'S YOU WHO'LL BE DOING IT!

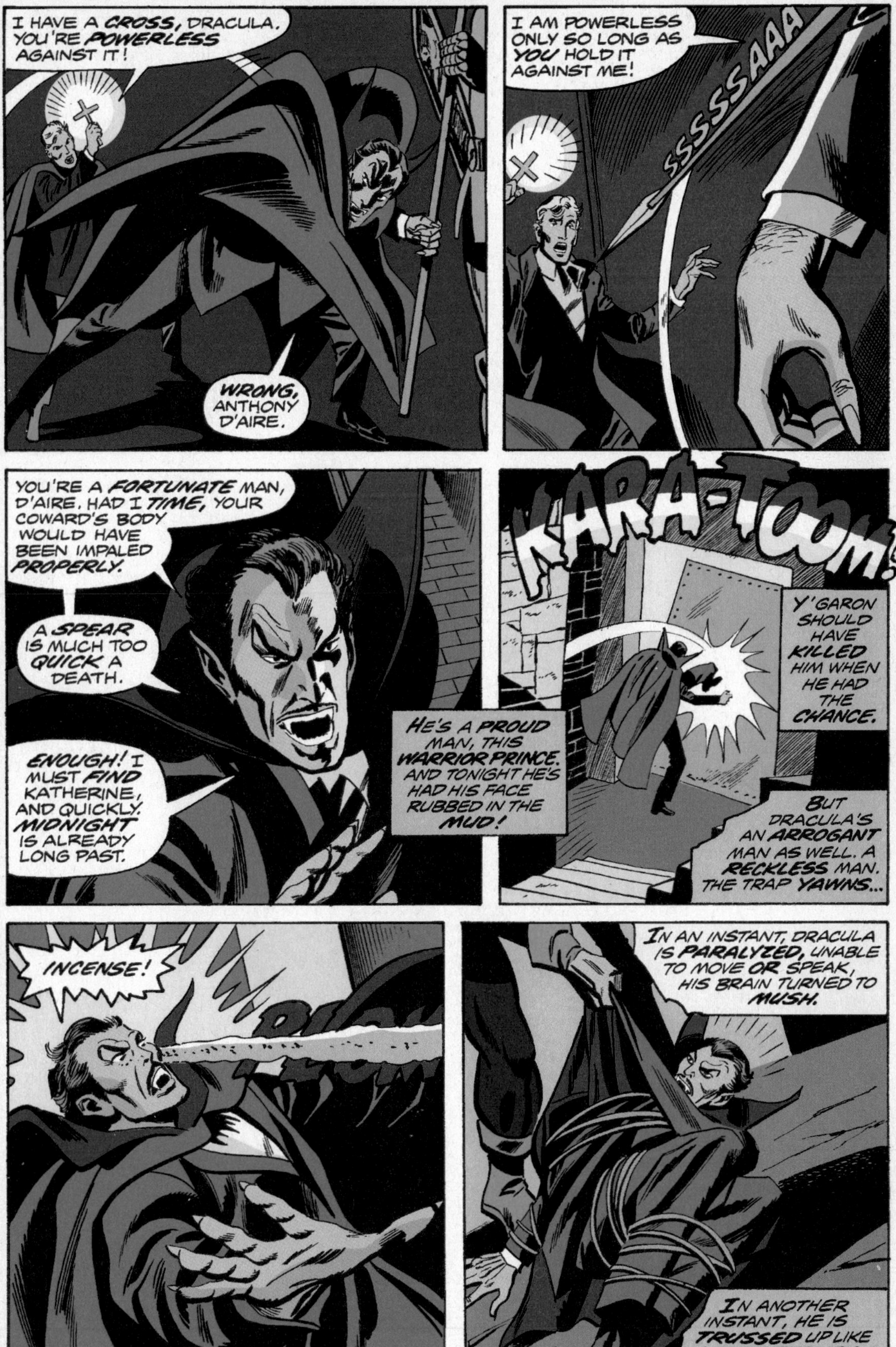
I HAVE A CROSS, DRACULA. YOU'RE POWERLESS AGAINST IT!
WRONG, ANTHONY D'AIRE.
I AM POWERLESS ONLY SO LONG AS YOU HOLD IT AGAINST ME!
SSSSSSAAA
YOU'RE A FORTUNATE MAN, D'AIRE. HAD I TIME, YOUR COWARD'S BODY WOULD HAVE BEEN IMPALED PROPERLY.
A SPEAR IS MUCH TOO QUICK A DEATH.
ENOUGH! I MUST FIND KATHERINE, AND QUICKLY. MIDNIGHT IS ALREADY LONG PAST.
HE'S A PROUD MAN, THIS WARRIOR PRINCE. AND TONIGHT HE'S HAD HIS FACE RUBBED IN THE MUD!
KARA-TOOM!
Y'GARON SHOULD HAVE KILLED HIM WHEN HE HAD THE CHANCE.
BUT DRACULA'S AN ARROGANT MAN AS WELL. A RECKLESS MAN. THE TRAP YAWNS...
INCENSE!
IN AN INSTANT, DRACULA IS PARALYZED, UNABLE TO MOVE OR SPEAK, HIS BRAIN TURNED TO MUSH.
IN ANOTHER INSTANT, HE IS TRUSSED UP LIKE A PRIZE TURKEY.

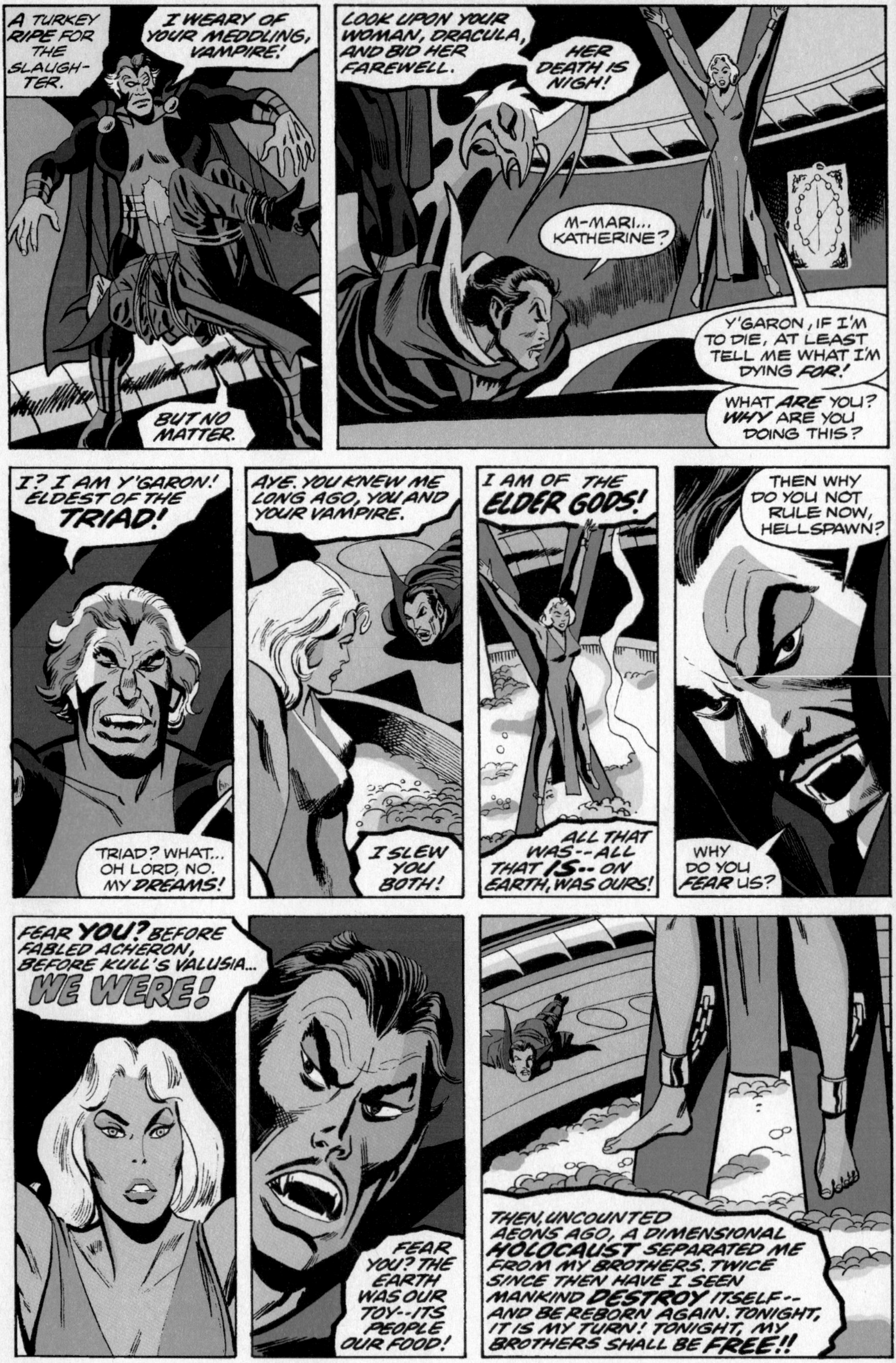
A TURKEY RIPE FOR THE SLAUGHTER.
I WEARY OF YOUR MEDDLING, VAMPIRE!
BUT NO MATTER.
LOOK UPON YOUR WOMAN, DRACULA, AND BID HER FAREWELL.
HER DEATH IS NIGH!
M-MARI... KATHERINE?
Y'GARON, IF I'M TO DIE, AT LEAST TELL ME WHAT I'M DYING FOR!
WHAT ARE YOU? WHY ARE YOU DOING THIS?
I? I AM Y'GARON! ELDEST OF THE TRIAD!
TRIAD? WHAT... OH LORD, NO. MY DREAMS!
AYE. YOU KNEW ME LONG AGO, YOU AND YOUR VAMPIRE.
I SLEW YOU BOTH!
I AM OF THE ELDER GODS!
ALL THAT WAS--ALL THAT IS--ON EARTH, WAS OURS!
THEN WHY DO YOU NOT RULE NOW, HELLSPAWN?
WHY DO YOU FEAR US?
FEAR YOU? BEFORE FABLED ACHERON, BEFORE KULL'S VALUSIA... WE WERE!
FEAR YOU? THE EARTH WAS OUR TOY--ITS PEOPLE OUR FOOD!
THEN, UNCOUNTED AEONS AGO, A DIMENSIONAL HOLOCAUST SEPARATED ME FROM MY BROTHERS. TWICE SINCE THEN HAVE I SEEN MANKIND DESTROY ITSELF--AND BE REBORN AGAIN. TONIGHT, IT IS MY TURN! TONIGHT, MY BROTHERS SHALL BE FREE!!

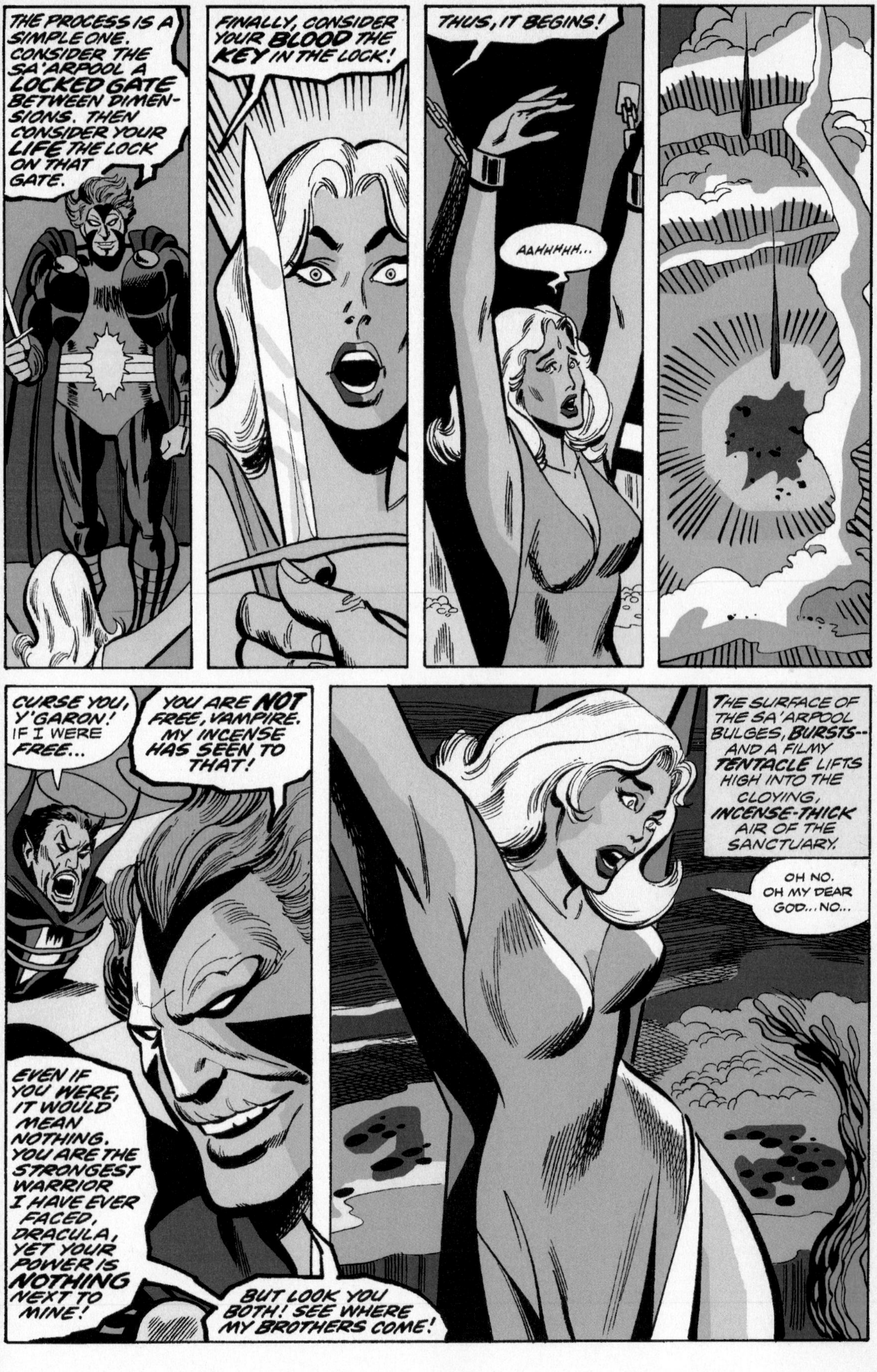
THE PROCESS IS A SIMPLE ONE. CONSIDER THE SA'ARPOOL A LOCKED GATE BETWEEN DIMENSIONS. THEN CONSIDER YOUR LIFE THE LOCK ON THAT GATE.
FINALLY, CONSIDER YOUR BLOOD THE KEY IN THE LOCK!
THUS, IT BEGINS!
AAHHHHH...
CURSE YOU, Y'GARON! IF I WERE FREE...
YOU ARE NOT FREE, VAMPIRE. MY INCENSE HAS SEEN TO THAT!
EVEN IF YOU WERE, IT WOULD MEAN NOTHING. YOU ARE THE STRONGEST WARRIOR I HAVE EVER FACED, DRACULA, YET YOUR POWER IS NOTHING NEXT TO MINE!
BUT LOOK YOU BOTH! SEE WHERE MY BROTHERS COME!
THE SURFACE OF THE SA'ARPOOL BULGES, BURSTS-- AND A FILMY TENTACLE LIFTS HIGH INTO THE CLOYING, INCENSE-THICK AIR OF THE SANCTUARY.
OH NO. OH MY DEAR GOD... NO...

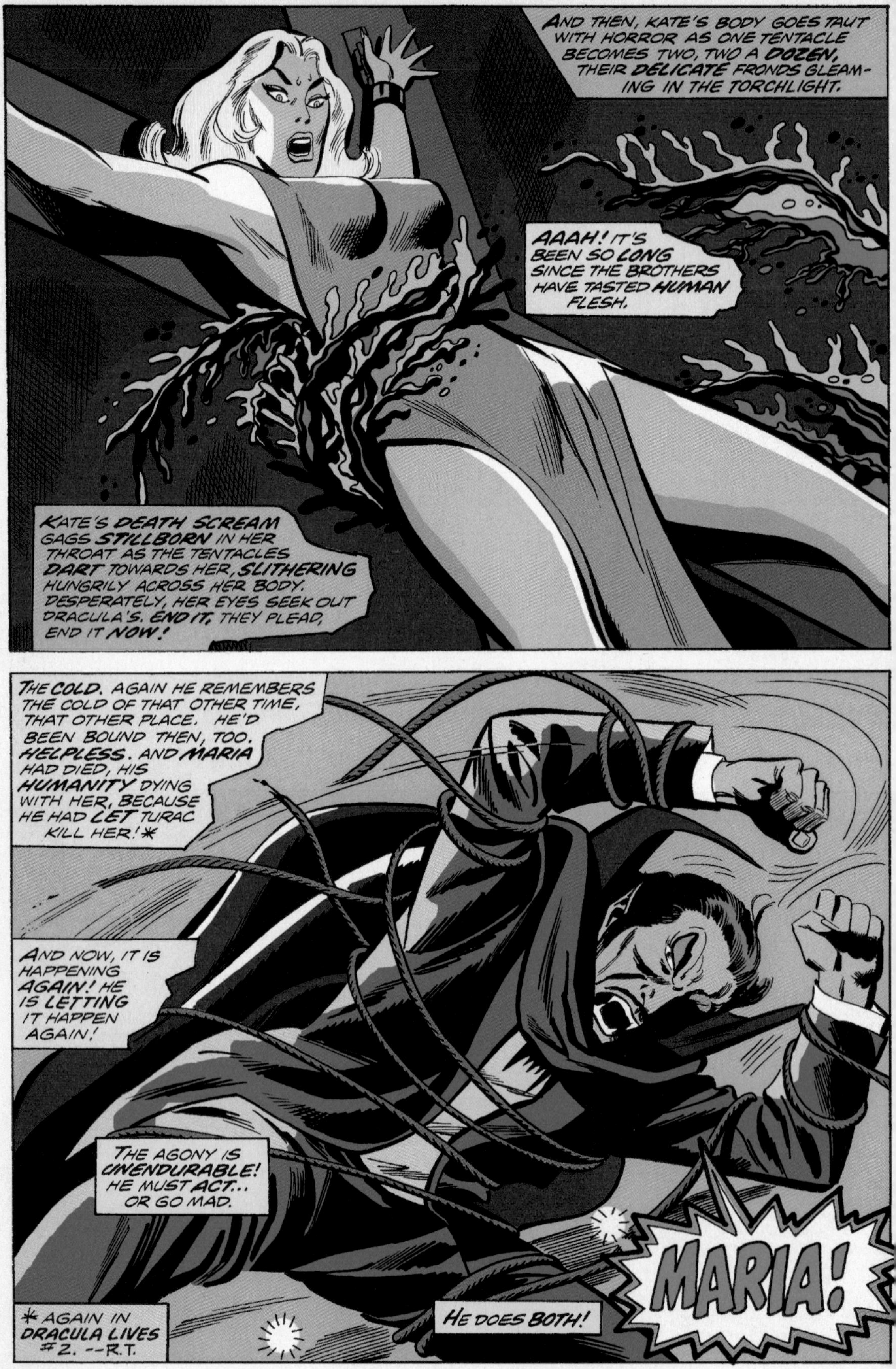
AND THEN, KATE'S BODY GOES TAUT WITH HORROR AS ONE TENTACLE BECOMES TWO, TWO A DOZEN, THEIR DELICATE FRONDS GLEAMING IN THE TORCHLIGHT.
AAAH! IT'S BEEN SO LONG SINCE THE BROTHERS HAVE TASTED HUMAN FLESH.
KATE'S DEATH SCREAM GAGS STILLBORN IN HER THROAT AS THE TENTACLES DART TOWARDS HER, SLITHERING HUNGRILY ACROSS HER BODY. DESPERATELY, HER EYES SEEK OUT DRACULA'S. END IT, THEY PLEAD, END IT NOW!
THE COLD. AGAIN HE REMEMBERS THE COLD OF THAT OTHER TIME, THAT OTHER PLACE. HE'D BEEN BOUND THEN, TOO. HELPLESS. AND MARIA HAD DIED, HIS HUMANITY DYING WITH HER, BECAUSE HE HAD LET TURAC KILL HER!*
AND NOW, IT IS HAPPENING AGAIN! HE IS LETTING IT HAPPEN AGAIN!
THE AGONY IS UNENDURABLE! HE MUST ACT.. OR GO MAD.
MARIA!
HE DOES BOTH!
* AGAIN IN DRACULA LIVES #2. --R.T.

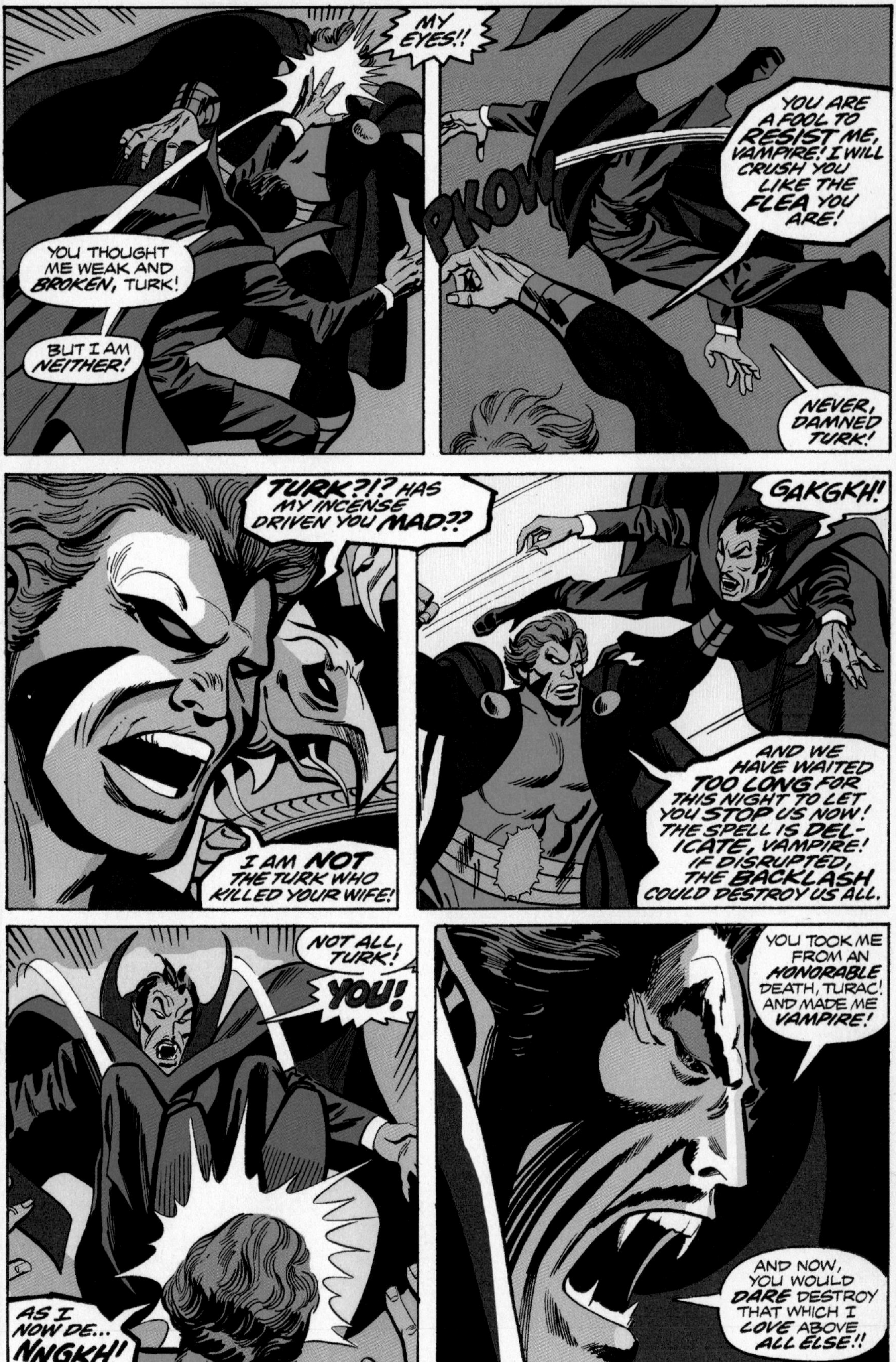
MY EYES!!
YOU THOUGHT ME WEAK AND BROKEN, TURK!
BUT I AM NEITHER!
PKOW
YOU ARE A FOOL TO RESIST ME, VAMPIRE! I WILL CRUSH YOU LIKE THE FLEA YOU ARE!
NEVER, DAMNED TURK!
TURK?!? HAS MY INCENSE DRIVEN YOU MAD??
I AM NOT THE TURK WHO KILLED YOUR WIFE!
GAKGKH!
AND WE HAVE WAITED TOO LONG FOR THIS NIGHT TO LET YOU STOP US NOW! THE SPELL IS DEL-ICATE, VAMPIRE! IF DISRUPTED, THE BACKLASH COULD DESTROY US ALL.
NOT ALL, TURK!
YOU!
AS I NOW DE... NNGKH!
YOU TOOK ME FROM AN HONORABLE DEATH, TURAC! AND MADE ME VAMPIRE!
AND NOW, YOU WOULD DARE DESTROY THAT WHICH I LOVE ABOVE ALL ELSE!!

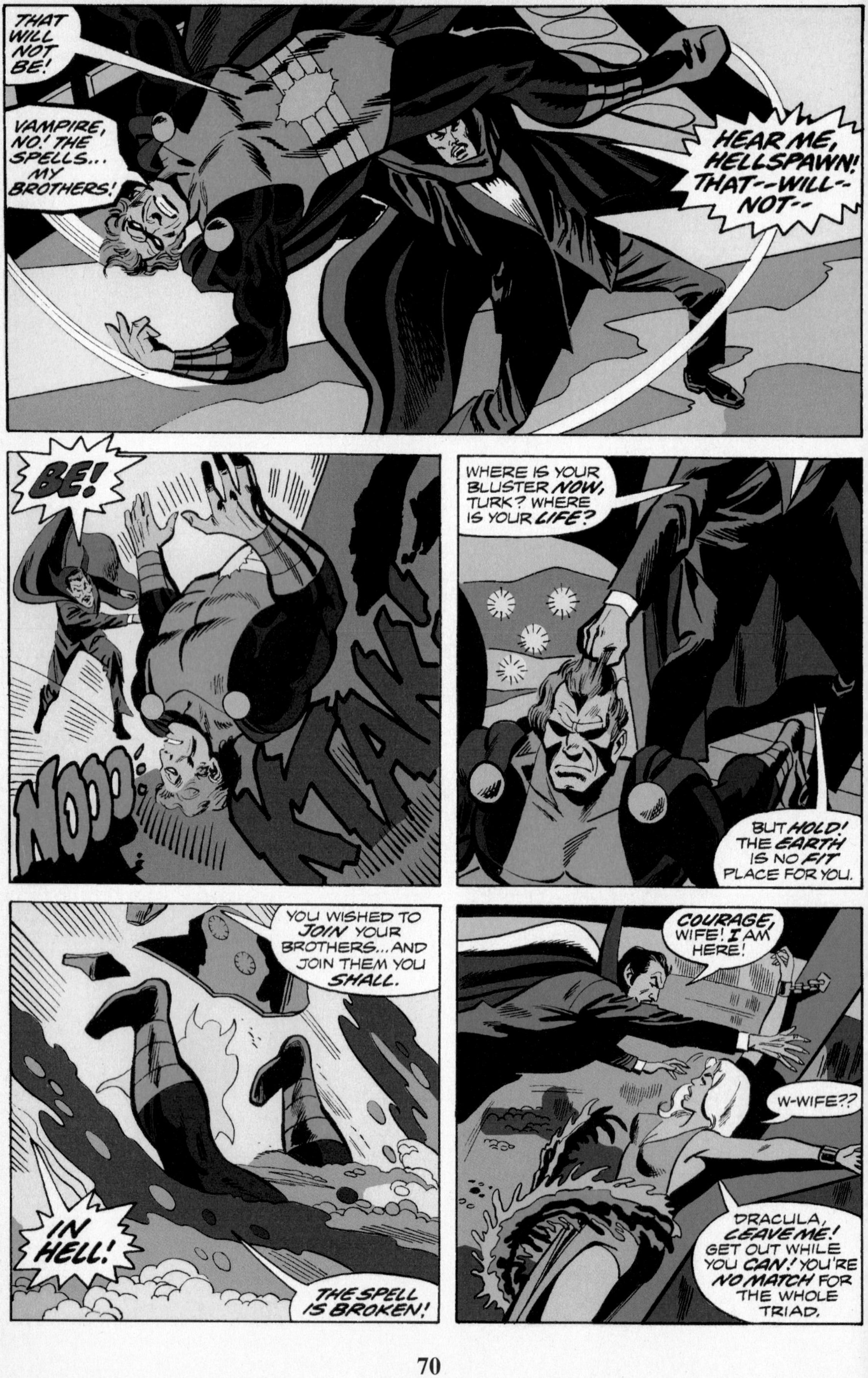
THAT WILL NOT BE!
VAMPIRE, NO! THE SPELLS... MY BROTHERS!
HEAR ME, HELLSPAWN! THAT--WILL--NOT--
BE!
NOOO
WHERE IS YOUR BLUSTER NOW, TURK? WHERE IS YOUR LIFE?
BUT HOLD! THE EARTH IS NO FIT PLACE FOR YOU.
YOU WISHED TO JOIN YOUR BROTHERS...AND JOIN THEM YOU SHALL.
IN HELL!
THE SPELL IS BROKEN!
COURAGE, WIFE! I AM HERE!
W-WIFE??
DRACULA, LEAVE ME! GET OUT WHILE YOU CAN! YOU'RE NO MATCH FOR THE WHOLE TRIAD.

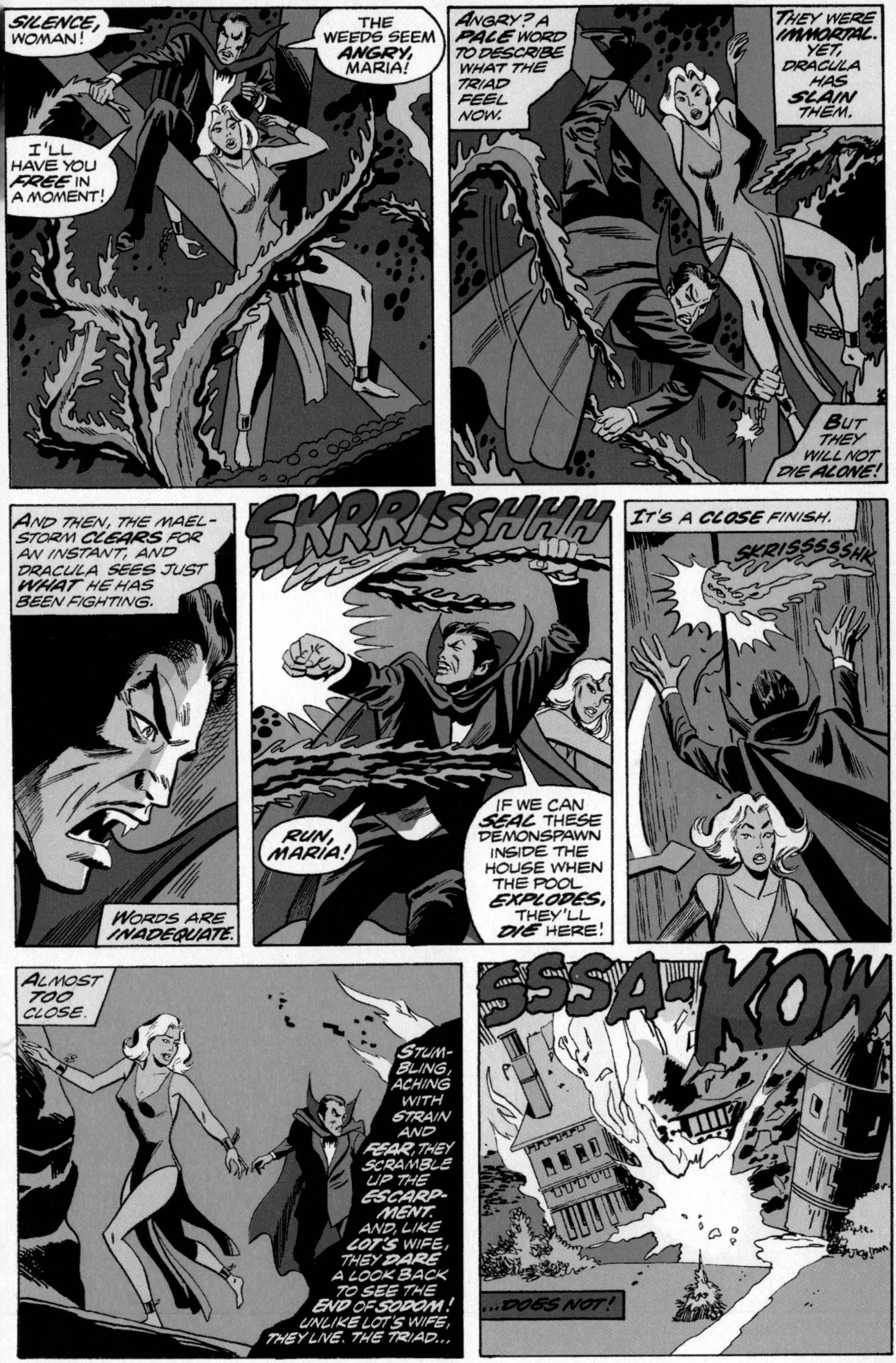
SILENCE, WOMAN!
THE WEEDS SEEM ANGRY, MARIA!
I'LL HAVE YOU FREE IN A MOMENT!
ANGRY? A PALE WORD TO DESCRIBE WHAT THE TRIAD FEEL NOW.
THEY WERE IMMORTAL. YET, DRACULA HAS SLAIN THEM.
BUT THEY WILL NOT DIE ALONE!
AND THEN, THE MAEL-STORM CLEARS FOR AN INSTANT, AND DRACULA SEES JUST WHAT HE HAS BEEN FIGHTING.
WORDS ARE INADEQUATE.
SKRRISSHHH
RUN, MARIA!
IF WE CAN SEAL THESE DEMONSPAWN INSIDE THE HOUSE WHEN THE POOL EXPLODES, THEY'LL DIE HERE!
IT'S A CLOSE FINISH.
SKRISSSSSHK
ALMOST TOO CLOSE.
STUM-BLING, ACHING WITH STRAIN AND FEAR, THEY SCRAMBLE UP THE ESCARP-MENT. AND, LIKE LOT'S WIFE, THEY DARE A LOOK BACK TO SEE THE END OF SODOM! UNLIKE LOT'S WIFE, THEY LIVE. THE TRIAD...
SSSA-KOW
...DOES NOT!

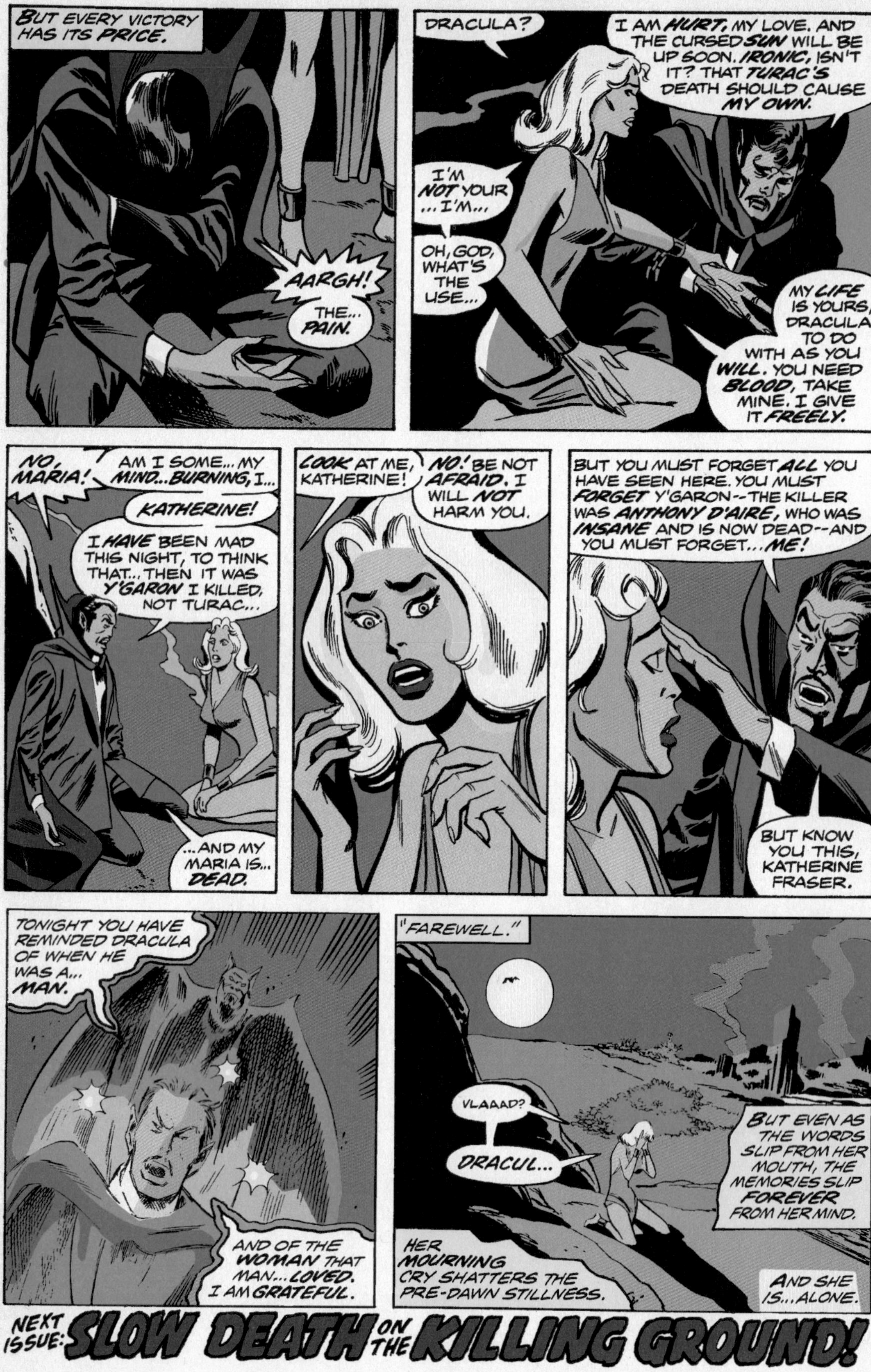

BUT EVERY VICTORY HAS ITS PRICE.
AARGH!
THE... PAIN.
DRACULA?
I AM HURT, MY LOVE. AND THE CURSED SUN WILL BE UP SOON. IRONIC, ISN'T IT? THAT TURAC'S DEATH SHOULD CAUSE MY OWN.
I'M NOT YOUR ...I'M...
OH, GOD, WHAT'S THE USE...
MY LIFE IS YOURS, DRACULA, TO DO WITH AS YOU WILL. YOU NEED BLOOD, TAKE MINE. I GIVE IT FREELY.
NO, MARIA!
AM I SOME... MY MIND...BURNING, I...
KATHERINE!
I HAVE BEEN MAD THIS NIGHT, TO THINK THAT... THEN IT WAS Y'GARON I KILLED, NOT TURAC...
...AND MY MARIA IS... DEAD.
LOOK AT ME, KATHERINE!
NO! BE NOT AFRAID. I WILL NOT HARM YOU.
BUT YOU MUST FORGET ALL YOU HAVE SEEN HERE. YOU MUST FORGET Y'GARON--THE KILLER WAS ANTHONY D'AIRE, WHO WAS INSANE AND IS NOW DEAD--AND YOU MUST FORGET... ME!
BUT KNOW YOU THIS, KATHERINE FRASER.
TONIGHT YOU HAVE REMINDED DRACULA OF WHEN HE WAS A... MAN.
AND OF THE WOMAN THAT MAN... LOVED. I AM GRATEFUL.
"FAREWELL."
VLAAAD?
DRACUL...
BUT EVEN AS THE WORDS SLIP FROM HER MOUTH, THE MEMORIES SLIP FOREVER FROM HER MIND.
HER MOURNING CRY SHATTERS THE PRE-DAWN STILLNESS.
AND SHE IS... ALONE.
NEXT ISSUE: SLOW DEATH ON THE KILLING GROUND!

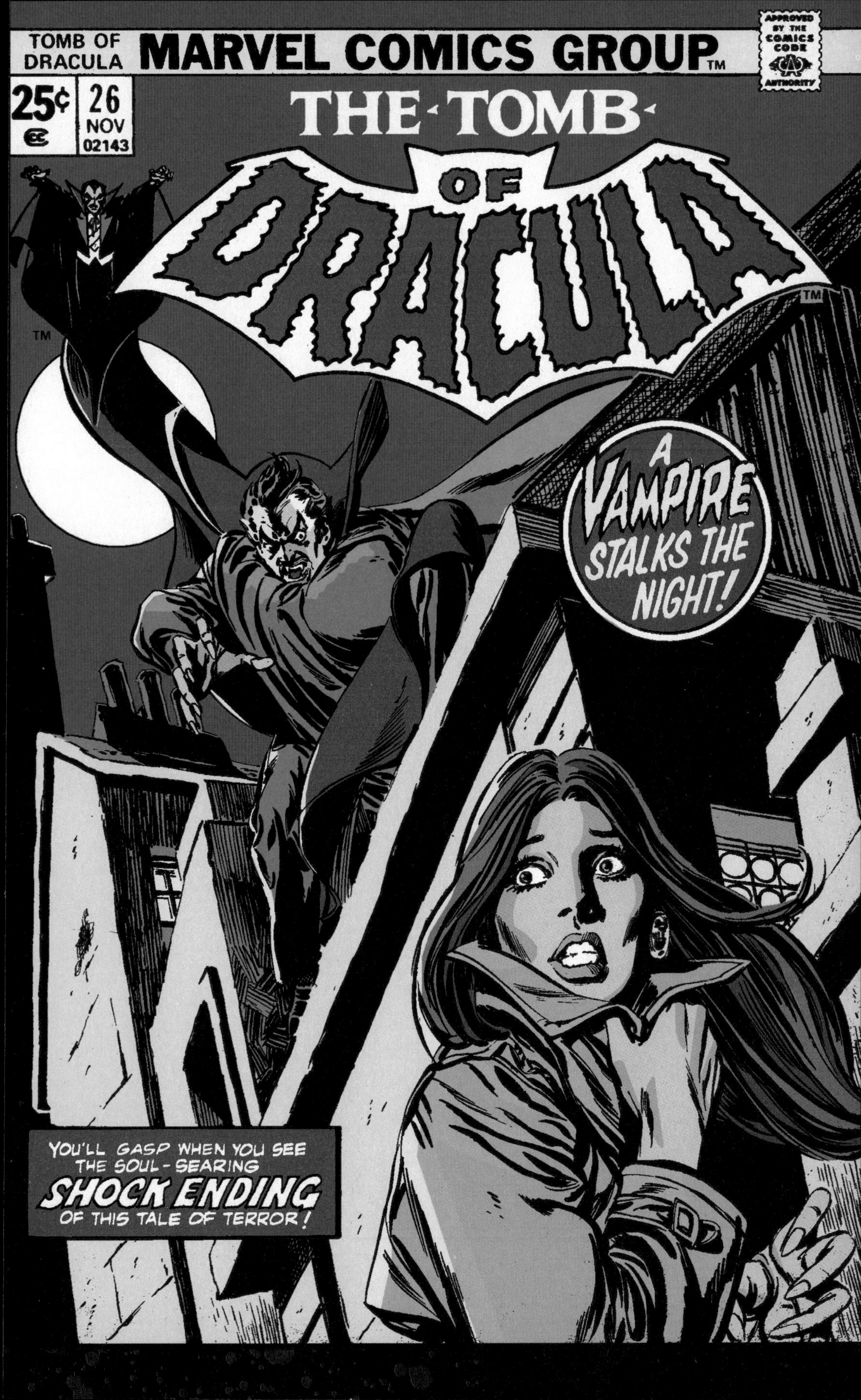

TOMB OF DRACULA
MARVEL COMICS GROUP™
APPROVED BY THE COMICS CODE AUTHORITY
25¢
26 NOV 02143
THE TOMB OF DRACULA™
A VAMPIRE STALKS THE NIGHT!
YOU'LL GASP WHEN YOU SEE THE SOUL-SEARING SHOCK ENDING OF THIS TALE OF TERROR!

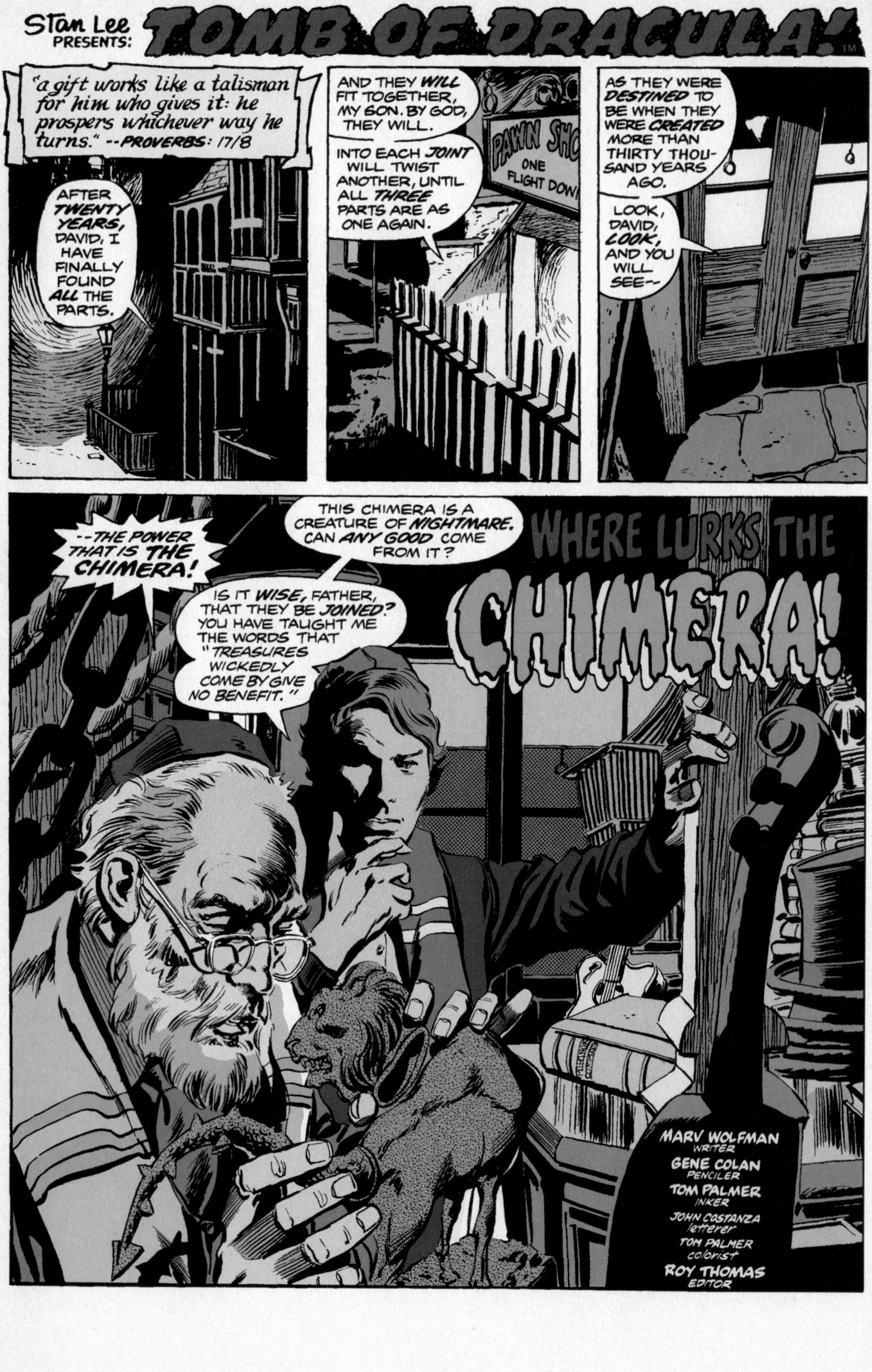

Stan Lee PRESENTS: TOMB OF DRACULA!
"a gift works like a talisman for him who gives it: he prospers whichever way he turns." --PROVERBS: 17/8
AFTER TWENTY YEARS, DAVID, I HAVE FINALLY FOUND ALL THE PARTS.
AND THEY WILL FIT TOGETHER, MY SON. BY GOD, THEY WILL.
INTO EACH JOINT WILL TWIST ANOTHER, UNTIL ALL THREE PARTS ARE AS ONE AGAIN.
PAWN SHO
ONE FLIGHT DOW
AS THEY WERE DESTINED TO BE WHEN THEY WERE CREATED MORE THAN THIRTY THOUSAND YEARS AGO.
LOOK, DAVID, LOOK, AND YOU WILL SEE--
--THE POWER THAT IS THE CHIMERA!
THIS CHIMERA IS A CREATURE OF NIGHTMARE. CAN ANY GOOD COME FROM IT?
IS IT WISE, FATHER, THAT THEY BE JOINED? YOU HAVE TAUGHT ME THE WORDS THAT "TREASURES WICKEDLY COME BY GIVE NO BENEFIT."
WHERE LURKS THE CHIMERA!
MARV WOLFMAN WRITER
GENE COLAN PENCILER
TOM PALMER INKER
JOHN COSTANZA letterer
TOM PALMER colorist
ROY THOMAS EDITOR

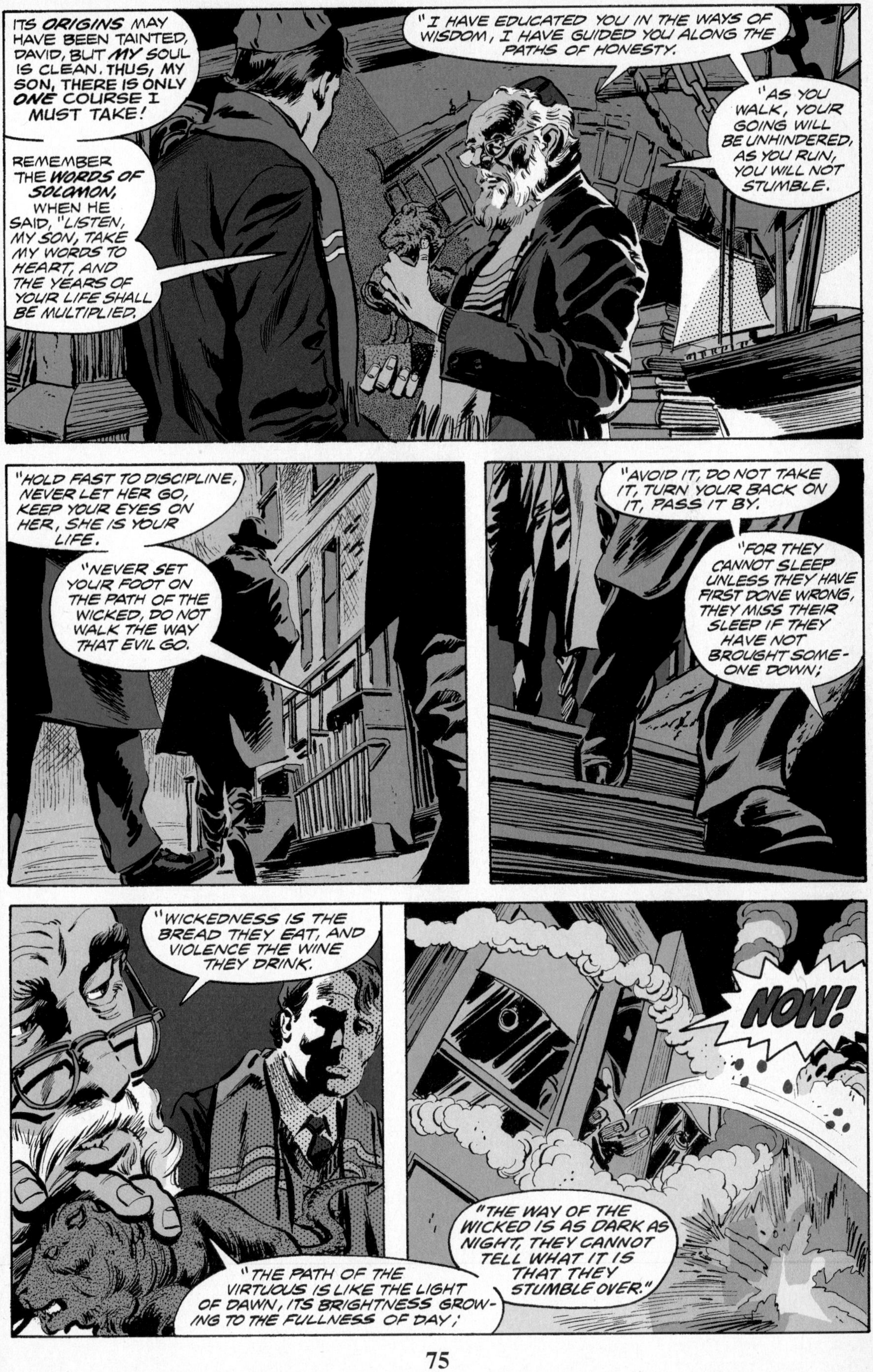
ITS ORIGINS MAY HAVE BEEN TAINTED, DAVID, BUT MY SOUL IS CLEAN. THUS, MY SON, THERE IS ONLY ONE COURSE I MUST TAKE!
REMEMBER THE WORDS OF SOLOMON, WHEN HE SAID, "LISTEN, MY SON, TAKE MY WORDS TO HEART, AND THE YEARS OF YOUR LIFE SHALL BE MULTIPLIED.
"I HAVE EDUCATED YOU IN THE WAYS OF WISDOM, I HAVE GUIDED YOU ALONG THE PATHS OF HONESTY.
"AS YOU WALK, YOUR GOING WILL BE UNHINDERED, AS YOU RUN, YOU WILL NOT STUMBLE.
"HOLD FAST TO DISCIPLINE, NEVER LET HER GO, KEEP YOUR EYES ON HER, SHE IS YOUR LIFE.
"NEVER SET YOUR FOOT ON THE PATH OF THE WICKED, DO NOT WALK THE WAY THAT EVIL GO.
"AVOID IT, DO NOT TAKE IT, TURN YOUR BACK ON IT, PASS IT BY.
"FOR THEY CANNOT SLEEP UNLESS THEY HAVE FIRST DONE WRONG, THEY MISS THEIR SLEEP IF THEY HAVE NOT BROUGHT SOME-ONE DOWN;
"WICKEDNESS IS THE BREAD THEY EAT, AND VIOLENCE THE WINE THEY DRINK.
"THE PATH OF THE VIRTUOUS IS LIKE THE LIGHT OF DAWN, ITS BRIGHTNESS GROW-ING TO THE FULLNESS OF DAY;
"THE WAY OF THE WICKED IS AS DARK AS NIGHT, THEY CANNOT TELL WHAT IT IS THAT THEY STUMBLE OVER."
NOW!

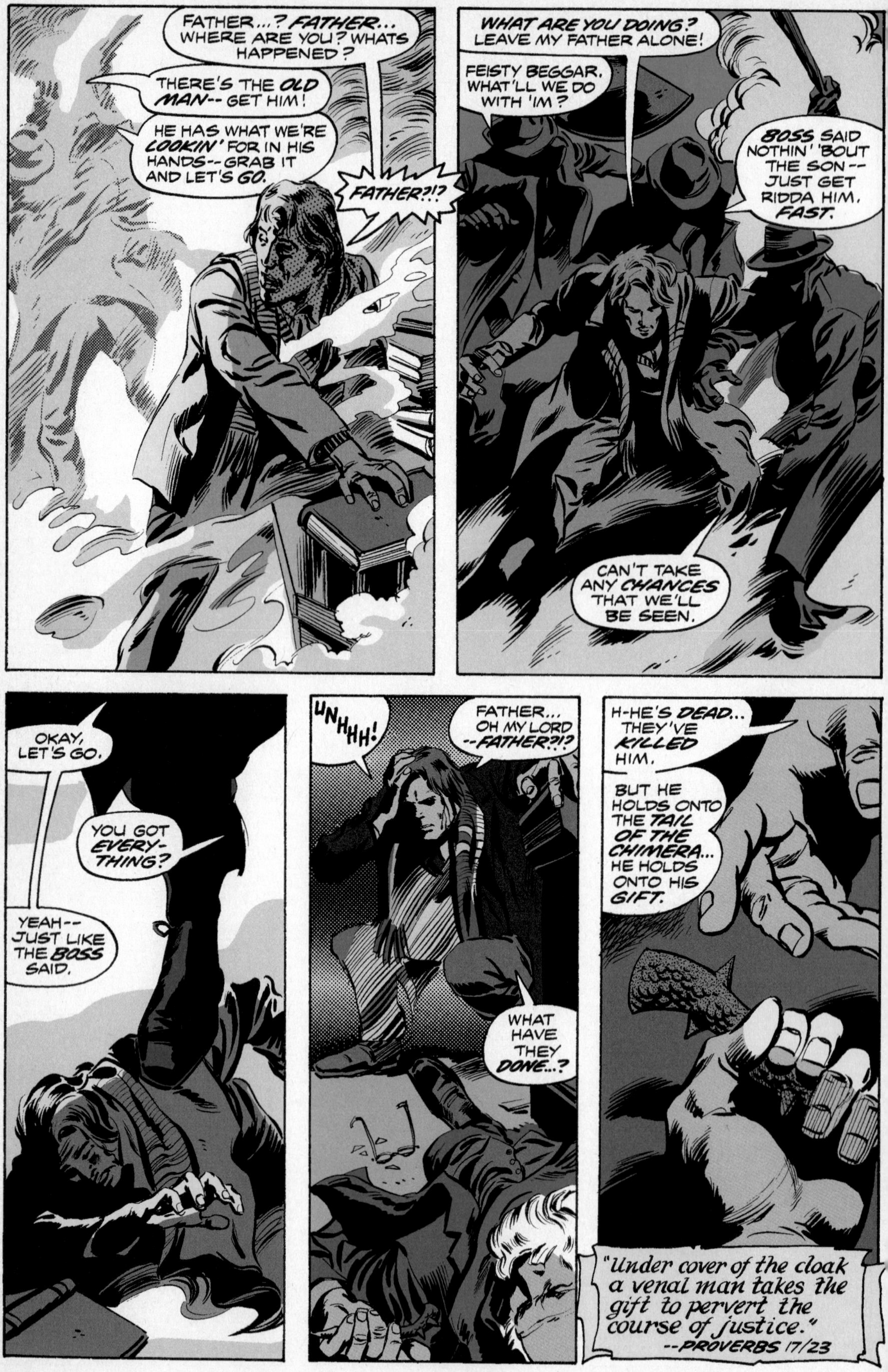
FATHER...? FATHER... WHERE ARE YOU? WHATS HAPPENED?
THERE'S THE OLD MAN-- GET HIM!
HE HAS WHAT WE'RE COOKIN' FOR IN HIS HANDS--GRAB IT AND LET'S GO.
FATHER?!?
WHAT ARE YOU DOING? LEAVE MY FATHER ALONE!
FEISTY BEGGAR. WHAT'LL WE DO WITH 'IM?
BOSS SAID NOTHIN' 'BOUT THE SON-- JUST GET RIDDA HIM. FAST.
CAN'T TAKE ANY CHANCES THAT WE'LL BE SEEN.
OKAY, LET'S GO.
YOU GOT EVERY-THING?
YEAH-- JUST LIKE THE BOSS SAID.
UNHHH!
FATHER... OH MY LORD --FATHER?!?
WHAT HAVE THEY DONE...?
H-HE'S DEAD... THEY'VE KILLED HIM.
BUT HE HOLDS ONTO THE TAIL OF THE CHIMERA... HE HOLDS ONTO HIS GIFT.
"Under cover of the cloak a venal man takes the gift to pervert the course of justice."
--PROVERBS 17/23

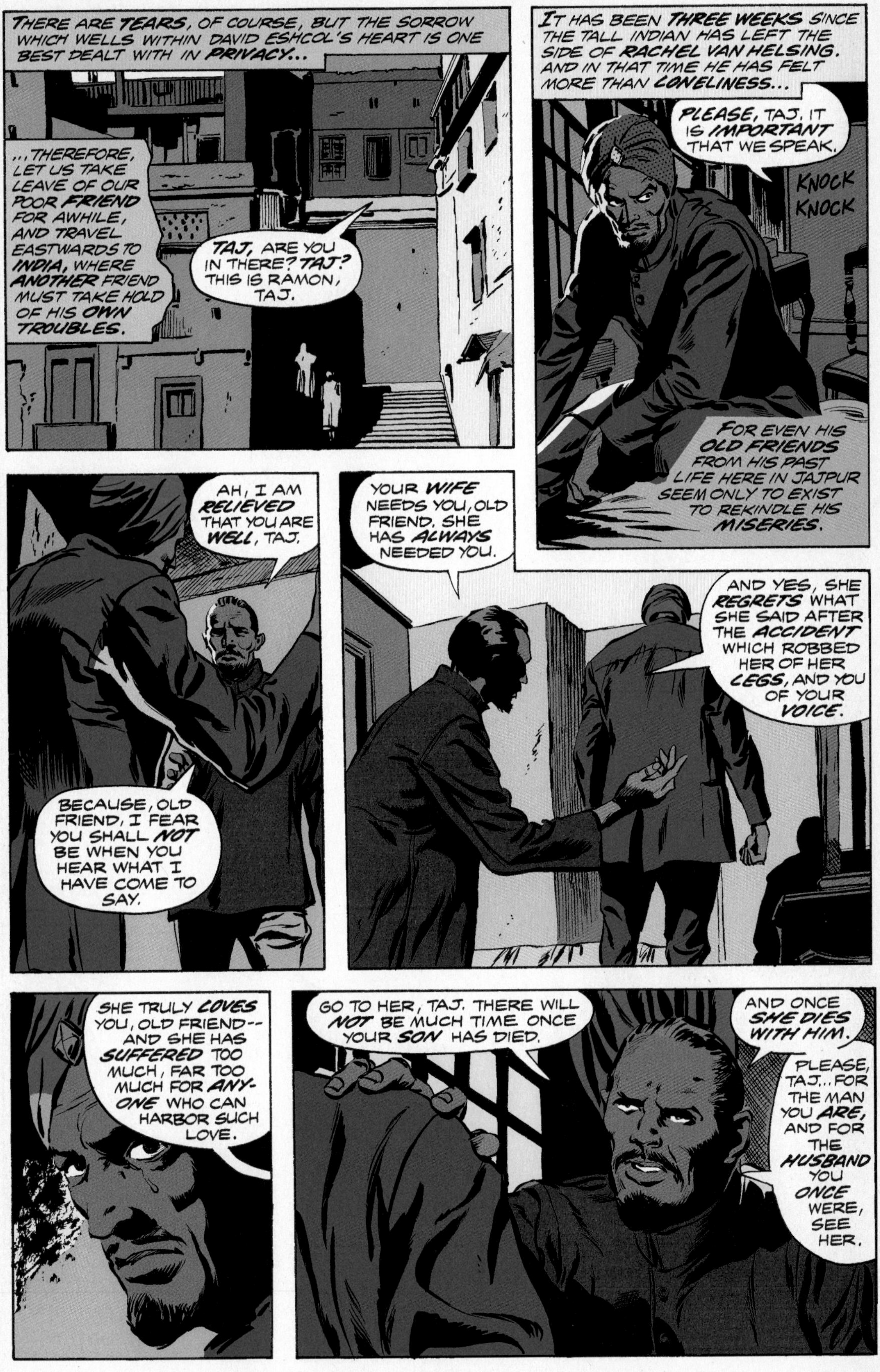
THERE ARE TEARS, OF COURSE, BUT THE SORROW WHICH WELLS WITHIN DAVID ESHCOL'S HEART IS ONE BEST DEALT WITH IN PRIVACY...
...THEREFORE, LET US TAKE LEAVE OF OUR POOR FRIEND FOR AWHILE, AND TRAVEL EASTWARDS TO INDIA, WHERE ANOTHER FRIEND MUST TAKE HOLD OF HIS OWN TROUBLES.
TAJ, ARE YOU IN THERE? TAJ? THIS IS RAMON, TAJ.
IT HAS BEEN THREE WEEKS SINCE THE TALL INDIAN HAS LEFT THE SIDE OF RACHEL VAN HELSING. AND IN THAT TIME HE HAS FELT MORE THAN LONELINESS...
PLEASE, TAJ, IT IS IMPORTANT THAT WE SPEAK.
KNOCK KNOCK
FOR EVEN HIS OLD FRIENDS FROM HIS PAST LIFE HERE IN JAJPUR SEEM ONLY TO EXIST TO REKINDLE HIS MISERIES.
AH, I AM RELIEVED THAT YOU ARE WELL, TAJ.
BECAUSE, OLD FRIEND, I FEAR YOU SHALL NOT BE WHEN YOU HEAR WHAT I HAVE COME TO SAY.
YOUR WIFE NEEDS YOU, OLD FRIEND. SHE HAS ALWAYS NEEDED YOU.
AND YES, SHE REGRETS WHAT SHE SAID AFTER THE ACCIDENT WHICH ROBBED HER OF HER LEGS, AND YOU OF YOUR VOICE.
SHE TRULY LOVES YOU, OLD FRIEND-- AND SHE HAS SUFFERED TOO MUCH, FAR TOO MUCH FOR ANY-ONE WHO CAN HARBOR SUCH LOVE.
GO TO HER, TAJ. THERE WILL NOT BE MUCH TIME ONCE YOUR SON HAS DIED.
AND ONCE SHE DIES WITH HIM.
PLEASE, TAJ...FOR THE MAN YOU ARE, AND FOR THE HUSBAND YOU ONCE WERE, SEE HER.

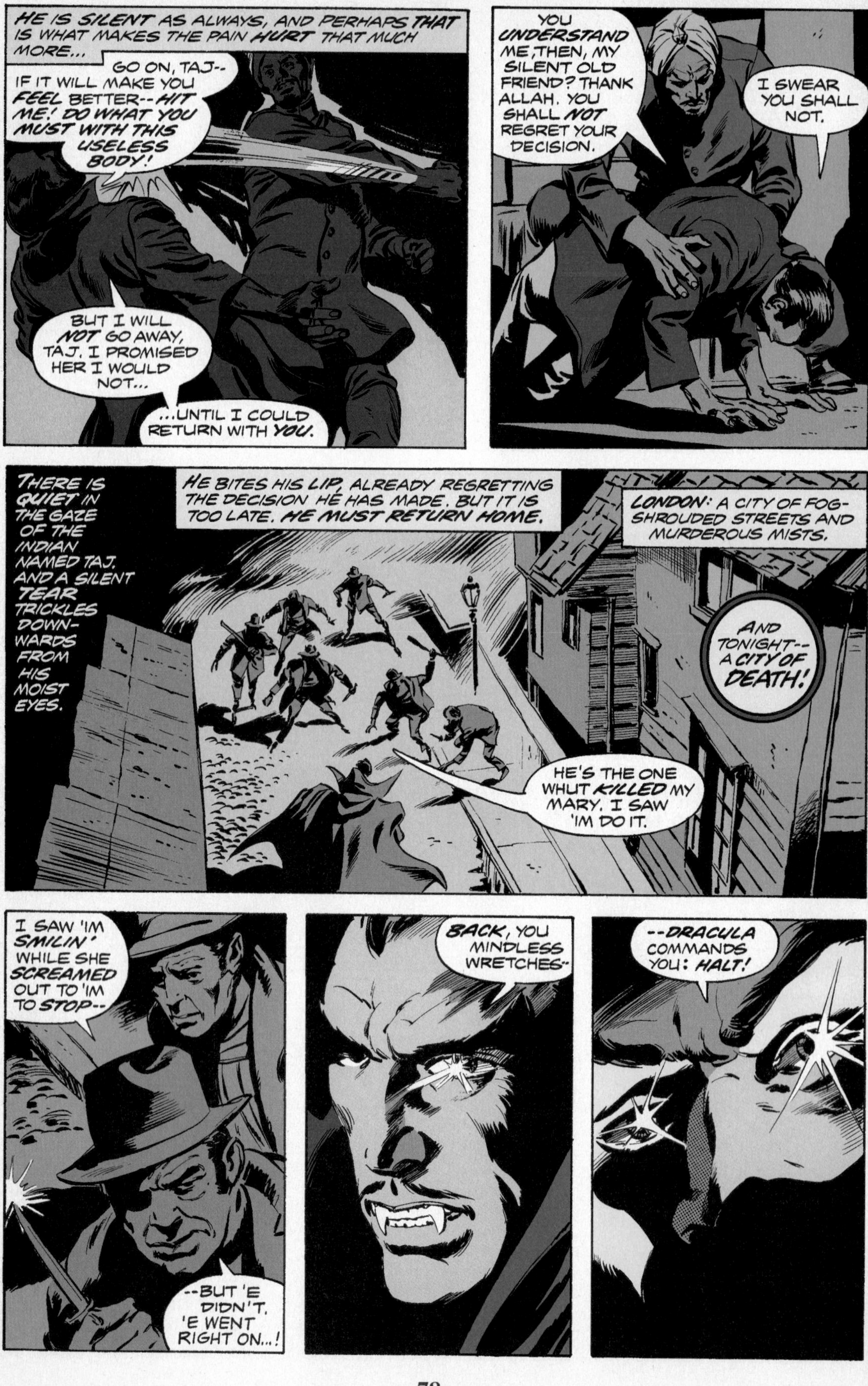
HE IS SILENT AS ALWAYS, AND PERHAPS THAT IS WHAT MAKES THE PAIN HURT THAT MUCH MORE...
GO ON, TAJ-- IF IT WILL MAKE YOU FEEL BETTER--HIT ME! DO WHAT YOU MUST WITH THIS USELESS BODY!
BUT I WILL NOT GO AWAY, TAJ. I PROMISED HER I WOULD NOT...
...UNTIL I COULD RETURN WITH YOU.
YOU UNDERSTAND ME, THEN, MY SILENT OLD FRIEND? THANK ALLAH. YOU SHALL NOT REGRET YOUR DECISION.
I SWEAR YOU SHALL NOT.
THERE IS QUIET IN THE GAZE OF THE INDIAN NAMED TAJ. AND A SILENT TEAR TRICKLES DOWNWARDS FROM HIS MOIST EYES.
HE BITES HIS LIP, ALREADY REGRETTING THE DECISION HE HAS MADE. BUT IT IS TOO LATE. HE MUST RETURN HOME.
LONDON: A CITY OF FOG-SHROUDED STREETS AND MURDEROUS MISTS.
AND TONIGHT--A CITY OF DEATH!
HE'S THE ONE WHUT KILLED MY MARY. I SAW 'IM DO IT.
I SAW 'IM SMILIN' WHILE SHE SCREAMED OUT TO 'IM TO STOP--
--BUT 'E DIDN'T. 'E WENT RIGHT ON...!
BACK, YOU MINDLESS WRETCHES--
--DRACULA COMMANDS YOU: HALT!

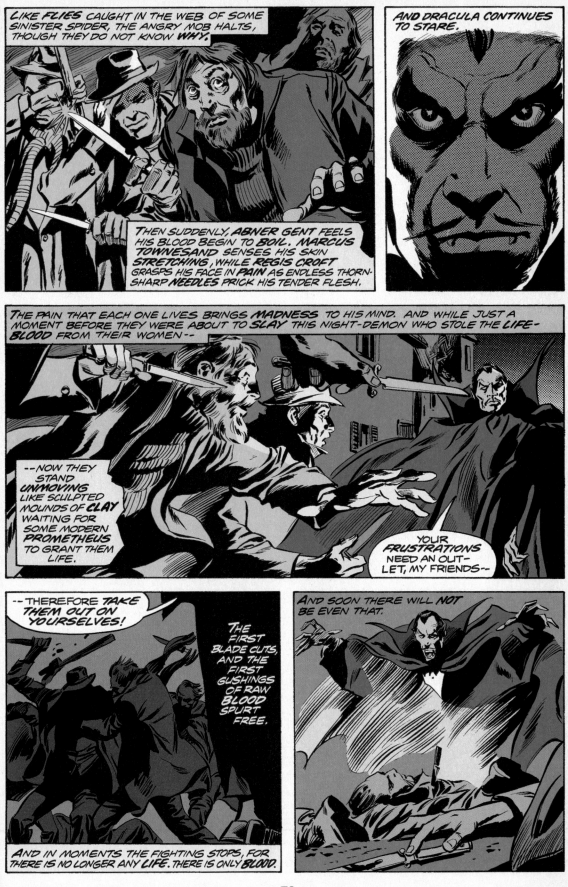

LIKE FLIES CAUGHT IN THE WEB OF SOME SINISTER SPIDER, THE ANGRY MOB HALTS, THOUGH THEY DO NOT KNOW WHY.

THEN SUDDENLY, ABNER GENT FEELS HIS BLOOD BEGIN TO BOIL. MARCUS TOWNESAND SENSES HIS SKIN STRETCHING, WHILE REGIS CROFT GRASPS HIS FACE IN PAIN AS ENDLESS THORN-SHARP NEEDLES PRICK HIS TENDER FLESH.

AND DRACULA CONTINUES TO STARE.

THE PAIN THAT EACH ONE LIVES BRINGS MADNESS TO HIS MIND. AND WHILE JUST A MOMENT BEFORE THEY WERE ABOUT TO SLAY THIS NIGHT-DEMON WHO STOLE THE LIFE-BLOOD FROM THEIR WOMEN--

--NOW THEY STAND UNMOVING LIKE SCULPTED MOUNDS OF CLAY WAITING FOR SOME MODERN PROMETHEUS TO GRANT THEM LIFE.

YOUR FRUSTRATIONS NEED AN OUT-LET, MY FRIENDS--

--THEREFORE TAKE THEM OUT ON YOURSELVES!

THE FIRST BLADE CUTS, AND THE FIRST GUSHINGS OF RAW BLOOD SPURT FREE.

AND IN MOMENTS THE FIGHTING STOPS, FOR THERE IS NO LONGER ANY LIFE. THERE IS ONLY BLOOD.

AND SOON THERE WILL NOT BE EVEN THAT.

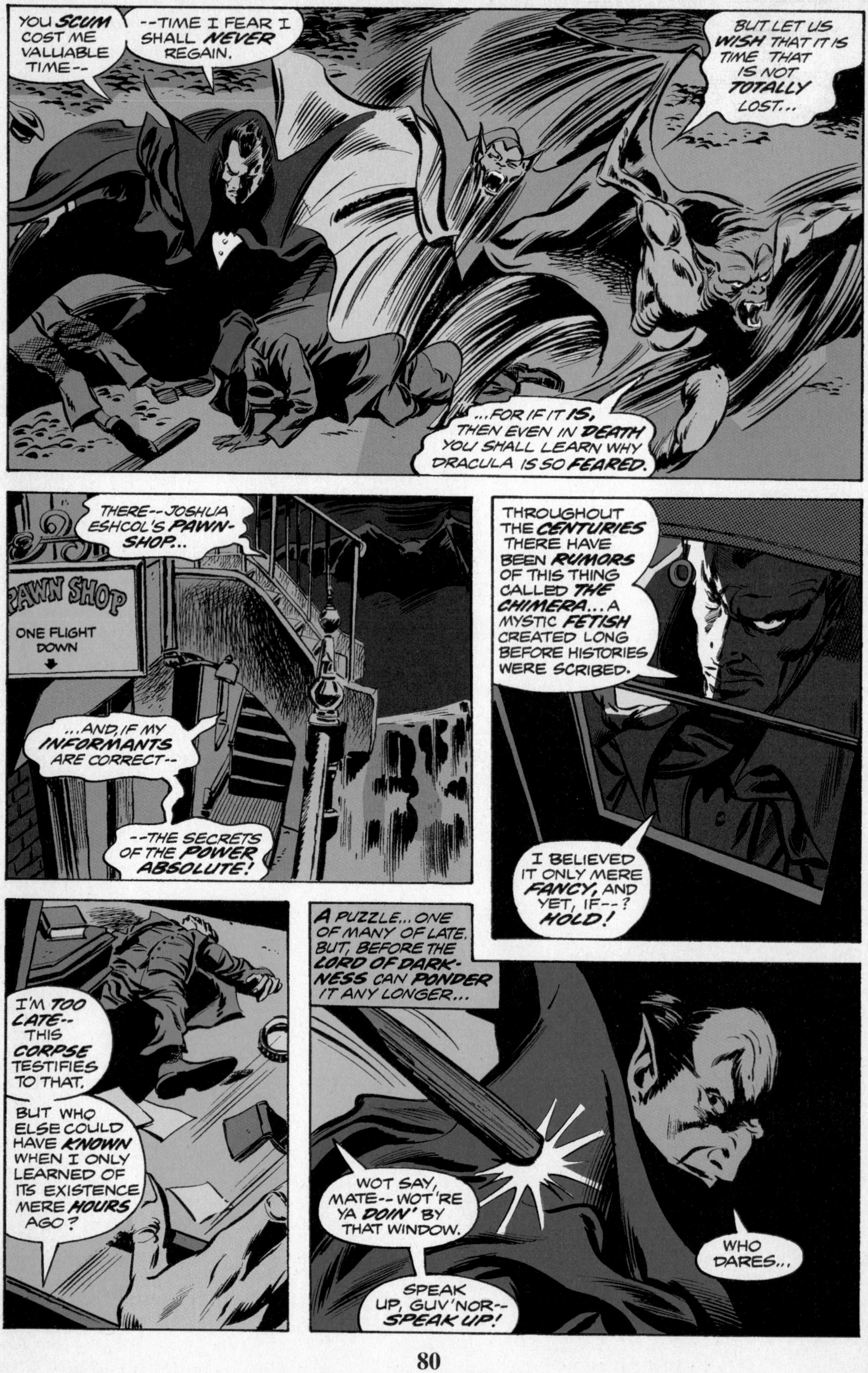

YOU SCUM COST ME VALUABLE TIME--
--TIME I FEAR I SHALL NEVER REGAIN.
BUT LET US WISH THAT IT IS TIME THAT IS NOT TOTALLY LOST...
...FOR IF IT IS, THEN EVEN IN DEATH YOU SHALL LEARN WHY DRACULA IS SO FEARED.
THERE--JOSHUA ESHCOL'S PAWN-SHOP...
PAWN SHOP
ONE FLIGHT DOWN
...AND, IF MY INFORMANTS ARE CORRECT--
--THE SECRETS OF THE POWER ABSOLUTE!
THROUGHOUT THE CENTURIES THERE HAVE BEEN RUMORS OF THIS THING CALLED THE CHIMERA... A MYSTIC FETISH CREATED LONG BEFORE HISTORIES WERE SCRIBED.
I BELIEVED IT ONLY MERE FANCY, AND YET, IF--? HOLD!
I'M TOO LATE-- THIS CORPSE TESTIFIES TO THAT.
BUT WHO ELSE COULD HAVE KNOWN WHEN I ONLY LEARNED OF ITS EXISTENCE MERE HOURS AGO?
A PUZZLE... ONE OF MANY OF LATE. BUT, BEFORE THE LORD OF DARK-NESS CAN PONDER IT ANY LONGER...
WOT SAY, MATE-- WOT'RE YA DOIN' BY THAT WINDOW.
SPEAK UP, GUV'NOR-- SPEAK UP!
WHO DARES...

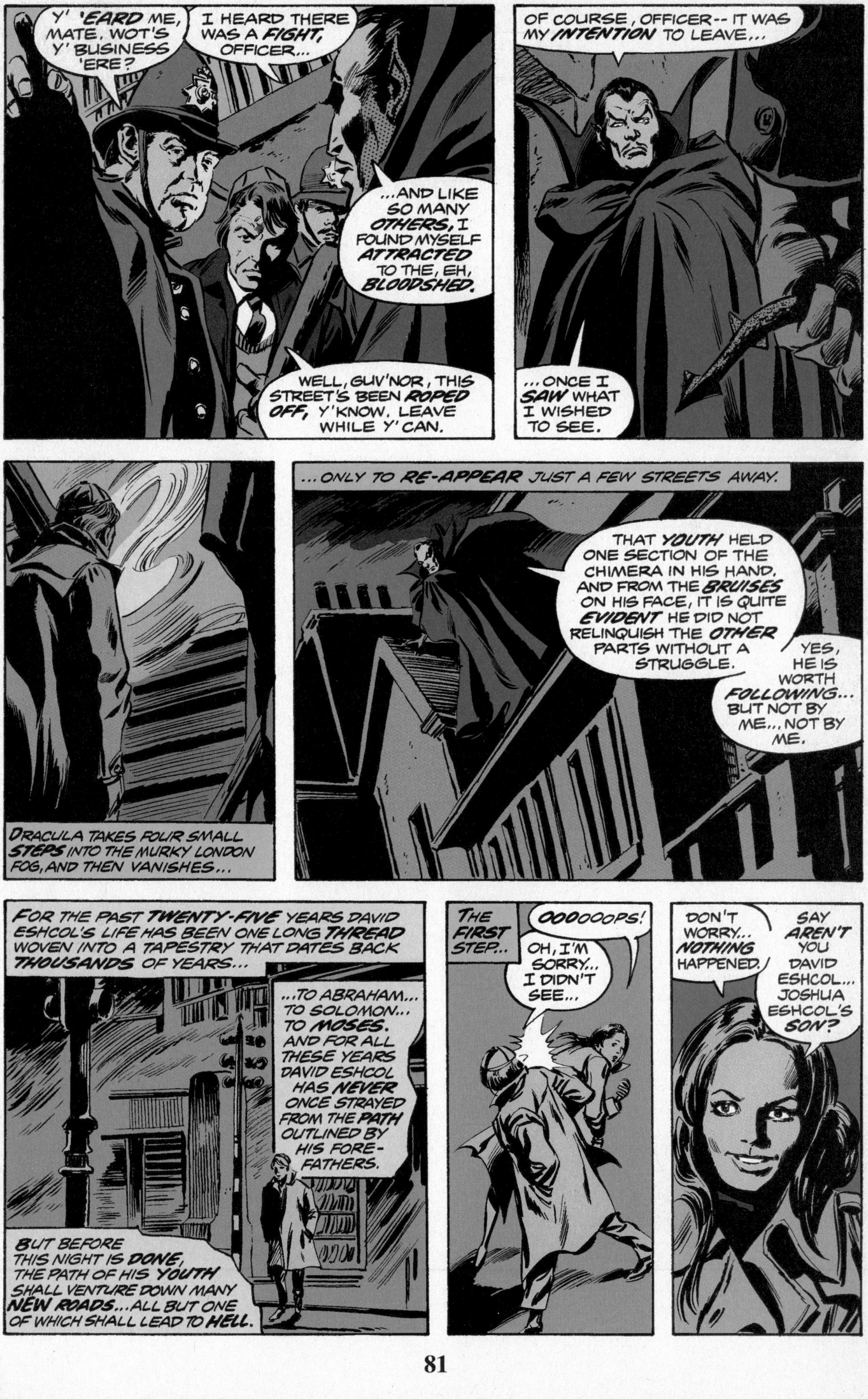
Y' 'EARD ME, MATE. WOT'S Y' BUSINESS 'ERE?
I HEARD THERE WAS A FIGHT, OFFICER...
...AND LIKE SO MANY OTHERS, I FOUND MYSELF ATTRACTED TO THE, EH, BLOODSHED.
WELL, GUV'NOR, THIS STREET'S BEEN ROPED OFF, Y'KNOW. LEAVE WHILE Y' CAN.
OF COURSE, OFFICER-- IT WAS MY INTENTION TO LEAVE...
...ONCE I SAW WHAT I WISHED TO SEE.
DRACULA TAKES FOUR SMALL STEPS INTO THE MURKY LONDON FOG, AND THEN VANISHES...
...ONLY TO RE-APPEAR JUST A FEW STREETS AWAY.
THAT YOUTH HELD ONE SECTION OF THE CHIMERA IN HIS HAND. AND FROM THE BRUISES ON HIS FACE, IT IS QUITE EVIDENT HE DID NOT RELINQUISH THE OTHER PARTS WITHOUT A STRUGGLE.
YES, HE IS WORTH FOLLOWING... BUT NOT BY ME... NOT BY ME.
FOR THE PAST TWENTY-FIVE YEARS DAVID ESHCOL'S LIFE HAS BEEN ONE LONG THREAD WOVEN INTO A TAPESTRY THAT DATES BACK THOUSANDS OF YEARS...
...TO ABRAHAM... TO SOLOMON... TO MOSES. AND FOR ALL THESE YEARS DAVID ESHCOL HAS NEVER ONCE STRAYED FROM THE PATH OUTLINED BY HIS FORE-FATHERS.
BUT BEFORE THIS NIGHT IS DONE, THE PATH OF HIS YOUTH SHALL VENTURE DOWN MANY NEW ROADS... ALL BUT ONE OF WHICH SHALL LEAD TO HELL.
THE FIRST STEP...
OOOOOOOPS!
OH, I'M SORRY... I DIDN'T SEE...
DON'T WORRY... NOTHING HAPPENED.
SAY AREN'T YOU DAVID ESHCOL... JOSHUA ESHCOL'S SON?

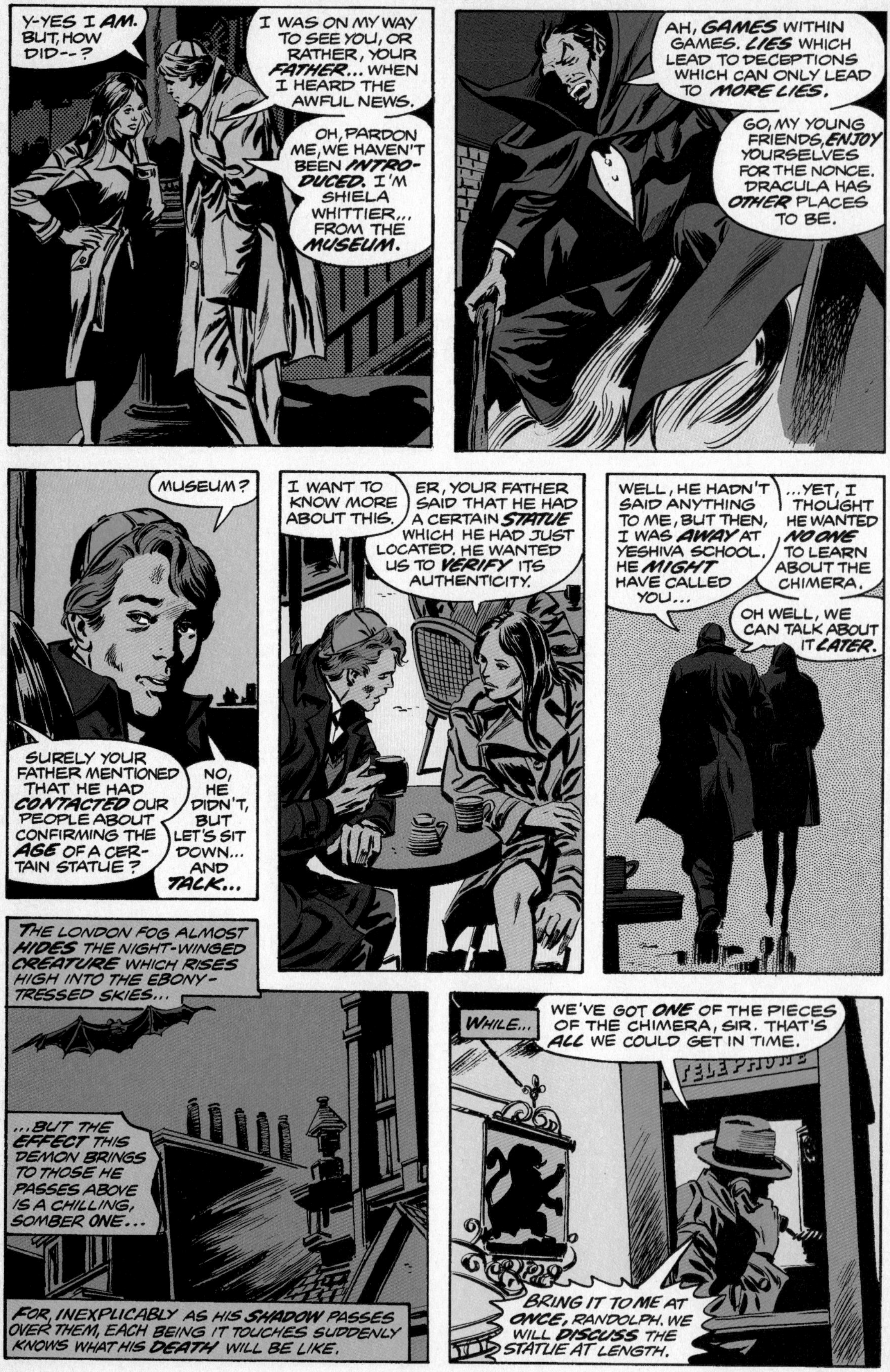

Y-YES I AM. BUT, HOW DID--?
I WAS ON MY WAY TO SEE YOU, OR RATHER, YOUR FATHER... WHEN I HEARD THE AWFUL NEWS.
OH, PARDON ME, WE HAVEN'T BEEN INTRO-DUCED. I'M SHIELA WHITTIER... FROM THE MUSEUM.
AH, GAMES WITHIN GAMES. LIES WHICH LEAD TO DECEPTIONS WHICH CAN ONLY LEAD TO MORE LIES.
GO, MY YOUNG FRIENDS, ENJOY YOURSELVES FOR THE NONCE. DRACULA HAS OTHER PLACES TO BE.
MUSEUM?
SURELY YOUR FATHER MENTIONED THAT HE HAD CONTACTED OUR PEOPLE ABOUT CONFIRMING THE AGE OF A CER-TAIN STATUE?
NO, HE DIDN'T, BUT LET'S SIT DOWN... AND TALK...
I WANT TO KNOW MORE ABOUT THIS.
ER, YOUR FATHER SAID THAT HE HAD A CERTAIN STATUE WHICH HE HAD JUST LOCATED. HE WANTED US TO VERIFY ITS AUTHENTICITY.
WELL, HE HADN'T SAID ANYTHING TO ME, BUT THEN, I WAS AWAY AT YESHIVA SCHOOL. HE MIGHT HAVE CALLED YOU...
...YET, I THOUGHT HE WANTED NO ONE TO LEARN ABOUT THE CHIMERA.
OH WELL, WE CAN TALK ABOUT IT LATER.
THE LONDON FOG ALMOST HIDES THE NIGHT-WINGED CREATURE WHICH RISES HIGH INTO THE EBONY-TRESSED SKIES...
...BUT THE EFFECT THIS DEMON BRINGS TO THOSE HE PASSES ABOVE IS A CHILLING, SOMBER ONE...
FOR, INEXPLICABLY AS HIS SHADOW PASSES OVER THEM, EACH BEING IT TOUCHES SUDDENLY KNOWS WHAT HIS DEATH WILL BE LIKE.
WHILE...
WE'VE GOT ONE OF THE PIECES OF THE CHIMERA, SIR. THAT'S ALL WE COULD GET IN TIME.
TELEPHONE
BRING IT TO ME AT ONCE, RANDOLPH. WE WILL DISCUSS THE STATUE AT LENGTH.

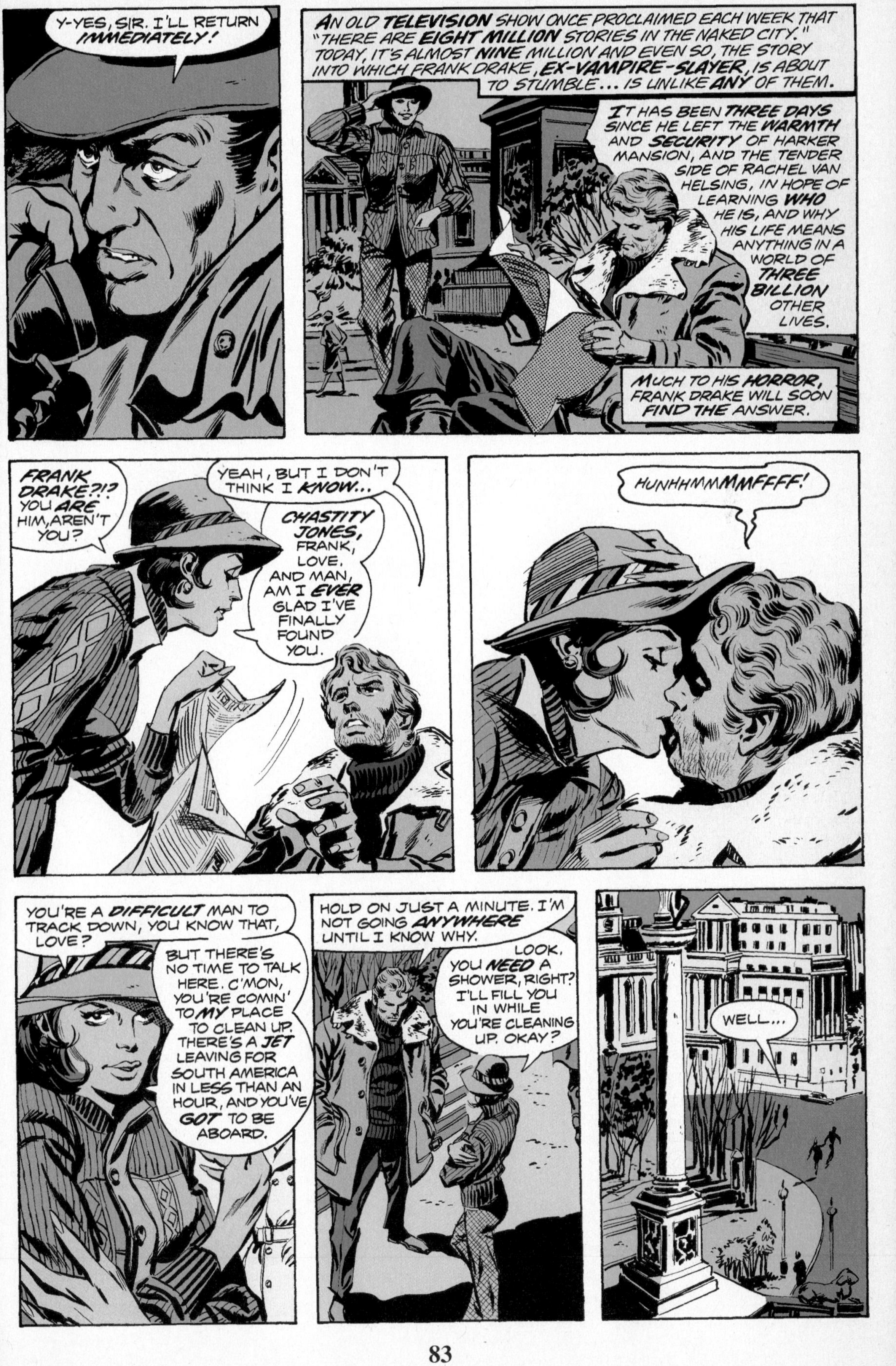
Y-YES, SIR. I'LL RETURN IMMEDIATELY!
AN OLD TELEVISION SHOW ONCE PROCLAIMED EACH WEEK THAT "THERE ARE EIGHT MILLION STORIES IN THE NAKED CITY." TODAY, IT'S ALMOST NINE MILLION AND EVEN SO, THE STORY INTO WHICH FRANK DRAKE, EX-VAMPIRE-SLAYER, IS ABOUT TO STUMBLE... IS UNLIKE ANY OF THEM.
IT HAS BEEN THREE DAYS SINCE HE LEFT THE WARMTH AND SECURITY OF HARKER MANSION, AND THE TENDER SIDE OF RACHEL VAN HELSING, IN HOPE OF LEARNING WHO HE IS, AND WHY HIS LIFE MEANS ANYTHING IN A WORLD OF THREE BILLION OTHER LIVES.
MUCH TO HIS HORROR, FRANK DRAKE WILL SOON FIND THE ANSWER.
FRANK DRAKE?!? YOU ARE HIM, AREN'T YOU?
YEAH, BUT I DON'T THINK I KNOW...
CHASTITY JONES, FRANK, LOVE. AND MAN, AM I EVER GLAD I'VE FINALLY FOUND YOU.
HUNHHMMMMMFFFF!
YOU'RE A DIFFICULT MAN TO TRACK DOWN, YOU KNOW THAT, LOVE?
BUT THERE'S NO TIME TO TALK HERE. C'MON, YOU'RE COMIN' TO MY PLACE TO CLEAN UP. THERE'S A JET LEAVING FOR SOUTH AMERICA IN LESS THAN AN HOUR, AND YOU'VE GOT TO BE ABOARD.
HOLD ON JUST A MINUTE. I'M NOT GOING ANYWHERE UNTIL I KNOW WHY.
LOOK, YOU NEED A SHOWER, RIGHT? I'LL FILL YOU IN WHILE YOU'RE CLEANING UP. OKAY?
WELL...

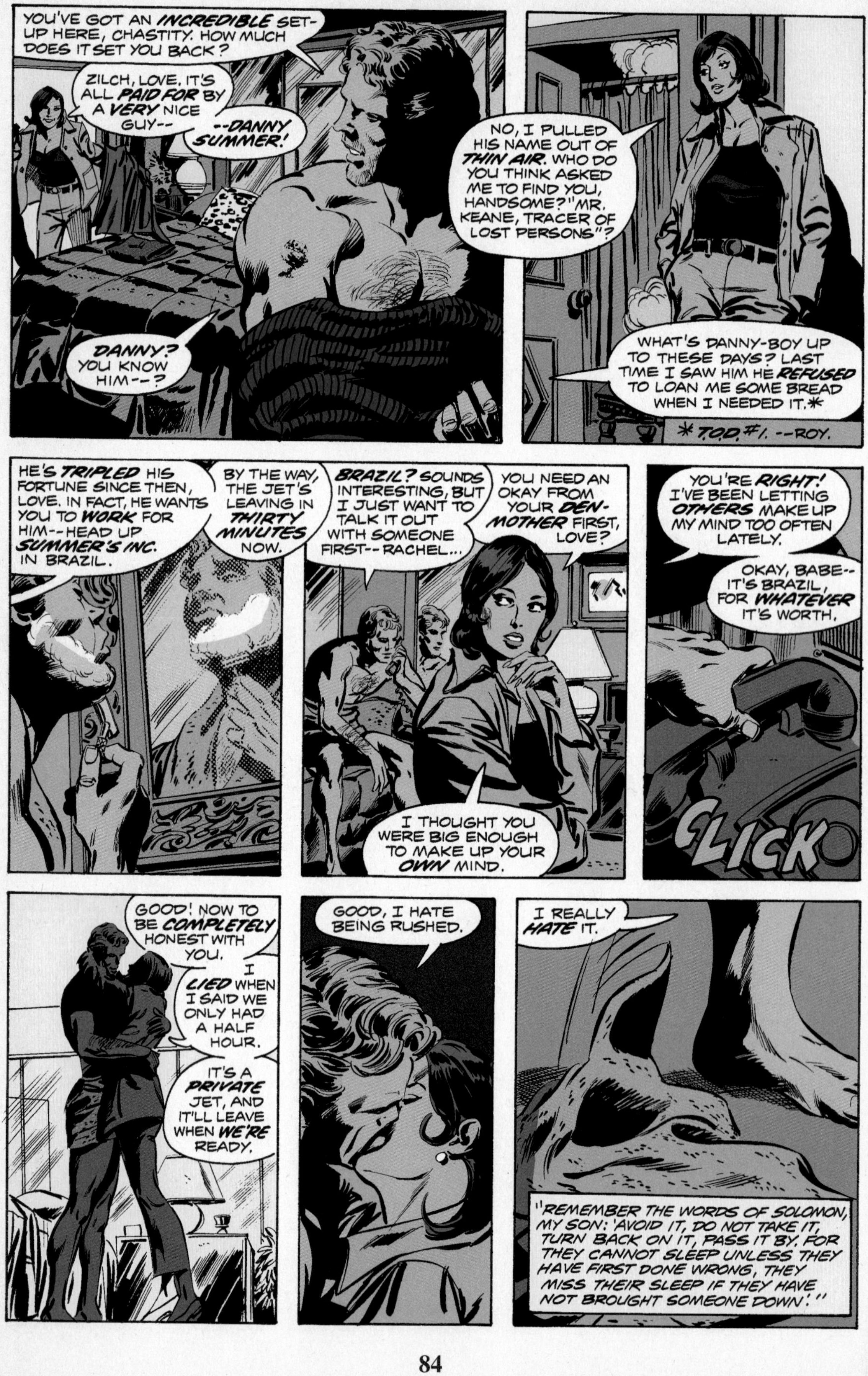
YOU'VE GOT AN INCREDIBLE SET-UP HERE, CHASTITY. HOW MUCH DOES IT SET YOU BACK?
ZILCH, LOVE. IT'S ALL PAID FOR BY A VERY NICE GUY--
--DANNY SUMMER!
DANNY? YOU KNOW HIM--?
NO, I PULLED HIS NAME OUT OF THIN AIR. WHO DO YOU THINK ASKED ME TO FIND YOU, HANDSOME? "MR. KEANE, TRACER OF LOST PERSONS"?
WHAT'S DANNY-BOY UP TO THESE DAYS? LAST TIME I SAW HIM HE REFUSED TO LOAN ME SOME BREAD WHEN I NEEDED IT.*
* T.O.D. #1. --ROY.
HE'S TRIPLED HIS FORTUNE SINCE THEN, LOVE. IN FACT, HE WANTS YOU TO WORK FOR HIM--HEAD UP SUMMER'S INC. IN BRAZIL.
BY THE WAY, THE JET'S LEAVING IN THIRTY MINUTES NOW.
BRAZIL? SOUNDS INTERESTING, BUT I JUST WANT TO TALK IT OUT WITH SOMEONE FIRST-- RACHEL...
YOU NEED AN OKAY FROM YOUR DEN-MOTHER FIRST, LOVE?
I THOUGHT YOU WERE BIG ENOUGH TO MAKE UP YOUR OWN MIND.
YOU'RE RIGHT! I'VE BEEN LETTING OTHERS MAKE UP MY MIND TOO OFTEN LATELY.
OKAY, BABE-- IT'S BRAZIL, FOR WHATEVER IT'S WORTH.
CLICK
GOOD! NOW TO BE COMPLETELY HONEST WITH YOU.
I LIED WHEN I SAID WE ONLY HAD A HALF HOUR.
IT'S A PRIVATE JET, AND IT'LL LEAVE WHEN WE'RE READY.
GOOD, I HATE BEING RUSHED.
I REALLY HATE IT.
"REMEMBER THE WORDS OF SOLOMON, MY SON: 'AVOID IT, DO NOT TAKE IT, TURN BACK ON IT, PASS IT BY. FOR THEY CANNOT SLEEP UNLESS THEY HAVE FIRST DONE WRONG, THEY MISS THEIR SLEEP IF THEY HAVE NOT BROUGHT SOMEONE DOWN'."

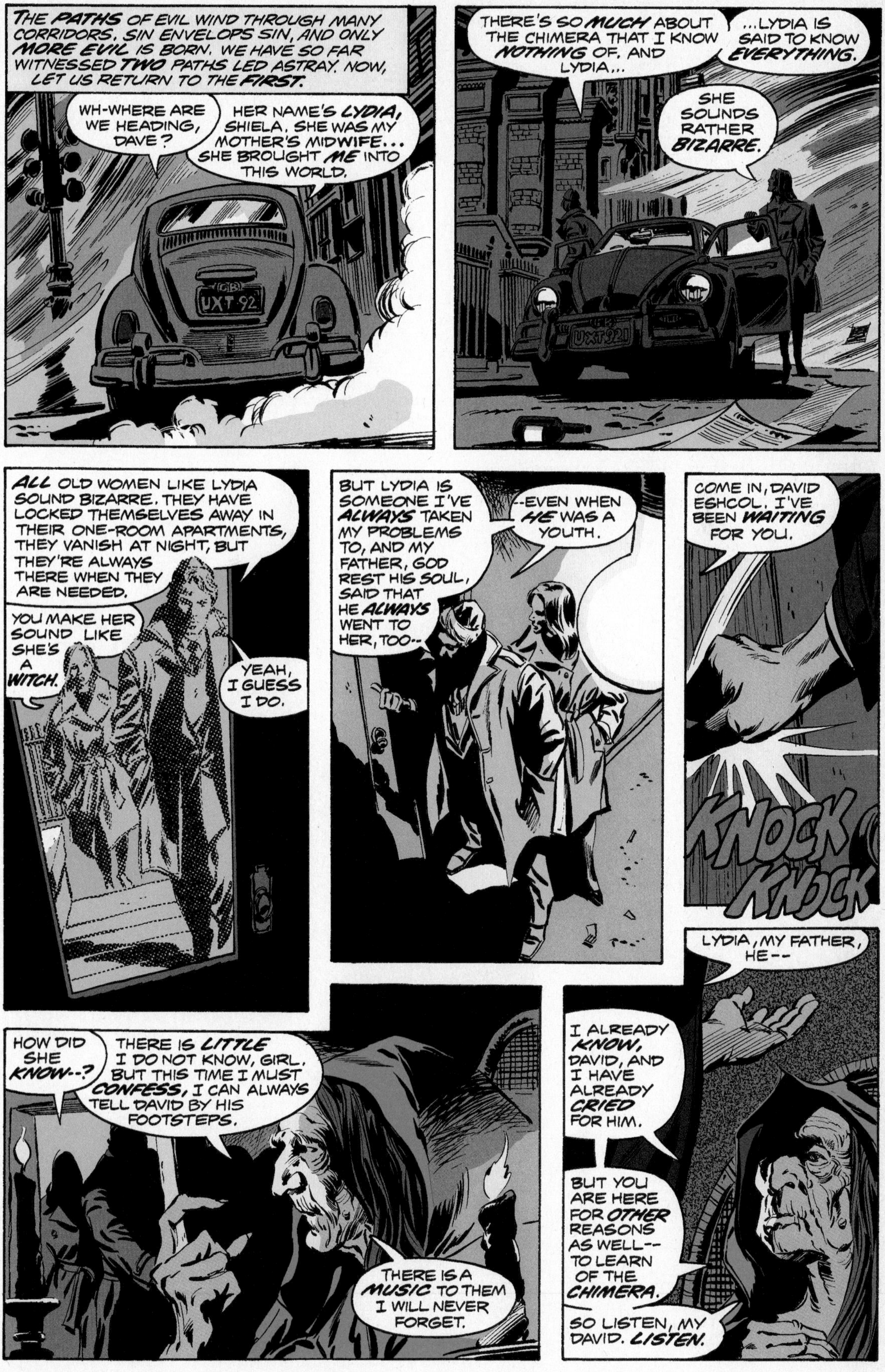
THE PATHS OF EVIL WIND THROUGH MANY CORRIDORS. SIN ENVELOPS SIN, AND ONLY MORE EVIL IS BORN. WE HAVE SO FAR WITNESSED TWO PATHS LED ASTRAY. NOW, LET US RETURN TO THE FIRST.
WH-WHERE ARE WE HEADING, DAVE?
HER NAME'S LYDIA, SHIELA. SHE WAS MY MOTHER'S MIDWIFE... SHE BROUGHT ME INTO THIS WORLD.
UXT 92
THERE'S SO MUCH ABOUT THE CHIMERA THAT I KNOW NOTHING OF. AND LYDIA...
...LYDIA IS SAID TO KNOW EVERYTHING.
SHE SOUNDS RATHER BIZARRE.
UXT 92
ALL OLD WOMEN LIKE LYDIA SOUND BIZARRE. THEY HAVE LOCKED THEMSELVES AWAY IN THEIR ONE-ROOM APARTMENTS, THEY VANISH AT NIGHT, BUT THEY'RE ALWAYS THERE WHEN THEY ARE NEEDED.
YOU MAKE HER SOUND LIKE SHE'S A WITCH.
YEAH, I GUESS I DO.
BUT LYDIA IS SOMEONE I'VE ALWAYS TAKEN MY PROBLEMS TO, AND MY FATHER, GOD REST HIS SOUL, SAID THAT HE ALWAYS WENT TO HER, TOO--
--EVEN WHEN HE WAS A YOUTH.
COME IN, DAVID ESHCOL. I'VE BEEN WAITING FOR YOU.
KNOCK KNOCK
HOW DID SHE KNOW--?
THERE IS LITTLE I DO NOT KNOW, GIRL. BUT THIS TIME I MUST CONFESS, I CAN ALWAYS TELL DAVID BY HIS FOOTSTEPS.
THERE IS A MUSIC TO THEM I WILL NEVER FORGET.
LYDIA, MY FATHER, HE--
I ALREADY KNOW, DAVID, AND I HAVE ALREADY CRIED FOR HIM.
BUT YOU ARE HERE FOR OTHER REASONS AS WELL-- TO LEARN OF THE CHIMERA.
SO LISTEN, MY DAVID. LISTEN.

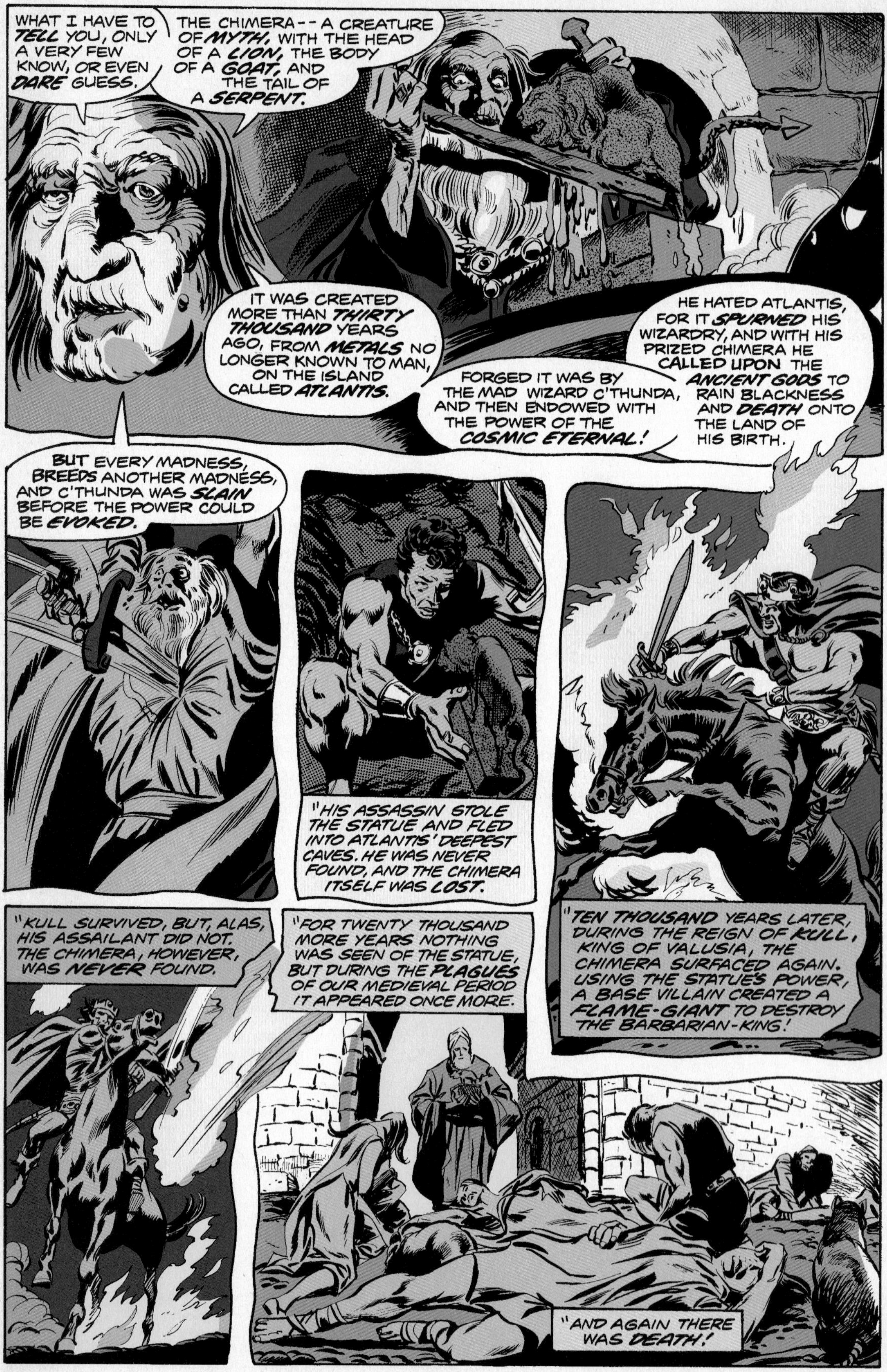
WHAT I HAVE TO TELL YOU, ONLY A VERY FEW KNOW, OR EVEN DARE GUESS.
THE CHIMERA--A CREATURE OF MYTH, WITH THE HEAD OF A LION, THE BODY OF A GOAT, AND THE TAIL OF A SERPENT.
IT WAS CREATED MORE THAN THIRTY THOUSAND YEARS AGO, FROM METALS NO LONGER KNOWN TO MAN, ON THE ISLAND CALLED ATLANTIS.
FORGED IT WAS BY THE MAD WIZARD C'THUNDA, AND THEN ENDOWED WITH THE POWER OF THE COSMIC ETERNAL!
HE HATED ATLANTIS, FOR IT SPURNED HIS WIZARDRY, AND WITH HIS PRIZED CHIMERA HE CALLED UPON THE ANCIENT GODS TO RAIN BLACKNESS AND DEATH ONTO THE LAND OF HIS BIRTH.
BUT EVERY MADNESS, BREEDS ANOTHER MADNESS, AND C'THUNDA WAS SLAIN BEFORE THE POWER COULD BE EVOKED.
"HIS ASSASSIN STOLE THE STATUE AND FLED INTO ATLANTIS' DEEPEST CAVES. HE WAS NEVER FOUND, AND THE CHIMERA ITSELF WAS LOST.
"TEN THOUSAND YEARS LATER, DURING THE REIGN OF KULL, KING OF VALUSIA, THE CHIMERA SURFACED AGAIN. USING THE STATUE'S POWER, A BASE VILLAIN CREATED A FLAME-GIANT TO DESTROY THE BARBARIAN-KING!
"KULL SURVIVED, BUT, ALAS, HIS ASSAILANT DID NOT. THE CHIMERA, HOWEVER, WAS NEVER FOUND.
"FOR TWENTY THOUSAND MORE YEARS NOTHING WAS SEEN OF THE STATUE, BUT DURING THE PLAGUES OF OUR MEDIEVAL PERIOD IT APPEARED ONCE MORE.
"AND AGAIN THERE WAS DEATH!

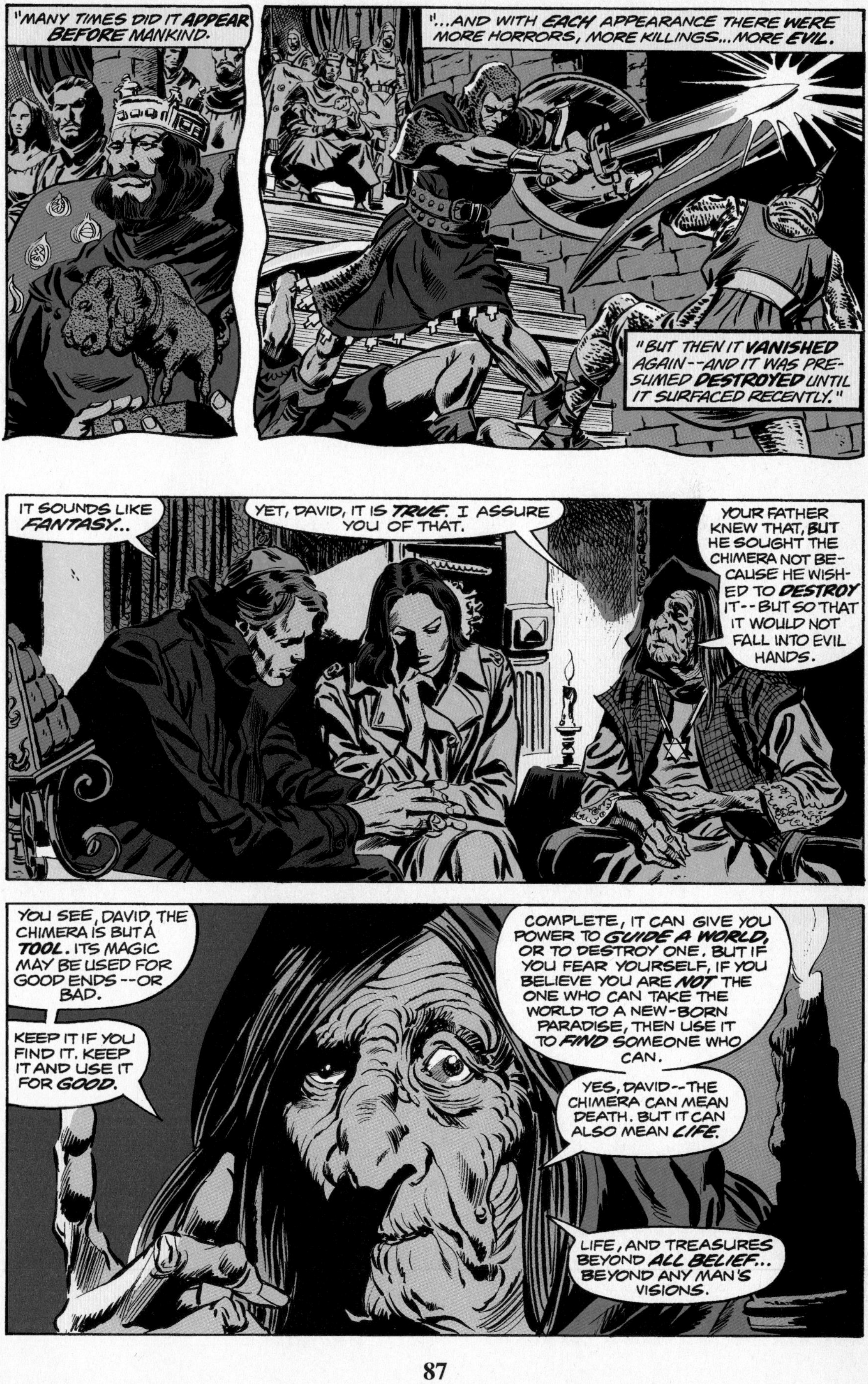
"MANY TIMES DID IT APPEAR BEFORE MANKIND.
"...AND WITH EACH APPEARANCE THERE WERE MORE HORRORS, MORE KILLINGS... MORE EVIL.
"BUT THEN IT VANISHED AGAIN--AND IT WAS PRESUMED DESTROYED UNTIL IT SURFACED RECENTLY."
IT SOUNDS LIKE FANTASY...
YET, DAVID, IT IS TRUE. I ASSURE YOU OF THAT.
YOUR FATHER KNEW THAT, BUT HE SOUGHT THE CHIMERA NOT BECAUSE HE WISHED TO DESTROY IT--BUT SO THAT IT WOULD NOT FALL INTO EVIL HANDS.
YOU SEE, DAVID, THE CHIMERA IS BUT A TOOL. ITS MAGIC MAY BE USED FOR GOOD ENDS --OR BAD.
KEEP IT IF YOU FIND IT. KEEP IT AND USE IT FOR GOOD.
COMPLETE, IT CAN GIVE YOU POWER TO GUIDE A WORLD, OR TO DESTROY ONE. BUT IF YOU FEAR YOURSELF, IF YOU BELIEVE YOU ARE NOT THE ONE WHO CAN TAKE THE WORLD TO A NEW-BORN PARADISE, THEN USE IT TO FIND SOMEONE WHO CAN.
YES, DAVID--THE CHIMERA CAN MEAN DEATH. BUT IT CAN ALSO MEAN LIFE.
LIFE, AND TREASURES BEYOND ALL BELIEF... BEYOND ANY MAN'S VISIONS.

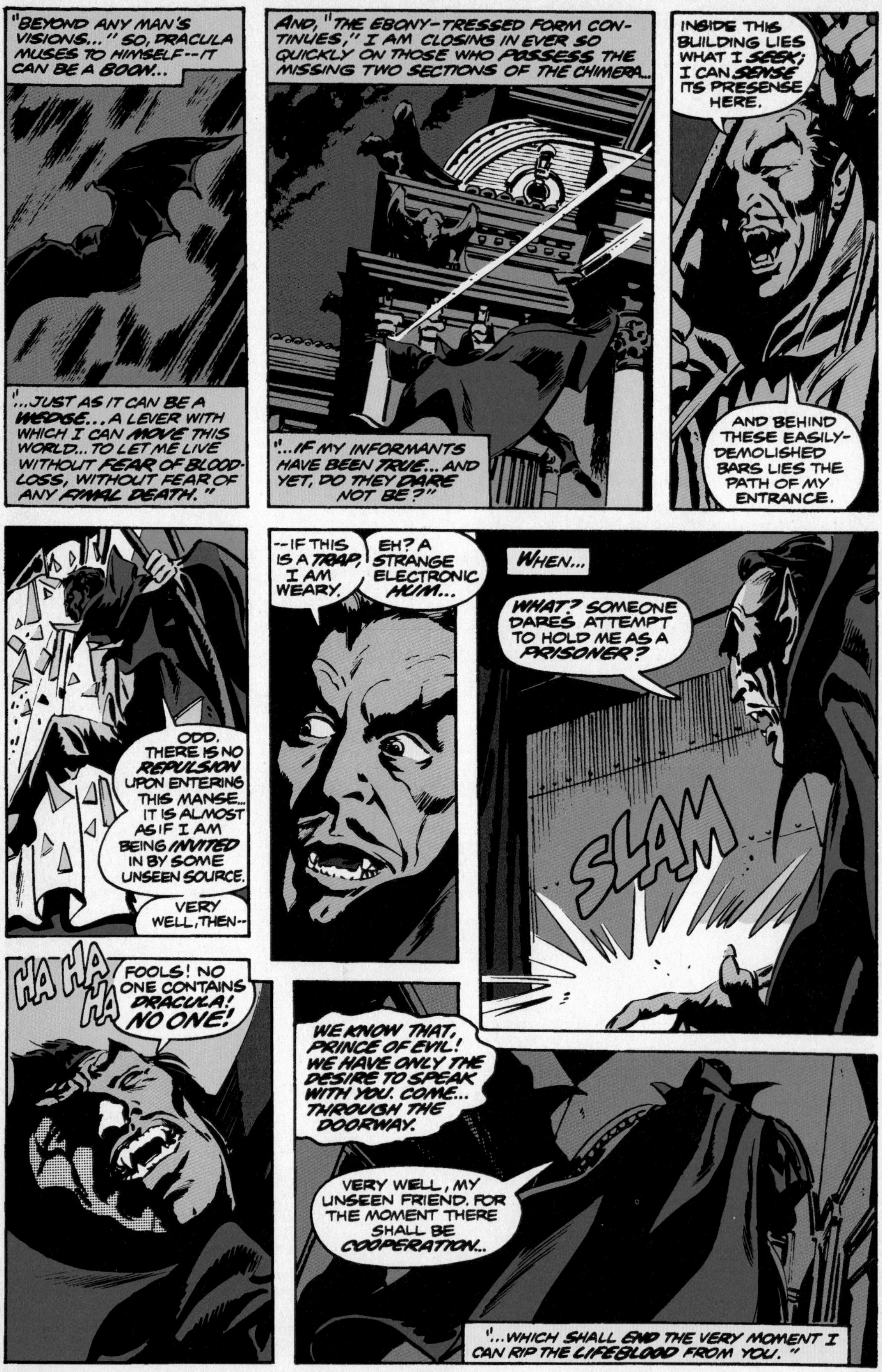
"BEYOND ANY MAN'S VISIONS..." SO, DRACULA MUSES TO HIMSELF--IT CAN BE A BOON...
"...JUST AS IT CAN BE A WEDGE...A LEVER WITH WHICH I CAN MOVE THIS WORLD...TO LET ME LIVE WITHOUT FEAR OF BLOOD-LOSS, WITHOUT FEAR OF ANY FINAL DEATH."
AND," THE EBONY-TRESSED FORM CONTINUES," I AM CLOSING IN EVER SO QUICKLY ON THOSE WHO POSSESS THE MISSING TWO SECTIONS OF THE CHIMERA...
"...IF MY INFORMANTS HAVE BEEN TRUE...AND YET, DO THEY DARE NOT BE?"
INSIDE THIS BUILDING LIES WHAT I SEEK; I CAN SENSE ITS PRESENSE HERE.
AND BEHIND THESE EASILY-DEMOLISHED BARS LIES THE PATH OF MY ENTRANCE.
ODD. THERE IS NO REPULSION UPON ENTERING THIS MANSE... IT IS ALMOST AS IF I AM BEING INVITED IN BY SOME UNSEEN SOURCE.
VERY WELL, THEN--
--IF THIS IS A TRAP, I AM WEARY.
EH? A STRANGE ELECTRONIC HUM...
WHEN...
WHAT? SOMEONE DARES ATTEMPT TO HOLD ME AS A PRISONER?
SLAM
HA HA HA
FOOLS! NO ONE CONTAINS DRACULA! NO ONE!
WE KNOW THAT, PRINCE OF EVIL! WE HAVE ONLY THE DESIRE TO SPEAK WITH YOU. COME... THROUGH THE DOORWAY.
VERY WELL, MY UNSEEN FRIEND. FOR THE MOMENT THERE SHALL BE COOPERATION...
"...WHICH SHALL END THE VERY MOMENT I CAN RIP THE LIFEBLOOD FROM YOU."

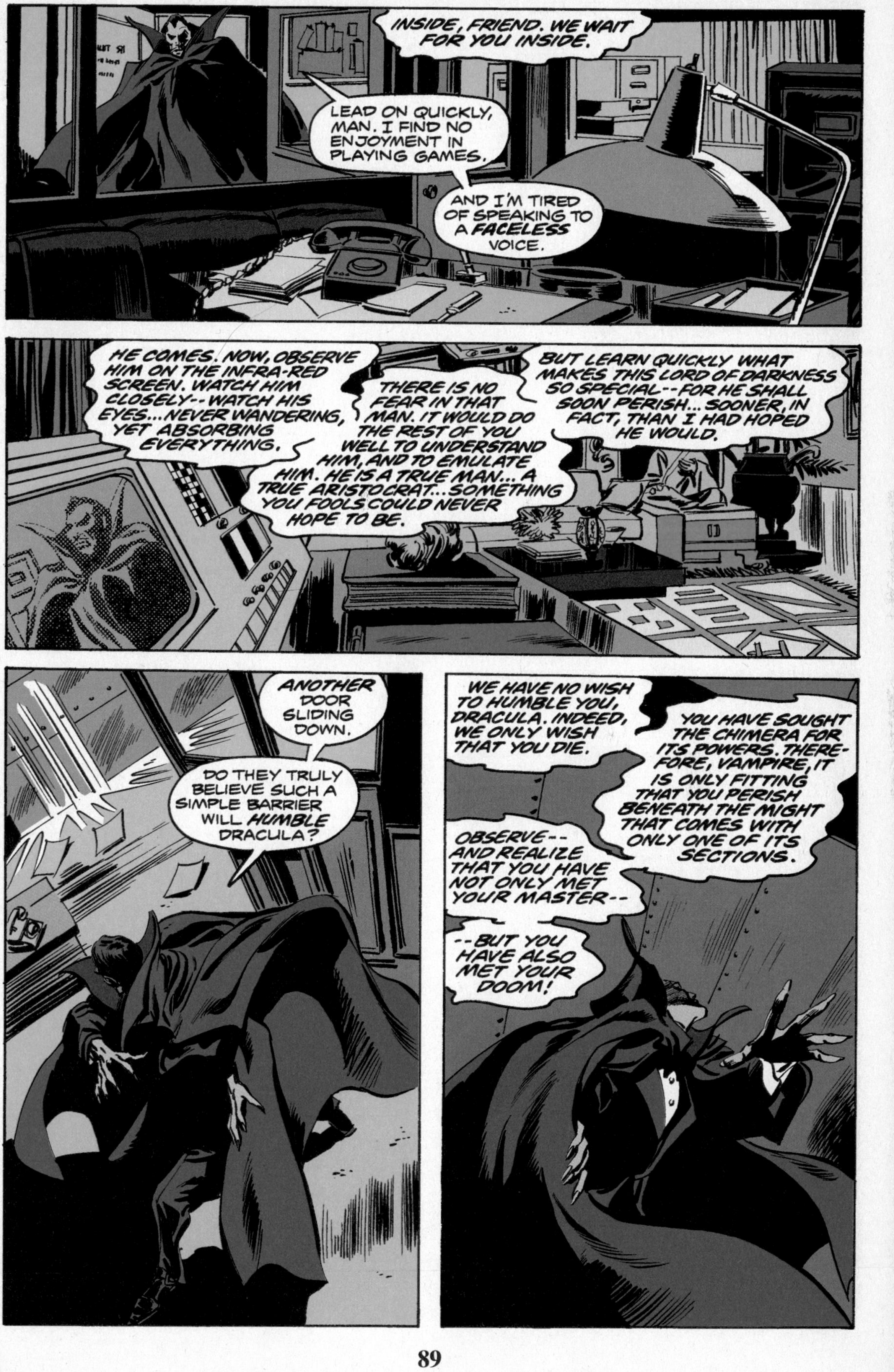
INSIDE, FRIEND. WE WAIT FOR YOU INSIDE.
LEAD ON QUICKLY, MAN. I FIND NO ENJOYMENT IN PLAYING GAMES.
AND I'M TIRED OF SPEAKING TO A FACELESS VOICE.
HE COMES. NOW, OBSERVE HIM ON THE INFRA-RED SCREEN. WATCH HIM CLOSELY-- WATCH HIS EYES... NEVER WANDERING, YET ABSORBING EVERYTHING.
THERE IS NO FEAR IN THAT MAN. IT WOULD DO THE REST OF YOU WELL TO UNDERSTAND HIM, AND TO EMULATE HIM. HE IS A TRUE MAN... A TRUE ARISTOCRAT... SOMETHING YOU FOOLS COULD NEVER HOPE TO BE.
BUT LEARN QUICKLY WHAT MAKES THIS LORD OF DARKNESS SO SPECIAL--FOR HE SHALL SOON PERISH... SOONER, IN FACT, THAN I HAD HOPED HE WOULD.
ANOTHER DOOR SLIDING DOWN.
DO THEY TRULY BELIEVE SUCH A SIMPLE BARRIER WILL HUMBLE DRACULA?
WE HAVE NO WISH TO HUMBLE YOU, DRACULA. INDEED, WE ONLY WISH THAT YOU DIE.
YOU HAVE SOUGHT THE CHIMERA FOR ITS POWERS. THEREFORE, VAMPIRE, IT IS ONLY FITTING THAT YOU PERISH BENEATH THE MIGHT THAT COMES WITH ONLY ONE OF ITS SECTIONS.
OBSERVE-- AND REALIZE THAT YOU HAVE NOT ONLY MET YOUR MASTER--
--BUT YOU HAVE ALSO MET YOUR DOOM!

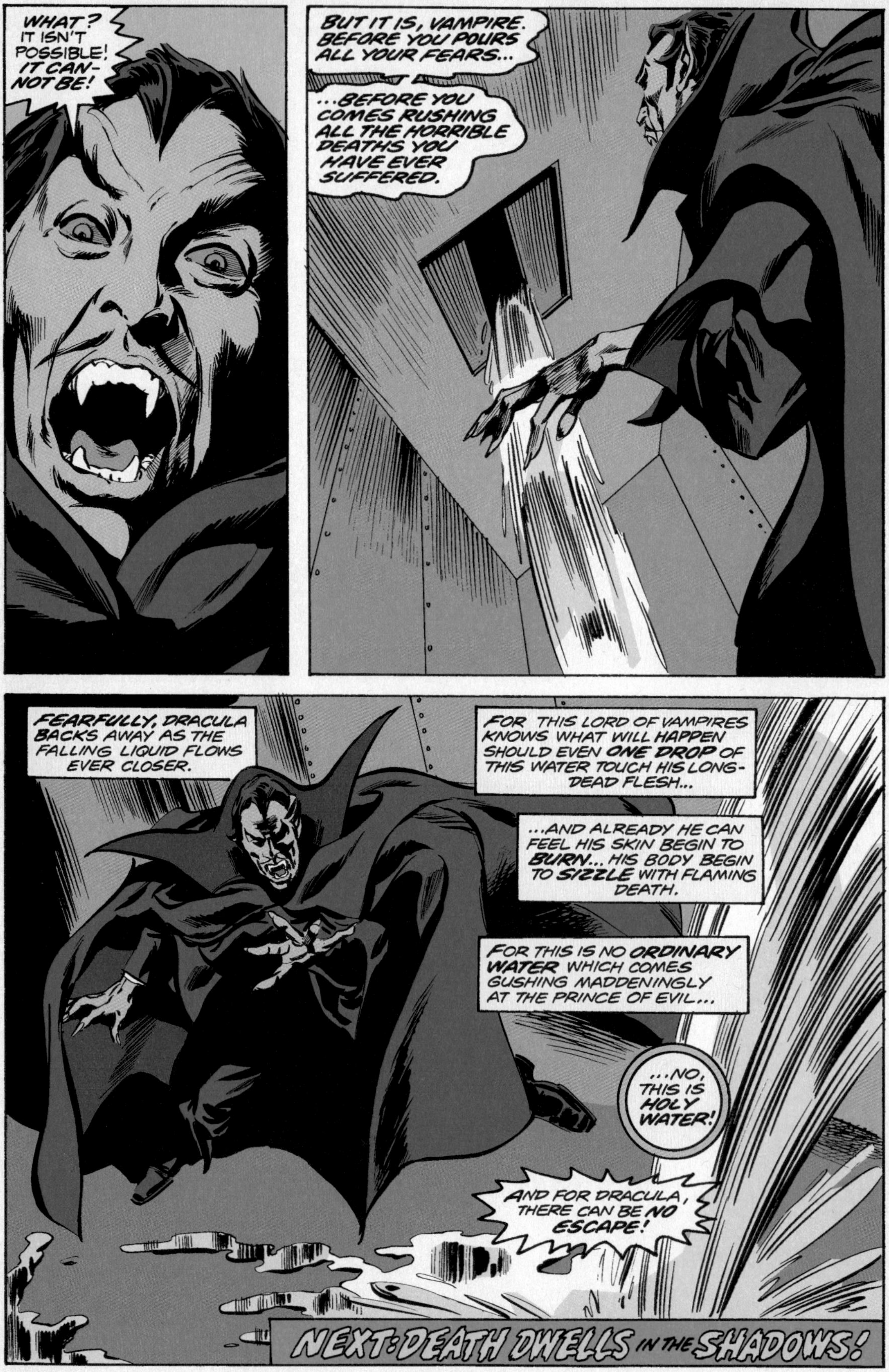
WHAT? IT ISN'T POSSIBLE! IT CAN-NOT BE!
BUT IT IS, VAMPIRE. BEFORE YOU POURS ALL YOUR FEARS...
...BEFORE YOU COMES RUSHING ALL THE HORRIBLE DEATHS YOU HAVE EVER SUFFERED.
FEARFULLY, DRACULA BACKS AWAY AS THE FALLING LIQUID FLOWS EVER CLOSER.
FOR THIS LORD OF VAMPIRES KNOWS WHAT WILL HAPPEN SHOULD EVEN ONE DROP OF THIS WATER TOUCH HIS LONG-DEAD FLESH...
...AND ALREADY HE CAN FEEL HIS SKIN BEGIN TO BURN... HIS BODY BEGIN TO SIZZLE WITH FLAMING DEATH.
FOR THIS IS NO ORDINARY WATER WHICH COMES GUSHING MADDENINGLY AT THE PRINCE OF EVIL...
...NO, THIS IS HOLY WATER!
AND FOR DRACULA, THERE CAN BE NO ESCAPE!
NEXT: DEATH DWELLS IN THE SHADOWS!

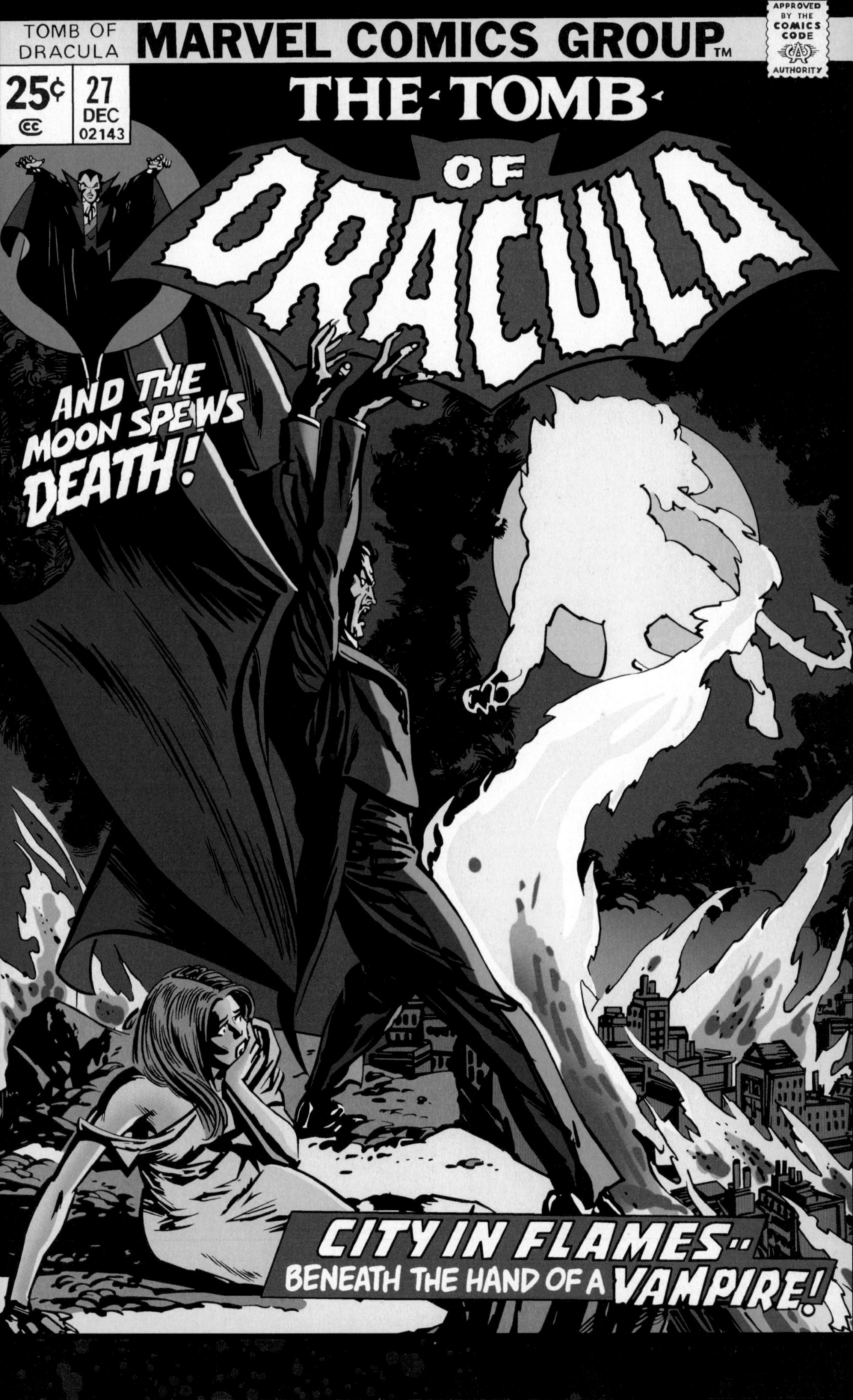
TOMB OF DRACULA
MARVEL COMICS GROUP TM
APPROVED BY THE COMICS CODE AUTHORITY
25¢
27 DEC 02143
THE TOMB OF DRACULA
AND THE MOON SPEWS DEATH!
CITY IN FLAMES.. BENEATH THE HAND OF A VAMPIRE!

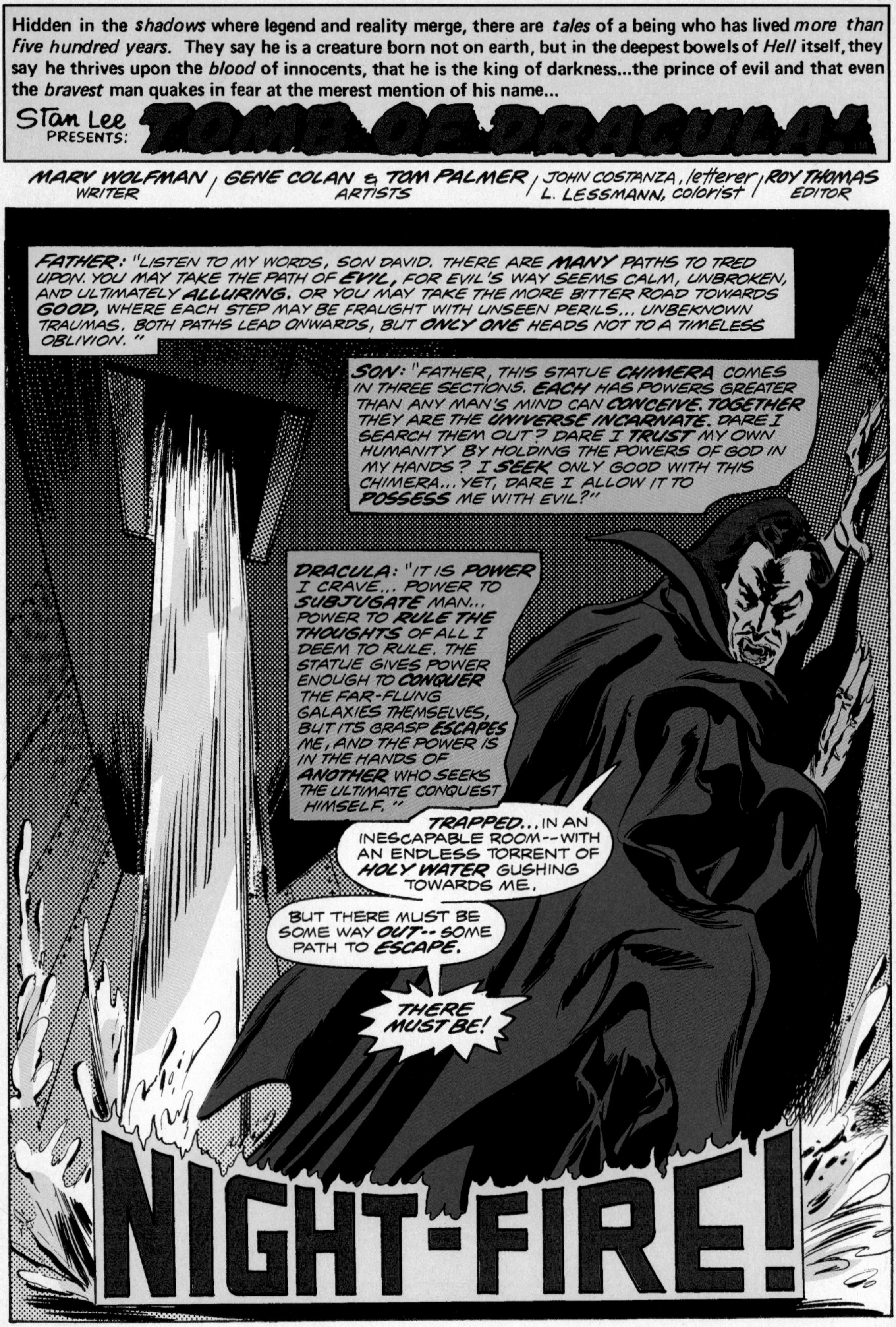
Hidden in the *shadows* where legend and reality merge, there are *tales* of a being who has lived *more than five hundred years.* They say he is a creature born not on earth, but in the deepest bowels of *Hell* itself, they say he thrives upon the *blood* of innocents, that he is the king of darkness...the prince of evil and that even the *bravest* man quakes in fear at the merest mention of his name...
Stan Lee PRESENTS: TOMB OF DRACULA
MARV WOLFMAN WRITER / GENE COLAN & TOM PALMER ARTISTS / JOHN COSTANZA, letterer L. LESSMANN, colorist / ROY THOMAS EDITOR
FATHER: "LISTEN TO MY WORDS, SON DAVID. THERE ARE MANY PATHS TO TRED UPON. YOU MAY TAKE THE PATH OF EVIL, FOR EVIL'S WAY SEEMS CALM, UNBROKEN, AND ULTIMATELY ALLURING. OR YOU MAY TAKE THE MORE BITTER ROAD TOWARDS GOOD, WHERE EACH STEP MAY BE FRAUGHT WITH UNSEEN PERILS... UNBEKNOWN TRAUMAS. BOTH PATHS LEAD ONWARDS, BUT ONLY ONE HEADS NOT TO A TIMELESS OBLIVION."
SON: "FATHER, THIS STATUE CHIMERA COMES IN THREE SECTIONS. EACH HAS POWERS GREATER THAN ANY MAN'S MIND CAN CONCEIVE. TOGETHER THEY ARE THE UNIVERSE INCARNATE. DARE I SEARCH THEM OUT? DARE I TRUST MY OWN HUMANITY BY HOLDING THE POWERS OF GOD IN MY HANDS? I SEEK ONLY GOOD WITH THIS CHIMERA... YET, DARE I ALLOW IT TO POSSESS ME WITH EVIL?"
DRACULA: "IT IS POWER I CRAVE... POWER TO SUBJUGATE MAN... POWER TO RULE THE THOUGHTS OF ALL I DEEM TO RULE. THE STATUE GIVES POWER ENOUGH TO CONQUER THE FAR-FLUNG GALAXIES THEMSELVES, BUT ITS GRASP ESCAPES ME, AND THE POWER IS IN THE HANDS OF ANOTHER WHO SEEKS THE ULTIMATE CONQUEST HIMSELF."
TRAPPED... IN AN INESCAPABLE ROOM--WITH AN ENDLESS TORRENT OF HOLY WATER GUSHING TOWARDS ME.
BUT THERE MUST BE SOME WAY OUT-- SOME PATH TO ESCAPE.
THERE MUST BE!
NIGHT-FIRE!

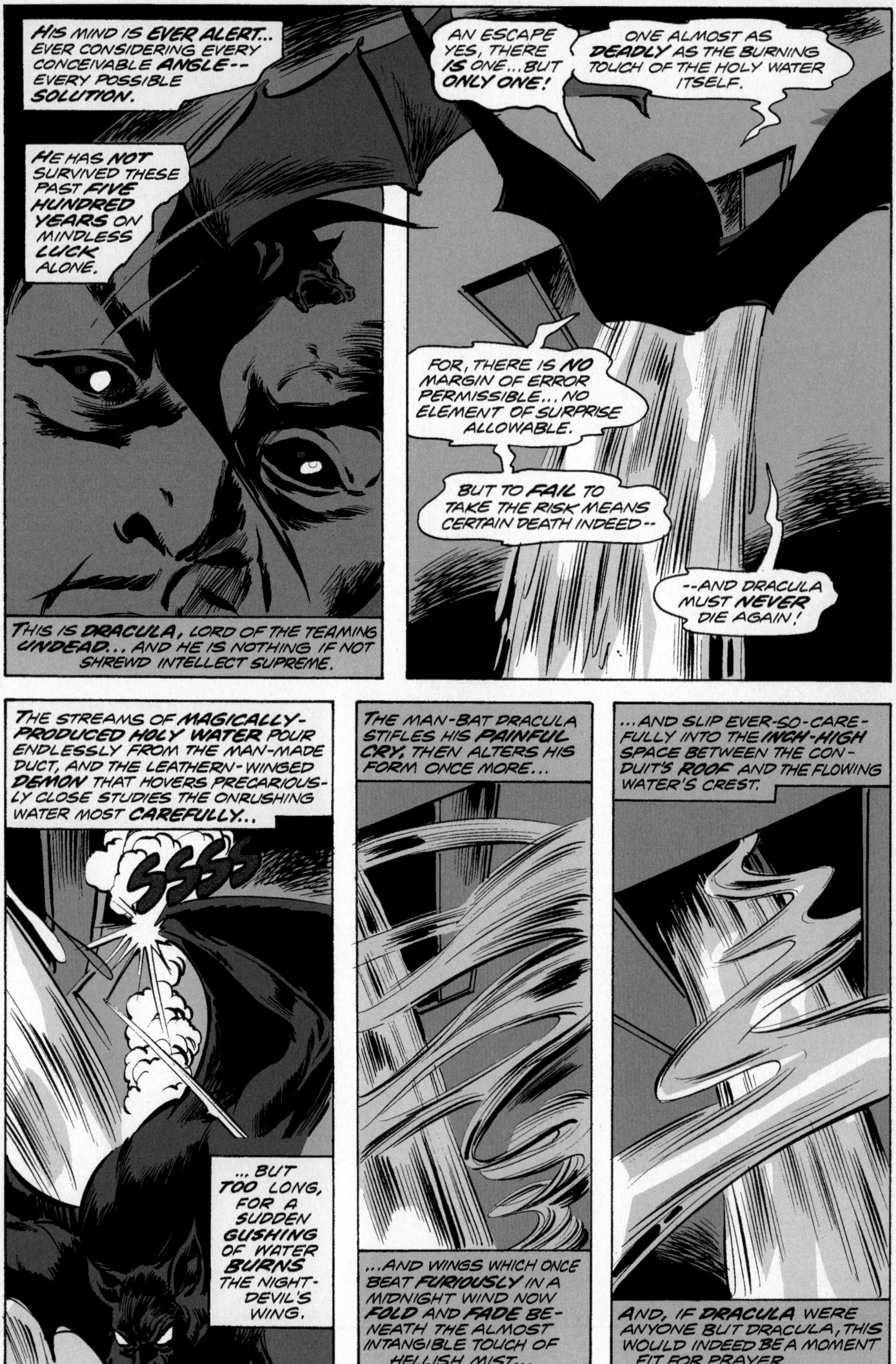
HIS MIND IS EVER ALERT... EVER CONSIDERING EVERY CONCEIVABLE ANGLE-- EVERY POSSIBLE SOLUTION.
HE HAS NOT SURVIVED THESE PAST FIVE HUNDRED YEARS ON MINDLESS LUCK ALONE.
THIS IS DRACULA, LORD OF THE TEAMING UNDEAD... AND HE IS NOTHING IF NOT SHREWD INTELLECT SUPREME.
AN ESCAPE YES, THERE IS ONE... BUT ONLY ONE!
ONE ALMOST AS DEADLY AS THE BURNING TOUCH OF THE HOLY WATER ITSELF.
FOR, THERE IS NO MARGIN OF ERROR PERMISSIBLE... NO ELEMENT OF SURPRISE ALLOWABLE.
BUT TO FAIL TO TAKE THE RISK MEANS CERTAIN DEATH INDEED--
--AND DRACULA MUST NEVER DIE AGAIN!
THE STREAMS OF MAGICALLY-PRODUCED HOLY WATER POUR ENDLESSLY FROM THE MAN-MADE DUCT, AND THE LEATHERN-WINGED DEMON THAT HOVERS PRECARIOUSLY CLOSE STUDIES THE ONRUSHING WATER MOST CAREFULLY...
SSSS
...BUT TOO LONG, FOR A SUDDEN GUSHING OF WATER BURNS THE NIGHT-DEVIL'S WING.
THE MAN-BAT DRACULA STIFLES HIS PAINFUL CRY, THEN ALTERS HIS FORM ONCE MORE...
...AND WINGS WHICH ONCE BEAT FURIOUSLY IN A MIDNIGHT WIND NOW FOLD AND FADE BENEATH THE ALMOST INTANGIBLE TOUCH OF HELLISH MIST...
...AND SLIP EVER-SO-CAREFULLY INTO THE INCH-HIGH SPACE BETWEEN THE CONDUIT'S ROOF AND THE FLOWING WATER'S CREST.
AND, IF DRACULA WERE ANYONE BUT DRACULA, THIS WOULD INDEED BE A MOMENT FIT FOR PRAYER.

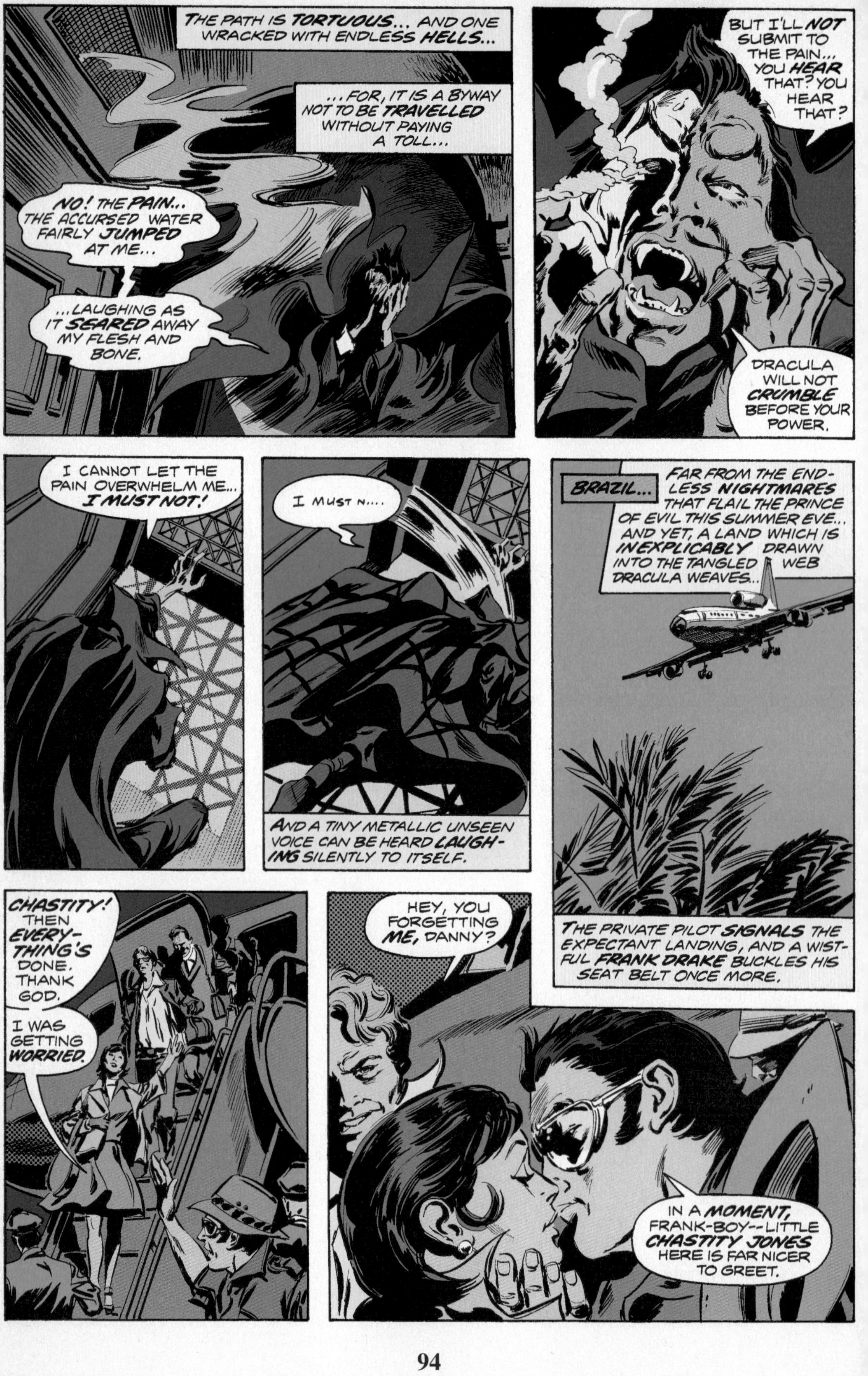

THE PATH IS TORTUOUS... AND ONE WRACKED WITH ENDLESS HELLS...
...FOR, IT IS A BYWAY NOT TO BE TRAVELLED WITHOUT PAYING A TOLL...
NO! THE PAIN... THE ACCURSED WATER FAIRLY JUMPED AT ME...
...LAUGHING AS IT SEARED AWAY MY FLESH AND BONE.
BUT I'LL NOT SUBMIT TO THE PAIN... YOU HEAR THAT? YOU HEAR THAT?
DRACULA WILL NOT CRUMBLE BEFORE YOUR POWER.
I CANNOT LET THE PAIN OVERWHELM ME... I MUST NOT!
I MUST N....
AND A TINY METALLIC UNSEEN VOICE CAN BE HEARD LAUGHING SILENTLY TO ITSELF.
BRAZIL...
FAR FROM THE ENDLESS NIGHTMARES THAT FLAIL THE PRINCE OF EVIL THIS SUMMER EVE... AND YET, A LAND WHICH IS INEXPLICABLY DRAWN INTO THE TANGLED WEB DRACULA WEAVES..
THE PRIVATE PILOT SIGNALS THE EXPECTANT LANDING, AND A WISTFUL FRANK DRAKE BUCKLES HIS SEAT BELT ONCE MORE.
CHASTITY! THEN EVERYTHING'S DONE. THANK GOD.
I WAS GETTING WORRIED.
HEY, YOU FORGETTING ME, DANNY?
IN A MOMENT, FRANK-BOY--LITTLE CHASTITY JONES HERE IS FAR NICER TO GREET.

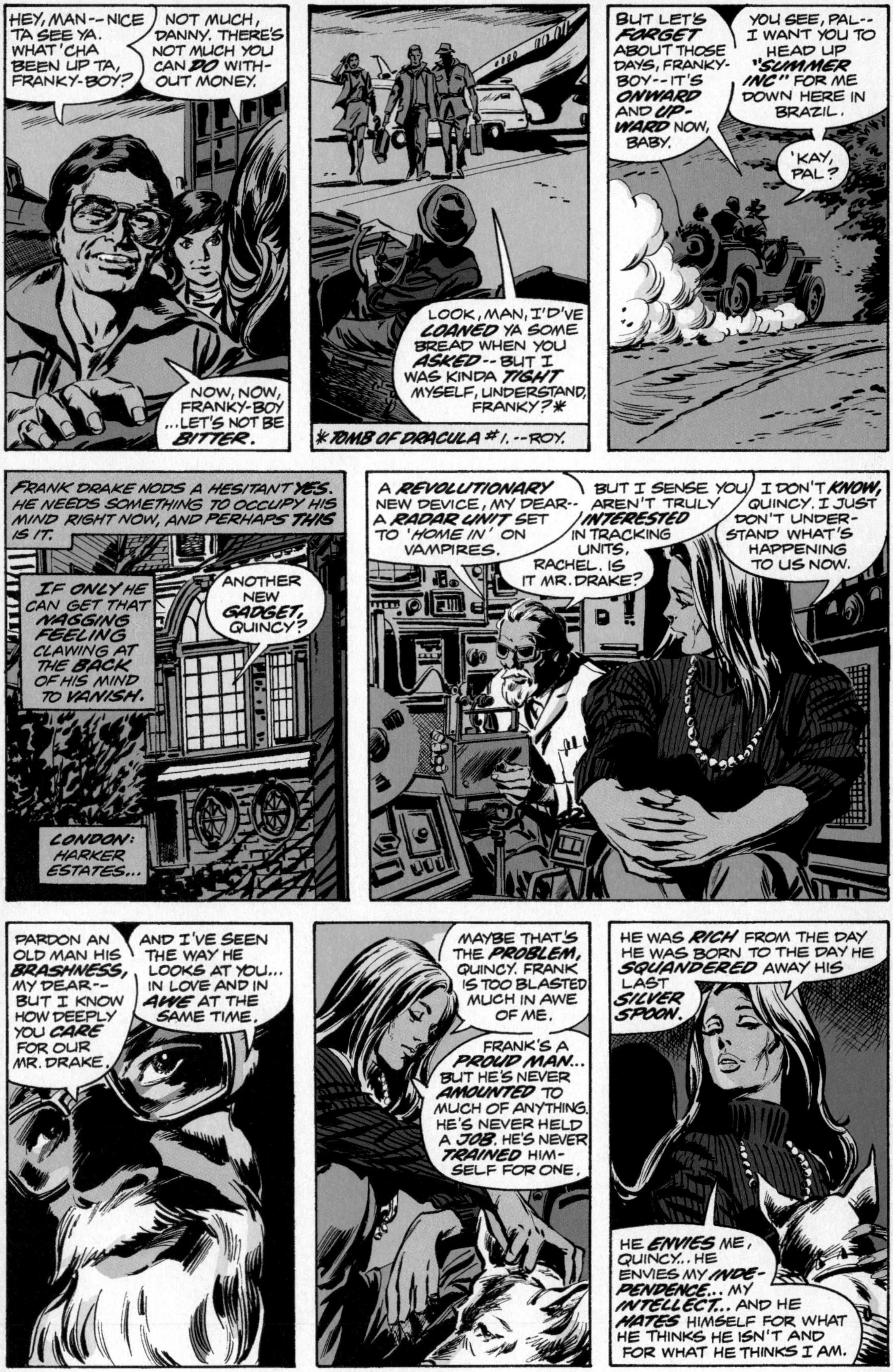
HEY, MAN--NICE TA SEE YA. WHAT'CHA BEEN UP TA, FRANKY-BOY?
NOT MUCH, DANNY. THERE'S NOT MUCH YOU CAN DO WITH-OUT MONEY.
NOW, NOW, FRANKY-BOY ...LET'S NOT BE BITTER.
LOOK, MAN, I'D'VE LOANED YA SOME BREAD WHEN YOU ASKED--BUT I WAS KINDA TIGHT MYSELF, UNDERSTAND, FRANKY?*
*TOMB OF DRACULA #1. --ROY.
BUT LET'S FORGET ABOUT THOSE DAYS, FRANKY-BOY--IT'S ONWARD AND UP-WARD NOW, BABY.
YOU SEE, PAL--I WANT YOU TO HEAD UP "SUMMER INC" FOR ME DOWN HERE IN BRAZIL.
'KAY, PAL?
FRANK DRAKE NODS A HESITANT YES. HE NEEDS SOMETHING TO OCCUPY HIS MIND RIGHT NOW, AND PERHAPS THIS IS IT.
IF ONLY HE CAN GET THAT NAGGING FEELING CLAWING AT THE BACK OF HIS MIND TO VANISH.
LONDON: HARKER ESTATES...
ANOTHER NEW GADGET, QUINCY?
A REVOLUTIONARY NEW DEVICE, MY DEAR--A RADAR UNIT SET TO 'HOME IN' ON VAMPIRES.
BUT I SENSE YOU AREN'T TRULY INTERESTED IN TRACKING UNITS, RACHEL. IS IT MR. DRAKE?
I DON'T KNOW, QUINCY. I JUST DON'T UNDER-STAND WHAT'S HAPPENING TO US NOW.
PARDON AN OLD MAN HIS BRASHNESS, MY DEAR--BUT I KNOW HOW DEEPLY YOU CARE FOR OUR MR. DRAKE.
AND I'VE SEEN THE WAY HE LOOKS AT YOU... IN LOVE AND IN AWE AT THE SAME TIME.
MAYBE THAT'S THE PROBLEM, QUINCY. FRANK IS TOO BLASTED MUCH IN AWE OF ME.
FRANK'S A PROUD MAN... BUT HE'S NEVER AMOUNTED TO MUCH OF ANYTHING. HE'S NEVER HELD A JOB. HE'S NEVER TRAINED HIM-SELF FOR ONE.
HE WAS RICH FROM THE DAY HE WAS BORN TO THE DAY HE SQUANDERED AWAY HIS LAST SILVER SPOON.
HE ENVIES ME, QUINCY... HE ENVIES MY INDE-PENDENCE... MY INTELLECT... AND HE HATES HIMSELF FOR WHAT HE THINKS HE ISN'T AND FOR WHAT HE THINKS I AM.

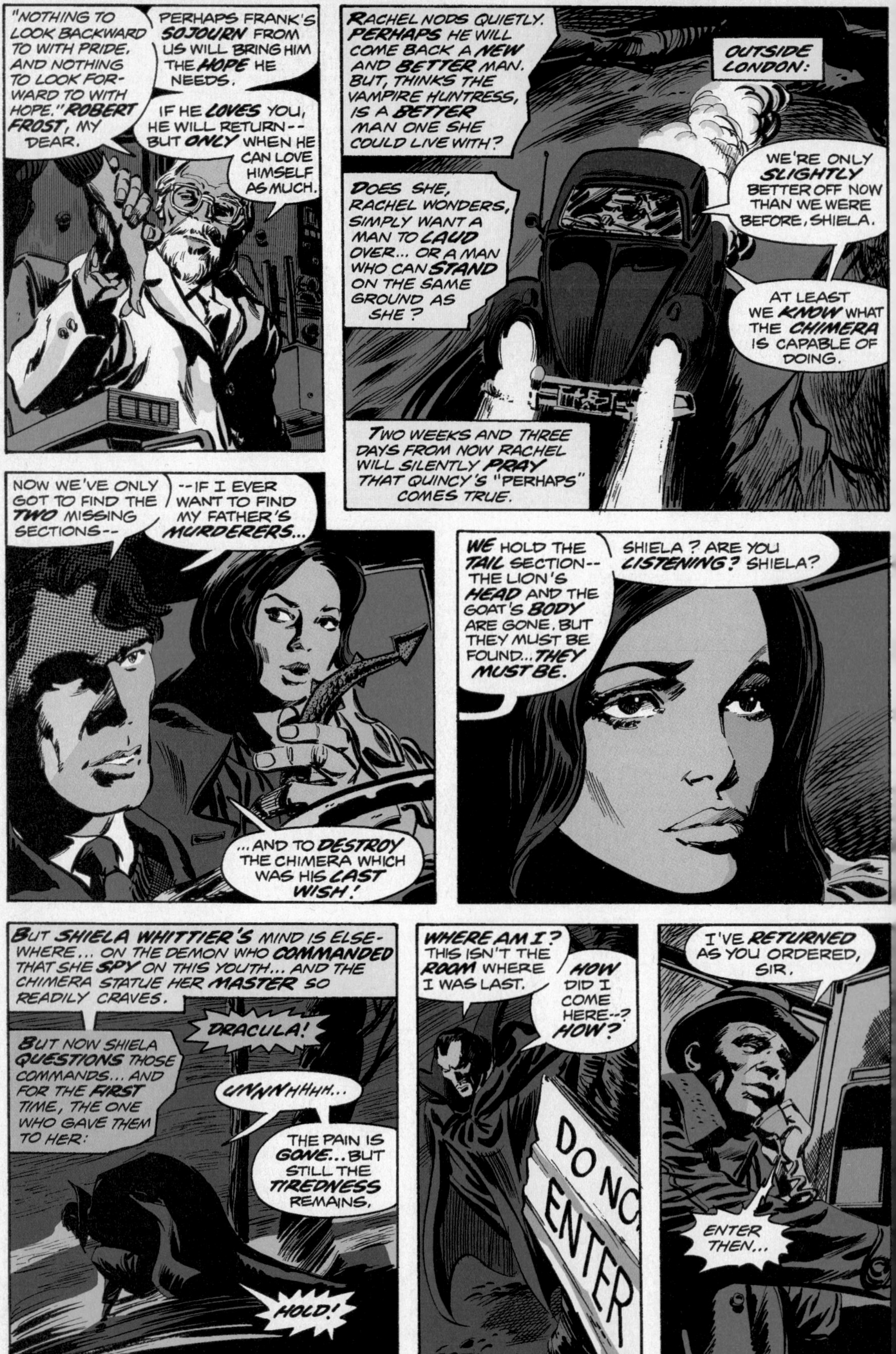
"NOTHING TO LOOK BACKWARD TO WITH PRIDE, AND NOTHING TO LOOK FORWARD TO WITH HOPE." ROBERT FROST, MY DEAR.
PERHAPS FRANK'S SOJOURN FROM US WILL BRING HIM THE HOPE HE NEEDS.
IF HE LOVES YOU, HE WILL RETURN-- BUT ONLY WHEN HE CAN LOVE HIMSELF AS MUCH.
RACHEL NODS QUIETLY. PERHAPS HE WILL COME BACK A NEW AND BETTER MAN. BUT, THINKS THE VAMPIRE HUNTRESS, IS A BETTER MAN ONE SHE COULD LIVE WITH?
DOES SHE, RACHEL WONDERS, SIMPLY WANT A MAN TO LAUD OVER... OR A MAN WHO CAN STAND ON THE SAME GROUND AS SHE?
TWO WEEKS AND THREE DAYS FROM NOW RACHEL WILL SILENTLY PRAY THAT QUINCY'S "PERHAPS" COMES TRUE.
OUTSIDE LONDON:
WE'RE ONLY SLIGHTLY BETTER OFF NOW THAN WE WERE BEFORE, SHIELA.
AT LEAST WE KNOW WHAT THE CHIMERA IS CAPABLE OF DOING.
NOW WE'VE ONLY GOT TO FIND THE TWO MISSING SECTIONS--
--IF I EVER WANT TO FIND MY FATHER'S MURDERERS...
...AND TO DESTROY THE CHIMERA WHICH WAS HIS LAST WISH!
WE HOLD THE TAIL SECTION-- THE LION'S HEAD AND THE GOAT'S BODY ARE GONE. BUT THEY MUST BE FOUND... THEY MUST BE.
SHIELA? ARE YOU LISTENING? SHIELA?
BUT SHIELA WHITTIER'S MIND IS ELSEWHERE... ON THE DEMON WHO COMMANDED THAT SHE SPY ON THIS YOUTH... AND THE CHIMERA STATUE HER MASTER SO READILY CRAVES.
BUT NOW SHIELA QUESTIONS THOSE COMMANDS... AND FOR THE FIRST TIME, THE ONE WHO GAVE THEM TO HER:
DRACULA!
UNNNHHHH...
THE PAIN IS GONE... BUT STILL THE TIREDNESS REMAINS.
HOLD!
WHERE AM I? THIS ISN'T THE ROOM WHERE I WAS LAST.
HOW DID I COME HERE--? HOW?
DO NO
ENTER
I'VE RETURNED AS YOU ORDERED, SIR.
ENTER THEN...

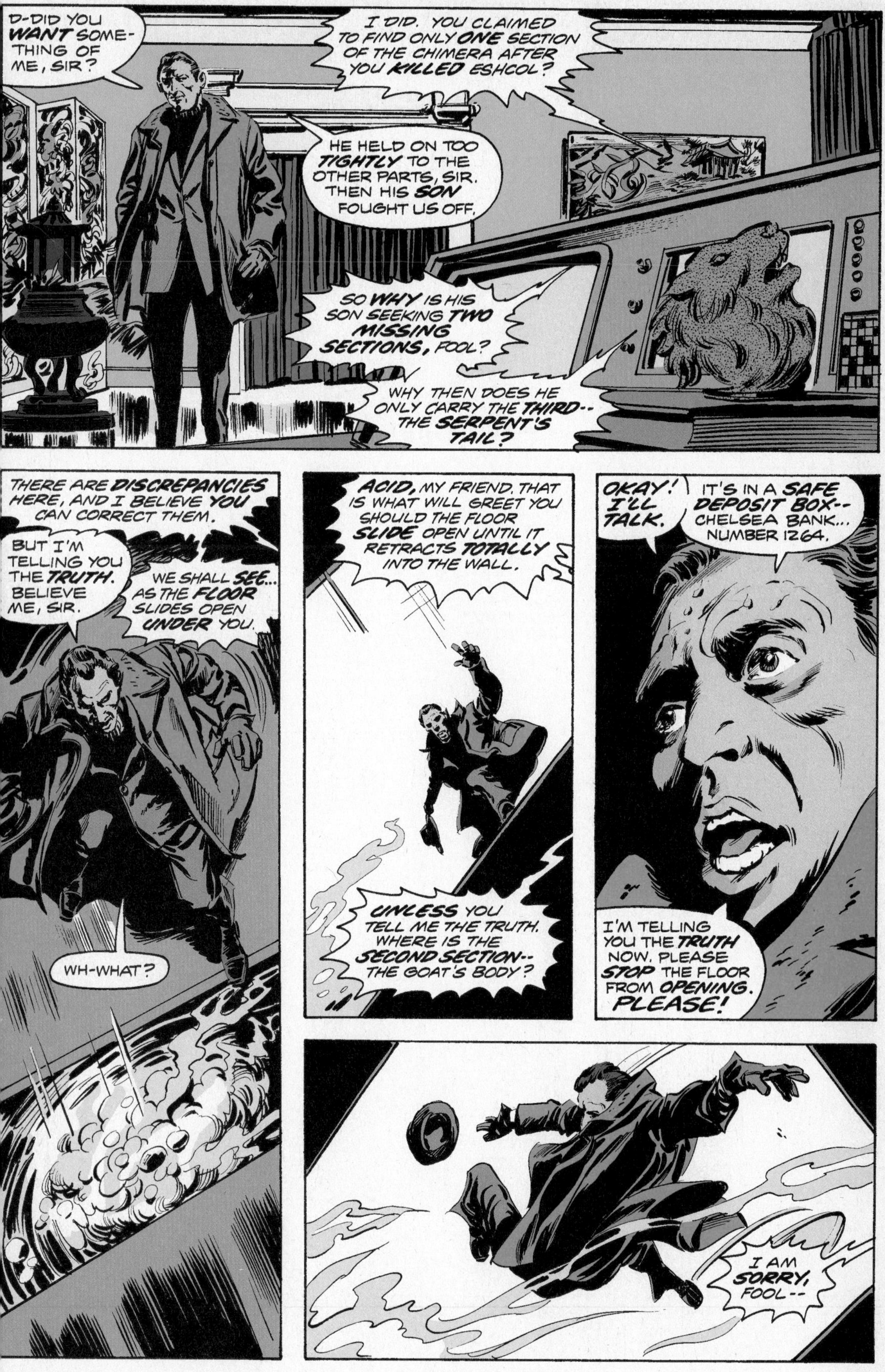
D-DID YOU WANT SOMETHING OF ME, SIR?
I DID. YOU CLAIMED TO FIND ONLY ONE SECTION OF THE CHIMERA AFTER YOU KILLED ESHCOL?
HE HELD ON TOO TIGHTLY TO THE OTHER PARTS, SIR. THEN HIS SON FOUGHT US OFF.
SO WHY IS HIS SON SEEKING TWO MISSING SECTIONS, FOOL?
WHY THEN DOES HE ONLY CARRY THE THIRD-- THE SERPENT'S TAIL?
THERE ARE DISCREPANCIES HERE, AND I BELIEVE YOU CAN CORRECT THEM.
BUT I'M TELLING YOU THE TRUTH. BELIEVE ME, SIR.
WE SHALL SEE... AS THE FLOOR SLIDES OPEN UNDER YOU.
WH-WHAT?
ACID, MY FRIEND. THAT IS WHAT WILL GREET YOU SHOULD THE FLOOR SLIDE OPEN UNTIL IT RETRACTS TOTALLY INTO THE WALL.
UNLESS YOU TELL ME THE TRUTH. WHERE IS THE SECOND SECTION-- THE GOAT'S BODY?
OKAY! I'LL TALK.
IT'S IN A SAFE DEPOSIT BOX-- CHELSEA BANK... NUMBER 1264.
I'M TELLING YOU THE TRUTH NOW. PLEASE STOP THE FLOOR FROM OPENING. PLEASE!
I AM SORRY, FOOL--

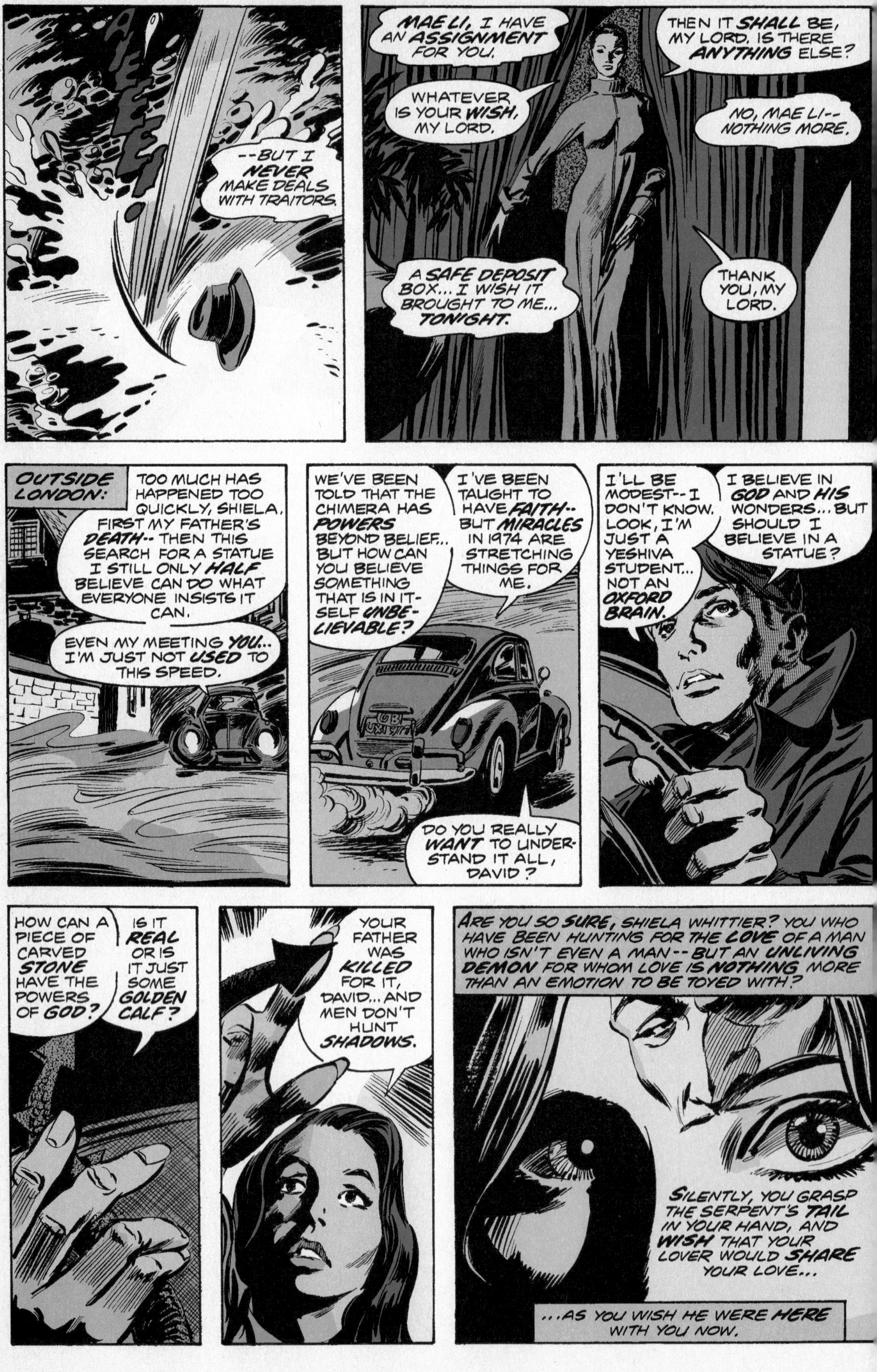
--BUT I NEVER MAKE DEALS WITH TRAITORS.
MAE LI, I HAVE AN ASSIGNMENT FOR YOU.
WHATEVER IS YOUR WISH, MY LORD.
A SAFE DEPOSIT BOX... I WISH IT BROUGHT TO ME... TONIGHT.
THEN IT SHALL BE, MY LORD. IS THERE ANYTHING ELSE?
NO, MAE LI-- NOTHING MORE.
THANK YOU, MY LORD.
OUTSIDE LONDON:
TOO MUCH HAS HAPPENED TOO QUICKLY, SHIELA. FIRST MY FATHER'S DEATH-- THEN THIS SEARCH FOR A STATUE I STILL ONLY HALF BELIEVE CAN DO WHAT EVERYONE INSISTS IT CAN.
EVEN MY MEETING YOU... I'M JUST NOT USED TO THIS SPEED.
WE'VE BEEN TOLD THAT THE CHIMERA HAS POWERS BEYOND BELIEF... BUT HOW CAN YOU BELIEVE SOMETHING THAT IS IN IT-SELF UNBE-LIEVABLE?
I'VE BEEN TAUGHT TO HAVE FAITH-- BUT MIRACLES IN 1974 ARE STRETCHING THINGS FOR ME.
DO YOU REALLY WANT TO UNDER-STAND IT ALL, DAVID?
I'LL BE MODEST-- I DON'T KNOW. LOOK, I'M JUST A YESHIVA STUDENT... NOT AN OXFORD BRAIN.
I BELIEVE IN GOD AND HIS WONDERS... BUT SHOULD I BELIEVE IN A STATUE?
HOW CAN A PIECE OF CARVED STONE HAVE THE POWERS OF GOD?
IS IT REAL OR IS IT JUST SOME GOLDEN CALF?
YOUR FATHER WAS KILLED FOR IT, DAVID... AND MEN DON'T HUNT SHADOWS.
ARE YOU SO SURE, SHIELA WHITTIER? YOU WHO HAVE BEEN HUNTING FOR THE LOVE OF A MAN WHO ISN'T EVEN A MAN-- BUT AN UNLIVING DEMON FOR WHOM LOVE IS NOTHING MORE THAN AN EMOTION TO BE TOYED WITH?
SILENTLY, YOU GRASP THE SERPENT'S TAIL IN YOUR HAND, AND WISH THAT YOUR LOVER WOULD SHARE YOUR LOVE...
...AS YOU WISH HE WERE HERE WITH YOU NOW.

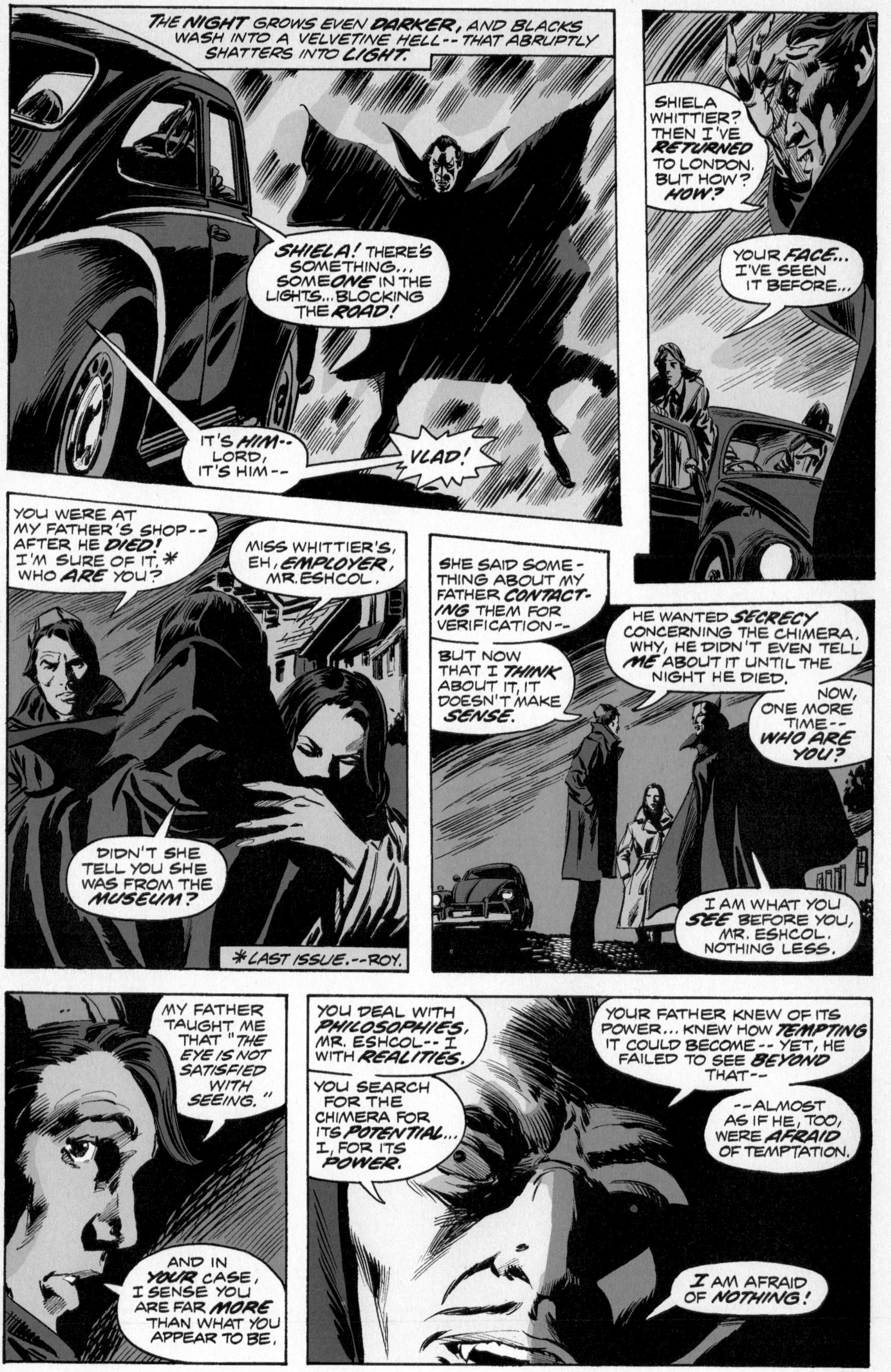
THE NIGHT GROWS EVEN DARKER, AND BLACKS WASH INTO A VELVETINE HELL-- THAT ABRUPTLY SHATTERS INTO LIGHT.
SHIELA! THERE'S SOMETHING... SOMEONE IN THE LIGHTS... BLOCKING THE ROAD!
IT'S HIM-- LORD, IT'S HIM --
VLAD!
SHIELA WHITTIER? THEN I'VE RETURNED TO LONDON. BUT HOW? HOW?
YOUR FACE... I'VE SEEN IT BEFORE...
YOU WERE AT MY FATHER'S SHOP-- AFTER HE DIED! I'M SURE OF IT.* WHO ARE YOU?
MISS WHITTIER'S, EH, EMPLOYER, MR. ESHCOL.
DIDN'T SHE TELL YOU SHE WAS FROM THE MUSEUM?
*LAST ISSUE.--ROY.
SHE SAID SOMETHING ABOUT MY FATHER CONTACTING THEM FOR VERIFICATION--
BUT NOW THAT I THINK ABOUT IT, IT DOESN'T MAKE SENSE.
HE WANTED SECRECY CONCERNING THE CHIMERA. WHY, HE DIDN'T EVEN TELL ME ABOUT IT UNTIL THE NIGHT HE DIED.
NOW, ONE MORE TIME-- WHO ARE YOU?
I AM WHAT YOU SEE BEFORE YOU, MR. ESHCOL. NOTHING LESS.
MY FATHER TAUGHT ME THAT "THE EYE IS NOT SATISFIED WITH SEEING."
AND IN YOUR CASE, I SENSE YOU ARE FAR MORE THAN WHAT YOU APPEAR TO BE.
YOU DEAL WITH PHILOSOPHIES, MR. ESHCOL-- I WITH REALITIES.
YOU SEARCH FOR THE CHIMERA FOR ITS POTENTIAL... I, FOR ITS POWER.
YOUR FATHER KNEW OF ITS POWER... KNEW HOW TEMPTING IT COULD BECOME-- YET, HE FAILED TO SEE BEYOND THAT--
--ALMOST AS IF HE, TOO, WERE AFRAID OF TEMPTATION.
I AM AFRAID OF NOTHING!

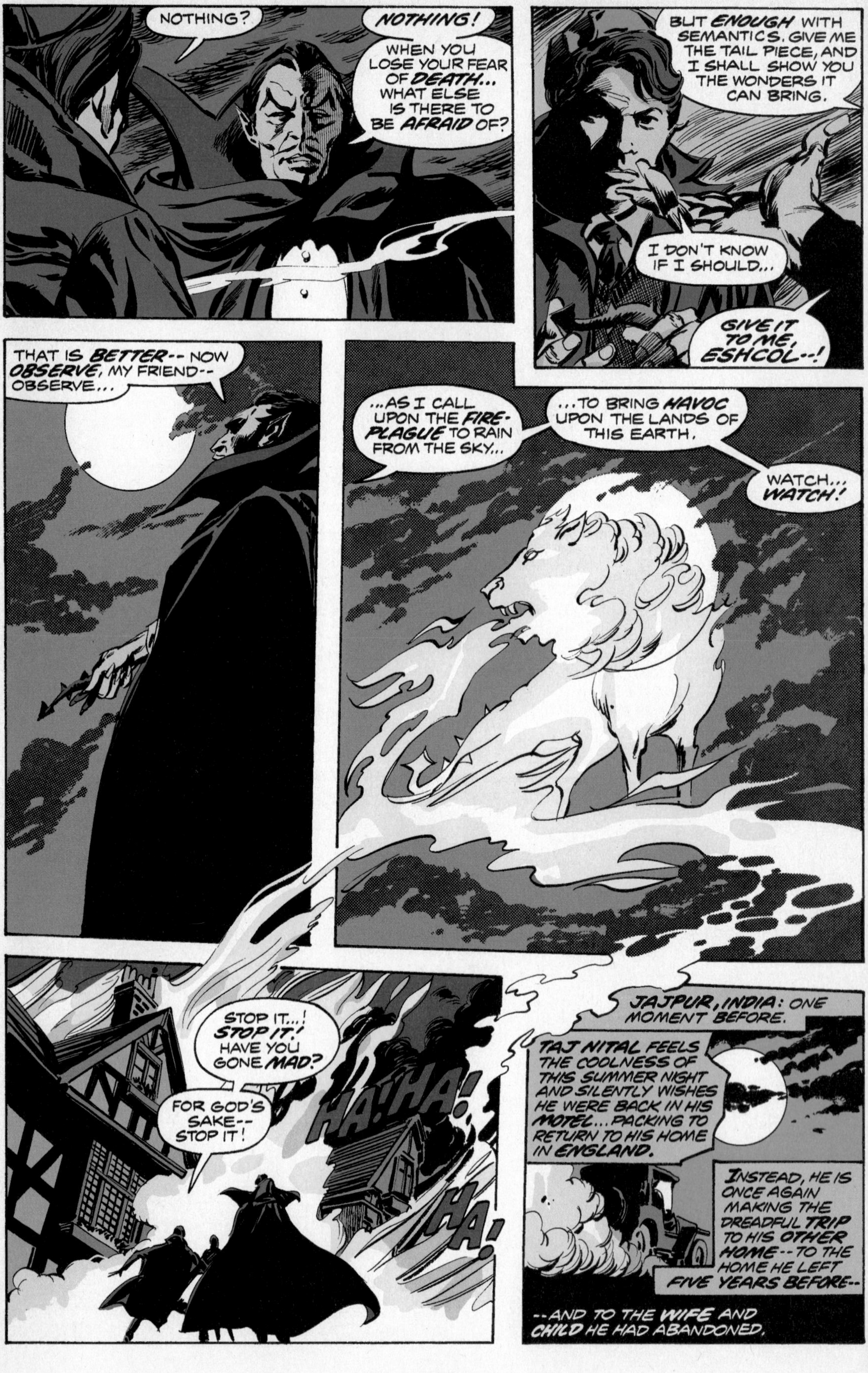
NOTHING?
NOTHING! WHEN YOU LOSE YOUR FEAR OF DEATH... WHAT ELSE IS THERE TO BE AFRAID OF?
BUT ENOUGH WITH SEMANTICS. GIVE ME THE TAIL PIECE, AND I SHALL SHOW YOU THE WONDERS IT CAN BRING.
I DON'T KNOW IF I SHOULD...
GIVE IT TO ME, ESHCOL--!
THAT IS BETTER-- NOW OBSERVE, MY FRIEND-- OBSERVE...
...AS I CALL UPON THE FIRE-PLAGUE TO RAIN FROM THE SKY...
...TO BRING HAVOC UPON THE LANDS OF THIS EARTH.
WATCH... WATCH!
STOP IT...! STOP IT! HAVE YOU GONE MAD?
FOR GOD'S SAKE-- STOP IT!
HA! HA!
HA!
JAJPUR, INDIA: ONE MOMENT BEFORE.
TAJ NITAL FEELS THE COOLNESS OF THIS SUMMER NIGHT AND SILENTLY WISHES HE WERE BACK IN HIS MOTEL... PACKING TO RETURN TO HIS HOME IN ENGLAND.
INSTEAD, HE IS ONCE AGAIN MAKING THE DREADFUL TRIP TO HIS OTHER HOME--TO THE HOME HE LEFT FIVE YEARS BEFORE--
--AND TO THE WIFE AND CHILD HE HAD ABANDONED.

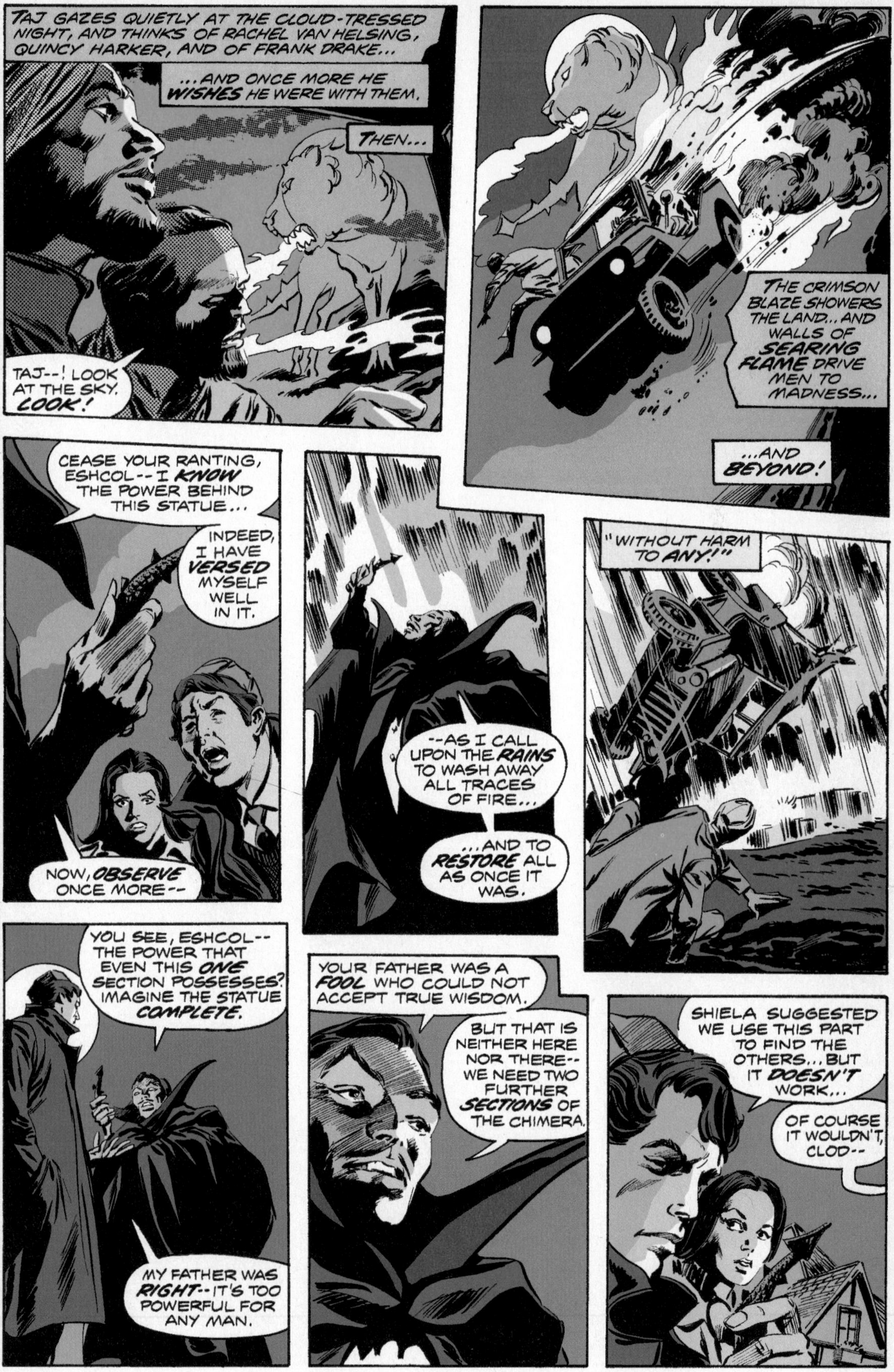
TAJ GAZES QUIETLY AT THE CLOUD-TRESSED NIGHT, AND THINKS OF RACHEL VAN HELSING, QUINCY HARKER, AND OF FRANK DRAKE...
...AND ONCE MORE HE WISHES HE WERE WITH THEM.
THEN...
TAJ--! LOOK AT THE SKY. LOOK!
THE CRIMSON BLAZE SHOWERS THE LAND... AND WALLS OF SEARING FLAME DRIVE MEN TO MADNESS...
...AND BEYOND!
CEASE YOUR RANTING, ESHCOL-- I KNOW THE POWER BEHIND THIS STATUE...
INDEED, I HAVE VERSED MYSELF WELL IN IT.
NOW, OBSERVE ONCE MORE--
--AS I CALL UPON THE RAINS TO WASH AWAY ALL TRACES OF FIRE...
...AND TO RESTORE ALL AS ONCE IT WAS.
"WITHOUT HARM TO ANY!"
YOU SEE, ESHCOL-- THE POWER THAT EVEN THIS ONE SECTION POSSESSES? IMAGINE THE STATUE COMPLETE.
MY FATHER WAS RIGHT-- IT'S TOO POWERFUL FOR ANY MAN.
YOUR FATHER WAS A FOOL WHO COULD NOT ACCEPT TRUE WISDOM.
BUT THAT IS NEITHER HERE NOR THERE-- WE NEED TWO FURTHER SECTIONS OF THE CHIMERA.
SHIELA SUGGESTED WE USE THIS PART TO FIND THE OTHERS... BUT IT DOESN'T WORK...
OF COURSE IT WOULDN'T, CLOD--

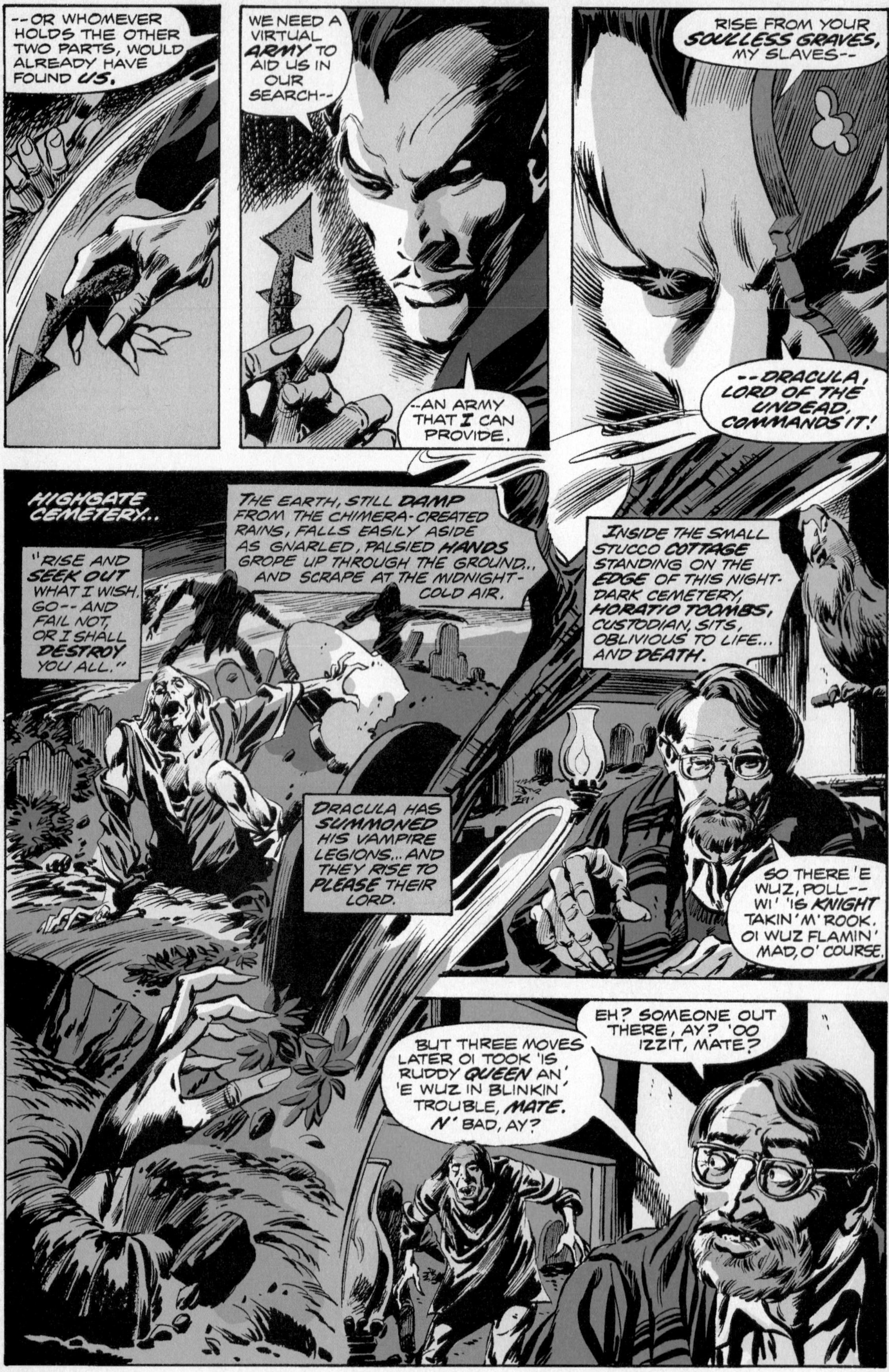

--OR WHOMEVER HOLDS THE OTHER TWO PARTS, WOULD ALREADY HAVE FOUND US.
WE NEED A VIRTUAL ARMY TO AID US IN OUR SEARCH--
--AN ARMY THAT I CAN PROVIDE.
RISE FROM YOUR SOULLESS GRAVES, MY SLAVES--
--DRACULA, LORD OF THE UNDEAD, COMMANDS IT!
HIGHGATE CEMETERY...
THE EARTH, STILL DAMP FROM THE CHIMERA-CREATED RAINS, FALLS EASILY ASIDE AS GNARLED, PALSIED HANDS GROPE UP THROUGH THE GROUND... AND SCRAPE AT THE MIDNIGHT-COLD AIR.
"RISE AND SEEK OUT WHAT I WISH. GO--AND FAIL NOT, OR I SHALL DESTROY YOU ALL."
DRACULA HAS SUMMONED HIS VAMPIRE LEGIONS... AND THEY RISE TO PLEASE THEIR LORD.
INSIDE THE SMALL STUCCO COTTAGE STANDING ON THE EDGE OF THIS NIGHT-DARK CEMETERY, HORATIO TOOMBS, CUSTODIAN, SITS, OBLIVIOUS TO LIFE... AND DEATH.
SO THERE 'E WUZ, POLL-- WI' 'IS KNIGHT TAKIN' M' ROOK. OI WUZ FLAMIN' MAD, O' COURSE.
BUT THREE MOVES LATER OI TOOK 'IS RUDDY QUEEN AN' 'E WUZ IN BLINKIN' TROUBLE, MATE. N' BAD, AY?
EH? SOMEONE OUT THERE, AY? 'OO IZZIT, MATE?

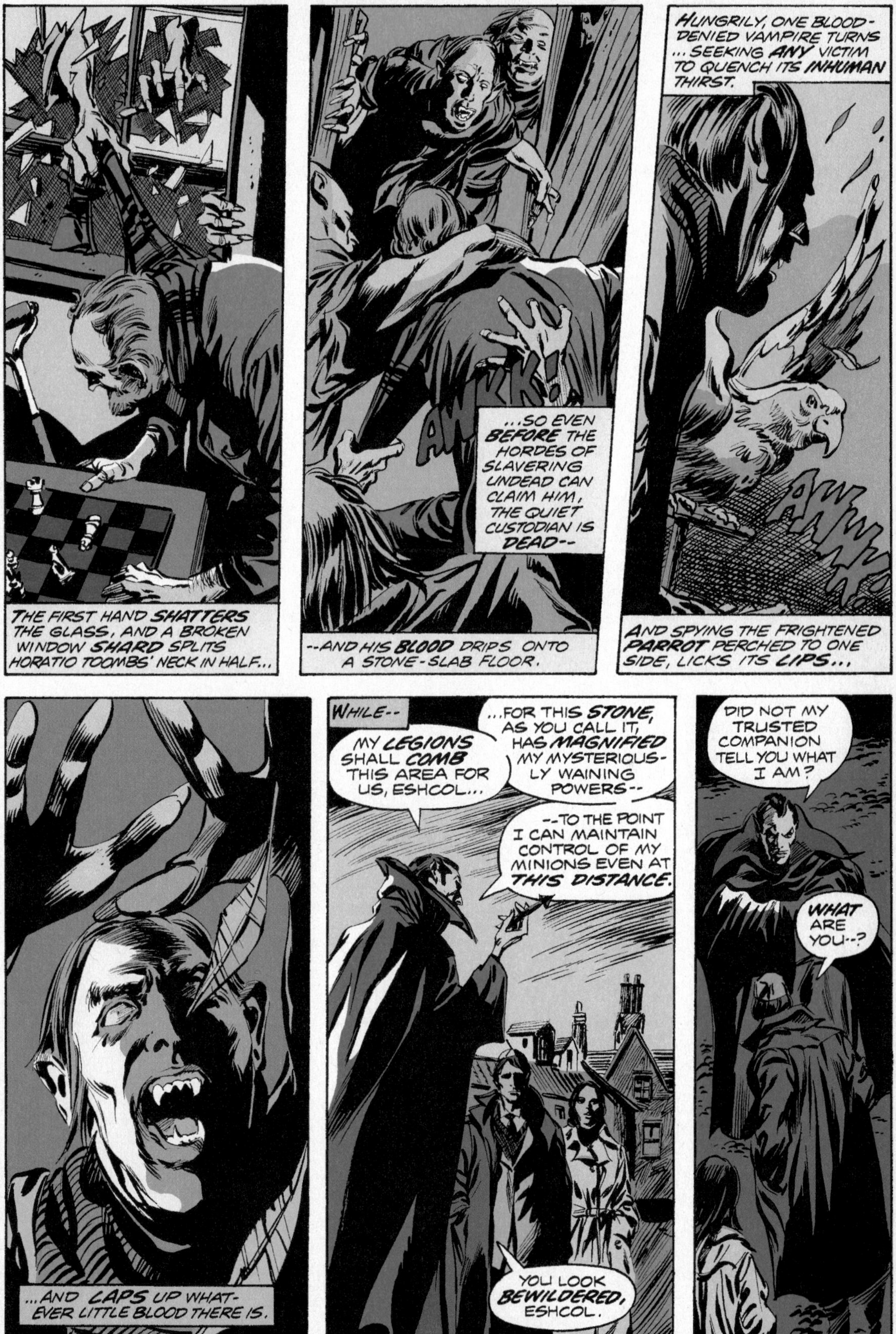
THE FIRST HAND SHATTERS THE GLASS, AND A BROKEN WINDOW SHARD SPLITS HORATIO TOOMBS' NECK IN HALF...
AWKK!
...SO EVEN BEFORE THE HORDES OF SLAVERING UNDEAD CAN CLAIM HIM, THE QUIET CUSTODIAN IS DEAD--
--AND HIS BLOOD DRIPS ONTO A STONE-SLAB FLOOR.
HUNGRILY, ONE BLOOD-DENIED VAMPIRE TURNS ...SEEKING ANY VICTIM TO QUENCH ITS INHUMAN THIRST.
AND SPYING THE FRIGHTENED PARROT PERCHED TO ONE SIDE, LICKS ITS LIPS...
...AND CAPS UP WHAT-EVER LITTLE BLOOD THERE IS.
WHILE--
MY LEGIONS SHALL COMB THIS AREA FOR US, ESHCOL...
...FOR THIS STONE, AS YOU CALL IT, HAS MAGNIFIED MY MYSTERIOUS-LY WAINING POWERS--
--TO THE POINT I CAN MAINTAIN CONTROL OF MY MINIONS EVEN AT THIS DISTANCE.
YOU LOOK BEWILDERED, ESHCOL.
DID NOT MY TRUSTED COMPANION TELL YOU WHAT I AM?
WHAT ARE YOU--?

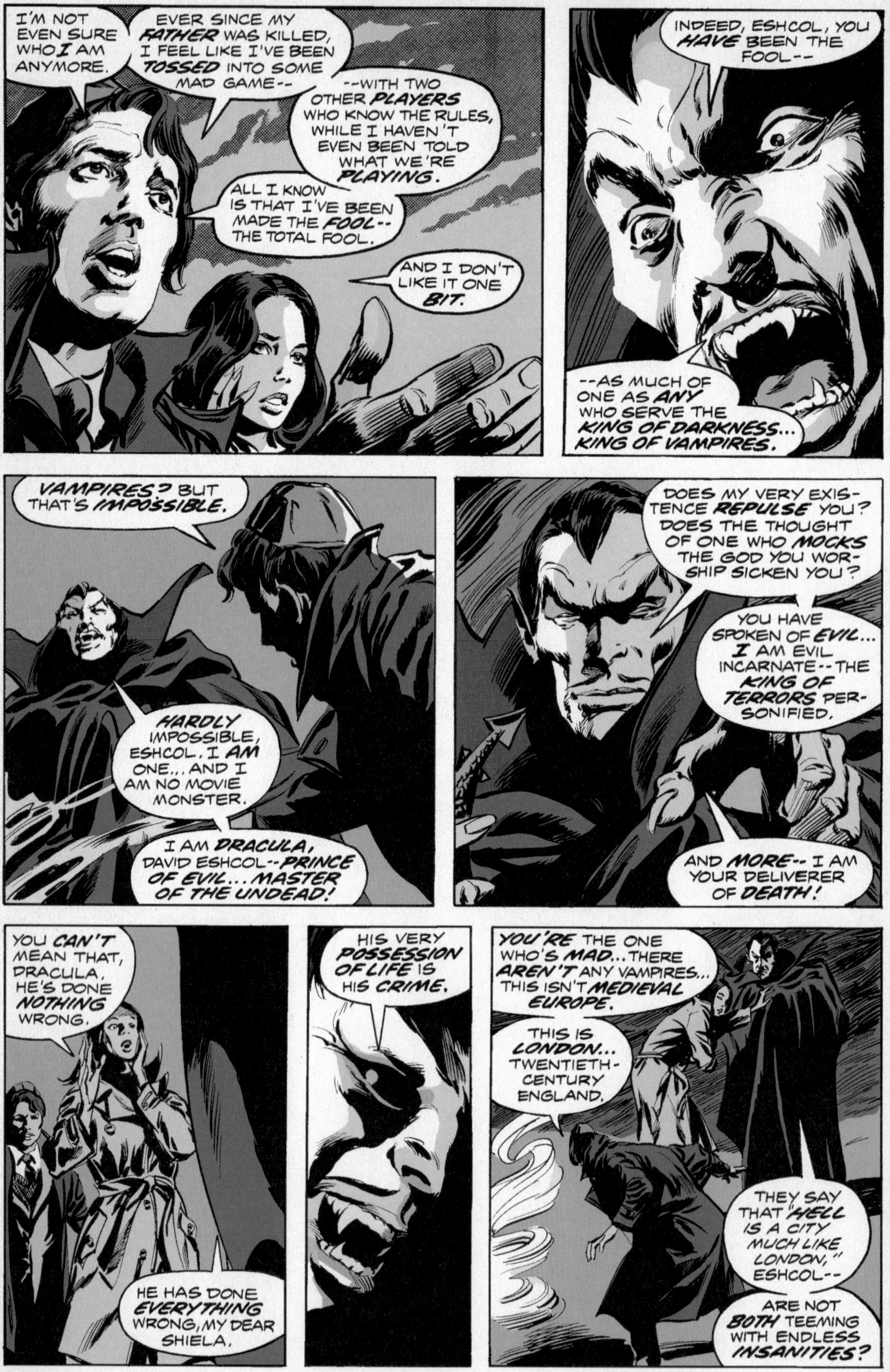

I'M NOT EVEN SURE WHO I AM ANYMORE.
EVER SINCE MY FATHER WAS KILLED, I FEEL LIKE I'VE BEEN TOSSED INTO SOME MAD GAME--
--WITH TWO OTHER PLAYERS WHO KNOW THE RULES, WHILE I HAVEN'T EVEN BEEN TOLD WHAT WE'RE PLAYING.
ALL I KNOW IS THAT I'VE BEEN MADE THE FOOL-- THE TOTAL FOOL.
AND I DON'T LIKE IT ONE BIT.
INDEED, ESHCOL, YOU HAVE BEEN THE FOOL--
--AS MUCH OF ONE AS ANY WHO SERVE THE KING OF DARKNESS... KING OF VAMPIRES.
VAMPIRES? BUT THAT'S IMPOSSIBLE.
HARDLY IMPOSSIBLE, ESHCOL. I AM ONE... AND I AM NO MOVIE MONSTER.
I AM DRACULA, DAVID ESHCOL-- PRINCE OF EVIL... MASTER OF THE UNDEAD!
DOES MY VERY EXISTENCE REPULSE YOU? DOES THE THOUGHT OF ONE WHO MOCKS THE GOD YOU WORSHIP SICKEN YOU?
YOU HAVE SPOKEN OF EVIL... I AM EVIL INCARNATE-- THE KING OF TERRORS PERSONIFIED.
AND MORE-- I AM YOUR DELIVERER OF DEATH!
YOU CAN'T MEAN THAT, DRACULA, HE'S DONE NOTHING WRONG.
HE HAS DONE EVERYTHING WRONG, MY DEAR SHIELA.
HIS VERY POSSESSION OF LIFE IS HIS CRIME.
YOU'RE THE ONE WHO'S MAD... THERE AREN'T ANY VAMPIRES... THIS ISN'T MEDIEVAL EUROPE.
THIS IS LONDON... TWENTIETH-CENTURY ENGLAND.
THEY SAY THAT "HELL IS A CITY MUCH LIKE LONDON," ESHCOL--
ARE NOT BOTH TEEMING WITH ENDLESS INSANITIES?

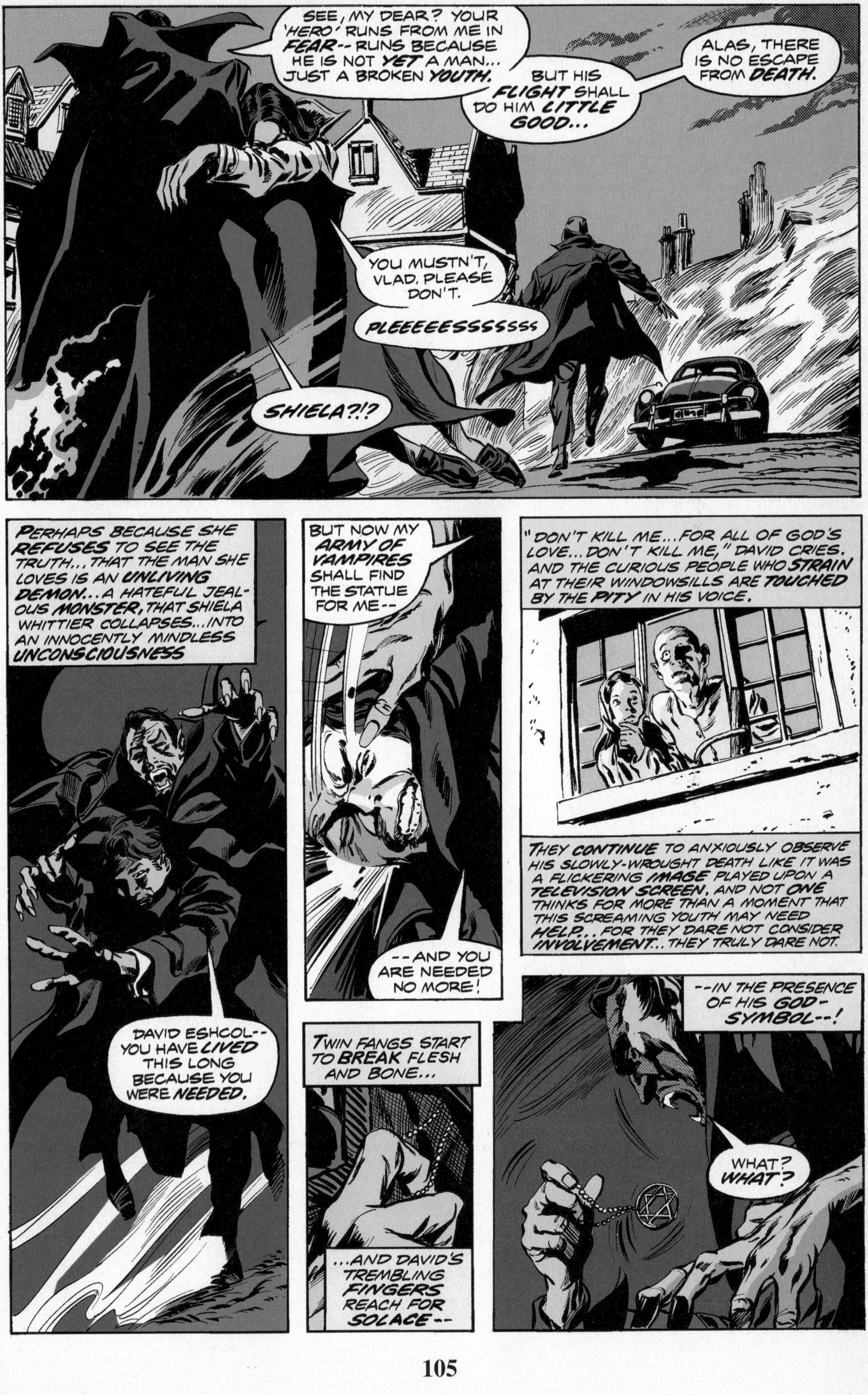
SEE, MY DEAR? YOUR 'HERO' RUNS FROM ME IN FEAR-- RUNS BECAUSE HE IS NOT YET A MAN... JUST A BROKEN YOUTH.
BUT HIS FLIGHT SHALL DO HIM LITTLE GOOD...
ALAS, THERE IS NO ESCAPE FROM DEATH.
YOU MUSTN'T, VLAD. PLEASE DON'T.
PLEEEEEESSSSSSS
SHIELA?!?
PERHAPS BECAUSE SHE REFUSES TO SEE THE TRUTH... THAT THE MAN SHE LOVES IS AN UNLIVING DEMON... A HATEFUL JEALOUS MONSTER, THAT SHIELA WHITTIER COLLAPSES... INTO AN INNOCENTLY MINDLESS UNCONSCIOUSNESS
DAVID ESHCOL-- YOU HAVE LIVED THIS LONG BECAUSE YOU WERE NEEDED.
BUT NOW MY ARMY OF VAMPIRES SHALL FIND THE STATUE FOR ME--
--AND YOU ARE NEEDED NO MORE!
"DON'T KILL ME... FOR ALL OF GOD'S LOVE... DON'T KILL ME," DAVID CRIES. AND THE CURIOUS PEOPLE WHO STRAIN AT THEIR WINDOWSILLS ARE TOUCHED BY THE PITY IN HIS VOICE.
THEY CONTINUE TO ANXIOUSLY OBSERVE HIS SLOWLY-WROUGHT DEATH LIKE IT WAS A FLICKERING IMAGE PLAYED UPON A TELEVISION SCREEN, AND NOT ONE THINKS FOR MORE THAN A MOMENT THAT THIS SCREAMING YOUTH MAY NEED HELP... FOR THEY DARE NOT CONSIDER INVOLVEMENT... THEY TRULY DARE NOT.
TWIN FANGS START TO BREAK FLESH AND BONE...
...AND DAVID'S TREMBLING FINGERS REACH FOR SOLACE--
--IN THE PRESENCE OF HIS GOD-SYMBOL--!
WHAT? WHAT?

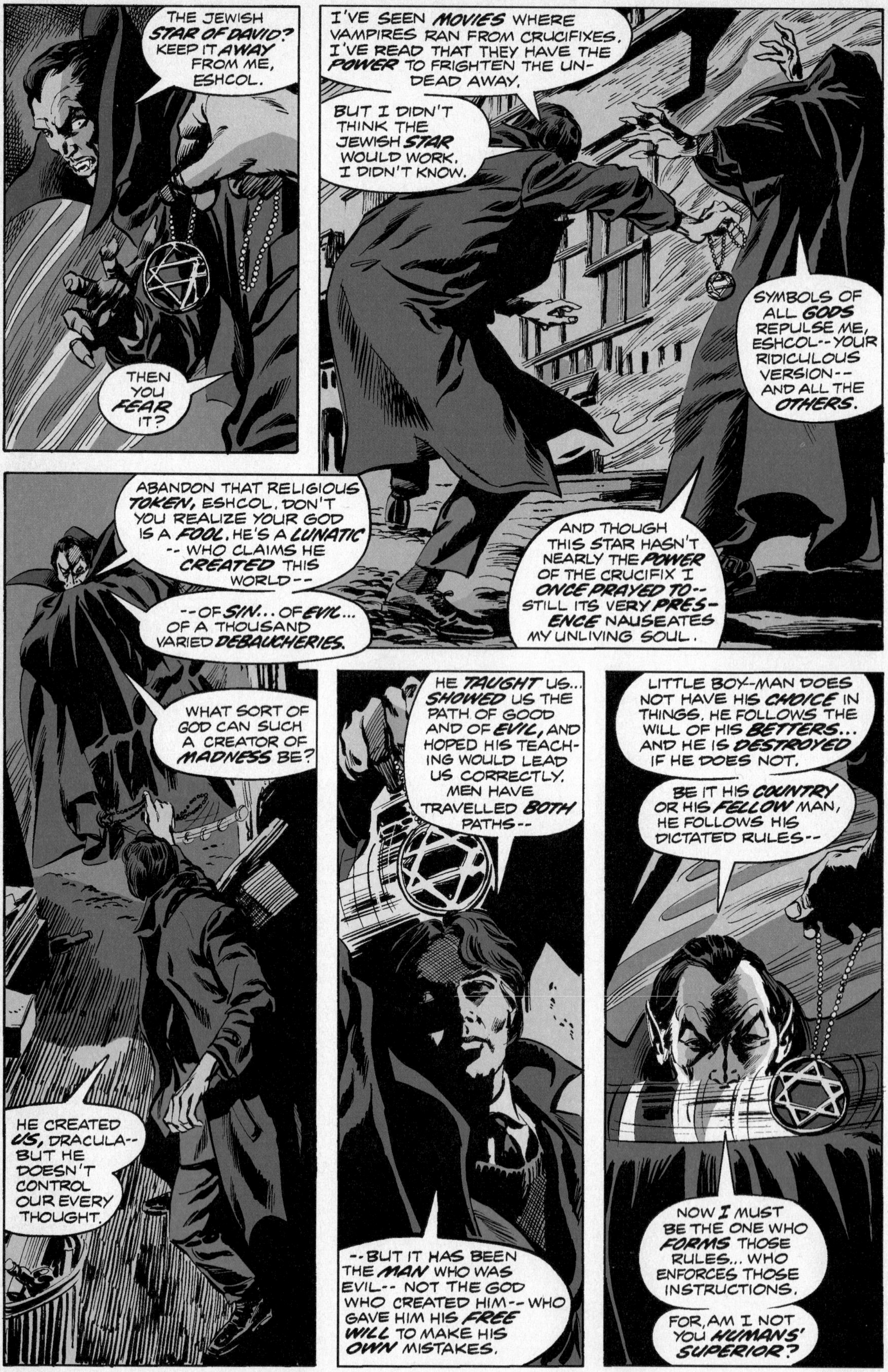
THE JEWISH STAR OF DAVID? KEEP IT AWAY FROM ME, ESHCOL.
THEN YOU FEAR IT?
I'VE SEEN MOVIES WHERE VAMPIRES RAN FROM CRUCIFIXES. I'VE READ THAT THEY HAVE THE POWER TO FRIGHTEN THE UN-DEAD AWAY.
BUT I DIDN'T THINK THE JEWISH STAR WOULD WORK. I DIDN'T KNOW.
SYMBOLS OF ALL GODS REPULSE ME, ESHCOL--YOUR RIDICULOUS VERSION--AND ALL THE OTHERS.
AND THOUGH THIS STAR HASN'T NEARLY THE POWER OF THE CRUCIFIX I ONCE PRAYED TO--STILL ITS VERY PRES-ENCE NAUSEATES MY UNLIVING SOUL.
ABANDON THAT RELIGIOUS TOKEN, ESHCOL. DON'T YOU REALIZE YOUR GOD IS A FOOL. HE'S A LUNATIC -- WHO CLAIMS HE CREATED THIS WORLD--
--OF SIN... OF EVIL... OF A THOUSAND VARIED DEBAUCHERIES.
WHAT SORT OF GOD CAN SUCH A CREATOR OF MADNESS BE?
HE CREATED US, DRACULA--BUT HE DOESN'T CONTROL OUR EVERY THOUGHT.
HE TAUGHT US... SHOWED US THE PATH OF GOOD AND OF EVIL, AND HOPED HIS TEACH-ING WOULD LEAD US CORRECTLY. MEN HAVE TRAVELLED BOTH PATHS--
--BUT IT HAS BEEN THE MAN WHO WAS EVIL-- NOT THE GOD WHO CREATED HIM--WHO GAVE HIM HIS FREE WILL TO MAKE HIS OWN MISTAKES.
LITTLE BOY-MAN DOES NOT HAVE HIS CHOICE IN THINGS. HE FOLLOWS THE WILL OF HIS BETTERS... AND HE IS DESTROYED IF HE DOES NOT.
BE IT HIS COUNTRY OR HIS FELLOW MAN, HE FOLLOWS HIS DICTATED RULES--
NOW I MUST BE THE ONE WHO FORMS THOSE RULES... WHO ENFORCES THOSE INSTRUCTIONS.
FOR, AM I NOT YOU HUMANS' SUPERIOR?

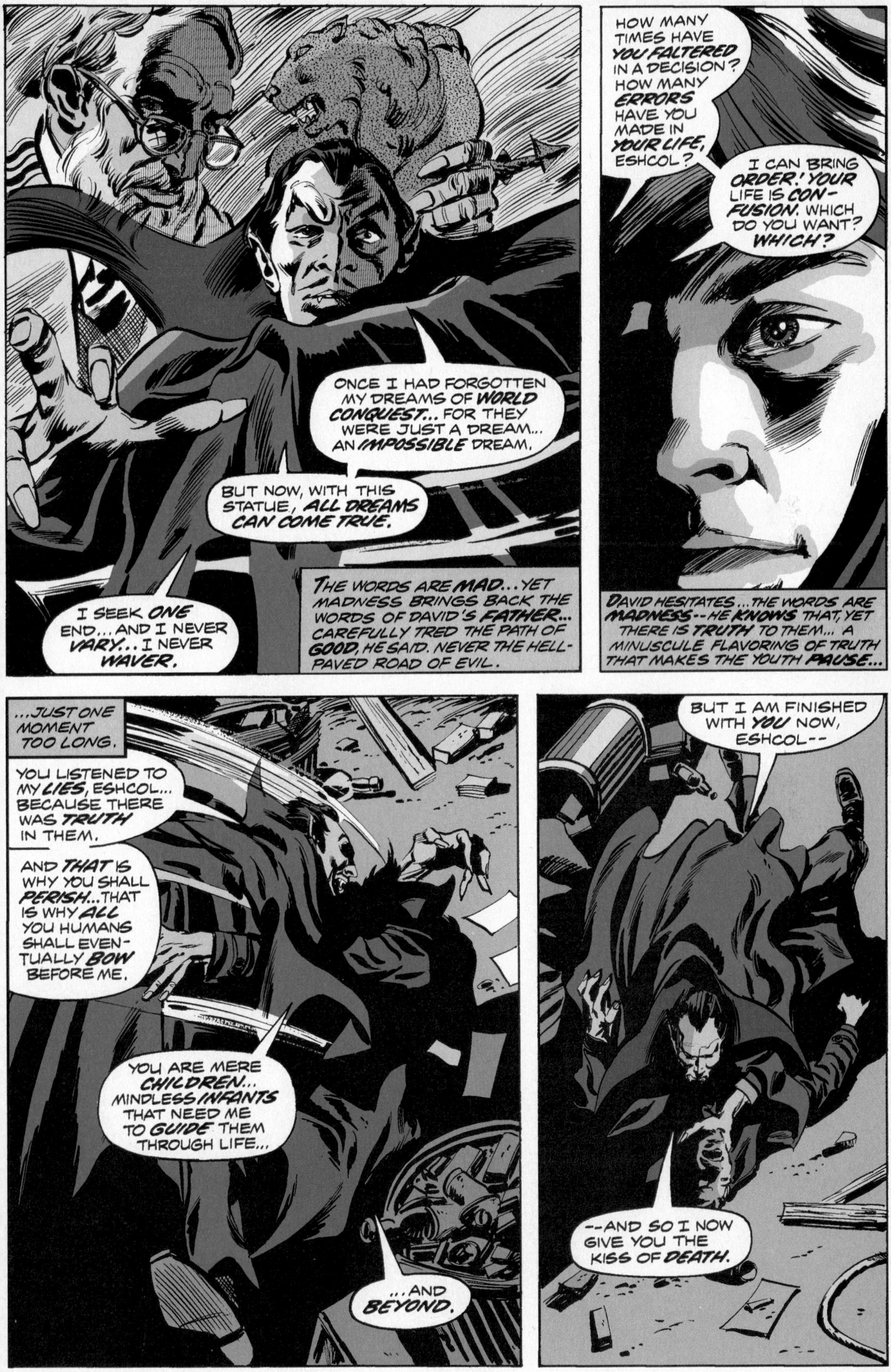
ONCE I HAD FORGOTTEN MY DREAMS OF WORLD CONQUEST... FOR THEY WERE JUST A DREAM... AN IMPOSSIBLE DREAM.
BUT NOW, WITH THIS STATUE, ALL DREAMS CAN COME TRUE.
I SEEK ONE END... AND I NEVER VARY... I NEVER WAVER.
THE WORDS ARE MAD... YET MADNESS BRINGS BACK THE WORDS OF DAVID'S FATHER... CAREFULLY TRED THE PATH OF GOOD, HE SAID. NEVER THE HELL-PAVED ROAD OF EVIL.
HOW MANY TIMES HAVE YOU FALTERED IN A DECISION? HOW MANY ERRORS HAVE YOU MADE IN YOUR LIFE, ESHCOL?
I CAN BRING ORDER! YOUR LIFE IS CON-FUSION. WHICH DO YOU WANT? WHICH?
DAVID HESITATES... THE WORDS ARE MADNESS--HE KNOWS THAT, YET THERE IS TRUTH TO THEM... A MINUSCULE FLAVORING OF TRUTH THAT MAKES THE YOUTH PAUSE...
...JUST ONE MOMENT TOO LONG.
YOU LISTENED TO MY LIES, ESHCOL... BECAUSE THERE WAS TRUTH IN THEM.
AND THAT IS WHY YOU SHALL PERISH... THAT IS WHY ALL YOU HUMANS SHALL EVEN-TUALLY BOW BEFORE ME.
YOU ARE MERE CHILDREN... MINDLESS INFANTS THAT NEED ME TO GUIDE THEM THROUGH LIFE...
...AND BEYOND.
BUT I AM FINISHED WITH YOU NOW, ESHCOL--
--AND SO I NOW GIVE YOU THE KISS OF DEATH.

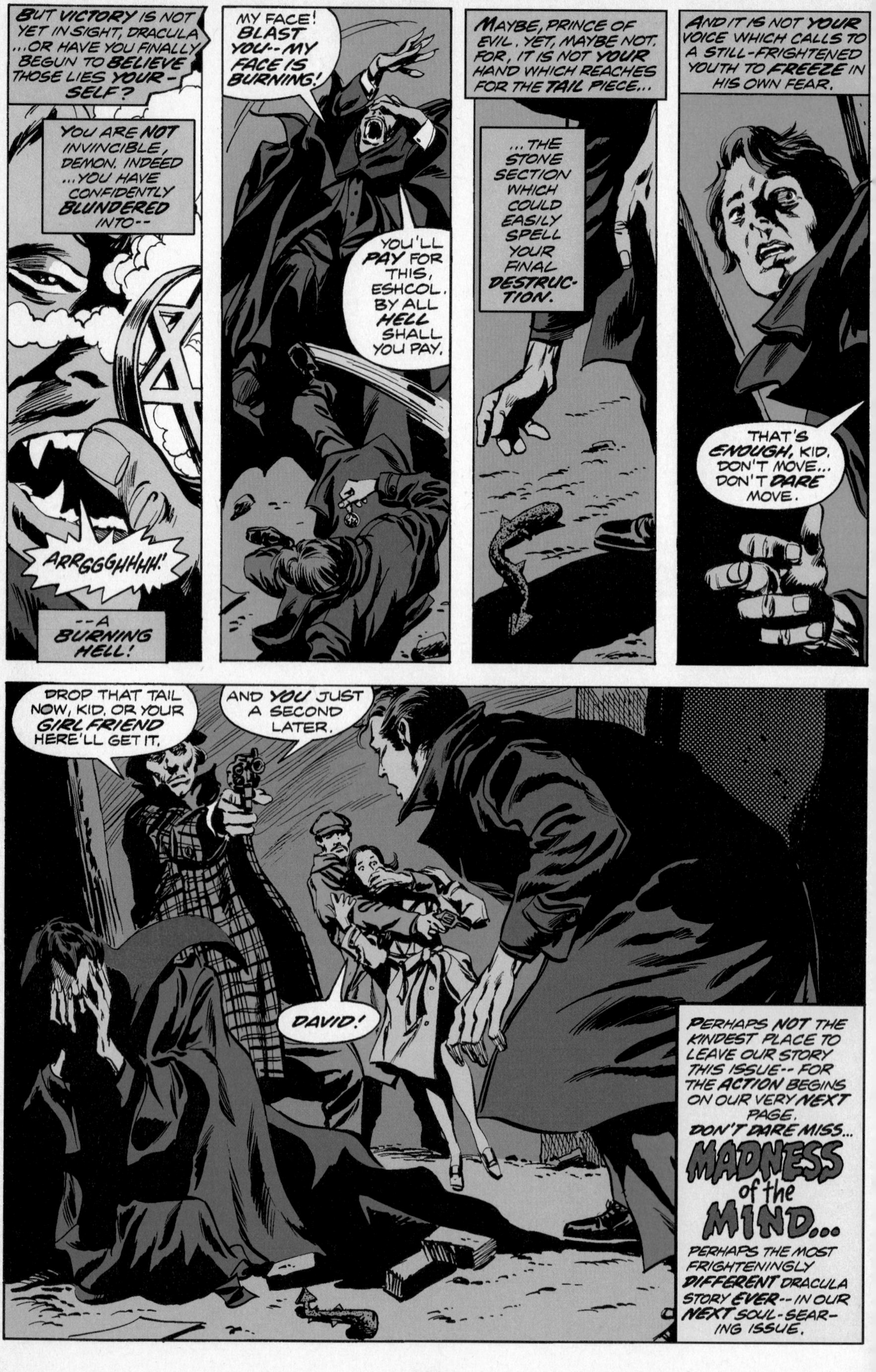
BUT VICTORY IS NOT YET IN SIGHT, DRACULA ...OR HAVE YOU FINALLY BEGUN TO BELIEVE THOSE LIES YOURSELF?
YOU ARE NOT INVINCIBLE, DEMON. INDEED ...YOU HAVE CONFIDENTLY BLUNDERED INTO--
ARRGGGHHHH!
--A BURNING HELL!
MY FACE! BLAST YOU--MY FACE IS BURNING!
YOU'LL PAY FOR THIS, ESHCOL. BY ALL HELL SHALL YOU PAY.
MAYBE, PRINCE OF EVIL. YET, MAYBE NOT. FOR, IT IS NOT YOUR HAND WHICH REACHES FOR THE TAIL PIECE...
...THE STONE SECTION WHICH COULD EASILY SPELL YOUR FINAL DESTRUCTION.
AND IT IS NOT YOUR VOICE WHICH CALLS TO A STILL-FRIGHTENED YOUTH TO FREEZE IN HIS OWN FEAR.
THAT'S ENOUGH, KID. DON'T MOVE... DON'T DARE MOVE.
DROP THAT TAIL NOW, KID, OR YOUR GIRL FRIEND HERE'LL GET IT.
AND YOU JUST A SECOND LATER.
DAVID!
PERHAPS NOT THE KINDEST PLACE TO LEAVE OUR STORY THIS ISSUE-- FOR THE ACTION BEGINS ON OUR VERY NEXT PAGE. DON'T DARE MISS...
MADNESS of the MIND...
PERHAPS THE MOST FRIGHTENINGLY DIFFERENT DRACULA STORY EVER--IN OUR NEXT SOUL-SEARING ISSUE.

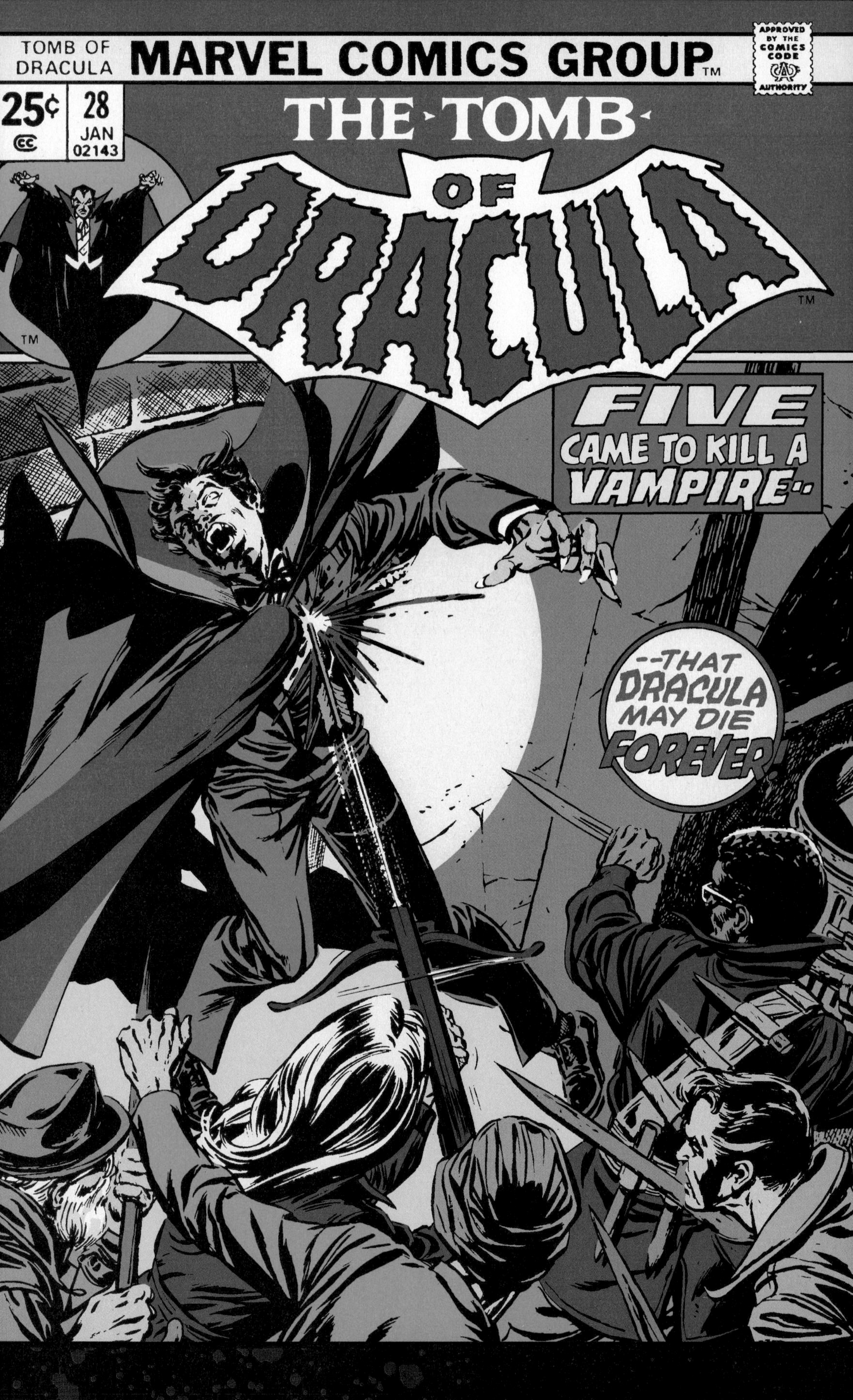
TOMB OF DRACULA
MARVEL COMICS GROUP™
APPROVED BY THE COMICS CODE AUTHORITY
25¢
28 JAN 02143
THE TOMB OF DRACULA™
FIVE CAME TO KILL A VAMPIRE..
--THAT DRACULA MAY DIE FOREVER!

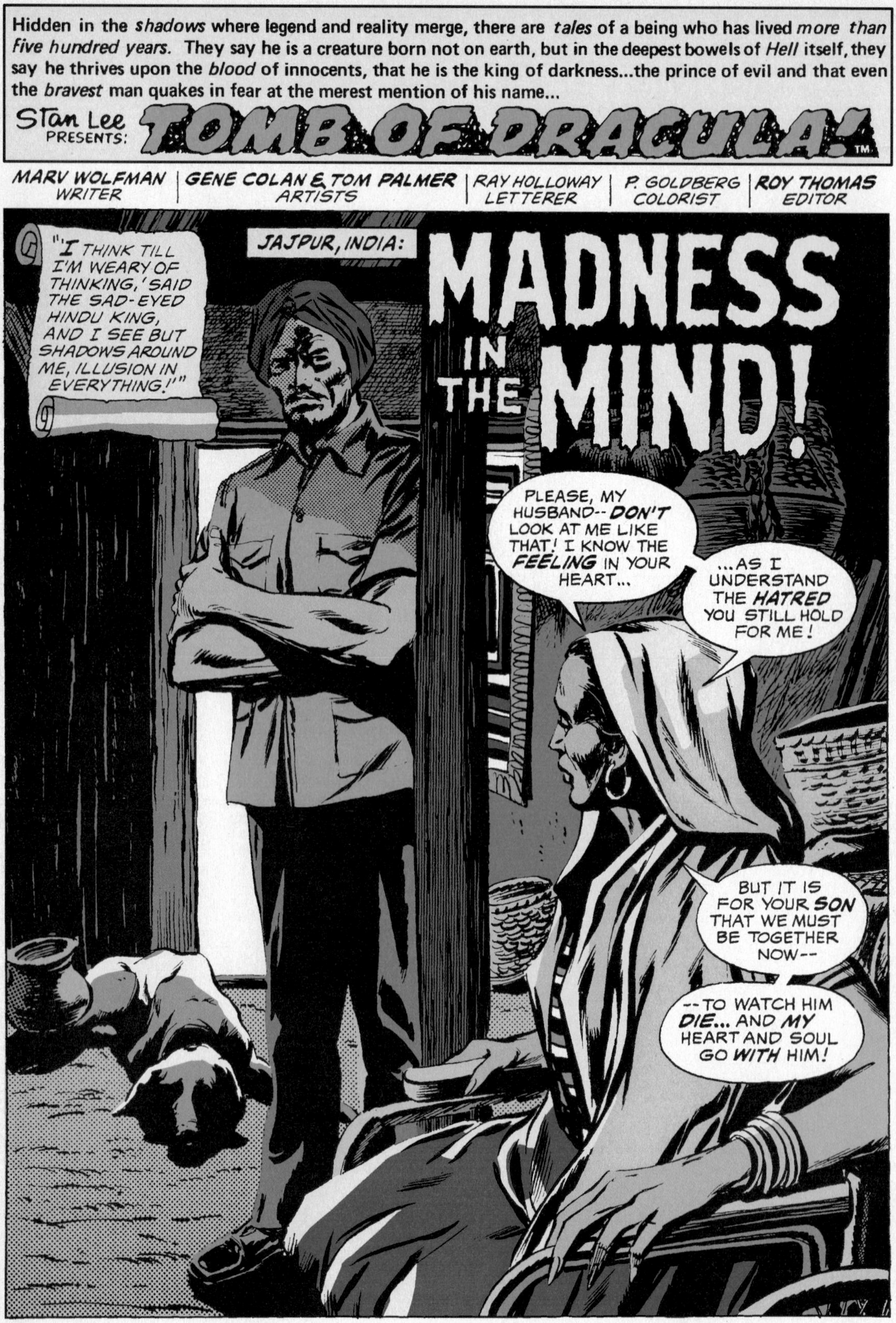
Hidden in the shadows where legend and reality merge, there are tales of a being who has lived more than five hundred years. They say he is a creature born not on earth, but in the deepest bowels of Hell itself, they say he thrives upon the blood of innocents, that he is the king of darkness...the prince of evil and that even the bravest man quakes in fear at the merest mention of his name...
Stan Lee PRESENTS: TOMB OF DRACULA! TM
MARV WOLFMAN WRITER
GENE COLAN & TOM PALMER ARTISTS
RAY HOLLOWAY LETTERER
P. GOLDBERG COLORIST
ROY THOMAS EDITOR
"I THINK TILL I'M WEARY OF THINKING,' SAID THE SAD-EYED HINDU KING, AND I SEE BUT SHADOWS AROUND ME, ILLUSION IN EVERYTHING!'"
JAJPUR, INDIA:
MADNESS IN THE MIND!
PLEASE, MY HUSBAND-- DON'T LOOK AT ME LIKE THAT! I KNOW THE FEELING IN YOUR HEART...
...AS I UNDERSTAND THE HATRED YOU STILL HOLD FOR ME!
BUT IT IS FOR YOUR SON THAT WE MUST BE TOGETHER NOW--
--TO WATCH HIM DIE... AND MY HEART AND SOUL GO WITH HIM!

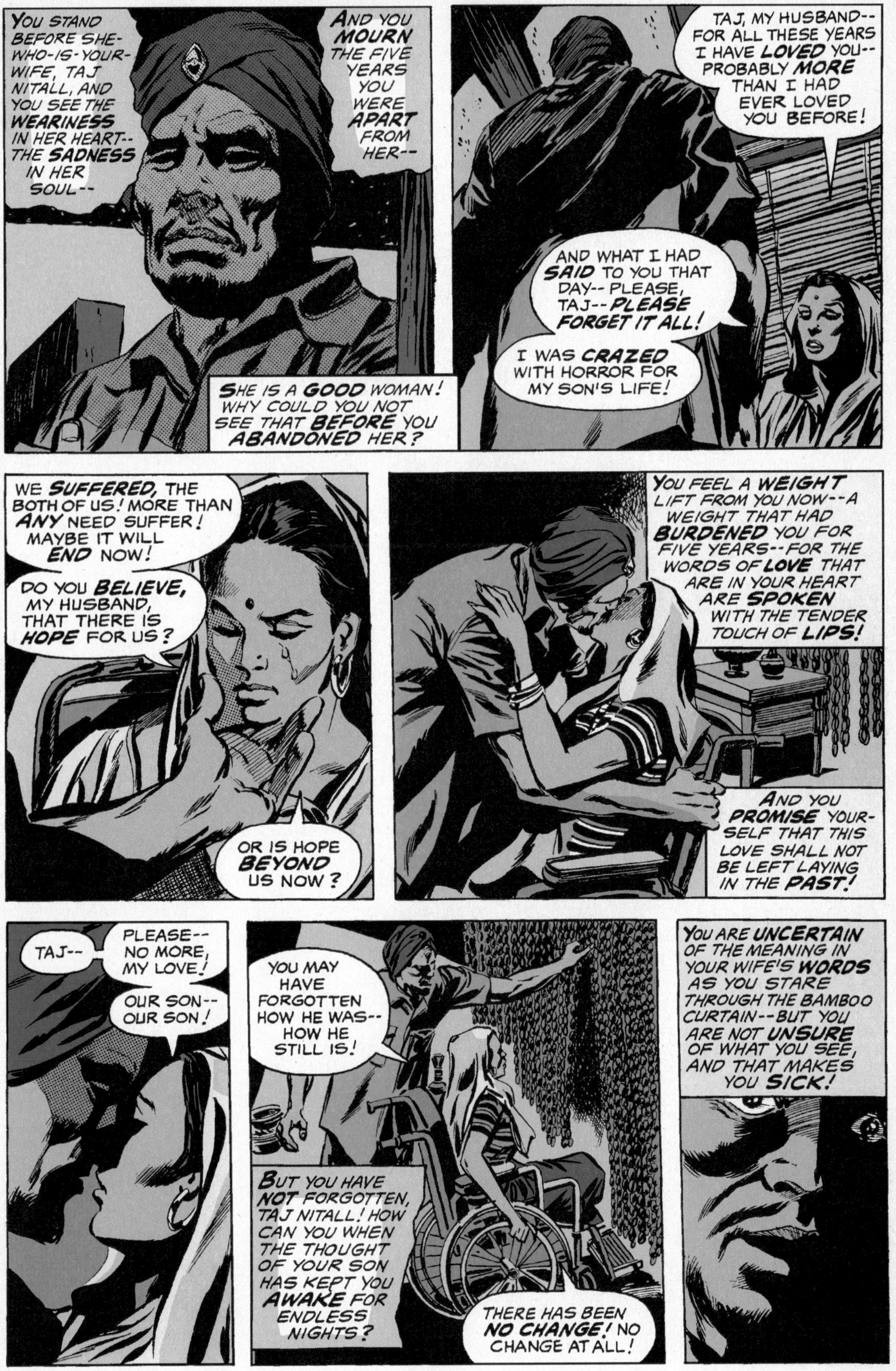
YOU STAND BEFORE SHE-WHO-IS-YOUR-WIFE, TAJ NITALL, AND YOU SEE THE WEARINESS IN HER HEART-- THE SADNESS IN HER SOUL--
AND YOU MOURN THE FIVE YEARS YOU WERE APART FROM HER--
SHE IS A GOOD WOMAN! WHY COULD YOU NOT SEE THAT BEFORE YOU ABANDONED HER?
TAJ, MY HUSBAND-- FOR ALL THESE YEARS I HAVE LOVED YOU-- PROBABLY MORE THAN I HAD EVER LOVED YOU BEFORE!
AND WHAT I HAD SAID TO YOU THAT DAY-- PLEASE, TAJ-- PLEASE FORGET IT ALL!
I WAS CRAZED WITH HORROR FOR MY SON'S LIFE!
WE SUFFERED, THE BOTH OF US! MORE THAN ANY NEED SUFFER! MAYBE IT WILL END NOW!
DO YOU BELIEVE, MY HUSBAND, THAT THERE IS HOPE FOR US?
OR IS HOPE BEYOND US NOW?
YOU FEEL A WEIGHT LIFT FROM YOU NOW--A WEIGHT THAT HAD BURDENED YOU FOR FIVE YEARS--FOR THE WORDS OF LOVE THAT ARE IN YOUR HEART ARE SPOKEN WITH THE TENDER TOUCH OF LIPS!
AND YOU PROMISE YOURSELF THAT THIS LOVE SHALL NOT BE LEFT LAYING IN THE PAST!
TAJ--
PLEASE-- NO MORE, MY LOVE!
OUR SON-- OUR SON!
YOU MAY HAVE FORGOTTEN HOW HE WAS-- HOW HE STILL IS!
BUT YOU HAVE NOT FORGOTTEN, TAJ NITALL! HOW CAN YOU WHEN THE THOUGHT OF YOUR SON HAS KEPT YOU AWAKE FOR ENDLESS NIGHTS?
THERE HAS BEEN NO CHANGE! NO CHANGE AT ALL!
YOU ARE UNCERTAIN OF THE MEANING IN YOUR WIFE'S WORDS AS YOU STARE THROUGH THE BAMBOO CURTAIN--BUT YOU ARE NOT UNSURE OF WHAT YOU SEE, AND THAT MAKES YOU SICK!

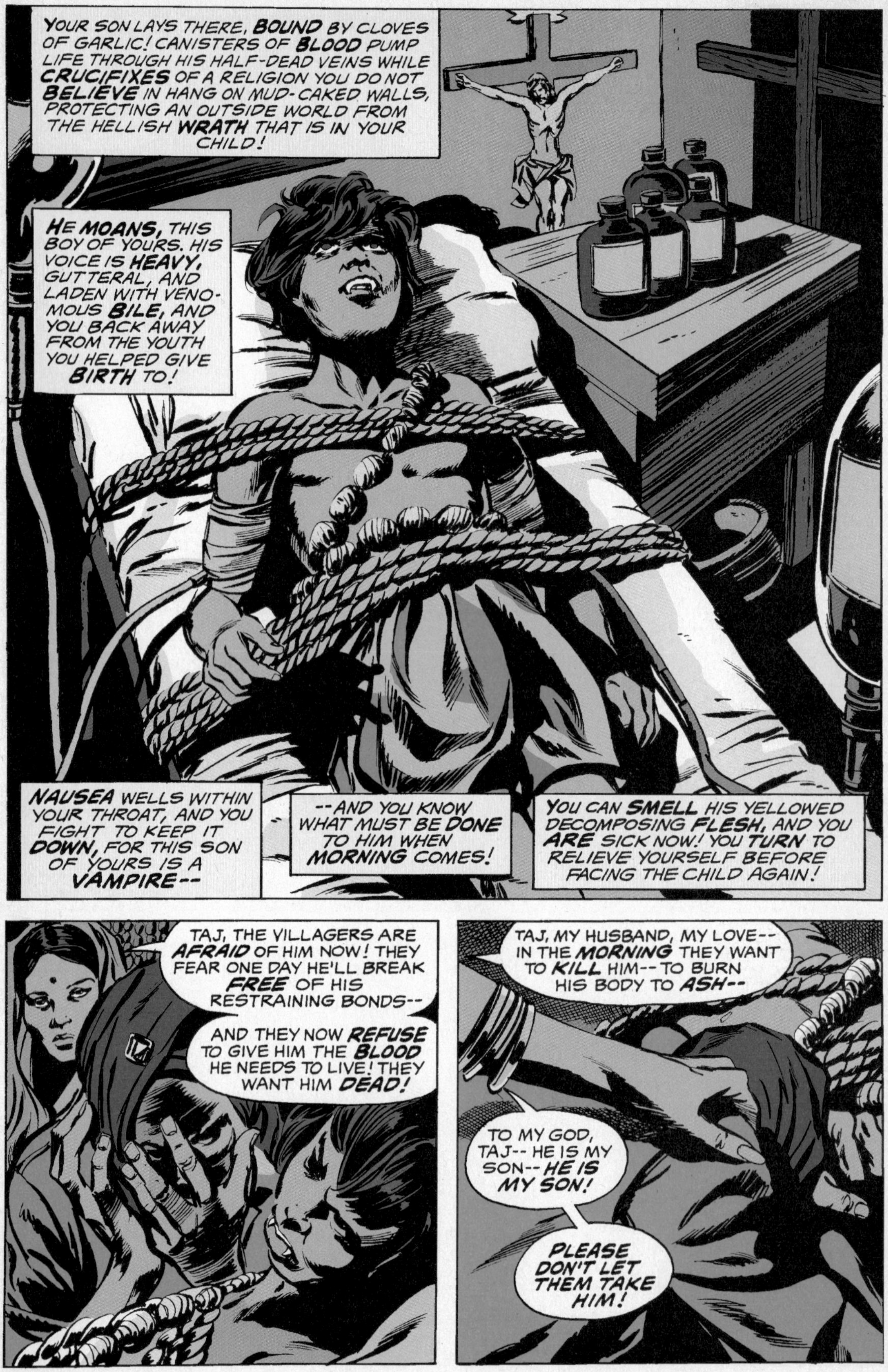
YOUR SON LAYS THERE, BOUND BY CLOVES OF GARLIC! CANISTERS OF BLOOD PUMP LIFE THROUGH HIS HALF-DEAD VEINS WHILE CRUCIFIXES OF A RELIGION YOU DO NOT BELIEVE IN HANG ON MUD-CAKED WALLS, PROTECTING AN OUTSIDE WORLD FROM THE HELLISH WRATH THAT IS IN YOUR CHILD!
HE MOANS, THIS BOY OF YOURS. HIS VOICE IS HEAVY, GUTTERAL, AND LADEN WITH VENOMOUS BILE, AND YOU BACK AWAY FROM THE YOUTH YOU HELPED GIVE BIRTH TO!
NAUSEA WELLS WITHIN YOUR THROAT, AND YOU FIGHT TO KEEP IT DOWN, FOR THIS SON OF YOURS IS A VAMPIRE--
--AND YOU KNOW WHAT MUST BE DONE TO HIM WHEN MORNING COMES!
YOU CAN SMELL HIS YELLOWED DECOMPOSING FLESH, AND YOU ARE SICK NOW! YOU TURN TO RELIEVE YOURSELF BEFORE FACING THE CHILD AGAIN!
TAJ, THE VILLAGERS ARE AFRAID OF HIM NOW! THEY FEAR ONE DAY HE'LL BREAK FREE OF HIS RESTRAINING BONDS--
AND THEY NOW REFUSE TO GIVE HIM THE BLOOD HE NEEDS TO LIVE! THEY WANT HIM DEAD!
TAJ, MY HUSBAND, MY LOVE-- IN THE MORNING THEY WANT TO KILL HIM-- TO BURN HIS BODY TO ASH--
TO MY GOD, TAJ-- HE IS MY SON-- HE IS MY SON!
PLEASE DON'T LET THEM TAKE HIM!

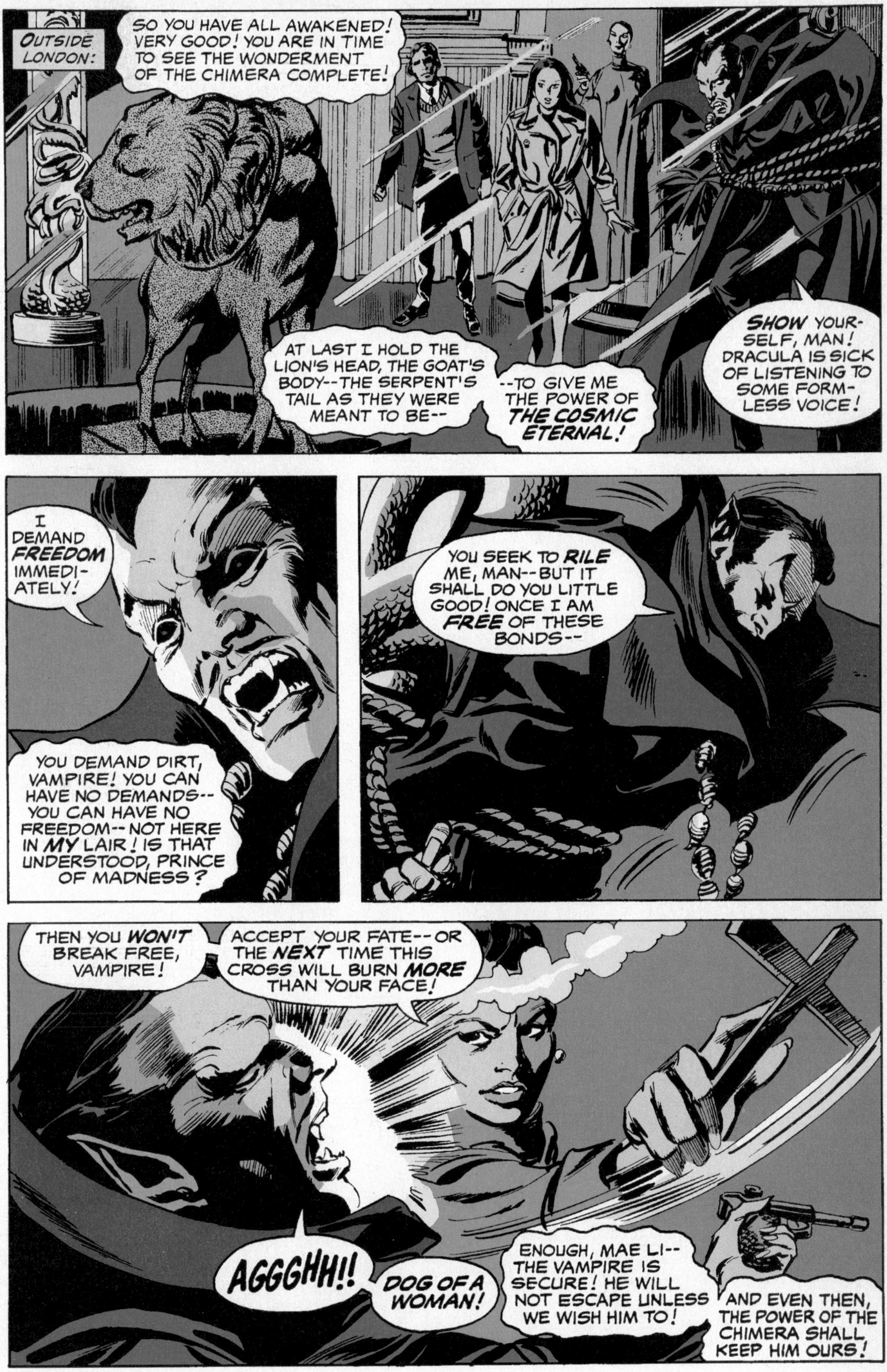
OUTSIDE LONDON:
SO YOU HAVE ALL AWAKENED! VERY GOOD! YOU ARE IN TIME TO SEE THE WONDERMENT OF THE CHIMERA COMPLETE!
AT LAST I HOLD THE LION'S HEAD, THE GOAT'S BODY--THE SERPENT'S TAIL AS THEY WERE MEANT TO BE--
--TO GIVE ME THE POWER OF THE COSMIC ETERNAL!
SHOW YOURSELF, MAN! DRACULA IS SICK OF LISTENING TO SOME FORMLESS VOICE!
I DEMAND FREEDOM IMMEDIATELY!
YOU DEMAND DIRT, VAMPIRE! YOU CAN HAVE NO DEMANDS--YOU CAN HAVE NO FREEDOM--NOT HERE IN MY LAIR! IS THAT UNDERSTOOD, PRINCE OF MADNESS?
YOU SEEK TO RILE ME, MAN--BUT IT SHALL DO YOU LITTLE GOOD! ONCE I AM FREE OF THESE BONDS--
THEN YOU WON'T BREAK FREE, VAMPIRE!
ACCEPT YOUR FATE--OR THE NEXT TIME THIS CROSS WILL BURN MORE THAN YOUR FACE!
AGGGHH!!
DOG OF A WOMAN!
ENOUGH, MAE LI--THE VAMPIRE IS SECURE! HE WILL NOT ESCAPE UNLESS WE WISH HIM TO!
AND EVEN THEN, THE POWER OF THE CHIMERA SHALL KEEP HIM OURS!

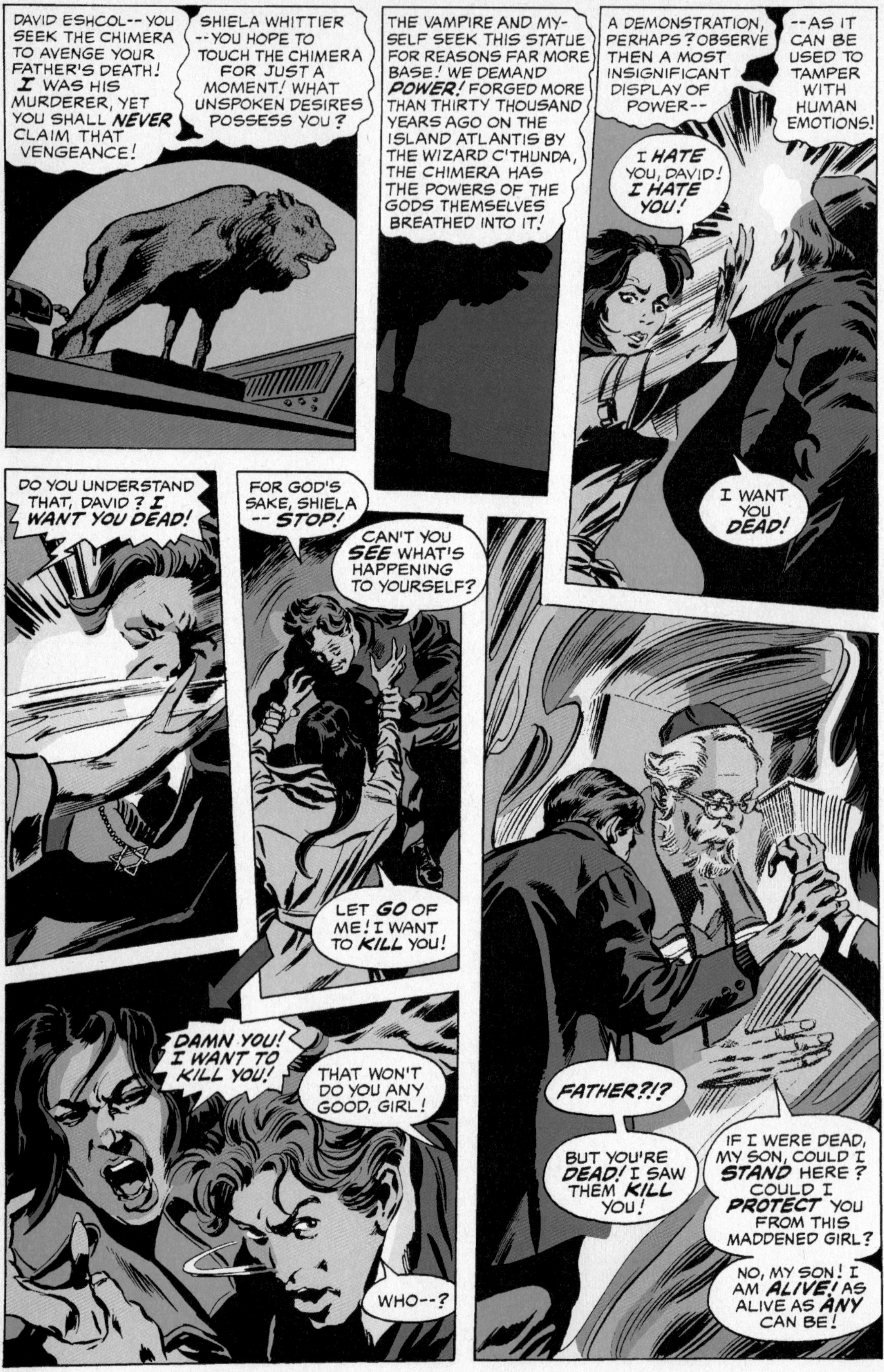
DAVID ESHCOL-- YOU SEEK THE CHIMERA TO AVENGE YOUR FATHER'S DEATH! I WAS HIS MURDERER, YET YOU SHALL NEVER CLAIM THAT VENGEANCE!
SHIELA WHITTIER --YOU HOPE TO TOUCH THE CHIMERA FOR JUST A MOMENT! WHAT UNSPOKEN DESIRES POSSESS YOU?
THE VAMPIRE AND MYSELF SEEK THIS STATUE FOR REASONS FAR MORE BASE! WE DEMAND POWER! FORGED MORE THAN THIRTY THOUSAND YEARS AGO ON THE ISLAND ATLANTIS BY THE WIZARD C'THUNDA, THE CHIMERA HAS THE POWERS OF THE GODS THEMSELVES BREATHED INTO IT!
A DEMONSTRATION, PERHAPS? OBSERVE THEN A MOST INSIGNIFICANT DISPLAY OF POWER--
--AS IT CAN BE USED TO TAMPER WITH HUMAN EMOTIONS!
I HATE YOU, DAVID! I HATE YOU!
I WANT YOU DEAD!
DO YOU UNDERSTAND THAT, DAVID? I WANT YOU DEAD!
FOR GOD'S SAKE, SHIELA -- STOP!
CAN'T YOU SEE WHAT'S HAPPENING TO YOURSELF?
LET GO OF ME! I WANT TO KILL YOU!
DAMN YOU! I WANT TO KILL YOU!
THAT WON'T DO YOU ANY GOOD, GIRL!
WHO--?
FATHER?!?
BUT YOU'RE DEAD! I SAW THEM KILL YOU!
IF I WERE DEAD, MY SON, COULD I STAND HERE? COULD I PROTECT YOU FROM THIS MADDENED GIRL?
NO, MY SON! I AM ALIVE! AS ALIVE AS ANY CAN BE!

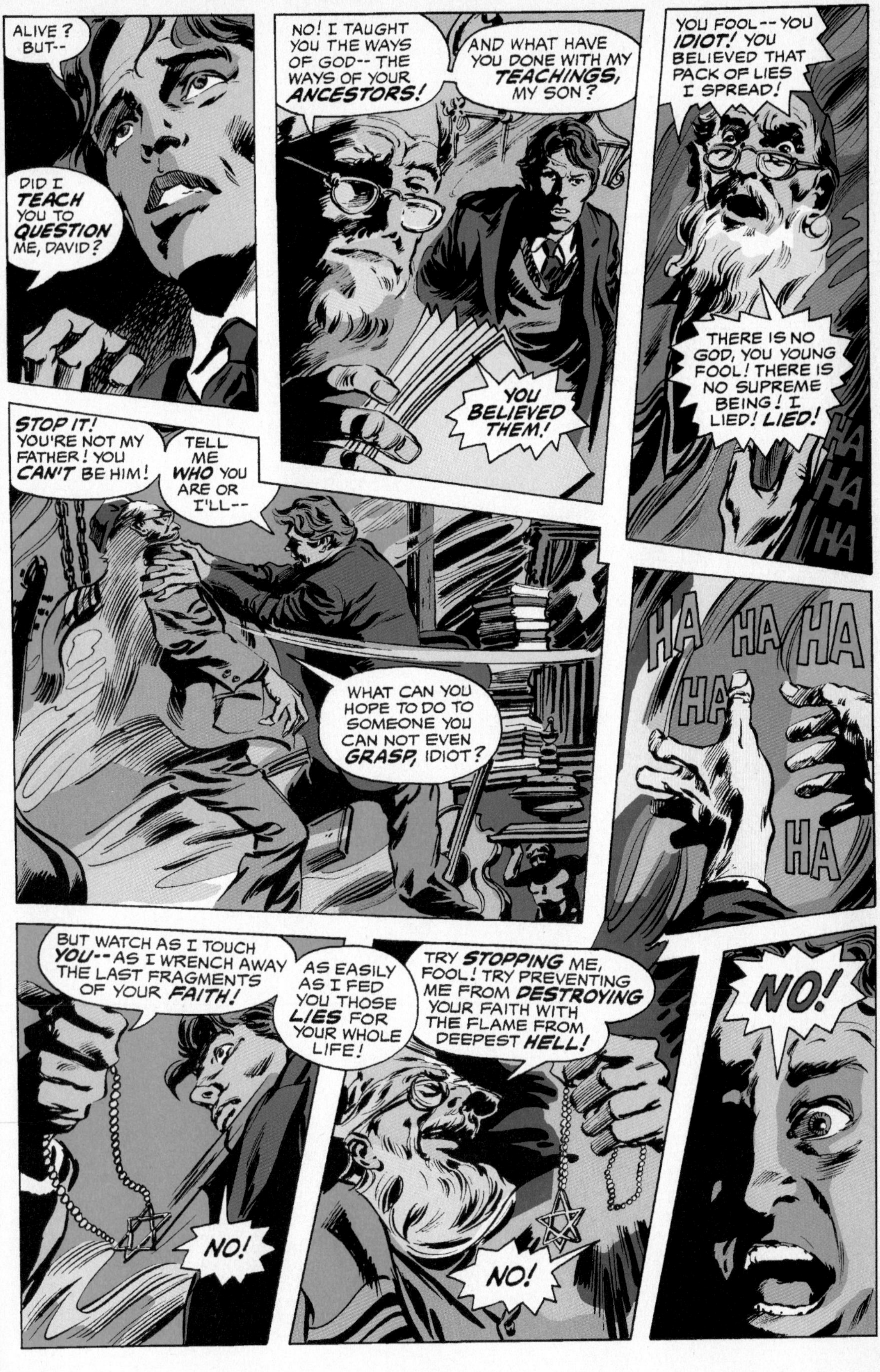
ALIVE? BUT--
DID I TEACH YOU TO QUESTION ME, DAVID?
NO! I TAUGHT YOU THE WAYS OF GOD-- THE WAYS OF YOUR ANCESTORS!
AND WHAT HAVE YOU DONE WITH MY TEACHINGS, MY SON?
YOU BELIEVED THEM!
YOU FOOL-- YOU IDIOT! YOU BELIEVED THAT PACK OF LIES I SPREAD!
THERE IS NO GOD, YOU YOUNG FOOL! THERE IS NO SUPREME BEING! I LIED! LIED!
HA HA HA HA
STOP IT! YOU'RE NOT MY FATHER! YOU CAN'T BE HIM!
TELL ME WHO YOU ARE OR I'LL--
WHAT CAN YOU HOPE TO DO TO SOMEONE YOU CAN NOT EVEN GRASP, IDIOT?
HA HA HA HA HA
BUT WATCH AS I TOUCH YOU-- AS I WRENCH AWAY THE LAST FRAGMENTS OF YOUR FAITH!
AS EASILY AS I FED YOU THOSE LIES FOR YOUR WHOLE LIFE!
NO!
TRY STOPPING ME, FOOL! TRY PREVENTING ME FROM DESTROYING YOUR FAITH WITH THE FLAME FROM DEEPEST HELL!
NO!
NO!

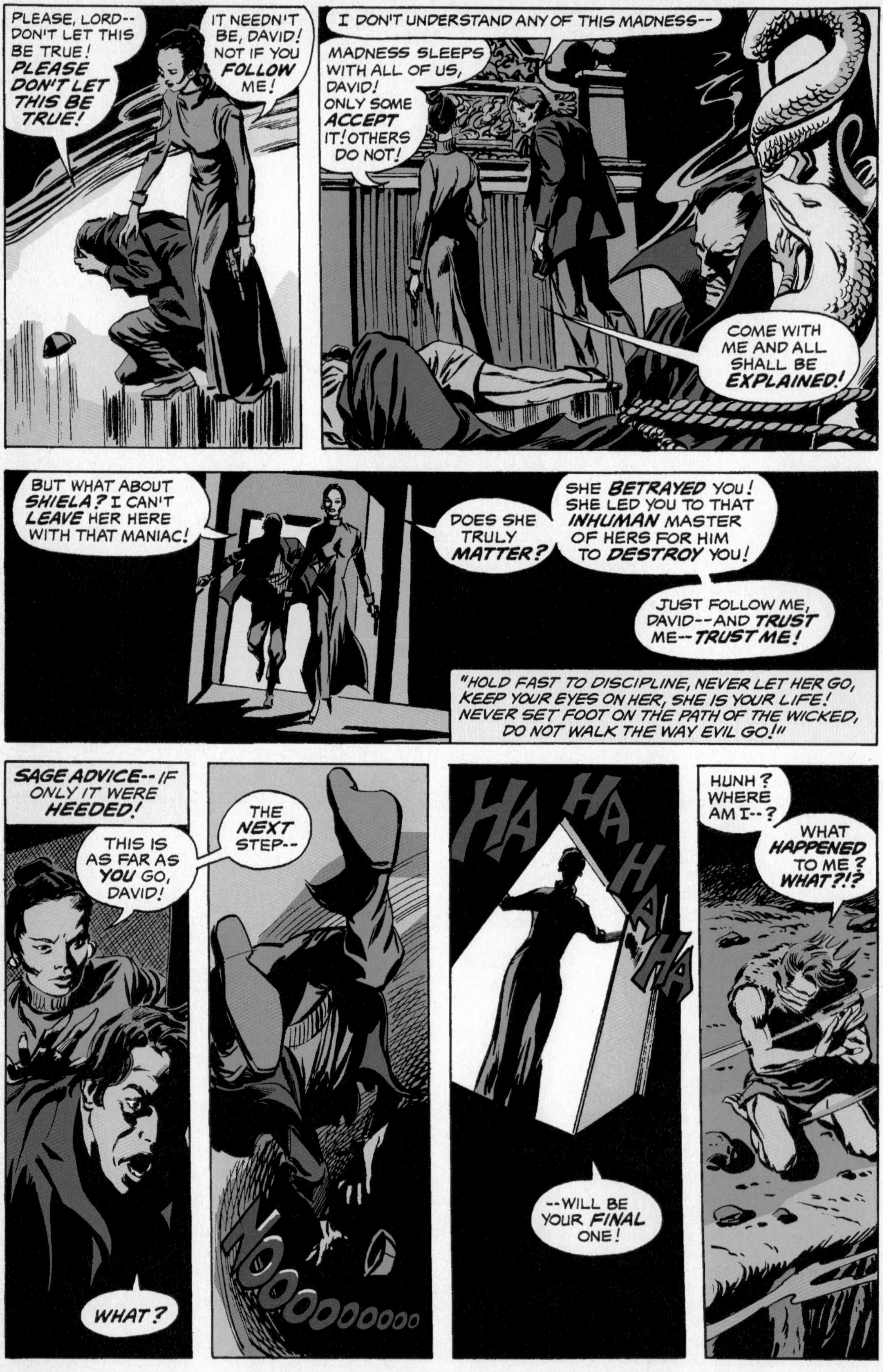
PLEASE, LORD-- DON'T LET THIS BE TRUE! PLEASE DON'T LET THIS BE TRUE!
IT NEEDN'T BE, DAVID! NOT IF YOU FOLLOW ME!
I DON'T UNDERSTAND ANY OF THIS MADNESS--
MADNESS SLEEPS WITH ALL OF US, DAVID! ONLY SOME ACCEPT IT! OTHERS DO NOT!
COME WITH ME AND ALL SHALL BE EXPLAINED!
BUT WHAT ABOUT SHIELA? I CAN'T LEAVE HER HERE WITH THAT MANIAC!
DOES SHE TRULY MATTER?
SHE BETRAYED YOU! SHE LED YOU TO THAT INHUMAN MASTER OF HERS FOR HIM TO DESTROY YOU!
JUST FOLLOW ME, DAVID--AND TRUST ME--TRUST ME!
"HOLD FAST TO DISCIPLINE, NEVER LET HER GO, KEEP YOUR EYES ON HER, SHE IS YOUR LIFE! NEVER SET FOOT ON THE PATH OF THE WICKED, DO NOT WALK THE WAY EVIL GO!"
SAGE ADVICE-- IF ONLY IT WERE HEEDED!
THIS IS AS FAR AS YOU GO, DAVID!
WHAT?
THE NEXT STEP--
NOOOOOOOOOO
HA HA HA HA HA
--WILL BE YOUR FINAL ONE!
HUNH? WHERE AM I--?
WHAT HAPPENED TO ME? WHAT?!?

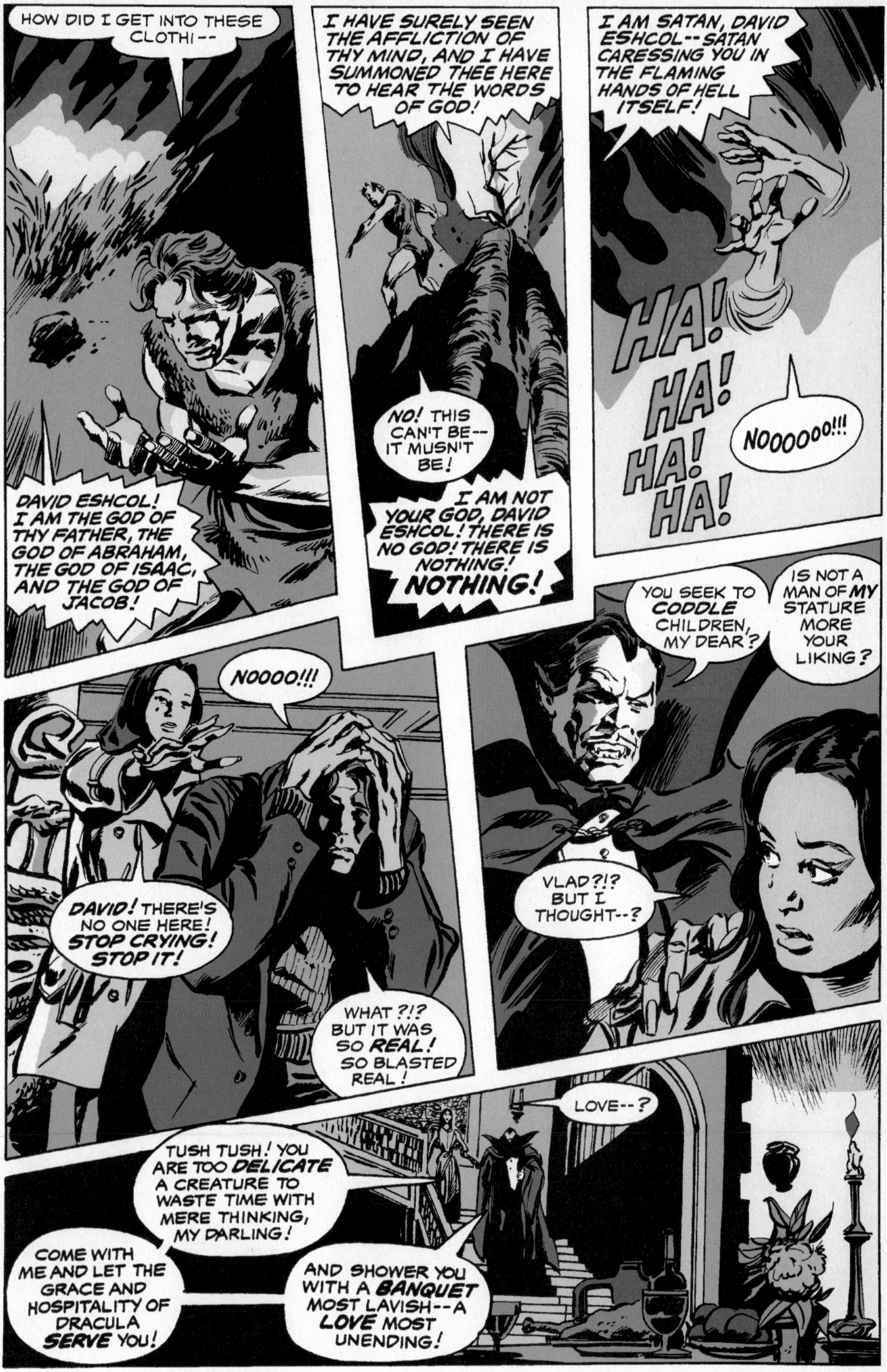
HOW DID I GET INTO THESE CLOTHI--
DAVID ESHCOL! I AM THE GOD OF THY FATHER, THE GOD OF ABRAHAM, THE GOD OF ISAAC, AND THE GOD OF JACOB!
I HAVE SURELY SEEN THE AFFLICTION OF THY MIND, AND I HAVE SUMMONED THEE HERE TO HEAR THE WORDS OF GOD!
NO! THIS CAN'T BE-- IT MUSN'T BE!
I AM NOT YOUR GOD, DAVID ESHCOL! THERE IS NO GOD! THERE IS NOTHING! NOTHING!
I AM SATAN, DAVID ESHCOL-- SATAN CARESSING YOU IN THE FLAMING HANDS OF HELL ITSELF!
HA! HA! HA! HA!
NOOOOOO!!!
NOOOO!!!
DAVID! THERE'S NO ONE HERE! STOP CRYING! STOP IT!
WHAT?!? BUT IT WAS SO REAL! SO BLASTED REAL!
YOU SEEK TO CODDLE CHILDREN, MY DEAR?
IS NOT A MAN OF MY STATURE MORE YOUR LIKING?
VLAD?!? BUT I THOUGHT--?
LOVE--?
TUSH TUSH! YOU ARE TOO DELICATE A CREATURE TO WASTE TIME WITH MERE THINKING, MY DARLING!
COME WITH ME AND LET THE GRACE AND HOSPITALITY OF DRACULA SERVE YOU!
AND SHOWER YOU WITH A BANQUET MOST LAVISH--A LOVE MOST UNENDING!

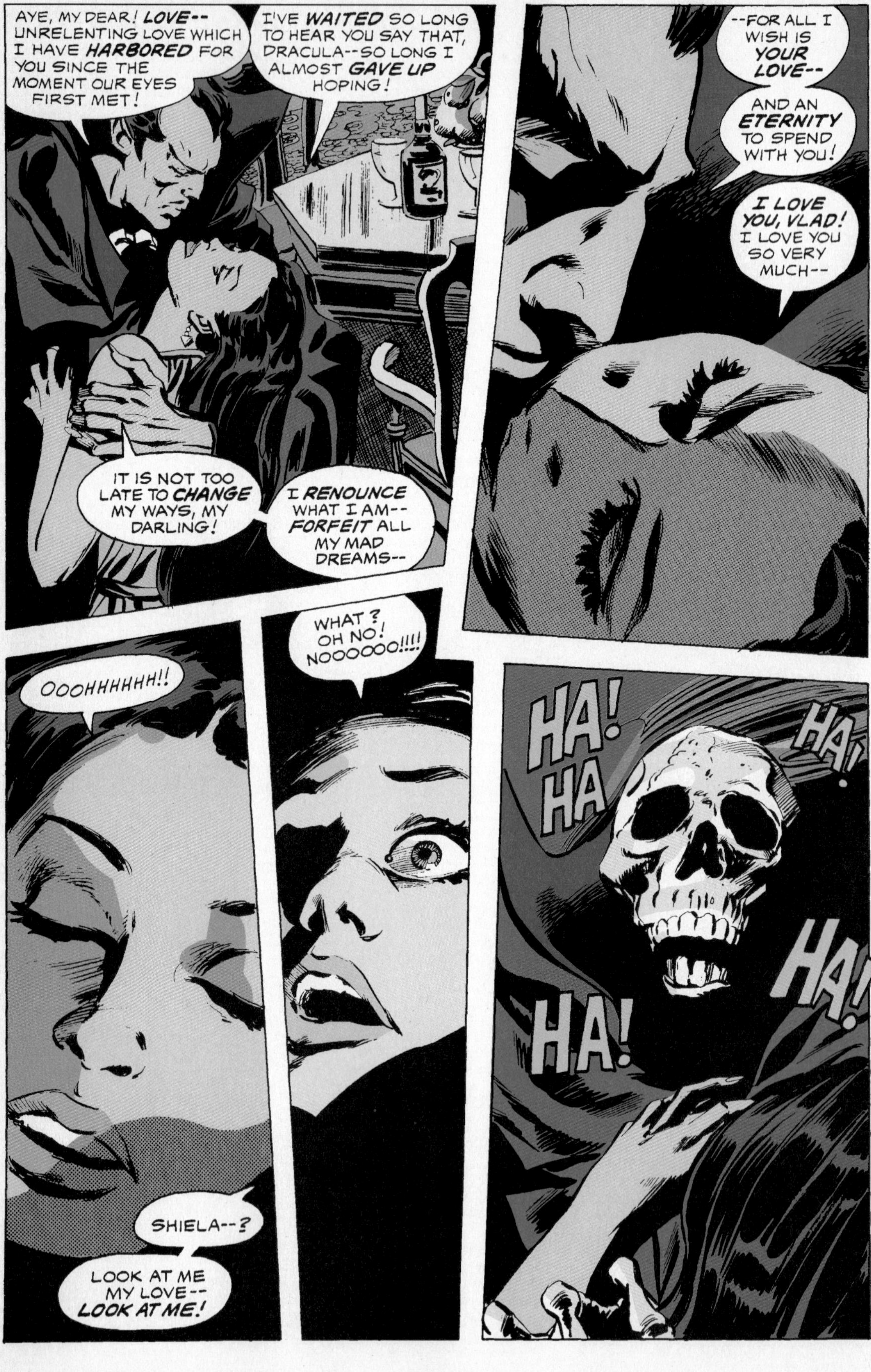

AYE, MY DEAR! LOVE-- UNRELENTING LOVE WHICH I HAVE HARBORED FOR YOU SINCE THE MOMENT OUR EYES FIRST MET!
I'VE WAITED SO LONG TO HEAR YOU SAY THAT, DRACULA--SO LONG I ALMOST GAVE UP HOPING!
IT IS NOT TOO LATE TO CHANGE MY WAYS, MY DARLING!
I RENOUNCE WHAT I AM-- FORFEIT ALL MY MAD DREAMS--
--FOR ALL I WISH IS YOUR LOVE--
AND AN ETERNITY TO SPEND WITH YOU!
I LOVE YOU, VLAD! I LOVE YOU SO VERY MUCH--
OOOHHHHHH!!
SHIELA--?
LOOK AT ME MY LOVE-- LOOK AT ME!
WHAT? OH NO! NOOOOOO!!!!
HA! HA
HA!
HA!
HA!

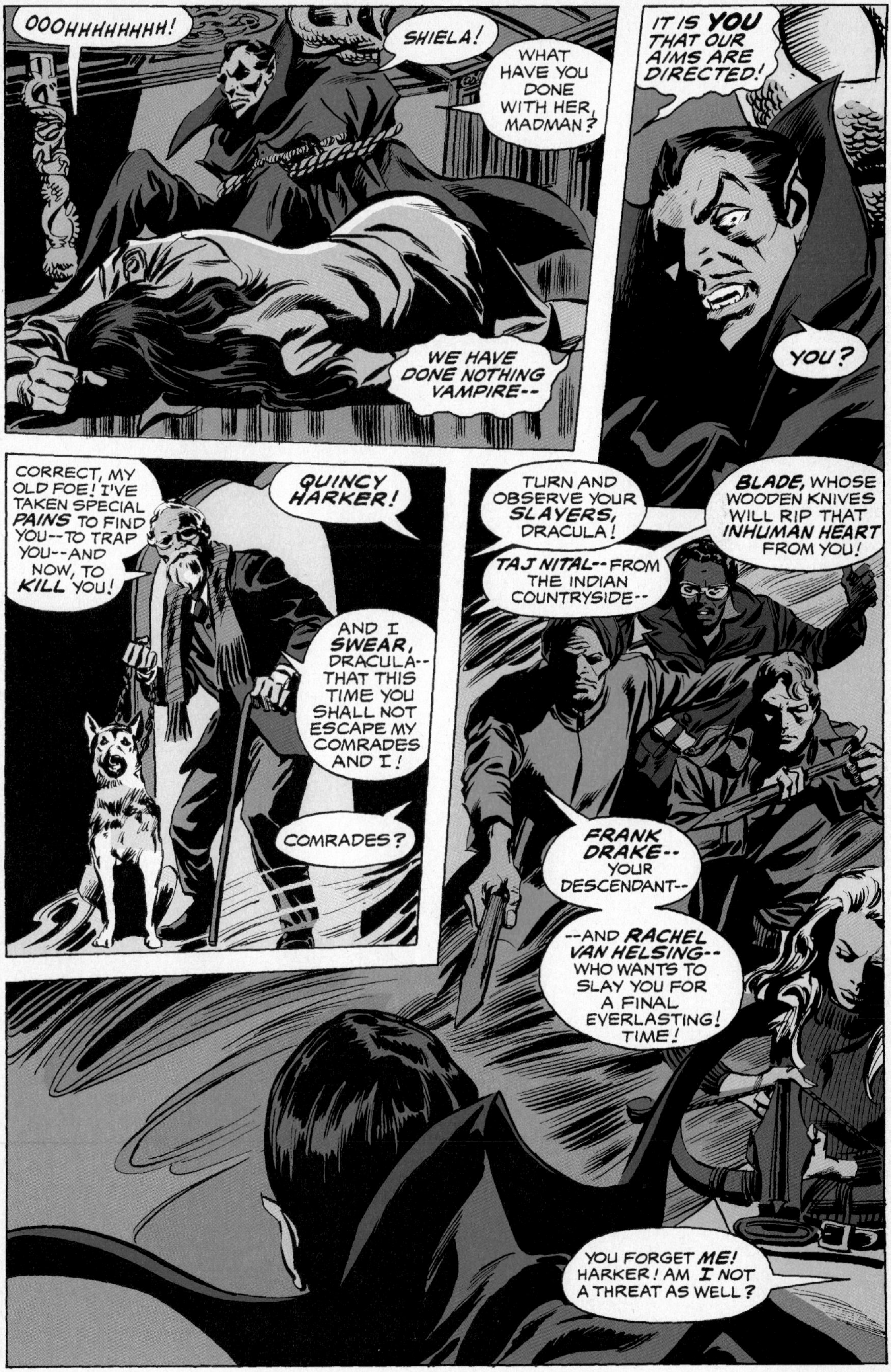
OOOHHHHHHHHH!
SHIELA!
WHAT HAVE YOU DONE WITH HER, MADMAN?
WE HAVE DONE NOTHING VAMPIRE--
IT IS YOU THAT OUR AIMS ARE DIRECTED!
YOU?
CORRECT, MY OLD FOE! I'VE TAKEN SPECIAL PAINS TO FIND YOU--TO TRAP YOU--AND NOW, TO KILL YOU!
QUINCY HARKER!
AND I SWEAR, DRACULA--THAT THIS TIME YOU SHALL NOT ESCAPE MY COMRADES AND I!
COMRADES?
TURN AND OBSERVE YOUR SLAYERS, DRACULA!
BLADE, WHOSE WOODEN KNIVES WILL RIP THAT INHUMAN HEART FROM YOU!
TAJ NITAL--FROM THE INDIAN COUNTRYSIDE--
FRANK DRAKE--YOUR DESCENDANT--
--AND RACHEL VAN HELSING--WHO WANTS TO SLAY YOU FOR A FINAL EVERLASTING! TIME!
YOU FORGET ME! HARKER! AM I NOT A THREAT AS WELL?

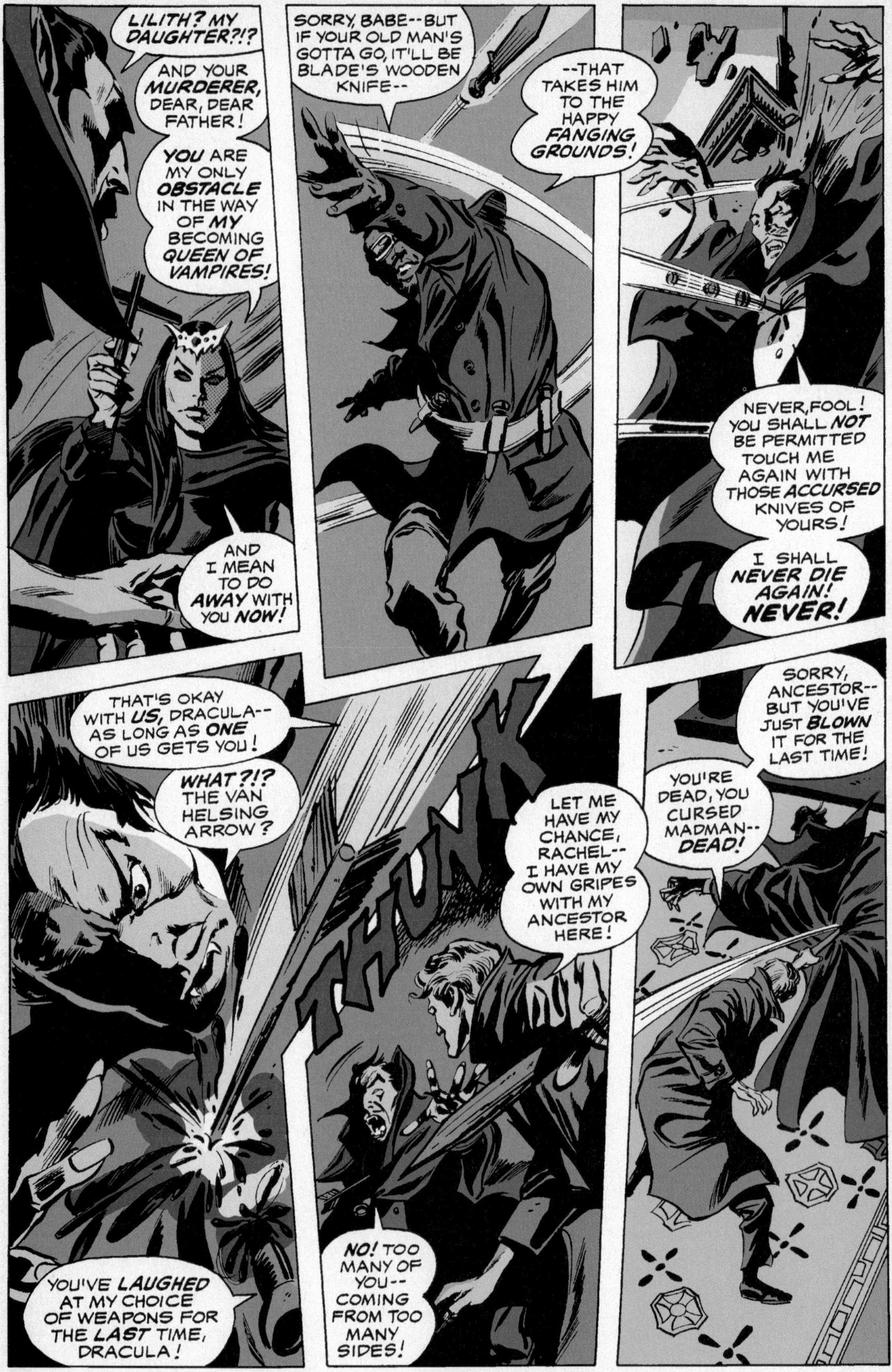

LILITH? MY DAUGHTER?!?
AND YOUR MURDERER, DEAR, DEAR FATHER!
YOU ARE MY ONLY OBSTACLE IN THE WAY OF MY BECOMING QUEEN OF VAMPIRES!
AND I MEAN TO DO AWAY WITH YOU NOW!
SORRY, BABE--BUT IF YOUR OLD MAN'S GOTTA GO, IT'LL BE BLADE'S WOODEN KNIFE--
--THAT TAKES HIM TO THE HAPPY FANGING GROUNDS!
NEVER, FOOL! YOU SHALL NOT BE PERMITTED TOUCH ME AGAIN WITH THOSE ACCURSED KNIVES OF YOURS!
I SHALL NEVER DIE AGAIN! NEVER!
THAT'S OKAY WITH US, DRACULA--AS LONG AS ONE OF US GETS YOU!
WHAT?!? THE VAN HELSING ARROW?
YOU'VE LAUGHED AT MY CHOICE OF WEAPONS FOR THE LAST TIME, DRACULA!
THUNK
LET ME HAVE MY CHANCE, RACHEL--I HAVE MY OWN GRIPES WITH MY ANCESTOR HERE!
NO! TOO MANY OF YOU--COMING FROM TOO MANY SIDES!
SORRY, ANCESTOR--BUT YOU'VE JUST BLOWN IT FOR THE LAST TIME!
YOU'RE DEAD, YOU CURSED MADMAN--DEAD!

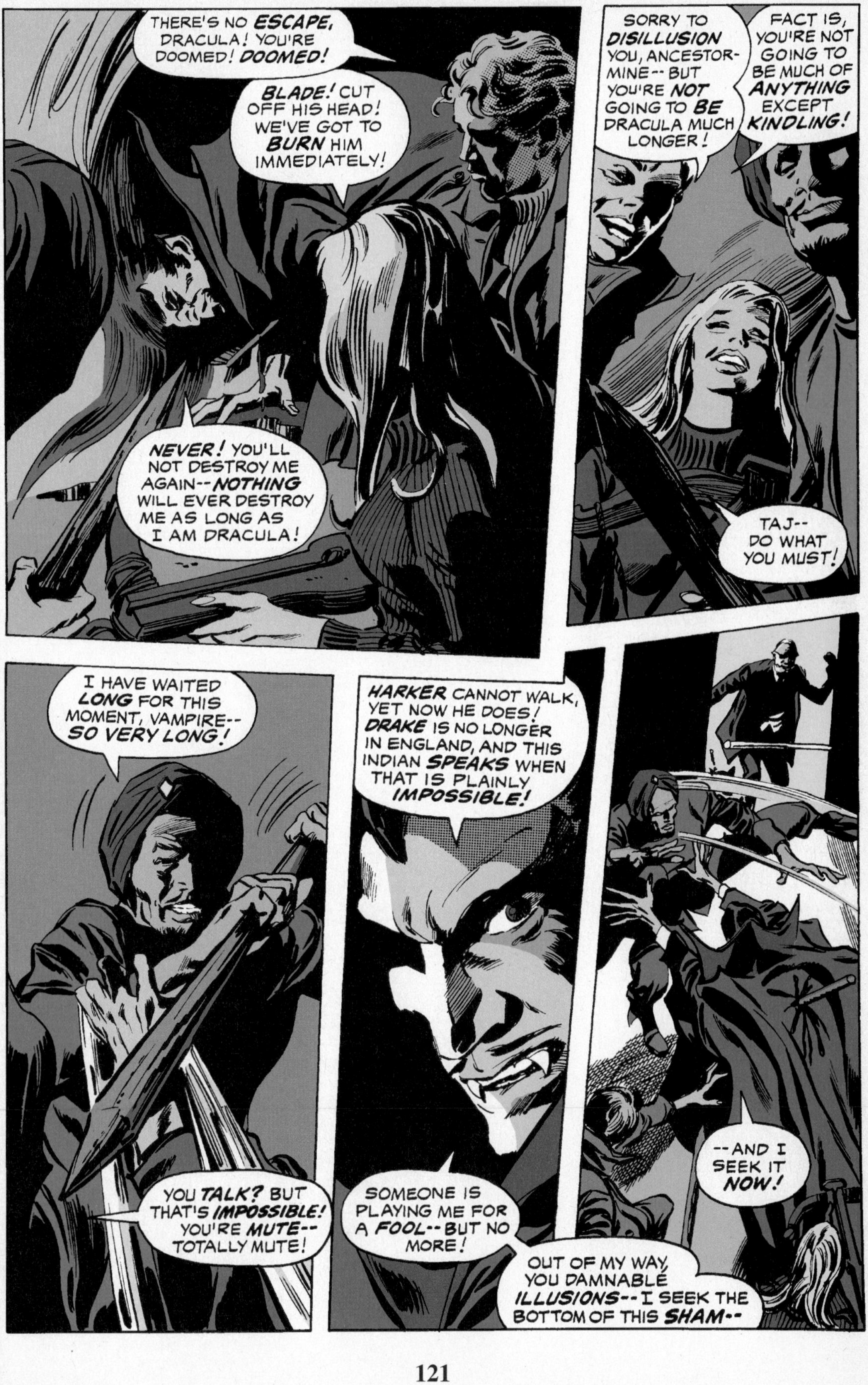
THERE'S NO ESCAPE, DRACULA! YOU'RE DOOMED! DOOMED!
BLADE! CUT OFF HIS HEAD! WE'VE GOT TO BURN HIM IMMEDIATELY!
NEVER! YOU'LL NOT DESTROY ME AGAIN--NOTHING WILL EVER DESTROY ME AS LONG AS I AM DRACULA!
SORRY TO DISILLUSION YOU, ANCESTOR-MINE--BUT YOU'RE NOT GOING TO BE DRACULA MUCH LONGER!
FACT IS, YOU'RE NOT GOING TO BE MUCH OF ANYTHING EXCEPT KINDLING!
TAJ--DO WHAT YOU MUST!
I HAVE WAITED LONG FOR THIS MOMENT, VAMPIRE--SO VERY LONG!
YOU TALK? BUT THAT'S IMPOSSIBLE! YOU'RE MUTE--TOTALLY MUTE!
HARKER CANNOT WALK, YET NOW HE DOES! DRAKE IS NO LONGER IN ENGLAND, AND THIS INDIAN SPEAKS WHEN THAT IS PLAINLY IMPOSSIBLE!
SOMEONE IS PLAYING ME FOR A FOOL--BUT NO MORE!
OUT OF MY WAY, YOU DAMNABLE ILLUSIONS--I SEEK THE BOTTOM OF THIS SHAM--
--AND I SEEK IT NOW!

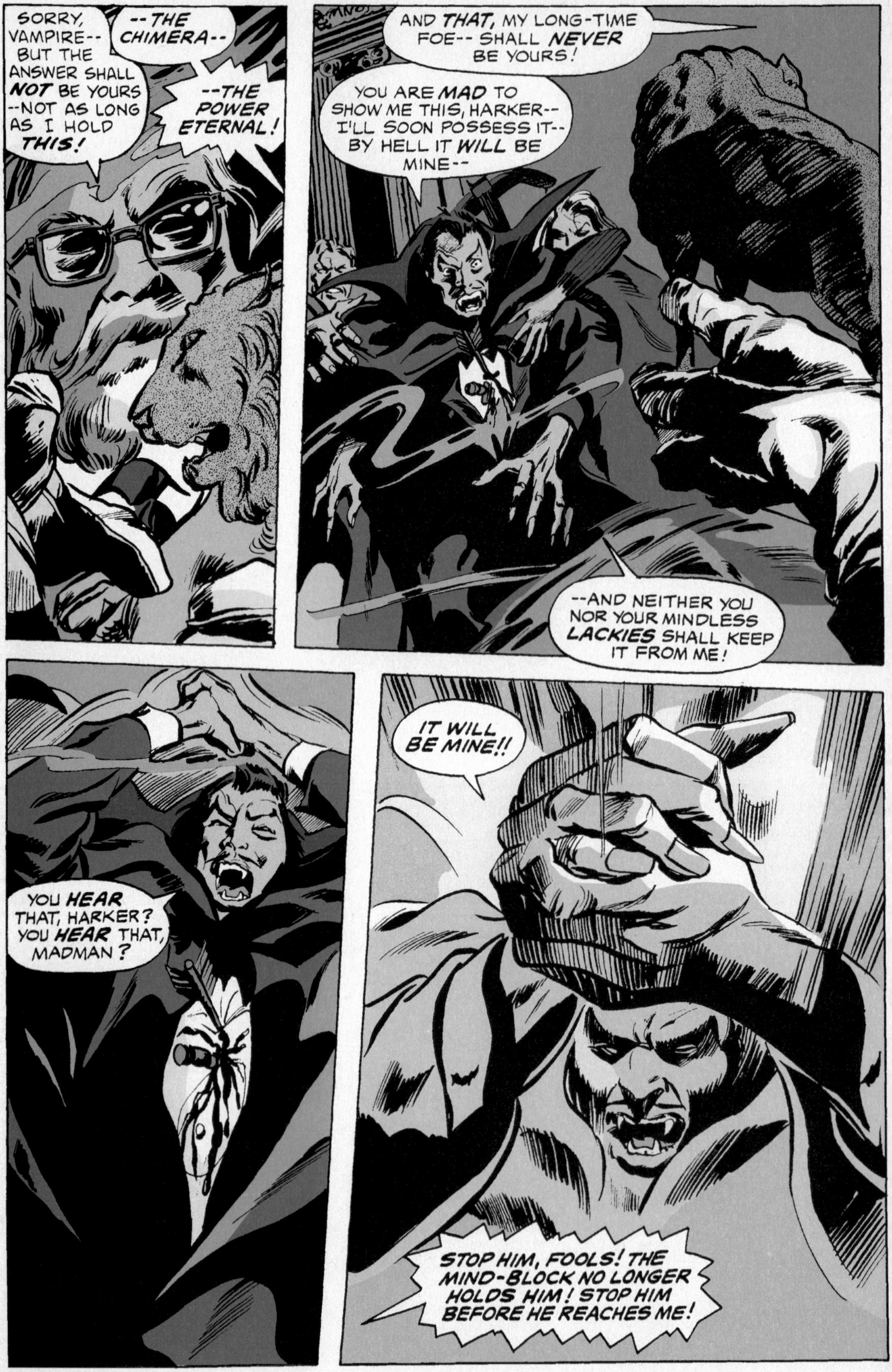
SORRY, VAMPIRE-- BUT THE ANSWER SHALL NOT BE YOURS --NOT AS LONG AS I HOLD THIS!
--THE CHIMERA--
--THE POWER ETERNAL!
AND THAT, MY LONG-TIME FOE-- SHALL NEVER BE YOURS!
YOU ARE MAD TO SHOW ME THIS, HARKER-- I'LL SOON POSSESS IT-- BY HELL IT WILL BE MINE--
--AND NEITHER YOU NOR YOUR MINDLESS LACKIES SHALL KEEP IT FROM ME!
YOU HEAR THAT, HARKER? YOU HEAR THAT, MADMAN?
IT WILL BE MINE!!
STOP HIM, FOOLS! THE MIND-BLOCK NO LONGER HOLDS HIM! STOP HIM BEFORE HE REACHES ME!

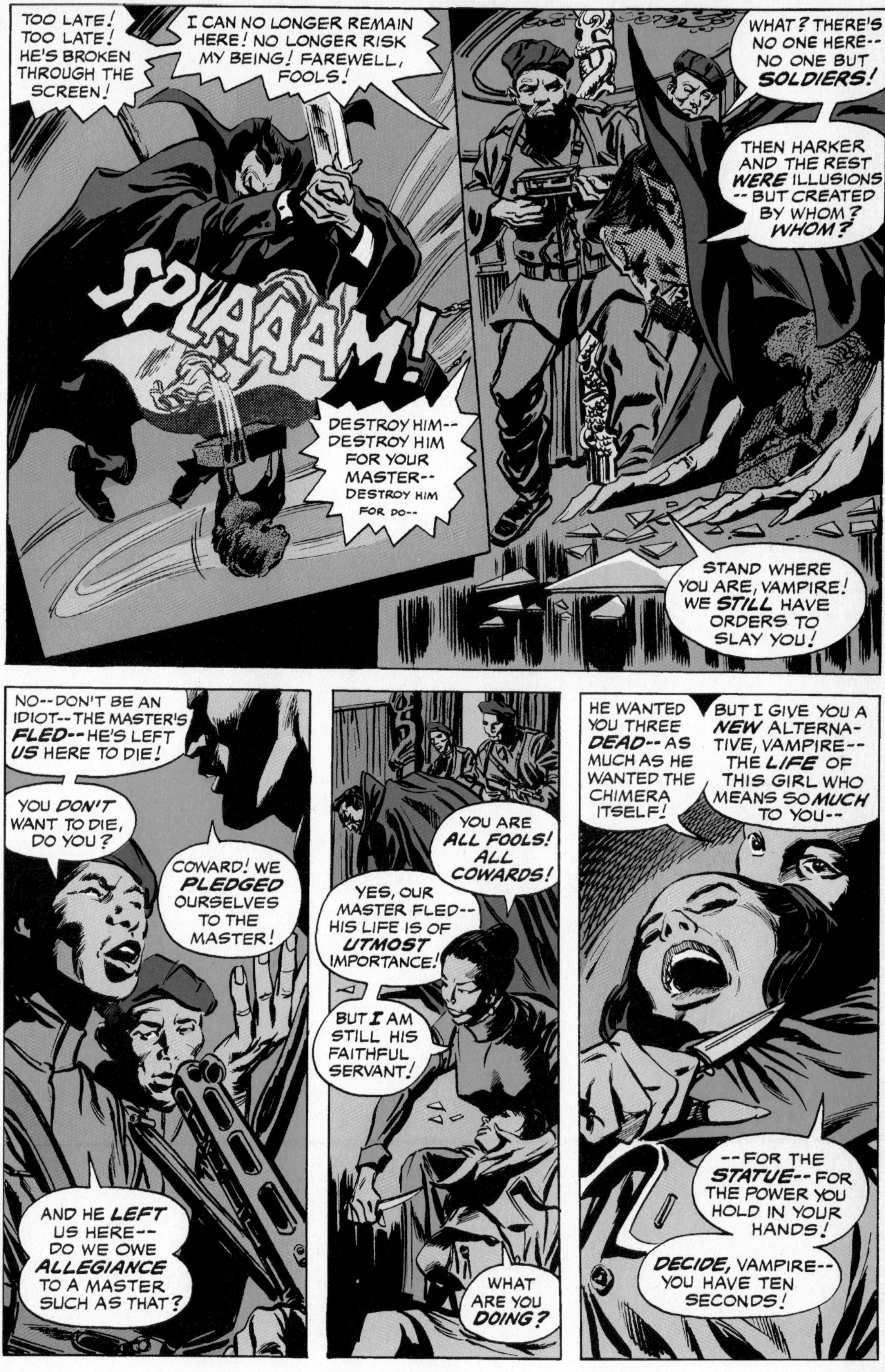
TOO LATE! TOO LATE! HE'S BROKEN THROUGH THE SCREEN!
I CAN NO LONGER REMAIN HERE! NO LONGER RISK MY BEING! FAREWELL, FOOLS!
SPLAAAM!
DESTROY HIM--DESTROY HIM FOR YOUR MASTER--DESTROY HIM FOR DO--
WHAT? THERE'S NO ONE HERE--NO ONE BUT SOLDIERS!
THEN HARKER AND THE REST WERE ILLUSIONS--BUT CREATED BY WHOM? WHOM?
STAND WHERE YOU ARE, VAMPIRE! WE STILL HAVE ORDERS TO SLAY YOU!
NO--DON'T BE AN IDIOT--THE MASTER'S FLED--HE'S LEFT US HERE TO DIE!
YOU DON'T WANT TO DIE, DO YOU?
COWARD! WE PLEDGED OURSELVES TO THE MASTER!
AND HE LEFT US HERE--DO WE OWE ALLEGIANCE TO A MASTER SUCH AS THAT?
YOU ARE ALL FOOLS! ALL COWARDS!
YES, OUR MASTER FLED--HIS LIFE IS OF UTMOST IMPORTANCE!
BUT I AM STILL HIS FAITHFUL SERVANT!
WHAT ARE YOU DOING?
HE WANTED YOU THREE DEAD--AS MUCH AS HE WANTED THE CHIMERA ITSELF!
BUT I GIVE YOU A NEW ALTERNATIVE, VAMPIRE--THE LIFE OF THIS GIRL WHO MEANS SO MUCH TO YOU--
--FOR THE STATUE--FOR THE POWER YOU HOLD IN YOUR HANDS!
DECIDE, VAMPIRE--YOU HAVE TEN SECONDS!

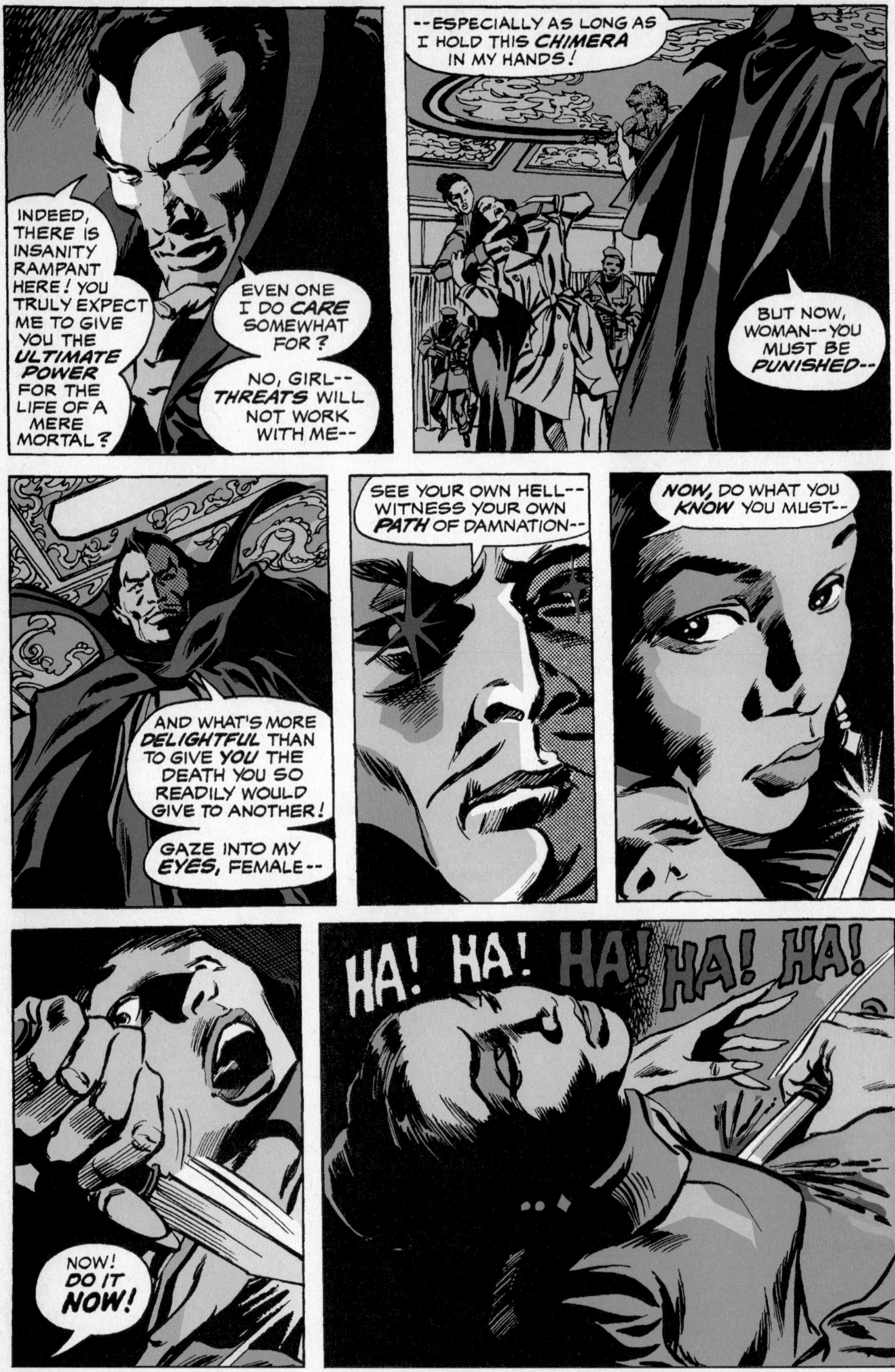
INDEED, THERE IS INSANITY RAMPANT HERE! YOU TRULY EXPECT ME TO GIVE YOU THE ULTIMATE POWER FOR THE LIFE OF A MERE MORTAL?
EVEN ONE I DO CARE SOMEWHAT FOR?
NO, GIRL-- THREATS WILL NOT WORK WITH ME--
--ESPECIALLY AS LONG AS I HOLD THIS CHIMERA IN MY HANDS!
BUT NOW, WOMAN--YOU MUST BE PUNISHED--
AND WHAT'S MORE DELIGHTFUL THAN TO GIVE YOU THE DEATH YOU SO READILY WOULD GIVE TO ANOTHER!
GAZE INTO MY EYES, FEMALE--
SEE YOUR OWN HELL-- WITNESS YOUR OWN PATH OF DAMNATION--
NOW, DO WHAT YOU KNOW YOU MUST--
NOW! DO IT NOW!
HA! HA! HA! HA! HA!

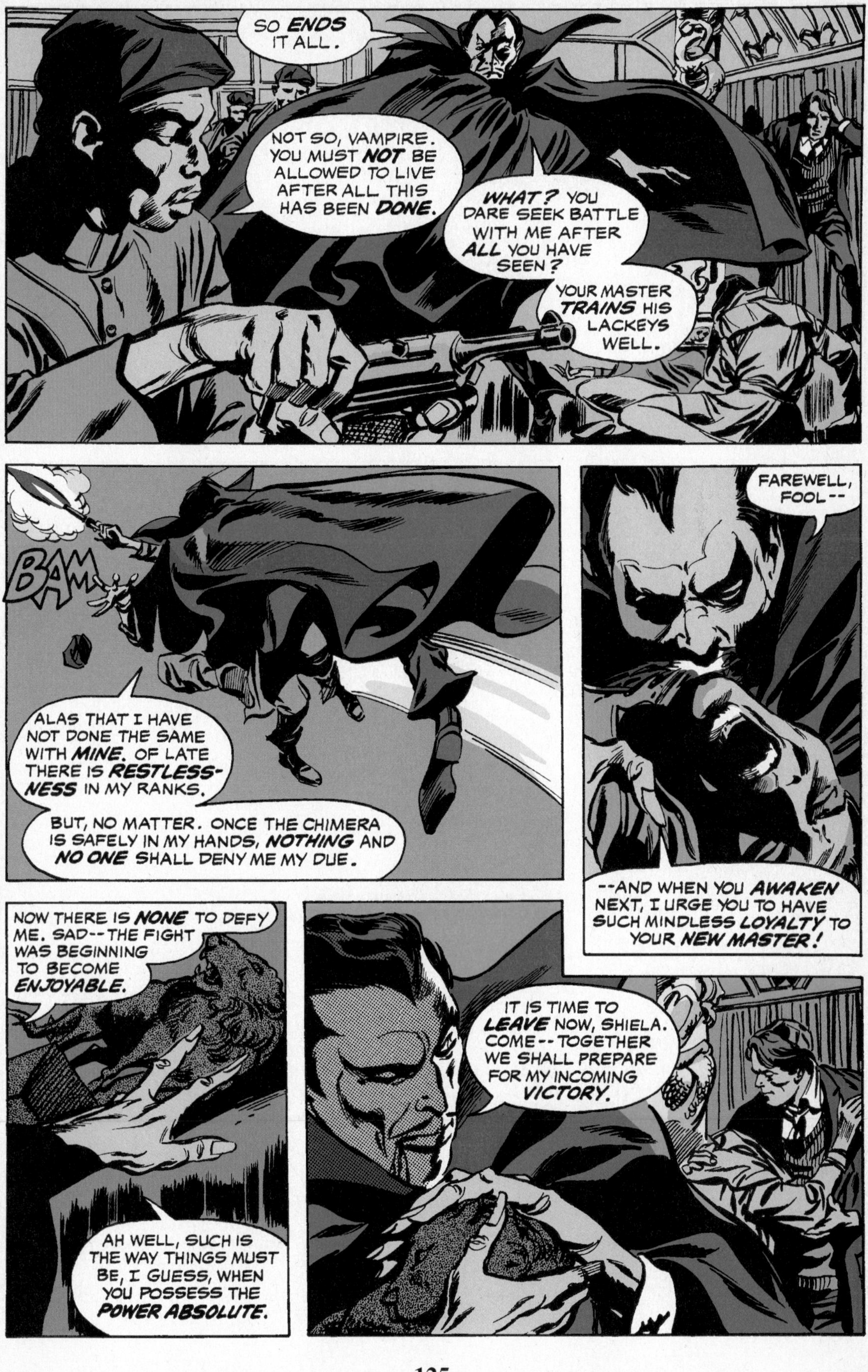
SO ENDS IT ALL.
NOT SO, VAMPIRE. YOU MUST NOT BE ALLOWED TO LIVE AFTER ALL THIS HAS BEEN DONE.
WHAT? YOU DARE SEEK BATTLE WITH ME AFTER ALL YOU HAVE SEEN?
YOUR MASTER TRAINS HIS LACKEYS WELL.
BAM
ALAS THAT I HAVE NOT DONE THE SAME WITH MINE. OF LATE THERE IS RESTLESS-NESS IN MY RANKS.
BUT, NO MATTER. ONCE THE CHIMERA IS SAFELY IN MY HANDS, NOTHING AND NO ONE SHALL DENY ME MY DUE.
FAREWELL, FOOL--
--AND WHEN YOU AWAKEN NEXT, I URGE YOU TO HAVE SUCH MINDLESS LOYALTY TO YOUR NEW MASTER!
NOW THERE IS NONE TO DEFY ME. SAD--THE FIGHT WAS BEGINNING TO BECOME ENJOYABLE.
AH WELL, SUCH IS THE WAY THINGS MUST BE, I GUESS, WHEN YOU POSSESS THE POWER ABSOLUTE.
IT IS TIME TO LEAVE NOW, SHIELA. COME--TOGETHER WE SHALL PREPARE FOR MY INCOMING VICTORY.

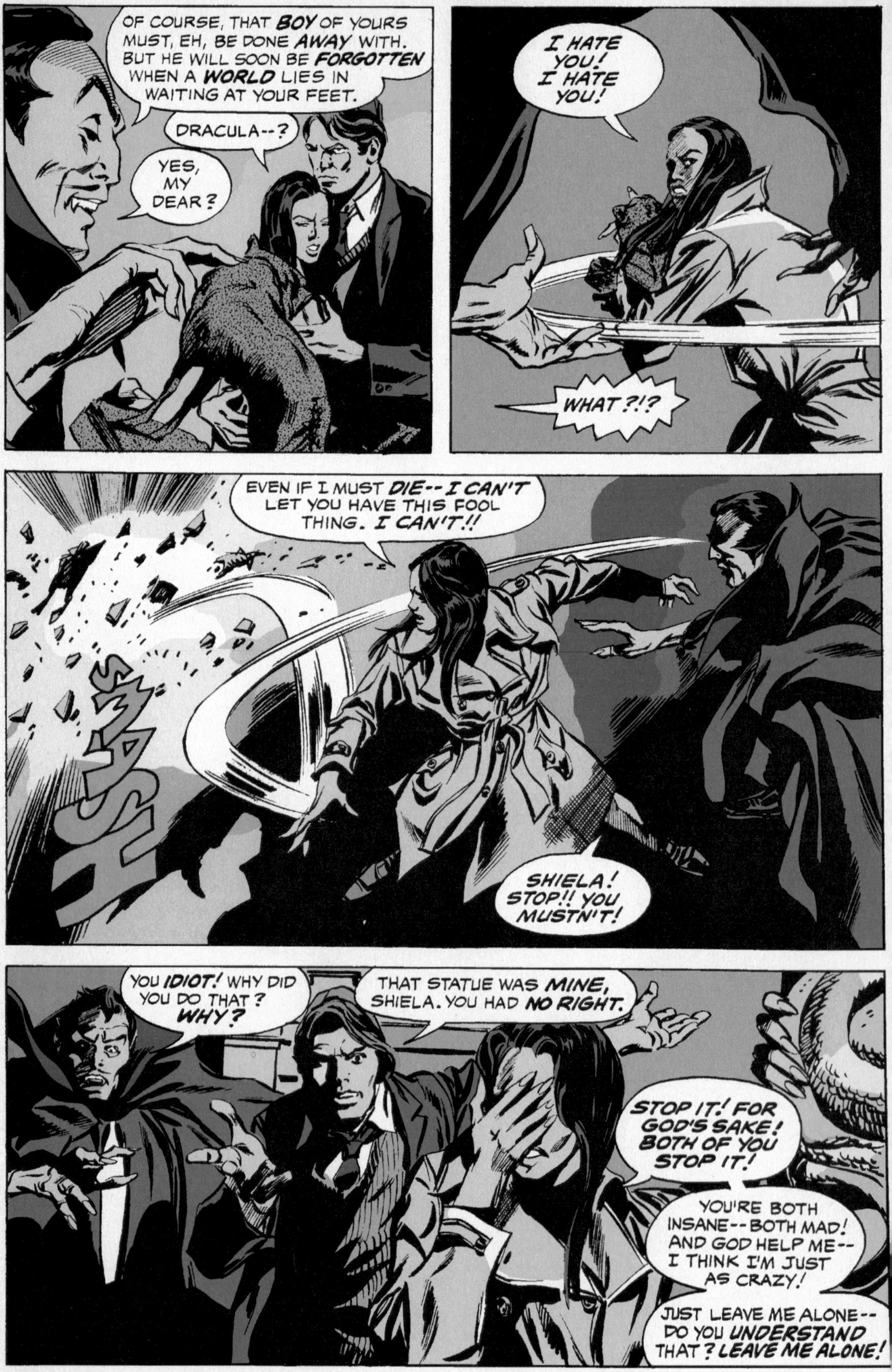
OF COURSE, THAT BOY OF YOURS MUST, EH, BE DONE AWAY WITH. BUT HE WILL SOON BE FORGOTTEN WHEN A WORLD LIES IN WAITING AT YOUR FEET.
DRACULA--?
YES, MY DEAR?
I HATE YOU! I HATE YOU!
WHAT?!?
EVEN IF I MUST DIE-- I CAN'T LET YOU HAVE THIS FOOL THING. I CAN'T!!
SMASH
SHIELA! STOP!! YOU MUSTN'T!
YOU IDIOT! WHY DID YOU DO THAT? WHY?
THAT STATUE WAS MINE, SHIELA. YOU HAD NO RIGHT.
STOP IT! FOR GOD'S SAKE! BOTH OF YOU STOP IT!
YOU'RE BOTH INSANE-- BOTH MAD! AND GOD HELP ME-- I THINK I'M JUST AS CRAZY!
JUST LEAVE ME ALONE-- DO YOU UNDERSTAND THAT? LEAVE ME ALONE!

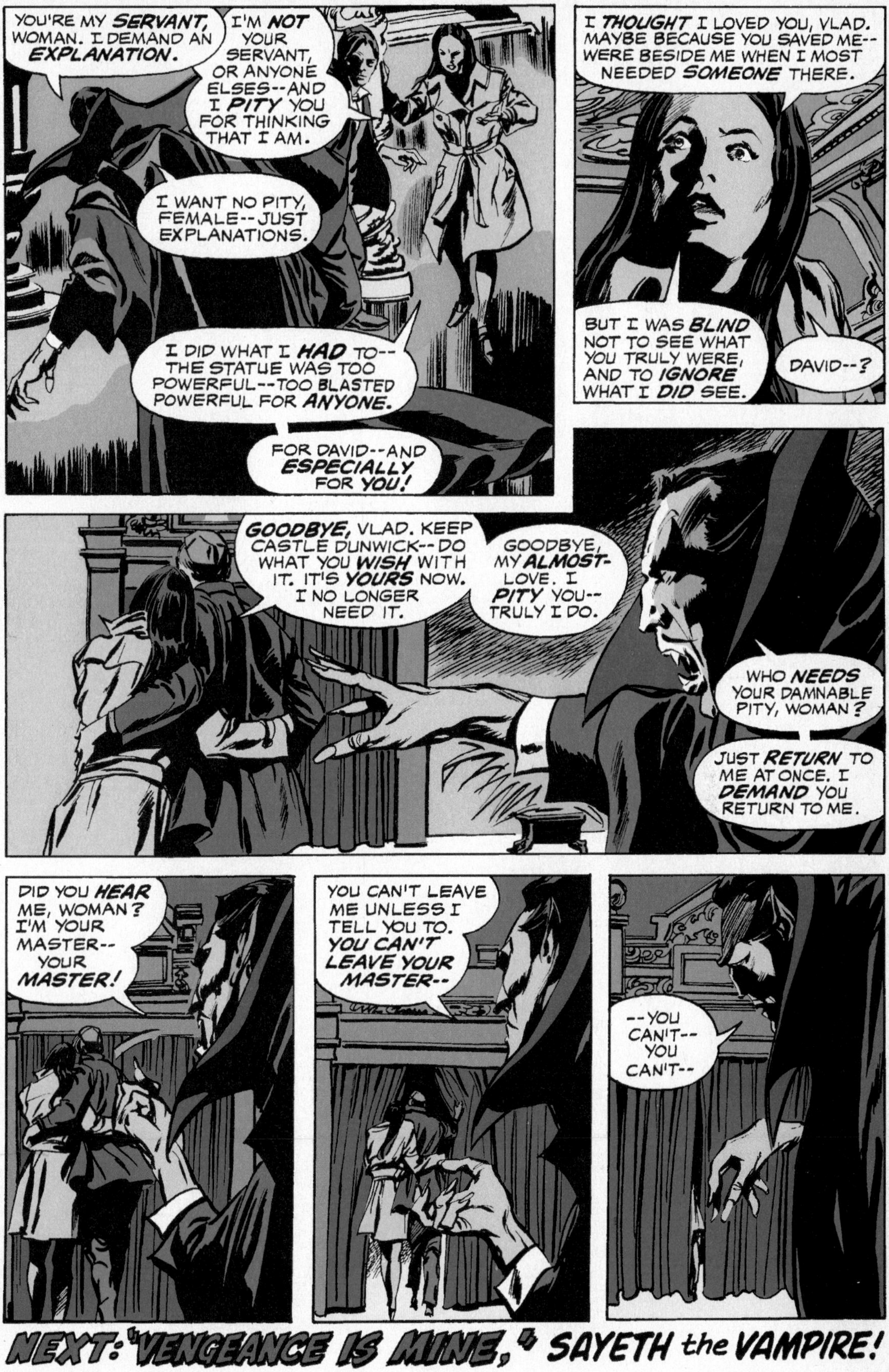
YOU'RE MY SERVANT, WOMAN. I DEMAND AN EXPLANATION.
I'M NOT YOUR SERVANT, OR ANYONE ELSES--AND I PITY YOU FOR THINKING THAT I AM.
I WANT NO PITY, FEMALE--JUST EXPLANATIONS.
I DID WHAT I HAD TO--THE STATUE WAS TOO POWERFUL--TOO BLASTED POWERFUL FOR ANYONE.
FOR DAVID--AND ESPECIALLY FOR YOU!
I THOUGHT I LOVED YOU, VLAD. MAYBE BECAUSE YOU SAVED ME--WERE BESIDE ME WHEN I MOST NEEDED SOMEONE THERE.
BUT I WAS BLIND NOT TO SEE WHAT YOU TRULY WERE, AND TO IGNORE WHAT I DID SEE.
DAVID--?
GOODBYE, VLAD. KEEP CASTLE DUNWICK--DO WHAT YOU WISH WITH IT. IT'S YOURS NOW. I NO LONGER NEED IT.
GOODBYE, MY ALMOST-LOVE. I PITY YOU--TRULY I DO.
WHO NEEDS YOUR DAMNABLE PITY, WOMAN?
JUST RETURN TO ME AT ONCE. I DEMAND YOU RETURN TO ME.
DID YOU HEAR ME, WOMAN? I'M YOUR MASTER--YOUR MASTER!
YOU CAN'T LEAVE ME UNLESS I TELL YOU TO. YOU CAN'T LEAVE YOUR MASTER--
--YOU CAN'T--YOU CAN'T--
NEXT: "VENGEANCE IS MINE," SAYETH the VAMPIRE!

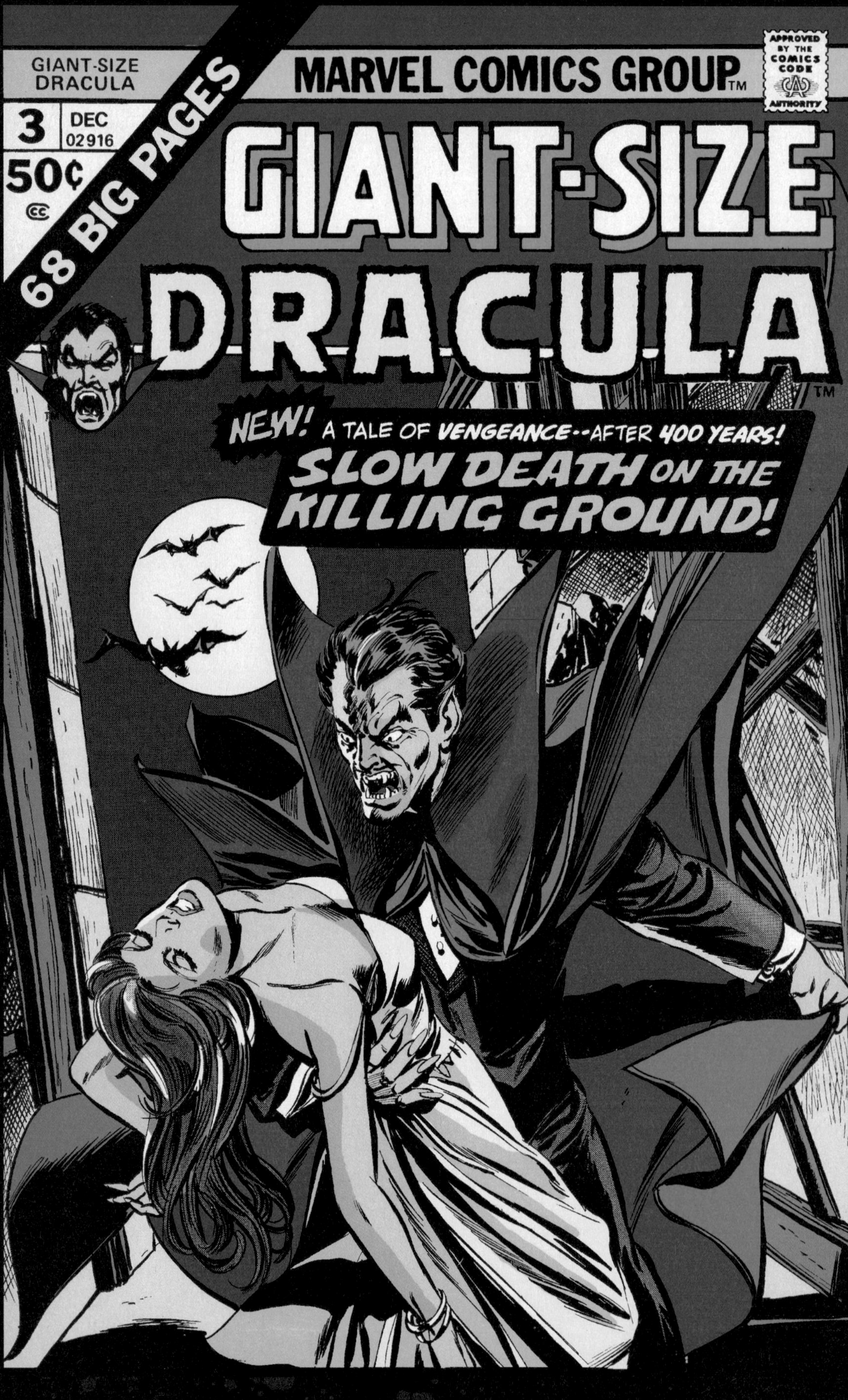
GIANT-SIZE DRACULA
MARVEL COMICS GROUP
APPROVED BY THE COMICS CODE AUTHORITY
3 DEC 02916
50¢
68 BIG PAGES
GIANT-SIZE DRACULA
NEW! A TALE OF VENGEANCE--AFTER 400 YEARS!
SLOW DEATH ON THE KILLING GROUND!

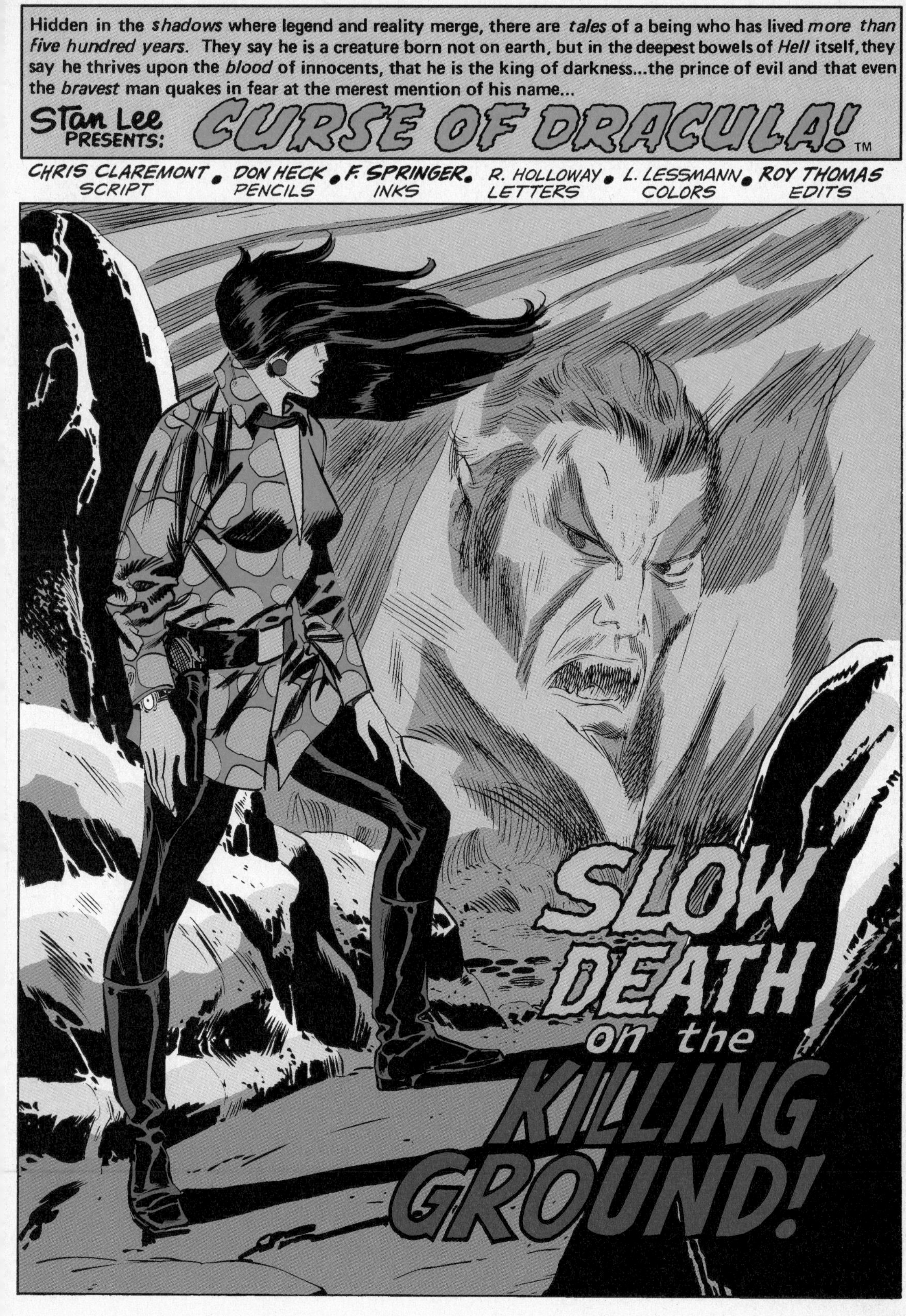

Hidden in the *shadows* where legend and reality merge, there are *tales* of a being who has lived *more than five hundred years*. They say he is a creature born not on earth, but in the deepest bowels of *Hell* itself, they say he thrives upon the *blood* of innocents, that he is the king of darkness...the prince of evil and that even the *bravest* man quakes in fear at the merest mention of his name...
Stan Lee PRESENTS:
CURSE OF DRACULA! TM
CHRIS CLAREMONT SCRIPT • DON HECK PENCILS • F. SPRINGER INKS • R. HOLLOWAY LETTERS • L. LESSMANN COLORS • ROY THOMAS EDITS
SLOW DEATH on the KILLING GROUND!

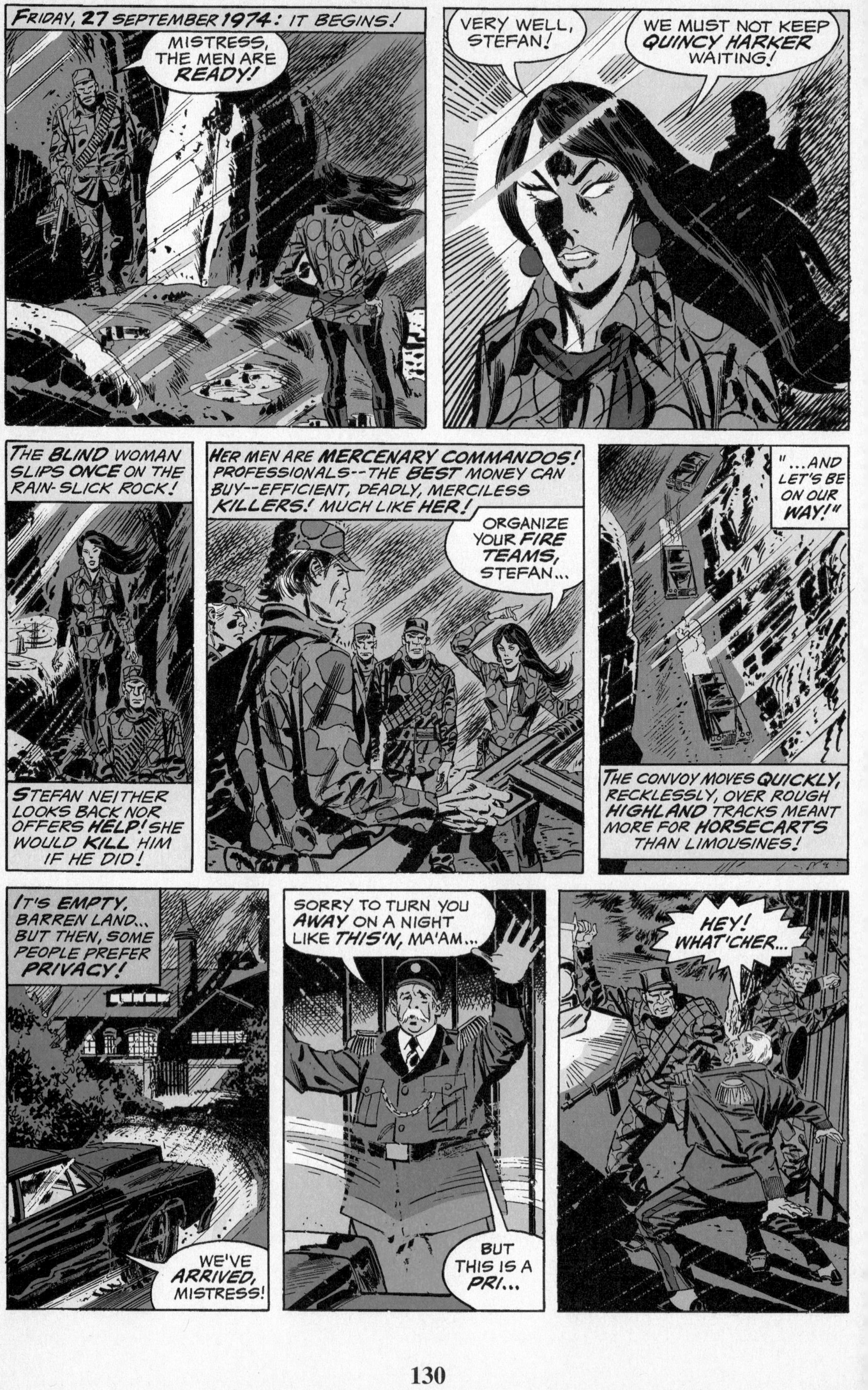
FRIDAY, 27 SEPTEMBER 1974: IT BEGINS!
MISTRESS, THE MEN ARE READY!
VERY WELL, STEFAN!
WE MUST NOT KEEP QUINCY HARKER WAITING!
THE BLIND WOMAN SLIPS ONCE ON THE RAIN-SLICK ROCK!
STEFAN NEITHER LOOKS BACK NOR OFFERS HELP! SHE WOULD KILL HIM IF HE DID!
HER MEN ARE MERCENARY COMMANDOS! PROFESSIONALS--THE BEST MONEY CAN BUY--EFFICIENT, DEADLY, MERCILESS KILLERS! MUCH LIKE HER!
ORGANIZE YOUR FIRE TEAMS, STEFAN...
"...AND LET'S BE ON OUR WAY!"
THE CONVOY MOVES QUICKLY, RECKLESSLY, OVER ROUGH HIGHLAND TRACKS MEANT MORE FOR HORSECARTS THAN LIMOUSINES!
IT'S EMPTY, BARREN LAND... BUT THEN, SOME PEOPLE PREFER PRIVACY!
WE'VE ARRIVED, MISTRESS!
SORRY TO TURN YOU AWAY ON A NIGHT LIKE THIS'N, MA'AM...
BUT THIS IS A PRI...
HEY! WHAT'CHER...

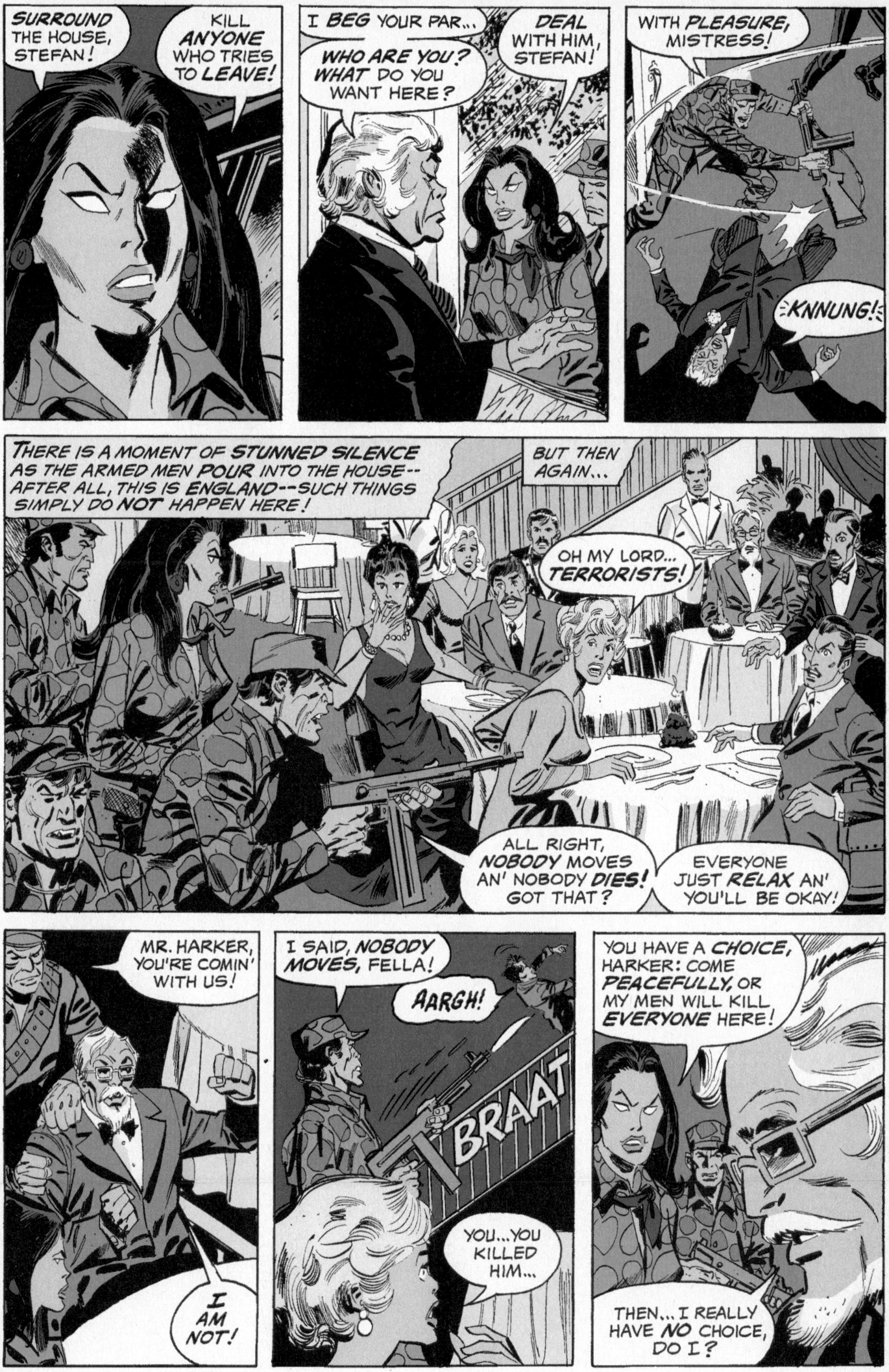
SURROUND THE HOUSE, STEFAN!
KILL ANYONE WHO TRIES TO LEAVE!
I BEG YOUR PAR...
WHO ARE YOU? WHAT DO YOU WANT HERE?
DEAL WITH HIM, STEFAN!
WITH PLEASURE, MISTRESS!
KNNUNG!
THERE IS A MOMENT OF STUNNED SILENCE AS THE ARMED MEN POUR INTO THE HOUSE-- AFTER ALL, THIS IS ENGLAND--SUCH THINGS SIMPLY DO NOT HAPPEN HERE!
BUT THEN AGAIN...
OH MY LORD... TERRORISTS!
ALL RIGHT, NOBODY MOVES AN' NOBODY DIES! GOT THAT?
EVERYONE JUST RELAX AN' YOU'LL BE OKAY!
MR. HARKER, YOU'RE COMIN' WITH US!
I AM NOT!
I SAID, NOBODY MOVES, FELLA!
AARGH!
BRAAT
YOU...YOU KILLED HIM...
YOU HAVE A CHOICE, HARKER: COME PEACEFULLY, OR MY MEN WILL KILL EVERYONE HERE!
THEN... I REALLY HAVE NO CHOICE, DO I?

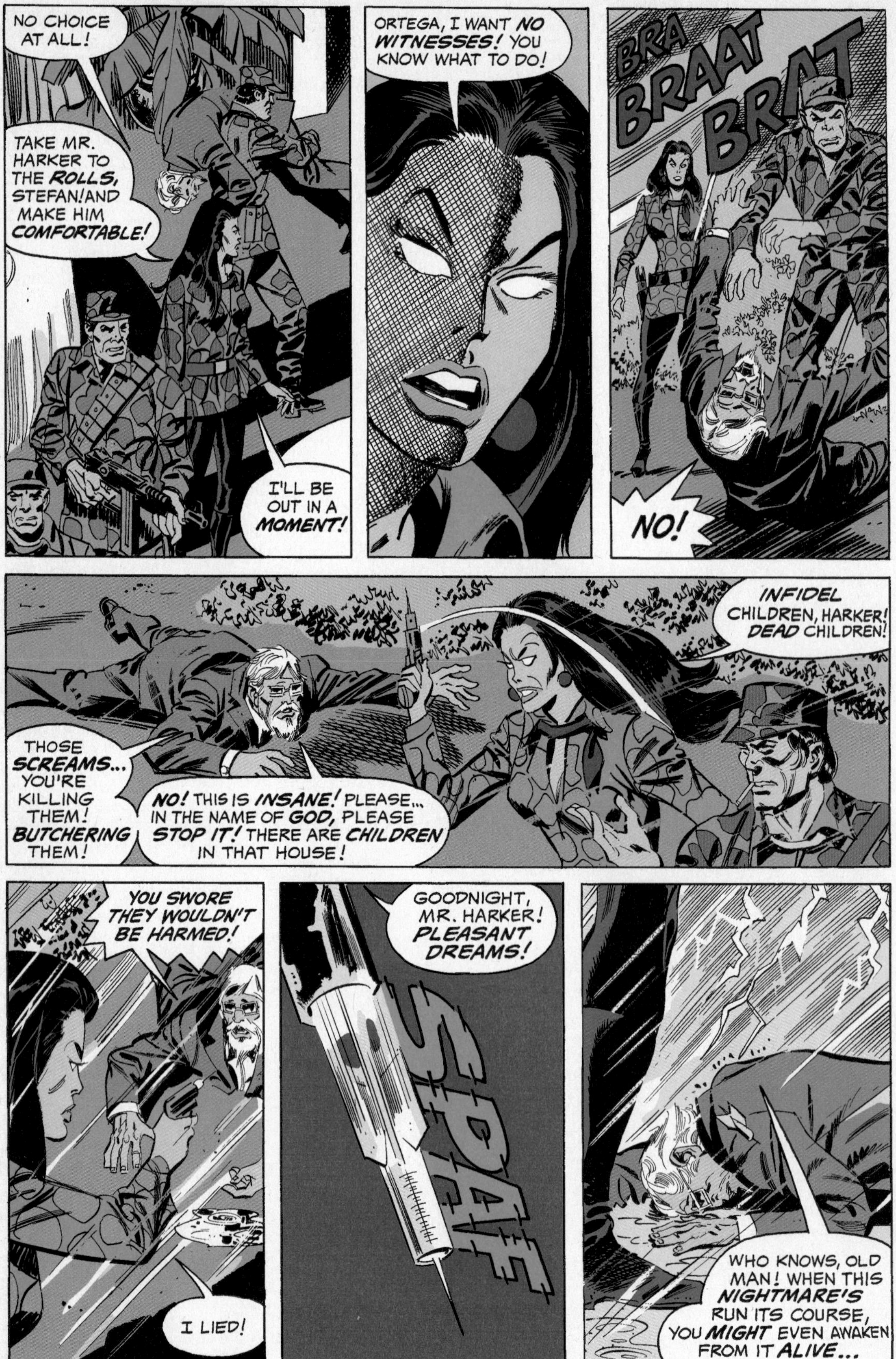
NO CHOICE AT ALL!
TAKE MR. HARKER TO THE ROLLS, STEFAN! AND MAKE HIM COMFORTABLE!
I'LL BE OUT IN A MOMENT!
ORTEGA, I WANT NO WITNESSES! YOU KNOW WHAT TO DO!
BRA BRAAT BRAT
NO!
INFIDEL CHILDREN, HARKER! DEAD CHILDREN!
THOSE SCREAMS... YOU'RE KILLING THEM! BUTCHERING THEM!
NO! THIS IS INSANE! PLEASE... IN THE NAME OF GOD, PLEASE STOP IT! THERE ARE CHILDREN IN THAT HOUSE!
YOU SWORE THEY WOULDN'T BE HARMED!
I LIED!
GOODNIGHT, MR. HARKER! PLEASANT DREAMS!
SPAF
WHO KNOWS, OLD MAN! WHEN THIS NIGHTMARE'S RUN ITS COURSE, YOU MIGHT EVEN AWAKEN FROM IT ALIVE...

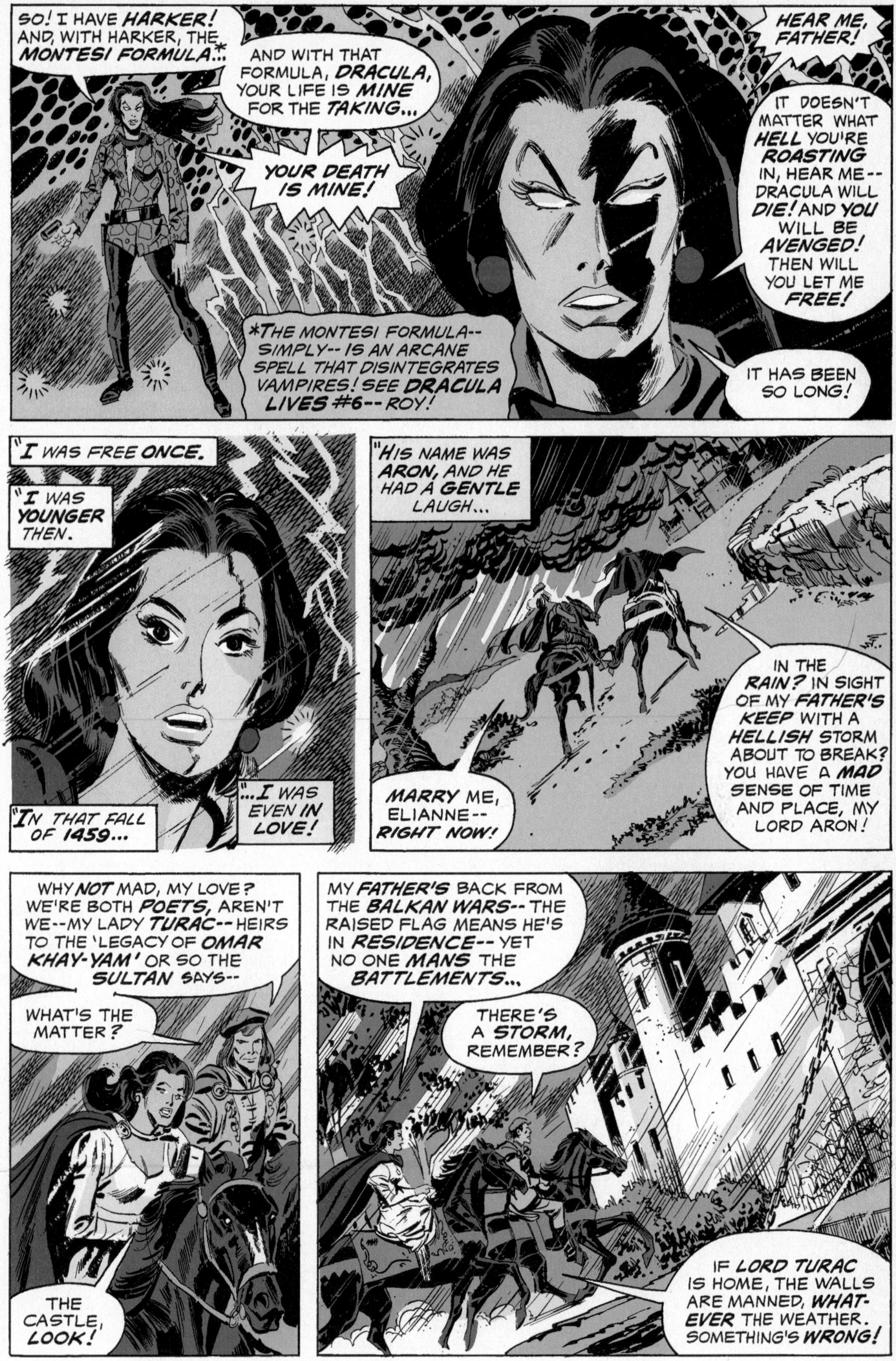
SO! I HAVE HARKER! AND, WITH HARKER, THE MONTESI FORMULA...*
AND WITH THAT FORMULA, DRACULA, YOUR LIFE IS MINE FOR THE TAKING...
YOUR DEATH IS MINE!
*THE MONTESI FORMULA-- SIMPLY-- IS AN ARCANE SPELL THAT DISINTEGRATES VAMPIRES! SEE DRACULA LIVES #6-- ROY!
HEAR ME, FATHER!
IT DOESN'T MATTER WHAT HELL YOU'RE ROASTING IN, HEAR ME-- DRACULA WILL DIE! AND YOU WILL BE AVENGED! THEN WILL YOU LET ME FREE!
IT HAS BEEN SO LONG!
"I WAS FREE ONCE.
"I WAS YOUNGER THEN.
"IN THAT FALL OF 1459...
"...I WAS EVEN IN LOVE!
"HIS NAME WAS ARON, AND HE HAD A GENTLE LAUGH...
MARRY ME, ELIANNE-- RIGHT NOW!
IN THE RAIN? IN SIGHT OF MY FATHER'S KEEP WITH A HELLISH STORM ABOUT TO BREAK? YOU HAVE A MAD SENSE OF TIME AND PLACE, MY LORD ARON!
WHY NOT MAD, MY LOVE? WE'RE BOTH POETS, AREN'T WE-- MY LADY TURAC-- HEIRS TO THE 'LEGACY OF OMAR KHAY-YAM' OR SO THE SULTAN SAYS--
WHAT'S THE MATTER?
THE CASTLE, LOOK!
MY FATHER'S BACK FROM THE BALKAN WARS-- THE RAISED FLAG MEANS HE'S IN RESIDENCE-- YET NO ONE MANS THE BATTLEMENTS...
THERE'S A STORM, REMEMBER?
IF LORD TURAC IS HOME, THE WALLS ARE MANNED, WHATEVER THE WEATHER. SOMETHING'S WRONG!

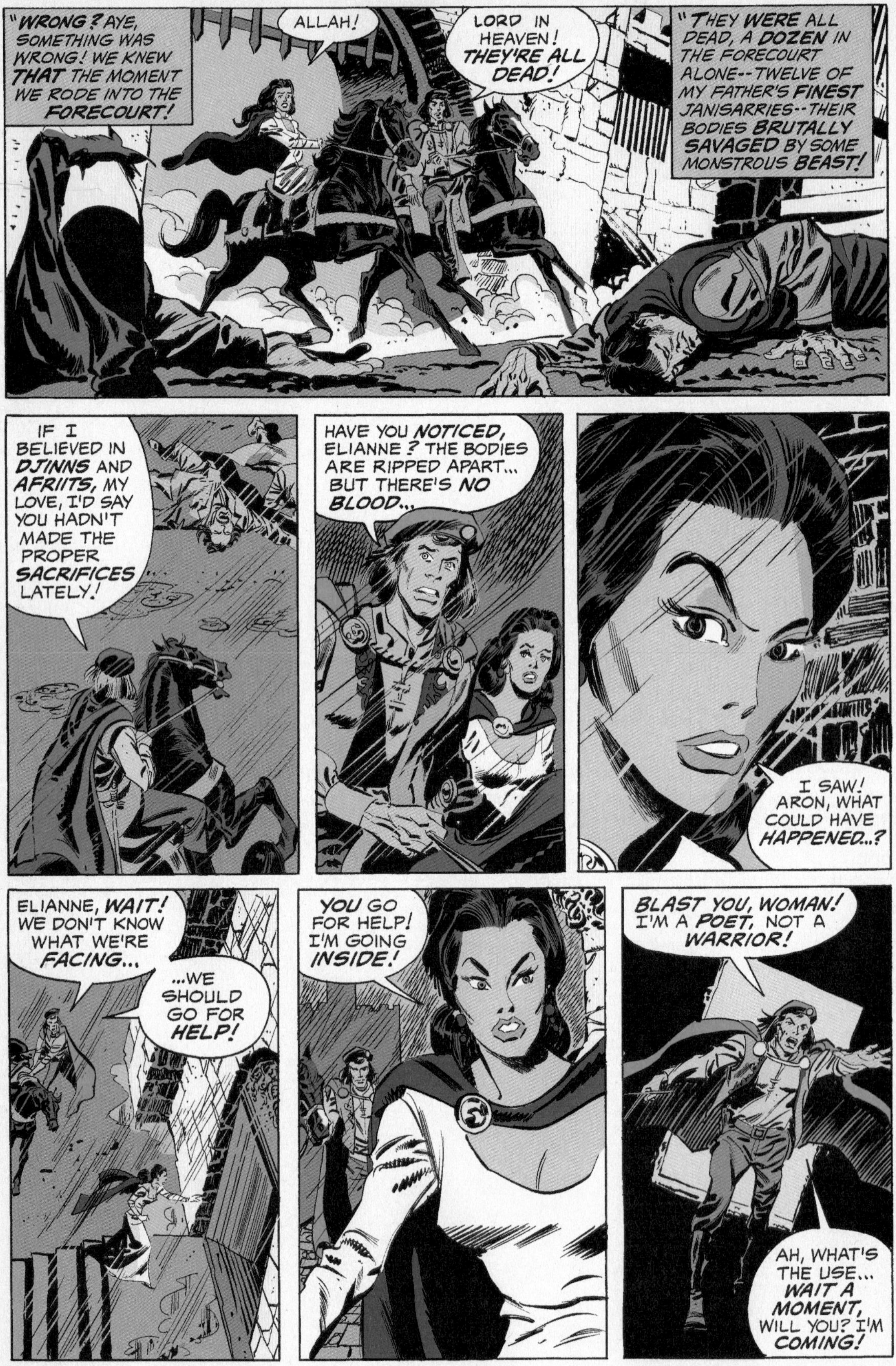
"WRONG? AYE, SOMETHING WAS WRONG! WE KNEW THAT THE MOMENT WE RODE INTO THE FORECOURT!
ALLAH!
LORD IN HEAVEN! THEY'RE ALL DEAD!
"THEY WERE ALL DEAD, A DOZEN IN THE FORECOURT ALONE--TWELVE OF MY FATHER'S FINEST JANISARRIES--THEIR BODIES BRUTALLY SAVAGED BY SOME MONSTROUS BEAST!
IF I BELIEVED IN DJINNS AND AFRIITS, MY LOVE, I'D SAY YOU HADN'T MADE THE PROPER SACRIFICES LATELY!
HAVE YOU NOTICED, ELIANNE? THE BODIES ARE RIPPED APART... BUT THERE'S NO BLOOD...
I SAW! ARON, WHAT COULD HAVE HAPPENED...?
ELIANNE, WAIT! WE DON'T KNOW WHAT WE'RE FACING...
...WE SHOULD GO FOR HELP!
YOU GO FOR HELP! I'M GOING INSIDE!
BLAST YOU, WOMAN! I'M A POET, NOT A WARRIOR!
AH, WHAT'S THE USE... WAIT A MOMENT, WILL YOU? I'M COMING!

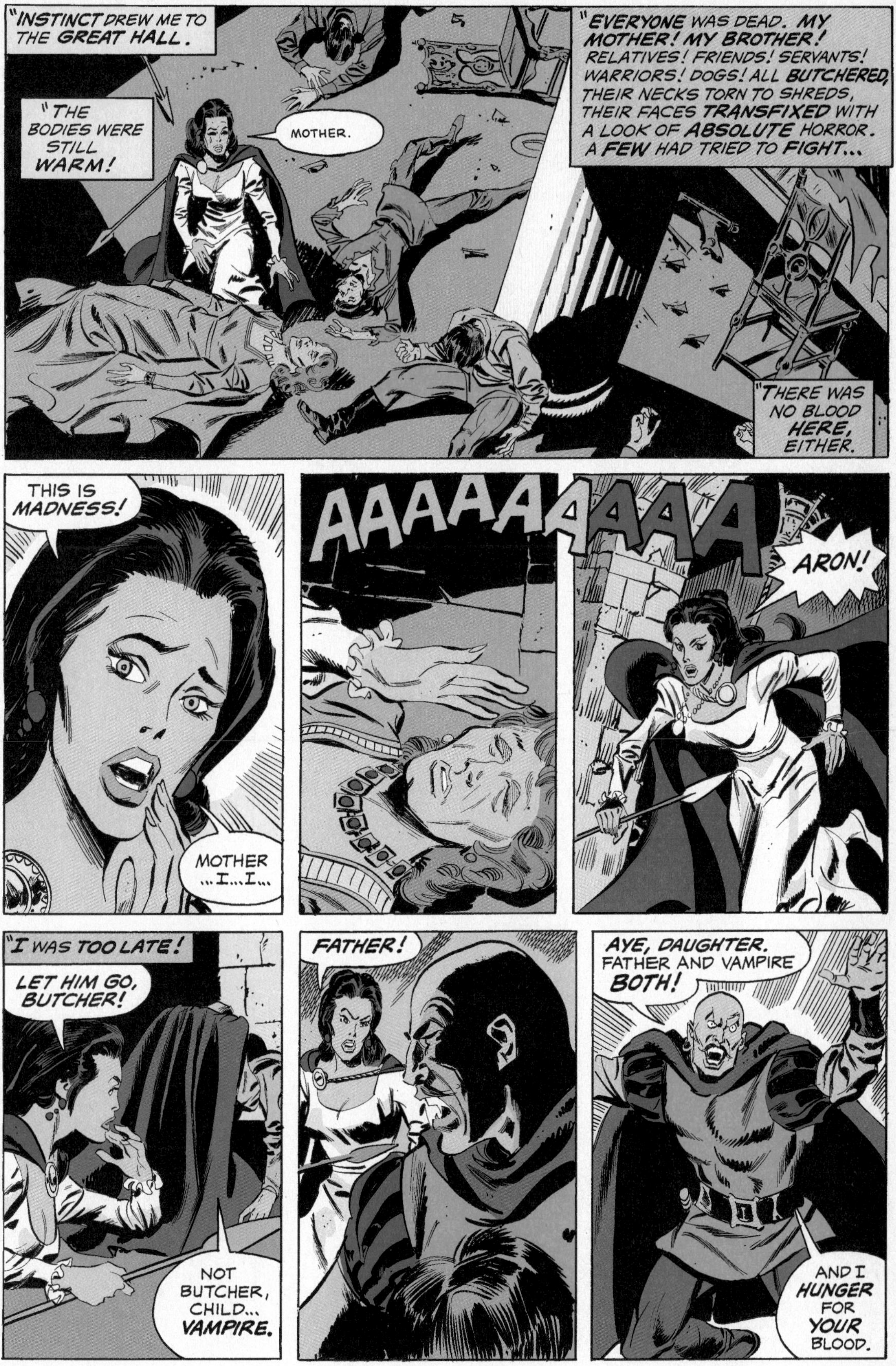
"INSTINCT DREW ME TO THE GREAT HALL.
"THE BODIES WERE STILL WARM!
MOTHER.
"EVERYONE WAS DEAD. MY MOTHER! MY BROTHER! RELATIVES! FRIENDS! SERVANTS! WARRIORS! DOGS! ALL BUTCHERED, THEIR NECKS TORN TO SHREDS, THEIR FACES TRANSFIXED WITH A LOOK OF ABSOLUTE HORROR. A FEW HAD TRIED TO FIGHT...
"THERE WAS NO BLOOD HERE, EITHER.
THIS IS MADNESS!
MOTHER ...I...I...
AAAAAAAAA
ARON!
"I WAS TOO LATE!
LET HIM GO, BUTCHER!
NOT BUTCHER, CHILD... VAMPIRE.
FATHER!
AYE, DAUGHTER. FATHER AND VAMPIRE BOTH!
AND I HUNGER FOR YOUR BLOOD.

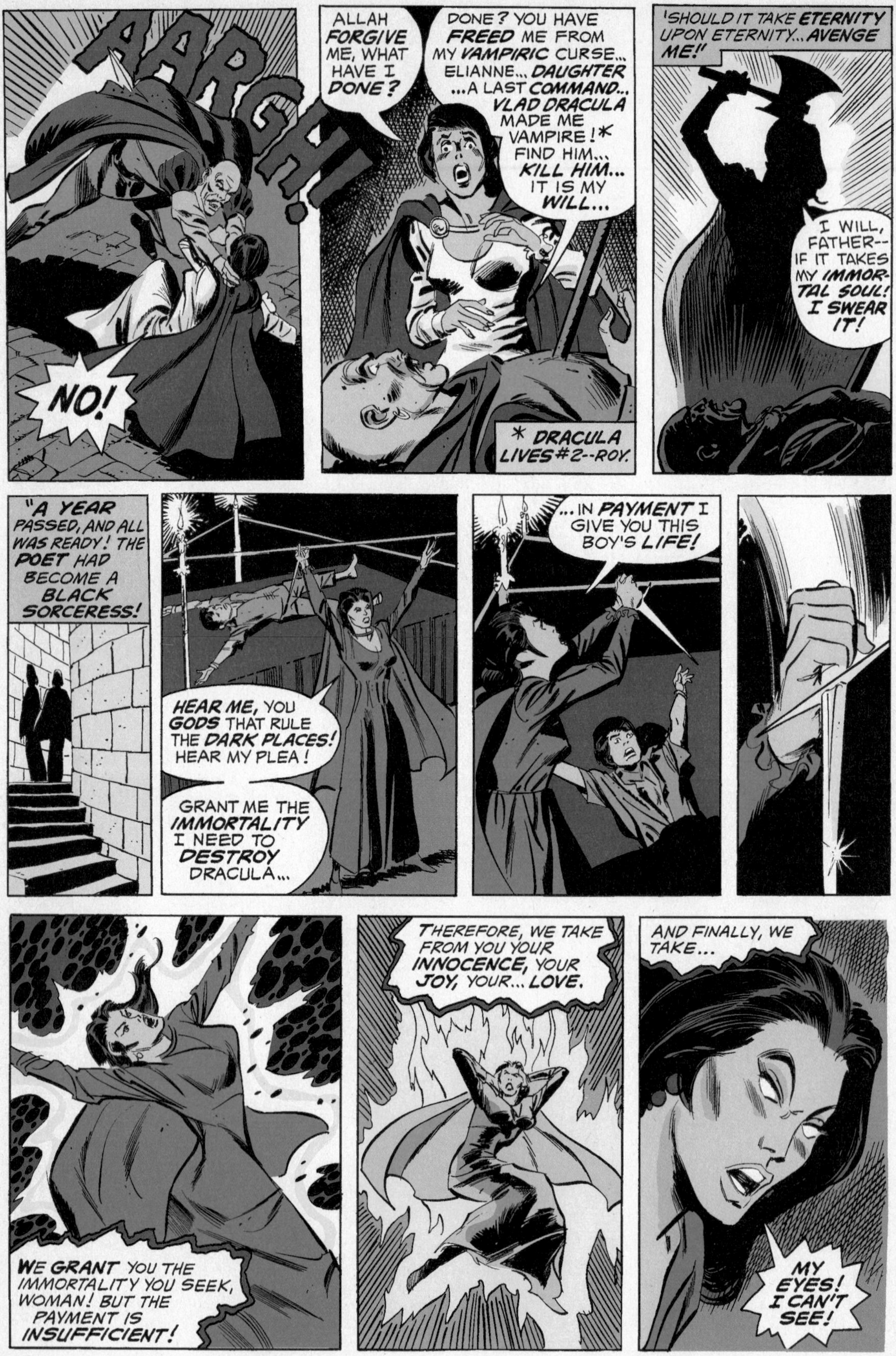
AARGH!
NO!
ALLAH FORGIVE ME, WHAT HAVE I DONE?
DONE? YOU HAVE FREED ME FROM MY VAMPIRIC CURSE... ELIANNE... DAUGHTER ...A LAST COMMAND... VLAD DRACULA MADE ME VAMPIRE!* FIND HIM... KILL HIM... IT IS MY WILL...
* DRACULA LIVES #2--ROY.
'SHOULD IT TAKE ETERNITY UPON ETERNITY... AVENGE ME!'
I WILL, FATHER-- IF IT TAKES MY IMMORTAL SOUL! I SWEAR IT!
"A YEAR PASSED, AND ALL WAS READY! THE POET HAD BECOME A BLACK SORCERESS!
HEAR ME, YOU GODS THAT RULE THE DARK PLACES! HEAR MY PLEA!
GRANT ME THE IMMORTALITY I NEED TO DESTROY DRACULA...
...IN PAYMENT I GIVE YOU THIS BOY'S LIFE!
WE GRANT YOU THE IMMORTALITY YOU SEEK, WOMAN! BUT THE PAYMENT IS INSUFFICIENT!
THEREFORE, WE TAKE FROM YOU YOUR INNOCENCE, YOUR JOY, YOUR... LOVE.
AND FINALLY, WE TAKE...
MY EYES! I CAN'T SEE!

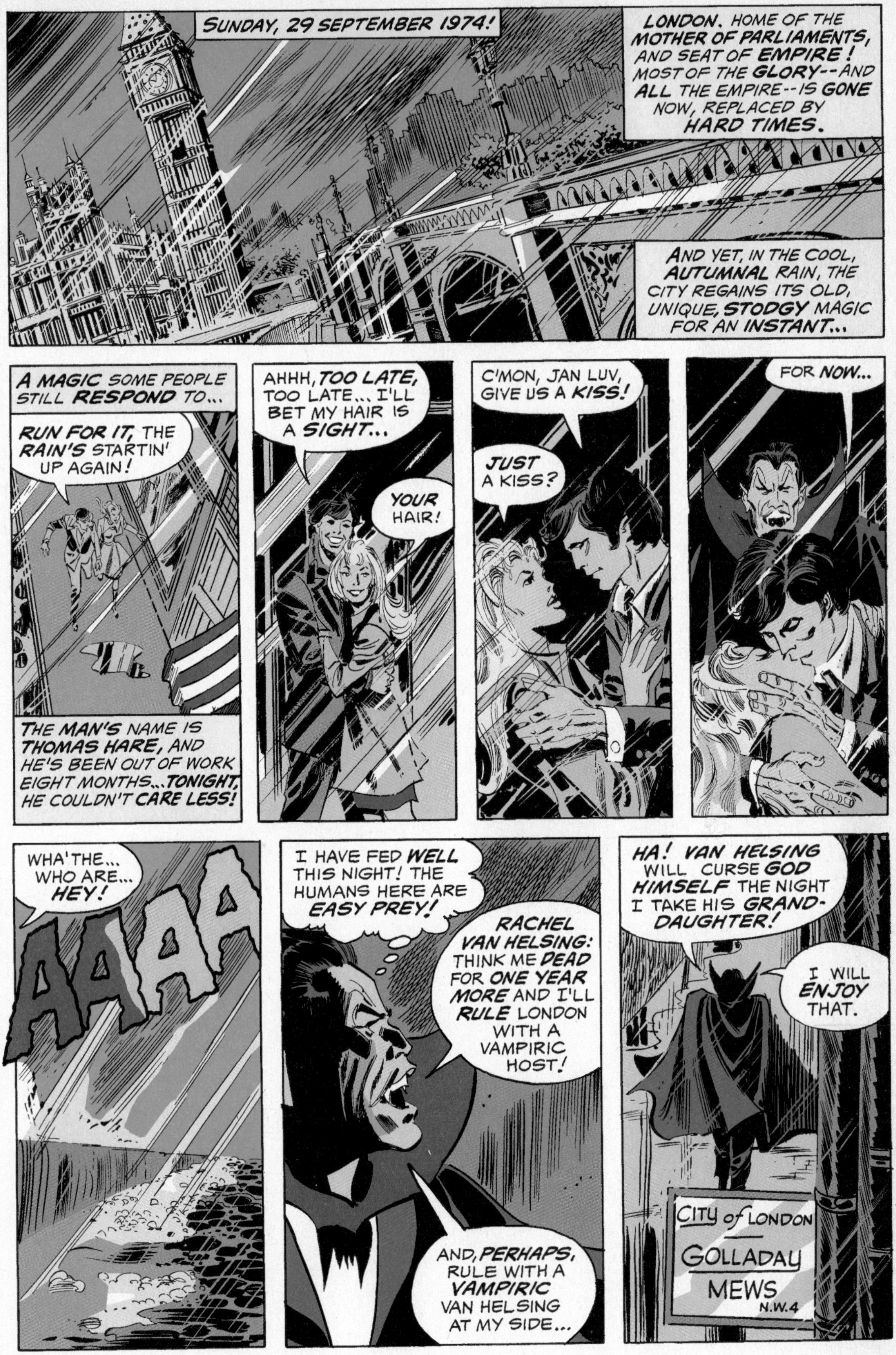
SUNDAY, 29 SEPTEMBER 1974!
LONDON. HOME OF THE MOTHER OF PARLIAMENTS, AND SEAT OF EMPIRE! MOST OF THE GLORY--AND ALL THE EMPIRE--IS GONE NOW, REPLACED BY HARD TIMES.
AND YET, IN THE COOL, AUTUMNAL RAIN, THE CITY REGAINS ITS OLD, UNIQUE, STODGY MAGIC FOR AN INSTANT...
A MAGIC SOME PEOPLE STILL RESPOND TO...
RUN FOR IT, THE RAIN'S STARTIN' UP AGAIN!
THE MAN'S NAME IS THOMAS HARE, AND HE'S BEEN OUT OF WORK EIGHT MONTHS...TONIGHT, HE COULDN'T CARE LESS!
AHHH, TOO LATE, TOO LATE... I'LL BET MY HAIR IS A SIGHT...
YOUR HAIR!
C'MON, JAN LUV, GIVE US A KISS!
JUST A KISS?
FOR NOW...
WHA'THE... WHO ARE... HEY!
AAAA
I HAVE FED WELL THIS NIGHT! THE HUMANS HERE ARE EASY PREY!
RACHEL VAN HELSING: THINK ME DEAD FOR ONE YEAR MORE AND I'LL RULE LONDON WITH A VAMPIRIC HOST!
AND, PERHAPS, RULE WITH A VAMPIRIC VAN HELSING AT MY SIDE...
HA! VAN HELSING WILL CURSE GOD HIMSELF THE NIGHT I TAKE HIS GRAND-DAUGHTER!
I WILL ENJOY THAT.
CITY of LONDON
GOLLADAY MEWS
N.W.4

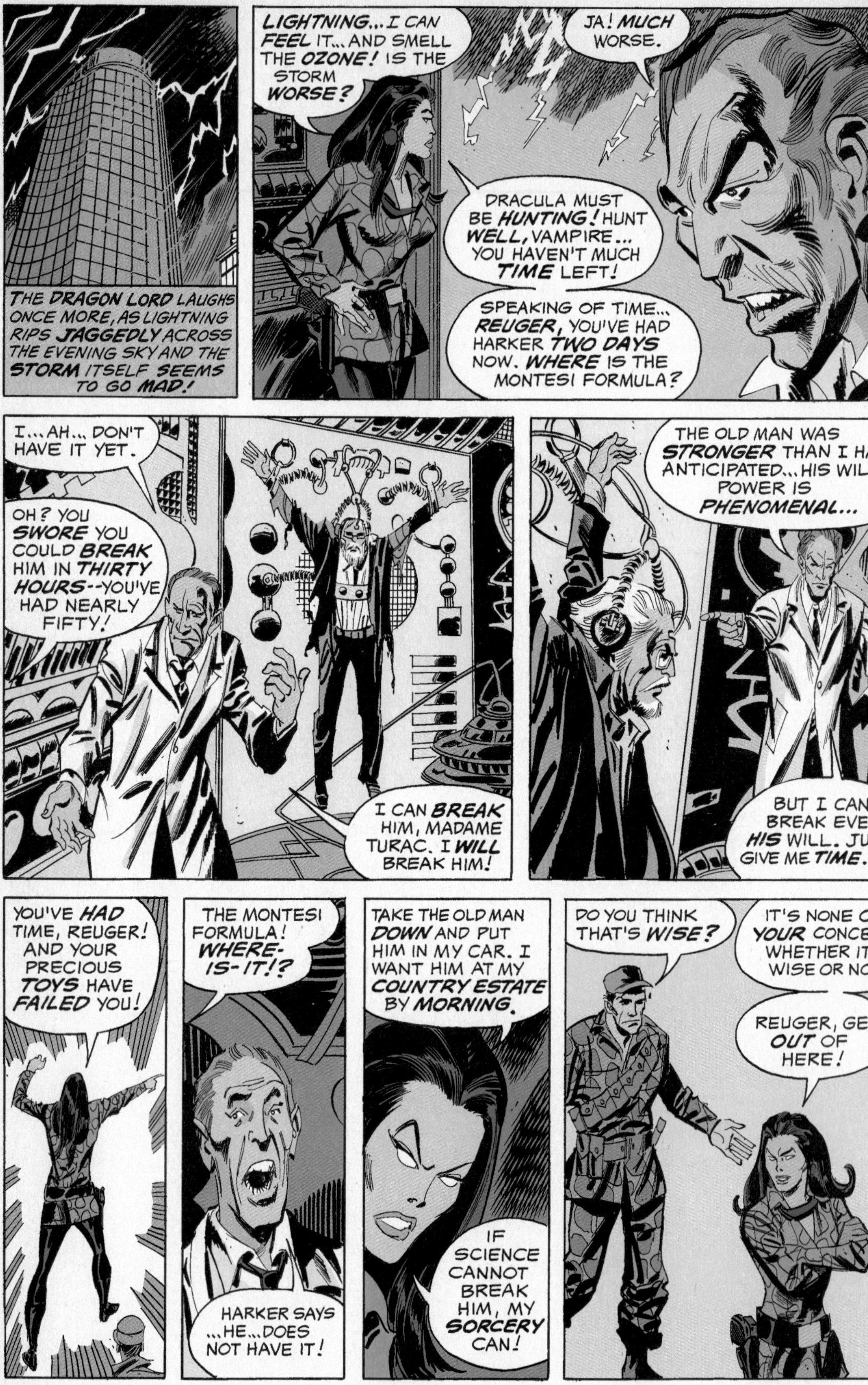
THE DRAGON LORD LAUGHS ONCE MORE, AS LIGHTNING RIPS JAGGEDLY ACROSS THE EVENING SKY AND THE STORM ITSELF SEEMS TO GO MAD!
LIGHTNING... I CAN FEEL IT... AND SMELL THE OZONE! IS THE STORM WORSE?
JA! MUCH WORSE.
DRACULA MUST BE HUNTING! HUNT WELL, VAMPIRE... YOU HAVEN'T MUCH TIME LEFT!
SPEAKING OF TIME... REUGER, YOU'VE HAD HARKER TWO DAYS NOW. WHERE IS THE MONTESI FORMULA?
I... AH... DON'T HAVE IT YET.
OH? YOU SWORE YOU COULD BREAK HIM IN THIRTY HOURS--YOU'VE HAD NEARLY FIFTY!
I CAN BREAK HIM, MADAME TURAC. I WILL BREAK HIM!
THE OLD MAN WAS STRONGER THAN I HAD ANTICIPATED... HIS WILL POWER IS PHENOMENAL...
BUT I CAN BREAK EVEN HIS WILL. JUST GIVE ME TIME...
YOU'VE HAD TIME, REUGER! AND YOUR PRECIOUS TOYS HAVE FAILED YOU!
THE MONTESI FORMULA! WHERE-IS-IT!?
HARKER SAYS ...HE...DOES NOT HAVE IT!
TAKE THE OLD MAN DOWN AND PUT HIM IN MY CAR. I WANT HIM AT MY COUNTRY ESTATE BY MORNING.
IF SCIENCE CANNOT BREAK HIM, MY SORCERY CAN!
DO YOU THINK THAT'S WISE?
IT'S NONE OF YOUR CONCERN WHETHER IT'S WISE OR NOT.
REUGER, GET OUT OF HERE!

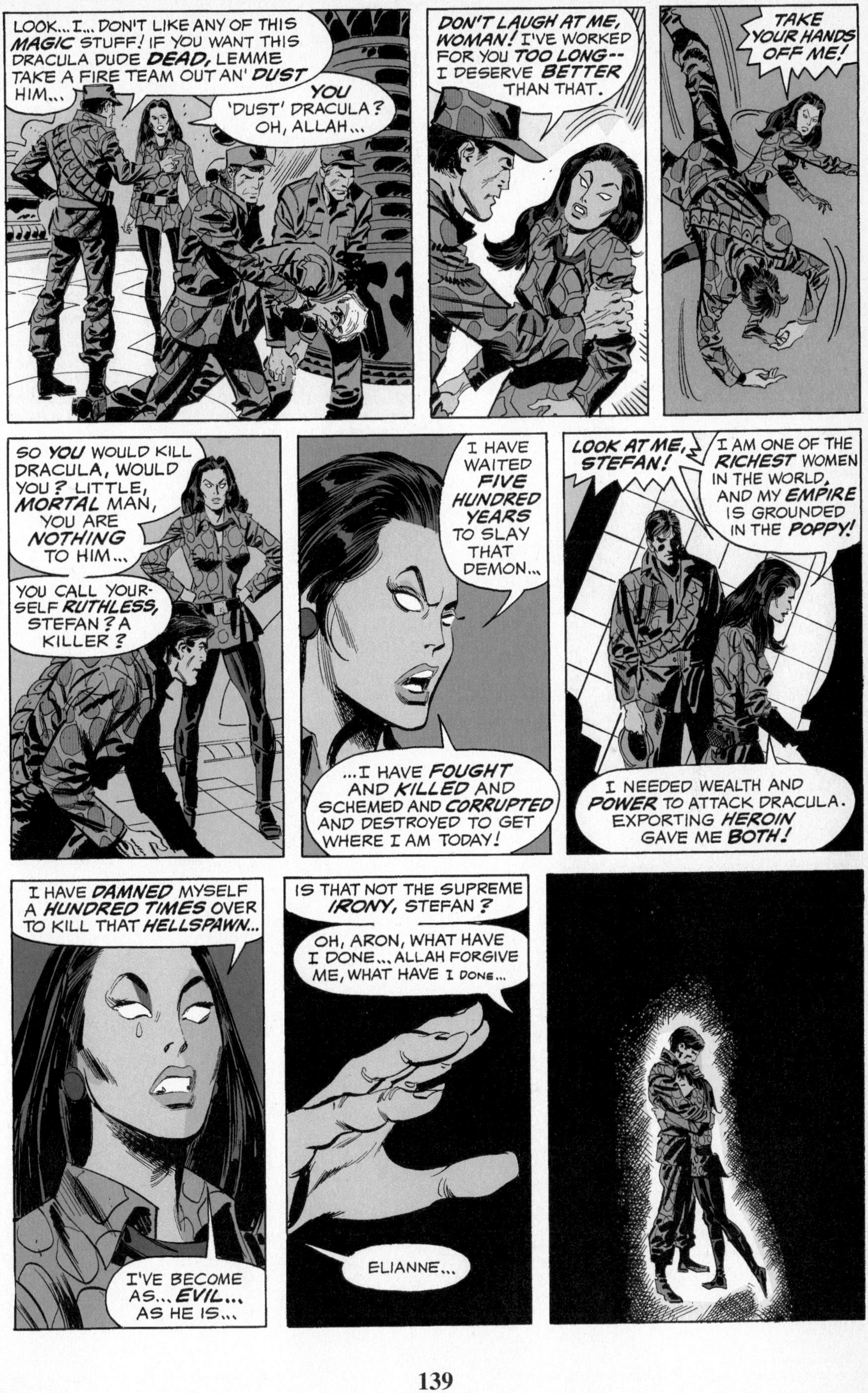
LOOK... I... DON'T LIKE ANY OF THIS MAGIC STUFF! IF YOU WANT THIS DRACULA DUDE DEAD, LEMME TAKE A FIRE TEAM OUT AN' DUST HIM...
YOU 'DUST' DRACULA? OH, ALLAH...
DON'T LAUGH AT ME, WOMAN! I'VE WORKED FOR YOU TOO LONG-- I DESERVE BETTER THAN THAT.
TAKE YOUR HANDS OFF ME!
SO YOU WOULD KILL DRACULA, WOULD YOU? LITTLE, MORTAL MAN, YOU ARE NOTHING TO HIM...
YOU CALL YOURSELF RUTHLESS, STEFAN? A KILLER?
I HAVE WAITED FIVE HUNDRED YEARS TO SLAY THAT DEMON...
...I HAVE FOUGHT AND KILLED AND SCHEMED AND CORRUPTED AND DESTROYED TO GET WHERE I AM TODAY!
LOOK AT ME, STEFAN!
I AM ONE OF THE RICHEST WOMEN IN THE WORLD, AND MY EMPIRE IS GROUNDED IN THE POPPY!
I NEEDED WEALTH AND POWER TO ATTACK DRACULA. EXPORTING HEROIN GAVE ME BOTH!
I HAVE DAMNED MYSELF A HUNDRED TIMES OVER TO KILL THAT HELLSPAWN...
I'VE BECOME AS... EVIL... AS HE IS...
IS THAT NOT THE SUPREME IRONY, STEFAN?
OH, ARON, WHAT HAVE I DONE... ALLAH FORGIVE ME, WHAT HAVE I DONE...
ELIANNE...

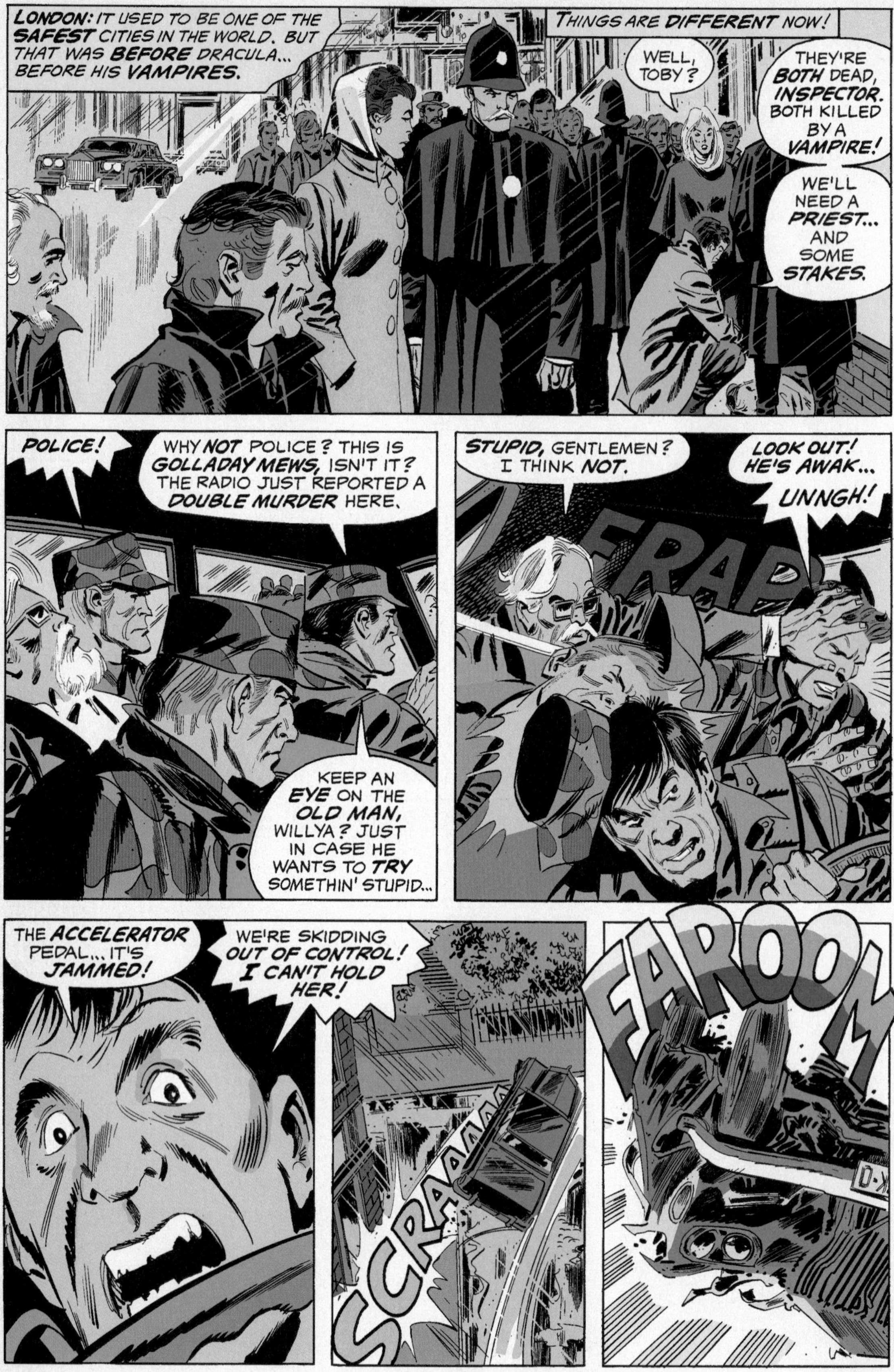
LONDON: IT USED TO BE ONE OF THE SAFEST CITIES IN THE WORLD. BUT THAT WAS BEFORE DRACULA... BEFORE HIS VAMPIRES.
THINGS ARE DIFFERENT NOW!
WELL, TOBY?
THEY'RE BOTH DEAD, INSPECTOR. BOTH KILLED BY A VAMPIRE!
WE'LL NEED A PRIEST... AND SOME STAKES.
POLICE!
WHY NOT POLICE? THIS IS GOLLADAY MEWS, ISN'T IT? THE RADIO JUST REPORTED A DOUBLE MURDER HERE.
KEEP AN EYE ON THE OLD MAN, WILLYA? JUST IN CASE HE WANTS TO TRY SOMETHIN' STUPID...
STUPID, GENTLEMEN? I THINK NOT.
FRAP
LOOK OUT! HE'S AWAK... UNNGH!
THE ACCELERATOR PEDAL... IT'S JAMMED!
WE'RE SKIDDING OUT OF CONTROL! I CAN'T HOLD HER!
SCRAAAAA
FAROOM

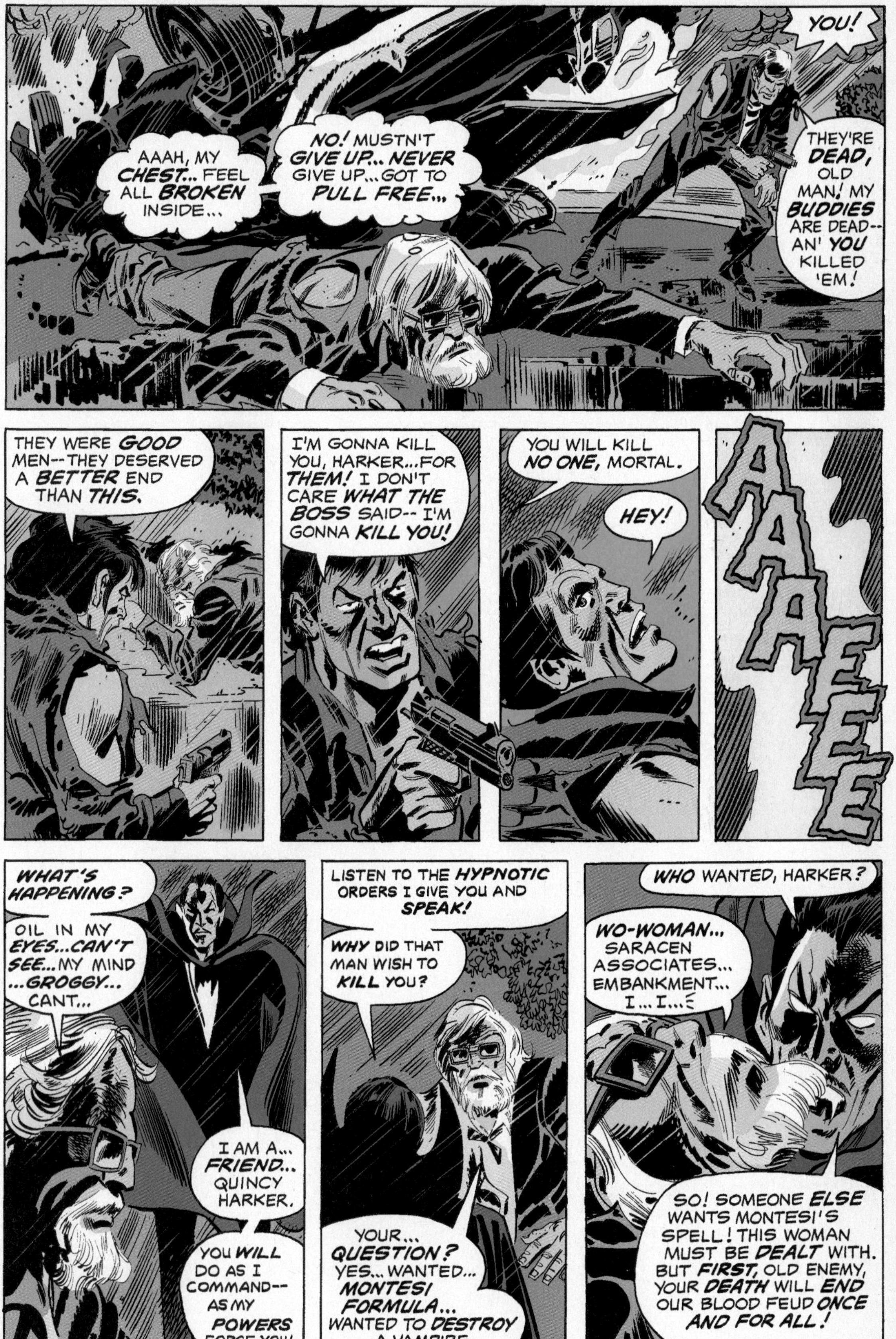
YOU!
AAAH, MY CHEST... FEEL ALL BROKEN INSIDE...
NO! MUSTN'T GIVE UP... NEVER GIVE UP... GOT TO PULL FREE...
THEY'RE DEAD, OLD MAN! MY BUDDIES ARE DEAD-- AN' YOU KILLED 'EM!
THEY WERE GOOD MEN--THEY DESERVED A BETTER END THAN THIS.
I'M GONNA KILL YOU, HARKER... FOR THEM! I DON'T CARE WHAT THE BOSS SAID-- I'M GONNA KILL YOU!
YOU WILL KILL NO ONE, MORTAL.
HEY!
AAAAEEEE
WHAT'S HAPPENING?
OIL IN MY EYES... CAN'T SEE... MY MIND ...GROGGY... CANT...
I AM A... FRIEND... QUINCY HARKER.
YOU WILL DO AS I COMMAND-- AS MY POWERS FORCE YOU!
LISTEN TO THE HYPNOTIC ORDERS I GIVE YOU AND SPEAK!
WHY DID THAT MAN WISH TO KILL YOU?
YOUR... QUESTION? YES... WANTED... MONTESI FORMULA... WANTED TO DESTROY A VAMPIRE...
WHO WANTED, HARKER?
WO-WOMAN... SARACEN ASSOCIATES... EMBANKMENT... I... I...
SO! SOMEONE ELSE WANTS MONTESI'S SPELL! THIS WOMAN MUST BE DEALT WITH. BUT FIRST, OLD ENEMY, YOUR DEATH WILL END OUR BLOOD FEUD ONCE AND FOR ALL!

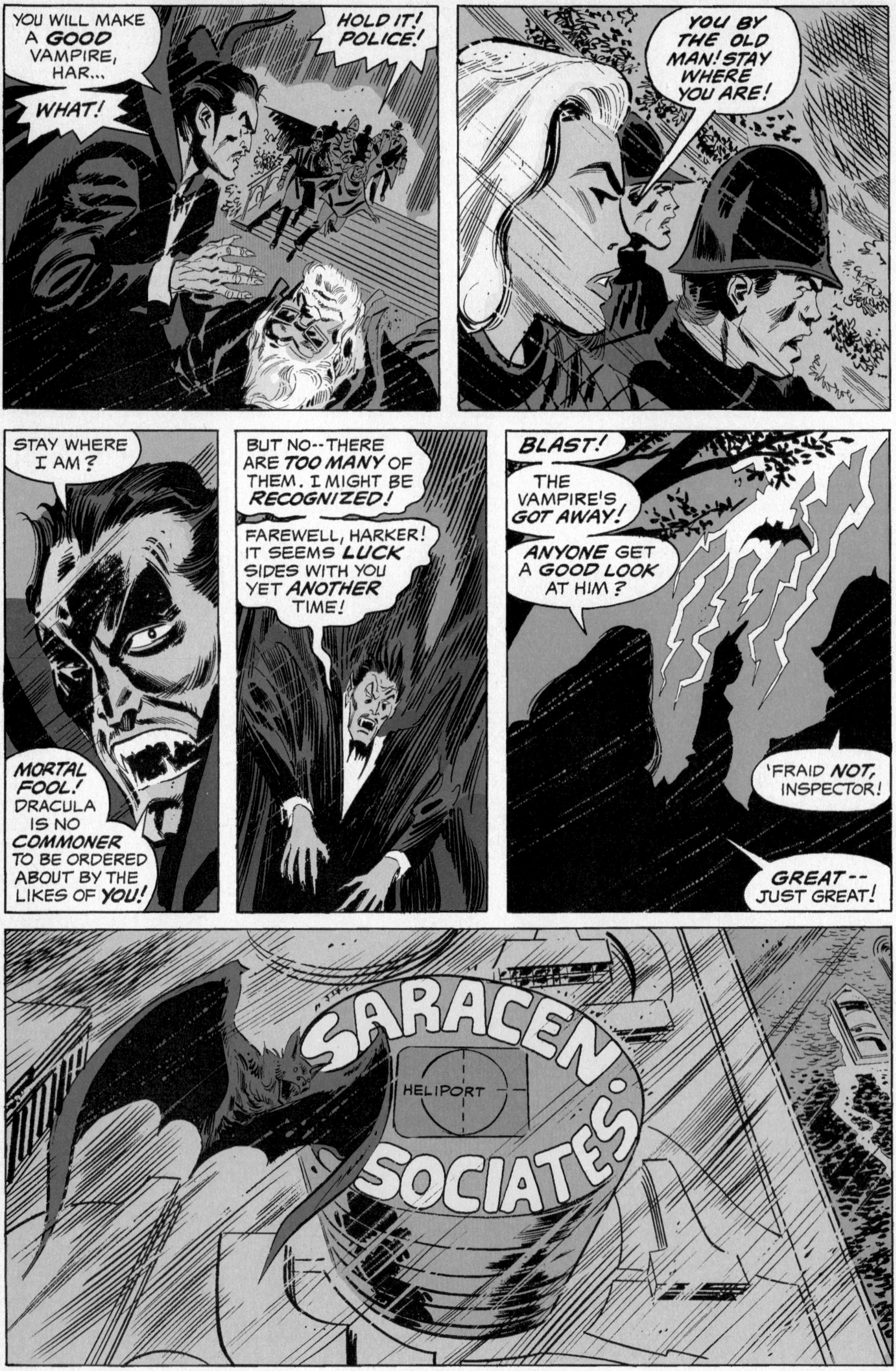

YOU WILL MAKE A GOOD VAMPIRE, HAR...
HOLD IT! POLICE!
WHAT!
YOU BY THE OLD MAN! STAY WHERE YOU ARE!
STAY WHERE I AM?
MORTAL FOOL! DRACULA IS NO COMMONER TO BE ORDERED ABOUT BY THE LIKES OF YOU!
BUT NO--THERE ARE TOO MANY OF THEM. I MIGHT BE RECOGNIZED!
FAREWELL, HARKER! IT SEEMS LUCK SIDES WITH YOU YET ANOTHER TIME!
BLAST!
THE VAMPIRE'S GOT AWAY!
ANYONE GET A GOOD LOOK AT HIM?
'FRAID NOT, INSPECTOR!
GREAT-- JUST GREAT!
SARACEN
SOCIATES
HELIPORT

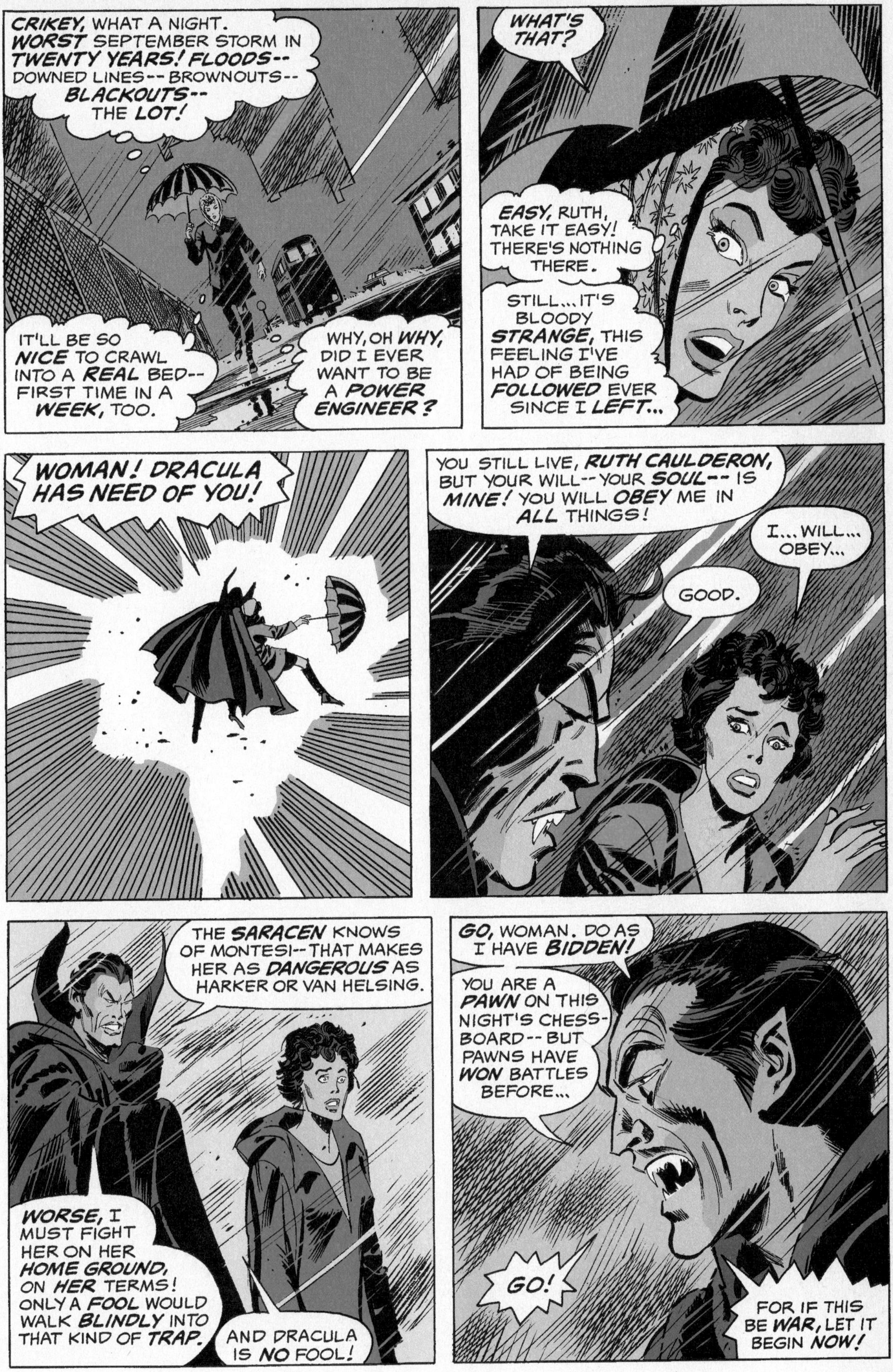
CRIKEY, WHAT A NIGHT. WORST SEPTEMBER STORM IN TWENTY YEARS! FLOODS-- DOWNED LINES-- BROWNOUTS-- BLACKOUTS-- THE LOT!
IT'LL BE SO NICE TO CRAWL INTO A REAL BED-- FIRST TIME IN A WEEK, TOO.
WHY, OH WHY, DID I EVER WANT TO BE A POWER ENGINEER?
WHAT'S THAT?
EASY, RUTH, TAKE IT EASY! THERE'S NOTHING THERE.
STILL... IT'S BLOODY STRANGE, THIS FEELING I'VE HAD OF BEING FOLLOWED EVER SINCE I LEFT...
WOMAN! DRACULA HAS NEED OF YOU!
YOU STILL LIVE, RUTH CAULDERON, BUT YOUR WILL-- YOUR SOUL-- IS MINE! YOU WILL OBEY ME IN ALL THINGS!
I... WILL... OBEY...
GOOD.
THE SARACEN KNOWS OF MONTESI--THAT MAKES HER AS DANGEROUS AS HARKER OR VAN HELSING.
WORSE, I MUST FIGHT HER ON HER HOME GROUND, ON HER TERMS! ONLY A FOOL WOULD WALK BLINDLY INTO THAT KIND OF TRAP.
AND DRACULA IS NO FOOL!
GO, WOMAN. DO AS I HAVE BIDDEN!
YOU ARE A PAWN ON THIS NIGHT'S CHESS-BOARD-- BUT PAWNS HAVE WON BATTLES BEFORE...
GO!
FOR IF THIS BE WAR, LET IT BEGIN NOW!

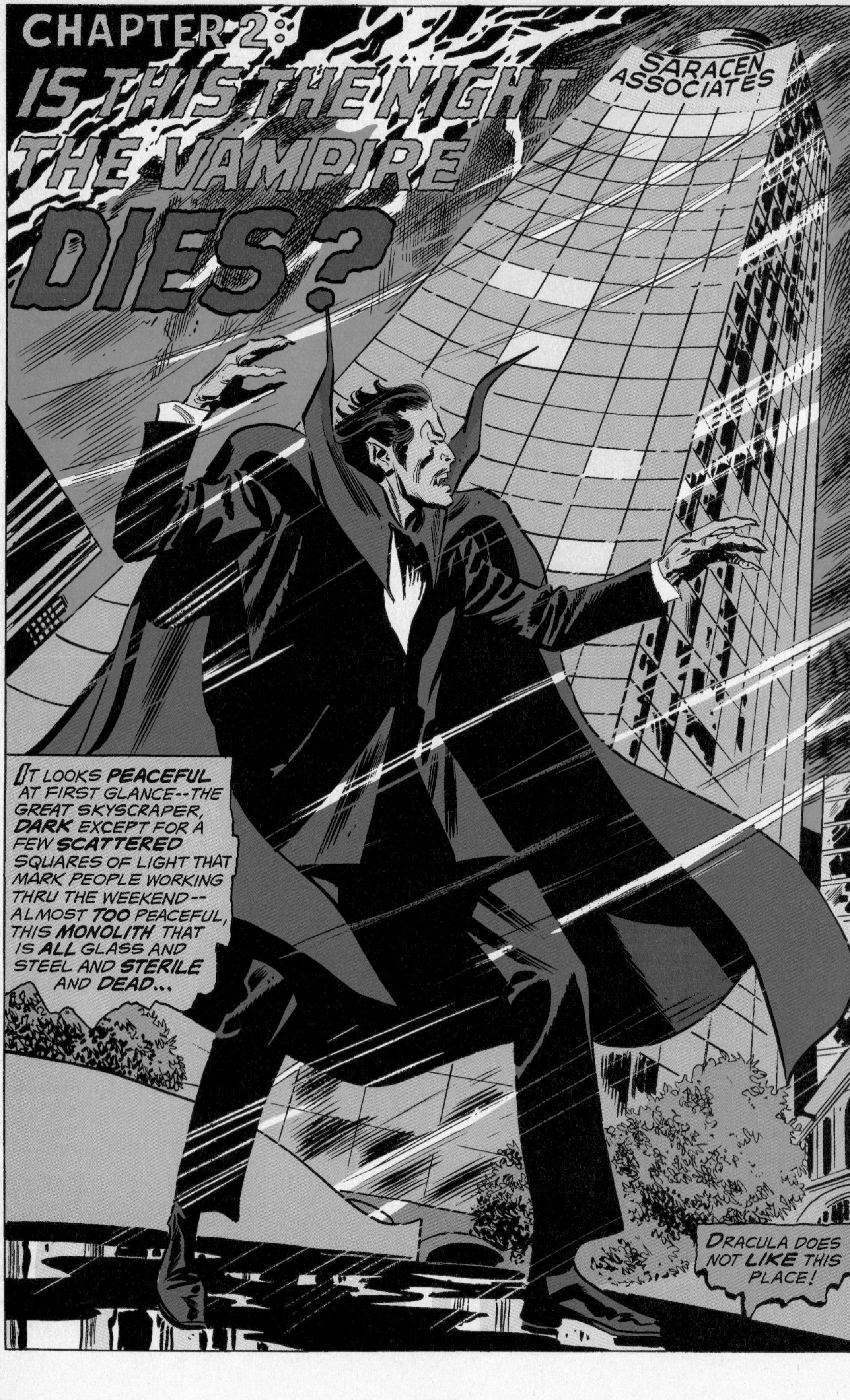
CHAPTER 2:
IS THIS THE NIGHT THE VAMPIRE DIES?
SARACEN ASSOCIATES
IT LOOKS PEACEFUL AT FIRST GLANCE--THE GREAT SKYSCRAPER, DARK EXCEPT FOR A FEW SCATTERED SQUARES OF LIGHT THAT MARK PEOPLE WORKING THRU THE WEEKEND--ALMOST TOO PEACEFUL, THIS MONOLITH THAT IS ALL GLASS AND STEEL AND STERILE AND DEAD...
DRACULA DOES NOT LIKE THIS PLACE!

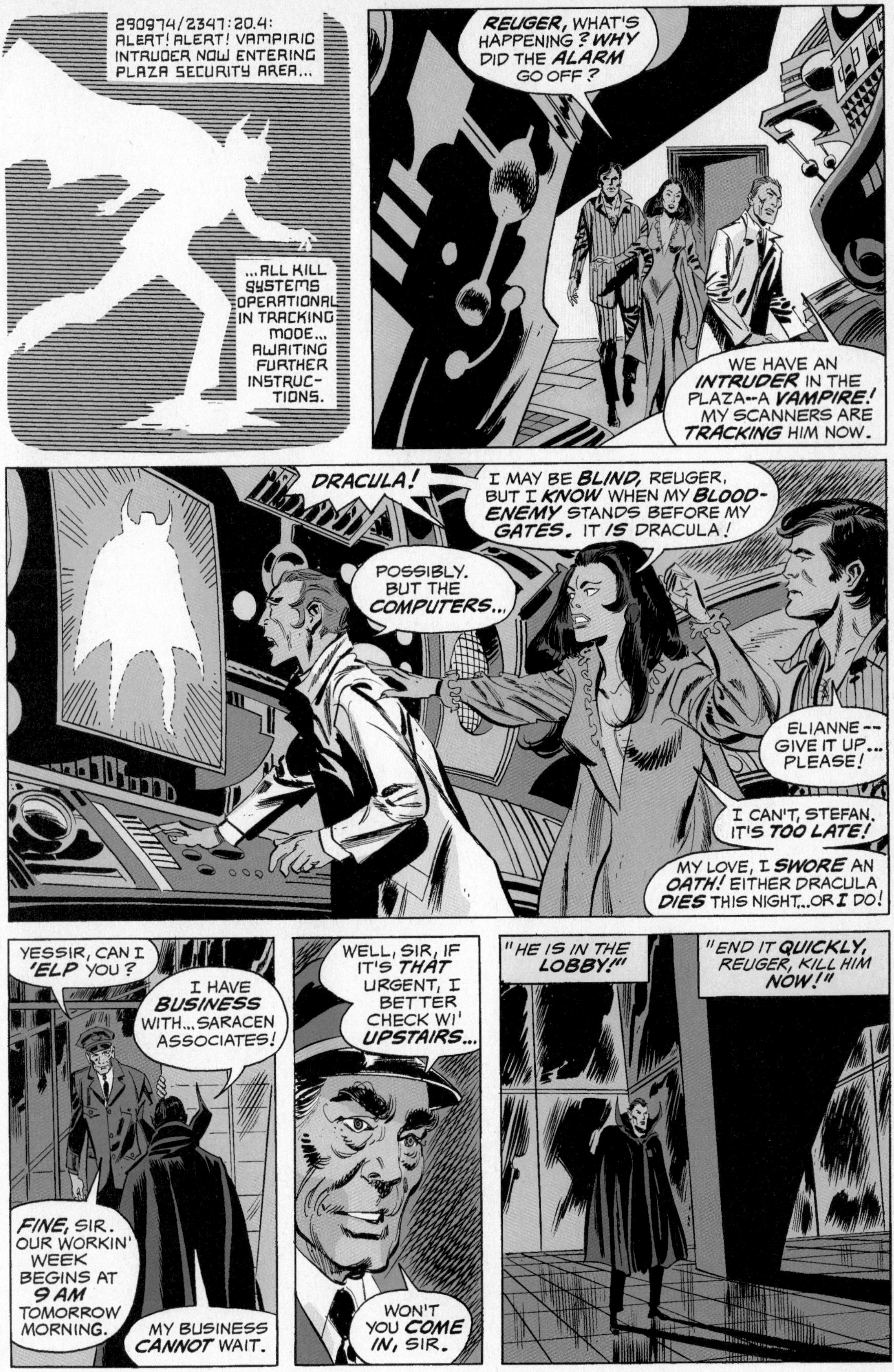
290974/2347:20.4: ALERT! ALERT! VAMPIRIC INTRUDER NOW ENTERING PLAZA SECURITY AREA...
...ALL KILL SYSTEMS OPERATIONAL IN TRACKING MODE... AWAITING FURTHER INSTRUC-TIONS.
REUGER, WHAT'S HAPPENING? WHY DID THE ALARM GO OFF?
WE HAVE AN INTRUDER IN THE PLAZA--A VAMPIRE! MY SCANNERS ARE TRACKING HIM NOW.
DRACULA!
I MAY BE BLIND, REUGER, BUT I KNOW WHEN MY BLOOD-ENEMY STANDS BEFORE MY GATES. IT IS DRACULA!
POSSIBLY. BUT THE COMPUTERS...
ELIANNE--GIVE IT UP... PLEASE!
I CAN'T, STEFAN. IT'S TOO LATE!
MY LOVE, I SWORE AN OATH! EITHER DRACULA DIES THIS NIGHT...OR I DO!
YESSIR, CAN I 'ELP YOU?
I HAVE BUSINESS WITH... SARACEN ASSOCIATES!
FINE, SIR. OUR WORKIN' WEEK BEGINS AT 9 AM TOMORROW MORNING.
MY BUSINESS CANNOT WAIT.
WELL, SIR, IF IT'S THAT URGENT, I BETTER CHECK WI' UPSTAIRS...
WON'T YOU COME IN, SIR.
"HE IS IN THE LOBBY!"
"END IT QUICKLY, REUGER, KILL HIM NOW!"

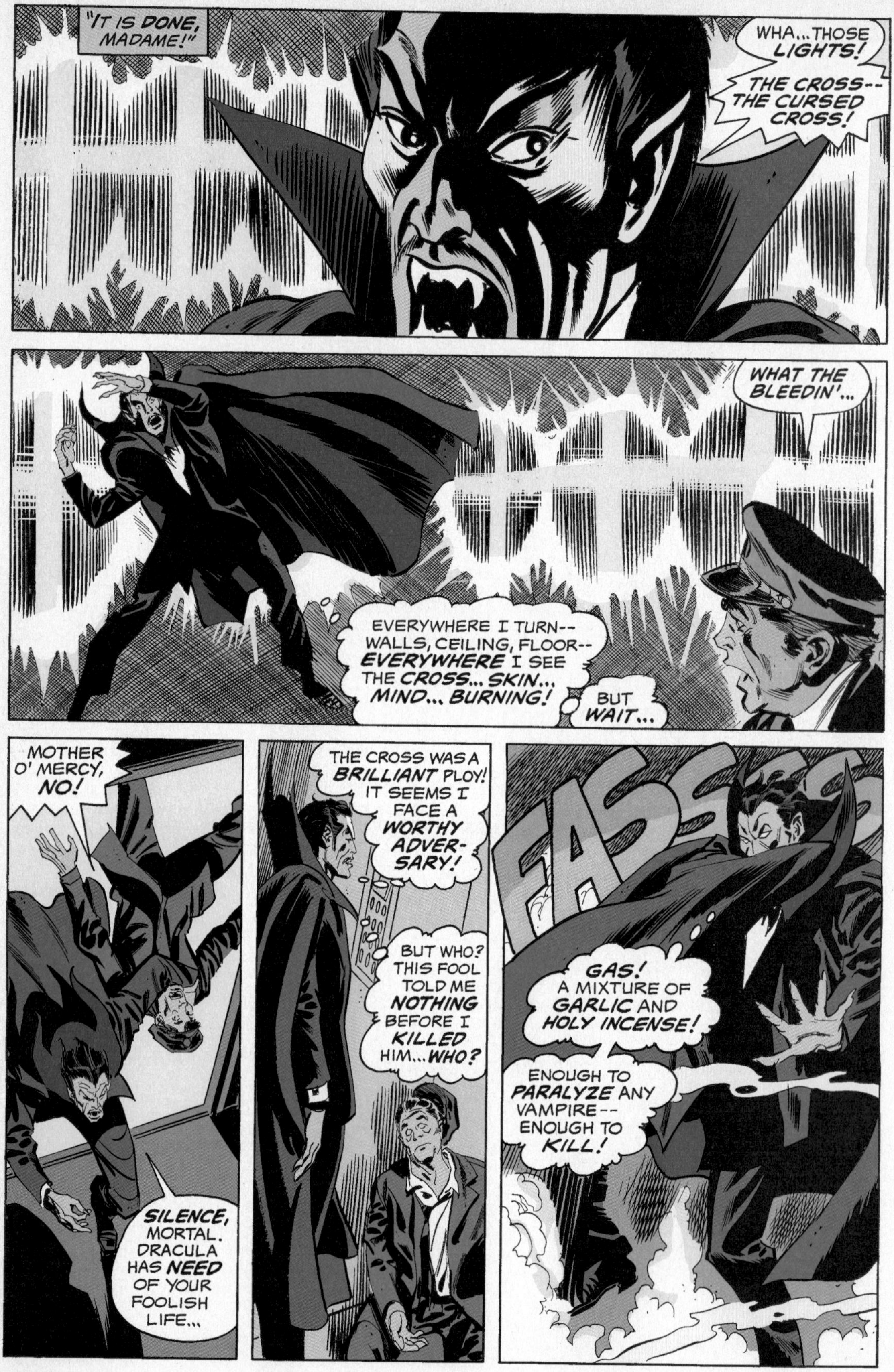
"IT IS DONE, MADAME!"
WHA... THOSE LIGHTS!
THE CROSS-- THE CURSED CROSS!
WHAT THE BLEEDIN'...
EVERYWHERE I TURN-- WALLS, CEILING, FLOOR-- EVERYWHERE I SEE THE CROSS... SKIN... MIND... BURNING!
BUT WAIT...
MOTHER O' MERCY, NO!
SILENCE, MORTAL. DRACULA HAS NEED OF YOUR FOOLISH LIFE...
THE CROSS WAS A BRILLIANT PLOY! IT SEEMS I FACE A WORTHY ADVERSARY!
BUT WHO? THIS FOOL TOLD ME NOTHING BEFORE I KILLED HIM... WHO?
FASSSS
GAS! A MIXTURE OF GARLIC AND HOLY INCENSE!
ENOUGH TO PARALYZE ANY VAMPIRE-- ENOUGH TO KILL!

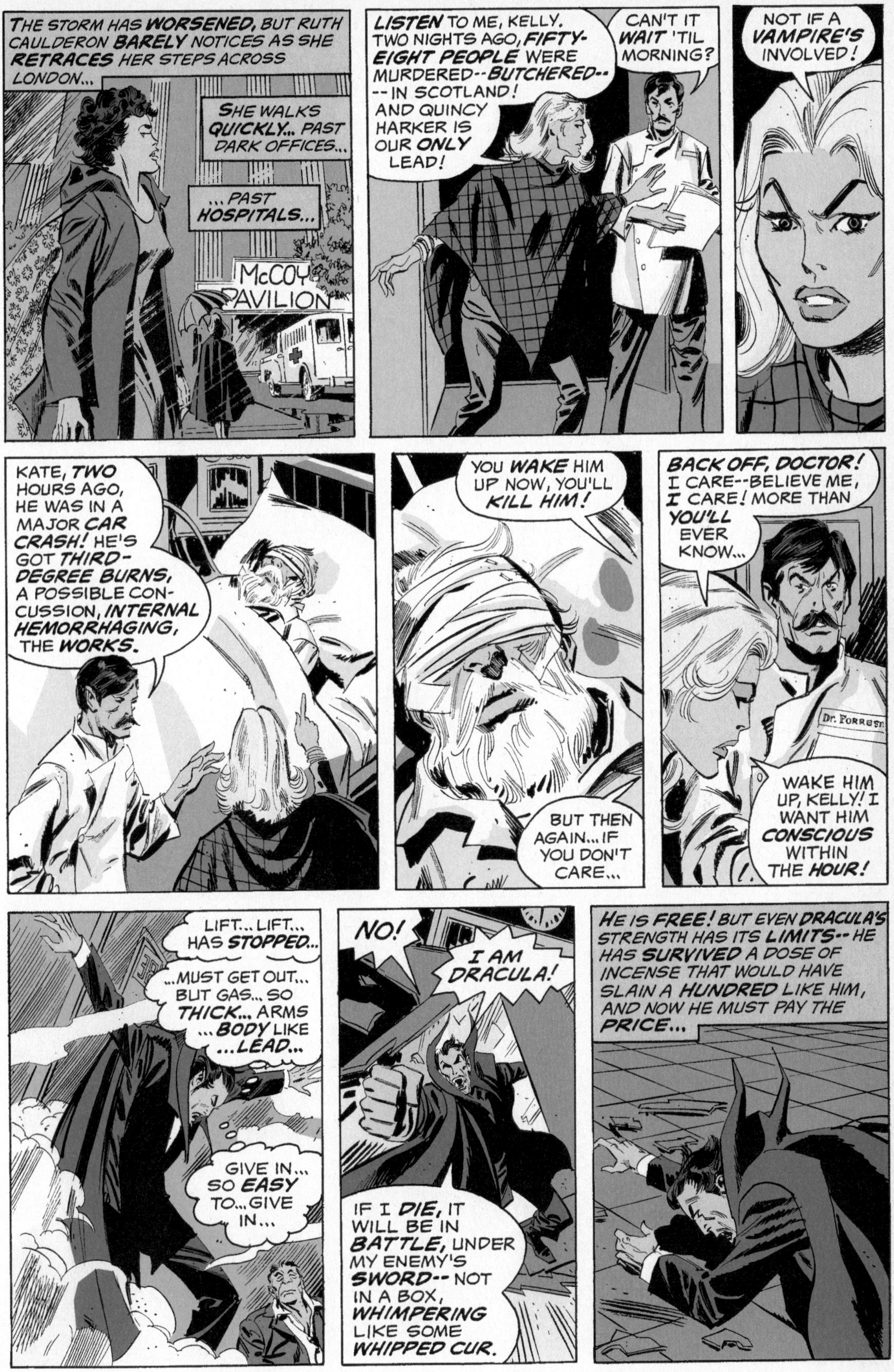
THE STORM HAS WORSENED, BUT RUTH CAULDERON BARELY NOTICES AS SHE RETRACES HER STEPS ACROSS LONDON...
SHE WALKS QUICKLY... PAST DARK OFFICES...
...PAST HOSPITALS...
McCOY PAVILION
LISTEN TO ME, KELLY. TWO NIGHTS AGO, FIFTY-EIGHT PEOPLE WERE MURDERED--BUTCHERED----IN SCOTLAND! AND QUINCY HARKER IS OUR ONLY LEAD!
CAN'T IT WAIT 'TIL MORNING?
NOT IF A VAMPIRE'S INVOLVED!
KATE, TWO HOURS AGO, HE WAS IN A MAJOR CAR CRASH! HE'S GOT THIRD-DEGREE BURNS, A POSSIBLE CON-CUSSION, INTERNAL HEMORRHAGING, THE WORKS.
YOU WAKE HIM UP NOW, YOU'LL KILL HIM!
BUT THEN AGAIN... IF YOU DON'T CARE...
BACK OFF, DOCTOR! I CARE--BELIEVE ME, I CARE! MORE THAN YOU'LL EVER KNOW...
Dr. Forrest
WAKE HIM UP, KELLY! I WANT HIM CONSCIOUS WITHIN THE HOUR!
LIFT... LIFT... HAS STOPPED...
...MUST GET OUT... BUT GAS... SO THICK... ARMS ...BODY LIKE ...LEAD...
GIVE IN... SO EASY TO... GIVE IN...
NO!
I AM DRACULA!
IF I DIE, IT WILL BE IN BATTLE, UNDER MY ENEMY'S SWORD-- NOT IN A BOX, WHIMPERING LIKE SOME WHIPPED CUR.
HE IS FREE! BUT EVEN DRACULA'S STRENGTH HAS ITS LIMITS-- HE HAS SURVIVED A DOSE OF INCENSE THAT WOULD HAVE SLAIN A HUNDRED LIKE HIM, AND NOW HE MUST PAY THE PRICE...

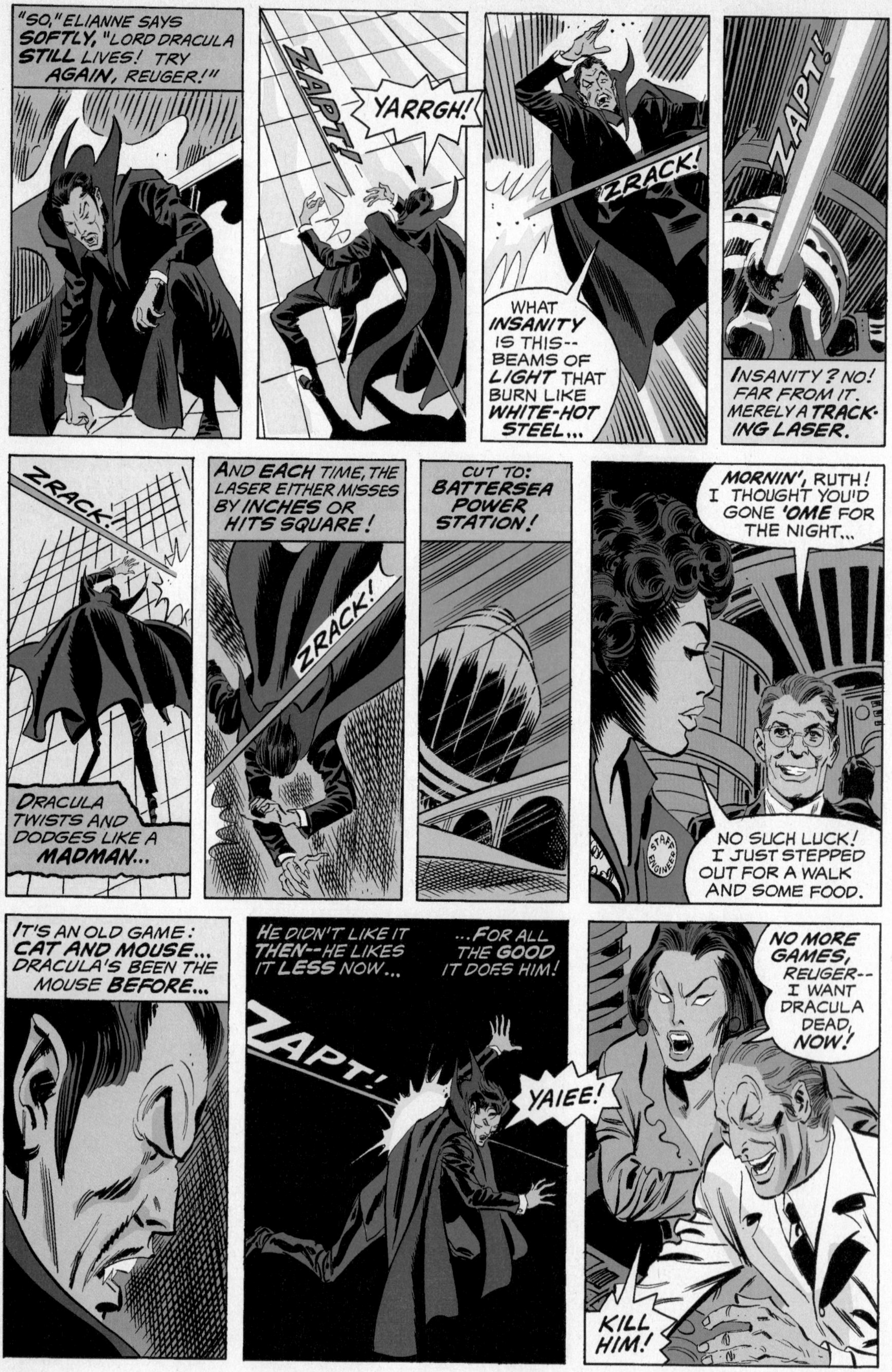
"SO," ELIANNE SAYS SOFTLY, "LORD DRACULA STILL LIVES! TRY AGAIN, REUGER!"
ZAPT!
YARRGH!
ZRACK!
WHAT INSANITY IS THIS-- BEAMS OF LIGHT THAT BURN LIKE WHITE-HOT STEEL...
ZAPT!
INSANITY? NO! FAR FROM IT. MERELY A TRACKING LASER.
ZRACK!
DRACULA TWISTS AND DODGES LIKE A MADMAN...
AND EACH TIME, THE LASER EITHER MISSES BY INCHES OR HITS SQUARE!
ZRACK!
CUT TO: BATTERSEA POWER STATION!
MORNIN', RUTH! I THOUGHT YOU'D GONE 'OME FOR THE NIGHT...
STAFF ENGINEER
NO SUCH LUCK! I JUST STEPPED OUT FOR A WALK AND SOME FOOD.
IT'S AN OLD GAME: CAT AND MOUSE... DRACULA'S BEEN THE MOUSE BEFORE...
HE DIDN'T LIKE IT THEN--HE LIKES IT LESS NOW...
...FOR ALL THE GOOD IT DOES HIM!
ZAPT!
YAIEE!
NO MORE GAMES, REUGER-- I WANT DRACULA DEAD, NOW!
KILL HIM!

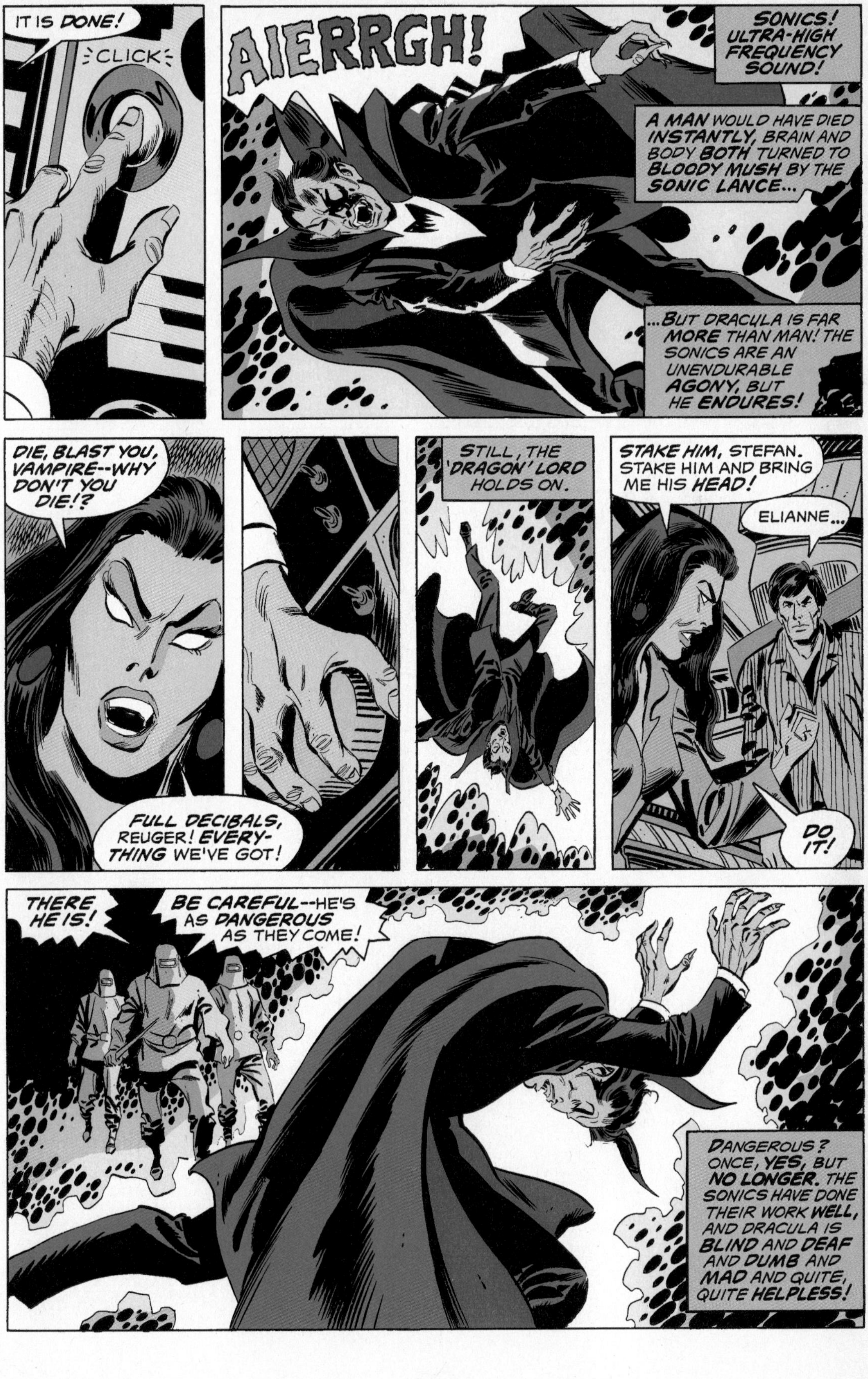
IT IS DONE!
CLICK
AIERRGH!
SONICS! ULTRA-HIGH FREQUENCY SOUND!
A MAN WOULD HAVE DIED INSTANTLY, BRAIN AND BODY BOTH TURNED TO BLOODY MUSH BY THE SONIC LANCE...
...BUT DRACULA IS FAR MORE THAN MAN! THE SONICS ARE AN UNENDURABLE AGONY, BUT HE ENDURES!
DIE, BLAST YOU, VAMPIRE--WHY DON'T YOU DIE!?
FULL DECIBALS, REUGER! EVERY-THING WE'VE GOT!
STILL, THE 'DRAGON' LORD HOLDS ON.
STAKE HIM, STEFAN. STAKE HIM AND BRING ME HIS HEAD!
ELIANNE...
DO IT!
THERE HE IS!
BE CAREFUL--HE'S AS DANGEROUS AS THEY COME!
DANGEROUS? ONCE, YES, BUT NO LONGER. THE SONICS HAVE DONE THEIR WORK WELL, AND DRACULA IS BLIND AND DEAF AND DUMB AND MAD AND QUITE, QUITE HELPLESS!

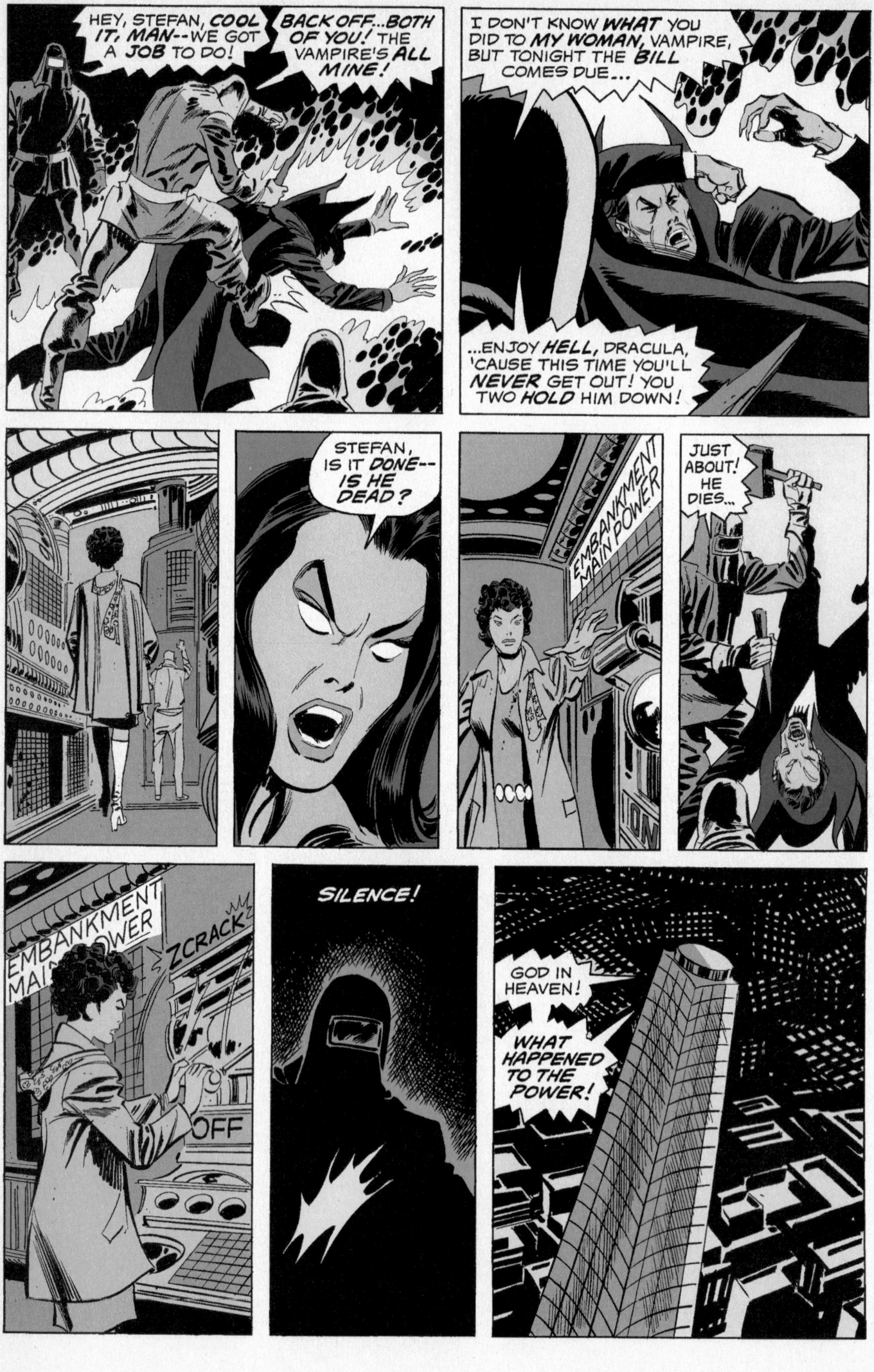
HEY, STEFAN, COOL IT, MAN--WE GOT A JOB TO DO!
BACK OFF...BOTH OF YOU! THE VAMPIRE'S ALL MINE!
I DON'T KNOW WHAT YOU DID TO MY WOMAN, VAMPIRE, BUT TONIGHT THE BILL COMES DUE...
...ENJOY HELL, DRACULA, 'CAUSE THIS TIME YOU'LL NEVER GET OUT! YOU TWO HOLD HIM DOWN!
STEFAN, IS IT DONE-- IS HE DEAD?
EMBANKMENT MAIN POWER
JUST ABOUT! HE DIES...
EMBANKMENT MAIN POWER
ZCRACK
OFF
SILENCE!
GOD IN HEAVEN!
WHAT HAPPENED TO THE POWER!

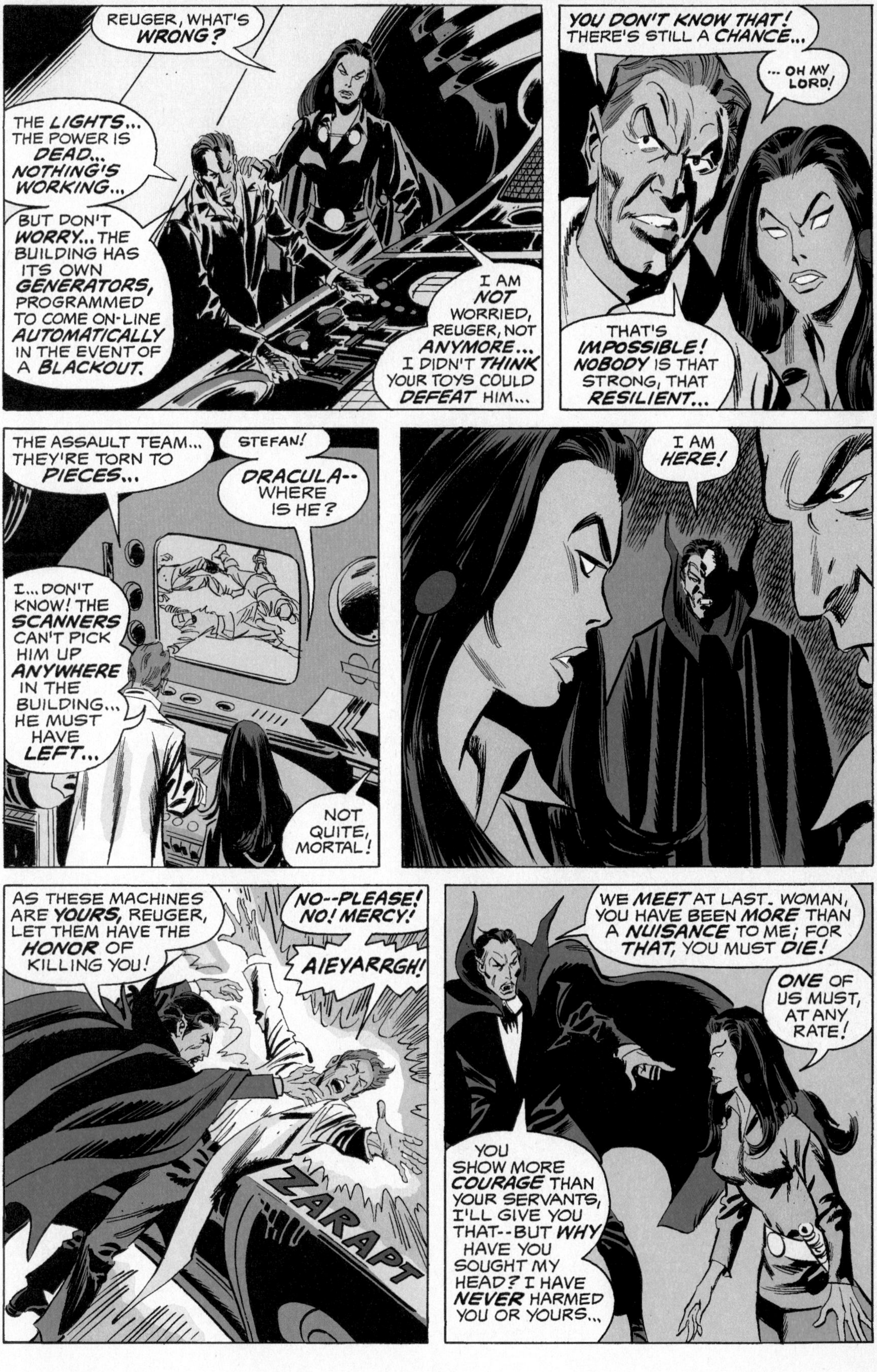
REUGER, WHAT'S WRONG?
THE LIGHTS... THE POWER IS DEAD... NOTHING'S WORKING...,
BUT DON'T WORRY... THE BUILDING HAS ITS OWN GENERATORS, PROGRAMMED TO COME ON-LINE AUTOMATICALLY IN THE EVENT OF A BLACKOUT.
I AM NOT WORRIED, REUGER, NOT ANYMORE... I DIDN'T THINK YOUR TOYS COULD DEFEAT HIM...
YOU DON'T KNOW THAT! THERE'S STILL A CHANCE...
... OH MY LORD!
THAT'S IMPOSSIBLE! NOBODY IS THAT STRONG, THAT RESILIENT...
THE ASSAULT TEAM... THEY'RE TORN TO PIECES...
STEFAN!
DRACULA-- WHERE IS HE?
I... DON'T KNOW! THE SCANNERS CAN'T PICK HIM UP ANYWHERE IN THE BUILDING... HE MUST HAVE LEFT...
NOT QUITE, MORTAL!
I AM HERE!
AS THESE MACHINES ARE YOURS, REUGER, LET THEM HAVE THE HONOR OF KILLING YOU!
NO--PLEASE! NO! MERCY!
AIEYARRGH!
ZARAPT
WE MEET AT LAST. WOMAN, YOU HAVE BEEN MORE THAN A NUISANCE TO ME; FOR THAT, YOU MUST DIE!
ONE OF US MUST, AT ANY RATE!
YOU SHOW MORE COURAGE THAN YOUR SERVANTS, I'LL GIVE YOU THAT--BUT WHY HAVE YOU SOUGHT MY HEAD? I HAVE NEVER HARMED YOU OR YOURS...

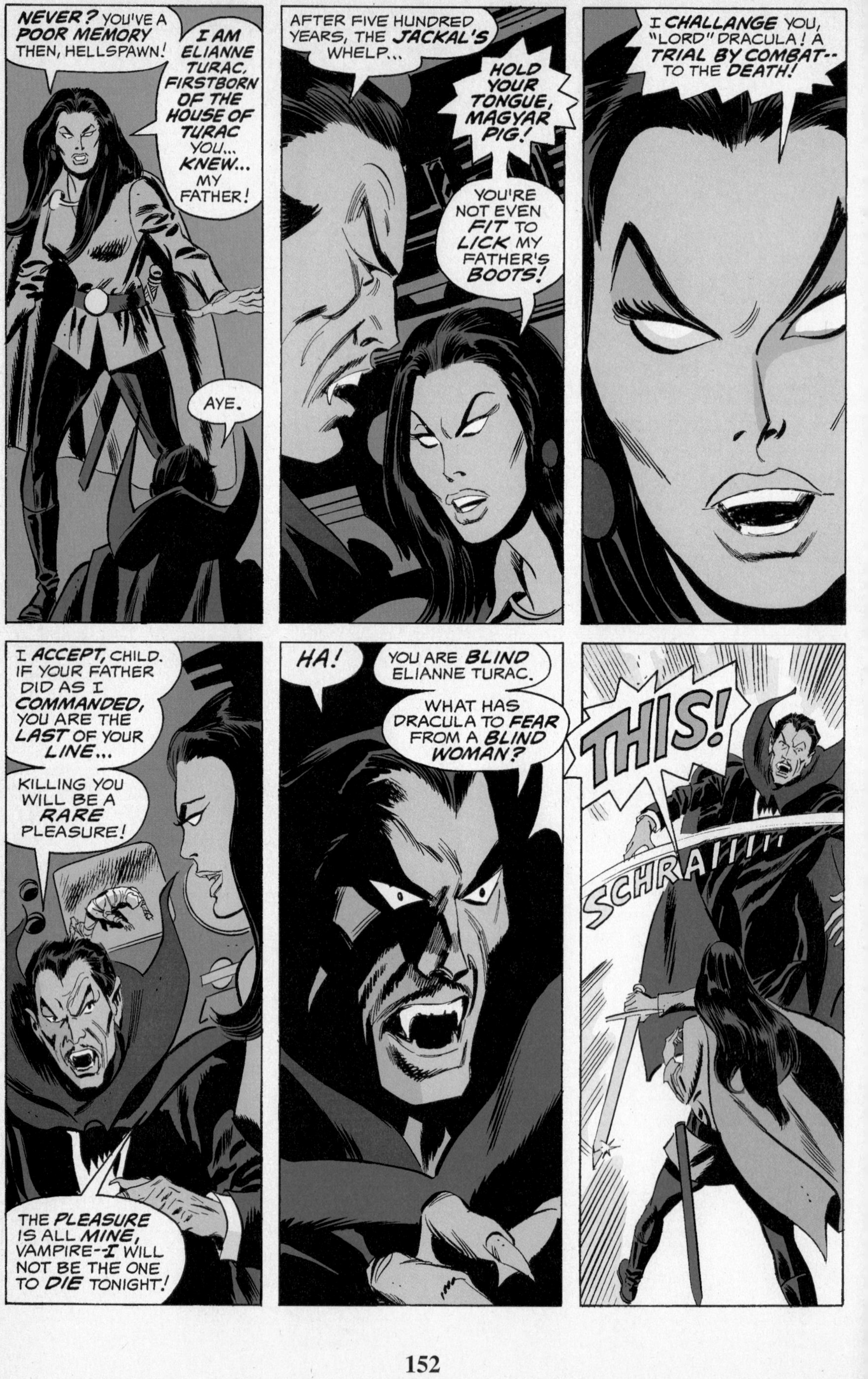

NEVER? YOU'VE A POOR MEMORY THEN, HELLSPAWN!
I AM ELIANNE TURAC, FIRSTBORN OF THE HOUSE OF TURAC YOU... KNEW... MY FATHER!
AYE.
AFTER FIVE HUNDRED YEARS, THE JACKAL'S WHELP...
HOLD YOUR TONGUE, MAGYAR PIG!
YOU'RE NOT EVEN FIT TO LICK MY FATHER'S BOOTS!
I CHALLANGE YOU, "LORD" DRACULA! A TRIAL BY COMBAT-- TO THE DEATH!
I ACCEPT, CHILD. IF YOUR FATHER DID AS I COMMANDED, YOU ARE THE LAST OF YOUR LINE...
KILLING YOU WILL BE A RARE PLEASURE!
THE PLEASURE IS ALL MINE, VAMPIRE--I WILL NOT BE THE ONE TO DIE TONIGHT!
HA!
YOU ARE BLIND ELIANNE TURAC.
WHAT HAS DRACULA TO FEAR FROM A BLIND WOMAN?
THIS!
SCHRAIIIII

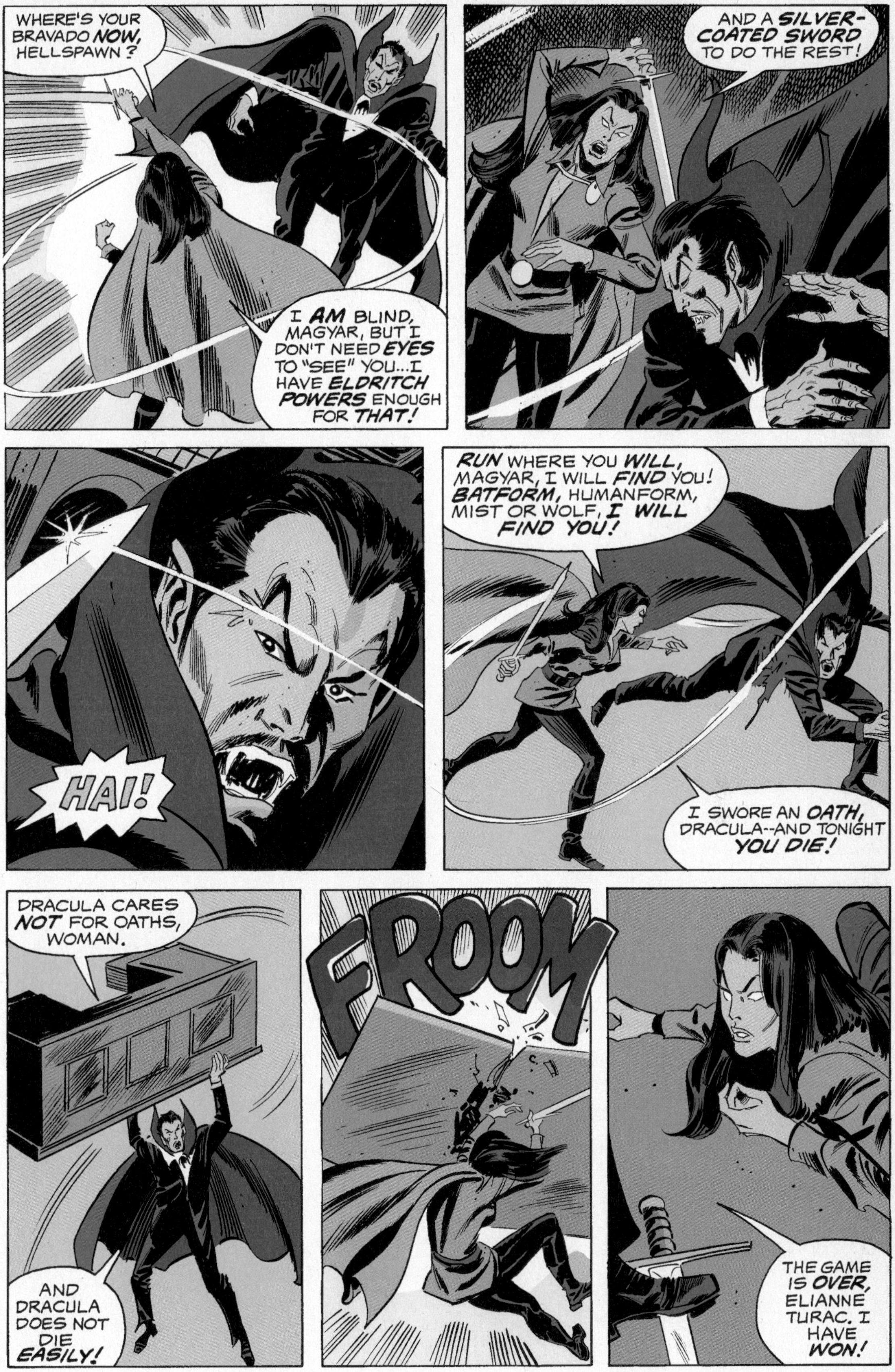
WHERE'S YOUR BRAVADO NOW, HELLSPAWN?
I AM BLIND, MAGYAR, BUT I DON'T NEED EYES TO "SEE" YOU...I HAVE ELDRITCH POWERS ENOUGH FOR THAT!
AND A SILVER-COATED SWORD TO DO THE REST!
HAI!
RUN WHERE YOU WILL, MAGYAR, I WILL FIND YOU! BATFORM, HUMANFORM, MIST OR WOLF, I WILL FIND YOU!
I SWORE AN OATH, DRACULA--AND TONIGHT YOU DIE!
DRACULA CARES NOT FOR OATHS, WOMAN.
AND DRACULA DOES NOT DIE EASILY!
FROOM
THE GAME IS OVER, ELIANNE TURAC. I HAVE WON!

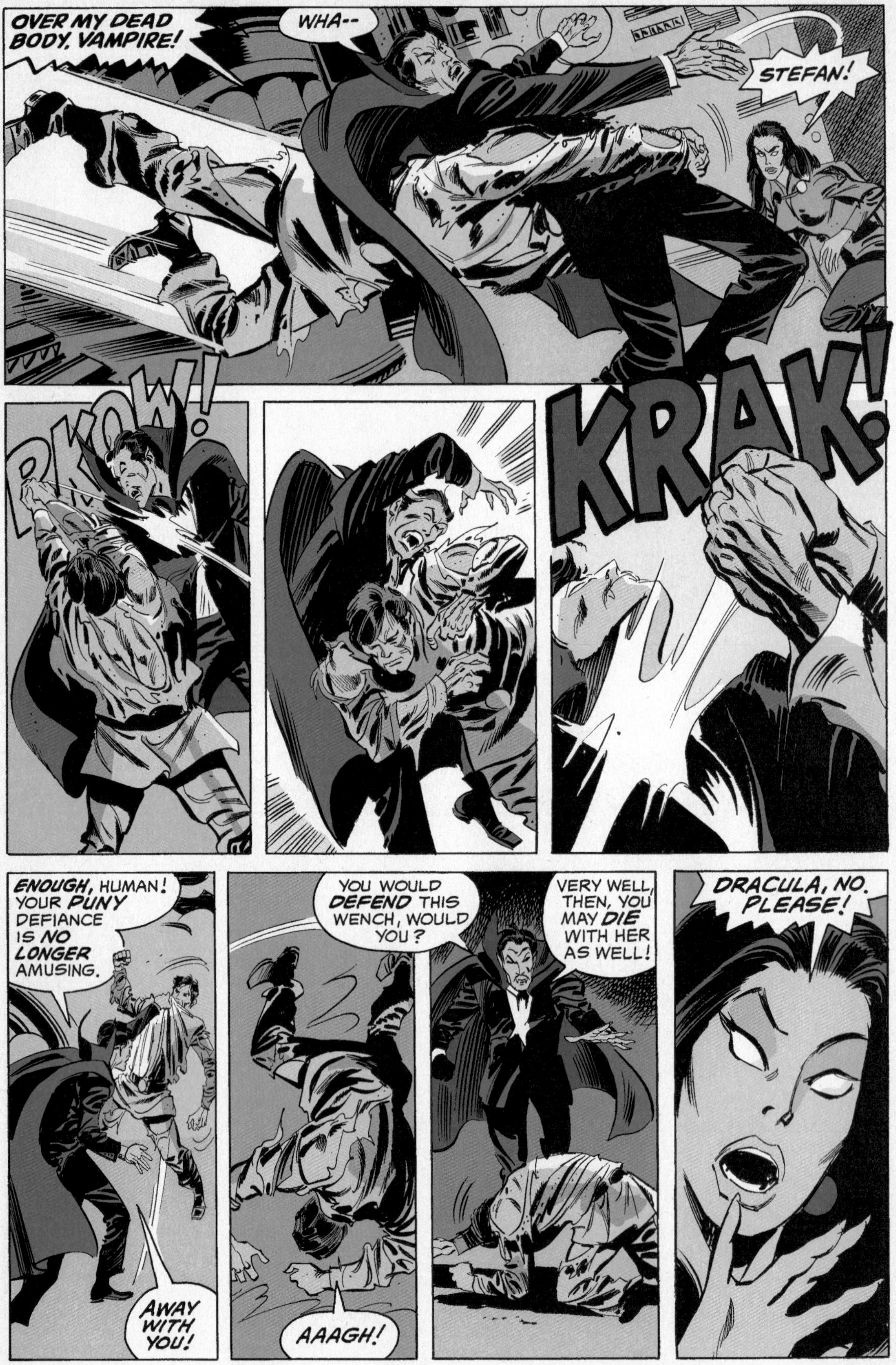
OVER MY DEAD BODY, VAMPIRE!
WHA--
STEFAN!
BKOW!
KRAK!
ENOUGH, HUMAN! YOUR PUNY DEFIANCE IS NO LONGER AMUSING.
AWAY WITH YOU!
YOU WOULD DEFEND THIS WENCH, WOULD YOU?
AAAGH!
VERY WELL, THEN, YOU MAY DIE WITH HER AS WELL!
DRACULA, NO. PLEASE!

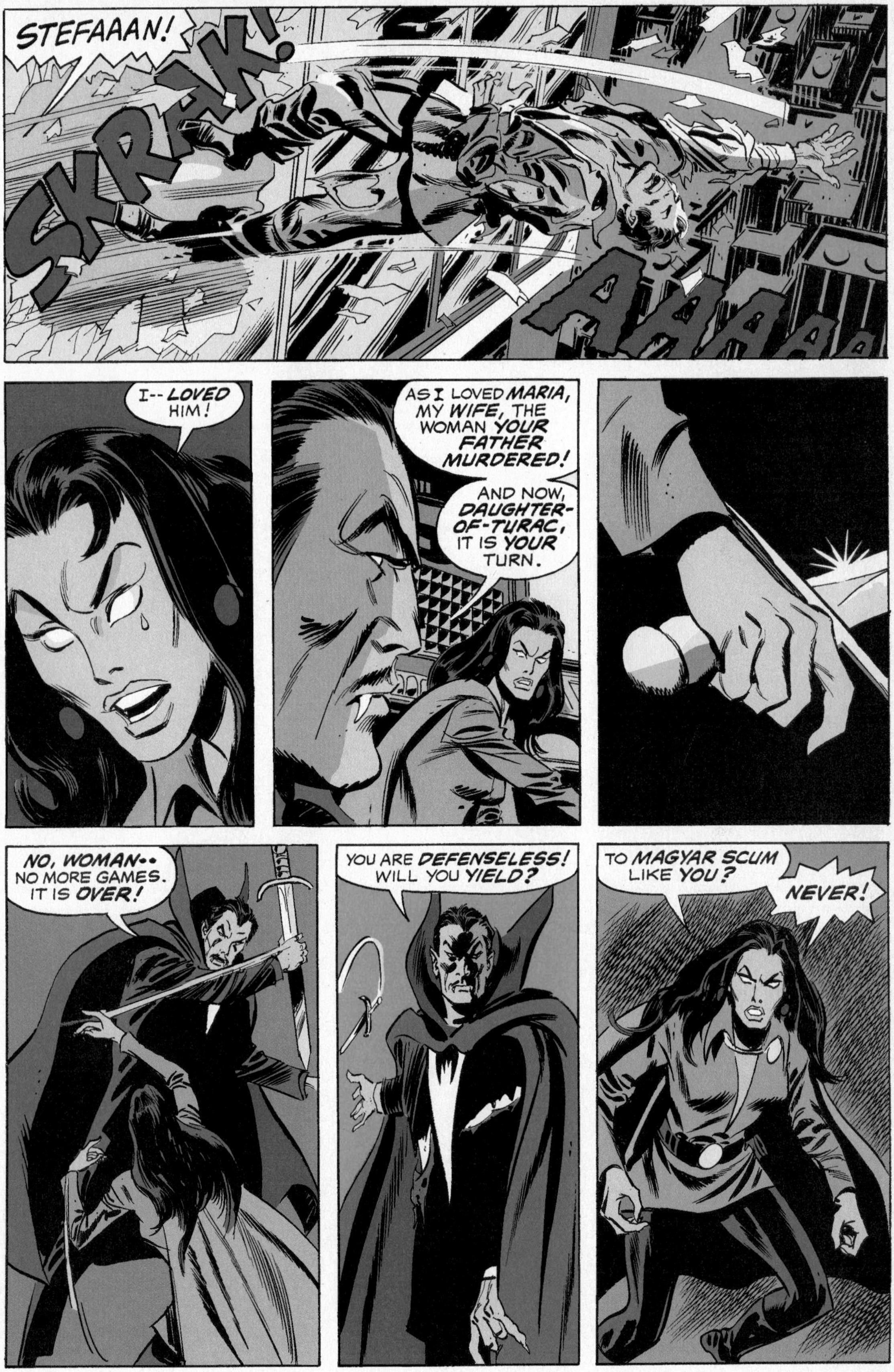
STEFAAAN!
SKRAK!
AAAAAA
I--LOVED HIM!
AS I LOVED MARIA, MY WIFE, THE WOMAN YOUR FATHER MURDERED!
AND NOW, DAUGHTER-OF-TURAC, IT IS YOUR TURN.
NO, WOMAN-- NO MORE GAMES. IT IS OVER!
YOU ARE DEFENSELESS! WILL YOU YIELD?
TO MAGYAR SCUM LIKE YOU?
NEVER!

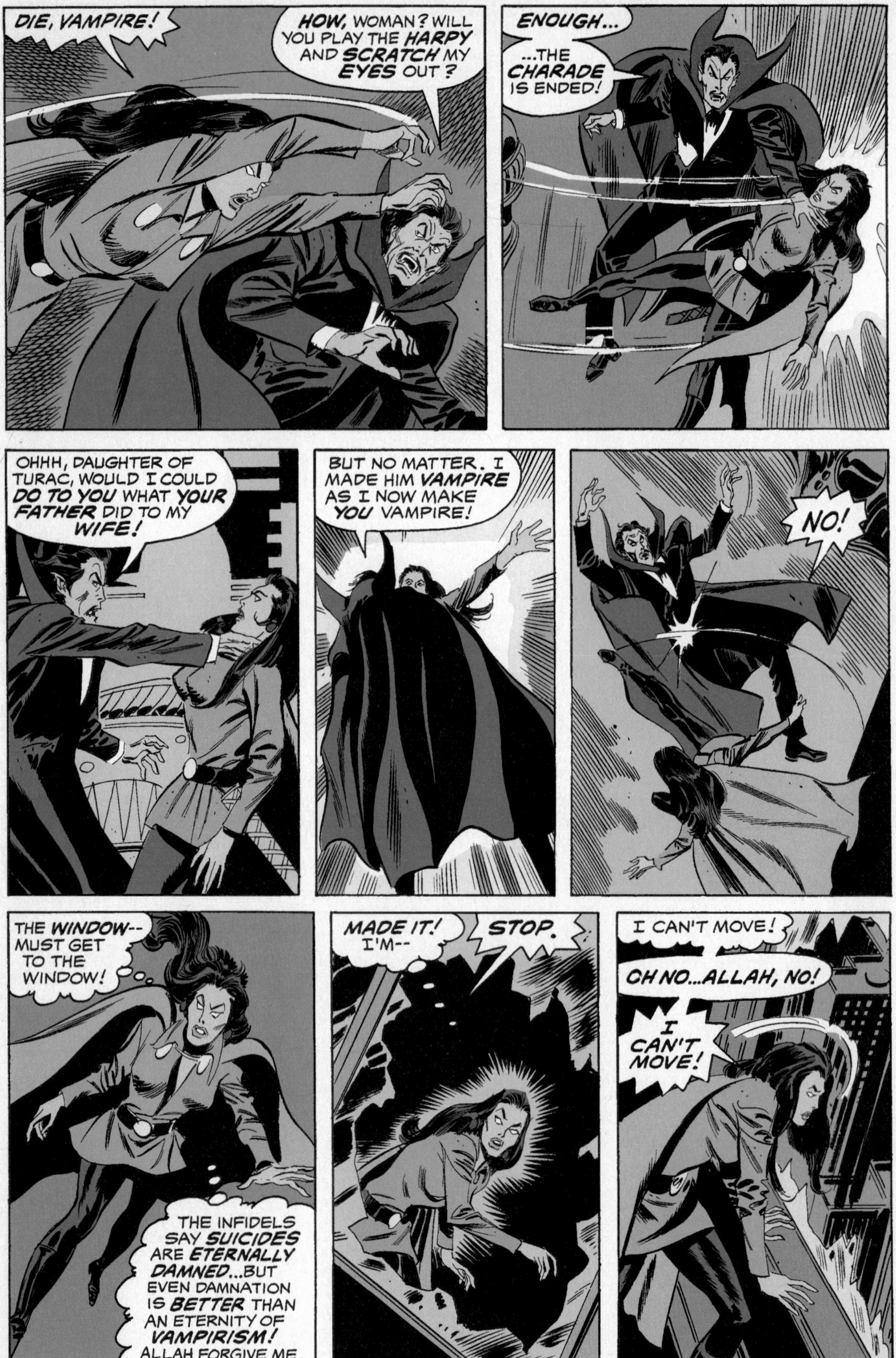
DIE, VAMPIRE!
HOW, WOMAN? WILL YOU PLAY THE HARPY AND SCRATCH MY EYES OUT?
ENOUGH...
...THE CHARADE IS ENDED!
OHHH, DAUGHTER OF TURAC, WOULD I COULD DO TO YOU WHAT YOUR FATHER DID TO MY WIFE!
BUT NO MATTER. I MADE HIM VAMPIRE AS I NOW MAKE YOU VAMPIRE!
NO!
THE WINDOW-- MUST GET TO THE WINDOW!
THE INFIDELS SAY SUICIDES ARE ETERNALLY DAMNED...BUT EVEN DAMNATION IS BETTER THAN AN ETERNITY OF VAMPIRISM! ALLAH FORGIVE ME.
MADE IT! I'M--
STOP.
I CAN'T MOVE!
OH NO...ALLAH, NO!
I CAN'T MOVE!

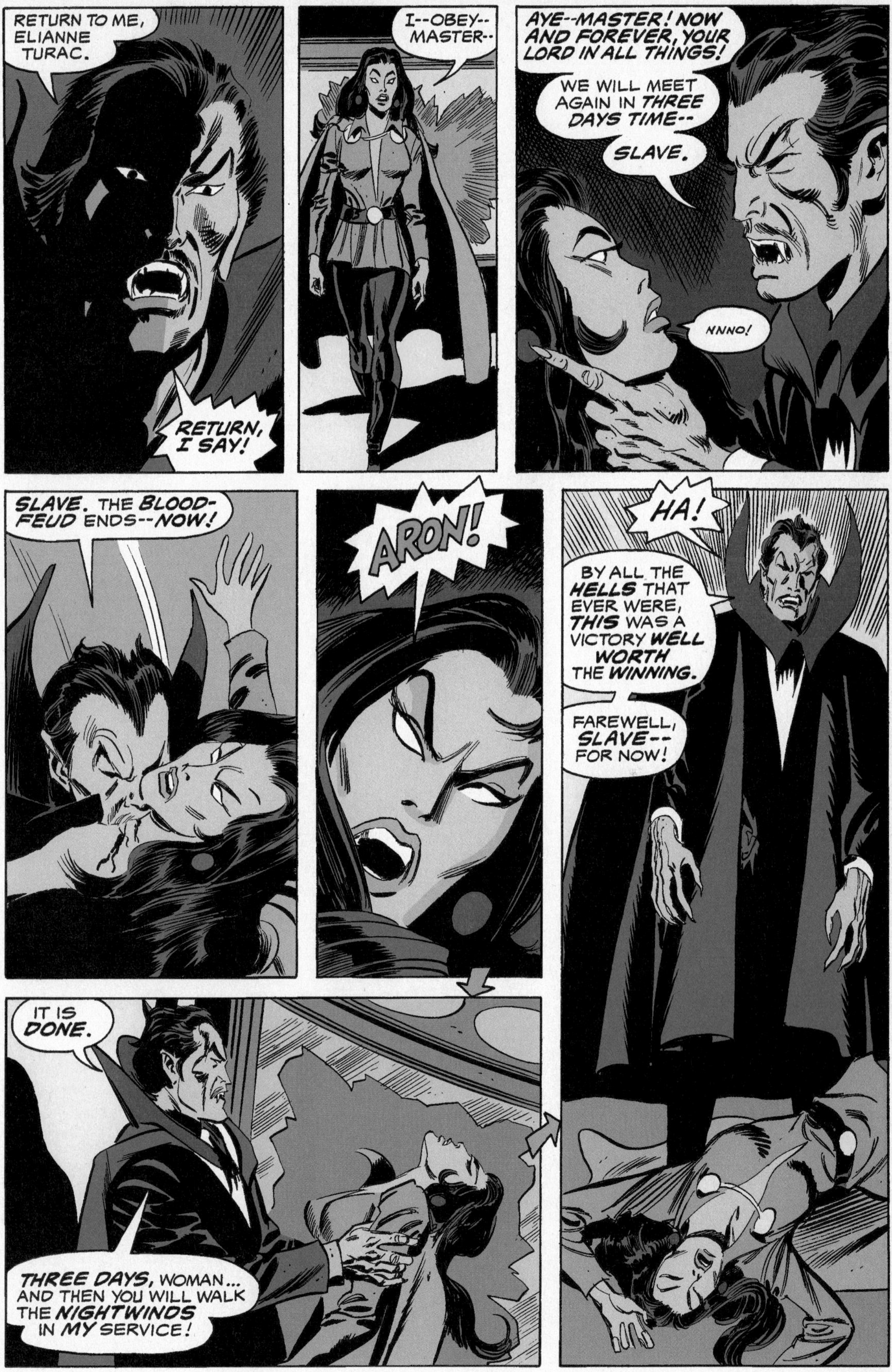

RETURN TO ME, ELIANNE TURAC.
RETURN, I SAY!
I--OBEY-- MASTER--
AYE--MASTER! NOW AND FOREVER, YOUR LORD IN ALL THINGS!
WE WILL MEET AGAIN IN THREE DAYS TIME--
SLAVE.
NNNO!
SLAVE. THE BLOOD-FEUD ENDS--NOW!
ARON!
HA!
BY ALL THE HELLS THAT EVER WERE, THIS WAS A VICTORY WELL WORTH THE WINNING.
FAREWELL, SLAVE-- FOR NOW!
IT IS DONE.
THREE DAYS, WOMAN... AND THEN YOU WILL WALK THE NIGHTWINDS IN MY SERVICE!

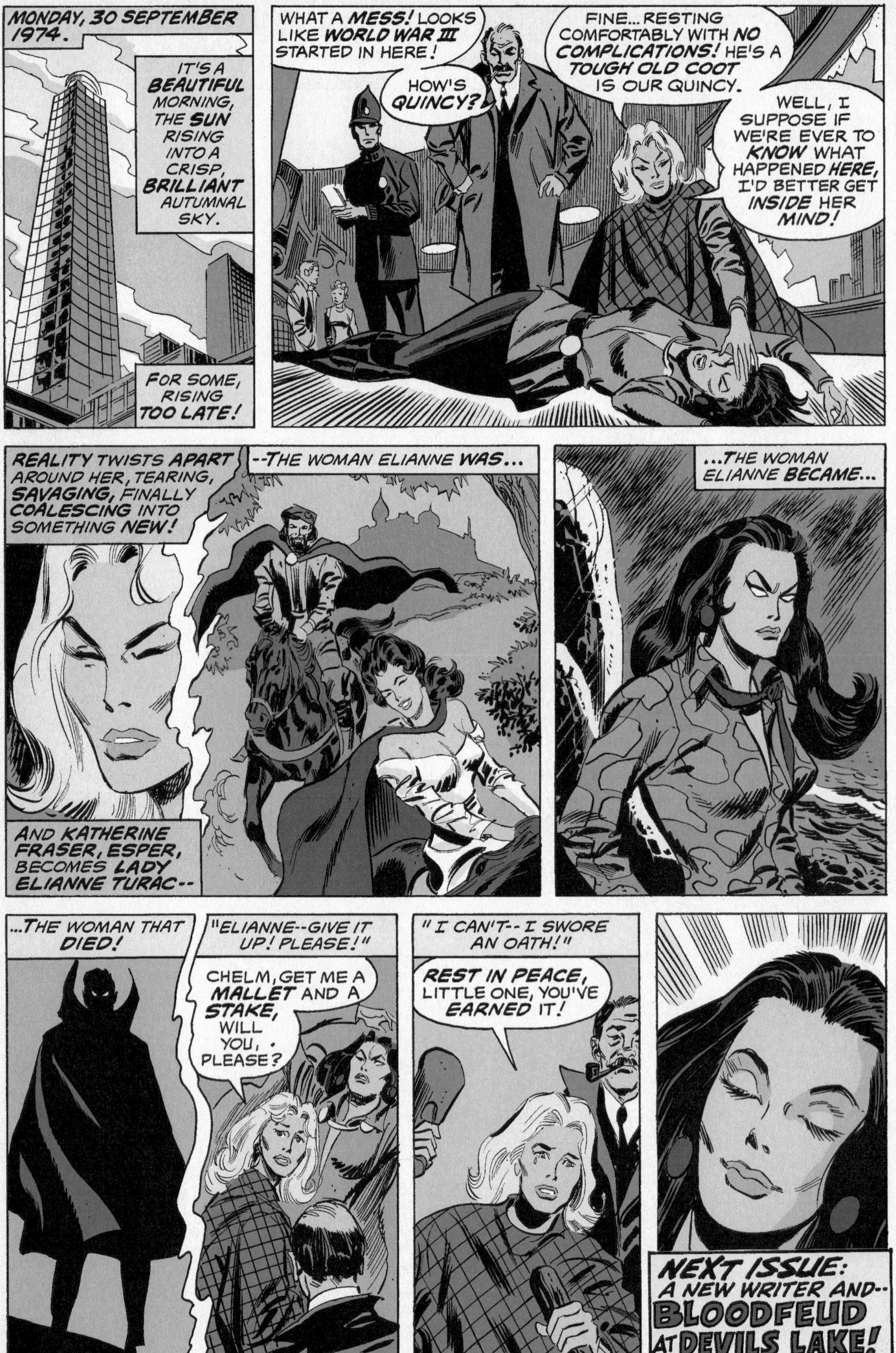
MONDAY, 30 SEPTEMBER 1974.
IT'S A BEAUTIFUL MORNING, THE SUN RISING INTO A CRISP, BRILLIANT AUTUMNAL SKY.
FOR SOME, RISING TOO LATE!
WHAT A MESS! LOOKS LIKE WORLD WAR III STARTED IN HERE!
HOW'S QUINCY?
FINE... RESTING COMFORTABLY WITH NO COMPLICATIONS! HE'S A TOUGH OLD COOT IS OUR QUINCY.
WELL, I SUPPOSE IF WE'RE EVER TO KNOW WHAT HAPPENED HERE, I'D BETTER GET INSIDE HER MIND!
REALITY TWISTS APART AROUND HER, TEARING, SAVAGING, FINALLY COALESCING INTO SOMETHING NEW!
AND KATHERINE FRASER, ESPER, BECOMES LADY ELIANNE TURAC--
--THE WOMAN ELIANNE WAS...
...THE WOMAN ELIANNE BECAME...
...THE WOMAN THAT DIED!
"ELIANNE--GIVE IT UP! PLEASE!"
CHELM, GET ME A MALLET AND A STAKE, WILL YOU, PLEASE?
"I CAN'T-- I SWORE AN OATH!"
REST IN PEACE, LITTLE ONE, YOU'VE EARNED IT!
NEXT ISSUE: A NEW WRITER AND-- BLOODFEUD AT DEVILS LAKE!

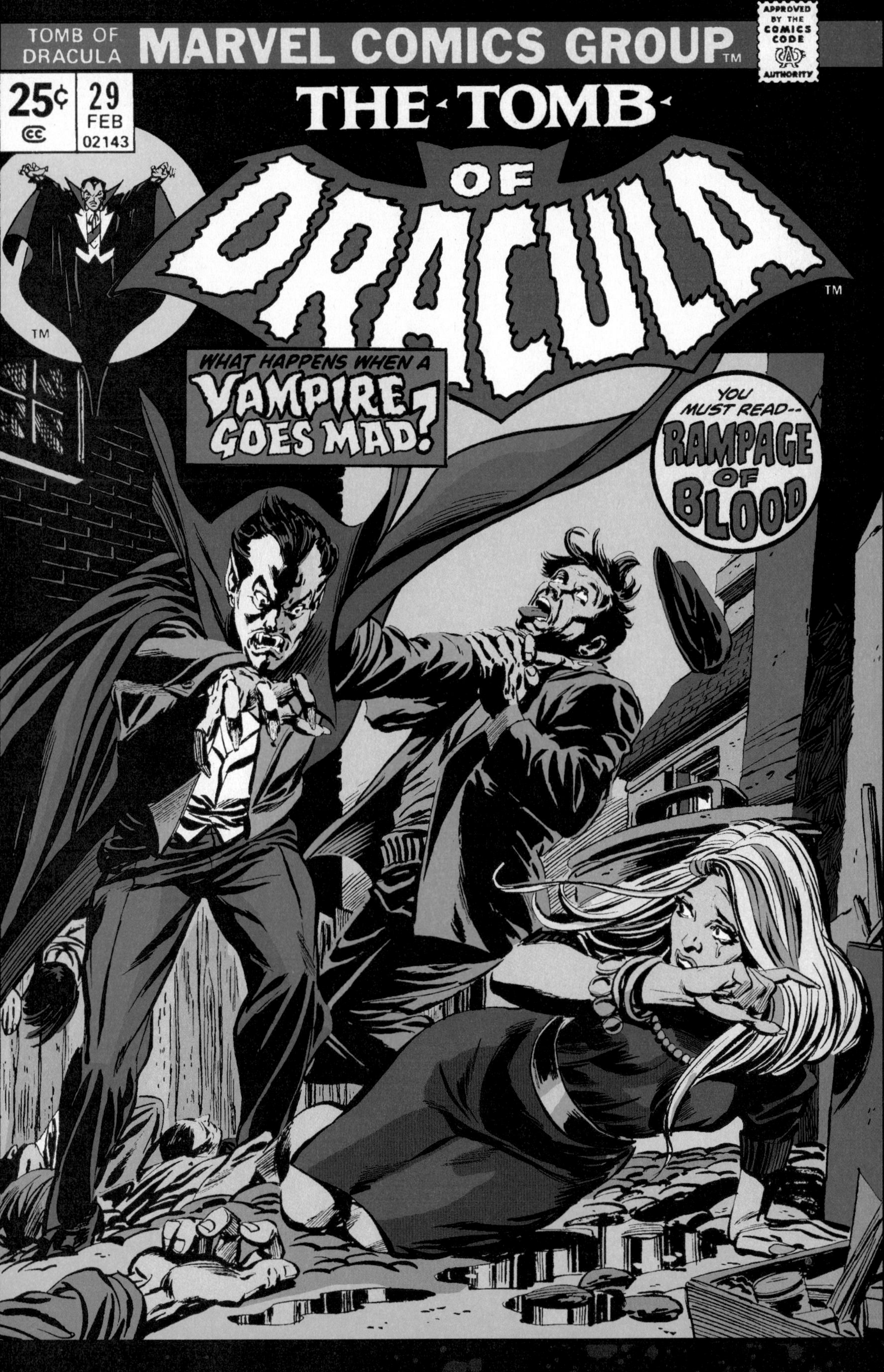
TOMB OF DRACULA
MARVEL COMICS GROUP™
APPROVED BY THE COMICS CODE AUTHORITY
25¢
29 FEB 02143
THE TOMB OF DRACULA™
WHAT HAPPENS WHEN A VAMPIRE GOES MAD?
YOU MUST READ-- RAMPAGE OF BLOOD

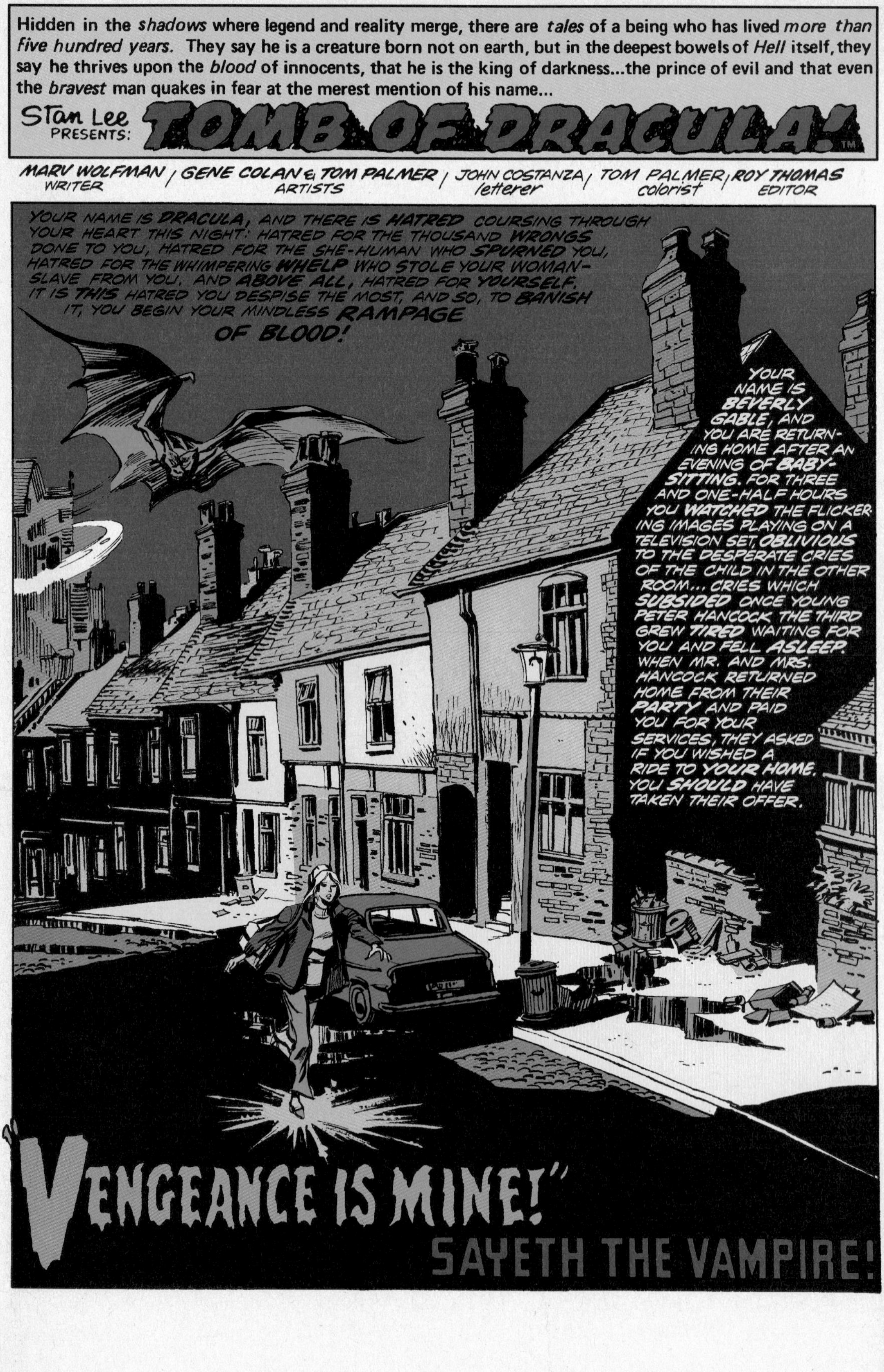
Hidden in the *shadows* where legend and reality merge, there are *tales* of a being who has lived *more than five hundred years.* They say he is a creature born not on earth, but in the deepest bowels of *Hell* itself, they say he thrives upon the *blood* of innocents, that he is the king of darkness...the prince of evil and that even the *bravest* man quakes in fear at the merest mention of his name...
Stan Lee PRESENTS: TOMB OF DRACULA!™
MARV WOLFMAN WRITER / GENE COLAN & TOM PALMER ARTISTS / JOHN COSTANZA letterer / TOM PALMER colorist / ROY THOMAS EDITOR
YOUR NAME IS DRACULA, AND THERE IS HATRED COURSING THROUGH YOUR HEART THIS NIGHT: HATRED FOR THE THOUSAND WRONGS DONE TO YOU, HATRED FOR THE SHE-HUMAN WHO SPURNED YOU, HATRED FOR THE WHIMPERING WHELP WHO STOLE YOUR WOMAN-SLAVE FROM YOU. AND ABOVE ALL, HATRED FOR YOURSELF. IT IS THIS HATRED YOU DESPISE THE MOST, AND SO, TO BANISH IT, YOU BEGIN YOUR MINDLESS RAMPAGE OF BLOOD!
YOUR NAME IS BEVERLY GABLE, AND YOU ARE RETURNING HOME AFTER AN EVENING OF BABY-SITTING. FOR THREE AND ONE-HALF HOURS YOU WATCHED THE FLICKERING IMAGES PLAYING ON A TELEVISION SET, OBLIVIOUS TO THE DESPERATE CRIES OF THE CHILD IN THE OTHER ROOM... CRIES WHICH SUBSIDED ONCE YOUNG PETER HANCOCK THE THIRD GREW TIRED WAITING FOR YOU AND FELL ASLEEP. WHEN MR. AND MRS. HANCOCK RETURNED HOME FROM THEIR PARTY AND PAID YOU FOR YOUR SERVICES, THEY ASKED IF YOU WISHED A RIDE TO YOUR HOME. YOU SHOULD HAVE TAKEN THEIR OFFER.
"VENGEANCE IS MINE!" SAYETH THE VAMPIRE!

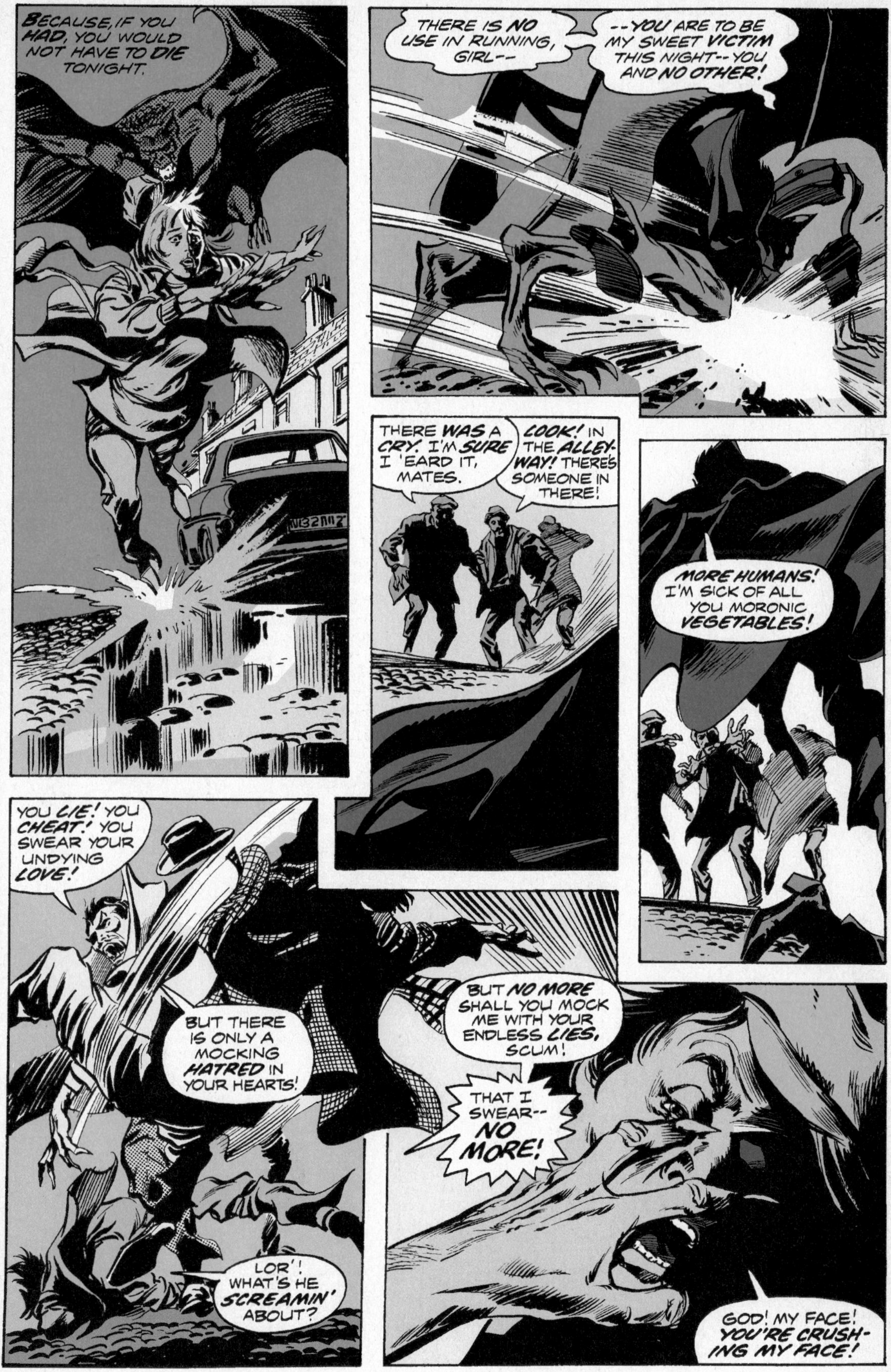
BECAUSE, IF YOU HAD, YOU WOULD NOT HAVE TO DIE TONIGHT.
THERE IS NO USE IN RUNNING, GIRL--
--YOU ARE TO BE MY SWEET VICTIM THIS NIGHT--YOU AND NO OTHER!
THERE WAS A CRY. I'M SURE I 'EARD IT, MATES.
LOOK! IN THE ALLEY-WAY! THERE'S SOMEONE IN THERE!
MORE HUMANS! I'M SICK OF ALL YOU MORONIC VEGETABLES!
YOU LIE! YOU CHEAT! YOU SWEAR YOUR UNDYING LOVE!
BUT THERE IS ONLY A MOCKING HATRED IN YOUR HEARTS!
LOR'! WHAT'S HE SCREAMIN' ABOUT?
BUT NO MORE SHALL YOU MOCK ME WITH YOUR ENDLESS LIES, SCUM!
THAT I SWEAR-- NO MORE!
GOD! MY FACE! YOU'RE CRUSH-ING MY FACE!

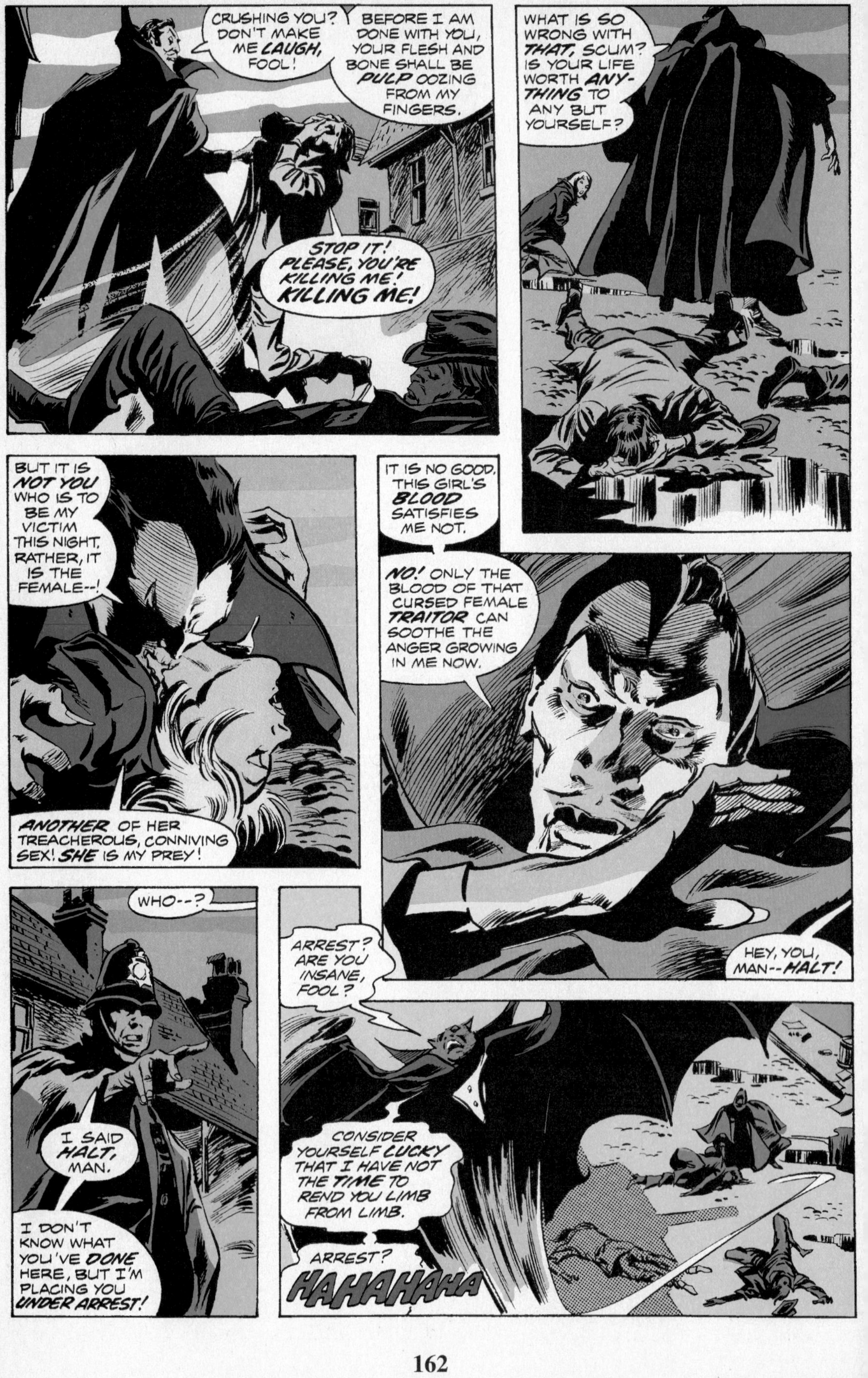
CRUSHING YOU? DON'T MAKE ME LAUGH, FOOL!
BEFORE I AM DONE WITH YOU, YOUR FLESH AND BONE SHALL BE PULP OOZING FROM MY FINGERS.
STOP IT! PLEASE, YOU'RE KILLING ME! KILLING ME!
WHAT IS SO WRONG WITH THAT, SCUM? IS YOUR LIFE WORTH ANYTHING TO ANY BUT YOURSELF?
BUT IT IS NOT YOU WHO IS TO BE MY VICTIM THIS NIGHT. RATHER, IT IS THE FEMALE--!
ANOTHER OF HER TREACHEROUS, CONNIVING SEX! SHE IS MY PREY!
IT IS NO GOOD. THIS GIRL'S BLOOD SATISFIES ME NOT.
NO! ONLY THE BLOOD OF THAT CURSED FEMALE TRAITOR CAN SOOTHE THE ANGER GROWING IN ME NOW.
HEY, YOU, MAN--HALT!
WHO--?
I SAID HALT, MAN.
I DON'T KNOW WHAT YOU'VE DONE HERE, BUT I'M PLACING YOU UNDER ARREST!
ARREST? ARE YOU INSANE, FOOL?
CONSIDER YOURSELF LUCKY THAT I HAVE NOT THE TIME TO REND YOU LIMB FROM LIMB.
ARREST?
HAHAHAHAHA

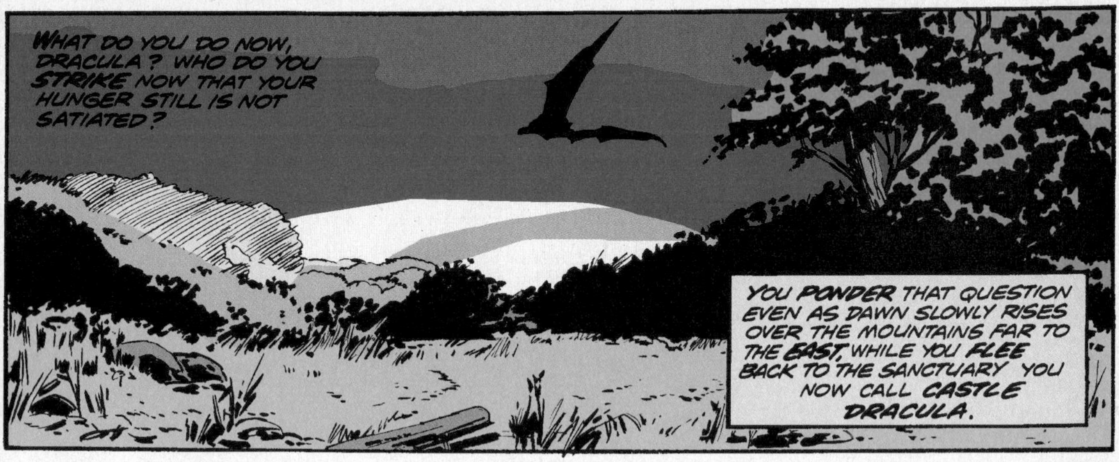
WHAT DO YOU DO NOW, DRACULA? WHO DO YOU STRIKE NOW THAT YOUR HUNGER STILL IS NOT SATIATED?
YOU PONDER THAT QUESTION EVEN AS DAWN SLOWLY RISES OVER THE MOUNTAINS FAR TO THE EAST, WHILE YOU FLEE BACK TO THE SANCTUARY YOU NOW CALL CASTLE DRACULA.

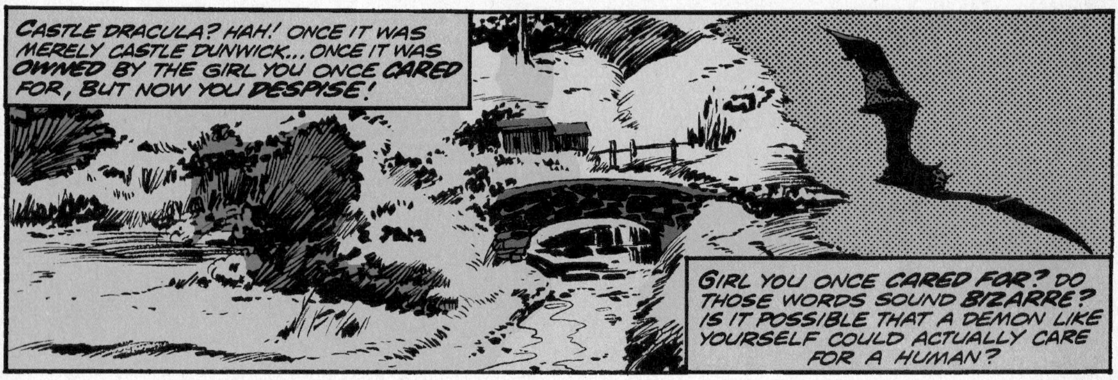
CASTLE DRACULA? HAH! ONCE IT WAS MERELY CASTLE DUNWICK... ONCE IT WAS OWNED BY THE GIRL YOU ONCE CARED FOR, BUT NOW YOU DESPISE!
GIRL YOU ONCE CARED FOR? DO THOSE WORDS SOUND BIZARRE? IS IT POSSIBLE THAT A DEMON LIKE YOURSELF COULD ACTUALLY CARE FOR A HUMAN?

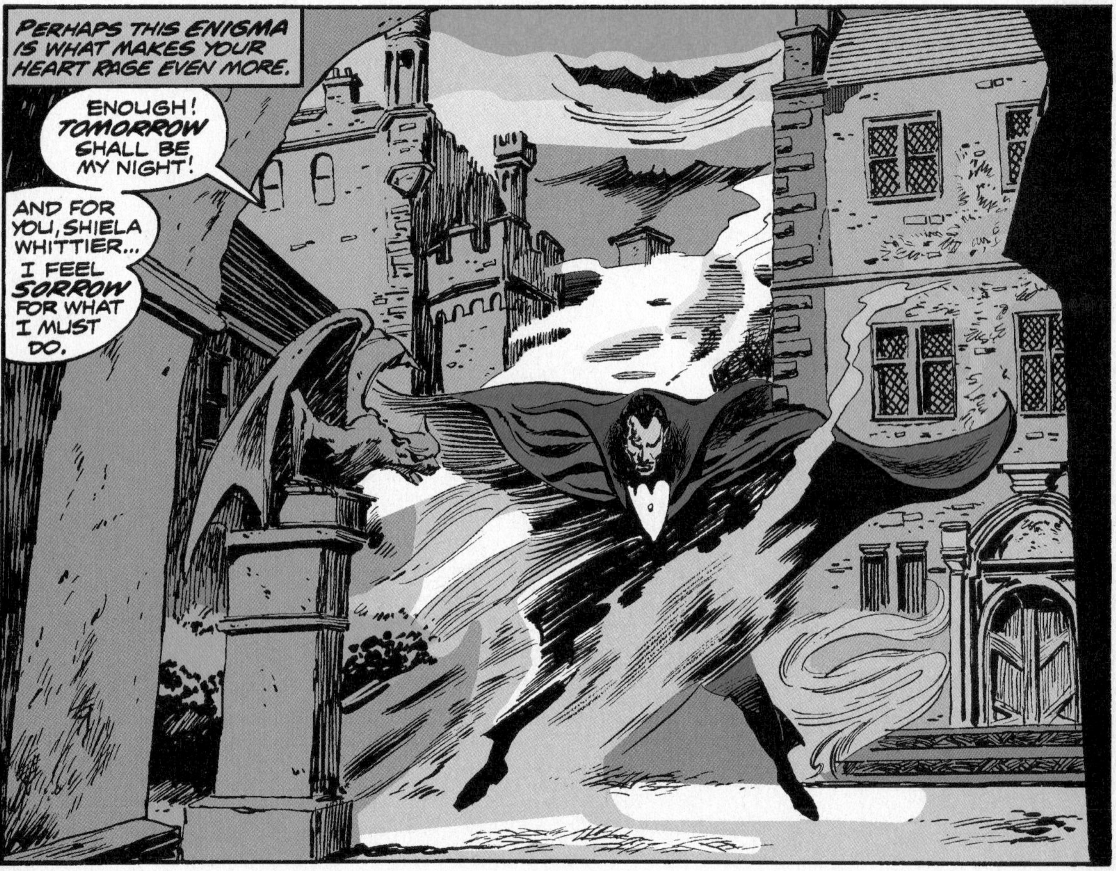
PERHAPS THIS ENIGMA IS WHAT MAKES YOUR HEART RAGE EVEN MORE.
ENOUGH! TOMORROW SHALL BE MY NIGHT!
AND FOR YOU, SHIELA WHITTIER... I FEEL SORROW FOR WHAT I MUST DO.

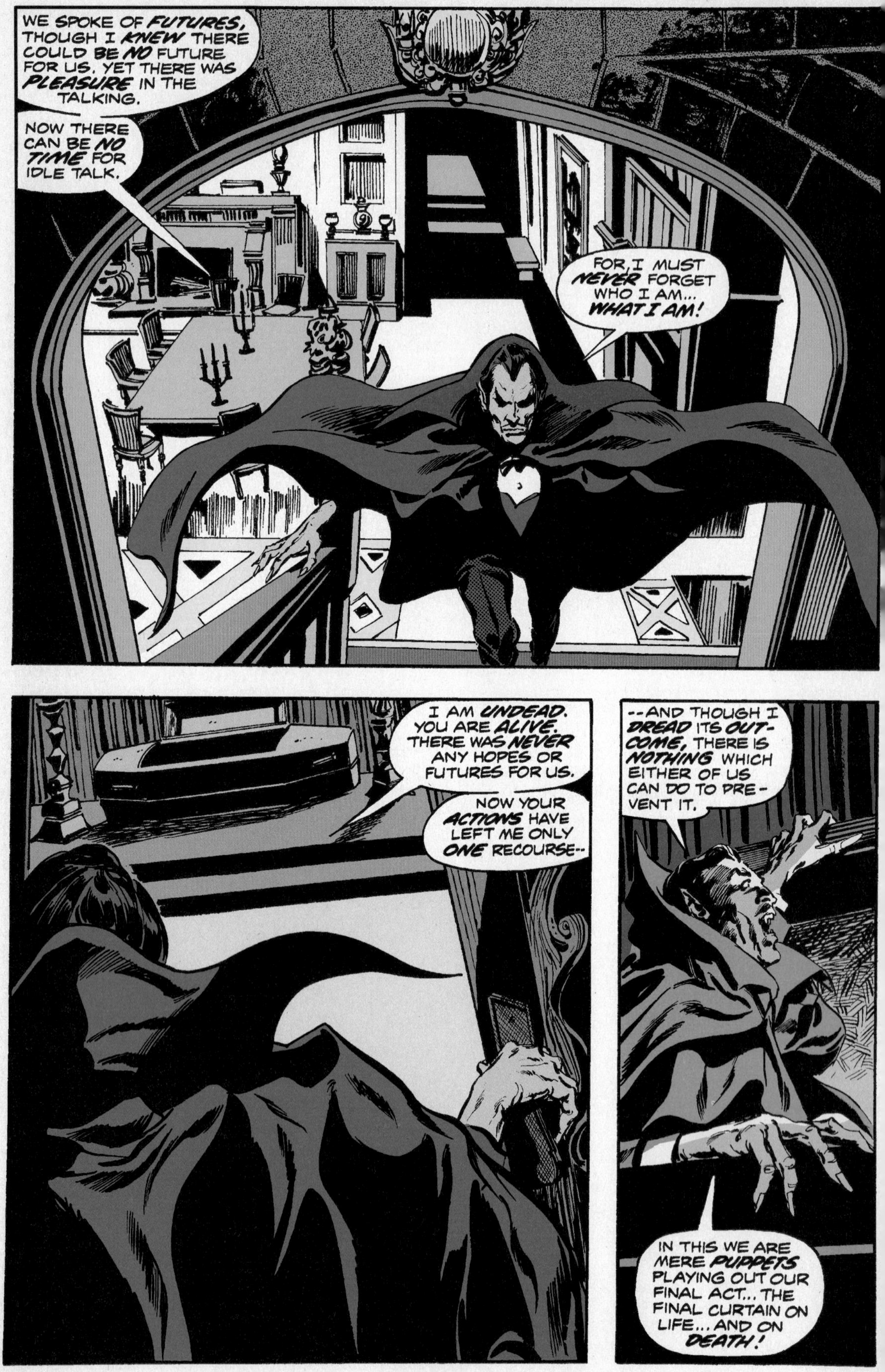
WE SPOKE OF FUTURES, THOUGH I KNEW THERE COULD BE NO FUTURE FOR US. YET THERE WAS PLEASURE IN THE TALKING.
NOW THERE CAN BE NO TIME FOR IDLE TALK.
FOR, I MUST NEVER FORGET WHO I AM... WHAT I AM!
I AM UNDEAD. YOU ARE ALIVE. THERE WAS NEVER ANY HOPES OR FUTURES FOR US.
NOW YOUR ACTIONS HAVE LEFT ME ONLY ONE RECOURSE--
--AND THOUGH I DREAD ITS OUT-COME, THERE IS NOTHING WHICH EITHER OF US CAN DO TO PRE-VENT IT.
IN THIS WE ARE MERE PUPPETS PLAYING OUT OUR FINAL ACT... THE FINAL CURTAIN ON LIFE... AND ON DEATH!

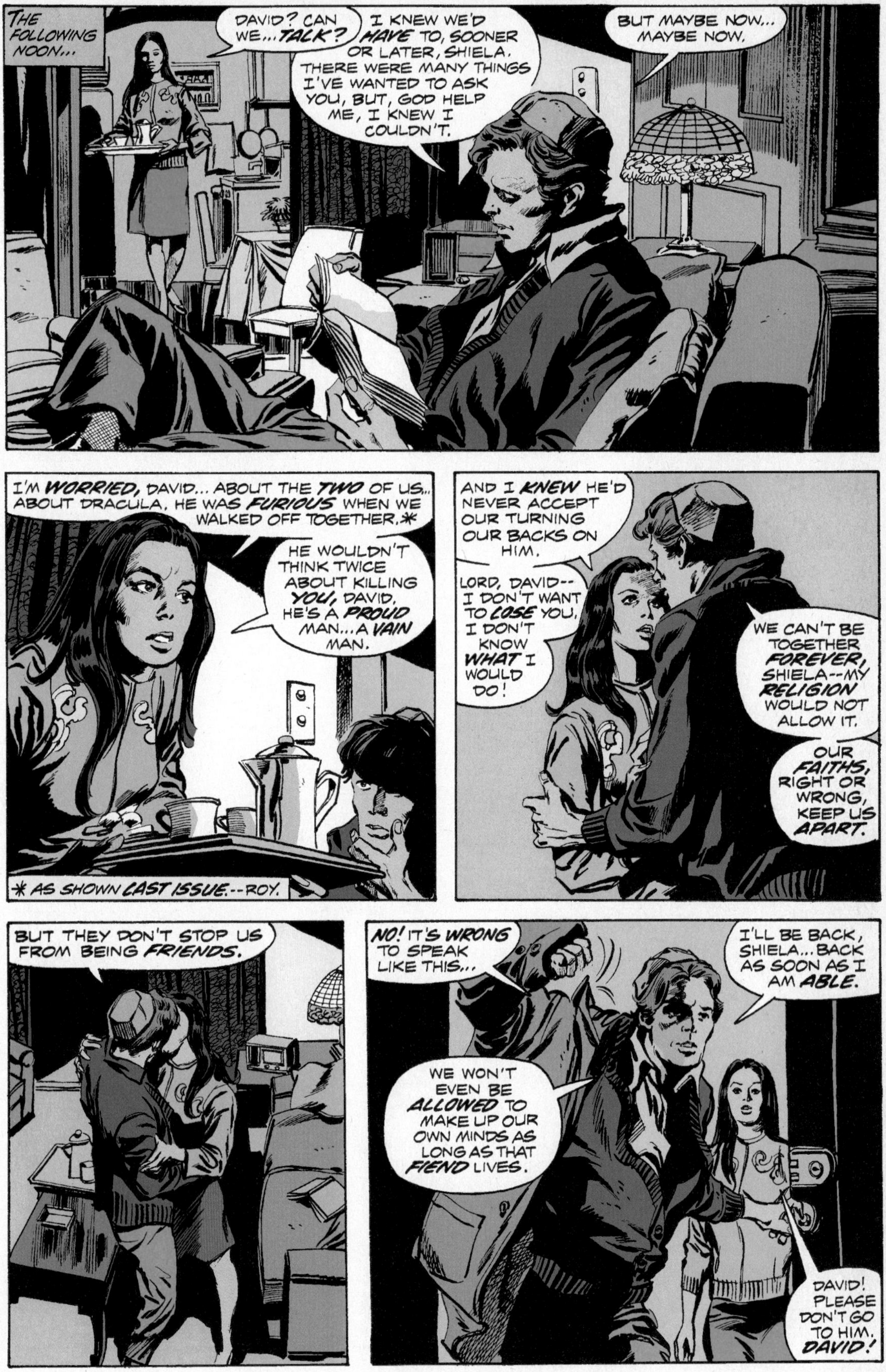
THE FOLLOWING NOON...
DAVID? CAN WE... TALK?
I KNEW WE'D HAVE TO, SOONER OR LATER, SHIELA. THERE WERE MANY THINGS I'VE WANTED TO ASK YOU, BUT, GOD HELP ME, I KNEW I COULDN'T.
BUT MAYBE NOW... MAYBE NOW.
I'M WORRIED, DAVID... ABOUT THE TWO OF US... ABOUT DRACULA. HE WAS FURIOUS WHEN WE WALKED OFF TOGETHER.*
HE WOULDN'T THINK TWICE ABOUT KILLING YOU, DAVID. HE'S A PROUD MAN... A VAIN MAN.
* AS SHOWN LAST ISSUE.--ROY.
AND I KNEW HE'D NEVER ACCEPT OUR TURNING OUR BACKS ON HIM.
LORD, DAVID-- I DON'T WANT TO LOSE YOU. I DON'T KNOW WHAT I WOULD DO!
WE CAN'T BE TOGETHER FOREVER, SHIELA--MY RELIGION WOULD NOT ALLOW IT.
OUR FAITHS, RIGHT OR WRONG, KEEP US APART.
BUT THEY DON'T STOP US FROM BEING FRIENDS.
NO! IT'S WRONG TO SPEAK LIKE THIS...
WE WON'T EVEN BE ALLOWED TO MAKE UP OUR OWN MINDS AS LONG AS THAT FIEND LIVES.
I'LL BE BACK, SHIELA... BACK AS SOON AS I AM ABLE.
DAVID! PLEASE DON'T GO TO HIM, DAVID!

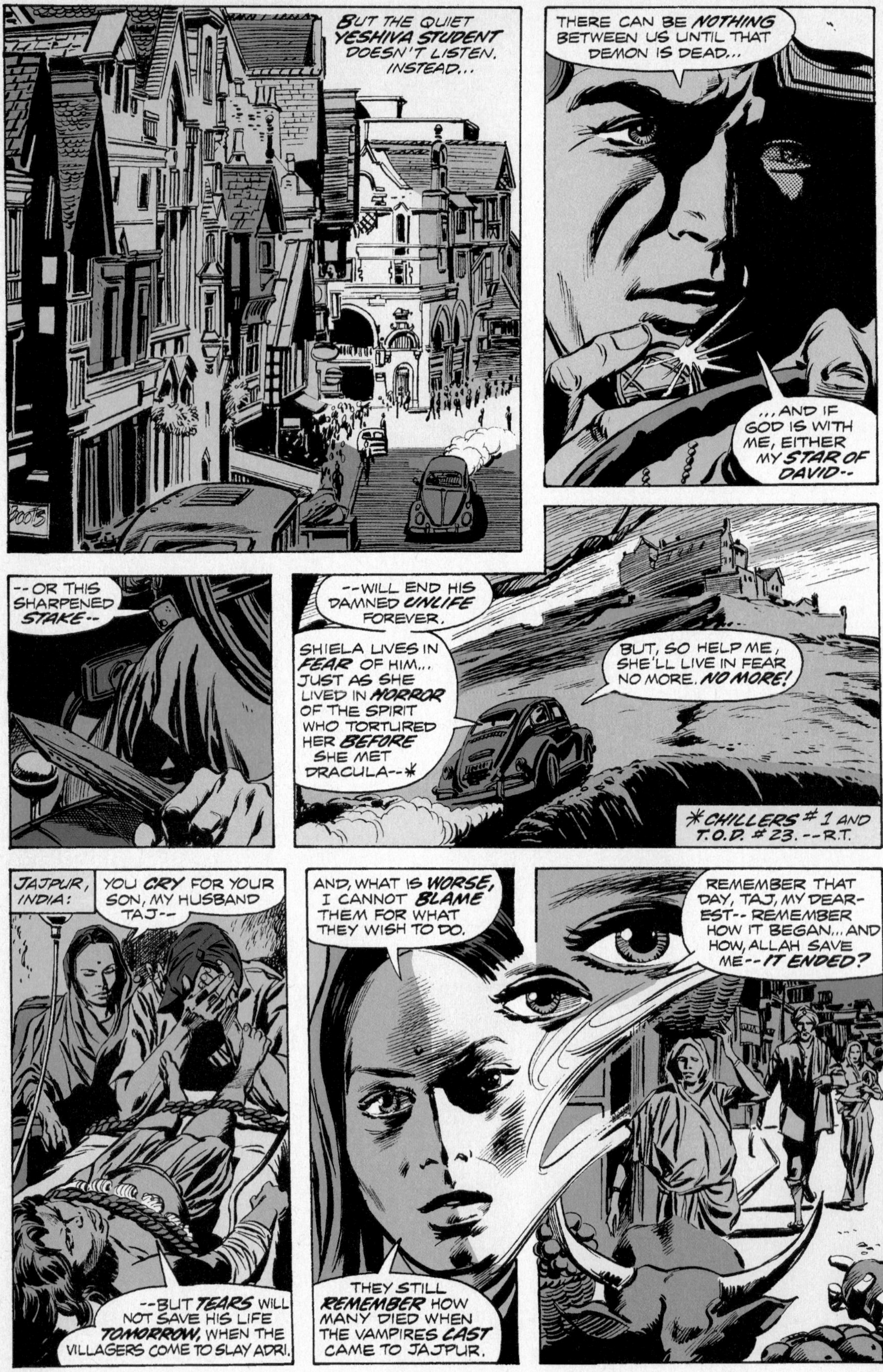
BUT THE QUIET YESHIVA STUDENT DOESN'T LISTEN. INSTEAD...
BOOTS
THERE CAN BE NOTHING BETWEEN US UNTIL THAT DEMON IS DEAD...
...AND IF GOD IS WITH ME, EITHER MY STAR OF DAVID--
--OR THIS SHARPENED STAKE--
--WILL END HIS DAMNED UNLIFE FOREVER.
SHIELA LIVES IN FEAR OF HIM... JUST AS SHE LIVED IN HORROR OF THE SPIRIT WHO TORTURED HER BEFORE SHE MET DRACULA--*
BUT, SO HELP ME, SHE'LL LIVE IN FEAR NO MORE. NO MORE!
*CHILLERS #1 AND T.O.D. #23. --R.T.
JAJPUR, INDIA:
YOU CRY FOR YOUR SON, MY HUSBAND TAJ--
--BUT TEARS WILL NOT SAVE HIS LIFE TOMORROW, WHEN THE VILLAGERS COME TO SLAY ADRI.
AND, WHAT IS WORSE, I CANNOT BLAME THEM FOR WHAT THEY WISH TO DO.
THEY STILL REMEMBER HOW MANY DIED WHEN THE VAMPIRES CAST CAME TO JAJPUR.
REMEMBER THAT DAY, TAJ, MY DEAREST-- REMEMBER HOW IT BEGAN... AND HOW, ALLAH SAVE ME-- IT ENDED?

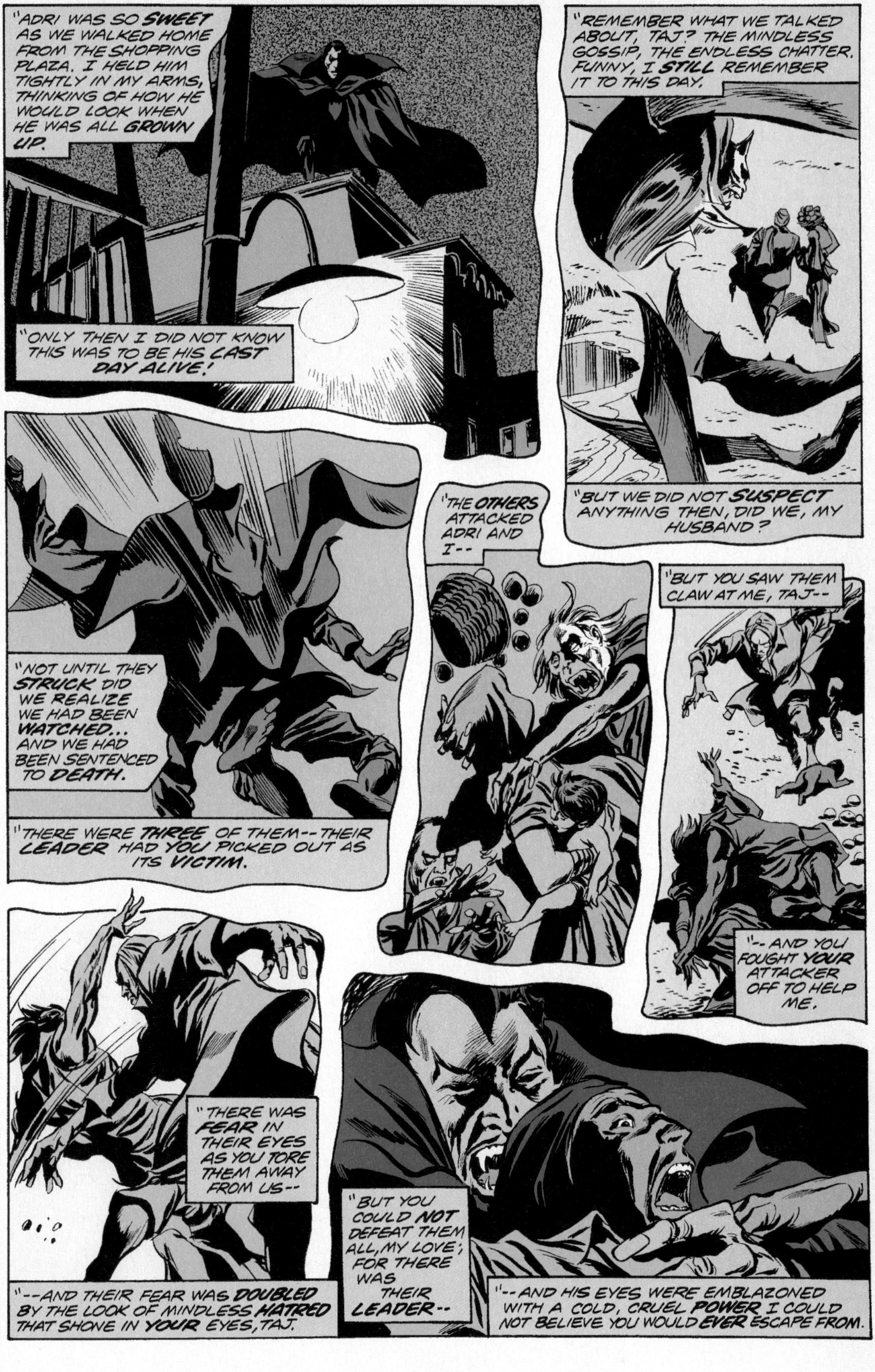
"ADRI WAS SO SWEET AS WE WALKED HOME FROM THE SHOPPING PLAZA. I HELD HIM TIGHTLY IN MY ARMS, THINKING OF HOW HE WOULD LOOK WHEN HE WAS ALL GROWN UP.
"ONLY THEN I DID NOT KNOW THIS WAS TO BE HIS LAST DAY ALIVE!
"REMEMBER WHAT WE TALKED ABOUT, TAJ? THE MINDLESS GOSSIP, THE ENDLESS CHATTER. FUNNY, I STILL REMEMBER IT TO THIS DAY.
"BUT WE DID NOT SUSPECT ANYTHING THEN, DID WE, MY HUSBAND?
"NOT UNTIL THEY STRUCK DID WE REALIZE WE HAD BEEN WATCHED... AND WE HAD BEEN SENTENCED TO DEATH.
"THERE WERE THREE OF THEM--THEIR LEADER HAD YOU PICKED OUT AS ITS VICTIM.
"THE OTHERS ATTACKED ADRI AND I--
"BUT YOU SAW THEM CLAW AT ME, TAJ--
"--AND YOU FOUGHT YOUR ATTACKER OFF TO HELP ME.
"THERE WAS FEAR IN THEIR EYES AS YOU TORE THEM AWAY FROM US--
"--AND THEIR FEAR WAS DOUBLED BY THE LOOK OF MINDLESS HATRED THAT SHONE IN YOUR EYES, TAJ.
"BUT YOU COULD NOT DEFEAT THEM ALL, MY LOVE; FOR THERE WAS THEIR LEADER--
"--AND HIS EYES WERE EMBLAZONED WITH A COLD, CRUEL POWER I COULD NOT BELIEVE YOU WOULD EVER ESCAPE FROM.

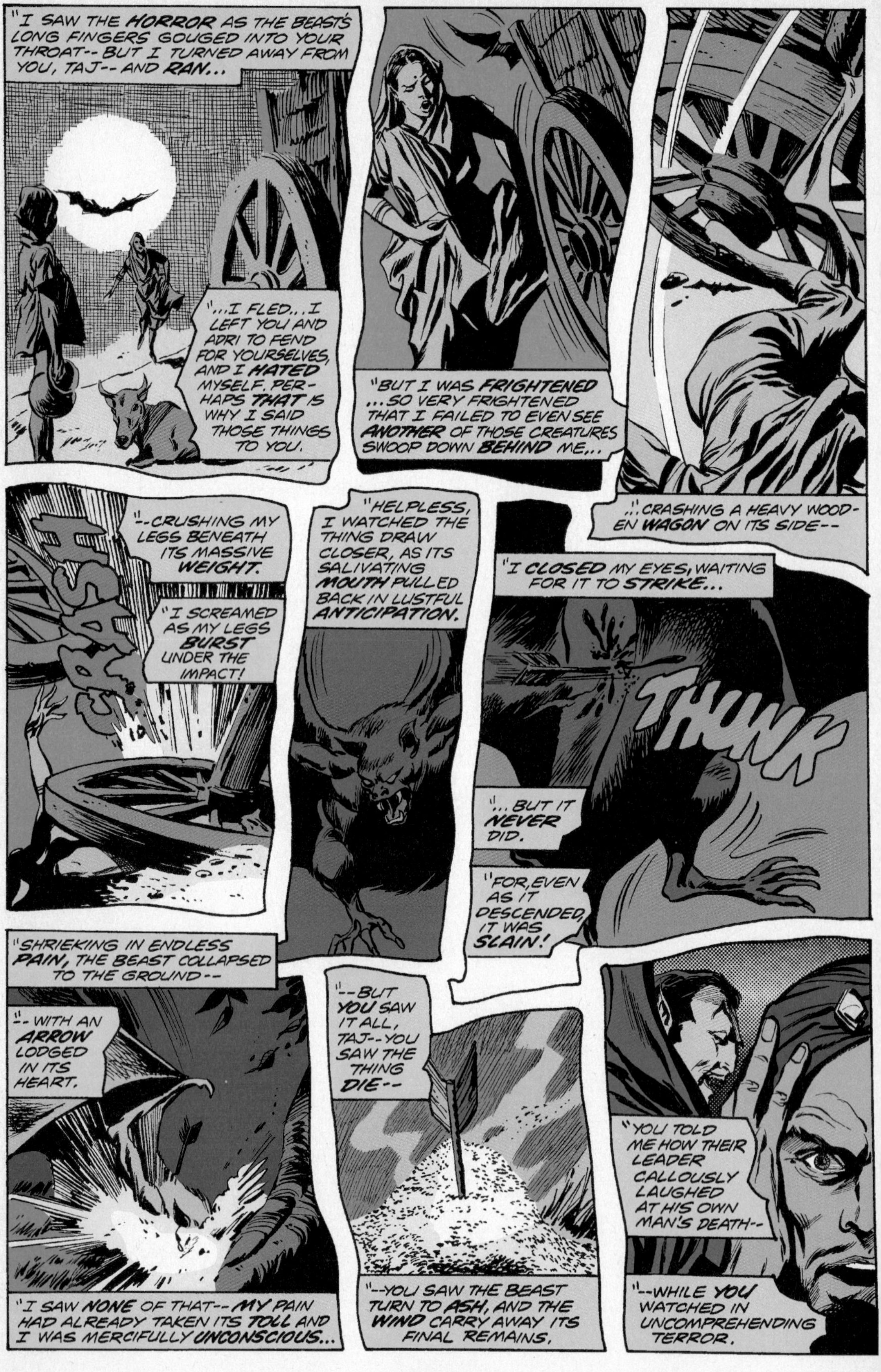
"I SAW THE HORROR AS THE BEAST'S LONG FINGERS GOUGED INTO YOUR THROAT-- BUT I TURNED AWAY FROM YOU, TAJ-- AND RAN...
"...I FLED... I LEFT YOU AND ADRI TO FEND FOR YOURSELVES, AND I HATED MYSELF. PERHAPS THAT IS WHY I SAID THOSE THINGS TO YOU.
"BUT I WAS FRIGHTENED ...SO VERY FRIGHTENED THAT I FAILED TO EVEN SEE ANOTHER OF THOSE CREATURES SWOOP DOWN BEHIND ME...
"...CRASHING A HEAVY WOODEN WAGON ON ITS SIDE--
"--CRUSHING MY LEGS BENEATH ITS MASSIVE WEIGHT.
CRASH
"I SCREAMED AS MY LEGS BURST UNDER THE IMPACT!
"HELPLESS, I WATCHED THE THING DRAW CLOSER, AS ITS SALIVATING MOUTH PULLED BACK IN LUSTFUL ANTICIPATION.
"I CLOSED MY EYES, WAITING FOR IT TO STRIKE...
THUNK
"...BUT IT NEVER DID.
"FOR, EVEN AS IT DESCENDED, IT WAS SLAIN!
"SHRIEKING IN ENDLESS PAIN, THE BEAST COLLAPSED TO THE GROUND--
"--WITH AN ARROW LODGED IN ITS HEART.
"I SAW NONE OF THAT-- MY PAIN HAD ALREADY TAKEN ITS TOLL AND I WAS MERCIFULLY UNCONSCIOUS...
"--BUT YOU SAW IT ALL, TAJ-- YOU SAW THE THING DIE--
"--YOU SAW THE BEAST TURN TO ASH, AND THE WIND CARRY AWAY ITS FINAL REMAINS.
"YOU TOLD ME HOW THEIR LEADER CALLOUSLY LAUGHED AT HIS OWN MAN'S DEATH--
"--WHILE YOU WATCHED IN UNCOMPREHENDING TERROR.

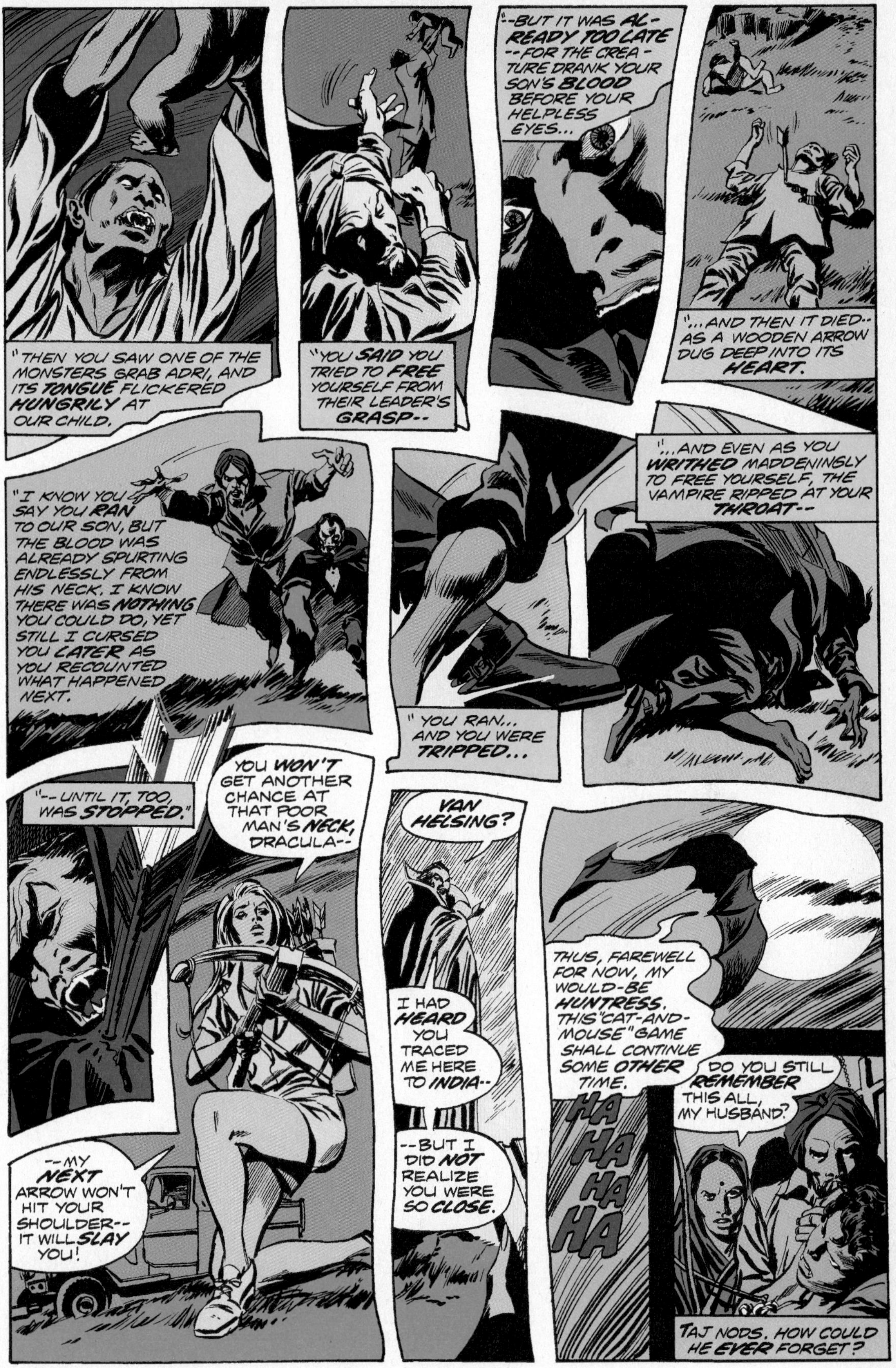
"THEN YOU SAW ONE OF THE MONSTERS GRAB ADRI, AND ITS TONGUE HUNGRILY FLICKERED AT OUR CHILD.
"YOU SAID YOU TRIED TO FREE YOURSELF FROM THEIR LEADER'S GRASP--
"--BUT IT WAS ALREADY TOO LATE--FOR THE CREATURE DRANK YOUR SON'S BLOOD BEFORE YOUR HELPLESS EYES...
"...AND THEN IT DIED--AS A WOODEN ARROW DUG DEEP INTO ITS HEART.
"I KNOW YOU SAY YOU RAN TO OUR SON, BUT THE BLOOD WAS ALREADY SPURTING ENDLESSLY FROM HIS NECK. I KNOW THERE WAS NOTHING YOU COULD DO, YET STILL I CURSED YOU LATER AS YOU RECOUNTED WHAT HAPPENED NEXT.
"...AND EVEN AS YOU WRITHED MADDENINGLY TO FREE YOURSELF, THE VAMPIRE RIPPED AT YOUR THROAT--
"YOU RAN... AND YOU WERE TRIPPED...
"--UNTIL IT, TOO, WAS STOPPED."
YOU WON'T GET ANOTHER CHANCE AT THAT POOR MAN'S NECK, DRACULA--
--MY NEXT ARROW WON'T HIT YOUR SHOULDER--IT WILL SLAY YOU!
VAN HELSING?
I HAD HEARD YOU TRACED ME HERE TO INDIA--
--BUT I DID NOT REALIZE YOU WERE SO CLOSE.
THUS, FAREWELL FOR NOW, MY WOULD-BE HUNTRESS. THIS "CAT-AND-MOUSE" GAME SHALL CONTINUE SOME OTHER TIME.
HA HA HA HA HA
DO YOU STILL REMEMBER THIS ALL, MY HUSBAND?
TAJ NODS. HOW COULD HE EVER FORGET?

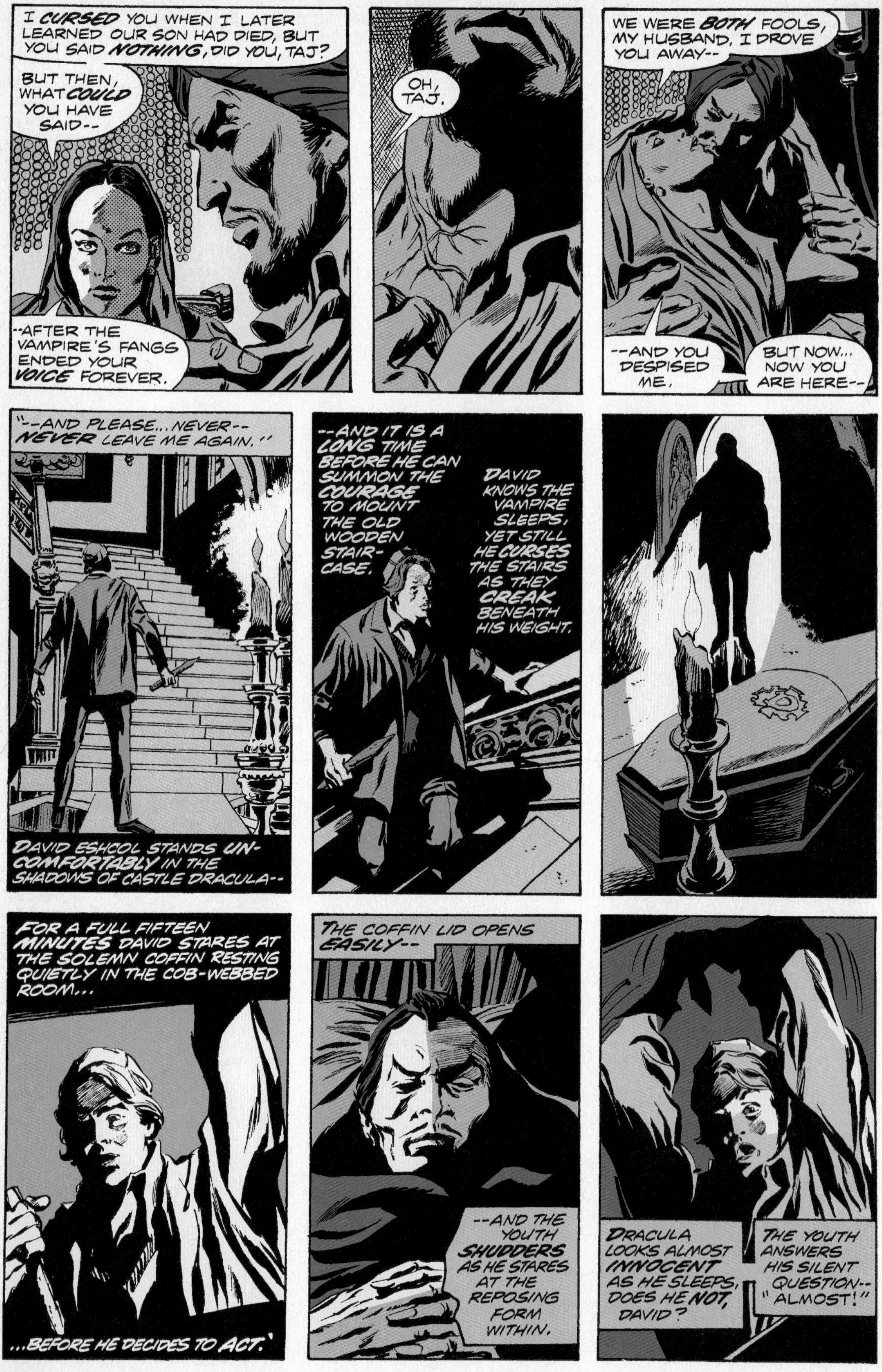

I CURSED YOU WHEN I LATER LEARNED OUR SON HAD DIED, BUT YOU SAID NOTHING, DID YOU, TAJ?
BUT THEN, WHAT COULD YOU HAVE SAID--
--AFTER THE VAMPIRE'S FANGS ENDED YOUR VOICE FOREVER.
OH, TAJ.
WE WERE BOTH FOOLS, MY HUSBAND. I DROVE YOU AWAY--
--AND YOU DESPISED ME.
BUT NOW... NOW YOU ARE HERE--
"--AND PLEASE... NEVER-- NEVER LEAVE ME AGAIN."
DAVID ESHCOL STANDS UNCOMFORTABLY IN THE SHADOWS OF CASTLE DRACULA--
--AND IT IS A LONG TIME BEFORE HE CAN SUMMON THE COURAGE TO MOUNT THE OLD WOODEN STAIRCASE.
DAVID KNOWS THE VAMPIRE SLEEPS, YET STILL HE CURSES THE STAIRS AS THEY CREAK BENEATH HIS WEIGHT.
FOR A FULL FIFTEEN MINUTES DAVID STARES AT THE SOLEMN COFFIN RESTING QUIETLY IN THE COB-WEBBED ROOM...
...BEFORE HE DECIDES TO ACT.
THE COFFIN LID OPENS EASILY--
--AND THE YOUTH SHUDDERS AS HE STARES AT THE REPOSING FORM WITHIN.
DRACULA LOOKS ALMOST INNOCENT AS HE SLEEPS, DOES HE NOT, DAVID?
THE YOUTH ANSWERS HIS SILENT QUESTION-- "ALMOST!"

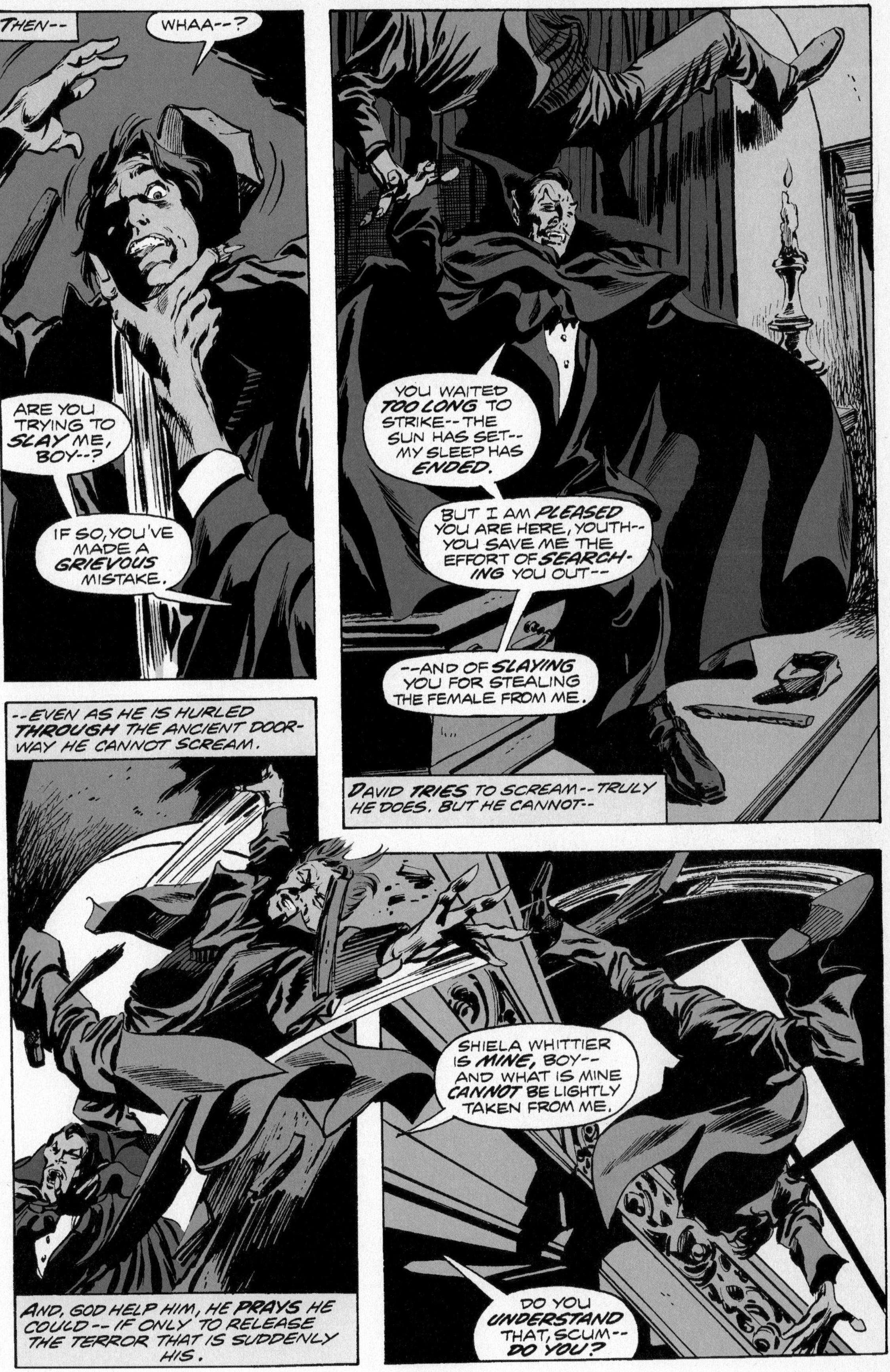
THEN--
WHAA--?
ARE YOU TRYING TO SLAY ME, BOY--?
IF SO, YOU'VE MADE A GRIEVOUS MISTAKE.
YOU WAITED TOO LONG TO STRIKE-- THE SUN HAS SET-- MY SLEEP HAS ENDED.
BUT I AM PLEASED YOU ARE HERE, YOUTH-- YOU SAVE ME THE EFFORT OF SEARCH-ING YOU OUT--
--AND OF SLAYING YOU FOR STEALING THE FEMALE FROM ME.
DAVID TRIES TO SCREAM-- TRULY HE DOES. BUT HE CANNOT--
--EVEN AS HE IS HURLED THROUGH THE ANCIENT DOOR-WAY HE CANNOT SCREAM.
AND, GOD HELP HIM, HE PRAYS HE COULD-- IF ONLY TO RELEASE THE TERROR THAT IS SUDDENLY HIS.
SHIELA WHITTIER IS MINE, BOY-- AND WHAT IS MINE CANNOT BE LIGHTLY TAKEN FROM ME.
DO YOU UNDERSTAND THAT, SCUM-- DO YOU?

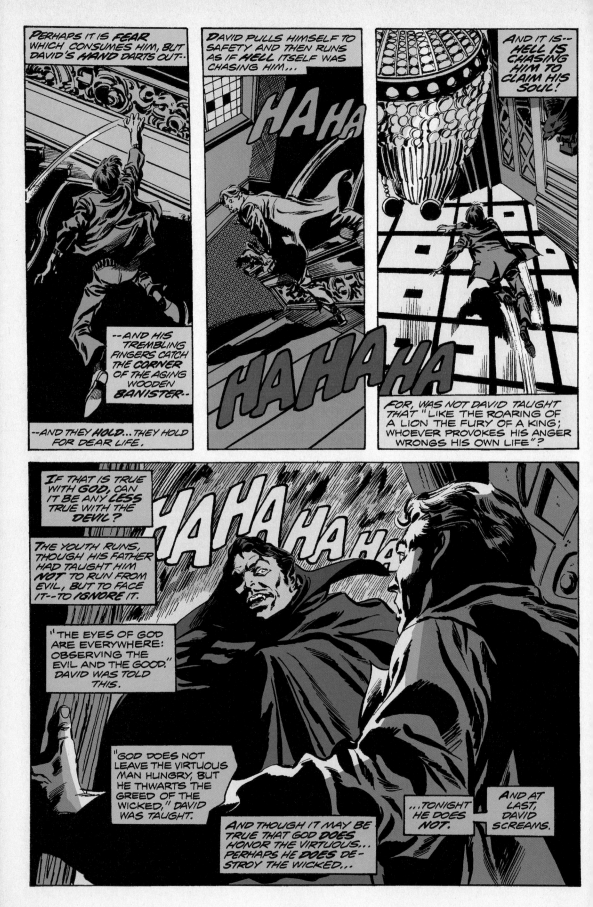

PERHAPS IT IS *FEAR* WHICH CONSUMES HIM, BUT DAVID'S *HAND* DARTS OUT--

--AND HIS TREMBLING FINGERS CATCH THE CORNER OF THE AGING WOODEN BANISTER--

--AND THEY *HOLD*...THEY HOLD FOR DEAR LIFE.

DAVID PULLS HIMSELF TO SAFETY AND THEN RUNS AS IF *HELL* ITSELF WAS CHASING HIM...

HA HA

HAHAHA

AND IT IS-- *HELL IS* CHASING HIM TO CLAIM HIS SOUL!

FOR, WAS NOT DAVID TAUGHT THAT "LIKE THE ROARING OF A LION THE FURY OF A KING; WHOEVER PROVOKES HIS ANGER WRONGS HIS OWN LIFE"?

IF THAT IS TRUE WITH *GOD*, CAN IT BE ANY *LESS* TRUE WITH THE *DEVIL*?

THE YOUTH RUNS, THOUGH HIS FATHER HAD TAUGHT HIM *NOT* TO RUN FROM EVIL, BUT TO FACE IT--TO *IGNORE* IT.

"THE EYES OF GOD ARE EVERYWHERE: OBSERVING THE EVIL AND THE GOOD," DAVID WAS TOLD THIS.

"GOD DOES NOT LEAVE THE VIRTUOUS MAN HUNGRY, BUT HE THWARTS THE GREED OF THE WICKED," DAVID WAS TAUGHT.

HAHA HA HA

AND THOUGH IT MAY BE TRUE THAT GOD *DOES* HONOR THE VIRTUOUS... PERHAPS HE *DOES* DE-STROY THE WICKED...

...TONIGHT HE DOES *NOT*.

AND AT LAST, DAVID SCREAMS.

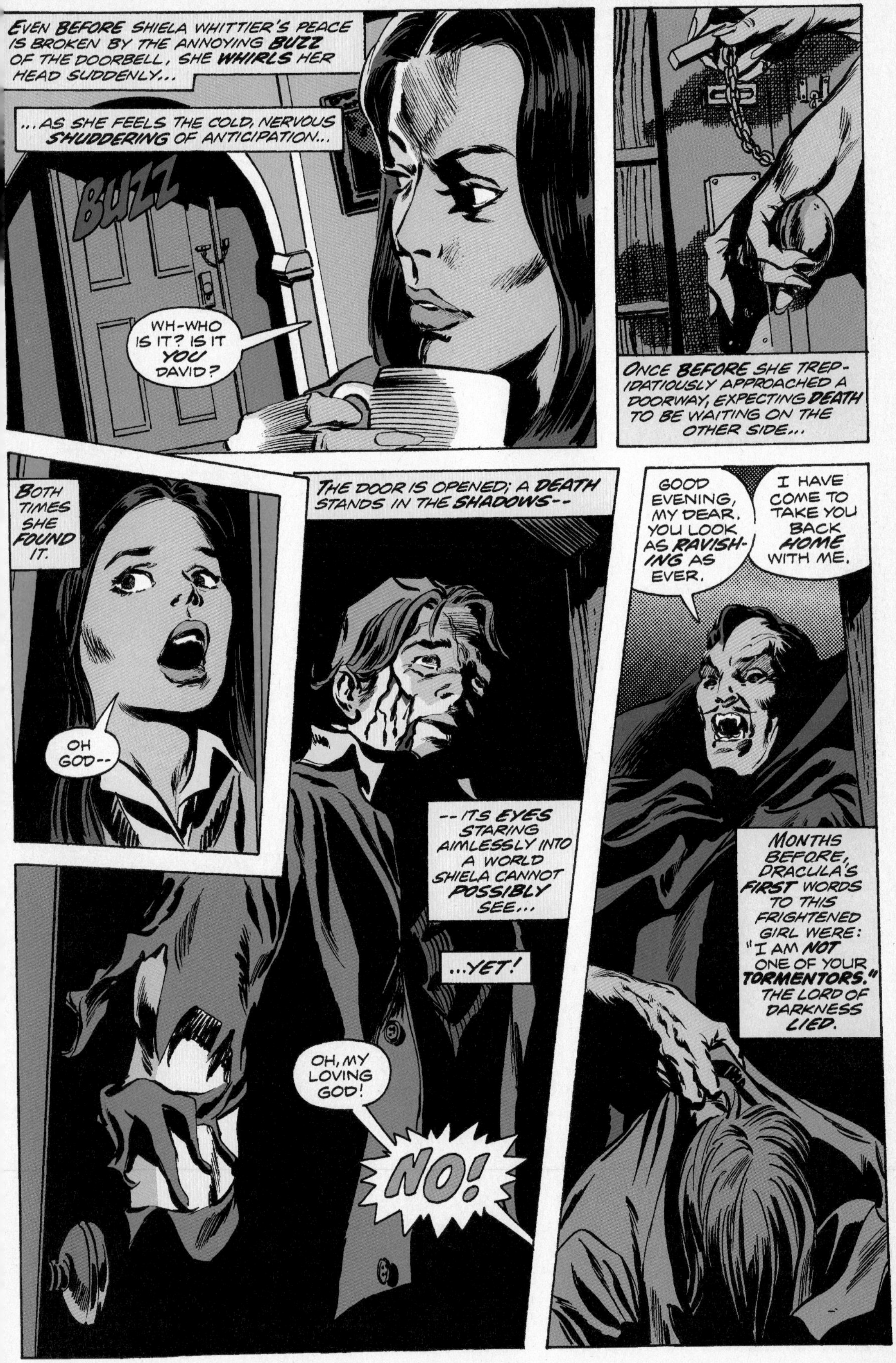
EVEN BEFORE SHIELA WHITTIER'S PEACE IS BROKEN BY THE ANNOYING BUZZ OF THE DOORBELL, SHE WHIRLS HER HEAD SUDDENLY...
...AS SHE FEELS THE COLD, NERVOUS SHUDDERING OF ANTICIPATION...
BUZZ
WH-WHO IS IT? IS IT YOU DAVID?
ONCE BEFORE SHE TREPIDATIOUSLY APPROACHED A DOORWAY, EXPECTING DEATH TO BE WAITING ON THE OTHER SIDE...
BOTH TIMES SHE FOUND IT.
OH GOD--
THE DOOR IS OPENED; A DEATH STANDS IN THE SHADOWS--
--ITS EYES STARING AIMLESSLY INTO A WORLD SHIELA CANNOT POSSIBLY SEE...
...YET!
OH, MY LOVING GOD!
NO!
GOOD EVENING, MY DEAR. YOU LOOK AS RAVISHING AS EVER.
I HAVE COME TO TAKE YOU BACK HOME WITH ME.
MONTHS BEFORE, DRACULA'S FIRST WORDS TO THIS FRIGHTENED GIRL WERE: "I AM NOT ONE OF YOUR TORMENTORS." THE LORD OF DARKNESS LIED.

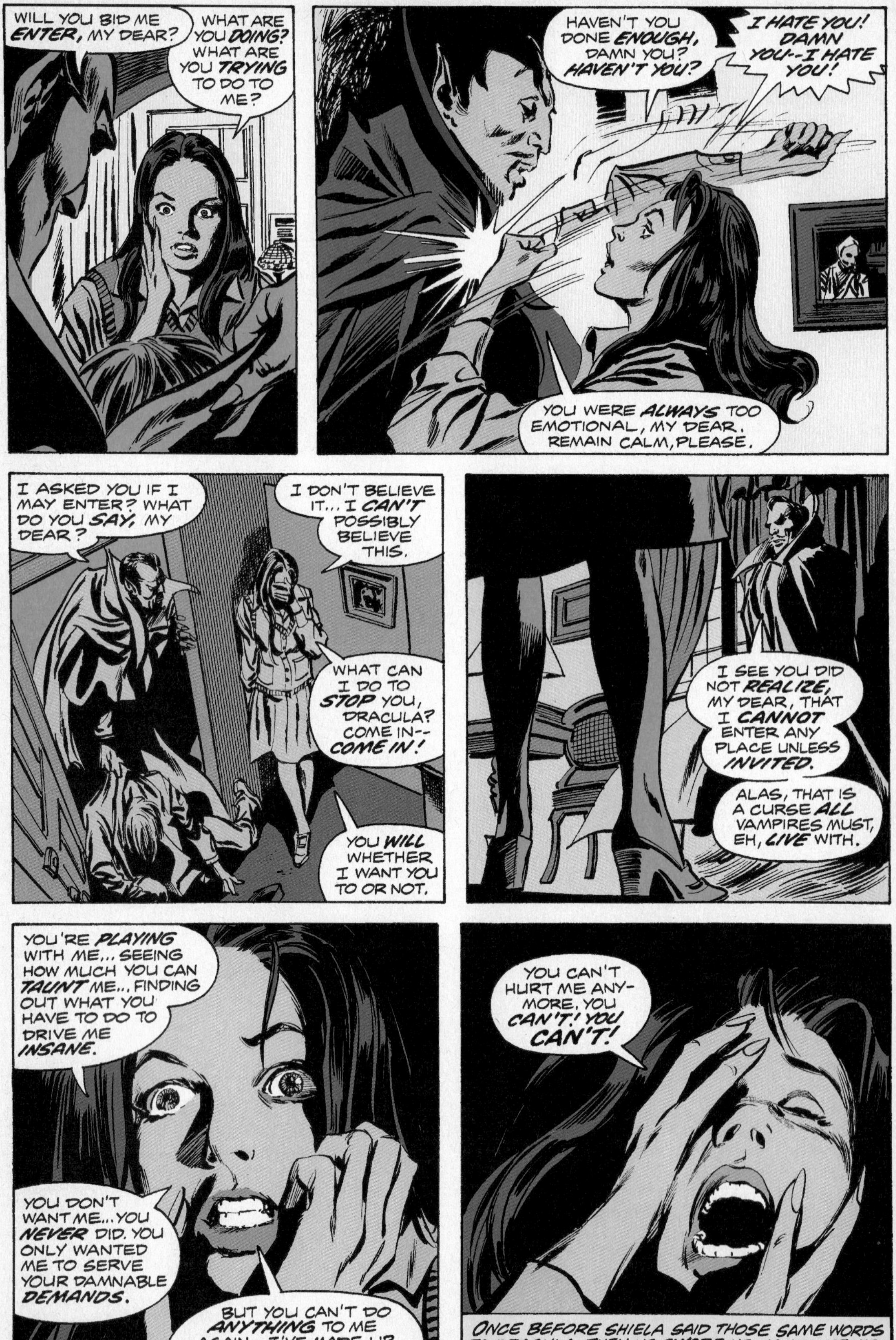
WILL YOU BID ME ENTER, MY DEAR?
WHAT ARE YOU DOING? WHAT ARE YOU TRYING TO DO TO ME?
HAVEN'T YOU DONE ENOUGH, DAMN YOU? HAVEN'T YOU?
I HATE YOU! DAMN YOU--I HATE YOU!
YOU WERE ALWAYS TOO EMOTIONAL, MY DEAR. REMAIN CALM, PLEASE.
I ASKED YOU IF I MAY ENTER? WHAT DO YOU SAY, MY DEAR?
I DON'T BELIEVE IT... I CAN'T POSSIBLY BELIEVE THIS.
WHAT CAN I DO TO STOP YOU, DRACULA? COME IN--COME IN!
YOU WILL WHETHER I WANT YOU TO OR NOT.
I SEE YOU DID NOT REALIZE, MY DEAR, THAT I CANNOT ENTER ANY PLACE UNLESS INVITED.
ALAS, THAT IS A CURSE ALL VAMPIRES MUST, EH, LIVE WITH.
YOU'RE PLAYING WITH ME... SEEING HOW MUCH YOU CAN TAUNT ME... FINDING OUT WHAT YOU HAVE TO DO TO DRIVE ME INSANE.
YOU DON'T WANT ME... YOU NEVER DID. YOU ONLY WANTED ME TO SERVE YOUR DAMNABLE DEMANDS.
BUT YOU CAN'T DO ANYTHING TO ME AGAIN... I'VE MADE UP MY MIND THAT YOU CAN'T.
YOU CAN'T HURT ME ANY-MORE. YOU CAN'T! YOU CAN'T!
ONCE BEFORE SHIELA SAID THOSE SAME WORDS TO DRACULA. THEN HE SWORE HE WOULD NOT HARM HER. YES, THE LORD OF DARKNESS LIED INDEED.

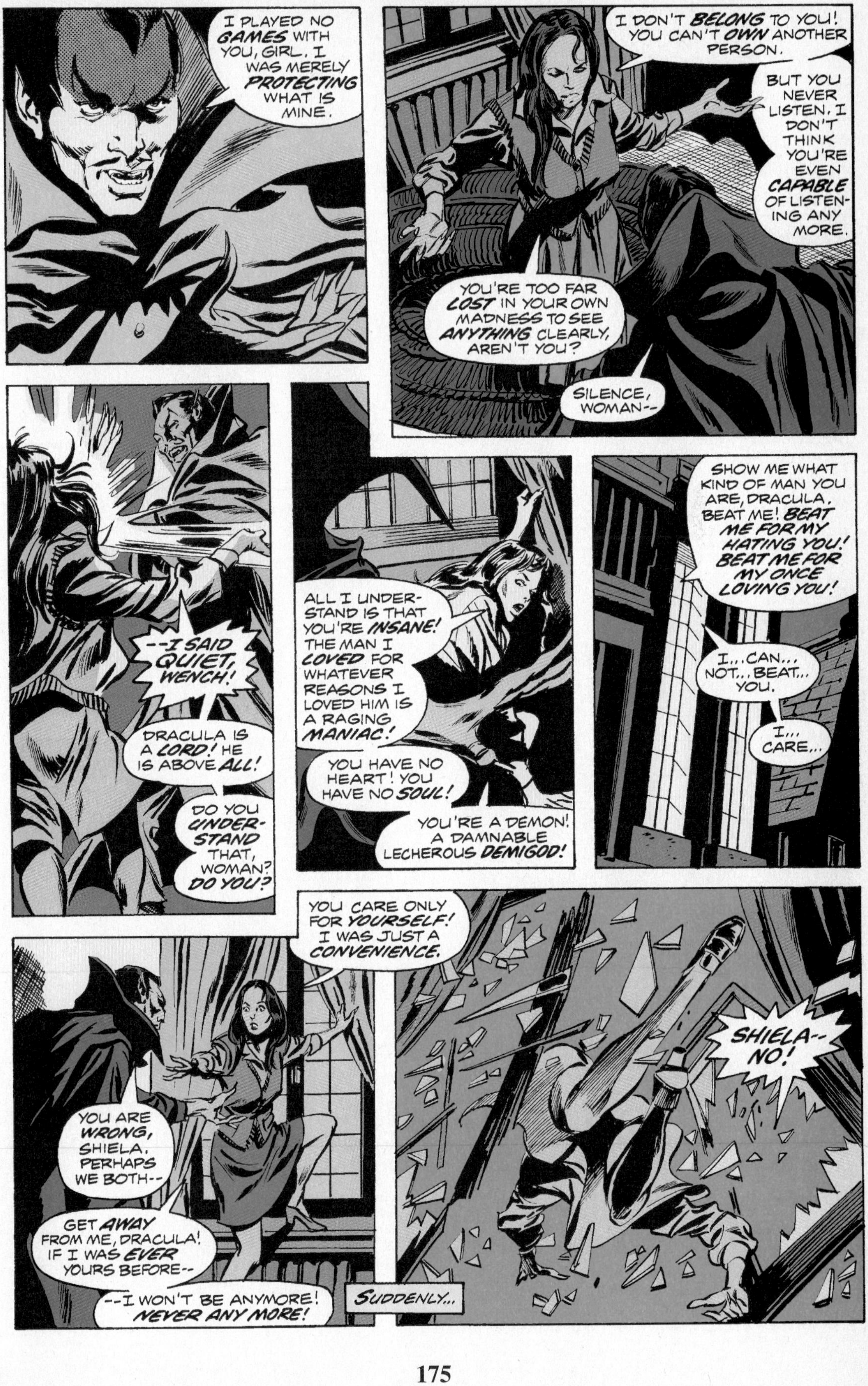
I PLAYED NO GAMES WITH YOU, GIRL. I WAS MERELY PROTECTING WHAT IS MINE.
I DON'T BELONG TO YOU! YOU CAN'T OWN ANOTHER PERSON.
BUT YOU NEVER LISTEN. I DON'T THINK YOU'RE EVEN CAPABLE OF LISTENING ANY MORE.
YOU'RE TOO FAR LOST IN YOUR OWN MADNESS TO SEE ANYTHING CLEARLY, AREN'T YOU?
SILENCE, WOMAN--
--I SAID QUIET, WENCH!
DRACULA IS A LORD! HE IS ABOVE ALL!
DO YOU UNDERSTAND THAT, WOMAN? DO YOU?
ALL I UNDERSTAND IS THAT YOU'RE INSANE! THE MAN I LOVED FOR WHATEVER REASONS I LOVED HIM IS A RAGING MANIAC!
YOU HAVE NO HEART! YOU HAVE NO SOUL!
YOU'RE A DEMON! A DAMNABLE LECHEROUS DEMIGOD!
SHOW ME WHAT KIND OF MAN YOU ARE, DRACULA. BEAT ME! BEAT ME FOR MY HATING YOU! BEAT ME FOR MY ONCE LOVING YOU!
I... CAN... NOT... BEAT... YOU.
I... CARE...
YOU CARE ONLY FOR YOURSELF! I WAS JUST A CONVENIENCE.
YOU ARE WRONG, SHIELA. PERHAPS WE BOTH--
GET AWAY FROM ME, DRACULA! IF I WAS EVER YOURS BEFORE--
--I WON'T BE ANYMORE! NEVER ANY MORE!
SUDDENLY...
SHIELA-- NO!

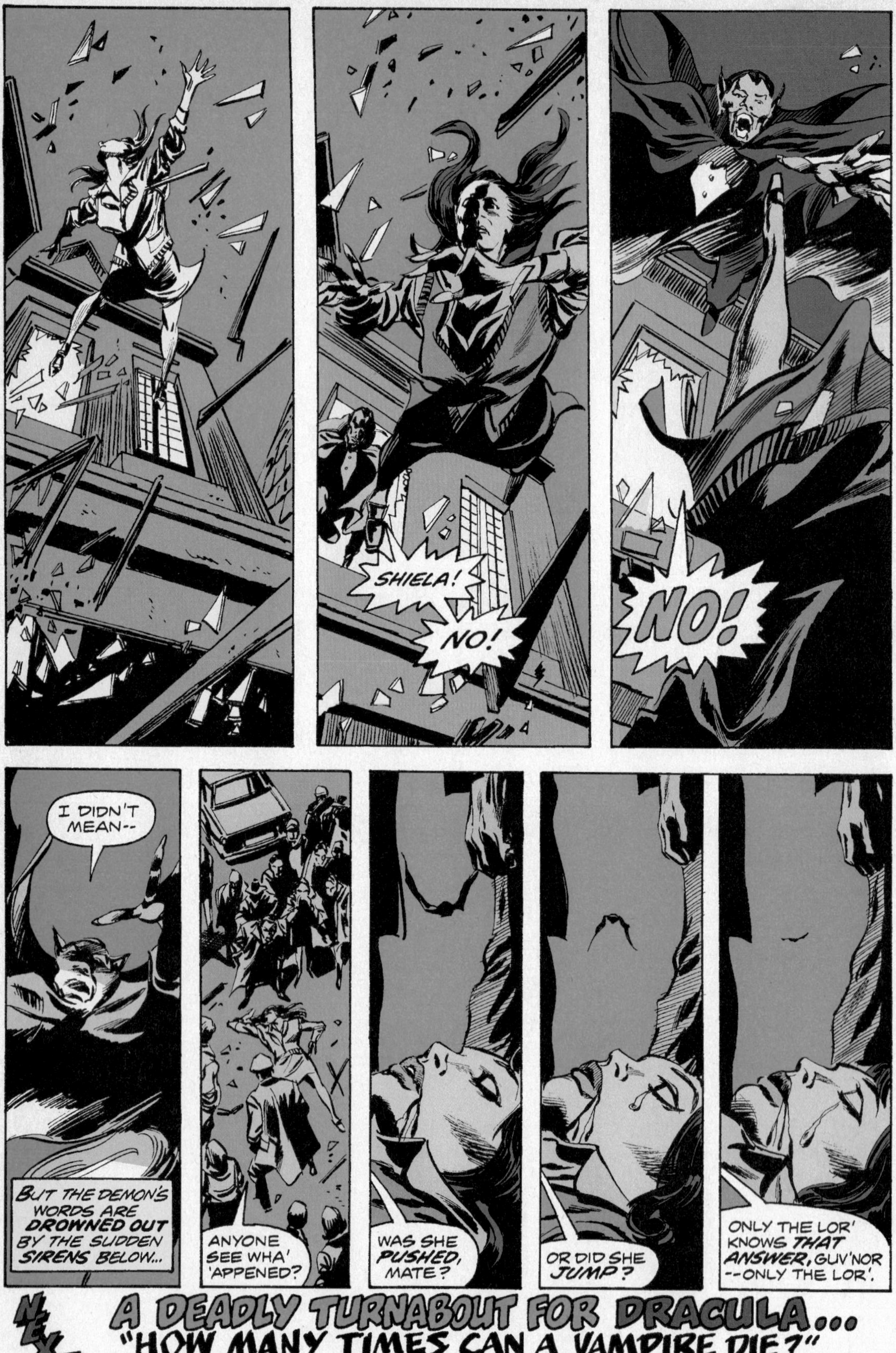

SHIELA!
NO!
NO!
I DIDN'T MEAN--
BUT THE DEMON'S WORDS ARE DROWNED OUT BY THE SUDDEN SIRENS BELOW...
ANYONE SEE WHA' 'APPENED?
WAS SHE PUSHED, MATE?
OR DID SHE JUMP?
ONLY THE LOR' KNOWS THAT ANSWER, GUV'NOR --ONLY THE LOR'.
NEXT
A DEADLY TURNABOUT FOR DRACULA...
"HOW MANY TIMES CAN A VAMPIRE DIE?"
and DRACULA'S JOURNAL.

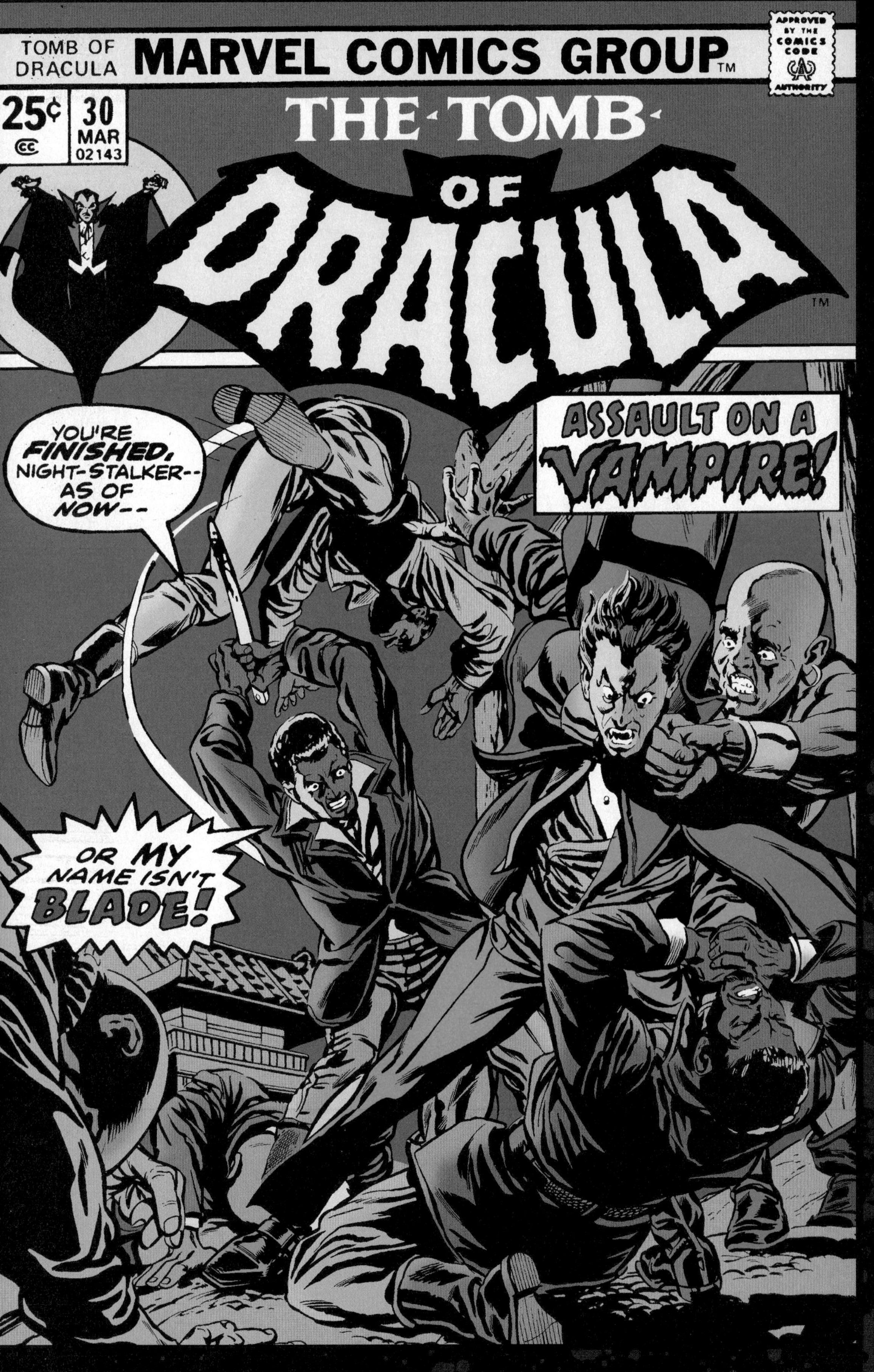
TOMB OF DRACULA
MARVEL COMICS GROUP™
APPROVED BY THE COMICS CODE AUTHORITY
25¢
30 MAR 02143
THE TOMB OF DRACULA™
ASSAULT ON A VAMPIRE!
YOU'RE FINISHED, NIGHT-STALKER-- AS OF NOW--
OR MY NAME ISN'T BLADE!

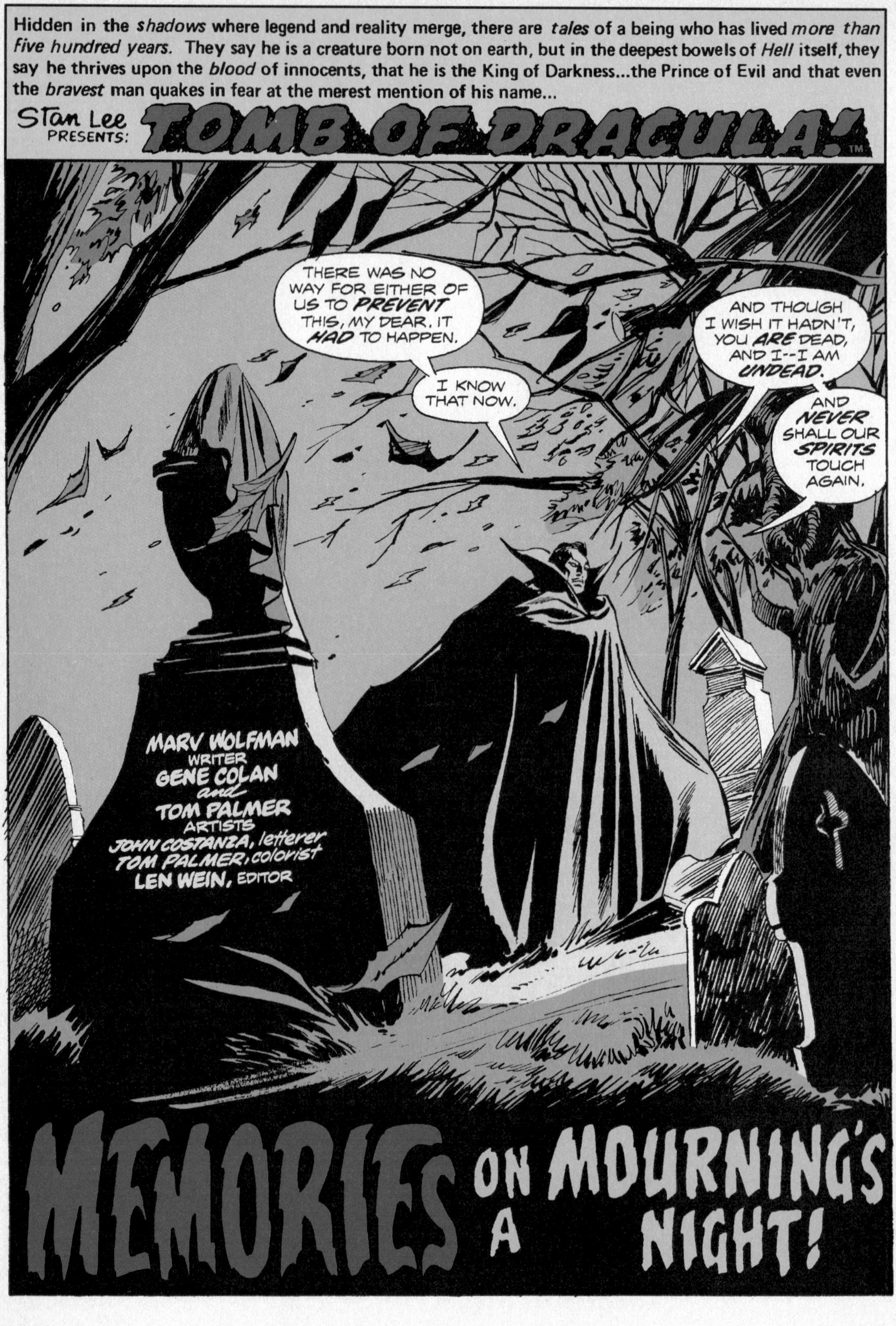
Hidden in the *shadows* where legend and reality merge, there are *tales* of a being who has lived *more than five hundred years.* They say he is a creature born not on earth, but in the deepest bowels of *Hell* itself, they say he thrives upon the *blood* of innocents, that he is the King of Darkness...the Prince of Evil and that even the *bravest* man quakes in fear at the merest mention of his name...
Stan Lee PRESENTS: TOMB OF DRACULA! ™
THERE WAS NO WAY FOR EITHER OF US TO PREVENT THIS, MY DEAR. IT HAD TO HAPPEN.
I KNOW THAT NOW.
AND THOUGH I WISH IT HADN'T, YOU ARE DEAD, AND I--I AM UNDEAD.
AND NEVER SHALL OUR SPIRITS TOUCH AGAIN.
MARV WOLFMAN WRITER GENE COLAN and TOM PALMER ARTISTS JOHN COSTANZA, letterer TOM PALMER, colorist LEN WEIN, EDITOR
MEMORIES ON A MOURNING'S NIGHT!

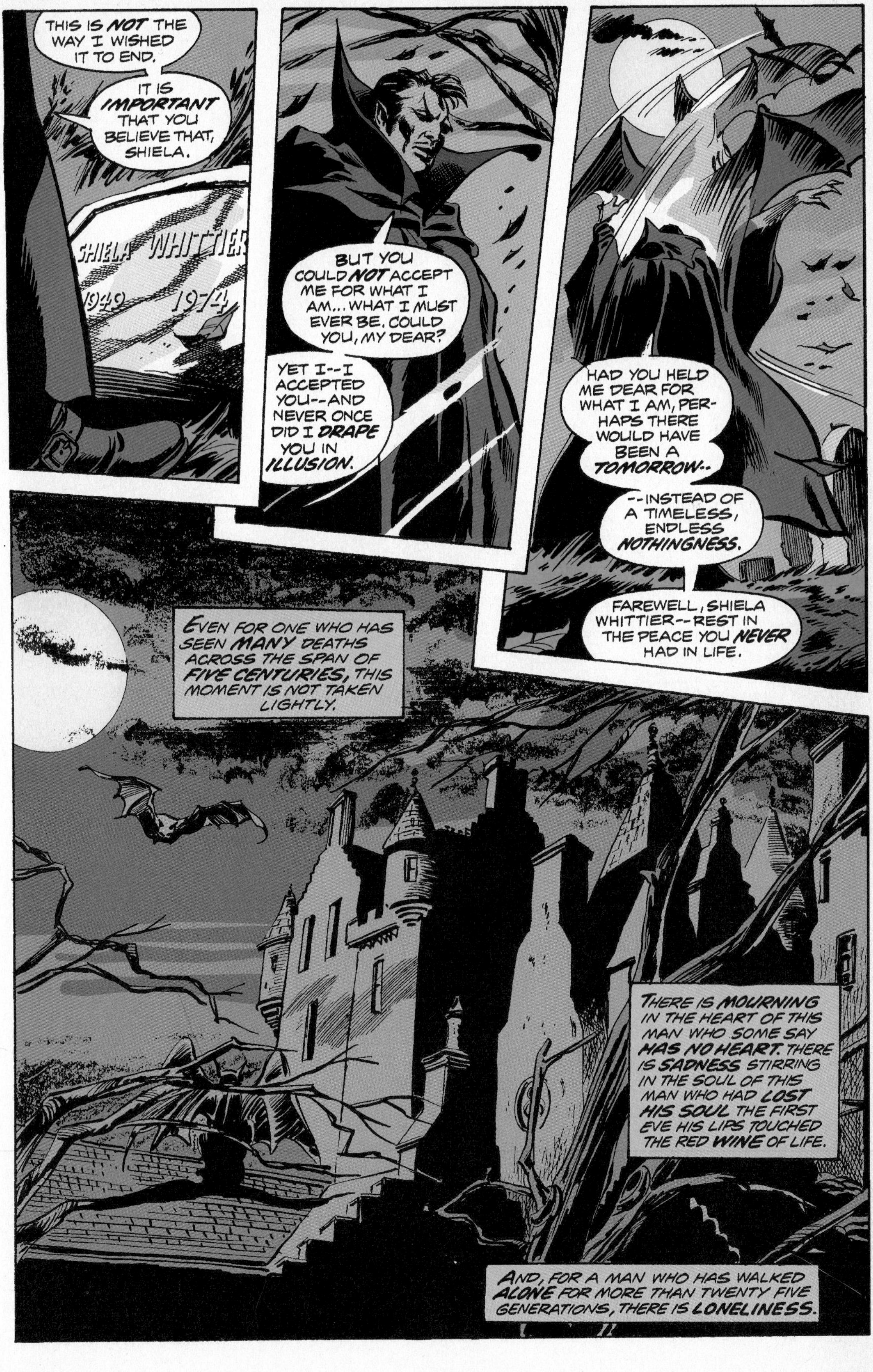

THIS IS NOT THE WAY I WISHED IT TO END.
IT IS IMPORTANT THAT YOU BELIEVE THAT, SHIELA.
SHIELA WHITTIER 1949 1974
BUT YOU COULD NOT ACCEPT ME FOR WHAT I AM... WHAT I MUST EVER BE. COULD YOU, MY DEAR?
YET I--I ACCEPTED YOU--AND NEVER ONCE DID I DRAPE YOU IN ILLUSION.
HAD YOU HELD ME DEAR FOR WHAT I AM, PER-HAPS THERE WOULD HAVE BEEN A TOMORROW--
--INSTEAD OF A TIMELESS, ENDLESS NOTHINGNESS.
FAREWELL, SHIELA WHITTIER--REST IN THE PEACE YOU NEVER HAD IN LIFE.
EVEN FOR ONE WHO HAS SEEN MANY DEATHS ACROSS THE SPAN OF FIVE CENTURIES, THIS MOMENT IS NOT TAKEN LIGHTLY.
THERE IS MOURNING IN THE HEART OF THIS MAN WHO SOME SAY HAS NO HEART. THERE IS SADNESS STIRRING IN THE SOUL OF THIS MAN WHO HAD LOST HIS SOUL THE FIRST EVE HIS LIPS TOUCHED THE RED WINE OF LIFE.
AND, FOR A MAN WHO HAS WALKED ALONE FOR MORE THAN TWENTY FIVE GENERATIONS, THERE IS LONELINESS.

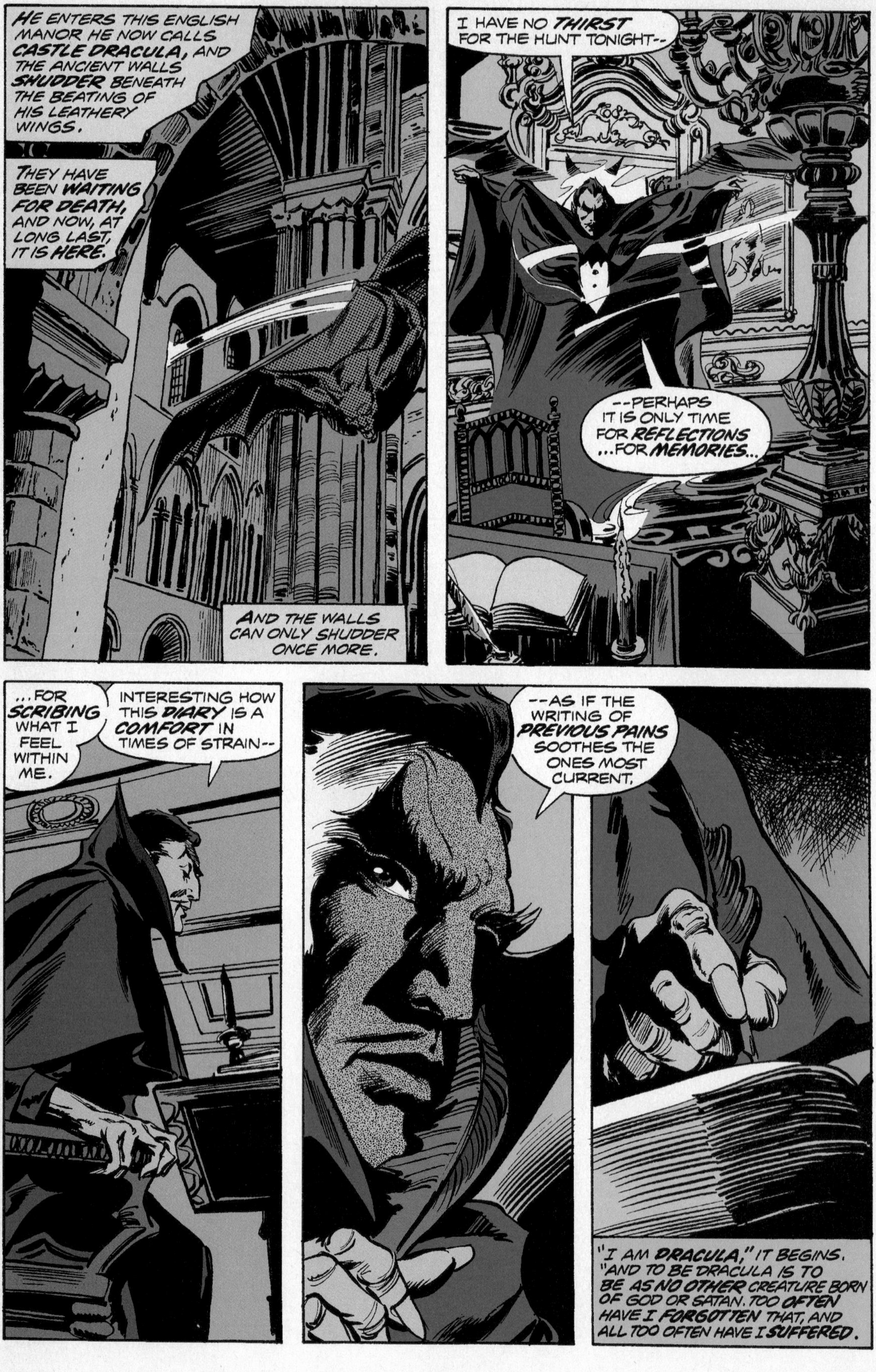
HE ENTERS THIS ENGLISH MANOR HE NOW CALLS CASTLE DRACULA, AND THE ANCIENT WALLS SHUDDER BENEATH THE BEATING OF HIS LEATHERY WINGS.
THEY HAVE BEEN WAITING FOR DEATH, AND NOW, AT LONG LAST, IT IS HERE.
AND THE WALLS CAN ONLY SHUDDER ONCE MORE.
I HAVE NO THIRST FOR THE HUNT TONIGHT--
--PERHAPS IT IS ONLY TIME FOR REFLECTIONS ...FOR MEMORIES...
...FOR SCRIBING WHAT I FEEL WITHIN ME.
INTERESTING HOW THIS DIARY IS A COMFORT IN TIMES OF STRAIN--
--AS IF THE WRITING OF PREVIOUS PAINS SOOTHES THE ONES MOST CURRENT.
"I AM DRACULA," IT BEGINS. "AND TO BE DRACULA IS TO BE AS NO OTHER CREATURE BORN OF GOD OR SATAN. TOO OFTEN HAVE I FORGOTTEN THAT, AND ALL TOO OFTEN HAVE I SUFFERED.

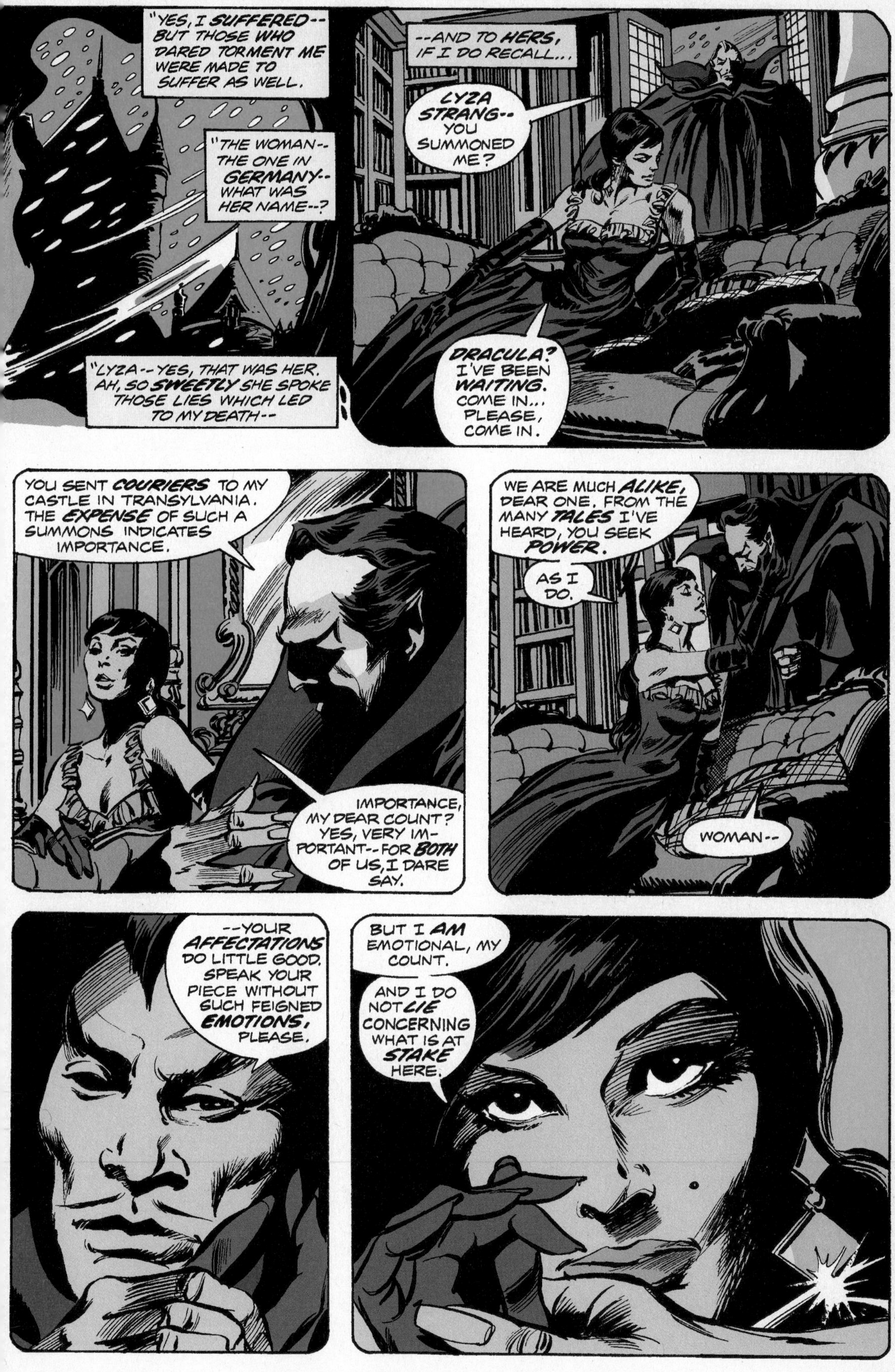
"YES, I SUFFERED-- BUT THOSE WHO DARED TORMENT ME WERE MADE TO SUFFER AS WELL.
"THE WOMAN-- THE ONE IN GERMANY-- WHAT WAS HER NAME--?
"LYZA--YES, THAT WAS HER. AH, SO SWEETLY SHE SPOKE THOSE LIES WHICH LED TO MY DEATH--
--AND TO HERS, IF I DO RECALL...
LYZA STRANG-- YOU SUMMONED ME?
DRACULA? I'VE BEEN WAITING. COME IN... PLEASE, COME IN.
YOU SENT COURIERS TO MY CASTLE IN TRANSYLVANIA. THE EXPENSE OF SUCH A SUMMONS INDICATES IMPORTANCE.
IMPORTANCE, MY DEAR COUNT? YES, VERY IMPORTANT--FOR BOTH OF US, I DARE SAY.
WE ARE MUCH ALIKE, DEAR ONE. FROM THE MANY TALES I'VE HEARD, YOU SEEK POWER.
AS I DO.
WOMAN--
--YOUR AFFECTATIONS DO LITTLE GOOD. SPEAK YOUR PIECE WITHOUT SUCH FEIGNED EMOTIONS, PLEASE.
BUT I AM EMOTIONAL, MY COUNT.
AND I DO NOT LIE CONCERNING WHAT IS AT STAKE HERE.

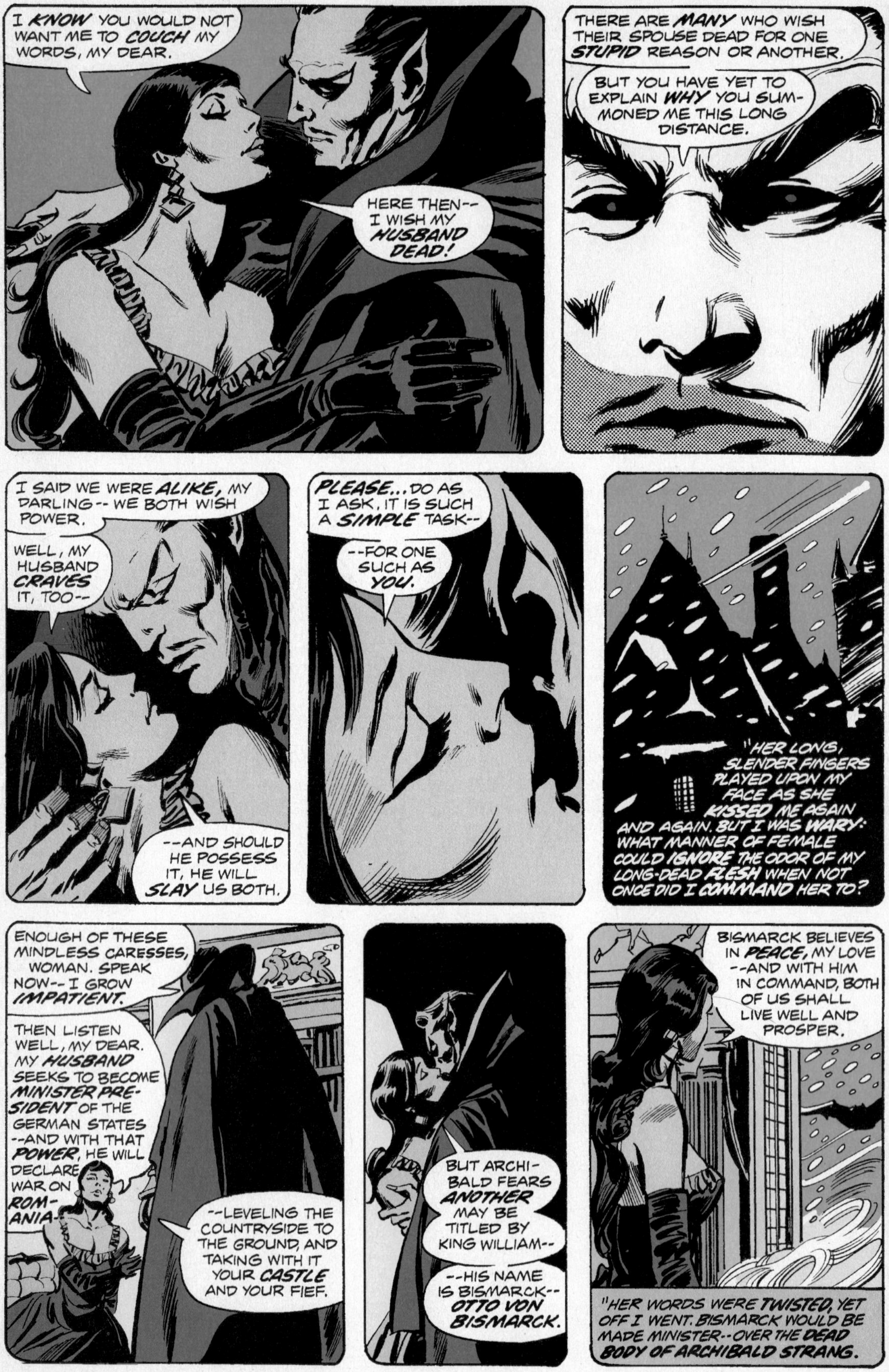

I KNOW YOU WOULD NOT WANT ME TO COUCH MY WORDS, MY DEAR.
HERE THEN-- I WISH MY HUSBAND DEAD!
THERE ARE MANY WHO WISH THEIR SPOUSE DEAD FOR ONE STUPID REASON OR ANOTHER.
BUT YOU HAVE YET TO EXPLAIN WHY YOU SUMMONED ME THIS LONG DISTANCE.
I SAID WE WERE ALIKE, MY DARLING-- WE BOTH WISH POWER.
WELL, MY HUSBAND CRAVES IT, TOO--
--AND SHOULD HE POSSESS IT, HE WILL SLAY US BOTH.
PLEASE... DO AS I ASK. IT IS SUCH A SIMPLE TASK--
--FOR ONE SUCH AS YOU.
"HER LONG, SLENDER FINGERS PLAYED UPON MY FACE AS SHE KISSED ME AGAIN AND AGAIN. BUT I WAS WARY: WHAT MANNER OF FEMALE COULD IGNORE THE ODOR OF MY LONG-DEAD FLESH WHEN NOT ONCE DID I COMMAND HER TO?
ENOUGH OF THESE MINDLESS CARESSES, WOMAN. SPEAK NOW-- I GROW IMPATIENT.
THEN LISTEN WELL, MY DEAR. MY HUSBAND SEEKS TO BECOME MINISTER PRESIDENT OF THE GERMAN STATES --AND WITH THAT POWER, HE WILL DECLARE WAR ON ROMANIA--
--LEVELING THE COUNTRYSIDE TO THE GROUND, AND TAKING WITH IT YOUR CASTLE AND YOUR FIEF.
BUT ARCHIBALD FEARS ANOTHER MAY BE TITLED BY KING WILLIAM--
--HIS NAME IS BISMARCK-- OTTO VON BISMARCK.
BISMARCK BELIEVES IN PEACE, MY LOVE --AND WITH HIM IN COMMAND, BOTH OF US SHALL LIVE WELL AND PROSPER.
"HER WORDS WERE TWISTED, YET OFF I WENT. BISMARCK WOULD BE MADE MINISTER--OVER THE DEAD BODY OF ARCHIBALD STRANG.

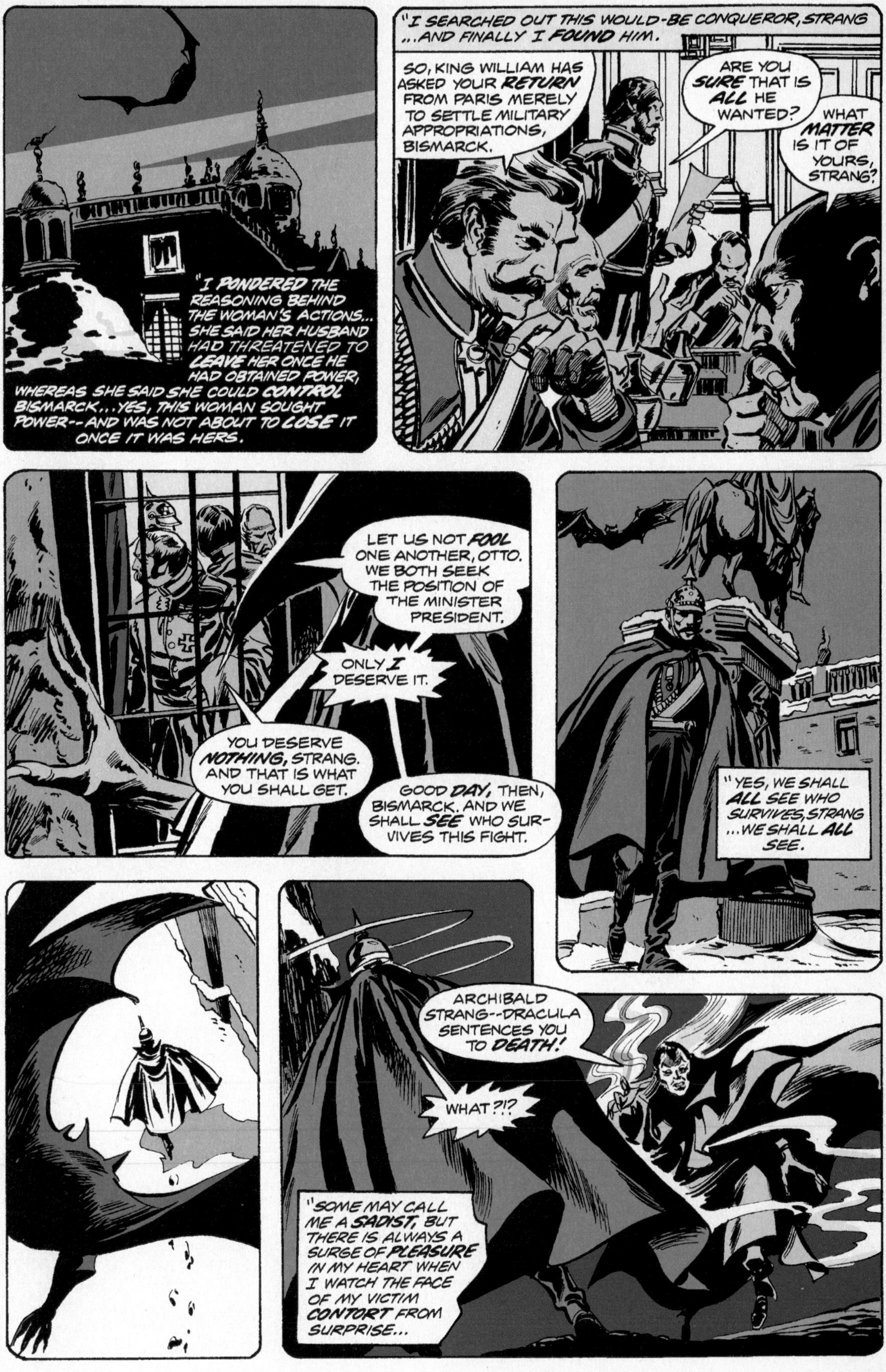
"I PONDERED THE REASONING BEHIND THE WOMAN'S ACTIONS... SHE SAID HER HUSBAND HAD THREATENED TO LEAVE HER ONCE HE HAD OBTAINED POWER, WHEREAS SHE SAID SHE COULD CONTROL BISMARCK...YES, THIS WOMAN SOUGHT POWER--AND WAS NOT ABOUT TO LOSE IT ONCE IT WAS HERS.
"I SEARCHED OUT THIS WOULD-BE CONQUEROR, STRANG ...AND FINALLY I FOUND HIM.
SO, KING WILLIAM HAS ASKED YOUR RETURN FROM PARIS MERELY TO SETTLE MILITARY APPROPRIATIONS, BISMARCK.
ARE YOU SURE THAT IS ALL HE WANTED?
WHAT MATTER IS IT OF YOURS, STRANG?
LET US NOT FOOL ONE ANOTHER, OTTO. WE BOTH SEEK THE POSITION OF THE MINISTER PRESIDENT.
ONLY I DESERVE IT.
YOU DESERVE NOTHING, STRANG. AND THAT IS WHAT YOU SHALL GET.
GOOD DAY, THEN, BISMARCK. AND WE SHALL SEE WHO SURVIVES THIS FIGHT.
"YES, WE SHALL ALL SEE WHO SURVIVES, STRANG ...WE SHALL ALL SEE.
ARCHIBALD STRANG--DRACULA SENTENCES YOU TO DEATH!
WHAT?!?
"SOME MAY CALL ME A SADIST, BUT THERE IS ALWAYS A SURGE OF PLEASURE IN MY HEART WHEN I WATCH THE FACE OF MY VICTIM CONTORT FROM SURPRISE...

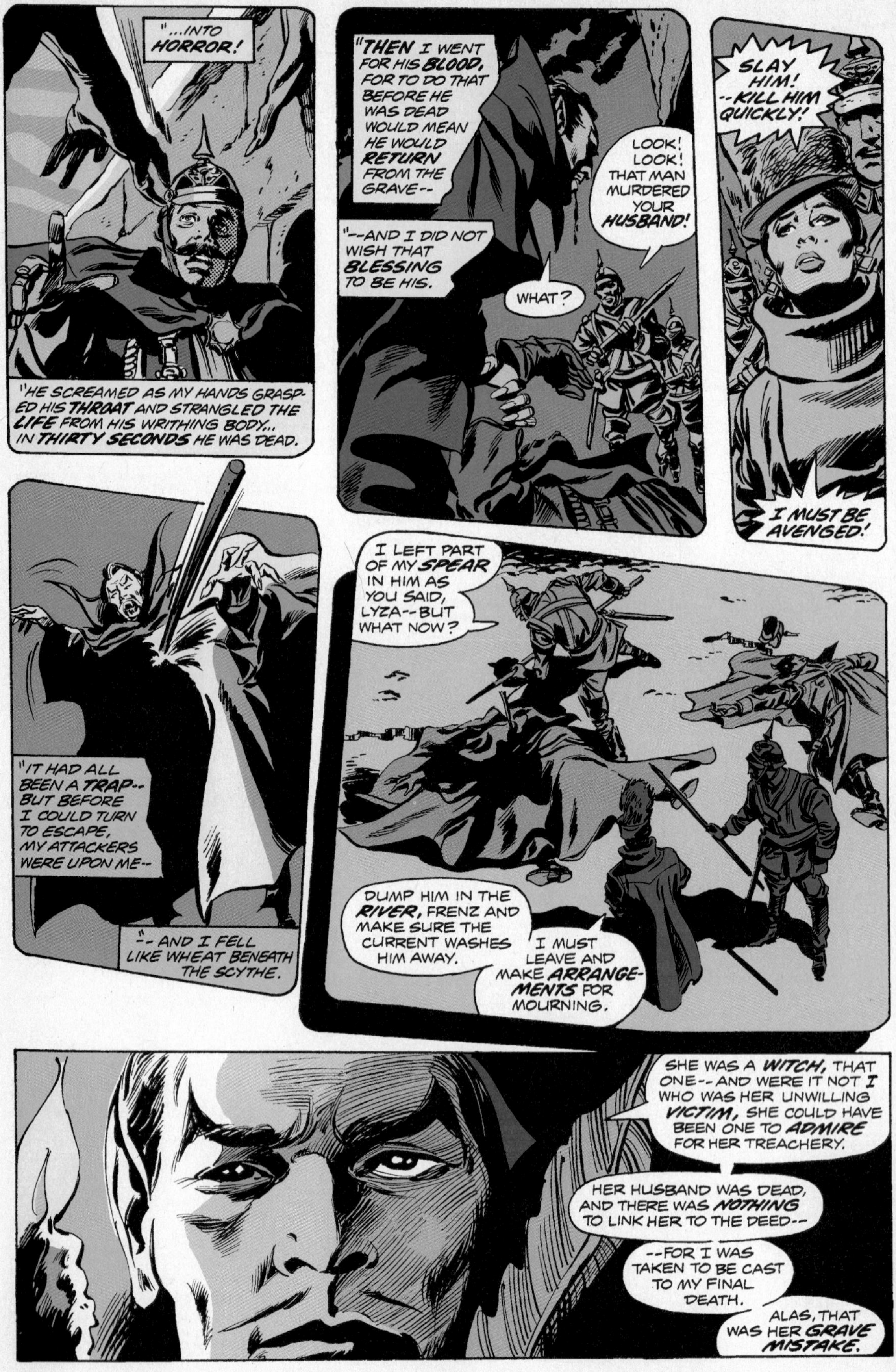
"...INTO HORROR!
"HE SCREAMED AS MY HANDS GRASPED HIS THROAT AND STRANGLED THE LIFE FROM HIS WRITHING BODY... IN THIRTY SECONDS HE WAS DEAD.
"THEN I WENT FOR HIS BLOOD, FOR TO DO THAT BEFORE HE WAS DEAD WOULD MEAN HE WOULD RETURN FROM THE GRAVE--
"--AND I DID NOT WISH THAT BLESSING TO BE HIS.
LOOK! LOOK! THAT MAN MURDERED YOUR HUSBAND!
WHAT?
SLAY HIM! --KILL HIM QUICKLY!
I MUST BE AVENGED!
"IT HAD ALL BEEN A TRAP-- BUT BEFORE I COULD TURN TO ESCAPE, MY ATTACKERS WERE UPON ME--
"-- AND I FELL LIKE WHEAT BENEATH THE SCYTHE.
I LEFT PART OF MY SPEAR IN HIM AS YOU SAID, LYZA--BUT WHAT NOW?
DUMP HIM IN THE RIVER, FRENZ AND MAKE SURE THE CURRENT WASHES HIM AWAY.
I MUST LEAVE AND MAKE ARRANGEMENTS FOR MOURNING.
SHE WAS A WITCH, THAT ONE-- AND WERE IT NOT I WHO WAS HER UNWILLING VICTIM, SHE COULD HAVE BEEN ONE TO ADMIRE FOR HER TREACHERY.
HER HUSBAND WAS DEAD, AND THERE WAS NOTHING TO LINK HER TO THE DEED--
--FOR I WAS TAKEN TO BE CAST TO MY FINAL DEATH.
ALAS, THAT WAS HER GRAVE MISTAKE.

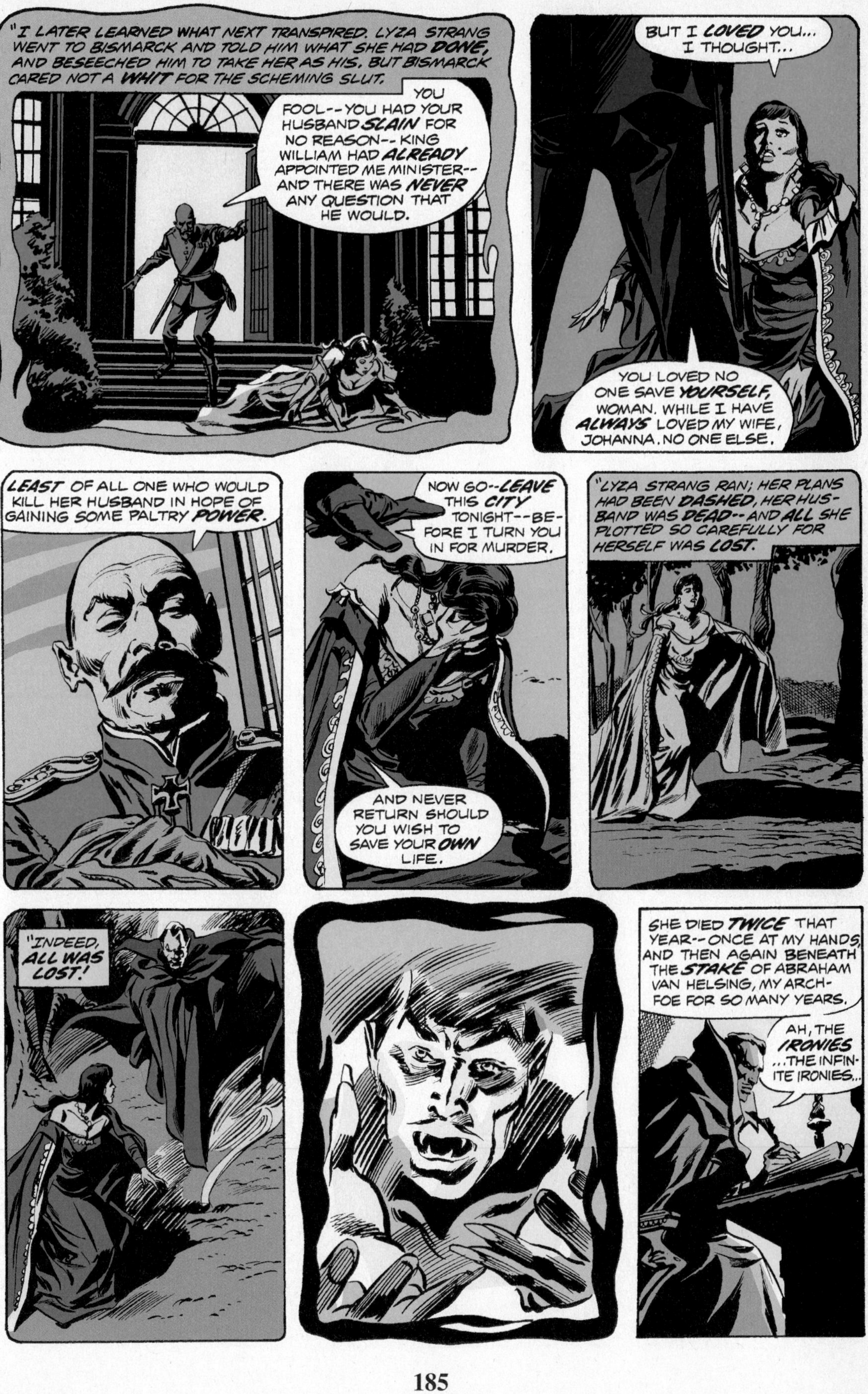
"I LATER LEARNED WHAT NEXT TRANSPIRED. LYZA STRANG WENT TO BISMARCK AND TOLD HIM WHAT SHE HAD DONE, AND BESEECHED HIM TO TAKE HER AS HIS. BUT BISMARCK CARED NOT A WHIT FOR THE SCHEMING SLUT.
YOU FOOL--YOU HAD YOUR HUSBAND SLAIN FOR NO REASON--KING WILLIAM HAD ALREADY APPOINTED ME MINISTER--AND THERE WAS NEVER ANY QUESTION THAT HE WOULD.
BUT I LOVED YOU... I THOUGHT...
YOU LOVED NO ONE SAVE YOURSELF, WOMAN. WHILE I HAVE ALWAYS LOVED MY WIFE, JOHANNA. NO ONE ELSE.
LEAST OF ALL ONE WHO WOULD KILL HER HUSBAND IN HOPE OF GAINING SOME PALTRY POWER.
NOW GO--LEAVE THIS CITY TONIGHT--BEFORE I TURN YOU IN FOR MURDER.
AND NEVER RETURN SHOULD YOU WISH TO SAVE YOUR OWN LIFE.
"LYZA STRANG RAN; HER PLANS HAD BEEN DASHED, HER HUSBAND WAS DEAD--AND ALL SHE PLOTTED SO CAREFULLY FOR HERSELF WAS LOST.
"INDEED, ALL WAS LOST!
SHE DIED TWICE THAT YEAR--ONCE AT MY HANDS, AND THEN AGAIN BENEATH THE STAKE OF ABRAHAM VAN HELSING, MY ARCH-FOE FOR SO MANY YEARS.
AH, THE IRONIES ...THE INFINITE IRONIES...

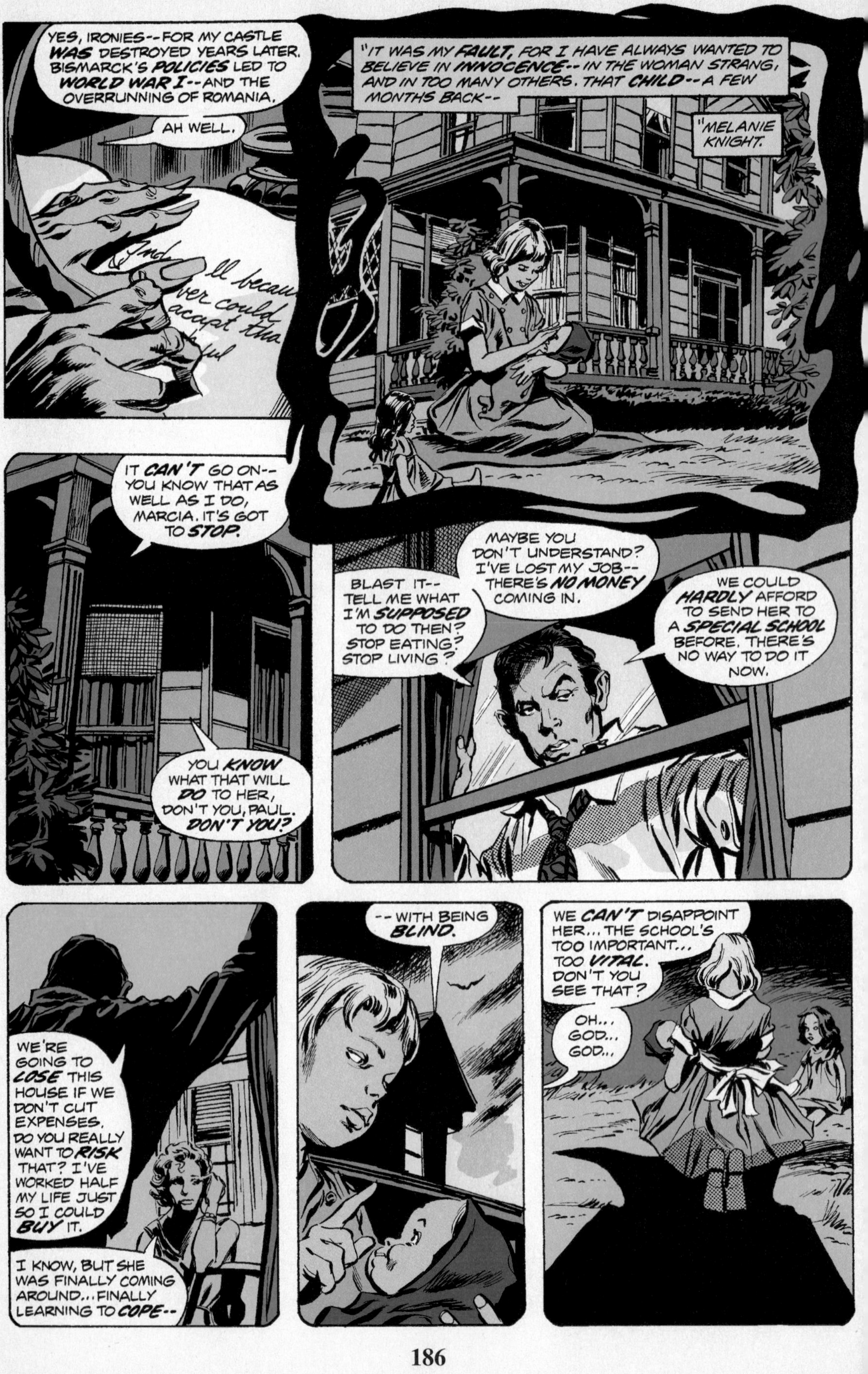
YES, IRONIES--FOR MY CASTLE WAS DESTROYED YEARS LATER. BISMARCK'S POLICIES LED TO WORLD WAR I--AND THE OVERRUNNING OF ROMANIA.
AH WELL.
"IT WAS MY FAULT, FOR I HAVE ALWAYS WANTED TO BELIEVE IN INNOCENCE-- IN THE WOMAN STRANG, AND IN TOO MANY OTHERS. THAT CHILD--A FEW MONTHS BACK--
"MELANIE KNIGHT.
IT CAN'T GO ON--YOU KNOW THAT AS WELL AS I DO, MARCIA. IT'S GOT TO STOP.
YOU KNOW WHAT THAT WILL DO TO HER, DON'T YOU, PAUL. DON'T YOU?
BLAST IT--TELL ME WHAT I'M SUPPOSED TO DO THEN? STOP EATING? STOP LIVING?
MAYBE YOU DON'T UNDERSTAND? I'VE LOST MY JOB--THERE'S NO MONEY COMING IN.
WE COULD HARDLY AFFORD TO SEND HER TO A SPECIAL SCHOOL BEFORE. THERE'S NO WAY TO DO IT NOW.
WE'RE GOING TO LOSE THIS HOUSE IF WE DON'T CUT EXPENSES. DO YOU REALLY WANT TO RISK THAT? I'VE WORKED HALF MY LIFE JUST SO I COULD BUY IT.
I KNOW, BUT SHE WAS FINALLY COMING AROUND... FINALLY LEARNING TO COPE--
--WITH BEING BLIND.
WE CAN'T DISAPPOINT HER... THE SCHOOL'S TOO IMPORTANT... TOO VITAL. DON'T YOU SEE THAT?
OH... GOD... GOD...

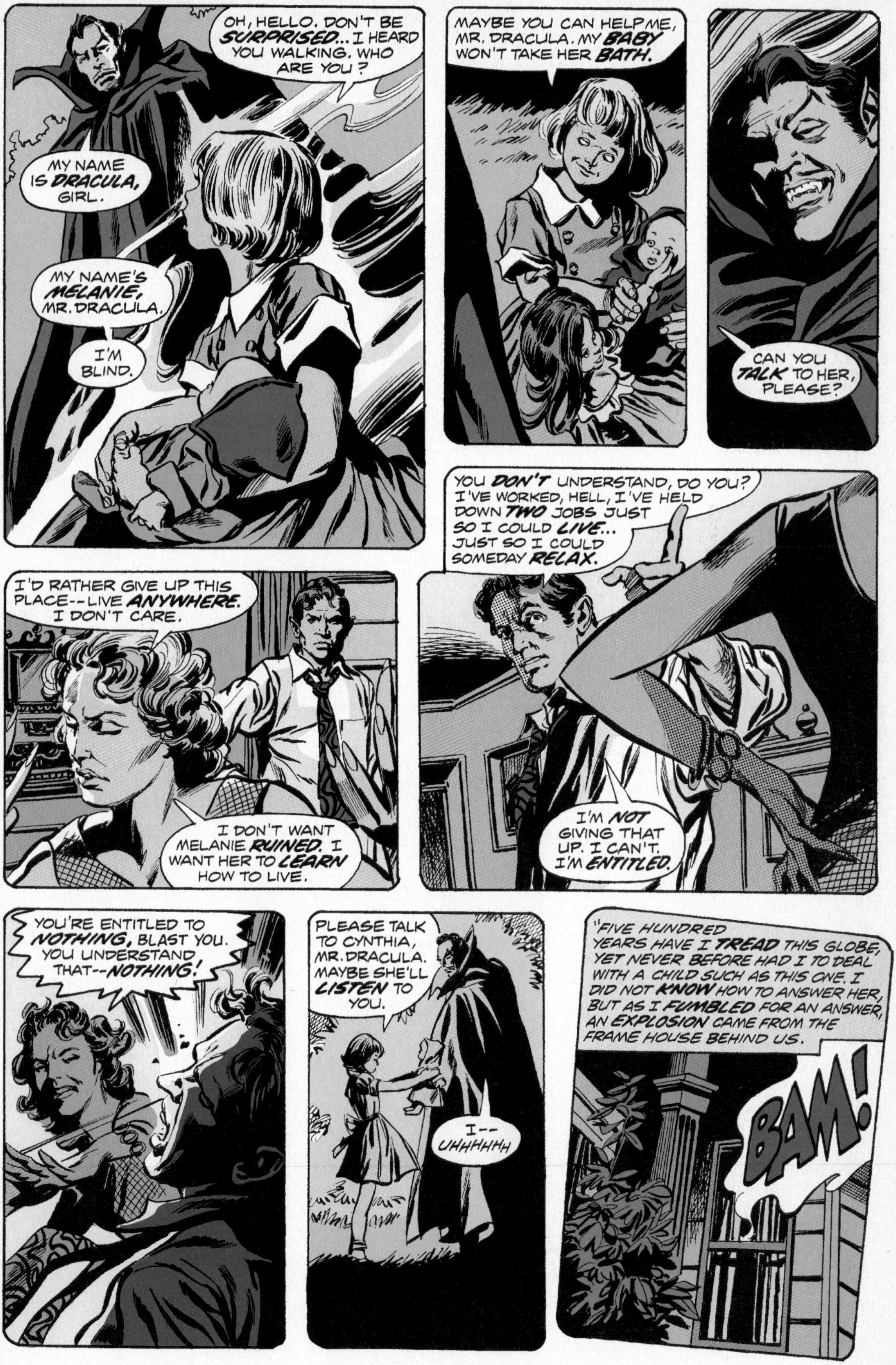
OH, HELLO. DON'T BE SURPRISED... I HEARD YOU WALKING. WHO ARE YOU?
MY NAME IS DRACULA, GIRL.
MY NAME'S MELANIE, MR. DRACULA.
I'M BLIND.
MAYBE YOU CAN HELP ME, MR. DRACULA. MY BABY WON'T TAKE HER BATH.
CAN YOU TALK TO HER, PLEASE?
YOU DON'T UNDERSTAND, DO YOU? I'VE WORKED, HELL, I'VE HELD DOWN TWO JOBS JUST SO I COULD LIVE... JUST SO I COULD SOMEDAY RELAX.
I'D RATHER GIVE UP THIS PLACE--LIVE ANYWHERE. I DON'T CARE.
I DON'T WANT MELANIE RUINED. I WANT HER TO LEARN HOW TO LIVE.
I'M NOT GIVING THAT UP. I CAN'T. I'M ENTITLED.
YOU'RE ENTITLED TO NOTHING, BLAST YOU. YOU UNDERSTAND THAT--NOTHING!
PLEASE TALK TO CYNTHIA, MR. DRACULA. MAYBE SHE'LL LISTEN TO YOU.
I-- UHHHHHH
"FIVE HUNDRED YEARS HAVE I TREAD THIS GLOBE, YET NEVER BEFORE HAD I TO DEAL WITH A CHILD SUCH AS THIS ONE. I DID NOT KNOW HOW TO ANSWER HER, BUT AS I FUMBLED FOR AN ANSWER, AN EXPLOSION CAME FROM THE FRAME HOUSE BEHIND US.
BAM!

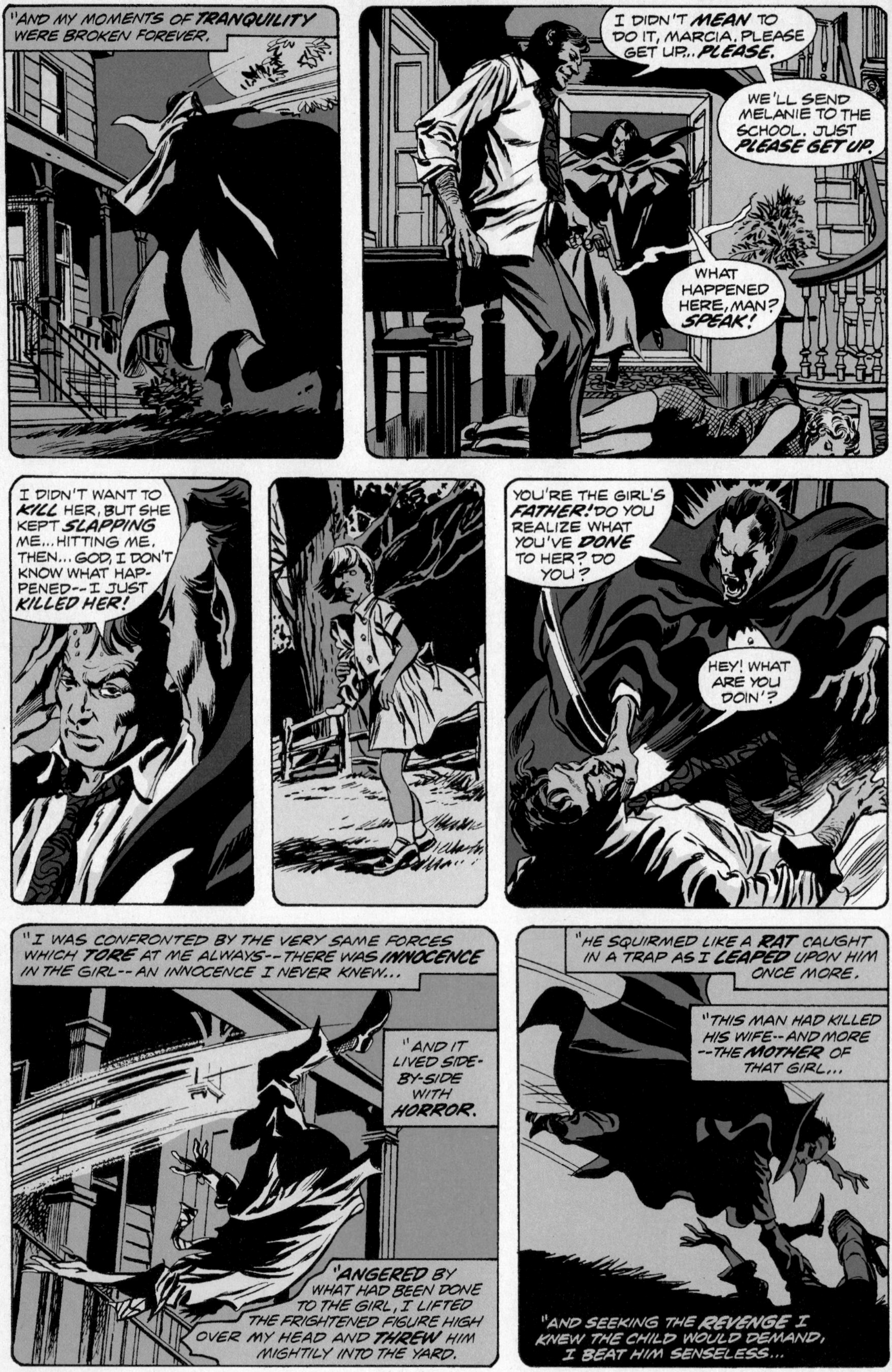
"AND MY MOMENTS OF TRANQUILITY WERE BROKEN FOREVER.
I DIDN'T MEAN TO DO IT, MARCIA. PLEASE GET UP... PLEASE.
WE'LL SEND MELANIE TO THE SCHOOL. JUST PLEASE GET UP.
WHAT HAPPENED HERE, MAN? SPEAK!
I DIDN'T WANT TO KILL HER, BUT SHE KEPT SLAPPING ME... HITTING ME. THEN... GOD, I DON'T KNOW WHAT HAP-PENED-- I JUST KILLED HER!
YOU'RE THE GIRL'S FATHER! DO YOU REALIZE WHAT YOU'VE DONE TO HER? DO YOU?
HEY! WHAT ARE YOU DOIN'?
"I WAS CONFRONTED BY THE VERY SAME FORCES WHICH TORE AT ME ALWAYS-- THERE WAS INNOCENCE IN THE GIRL-- AN INNOCENCE I NEVER KNEW...
"AND IT LIVED SIDE-BY-SIDE WITH HORROR.
"ANGERED BY WHAT HAD BEEN DONE TO THE GIRL, I LIFTED THE FRIGHTENED FIGURE HIGH OVER MY HEAD AND THREW HIM MIGHTILY INTO THE YARD.
"HE SQUIRMED LIKE A RAT CAUGHT IN A TRAP AS I LEAPED UPON HIM ONCE MORE.
"THIS MAN HAD KILLED HIS WIFE-- AND MORE --THE MOTHER OF THAT GIRL...
"AND SEEKING THE REVENGE I KNEW THE CHILD WOULD DEMAND, I BEAT HIM SENSELESS...

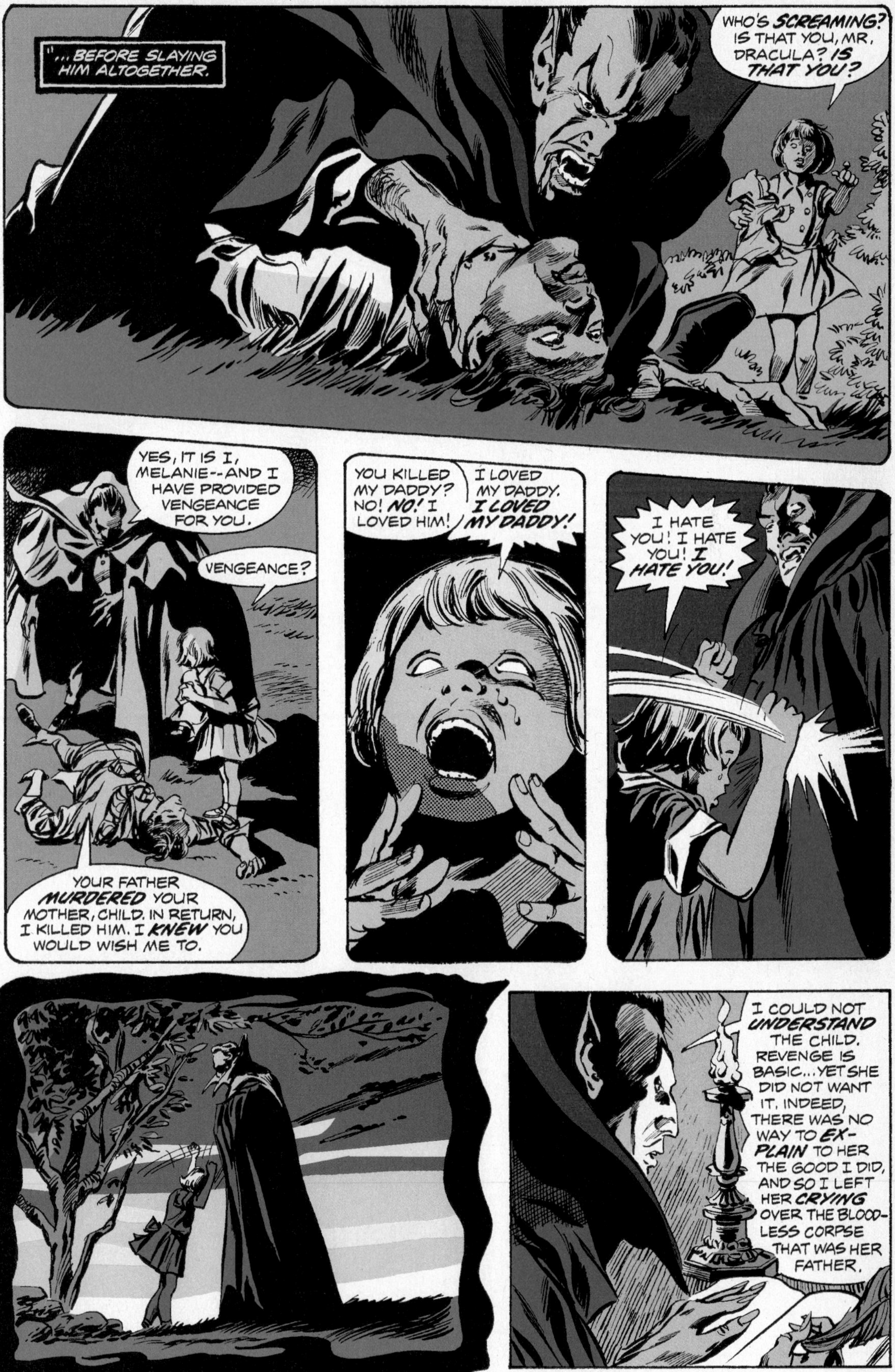
"...BEFORE SLAYING HIM ALTOGETHER.
WHO'S SCREAMING? IS THAT YOU, MR. DRACULA? IS THAT YOU?
YES, IT IS I, MELANIE--AND I HAVE PROVIDED VENGEANCE FOR YOU.
VENGEANCE?
YOUR FATHER MURDERED YOUR MOTHER, CHILD. IN RETURN, I KILLED HIM. I KNEW YOU WOULD WISH ME TO.
YOU KILLED MY DADDY? NO! NO! I LOVED HIM!
I LOVED MY DADDY. I LOVED MY DADDY!
I HATE YOU! I HATE YOU! I HATE YOU!
I COULD NOT UNDERSTAND THE CHILD. REVENGE IS BASIC...YET SHE DID NOT WANT IT. INDEED, THERE WAS NO WAY TO EX-PLAIN TO HER THE GOOD I DID, AND SO I LEFT HER CRYING OVER THE BLOOD-LESS CORPSE THAT WAS HER FATHER.

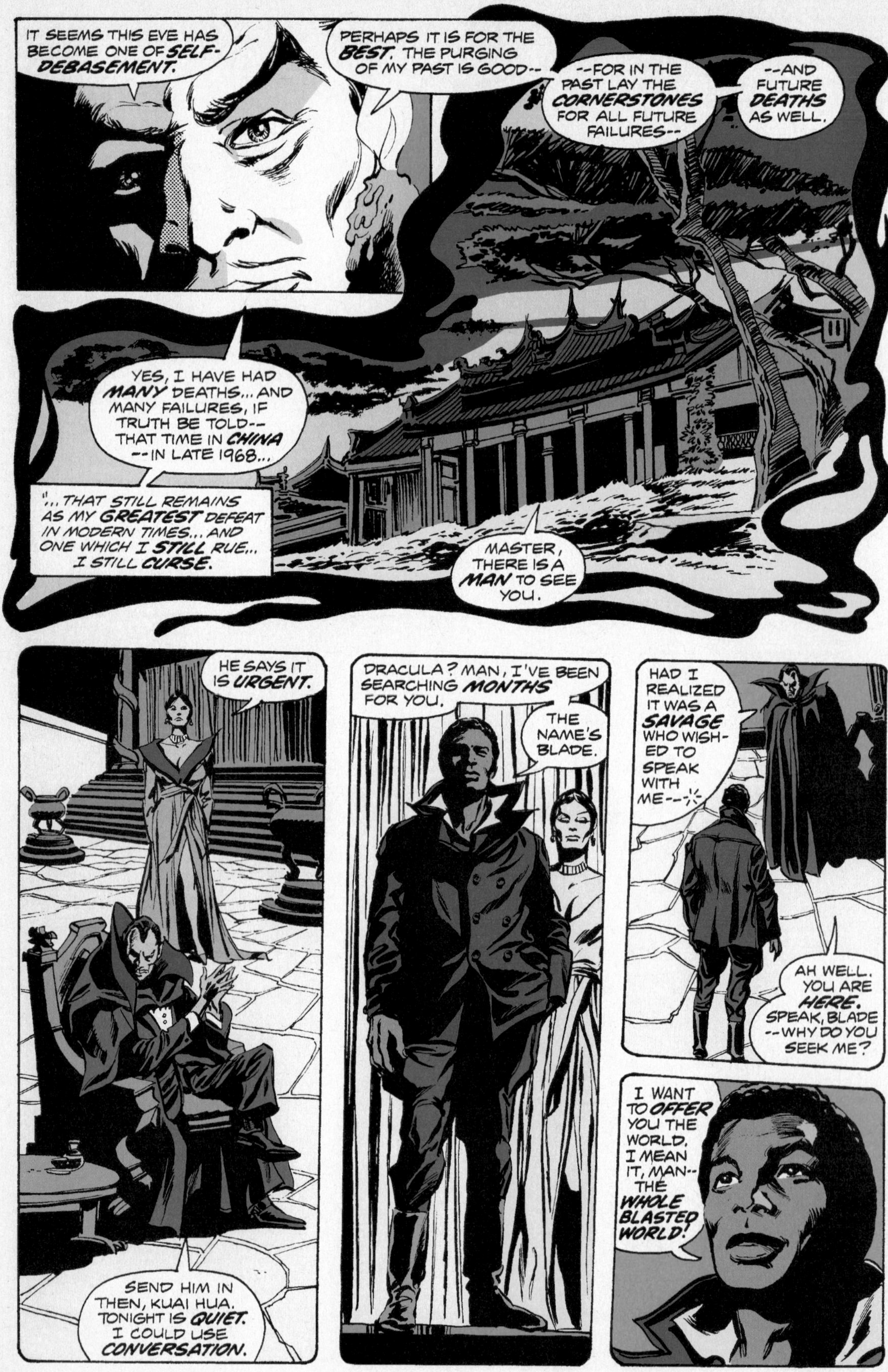

IT SEEMS THIS EVE HAS BECOME ONE OF SELF-DEBASEMENT.
PERHAPS IT IS FOR THE BEST. THE PURGING OF MY PAST IS GOOD--
--FOR IN THE PAST LAY THE CORNERSTONES FOR ALL FUTURE FAILURES--
--AND FUTURE DEATHS AS WELL.
YES, I HAVE HAD MANY DEATHS... AND MANY FAILURES, IF TRUTH BE TOLD-- THAT TIME IN CHINA --IN LATE 1968...
"...THAT STILL REMAINS AS MY GREATEST DEFEAT IN MODERN TIMES... AND ONE WHICH I STILL RUE... I STILL CURSE.
MASTER, THERE IS A MAN TO SEE YOU.
HE SAYS IT IS URGENT.
SEND HIM IN THEN, KUAI HUA. TONIGHT IS QUIET. I COULD USE CONVERSATION.
DRACULA? MAN, I'VE BEEN SEARCHING MONTHS FOR YOU.
THE NAME'S BLADE.
HAD I REALIZED IT WAS A SAVAGE WHO WISHED TO SPEAK WITH ME--
AH WELL. YOU ARE HERE. SPEAK, BLADE --WHY DO YOU SEEK ME?
I WANT TO OFFER YOU THE WORLD. I MEAN IT, MAN-- THE WHOLE BLASTED WORLD!

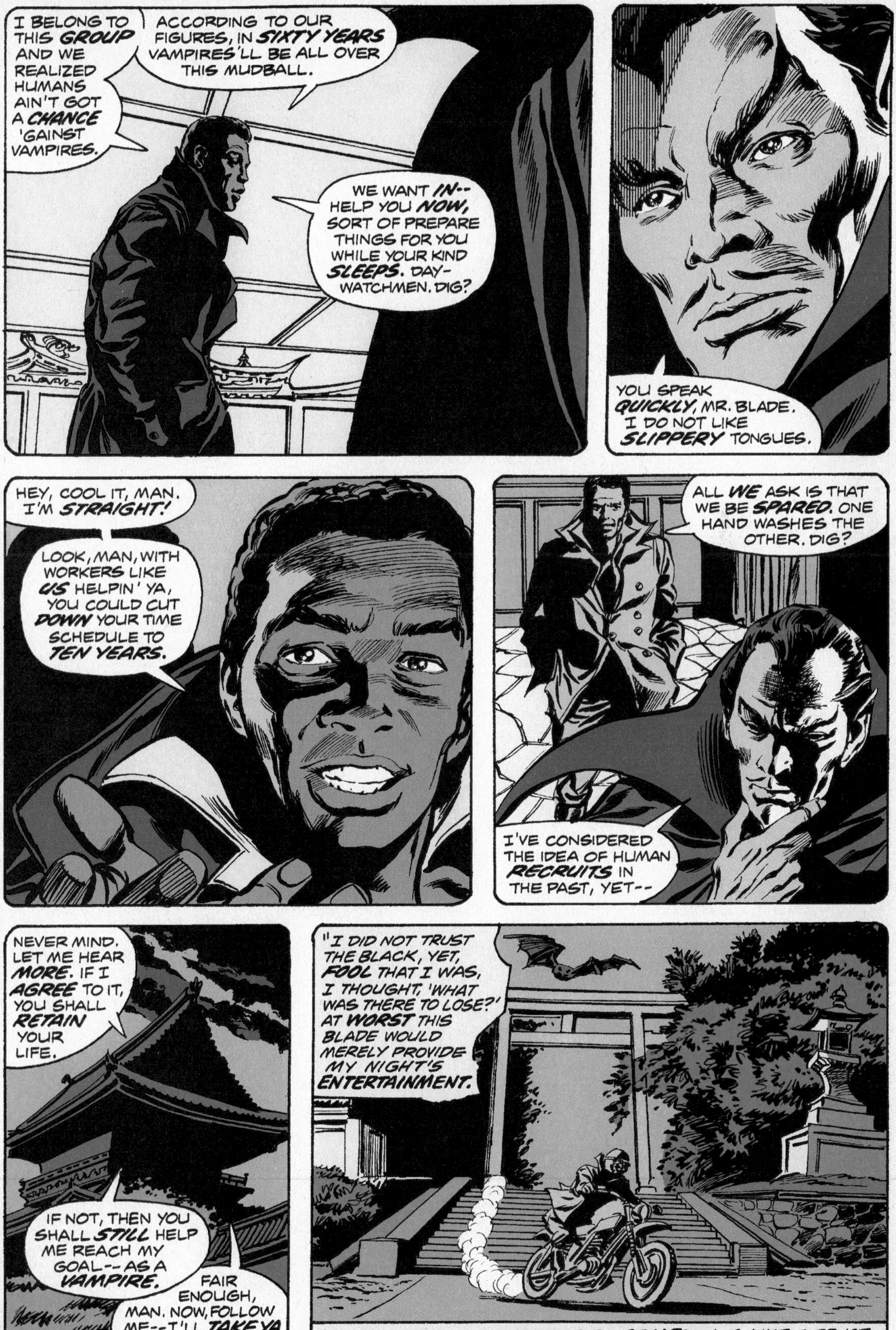
I BELONG TO THIS GROUP AND WE REALIZED HUMANS AIN'T GOT A CHANCE 'GAINST VAMPIRES.
ACCORDING TO OUR FIGURES, IN SIXTY YEARS VAMPIRES'LL BE ALL OVER THIS MUDBALL.
WE WANT IN-- HELP YOU NOW, SORT OF PREPARE THINGS FOR YOU WHILE YOUR KIND SLEEPS. DAY-WATCHMEN. DIG?
YOU SPEAK QUICKLY, MR. BLADE. I DO NOT LIKE SLIPPERY TONGUES.
HEY, COOL IT, MAN. I'M STRAIGHT!
LOOK, MAN, WITH WORKERS LIKE US HELPIN' YA, YOU COULD CUT DOWN YOUR TIME SCHEDULE TO TEN YEARS.
ALL WE ASK IS THAT WE BE SPARED. ONE HAND WASHES THE OTHER. DIG?
I'VE CONSIDERED THE IDEA OF HUMAN RECRUITS IN THE PAST, YET--
NEVER MIND. LET ME HEAR MORE. IF I AGREE TO IT, YOU SHALL RETAIN YOUR LIFE.
IF NOT, THEN YOU SHALL STILL HELP ME REACH MY GOAL--AS A VAMPIRE.
FAIR ENOUGH, MAN. NOW, FOLLOW ME--I'LL TAKE YA TO THE GROUP.
"I DID NOT TRUST THE BLACK, YET, FOOL THAT I WAS, I THOUGHT, 'WHAT WAS THERE TO LOSE?' AT WORST THIS BLADE WOULD MERELY PROVIDE MY NIGHT'S ENTERTAINMENT.
"I HAD NO IDEA OF WHAT WAS TO COME; THUS LIKE A TRUSTING BABY, I FOLLOWED THE PATH TO DEATH.

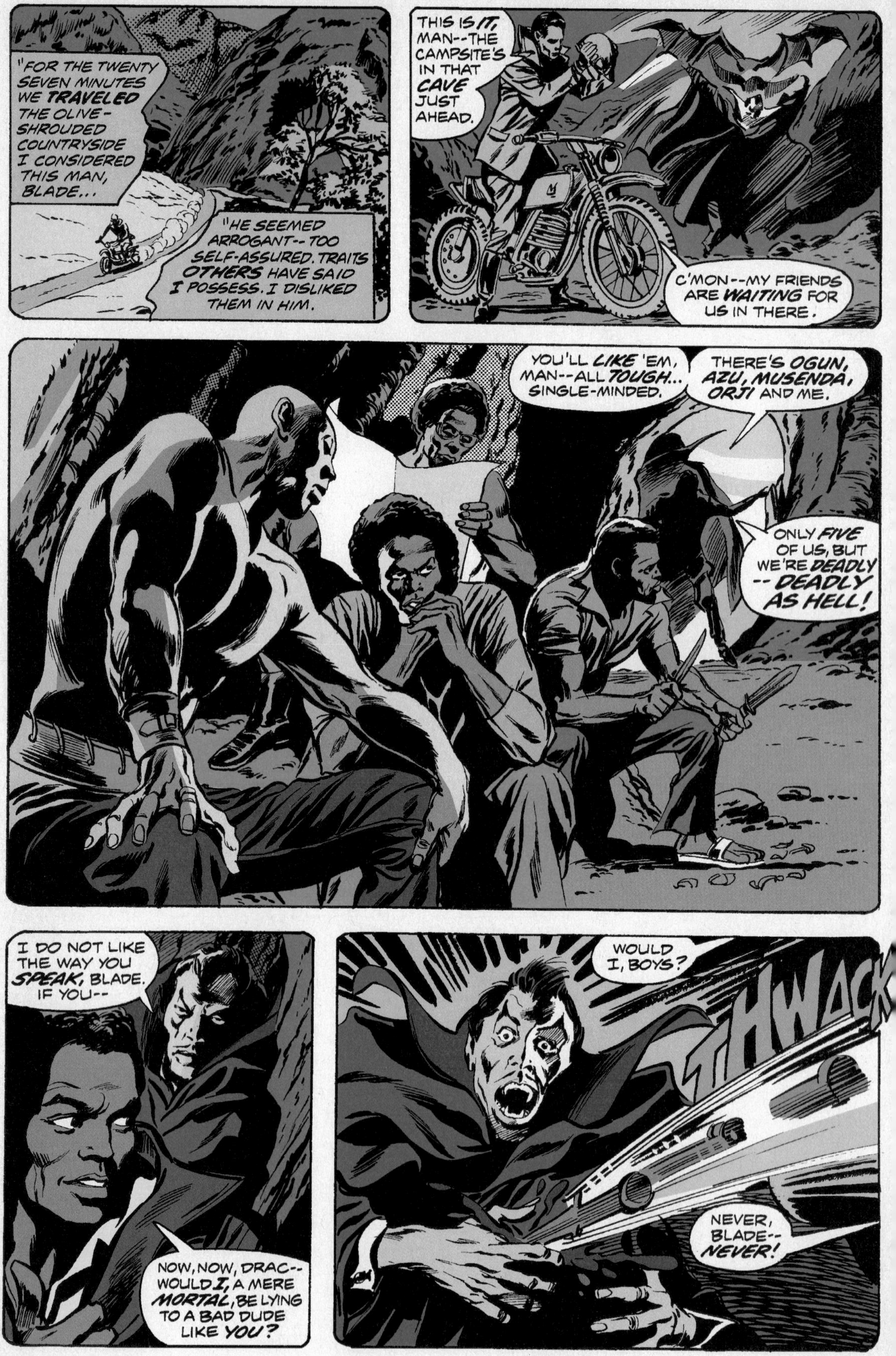
"FOR THE TWENTY SEVEN MINUTES WE TRAVELED THE OLIVE-SHROUDED COUNTRYSIDE I CONSIDERED THIS MAN, BLADE...
"HE SEEMED ARROGANT--TOO SELF-ASSURED. TRAITS OTHERS HAVE SAID I POSSESS. I DISLIKED THEM IN HIM.
THIS IS IT, MAN--THE CAMPSITE'S IN THAT CAVE JUST AHEAD.
C'MON--MY FRIENDS ARE WAITING FOR US IN THERE.
YOU'LL LIKE 'EM, MAN--ALL TOUGH... SINGLE-MINDED.
THERE'S OGUN, AZU, MUSENDA, ORJI AND ME.
ONLY FIVE OF US, BUT WE'RE DEADLY --DEADLY AS HELL!
I DO NOT LIKE THE WAY YOU SPEAK, BLADE. IF YOU--
NOW, NOW, DRAC--WOULD I, A MERE MORTAL, BE LYING TO A BAD DUDE LIKE YOU?
WOULD I, BOYS?
THWACK
NEVER, BLADE--NEVER!

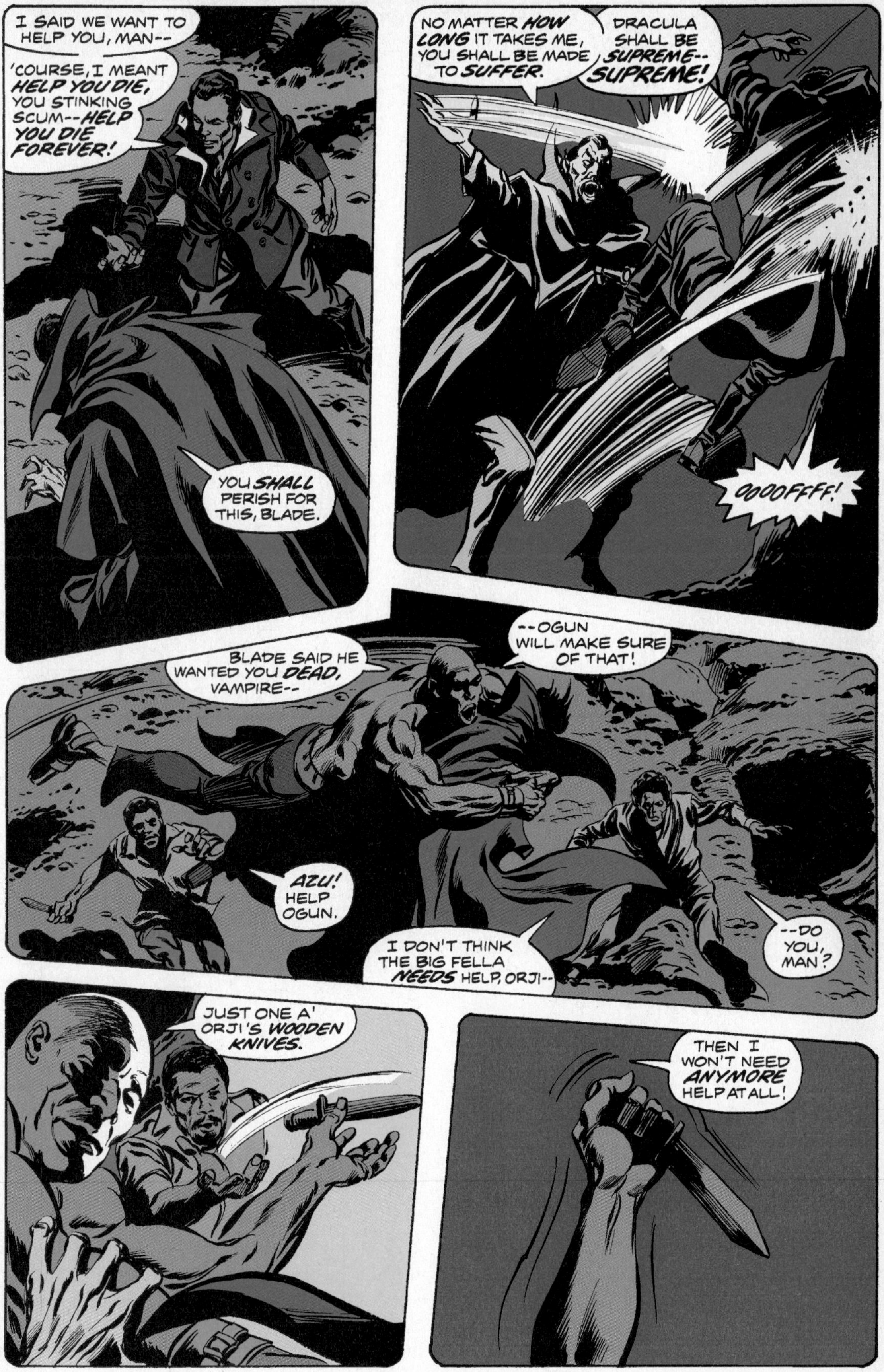

I SAID WE WANT TO HELP YOU, MAN--
'COURSE, I MEANT HELP YOU DIE, YOU STINKING SCUM--HELP YOU DIE FOREVER!
YOU SHALL PERISH FOR THIS, BLADE.
NO MATTER HOW LONG IT TAKES ME, YOU SHALL BE MADE TO SUFFER.
DRACULA SHALL BE SUPREME-- SUPREME!
OOOOFFFF!
BLADE SAID HE WANTED YOU DEAD, VAMPIRE--
--OGUN WILL MAKE SURE OF THAT!
AZU! HELP OGUN.
I DON'T THINK THE BIG FELLA NEEDS HELP, ORJI--
--DO YOU, MAN?
JUST ONE A' ORJI'S WOODEN KNIVES.
THEN I WON'T NEED ANYMORE HELP AT ALL!

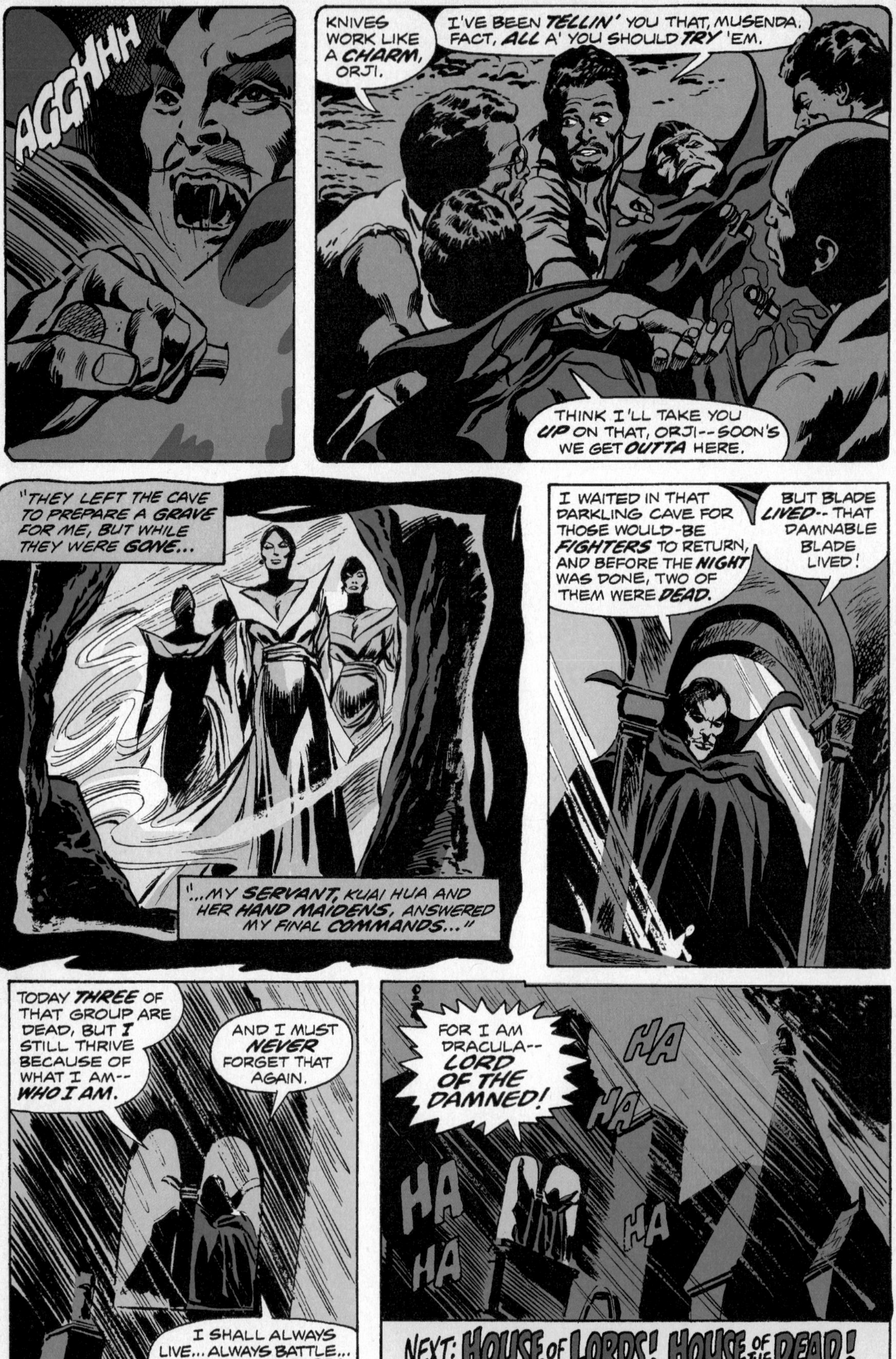
AGGHHH
KNIVES WORK LIKE A CHARM, ORJI.
I'VE BEEN TELLIN' YOU THAT, MUSENDA. FACT, ALL A' YOU SHOULD TRY 'EM.
THINK I'LL TAKE YOU UP ON THAT, ORJI-- SOON'S WE GET OUTTA HERE.
"THEY LEFT THE CAVE TO PREPARE A GRAVE FOR ME, BUT WHILE THEY WERE GONE...
"...MY SERVANT, KUAI HUA AND HER HAND MAIDENS, ANSWERED MY FINAL COMMANDS..."
I WAITED IN THAT DARKLING CAVE FOR THOSE WOULD-BE FIGHTERS TO RETURN, AND BEFORE THE NIGHT WAS DONE, TWO OF THEM WERE DEAD.
BUT BLADE LIVED-- THAT DAMNABLE BLADE LIVED!
TODAY THREE OF THAT GROUP ARE DEAD, BUT I STILL THRIVE BECAUSE OF WHAT I AM-- WHO I AM.
AND I MUST NEVER FORGET THAT AGAIN.
I SHALL ALWAYS LIVE... ALWAYS BATTLE... ALWAYS CONQUER!
FOR I AM DRACULA-- LORD OF THE DAMNED!
HA
HA
HA
HA
HA
NEXT: HOUSE OF LORDS! HOUSE OF THE DEAD!

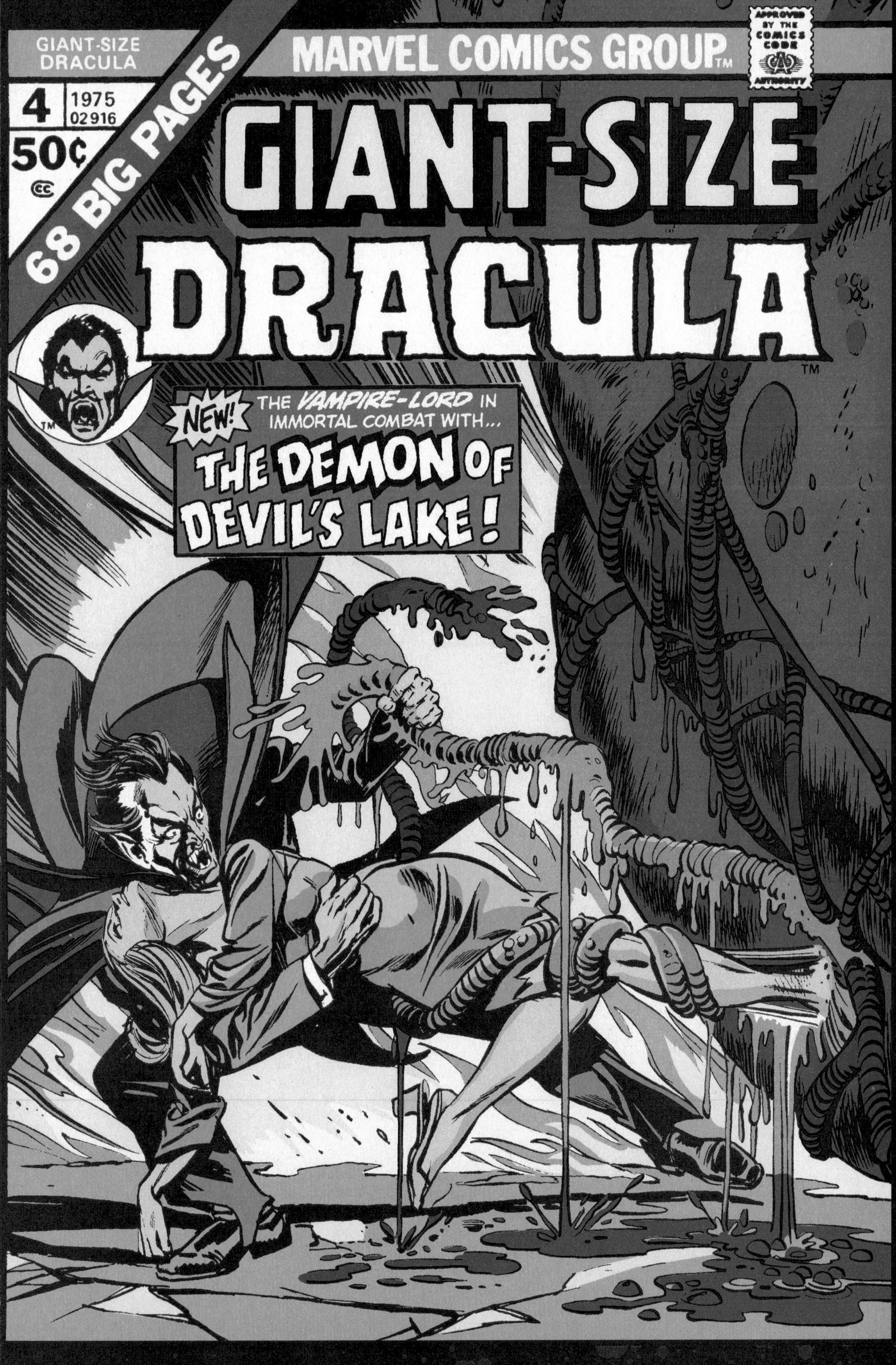
GIANT-SIZE DRACULA
MARVEL COMICS GROUP™
APPROVED BY THE COMICS CODE AUTHORITY
4
1975
02916
50¢
CC
68 BIG PAGES
GIANT-SIZE
DRACULA™
NEW!
THE VAMPIRE-LORD IN IMMORTAL COMBAT WITH...
THE DEMON OF DEVIL'S LAKE!

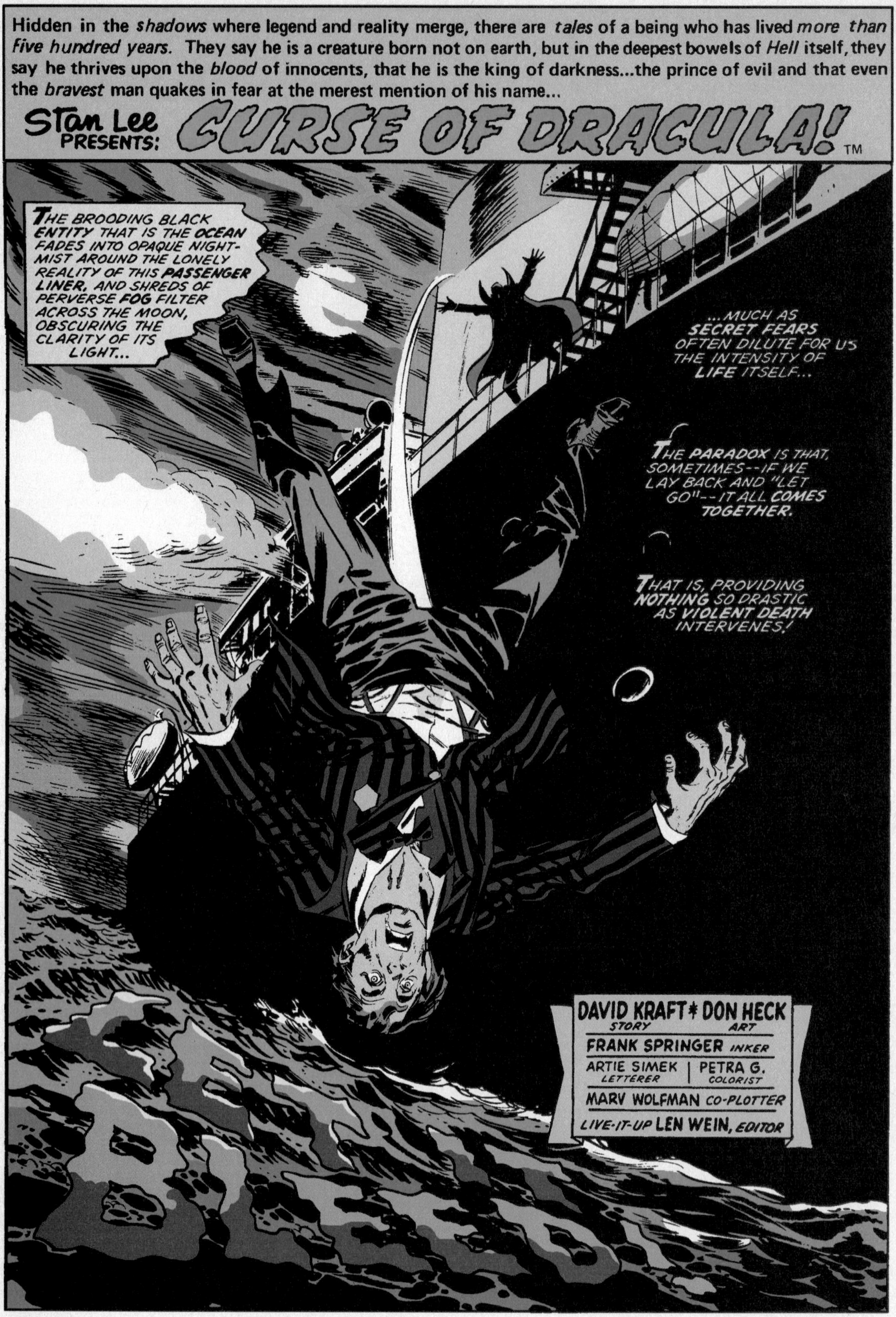

Hidden in the *shadows* where legend and reality merge, there are *tales* of a being who has lived *more than five hundred years.* They say he is a creature born not on earth, but in the deepest bowels of *Hell* itself, they say he thrives upon the *blood* of innocents, that he is the king of darkness...the prince of evil and that even the *bravest* man quakes in fear at the merest mention of his name...
Stan Lee PRESENTS: CURSE OF DRACULA! TM
THE BROODING BLACK ENTITY THAT IS THE OCEAN FADES INTO OPAQUE NIGHT-MIST AROUND THE LONELY REALITY OF THIS PASSENGER LINER, AND SHREDS OF PERVERSE FOG FILTER ACROSS THE MOON, OBSCURING THE CLARITY OF ITS LIGHT...
...MUCH AS SECRET FEARS OFTEN DILUTE FOR US THE INTENSITY OF LIFE ITSELF...
THE PARADOX IS THAT, SOMETIMES--IF WE LAY BACK AND "LET GO"--IT ALL COMES TOGETHER.
THAT IS, PROVIDING NOTHING SO DRASTIC AS VIOLENT DEATH INTERVENES!
DAVID KRAFT STORY * DON HECK ART
FRANK SPRINGER INKER
ARTIE SIMEK LETTERER | PETRA G. COLORIST
MARV WOLFMAN CO-PLOTTER
LIVE-IT-UP LEN WEIN, EDITOR

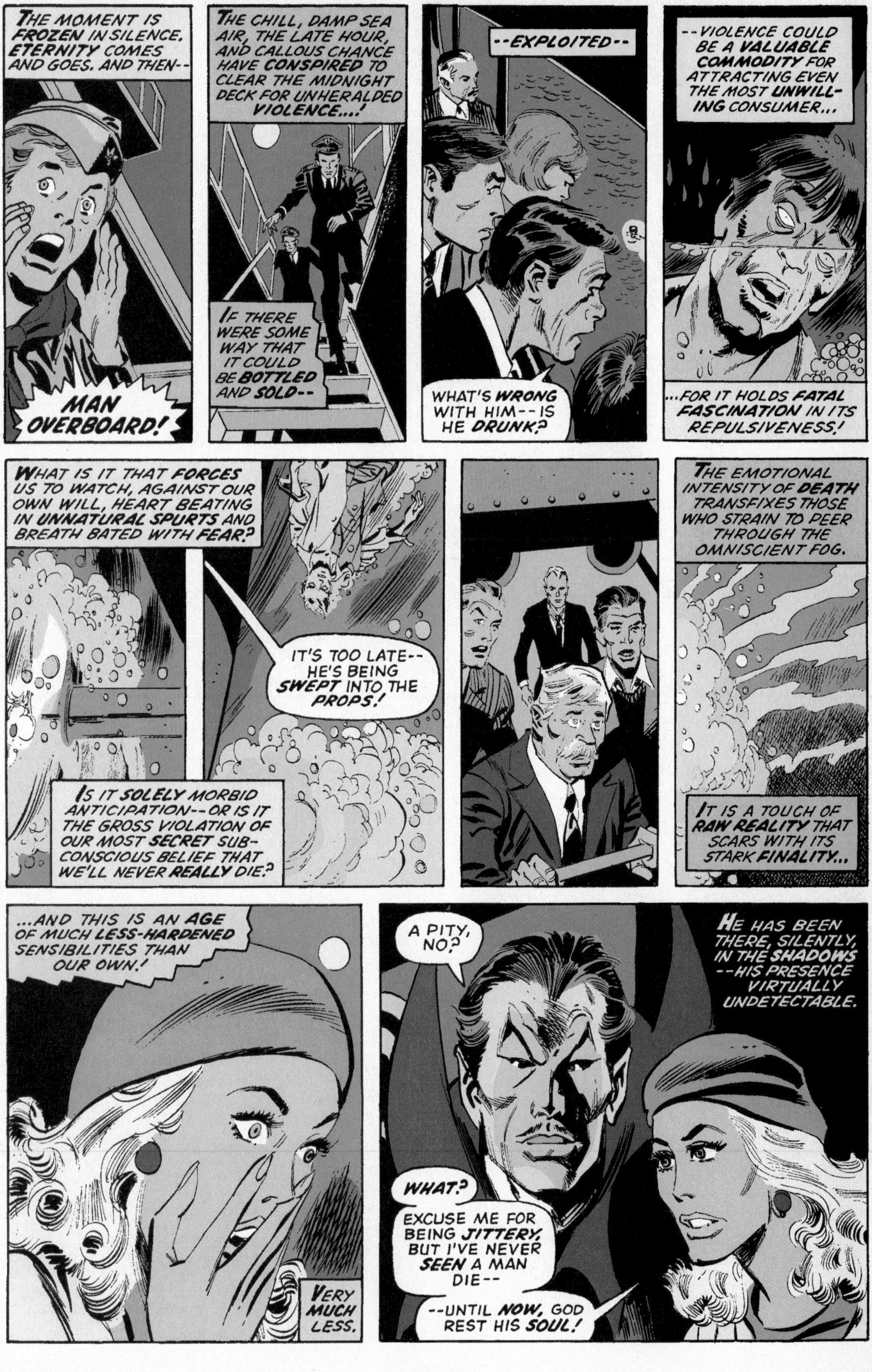
THE MOMENT IS FROZEN IN SILENCE. ETERNITY COMES AND GOES. AND THEN--
MAN OVERBOARD!
THE CHILL, DAMP SEA AIR, THE LATE HOUR, AND CALLOUS CHANCE HAVE CONSPIRED TO CLEAR THE MIDNIGHT DECK FOR UNHERALDED VIOLENCE...!
IF THERE WERE SOME WAY THAT IT COULD BE BOTTLED AND SOLD--
--EXPLOITED--
WHAT'S WRONG WITH HIM--IS HE DRUNK?
--VIOLENCE COULD BE A VALUABLE COMMODITY FOR ATTRACTING EVEN THE MOST UNWILLING CONSUMER...
...FOR IT HOLDS FATAL FASCINATION IN ITS REPULSIVENESS!
WHAT IS IT THAT FORCES US TO WATCH, AGAINST OUR OWN WILL, HEART BEATING IN UNNATURAL SPURTS AND BREATH BATED WITH FEAR?
IT'S TOO LATE--HE'S BEING SWEPT INTO THE PROPS!
IS IT SOLELY MORBID ANTICIPATION--OR IS IT THE GROSS VIOLATION OF OUR MOST SECRET SUB-CONSCIOUS BELIEF THAT WE'LL NEVER REALLY DIE?
THE EMOTIONAL INTENSITY OF DEATH TRANSFIXES THOSE WHO STRAIN TO PEER THROUGH THE OMNISCIENT FOG.
IT IS A TOUCH OF RAW REALITY THAT SCARS WITH ITS STARK FINALITY...
...AND THIS IS AN AGE OF MUCH LESS-HARDENED SENSIBILITIES THAN OUR OWN!
VERY MUCH LESS.
A PITY, NO?
HE HAS BEEN THERE, SILENTLY, IN THE SHADOWS --HIS PRESENCE VIRTUALLY UNDETECTABLE.
WHAT?
EXCUSE ME FOR BEING JITTERY, BUT I'VE NEVER SEEN A MAN DIE--
--UNTIL NOW, GOD REST HIS SOUL!

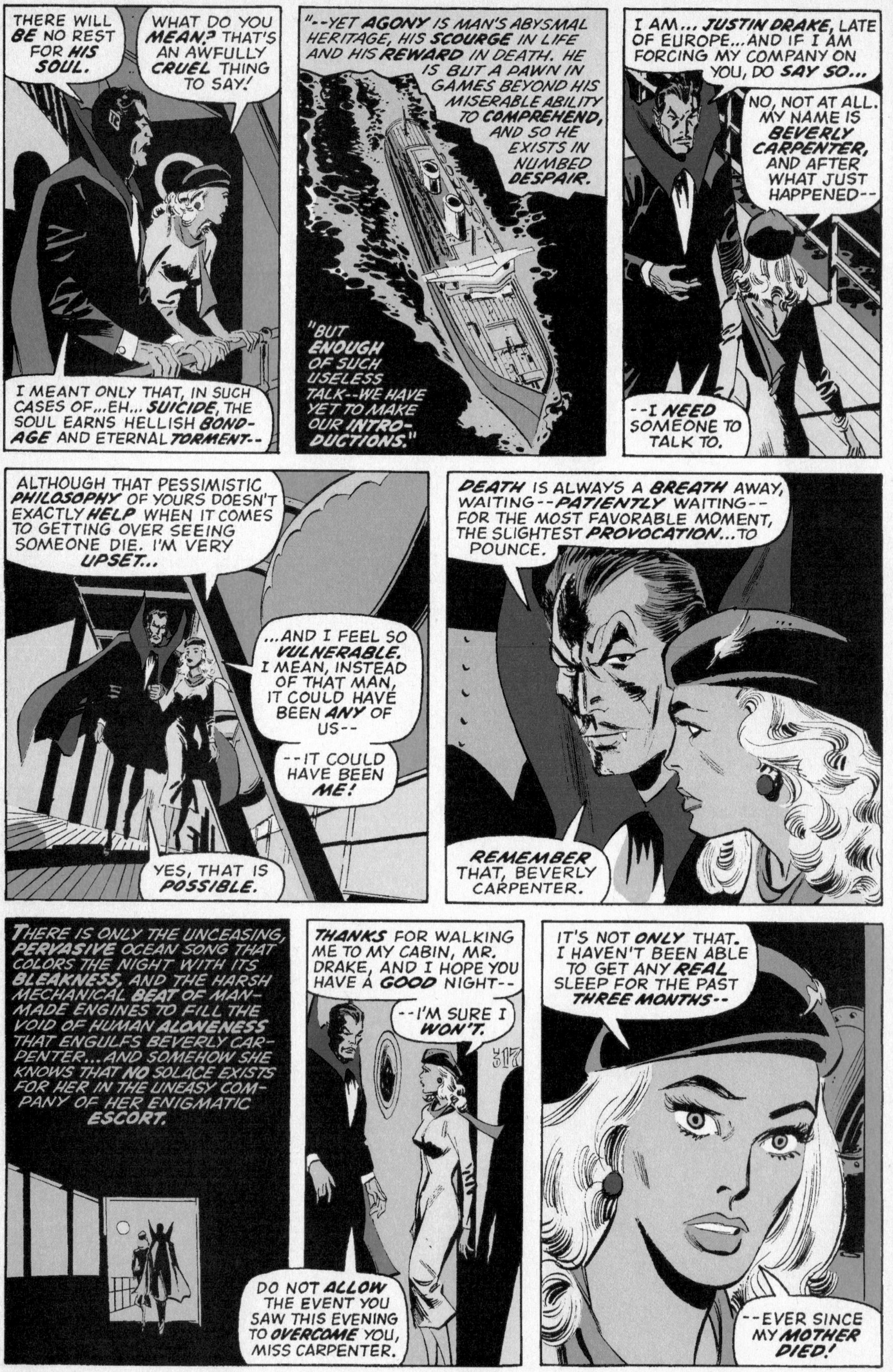
THERE WILL BE NO REST FOR HIS SOUL.
WHAT DO YOU MEAN? THAT'S AN AWFULLY CRUEL THING TO SAY!
I MEANT ONLY THAT, IN SUCH CASES OF...EH... SUICIDE, THE SOUL EARNS HELLISH BOND-AGE AND ETERNAL TORMENT--
"--YET AGONY IS MAN'S ABYSMAL HERITAGE, HIS SCOURGE IN LIFE AND HIS REWARD IN DEATH. HE IS BUT A PAWN IN GAMES BEYOND HIS MISERABLE ABILITY TO COMPREHEND, AND SO HE EXISTS IN NUMBED DESPAIR.
"BUT ENOUGH OF SUCH USELESS TALK--WE HAVE YET TO MAKE OUR INTRO-DUCTIONS."
I AM... JUSTIN DRAKE, LATE OF EUROPE...AND IF I AM FORCING MY COMPANY ON YOU, DO SAY SO...
NO, NOT AT ALL. MY NAME IS BEVERLY CARPENTER, AND AFTER WHAT JUST HAPPENED--
--I NEED SOMEONE TO TALK TO.
ALTHOUGH THAT PESSIMISTIC PHILOSOPHY OF YOURS DOESN'T EXACTLY HELP WHEN IT COMES TO GETTING OVER SEEING SOMEONE DIE. I'M VERY UPSET...
...AND I FEEL SO VULNERABLE. I MEAN, INSTEAD OF THAT MAN, IT COULD HAVE BEEN ANY OF US--
--IT COULD HAVE BEEN ME!
YES, THAT IS POSSIBLE.
DEATH IS ALWAYS A BREATH AWAY, WAITING--PATIENTLY WAITING--FOR THE MOST FAVORABLE MOMENT, THE SLIGHTEST PROVOCATION...TO POUNCE.
REMEMBER THAT, BEVERLY CARPENTER.
THERE IS ONLY THE UNCEASING, PERVASIVE OCEAN SONG THAT COLORS THE NIGHT WITH ITS BLEAKNESS, AND THE HARSH MECHANICAL BEAT OF MAN-MADE ENGINES TO FILL THE VOID OF HUMAN ALONENESS THAT ENGULFS BEVERLY CAR-PENTER...AND SOMEHOW SHE KNOWS THAT NO SOLACE EXISTS FOR HER IN THE UNEASY COM-PANY OF HER ENIGMATIC ESCORT.
THANKS FOR WALKING ME TO MY CABIN, MR. DRAKE, AND I HOPE YOU HAVE A GOOD NIGHT--
--I'M SURE I WON'T.
317
DO NOT ALLOW THE EVENT YOU SAW THIS EVENING TO OVERCOME YOU, MISS CARPENTER.
IT'S NOT ONLY THAT. I HAVEN'T BEEN ABLE TO GET ANY REAL SLEEP FOR THE PAST THREE MONTHS--
--EVER SINCE MY MOTHER DIED!

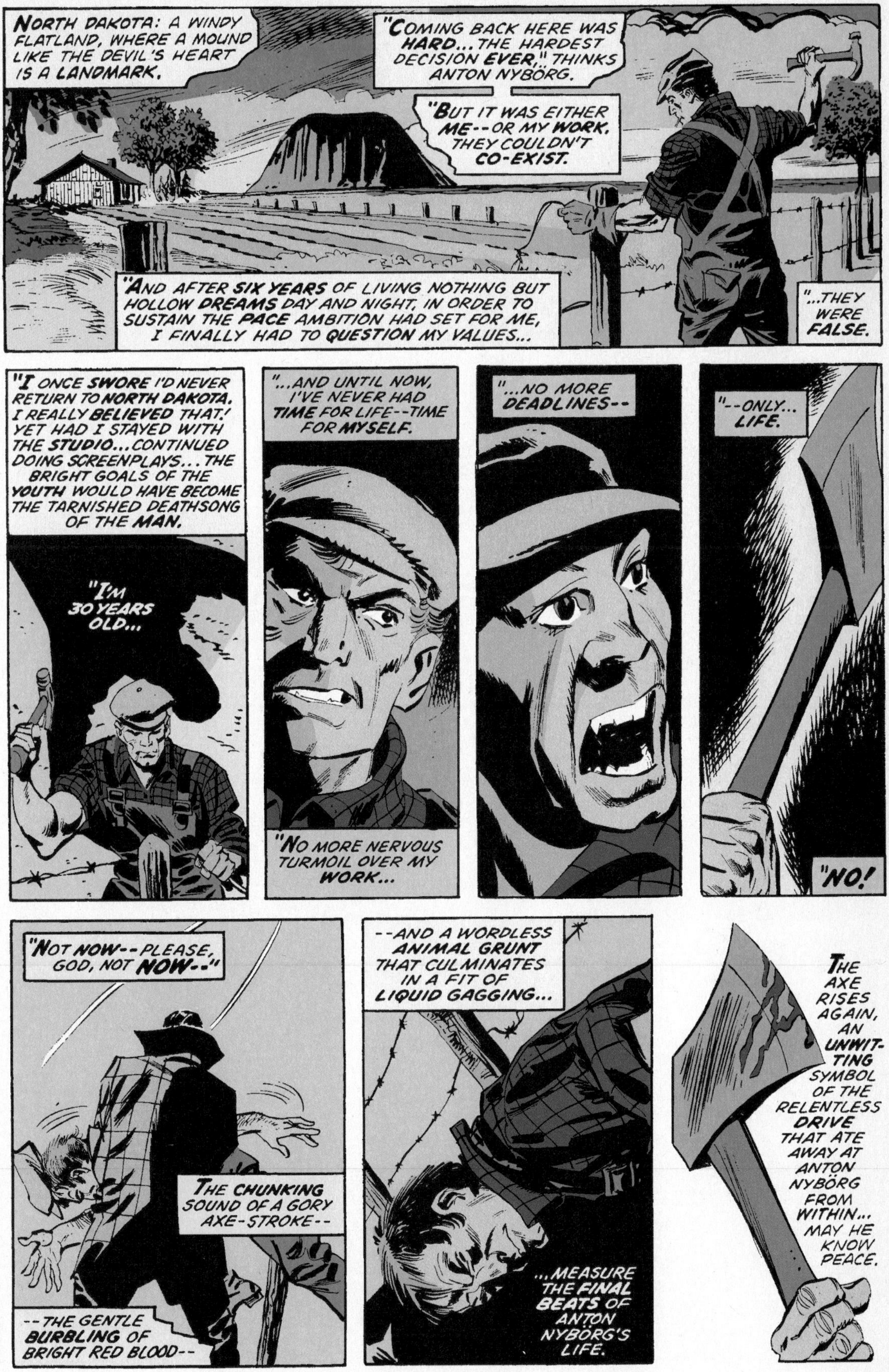
NORTH DAKOTA: A WINDY FLATLAND, WHERE A MOUND LIKE THE DEVIL'S HEART IS A LANDMARK.
"COMING BACK HERE WAS HARD... THE HARDEST DECISION EVER," THINKS ANTON NYBÖRG.
"BUT IT WAS EITHER ME--OR MY WORK. THEY COULDN'T CO-EXIST.
"AND AFTER SIX YEARS OF LIVING NOTHING BUT HOLLOW DREAMS DAY AND NIGHT, IN ORDER TO SUSTAIN THE PACE AMBITION HAD SET FOR ME, I FINALLY HAD TO QUESTION MY VALUES...
"...THEY WERE FALSE.
"I ONCE SWORE I'D NEVER RETURN TO NORTH DAKOTA. I REALLY BELIEVED THAT! YET HAD I STAYED WITH THE STUDIO... CONTINUED DOING SCREENPLAYS... THE BRIGHT GOALS OF THE YOUTH WOULD HAVE BECOME THE TARNISHED DEATHSONG OF THE MAN.
"I'M 30 YEARS OLD...
"...AND UNTIL NOW, I'VE NEVER HAD TIME FOR LIFE--TIME FOR MYSELF.
"NO MORE NERVOUS TURMOIL OVER MY WORK...
"...NO MORE DEADLINES--
"--ONLY... LIFE.
"NO!
"NOT NOW--PLEASE, GOD, NOT NOW--"
THE CHUNKING SOUND OF A GORY AXE-STROKE--
--THE GENTLE BURBLING OF BRIGHT RED BLOOD--
--AND A WORDLESS ANIMAL GRUNT THAT CULMINATES IN A FIT OF LIQUID GAGGING...
...MEASURE THE FINAL BEATS OF ANTON NYBÖRG'S LIFE.
THE AXE RISES AGAIN, AN UNWITTING SYMBOL OF THE RELENTLESS DRIVE THAT ATE AWAY AT ANTON NYBÖRG FROM WITHIN... MAY HE KNOW PEACE.

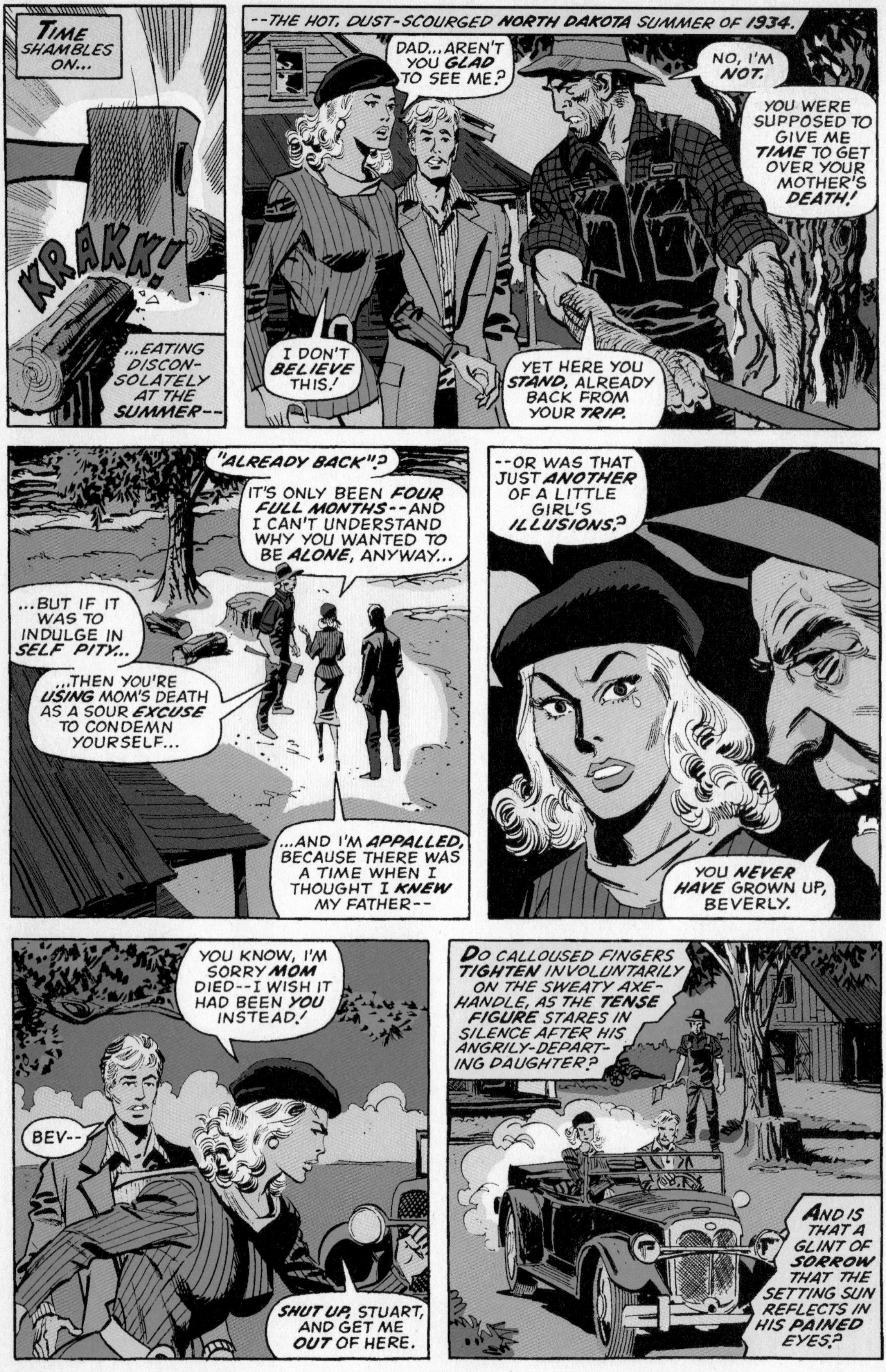
TIME SHAMBLES ON...
KRAKK!
...EATING DISCONSOLATELY AT THE SUMMER--
--THE HOT, DUST-SCOURGED NORTH DAKOTA SUMMER OF 1934.
DAD...AREN'T YOU GLAD TO SEE ME?
NO, I'M NOT.
YOU WERE SUPPOSED TO GIVE ME TIME TO GET OVER YOUR MOTHER'S DEATH!
I DON'T BELIEVE THIS.!
YET HERE YOU STAND, ALREADY BACK FROM YOUR TRIP.
"ALREADY BACK"?
IT'S ONLY BEEN FOUR FULL MONTHS--AND I CAN'T UNDERSTAND WHY YOU WANTED TO BE ALONE, ANYWAY...
...BUT IF IT WAS TO INDULGE IN SELF PITY...
...THEN YOU'RE USING MOM'S DEATH AS A SOUR EXCUSE TO CONDEMN YOURSELF...
...AND I'M APPALLED, BECAUSE THERE WAS A TIME WHEN I THOUGHT I KNEW MY FATHER--
--OR WAS THAT JUST ANOTHER OF A LITTLE GIRL'S ILLUSIONS?
YOU NEVER HAVE GROWN UP, BEVERLY.
YOU KNOW, I'M SORRY MOM DIED--I WISH IT HAD BEEN YOU INSTEAD.!
BEV--
SHUT UP, STUART, AND GET ME OUT OF HERE.
DO CALLOUSED FINGERS TIGHTEN INVOLUNTARILY ON THE SWEATY AXE-HANDLE, AS THE TENSE FIGURE STARES IN SILENCE AFTER HIS ANGRILY-DEPARTING DAUGHTER?
AND IS THAT A GLINT OF SORROW THAT THE SETTING SUN REFLECTS IN HIS PAINED EYES?

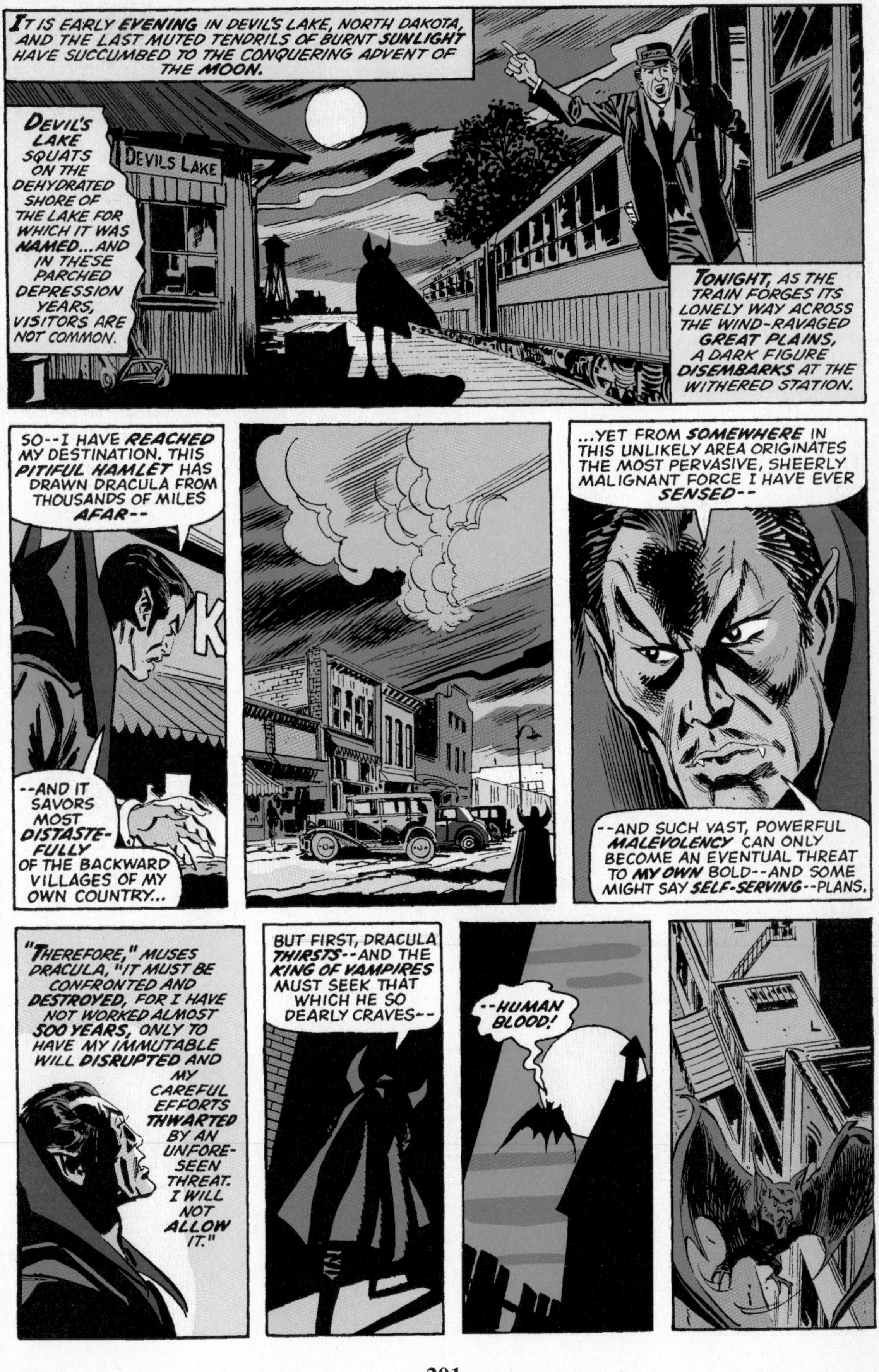

IT IS EARLY EVENING IN DEVIL'S LAKE, NORTH DAKOTA, AND THE LAST MUTED TENDRILS OF BURNT SUNLIGHT HAVE SUCCUMBED TO THE CONQUERING ADVENT OF THE MOON.
DEVIL'S LAKE SQUATS ON THE DEHYDRATED SHORE OF THE LAKE FOR WHICH IT WAS NAMED... AND IN THESE PARCHED DEPRESSION YEARS, VISITORS ARE NOT COMMON.
DEVILS LAKE
TONIGHT, AS THE TRAIN FORGES ITS LONELY WAY ACROSS THE WIND-RAVAGED GREAT PLAINS, A DARK FIGURE DISEMBARKS AT THE WITHERED STATION.
SO--I HAVE REACHED MY DESTINATION. THIS PITIFUL HAMLET HAS DRAWN DRACULA FROM THOUSANDS OF MILES AFAR--
--AND IT SAVORS MOST DISTASTEFULLY OF THE BACKWARD VILLAGES OF MY OWN COUNTRY...
...YET FROM SOMEWHERE IN THIS UNLIKELY AREA ORIGINATES THE MOST PERVASIVE, SHEERLY MALIGNANT FORCE I HAVE EVER SENSED--
--AND SUCH VAST, POWERFUL MALEVOLENCY CAN ONLY BECOME AN EVENTUAL THREAT TO MY OWN BOLD--AND SOME MIGHT SAY SELF-SERVING--PLANS.
"THEREFORE," MUSES DRACULA, "IT MUST BE CONFRONTED AND DESTROYED, FOR I HAVE NOT WORKED ALMOST 500 YEARS, ONLY TO HAVE MY IMMUTABLE WILL DISRUPTED AND MY CAREFUL EFFORTS THWARTED BY AN UNFORESEEN THREAT. I WILL NOT ALLOW IT."
BUT FIRST, DRACULA THIRSTS--AND THE KING OF VAMPIRES MUST SEEK THAT WHICH HE SO DEARLY CRAVES--
--HUMAN BLOOD!

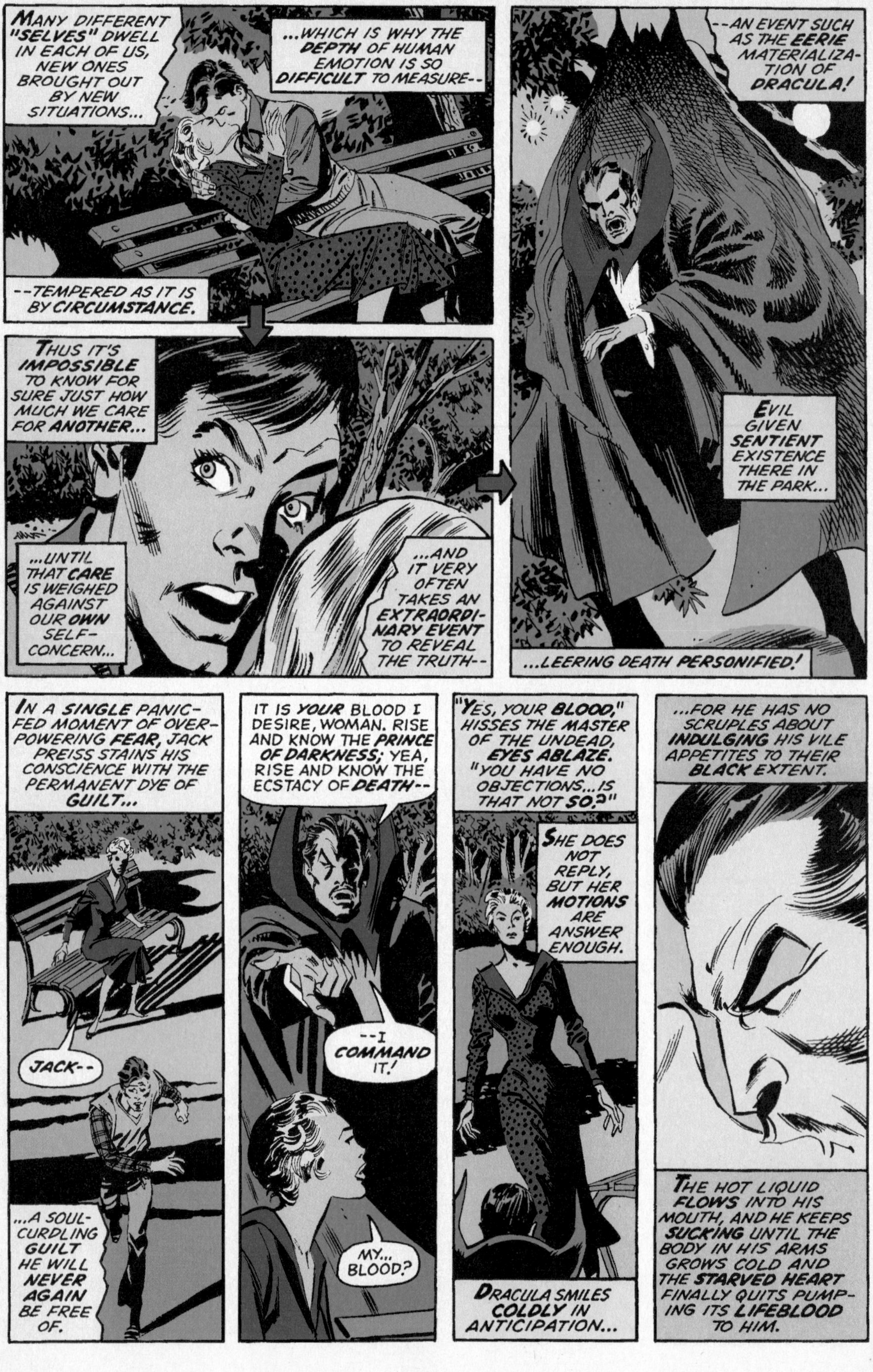
MANY DIFFERENT "SELVES" DWELL IN EACH OF US, NEW ONES BROUGHT OUT BY NEW SITUATIONS...
...WHICH IS WHY THE DEPTH OF HUMAN EMOTION IS SO DIFFICULT TO MEASURE--
--TEMPERED AS IT IS BY CIRCUMSTANCE.
THUS IT'S IMPOSSIBLE TO KNOW FOR SURE JUST HOW MUCH WE CARE FOR ANOTHER...
...UNTIL THAT CARE IS WEIGHED AGAINST OUR OWN SELF-CONCERN...
...AND IT VERY OFTEN TAKES AN EXTRAORDINARY EVENT TO REVEAL THE TRUTH--
--AN EVENT SUCH AS THE EERIE MATERIALIZATION OF DRACULA!
EVIL GIVEN SENTIENT EXISTENCE THERE IN THE PARK...
...LEERING DEATH PERSONIFIED!
IN A SINGLE PANIC-FED MOMENT OF OVERPOWERING FEAR, JACK PREISS STAINS HIS CONSCIENCE WITH THE PERMANENT DYE OF GUILT...
JACK--
...A SOUL-CURDLING GUILT HE WILL NEVER AGAIN BE FREE OF.
IT IS YOUR BLOOD I DESIRE, WOMAN. RISE AND KNOW THE PRINCE OF DARKNESS; YEA, RISE AND KNOW THE ECSTACY OF DEATH--
--I COMMAND IT!
MY... BLOOD?
"YES, YOUR BLOOD," HISSES THE MASTER OF THE UNDEAD, EYES ABLAZE. "YOU HAVE NO OBJECTIONS... IS THAT NOT SO?"
SHE DOES NOT REPLY, BUT HER MOTIONS ARE ANSWER ENOUGH.
DRACULA SMILES COLDLY IN ANTICIPATION...
...FOR HE HAS NO SCRUPLES ABOUT INDULGING HIS VILE APPETITES TO THEIR BLACK EXTENT.
THE HOT LIQUID FLOWS INTO HIS MOUTH, AND HE KEEPS SUCKING UNTIL THE BODY IN HIS ARMS GROWS COLD AND THE STARVED HEART FINALLY QUITS PUMPING ITS LIFEBLOOD TO HIM.

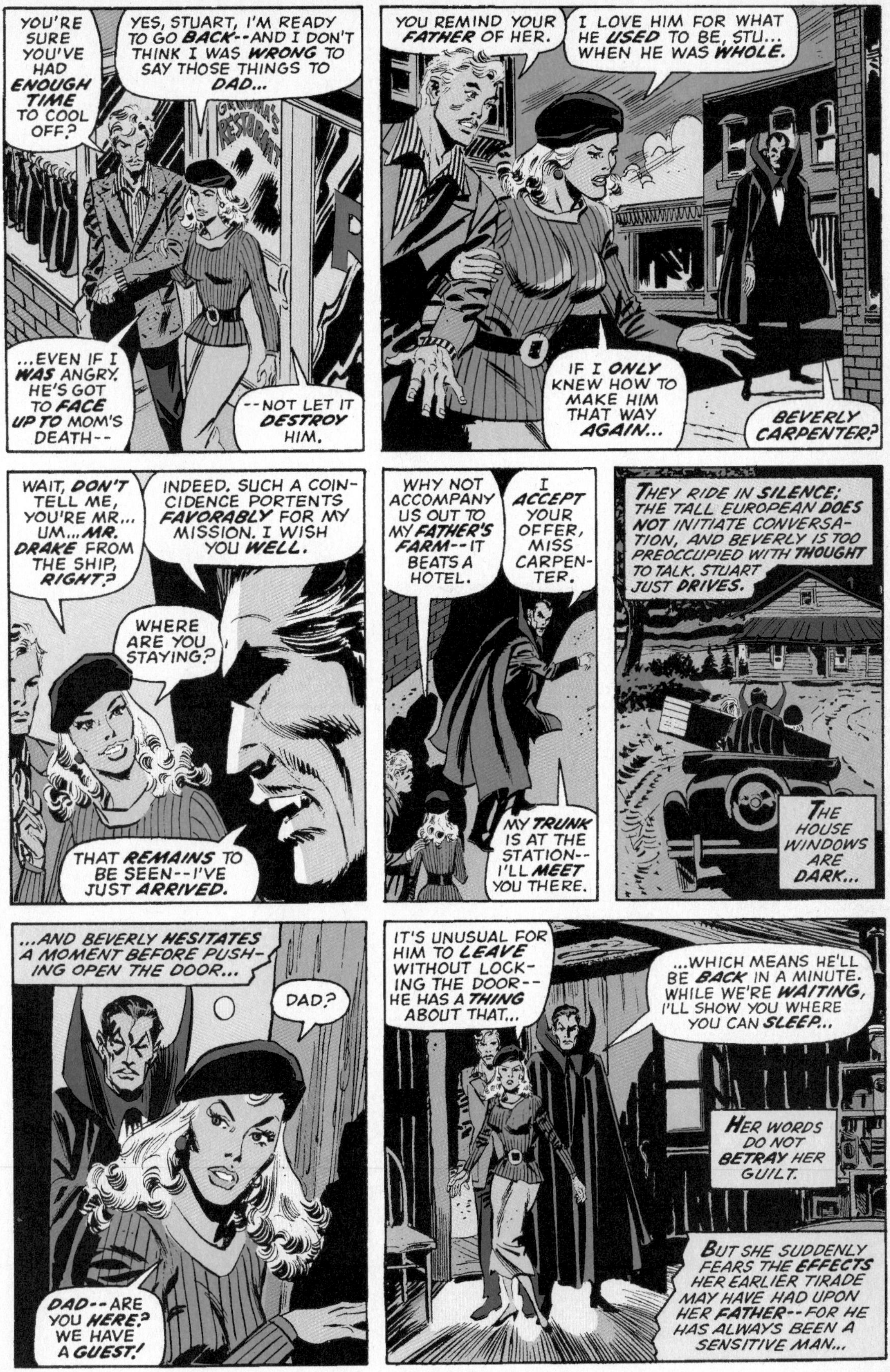
YOU'RE SURE YOU'VE HAD ENOUGH TIME TO COOL OFF?
YES, STUART, I'M READY TO GO BACK--AND I DON'T THINK I WAS WRONG TO SAY THOSE THINGS TO DAD...
...EVEN IF I WAS ANGRY. HE'S GOT TO FACE UP TO MOM'S DEATH--
--NOT LET IT DESTROY HIM.
YOU REMIND YOUR FATHER OF HER.
I LOVE HIM FOR WHAT HE USED TO BE, STU... WHEN HE WAS WHOLE.
IF I ONLY KNEW HOW TO MAKE HIM THAT WAY AGAIN...
BEVERLY CARPENTER?
WAIT, DON'T TELL ME, YOU'RE MR... UM...MR. DRAKE FROM THE SHIP, RIGHT?
INDEED. SUCH A COINCIDENCE PORTENTS FAVORABLY FOR MY MISSION. I WISH YOU WELL.
WHERE ARE YOU STAYING?
THAT REMAINS TO BE SEEN--I'VE JUST ARRIVED.
WHY NOT ACCOMPANY US OUT TO MY FATHER'S FARM--IT BEATS A HOTEL.
I ACCEPT YOUR OFFER, MISS CARPENTER.
MY TRUNK IS AT THE STATION--I'LL MEET YOU THERE.
THEY RIDE IN SILENCE: THE TALL EUROPEAN DOES NOT INITIATE CONVERSATION, AND BEVERLY IS TOO PREOCCUPIED WITH THOUGHT TO TALK. STUART JUST DRIVES.
THE HOUSE WINDOWS ARE DARK...
...AND BEVERLY HESITATES A MOMENT BEFORE PUSHING OPEN THE DOOR...
DAD?
DAD--ARE YOU HERE? WE HAVE A GUEST!
IT'S UNUSUAL FOR HIM TO LEAVE WITHOUT LOCKING THE DOOR--HE HAS A THING ABOUT THAT...
...WHICH MEANS HE'LL BE BACK IN A MINUTE. WHILE WE'RE WAITING, I'LL SHOW YOU WHERE YOU CAN SLEEP...
HER WORDS DO NOT BETRAY HER GUILT.
BUT SHE SUDDENLY FEARS THE EFFECTS HER EARLIER TIRADE MAY HAVE HAD UPON HER FATHER--FOR HE HAS ALWAYS BEEN A SENSITIVE MAN...

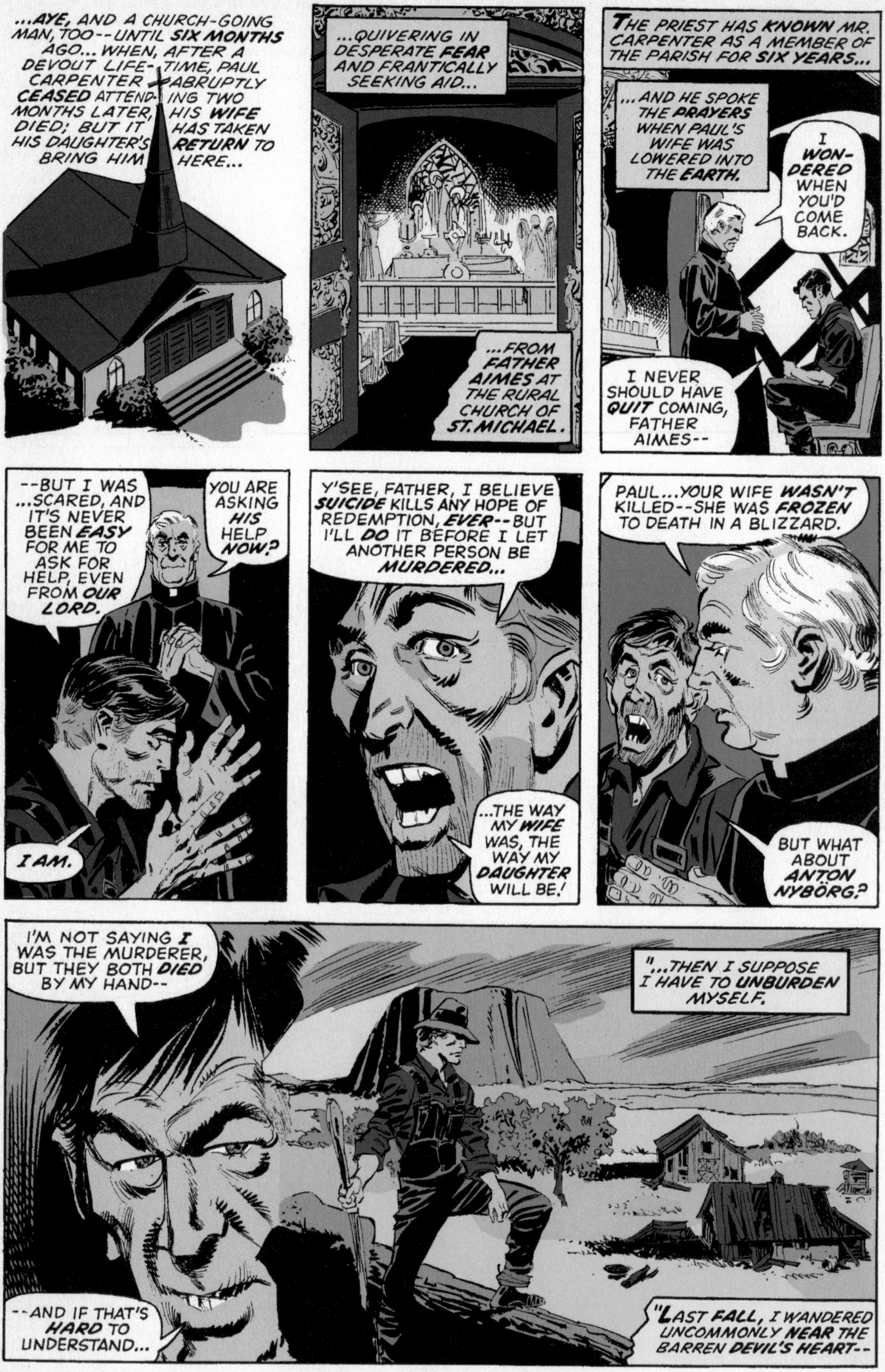
...AYE, AND A CHURCH-GOING MAN, TOO--UNTIL SIX MONTHS AGO... WHEN, AFTER A DEVOUT LIFE-TIME, PAUL CARPENTER ABRUPTLY CEASED ATTENDING TWO MONTHS LATER, HIS WIFE DIED; BUT IT HAS TAKEN HIS DAUGHTER'S RETURN TO BRING HIM HERE...
...QUIVERING IN DESPERATE FEAR AND FRANTICALLY SEEKING AID...
...FROM FATHER AIMES AT THE RURAL CHURCH OF ST. MICHAEL.
THE PRIEST HAS KNOWN MR. CARPENTER AS A MEMBER OF THE PARISH FOR SIX YEARS...
...AND HE SPOKE THE PRAYERS WHEN PAUL'S WIFE WAS LOWERED INTO THE EARTH.
I WONDERED WHEN YOU'D COME BACK.
I NEVER SHOULD HAVE QUIT COMING, FATHER AIMES--
--BUT I WAS ...SCARED, AND IT'S NEVER BEEN EASY FOR ME TO ASK FOR HELP, EVEN FROM OUR LORD.
YOU ARE ASKING HIS HELP NOW?
I AM.
Y'SEE, FATHER, I BELIEVE SUICIDE KILLS ANY HOPE OF REDEMPTION, EVER--BUT I'LL DO IT BEFORE I LET ANOTHER PERSON BE MURDERED...
...THE WAY MY WIFE WAS, THE WAY MY DAUGHTER WILL BE.!
PAUL...YOUR WIFE WASN'T KILLED--SHE WAS FROZEN TO DEATH IN A BLIZZARD.
BUT WHAT ABOUT ANTON NYBÖRG?
I'M NOT SAYING I WAS THE MURDERER, BUT THEY BOTH DIED BY MY HAND--
--AND IF THAT'S HARD TO UNDERSTAND...
"...THEN I SUPPOSE I HAVE TO UNBURDEN MYSELF.
"LAST FALL, I WANDERED UNCOMMONLY NEAR THE BARREN DEVIL'S HEART--

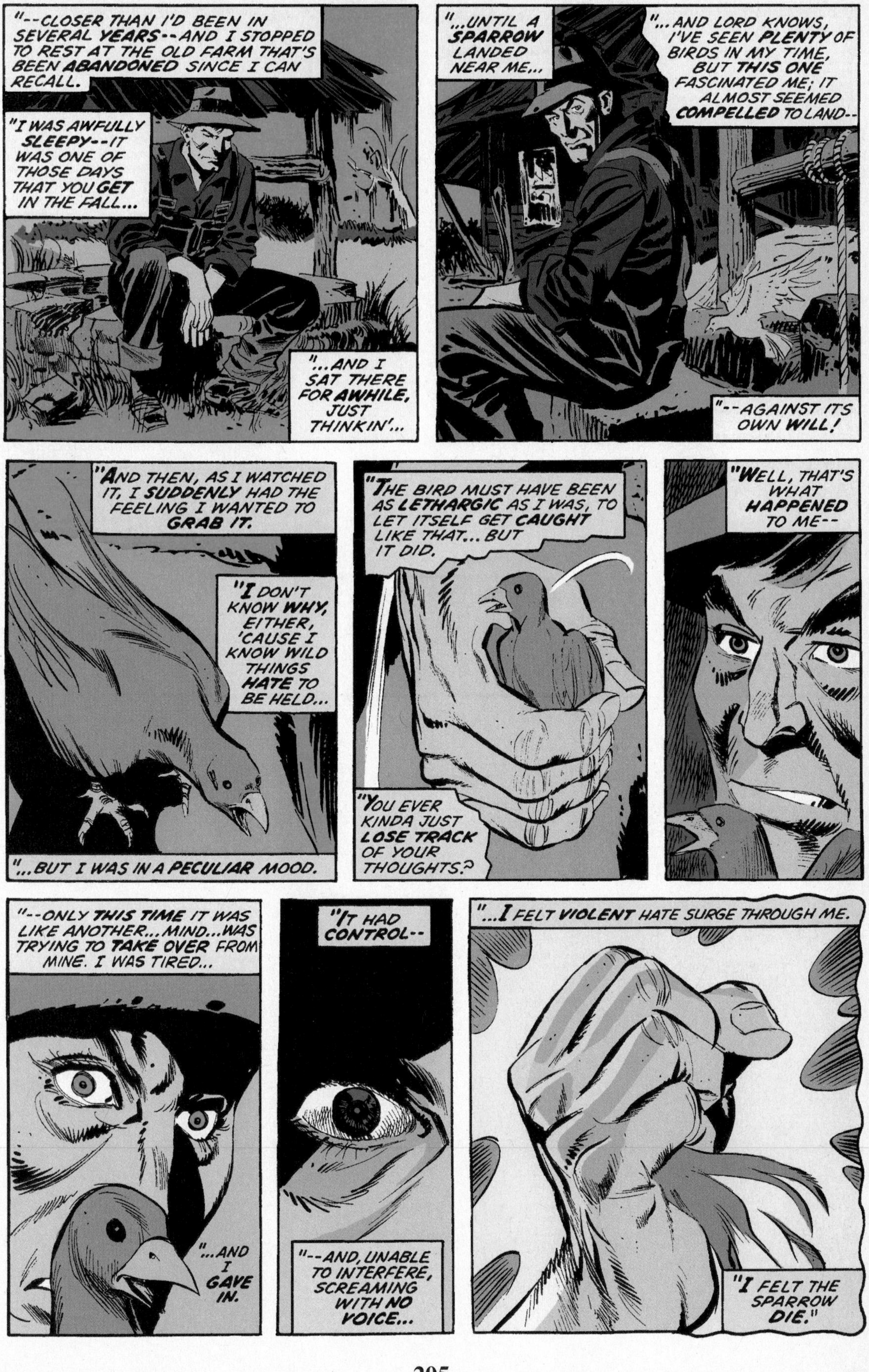
"--CLOSER THAN I'D BEEN IN SEVERAL YEARS--AND I STOPPED TO REST AT THE OLD FARM THAT'S BEEN ABANDONED SINCE I CAN RECALL.
"I WAS AWFULLY SLEEPY--IT WAS ONE OF THOSE DAYS THAT YOU GET IN THE FALL...
"...AND I SAT THERE FOR AWHILE, JUST THINKIN'...
"...UNTIL A SPARROW LANDED NEAR ME...
"...AND LORD KNOWS, I'VE SEEN PLENTY OF BIRDS IN MY TIME, BUT THIS ONE FASCINATED ME; IT ALMOST SEEMED COMPELLED TO LAND--
"--AGAINST ITS OWN WILL!
"AND THEN, AS I WATCHED IT, I SUDDENLY HAD THE FEELING I WANTED TO GRAB IT.
"I DON'T KNOW WHY, EITHER, 'CAUSE I KNOW WILD THINGS HATE TO BE HELD...
"...BUT I WAS IN A PECULIAR MOOD.
"THE BIRD MUST HAVE BEEN AS LETHARGIC AS I WAS, TO LET ITSELF GET CAUGHT LIKE THAT... BUT IT DID.
"YOU EVER KINDA JUST LOSE TRACK OF YOUR THOUGHTS?
"WELL, THAT'S WHAT HAPPENED TO ME--
"--ONLY THIS TIME IT WAS LIKE ANOTHER...MIND...WAS TRYING TO TAKE OVER FROM MINE. I WAS TIRED...
"...AND I GAVE IN.
"IT HAD CONTROL--
"--AND, UNABLE TO INTERFERE, SCREAMING WITH NO VOICE...
"...I FELT VIOLENT HATE SURGE THROUGH ME.
"I FELT THE SPARROW DIE."

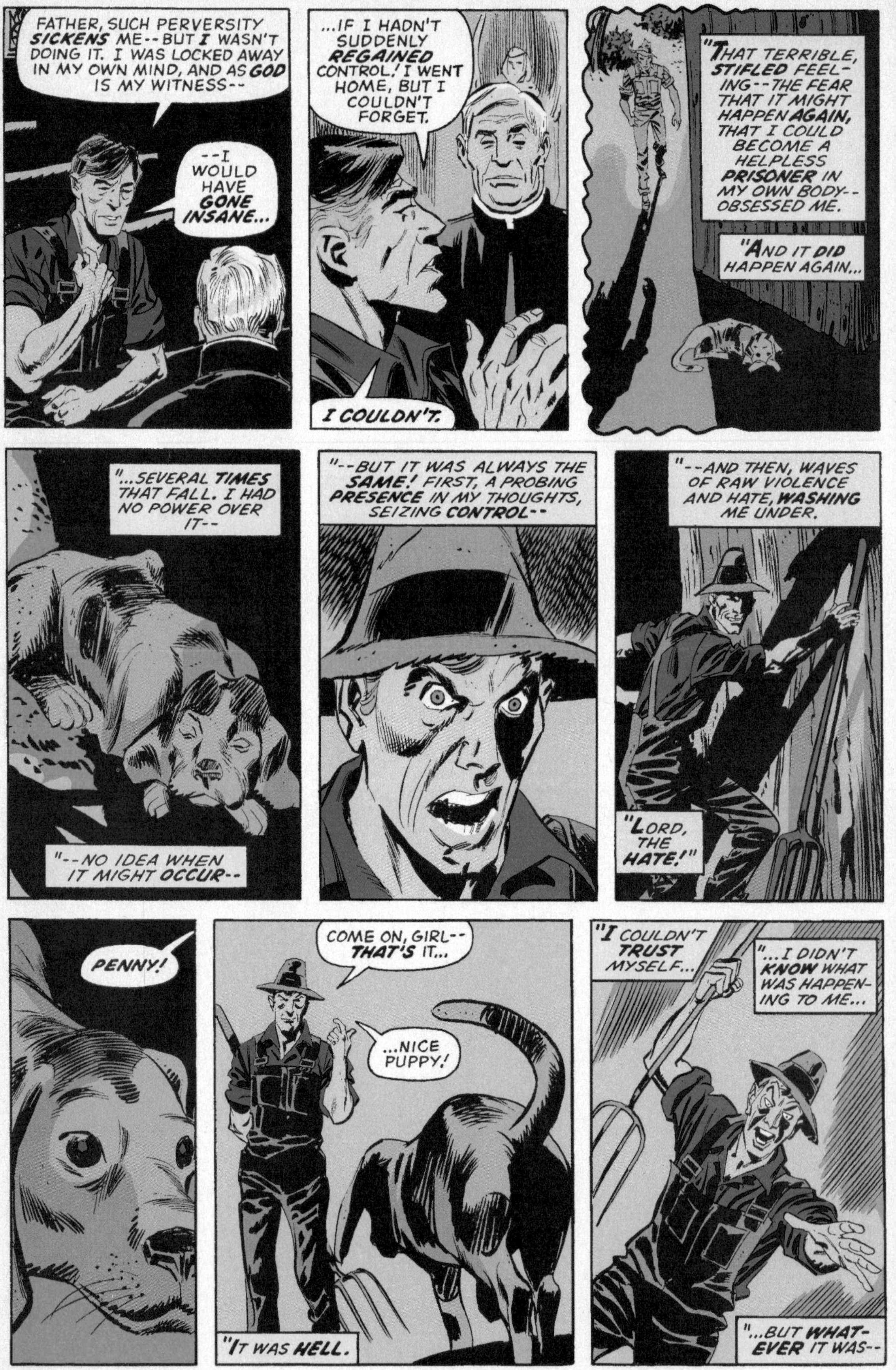

FATHER, SUCH PERVERSITY **SICKENS** ME--BUT **I** WASN'T DOING IT. I WAS LOCKED AWAY IN MY OWN MIND, AND AS **GOD** IS MY WITNESS--
--I WOULD HAVE **GONE INSANE...**
...IF I HADN'T SUDDENLY **REGAINED** CONTROL! I WENT HOME, BUT I COULDN'T FORGET.
I COULDN'T.
"THAT TERRIBLE, **STIFLED** FEEL-ING--THE FEAR THAT IT MIGHT HAPPEN **AGAIN,** THAT I COULD BECOME A HELPLESS **PRISONER** IN MY OWN BODY--OBSESSED ME.
"AND IT **DID** HAPPEN AGAIN...
"...SEVERAL **TIMES** THAT FALL. I HAD NO POWER OVER IT--
"--NO IDEA WHEN IT MIGHT **OCCUR**--
"--BUT IT WAS ALWAYS THE **SAME!** FIRST, A PROBING **PRESENCE** IN MY THOUGHTS, SEIZING **CONTROL**--
"--AND THEN, WAVES OF RAW VIOLENCE AND HATE, **WASHING** ME UNDER.
"LORD, THE **HATE!**"
PENNY!
"IT WAS **HELL.**
COME ON, GIRL--**THAT'S** IT...
...NICE PUPPY!
"I COULDN'T **TRUST** MYSELF...
"...I DIDN'T **KNOW** WHAT WAS HAPPEN-ING TO ME...
"...BUT **WHAT-EVER** IT WAS--

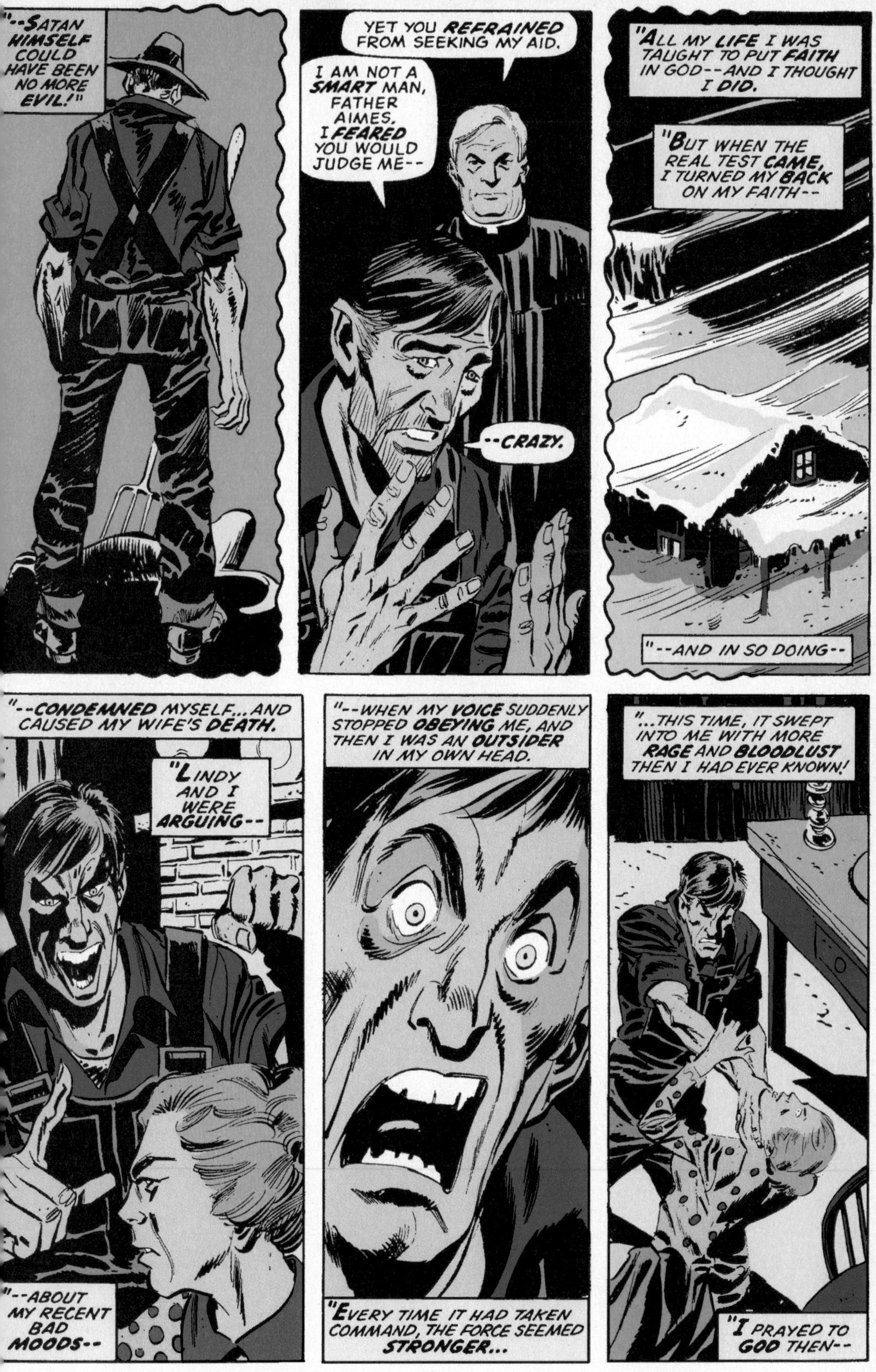

"--SATAN HIMSELF COULD HAVE BEEN NO MORE EVIL!"
YET YOU REFRAINED FROM SEEKING MY AID.
I AM NOT A SMART MAN, FATHER AIMES. I FEARED YOU WOULD JUDGE ME--
--CRAZY.
"ALL MY LIFE I WAS TAUGHT TO PUT FAITH IN GOD--AND I THOUGHT I DID.
"BUT WHEN THE REAL TEST CAME, I TURNED MY BACK ON MY FAITH--
"--AND IN SO DOING--
"--CONDEMNED MYSELF... AND CAUSED MY WIFE'S DEATH.
"LINDY AND I WERE ARGUING--
"--ABOUT MY RECENT BAD MOODS--
"--WHEN MY VOICE SUDDENLY STOPPED OBEYING ME, AND THEN I WAS AN OUTSIDER IN MY OWN HEAD.
"EVERY TIME IT HAD TAKEN COMMAND, THE FORCE SEEMED STRONGER...
"...THIS TIME, IT SWEPT INTO ME WITH MORE RAGE AND BLOODLUST THEN I HAD EVER KNOWN!
"I PRAYED TO GOD THEN--

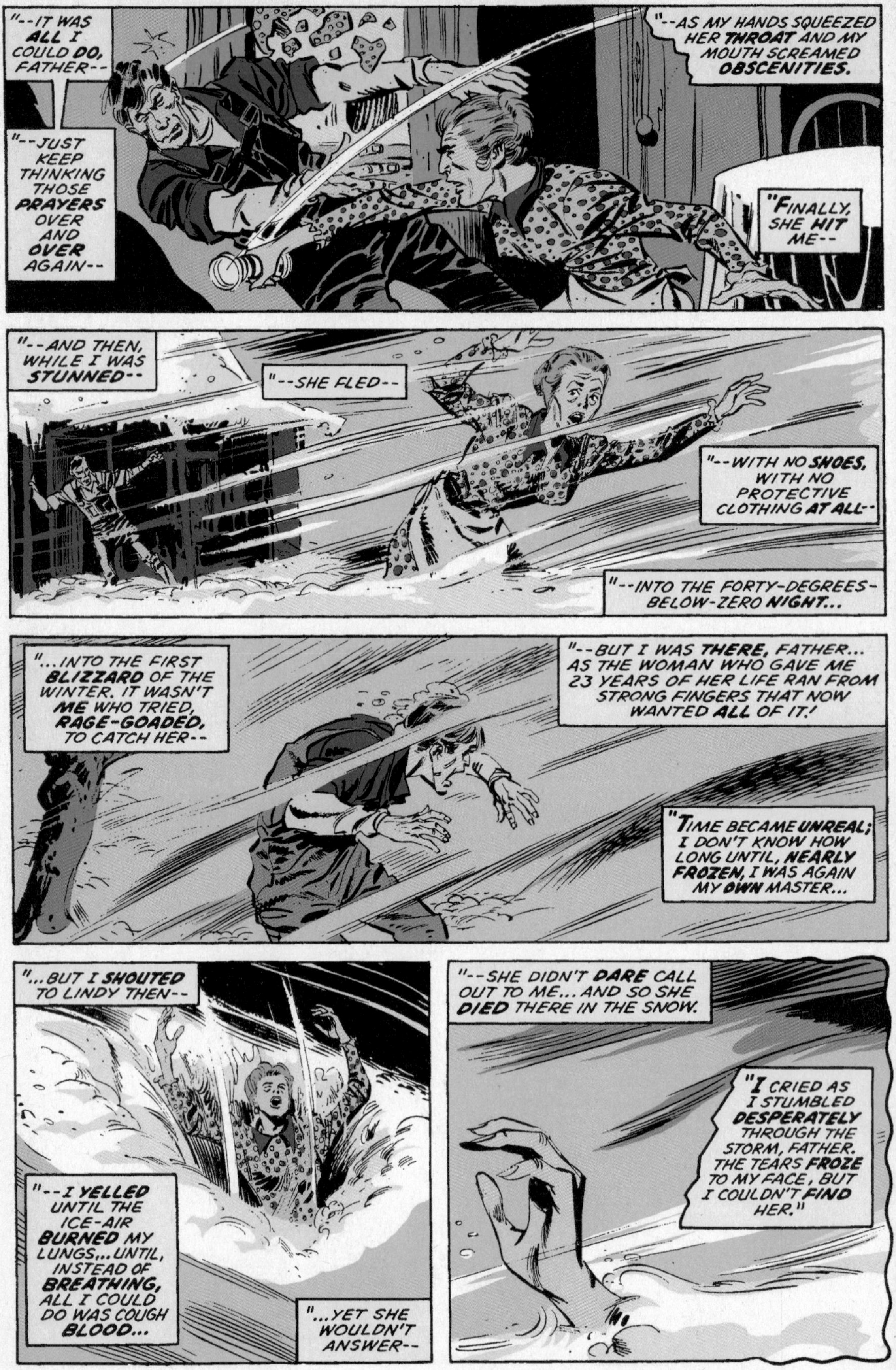

"--IT WAS ALL I COULD DO, FATHER--
"--JUST KEEP THINKING THOSE PRAYERS OVER AND OVER AGAIN--
"--AS MY HANDS SQUEEZED HER THROAT AND MY MOUTH SCREAMED OBSCENITIES.
"FINALLY, SHE HIT ME--
"--AND THEN, WHILE I WAS STUNNED--
"--SHE FLED--
"--WITH NO SHOES, WITH NO PROTECTIVE CLOTHING AT ALL--
"--INTO THE FORTY-DEGREES-BELOW-ZERO NIGHT...
"...INTO THE FIRST BLIZZARD OF THE WINTER. IT WASN'T ME WHO TRIED, RAGE-GOADED, TO CATCH HER--
"--BUT I WAS THERE, FATHER... AS THE WOMAN WHO GAVE ME 23 YEARS OF HER LIFE RAN FROM STRONG FINGERS THAT NOW WANTED ALL OF IT!
"TIME BECAME UNREAL; I DON'T KNOW HOW LONG UNTIL, NEARLY FROZEN, I WAS AGAIN MY OWN MASTER...
"...BUT I SHOUTED TO LINDY THEN--
"--I YELLED UNTIL THE ICE-AIR BURNED MY LUNGS... UNTIL, INSTEAD OF BREATHING, ALL I COULD DO WAS COUGH BLOOD...
"...YET SHE WOULDN'T ANSWER--
"--SHE DIDN'T DARE CALL OUT TO ME... AND SO SHE DIED THERE IN THE SNOW.
"I CRIED AS I STUMBLED DESPERATELY THROUGH THE STORM, FATHER. THE TEARS FROZE TO MY FACE, BUT I COULDN'T FIND HER."

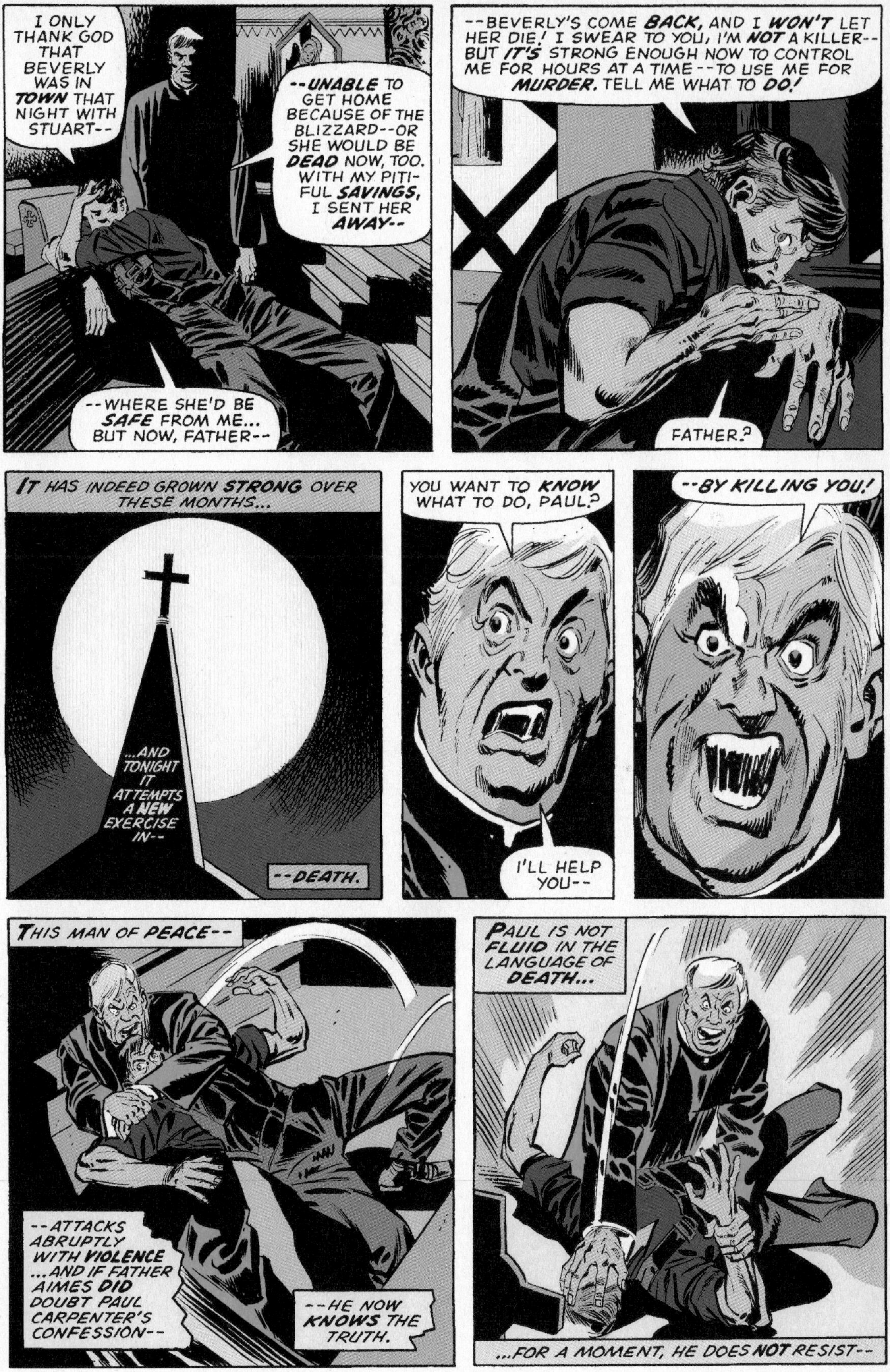
I ONLY THANK GOD THAT BEVERLY WAS IN TOWN THAT NIGHT WITH STUART--
--UNABLE TO GET HOME BECAUSE OF THE BLIZZARD--OR SHE WOULD BE DEAD NOW, TOO. WITH MY PITIFUL SAVINGS, I SENT HER AWAY--
--WHERE SHE'D BE SAFE FROM ME... BUT NOW, FATHER--
--BEVERLY'S COME BACK, AND I WON'T LET HER DIE! I SWEAR TO YOU, I'M NOT A KILLER--BUT IT'S STRONG ENOUGH NOW TO CONTROL ME FOR HOURS AT A TIME--TO USE ME FOR MURDER. TELL ME WHAT TO DO!
FATHER?
IT HAS INDEED GROWN STRONG OVER THESE MONTHS...
...AND TONIGHT IT ATTEMPTS A NEW EXERCISE IN--
--DEATH.
YOU WANT TO KNOW WHAT TO DO, PAUL?
I'LL HELP YOU--
--BY KILLING YOU!
THIS MAN OF PEACE--
--ATTACKS ABRUPTLY WITH VIOLENCE ...AND IF FATHER AIMES DID DOUBT PAUL CARPENTER'S CONFESSION--
--HE NOW KNOWS THE TRUTH.
PAUL IS NOT FLUID IN THE LANGUAGE OF DEATH...
...FOR A MOMENT, HE DOES NOT RESIST--

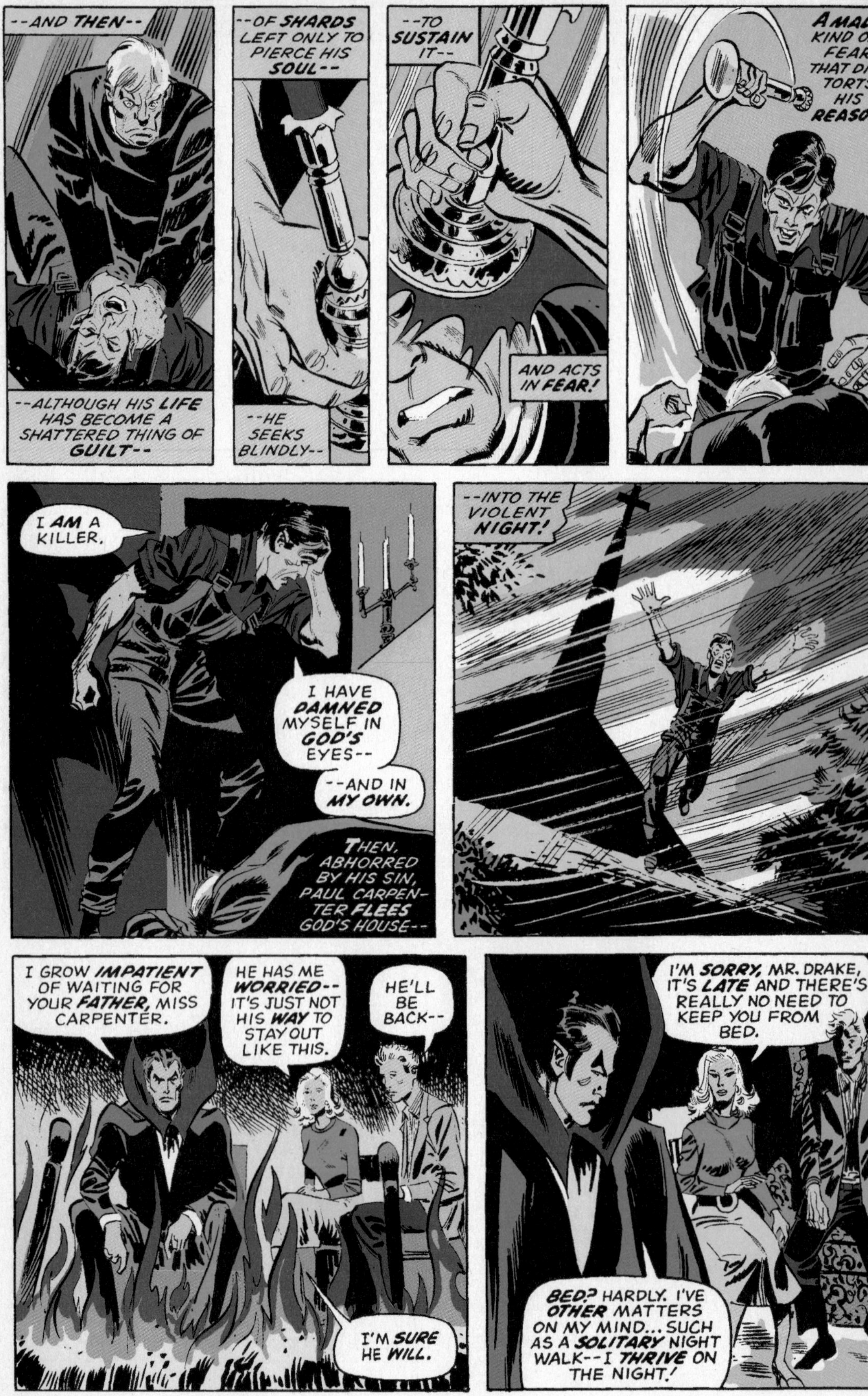
--AND THEN--
--ALTHOUGH HIS LIFE HAS BECOME A SHATTERED THING OF GUILT--
--OF SHARDS LEFT ONLY TO PIERCE HIS SOUL--
--HE SEEKS BLINDLY--
--TO SUSTAIN IT--
AND ACTS IN FEAR!
A MAD KIND OF FEAR THAT DISTORTS HIS REASON.
I AM A KILLER.
I HAVE DAMNED MYSELF IN GOD'S EYES--
--AND IN MY OWN.
THEN, ABHORRED BY HIS SIN, PAUL CARPENTER FLEES GOD'S HOUSE--
--INTO THE VIOLENT NIGHT!
I GROW IMPATIENT OF WAITING FOR YOUR FATHER, MISS CARPENTER.
HE HAS ME WORRIED--IT'S JUST NOT HIS WAY TO STAY OUT LIKE THIS.
HE'LL BE BACK--
I'M SURE HE WILL.
I'M SORRY, MR. DRAKE, IT'S LATE AND THERE'S REALLY NO NEED TO KEEP YOU FROM BED.
BED? HARDLY. I'VE OTHER MATTERS ON MY MIND... SUCH AS A SOLITARY NIGHT WALK--I THRIVE ON THE NIGHT!

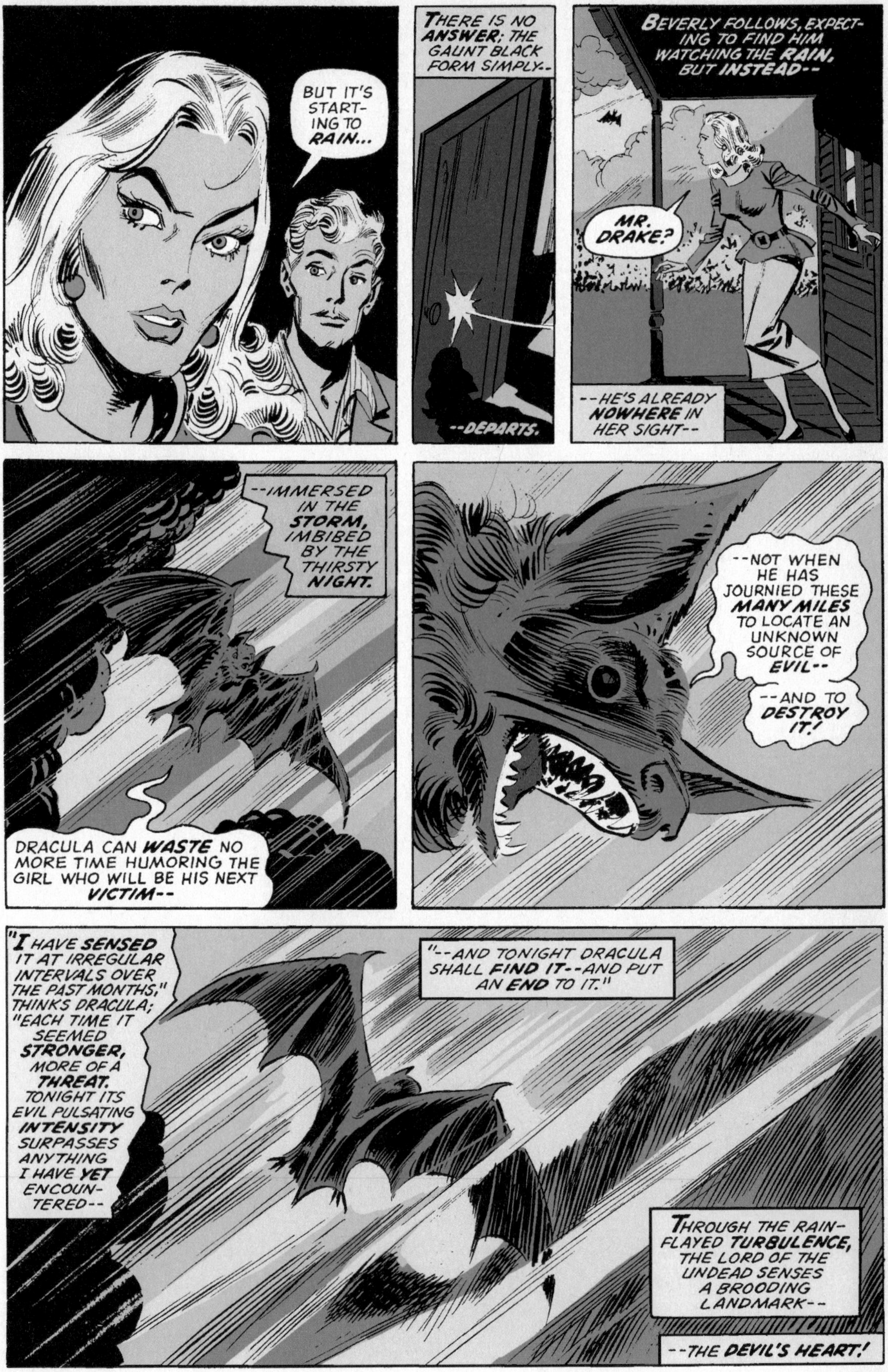

BUT IT'S START-ING TO RAIN...
THERE IS NO ANSWER; THE GAUNT BLACK FORM SIMPLY--
--DEPARTS.
BEVERLY FOLLOWS, EXPECT-ING TO FIND HIM WATCHING THE RAIN, BUT INSTEAD--
MR. DRAKE?
--HE'S ALREADY NOWHERE IN HER SIGHT--
--IMMERSED IN THE STORM, IMBIBED BY THE THIRSTY NIGHT.
DRACULA CAN WASTE NO MORE TIME HUMORING THE GIRL WHO WILL BE HIS NEXT VICTIM--
--NOT WHEN HE HAS JOURNIED THESE MANY MILES TO LOCATE AN UNKNOWN SOURCE OF EVIL--
--AND TO DESTROY IT!
"I HAVE SENSED IT AT IRREGULAR INTERVALS OVER THE PAST MONTHS," THINKS DRACULA; "EACH TIME IT SEEMED STRONGER, MORE OF A THREAT. TONIGHT ITS EVIL PULSATING INTENSITY SURPASSES ANYTHING I HAVE YET ENCOUN-TERED--
"--AND TONIGHT DRACULA SHALL FIND IT--AND PUT AN END TO IT."
THROUGH THE RAIN-FLAYED TURBULENCE, THE LORD OF THE UNDEAD SENSES A BROODING LANDMARK--
--THE DEVIL'S HEART!

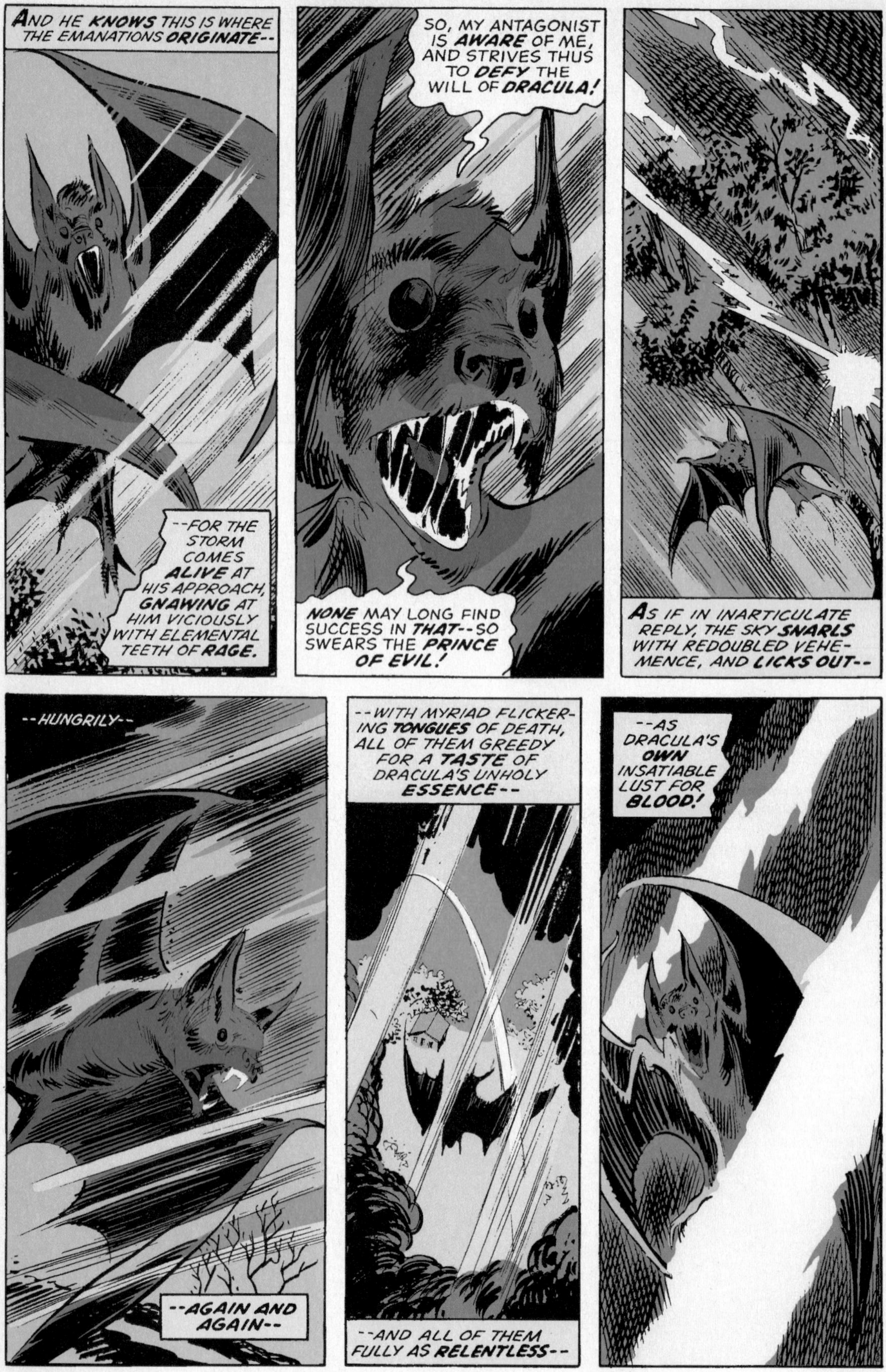
AND HE KNOWS THIS IS WHERE THE EMANATIONS ORIGINATE--
--FOR THE STORM COMES ALIVE AT HIS APPROACH, GNAWING AT HIM VICIOUSLY WITH ELEMENTAL TEETH OF RAGE.
SO, MY ANTAGONIST IS AWARE OF ME, AND STRIVES THUS TO DEFY THE WILL OF DRACULA!
NONE MAY LONG FIND SUCCESS IN THAT--SO SWEARS THE PRINCE OF EVIL!
AS IF IN INARTICULATE REPLY, THE SKY SNARLS WITH REDOUBLED VEHEMENCE, AND LICKS OUT--
--HUNGRILY--
--AGAIN AND AGAIN--
--WITH MYRIAD FLICKERING TONGUES OF DEATH, ALL OF THEM GREEDY FOR A TASTE OF DRACULA'S UNHOLY ESSENCE--
--AND ALL OF THEM FULLY AS RELENTLESS--
--AS DRACULA'S OWN INSATIABLE LUST FOR BLOOD!

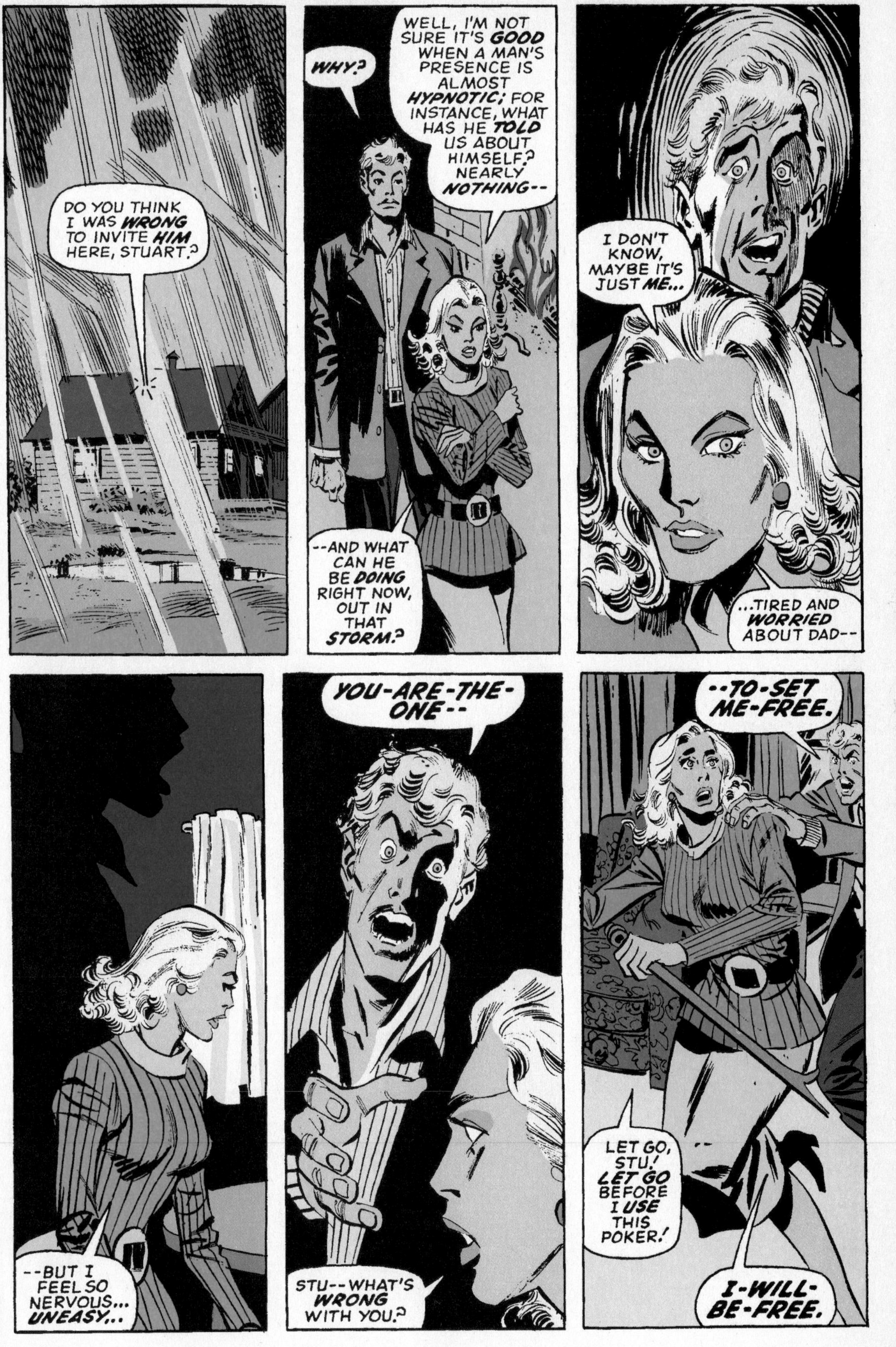
DO YOU THINK I WAS WRONG TO INVITE HIM HERE, STUART?
WHY?
WELL, I'M NOT SURE IT'S GOOD WHEN A MAN'S PRESENCE IS ALMOST HYPNOTIC; FOR INSTANCE, WHAT HAS HE TOLD US ABOUT HIMSELF? NEARLY NOTHING--
--AND WHAT CAN HE BE DOING RIGHT NOW, OUT IN THAT STORM?
I DON'T KNOW, MAYBE IT'S JUST ME...
...TIRED AND WORRIED ABOUT DAD--
--BUT I FEEL SO NERVOUS... UNEASY...
YOU-ARE-THE-ONE--
STU--WHAT'S WRONG WITH YOU?
--TO-SET ME-FREE.
LET GO, STU! LET GO BEFORE I USE THIS POKER!
I-WILL-BE-FREE.

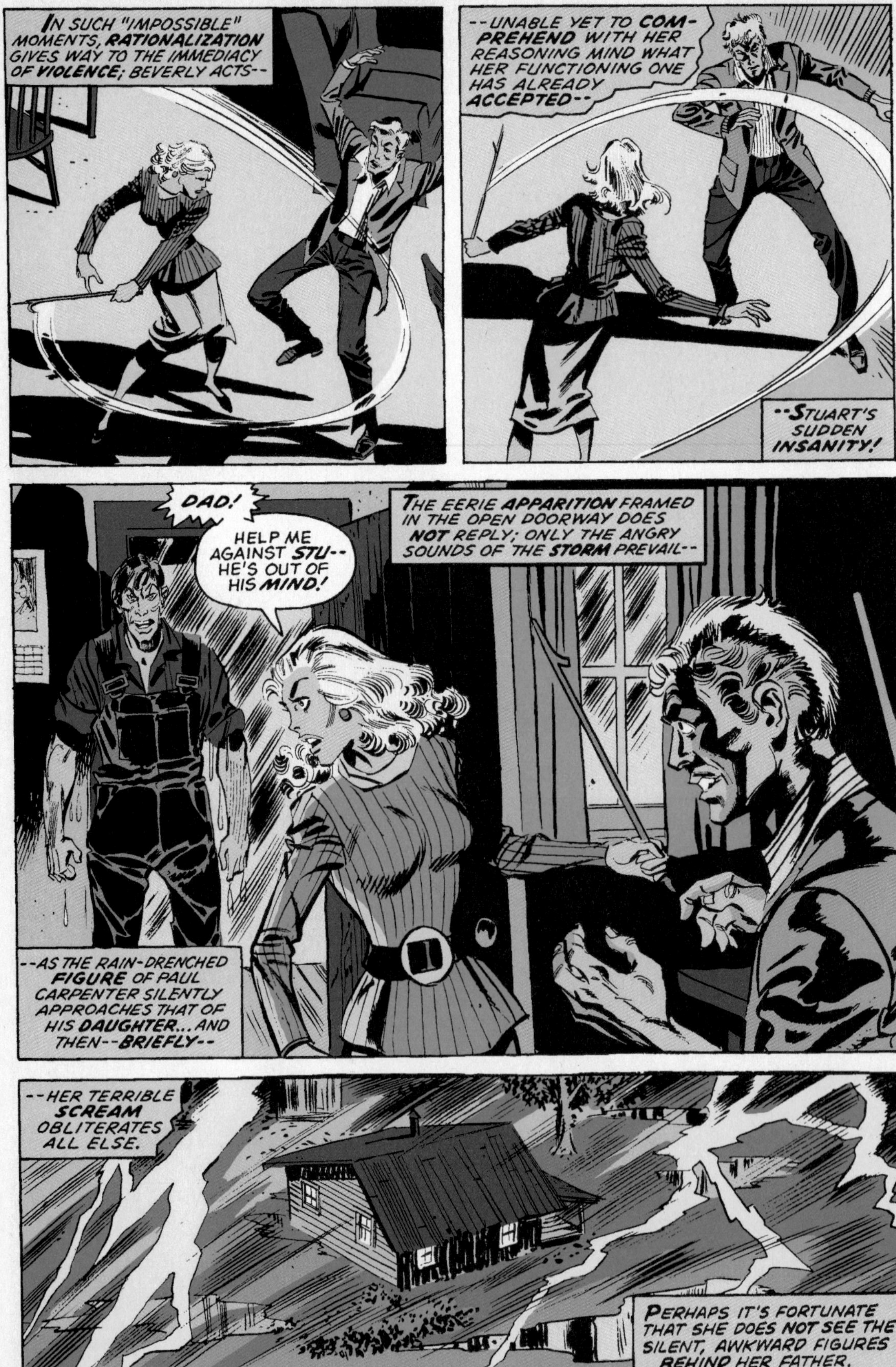
IN SUCH "IMPOSSIBLE" MOMENTS, RATIONALIZATION GIVES WAY TO THE IMMEDIACY OF VIOLENCE; BEVERLY ACTS--
--UNABLE YET TO COMPREHEND WITH HER REASONING MIND WHAT HER FUNCTIONING ONE HAS ALREADY ACCEPTED--
--STUART'S SUDDEN INSANITY!
DAD!
HELP ME AGAINST STU-- HE'S OUT OF HIS MIND!
THE EERIE APPARITION FRAMED IN THE OPEN DOORWAY DOES NOT REPLY; ONLY THE ANGRY SOUNDS OF THE STORM PREVAIL--
--AS THE RAIN-DRENCHED FIGURE OF PAUL CARPENTER SILENTLY APPROACHES THAT OF HIS DAUGHTER... AND THEN--BRIEFLY--
--HER TERRIBLE SCREAM OBLITERATES ALL ELSE.
PERHAPS IT'S FORTUNATE THAT SHE DOES NOT SEE THE SILENT, AWKWARD FIGURES BEHIND HER FATHER.

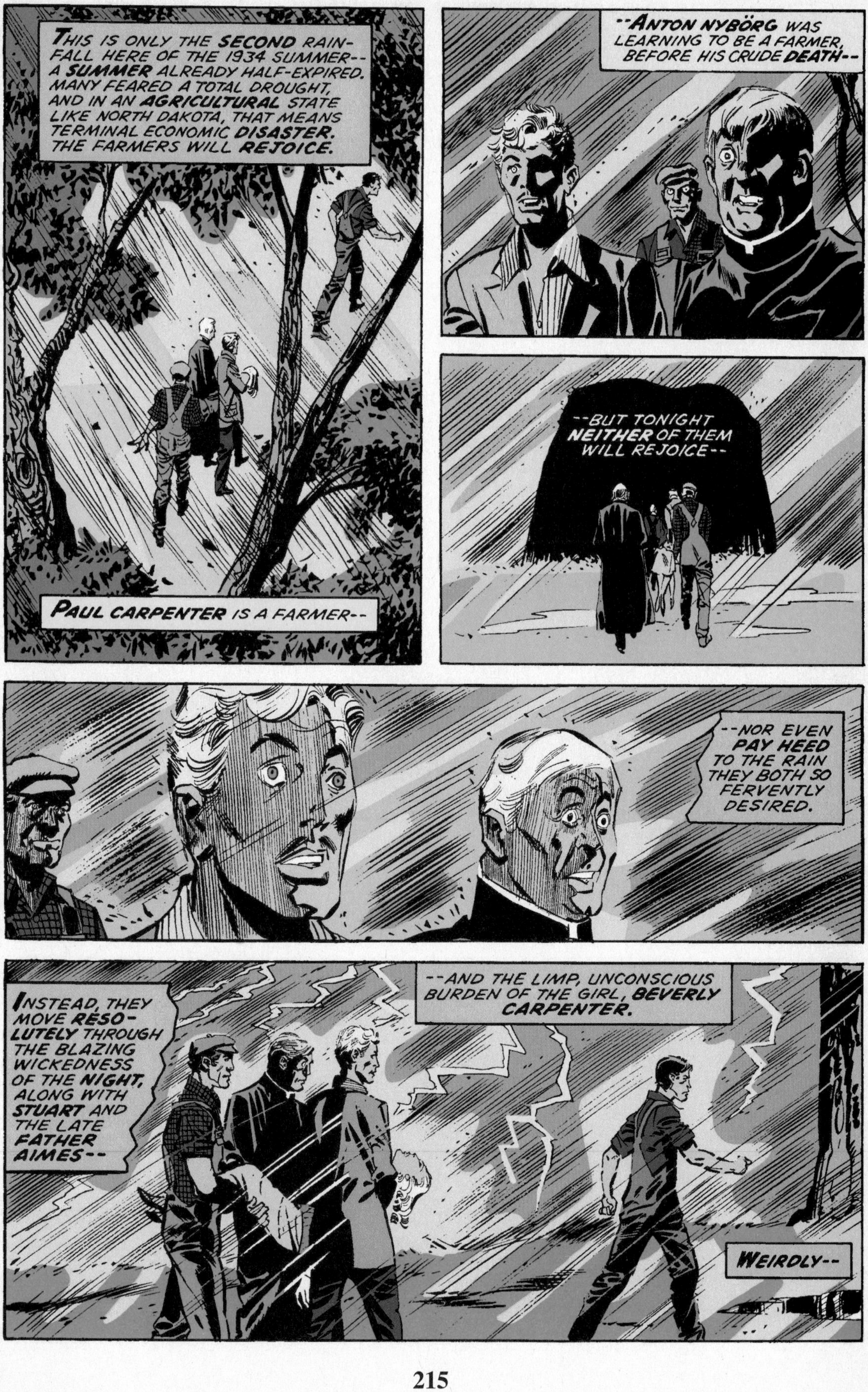
THIS IS ONLY THE SECOND RAIN-FALL HERE OF THE 1934 SUMMER--A SUMMER ALREADY HALF-EXPIRED. MANY FEARED A TOTAL DROUGHT, AND IN AN AGRICULTURAL STATE LIKE NORTH DAKOTA, THAT MEANS TERMINAL ECONOMIC DISASTER. THE FARMERS WILL REJOICE.
PAUL CARPENTER IS A FARMER--
--ANTON NYBÖRG WAS LEARNING TO BE A FARMER, BEFORE HIS CRUDE DEATH--
--BUT TONIGHT NEITHER OF THEM WILL REJOICE--
--NOR EVEN PAY HEED TO THE RAIN THEY BOTH SO FERVENTLY DESIRED.
INSTEAD, THEY MOVE RESOLUTELY THROUGH THE BLAZING WICKEDNESS OF THE NIGHT, ALONG WITH STUART AND THE LATE FATHER AIMES--
--AND THE LIMP, UNCONSCIOUS BURDEN OF THE GIRL, BEVERLY CARPENTER.
WEIRDLY--

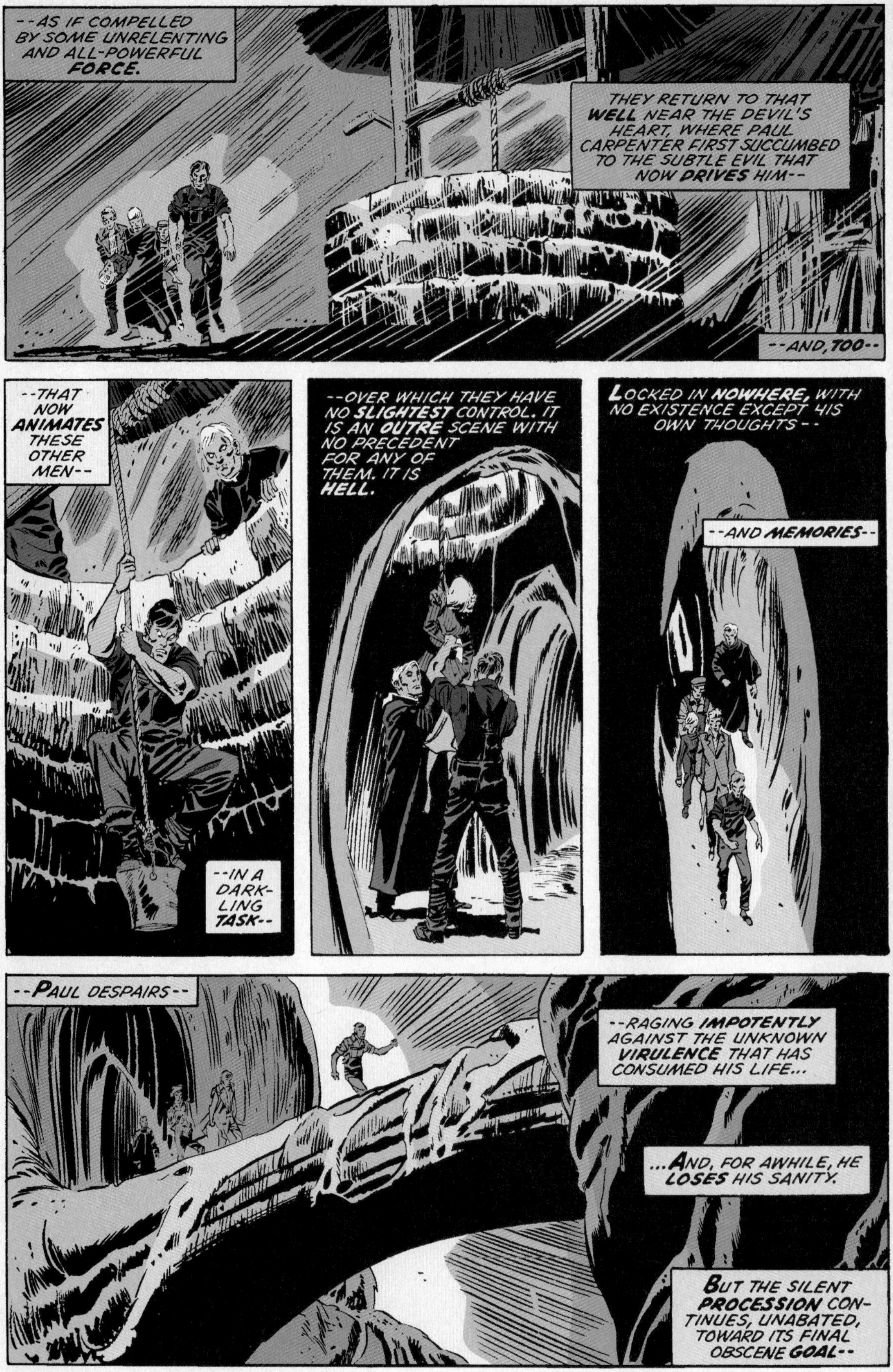
--AS IF COMPELLED BY SOME UNRELENTING AND ALL-POWERFUL FORCE.
THEY RETURN TO THAT WELL NEAR THE DEVIL'S HEART, WHERE PAUL CARPENTER FIRST SUCCUMBED TO THE SUBTLE EVIL THAT NOW DRIVES HIM--
--AND, TOO--
--THAT NOW ANIMATES THESE OTHER MEN--
--IN A DARK-LING TASK--
--OVER WHICH THEY HAVE NO SLIGHTEST CONTROL. IT IS AN OUTRE SCENE WITH NO PRECEDENT FOR ANY OF THEM. IT IS HELL.
LOCKED IN NOWHERE, WITH NO EXISTENCE EXCEPT HIS OWN THOUGHTS--
--AND MEMORIES--
--PAUL DESPAIRS--
--RAGING IMPOTENTLY AGAINST THE UNKNOWN VIRULENCE THAT HAS CONSUMED HIS LIFE...
...AND, FOR AWHILE, HE LOSES HIS SANITY.
BUT THE SILENT PROCESSION CON-TINUES, UNABATED, TOWARD ITS FINAL OBSCENE GOAL--

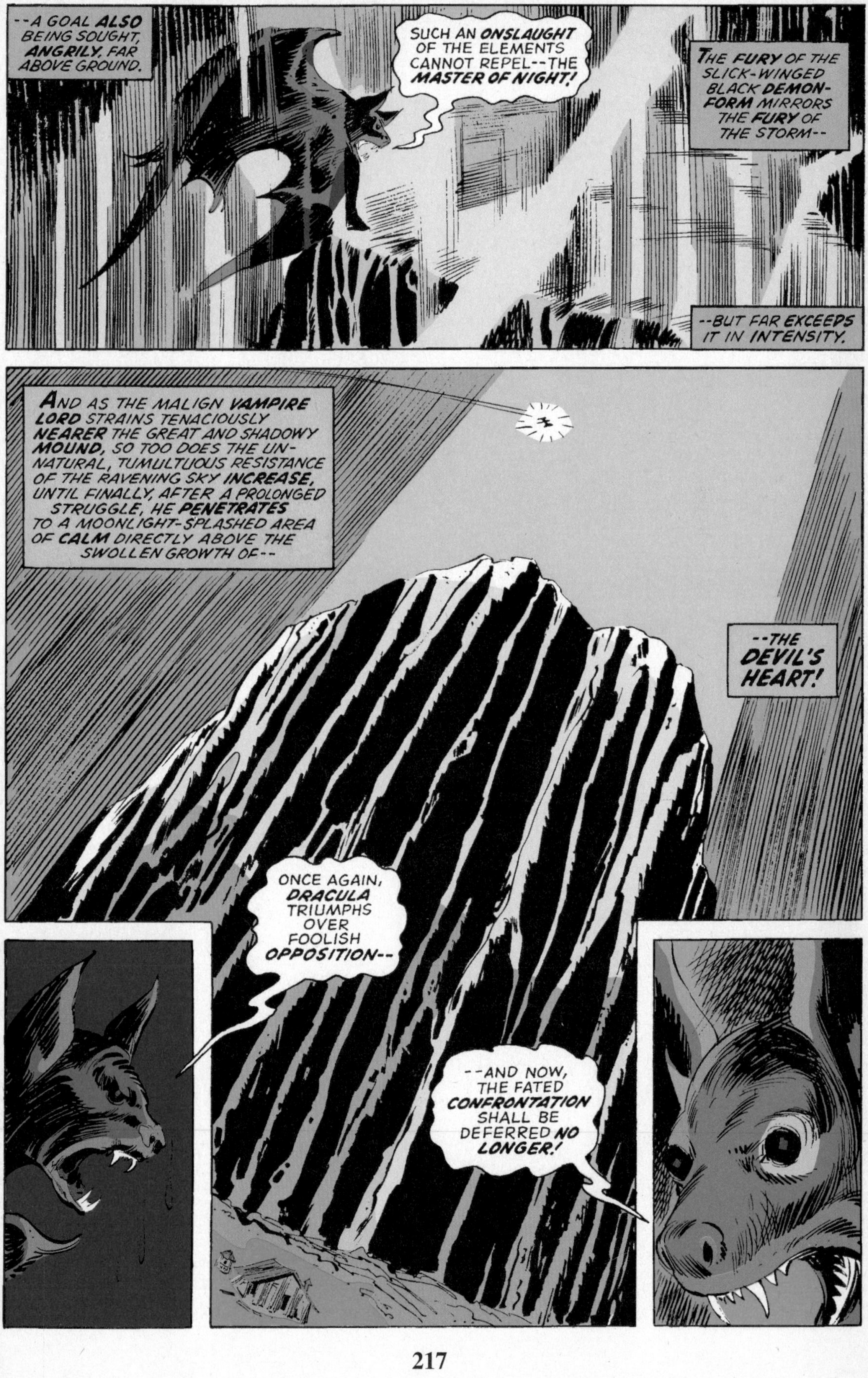

--A GOAL ALSO BEING SOUGHT, ANGRILY, FAR ABOVE GROUND.
SUCH AN ONSLAUGHT OF THE ELEMENTS CANNOT REPEL--THE MASTER OF NIGHT!
THE FURY OF THE SLICK-WINGED BLACK DEMON-FORM MIRRORS THE FURY OF THE STORM--
--BUT FAR EXCEEDS IT IN INTENSITY.
AND AS THE MALIGN VAMPIRE LORD STRAINS TENACIOUSLY NEARER THE GREAT AND SHADOWY MOUND, SO TOO DOES THE UN-NATURAL, TUMULTUOUS RESISTANCE OF THE RAVENING SKY INCREASE, UNTIL FINALLY, AFTER A PROLONGED STRUGGLE, HE PENETRATES TO A MOONLIGHT-SPLASHED AREA OF CALM DIRECTLY ABOVE THE SWOLLEN GROWTH OF--
--THE DEVIL'S HEART!
ONCE AGAIN, DRACULA TRIUMPHS OVER FOOLISH OPPOSITION--
--AND NOW, THE FATED CONFRONTATION SHALL BE DEFERRED NO LONGER!

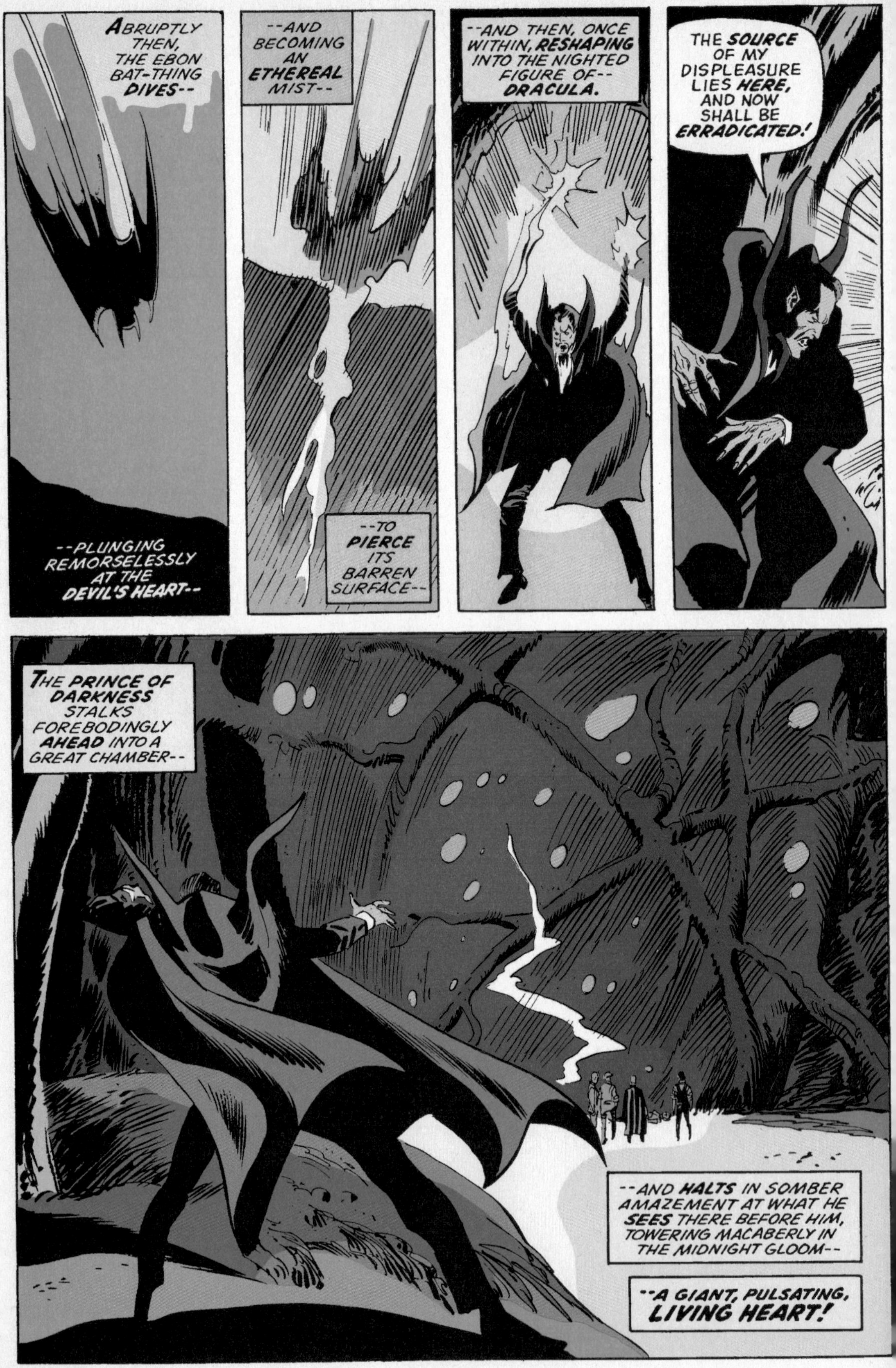
ABRUPTLY THEN, THE EBON BAT-THING DIVES--
--PLUNGING REMORSELESSLY AT THE DEVIL'S HEART--
--AND BECOMING AN ETHEREAL MIST--
--TO PIERCE ITS BARREN SURFACE--
--AND THEN, ONCE WITHIN, RESHAPING INTO THE NIGHTED FIGURE OF-- DRACULA.
THE SOURCE OF MY DISPLEASURE LIES HERE, AND NOW SHALL BE ERRADICATED!
THE PRINCE OF DARKNESS STALKS FOREBODINGLY AHEAD INTO A GREAT CHAMBER--
--AND HALTS IN SOMBER AMAZEMENT AT WHAT HE SEES THERE BEFORE HIM, TOWERING MACABERLY IN THE MIDNIGHT GLOOM--
--A GIANT, PULSATING, LIVING HEART!

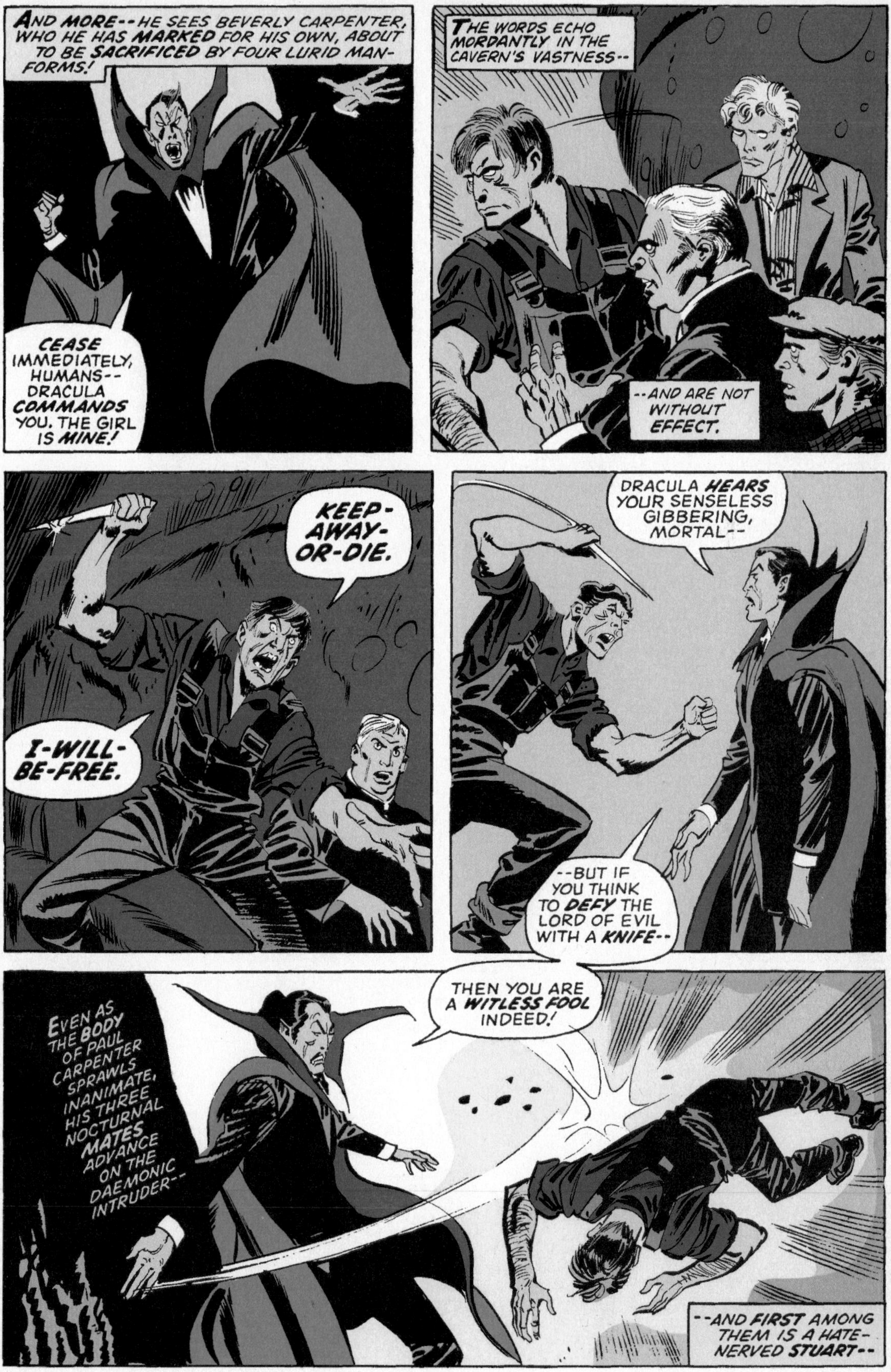
AND MORE--HE SEES BEVERLY CARPENTER, WHO HE HAS MARKED FOR HIS OWN, ABOUT TO BE SACRIFICED BY FOUR LURID MAN-FORMS!
CEASE IMMEDIATELY, HUMANS--DRACULA COMMANDS YOU. THE GIRL IS MINE!
THE WORDS ECHO MORDANTLY IN THE CAVERN'S VASTNESS--
--AND ARE NOT WITHOUT EFFECT.
KEEP-AWAY-OR-DIE.
I-WILL-BE-FREE.
DRACULA HEARS YOUR SENSELESS GIBBERING, MORTAL--
--BUT IF YOU THINK TO DEFY THE LORD OF EVIL WITH A KNIFE--
EVEN AS THE BODY OF PAUL CARPENTER SPRAWLS INANIMATE, HIS THREE NOCTURNAL MATES ADVANCE ON THE DAEMONIC INTRUDER--
THEN YOU ARE A WITLESS FOOL INDEED!
--AND FIRST AMONG THEM IS A HATE-NERVED STUART--

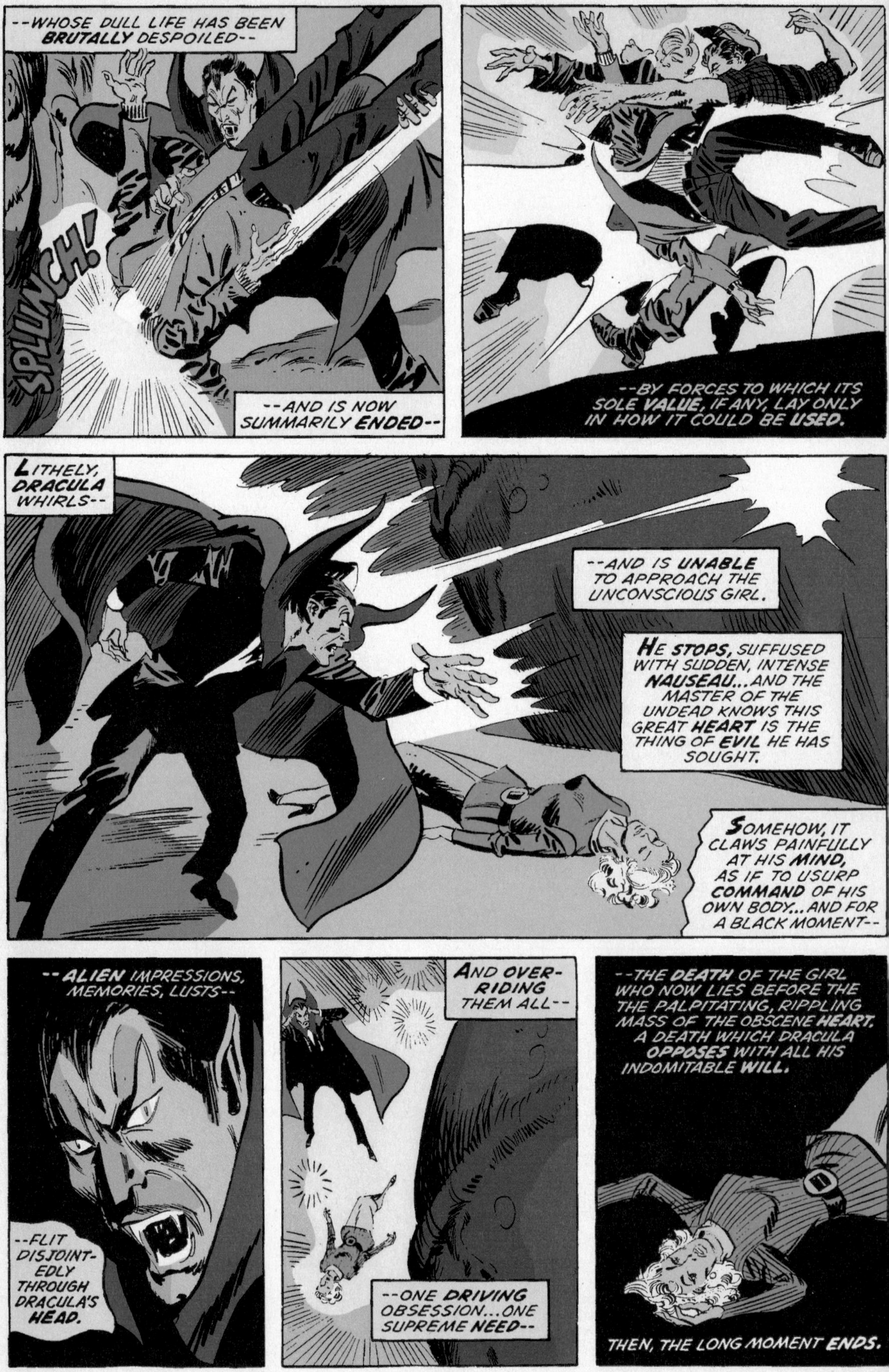
--WHOSE DULL LIFE HAS BEEN BRUTALLY DESPOILED--
SPLUNCH!
--AND IS NOW SUMMARILY ENDED--
--BY FORCES TO WHICH ITS SOLE VALUE, IF ANY, LAY ONLY IN HOW IT COULD BE USED.
LITHELY, DRACULA WHIRLS--
--AND IS UNABLE TO APPROACH THE UNCONSCIOUS GIRL.
HE STOPS, SUFFUSED WITH SUDDEN, INTENSE NAUSEAU...AND THE MASTER OF THE UNDEAD KNOWS THIS GREAT HEART IS THE THING OF EVIL HE HAS SOUGHT.
SOMEHOW, IT CLAWS PAINFULLY AT HIS MIND, AS IF TO USURP COMMAND OF HIS OWN BODY...AND FOR A BLACK MOMENT--
--ALIEN IMPRESSIONS, MEMORIES, LUSTS--
--FLIT DISJOINT-EDLY THROUGH DRACULA'S HEAD.
AND OVER-RIDING THEM ALL--
--ONE DRIVING OBSESSION...ONE SUPREME NEED--
--THE DEATH OF THE GIRL WHO NOW LIES BEFORE THE THE PALPITATING, RIPPLING MASS OF THE OBSCENE HEART. A DEATH WHICH DRACULA OPPOSES WITH ALL HIS INDOMITABLE WILL.
THEN, THE LONG MOMENT ENDS.

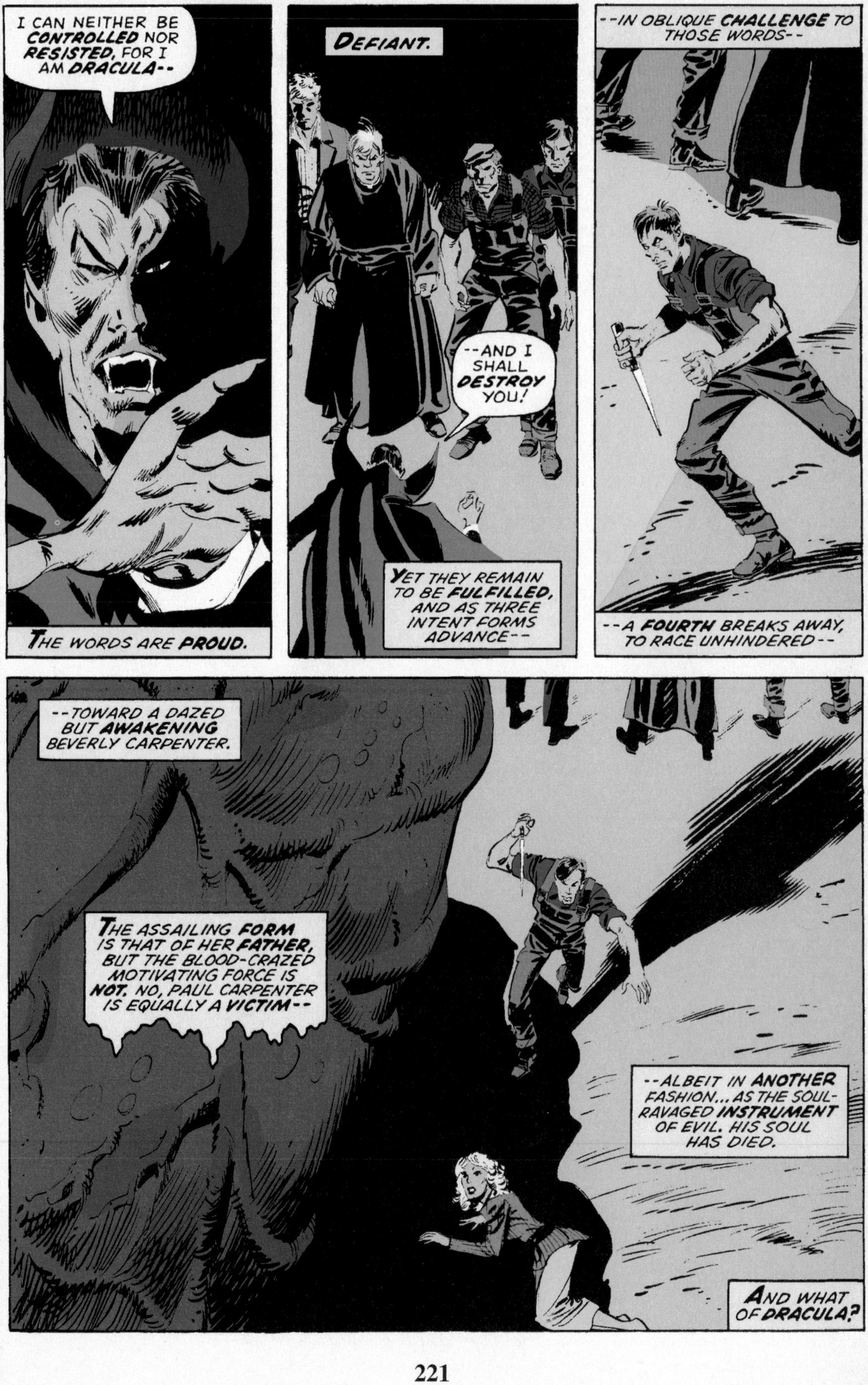
I CAN NEITHER BE CONTROLLED NOR RESISTED, FOR I AM DRACULA--
THE WORDS ARE PROUD.
DEFIANT.
--AND I SHALL DESTROY YOU!
YET THEY REMAIN TO BE FULFILLED, AND AS THREE INTENT FORMS ADVANCE--
--IN OBLIQUE CHALLENGE TO THOSE WORDS--
--A FOURTH BREAKS AWAY, TO RACE UNHINDERED--
--TOWARD A DAZED BUT AWAKENING BEVERLY CARPENTER.
THE ASSAILING FORM IS THAT OF HER FATHER, BUT THE BLOOD-CRAZED MOTIVATING FORCE IS NOT. NO, PAUL CARPENTER IS EQUALLY A VICTIM--
--ALBEIT IN ANOTHER FASHION... AS THE SOUL-RAVAGED INSTRUMENT OF EVIL. HIS SOUL HAS DIED.
AND WHAT OF DRACULA?

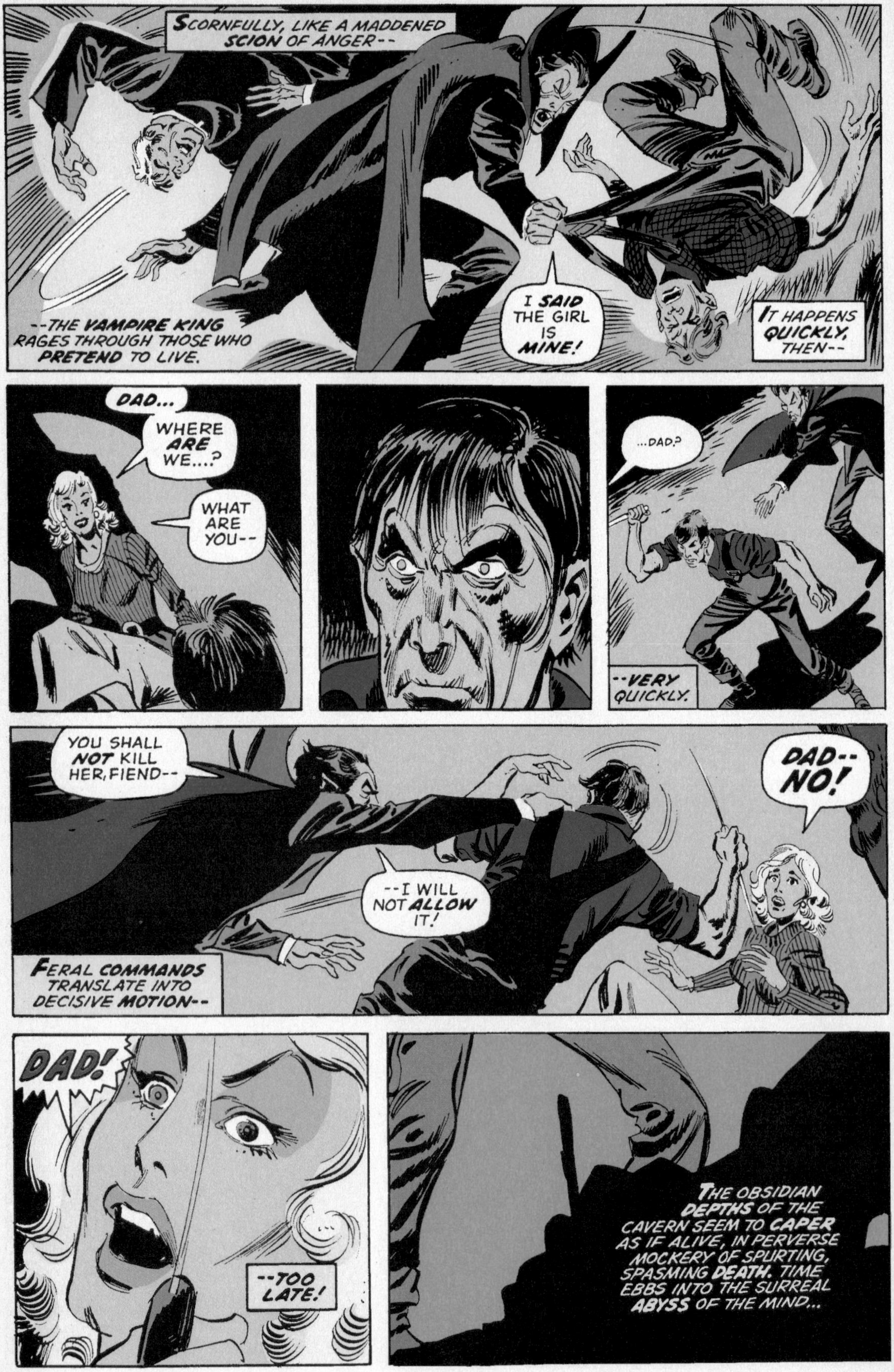
SCORNFULLY, LIKE A MADDENED SCION OF ANGER--
--THE VAMPIRE KING RAGES THROUGH THOSE WHO PRETEND TO LIVE.
I SAID THE GIRL IS MINE!
IT HAPPENS QUICKLY, THEN--
DAD...
WHERE ARE WE...?
WHAT ARE YOU--
...DAD?
--VERY QUICKLY.
YOU SHALL NOT KILL HER, FIEND--
DAD-- NO!
--I WILL NOT ALLOW IT!
FERAL COMMANDS TRANSLATE INTO DECISIVE MOTION--
DAD!
--TOO LATE!
THE OBSIDIAN DEPTHS OF THE CAVERN SEEM TO CAPER AS IF ALIVE, IN PERVERSE MOCKERY OF SPURTING, SPASMING DEATH. TIME EBBS INTO THE SURREAL ABYSS OF THE MIND...

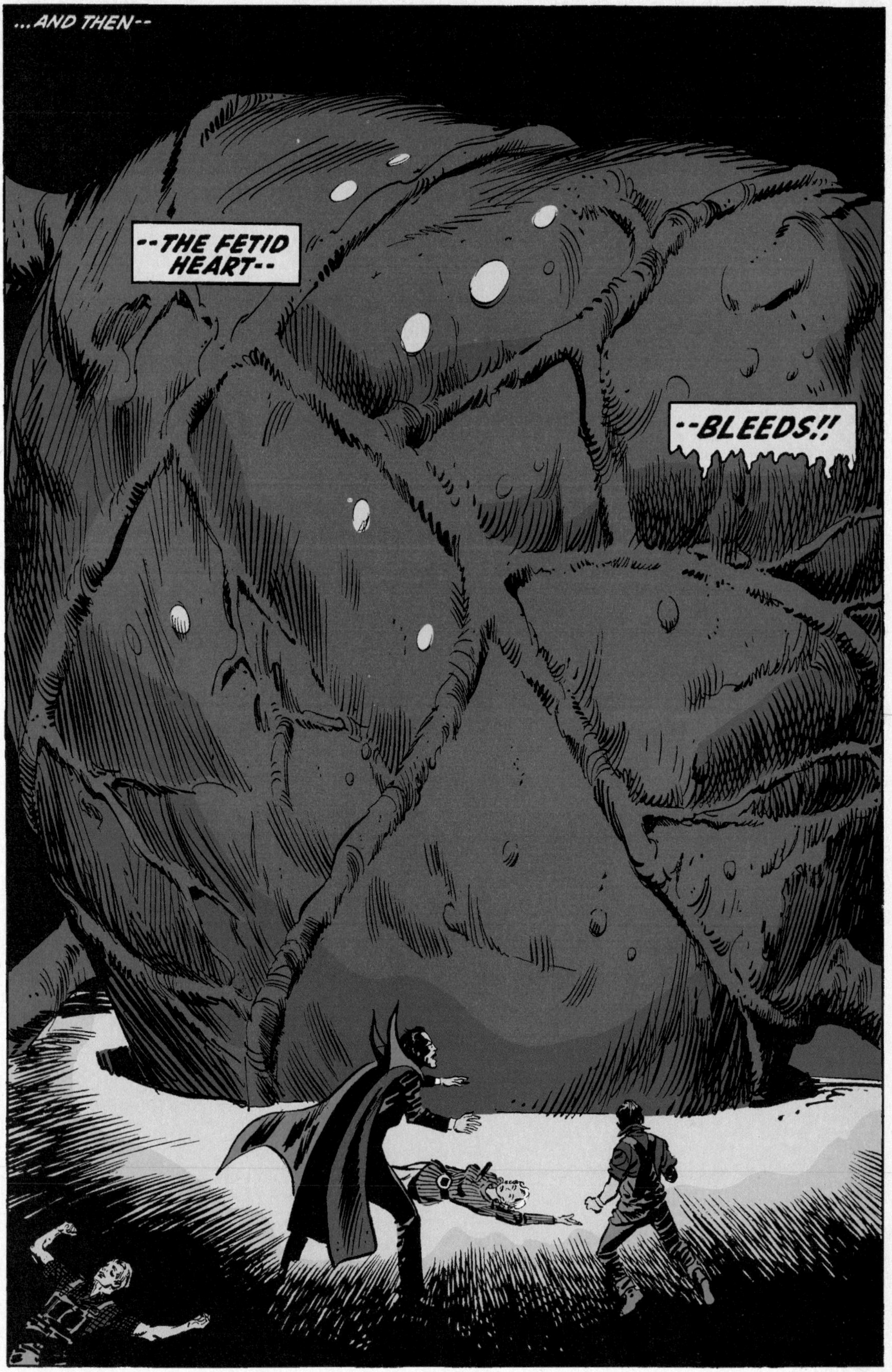
...AND THEN--
--THE FETID HEART--
--BLEEDS!!

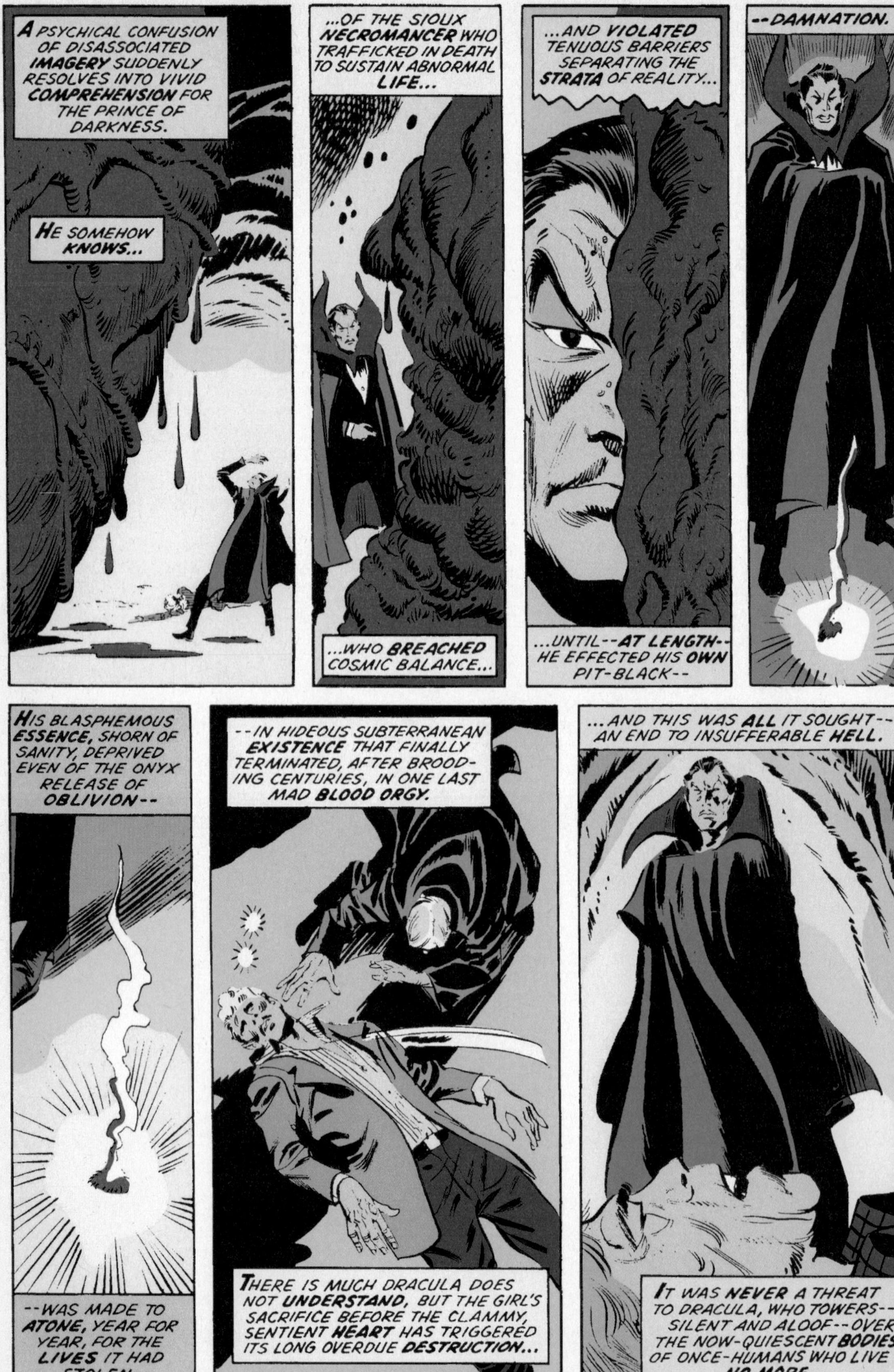
A PSYCHICAL CONFUSION OF DISASSOCIATED IMAGERY SUDDENLY RESOLVES INTO VIVID COMPREHENSION FOR THE PRINCE OF DARKNESS.
HE SOMEHOW KNOWS...
...OF THE SIOUX NECROMANCER WHO TRAFFICKED IN DEATH TO SUSTAIN ABNORMAL LIFE...
...WHO BREACHED COSMIC BALANCE...
...AND VIOLATED TENUOUS BARRIERS SEPARATING THE STRATA OF REALITY...
...UNTIL--AT LENGTH--HE EFFECTED HIS OWN PIT-BLACK--
--DAMNATION.
HIS BLASPHEMOUS ESSENCE, SHORN OF SANITY, DEPRIVED EVEN OF THE ONYX RELEASE OF OBLIVION--
--WAS MADE TO ATONE, YEAR FOR YEAR, FOR THE LIVES IT HAD STOLEN--
--IN HIDEOUS SUBTERRANEAN EXISTENCE THAT FINALLY TERMINATED, AFTER BROODING CENTURIES, IN ONE LAST MAD BLOOD ORGY.
THERE IS MUCH DRACULA DOES NOT UNDERSTAND, BUT THE GIRL'S SACRIFICE BEFORE THE CLAMMY, SENTIENT HEART HAS TRIGGERED ITS LONG OVERDUE DESTRUCTION...
...AND THIS WAS ALL IT SOUGHT--AN END TO INSUFFERABLE HELL.
IT WAS NEVER A THREAT TO DRACULA, WHO TOWERS--SILENT AND ALOOF--OVER THE NOW-QUIESCENT BODIES OF ONCE-HUMANS WHO LIVE NO MORE.

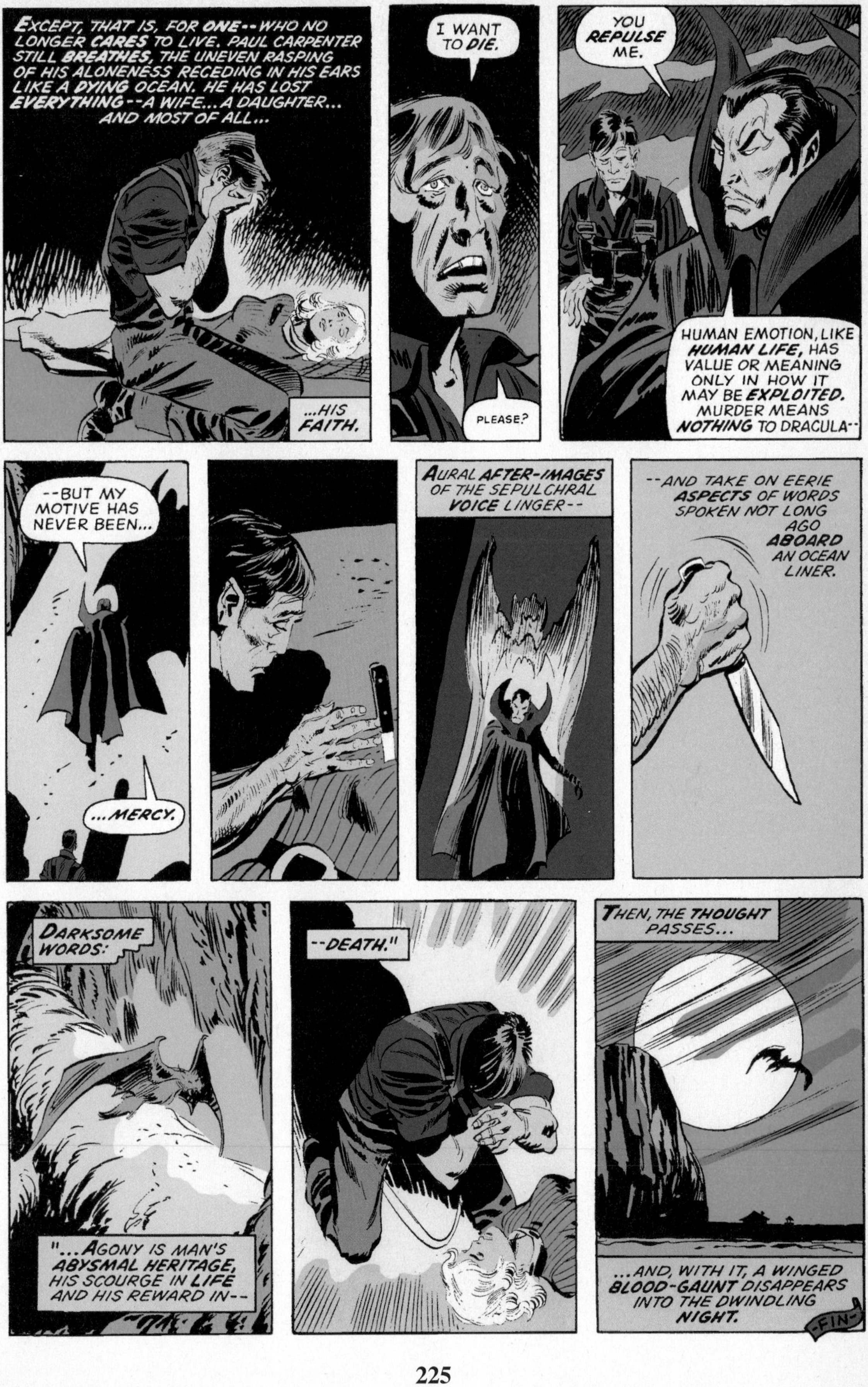
EXCEPT, THAT IS, FOR ONE--WHO NO LONGER CARES TO LIVE. PAUL CARPENTER STILL BREATHES, THE UNEVEN RASPING OF HIS ALONENESS RECEDING IN HIS EARS LIKE A DYING OCEAN. HE HAS LOST EVERYTHING--A WIFE... A DAUGHTER... AND MOST OF ALL...
...HIS FAITH.
I WANT TO DIE.
PLEASE?
YOU REPULSE ME.
HUMAN EMOTION, LIKE HUMAN LIFE, HAS VALUE OR MEANING ONLY IN HOW IT MAY BE EXPLOITED. MURDER MEANS NOTHING TO DRACULA--
--BUT MY MOTIVE HAS NEVER BEEN...
...MERCY.
AURAL AFTER-IMAGES OF THE SEPULCHRAL VOICE LINGER--
--AND TAKE ON EERIE ASPECTS OF WORDS SPOKEN NOT LONG AGO ABOARD AN OCEAN LINER.
DARKSOME WORDS:
"...AGONY IS MAN'S ABYSMAL HERITAGE, HIS SCOURGE IN LIFE AND HIS REWARD IN--
--DEATH."
THEN, THE THOUGHT PASSES...
...AND, WITH IT, A WINGED BLOOD-GAUNT DISAPPEARS INTO THE DWINDLING NIGHT.
-FIN-

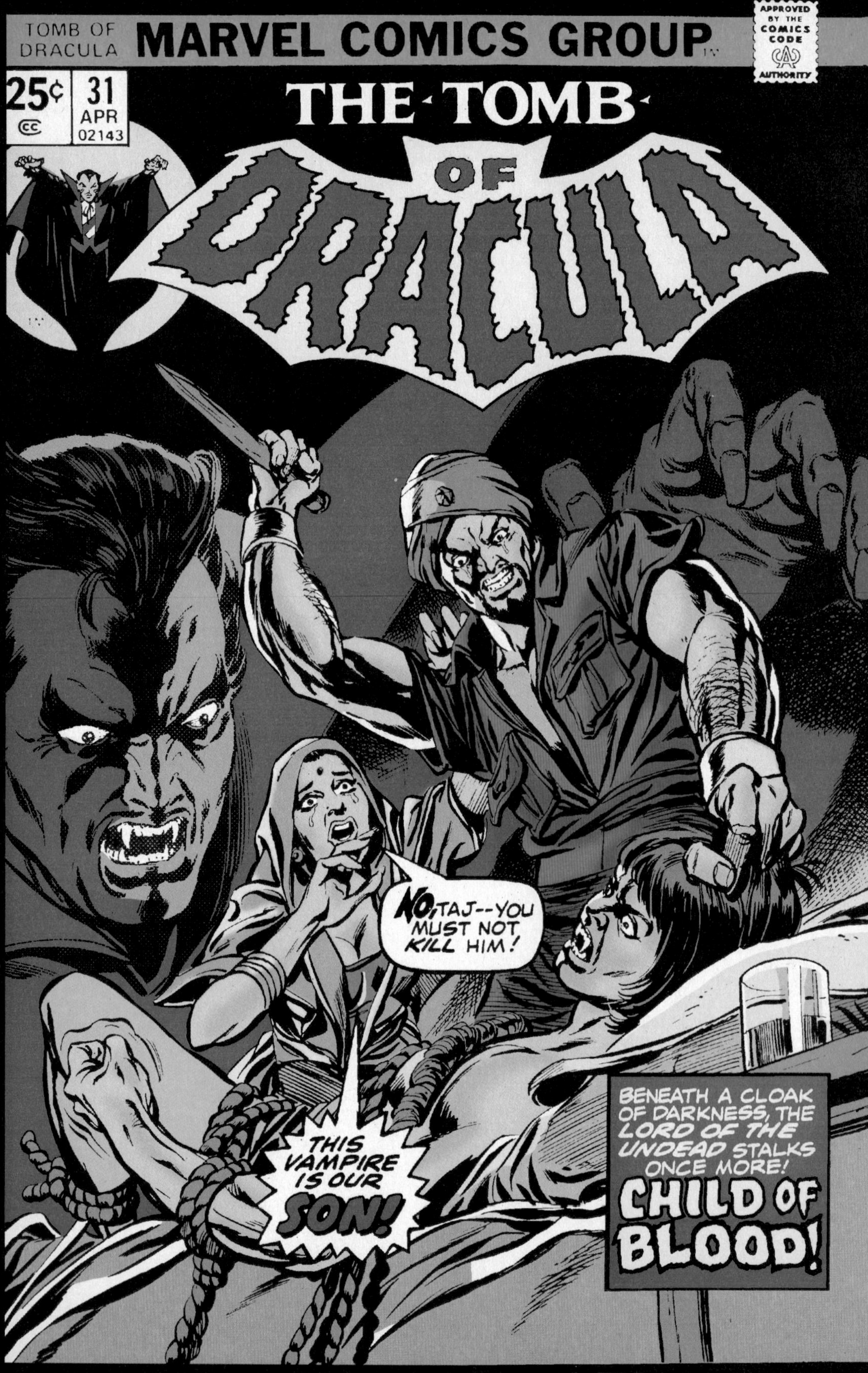
TOMB OF DRACULA
MARVEL COMICS GROUP
APPROVED BY THE COMICS CODE AUTHORITY
25¢
31
APR
02143
THE TOMB OF DRACULA
NO, TAJ--YOU MUST NOT KILL HIM!
THIS VAMPIRE IS OUR SON!
BENEATH A CLOAK OF DARKNESS, THE LORD OF THE UNDEAD STALKS ONCE MORE!
CHILD OF BLOOD!

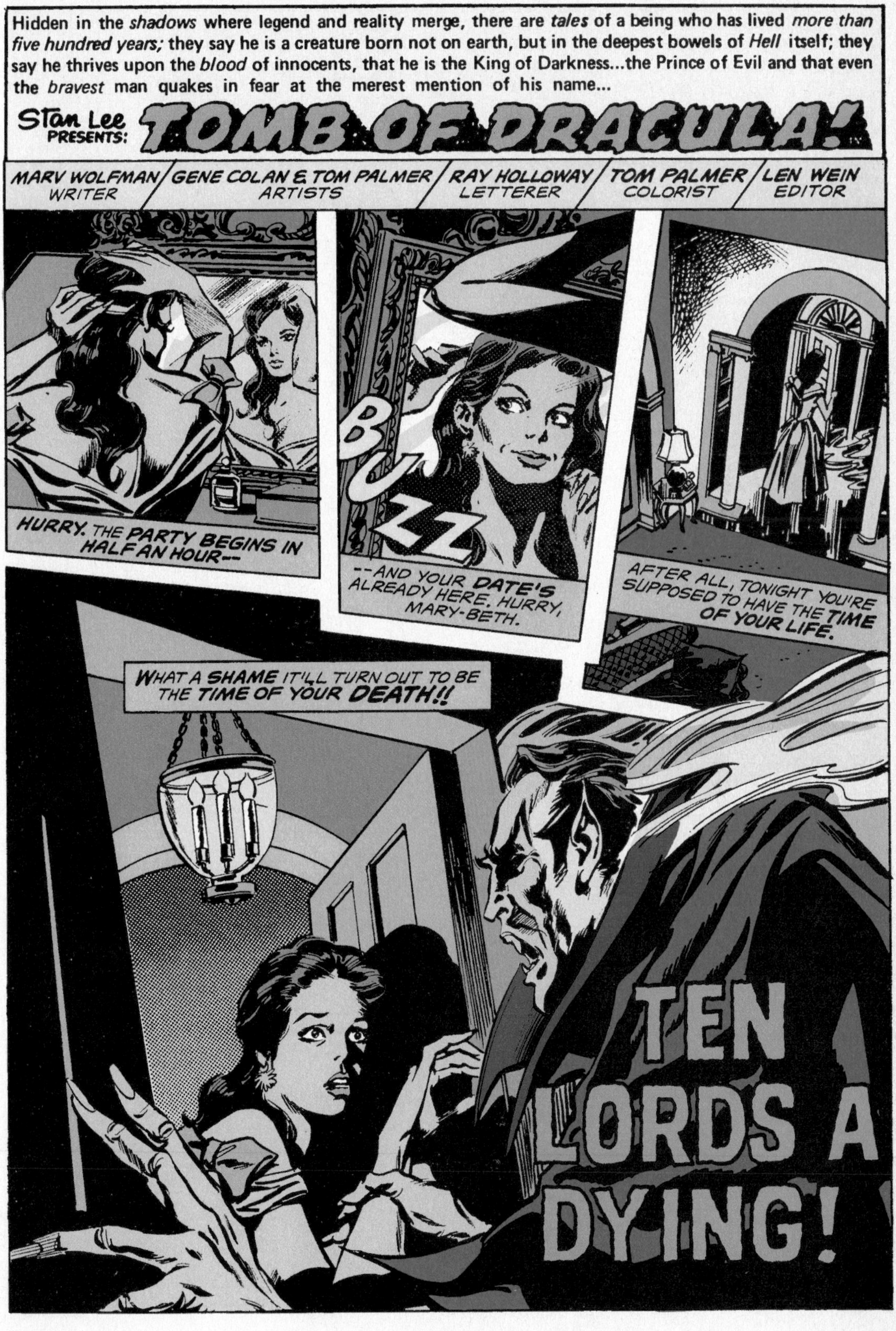
Hidden in the *shadows* where legend and reality merge, there are *tales* of a being who has lived *more than five hundred years;* they say he is a creature born not on earth, but in the deepest bowels of *Hell* itself; they say he thrives upon the *blood* of innocents, that he is the King of Darkness...the Prince of Evil and that even the *bravest* man quakes in fear at the merest mention of his name...
Stan Lee PRESENTS: TOMB OF DRACULA!
MARV WOLFMAN WRITER
GENE COLAN & TOM PALMER ARTISTS
RAY HOLLOWAY LETTERER
TOM PALMER COLORIST
LEN WEIN EDITOR
HURRY. THE PARTY BEGINS IN HALF AN HOUR--
BUZZ
--AND YOUR DATE'S ALREADY HERE. HURRY, MARY-BETH.
AFTER ALL, TONIGHT YOU'RE SUPPOSED TO HAVE THE TIME OF YOUR LIFE.
WHAT A SHAME IT'LL TURN OUT TO BE THE TIME OF YOUR DEATH!!
TEN LORDS A DYING!

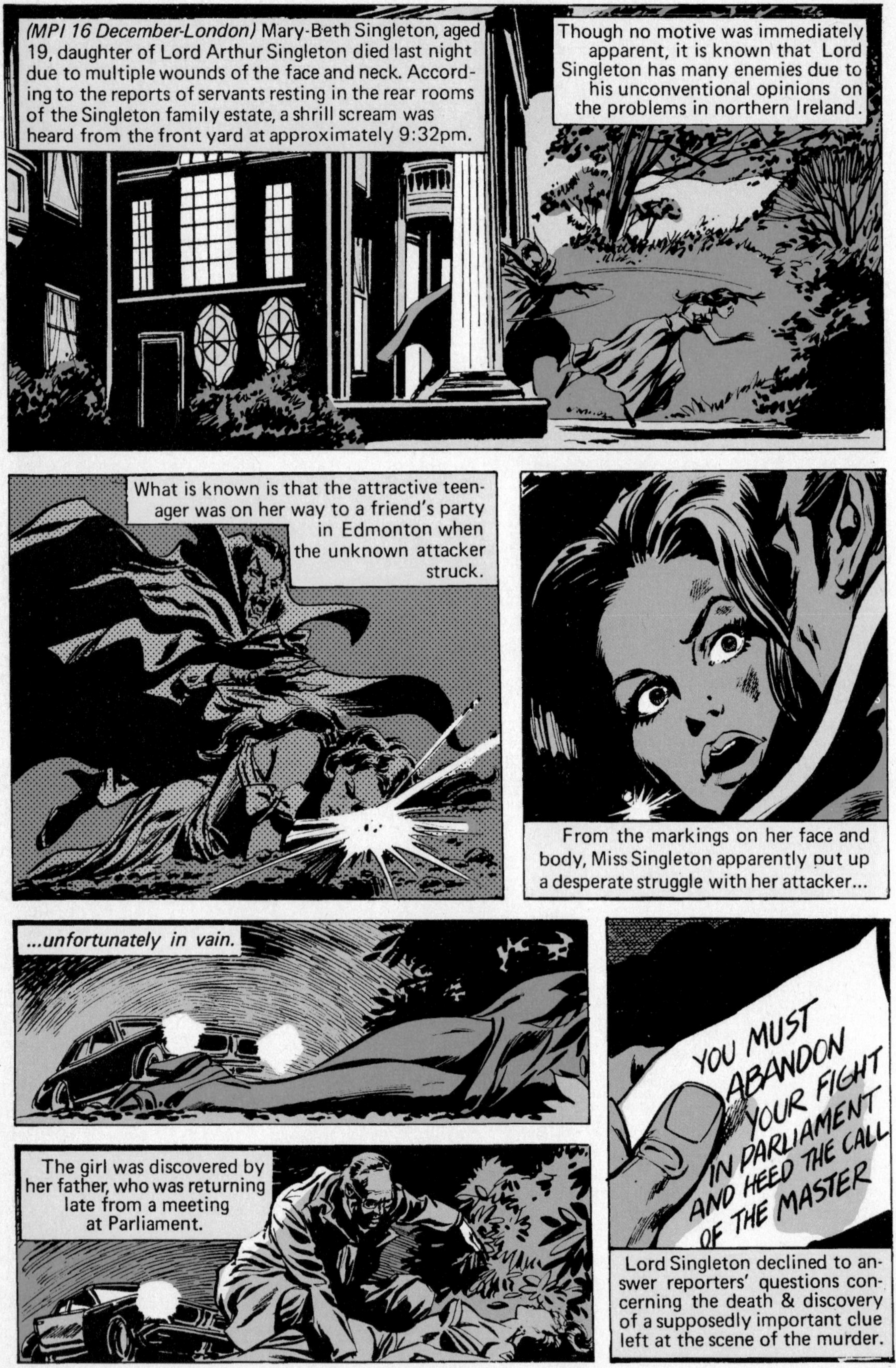
(MPI 16 December-London) Mary-Beth Singleton, aged 19, daughter of Lord Arthur Singleton died last night due to multiple wounds of the face and neck. According to the reports of servants resting in the rear rooms of the Singleton family estate, a shrill scream was heard from the front yard at approximately 9:32pm.
Though no motive was immediately apparent, it is known that Lord Singleton has many enemies due to his unconventional opinions on the problems in northern Ireland.
What is known is that the attractive teenager was on her way to a friend's party in Edmonton when the unknown attacker struck.
From the markings on her face and body, Miss Singleton apparently put up a desperate struggle with her attacker...
...unfortunately in vain.
YOU MUST ABANDON YOUR FIGHT IN PARLIAMENT AND HEED THE CALL OF THE MASTER
The girl was discovered by her father, who was returning late from a meeting at Parliament.
Lord Singleton declined to answer reporters' questions concerning the death & discovery of a supposedly important clue left at the scene of the murder.

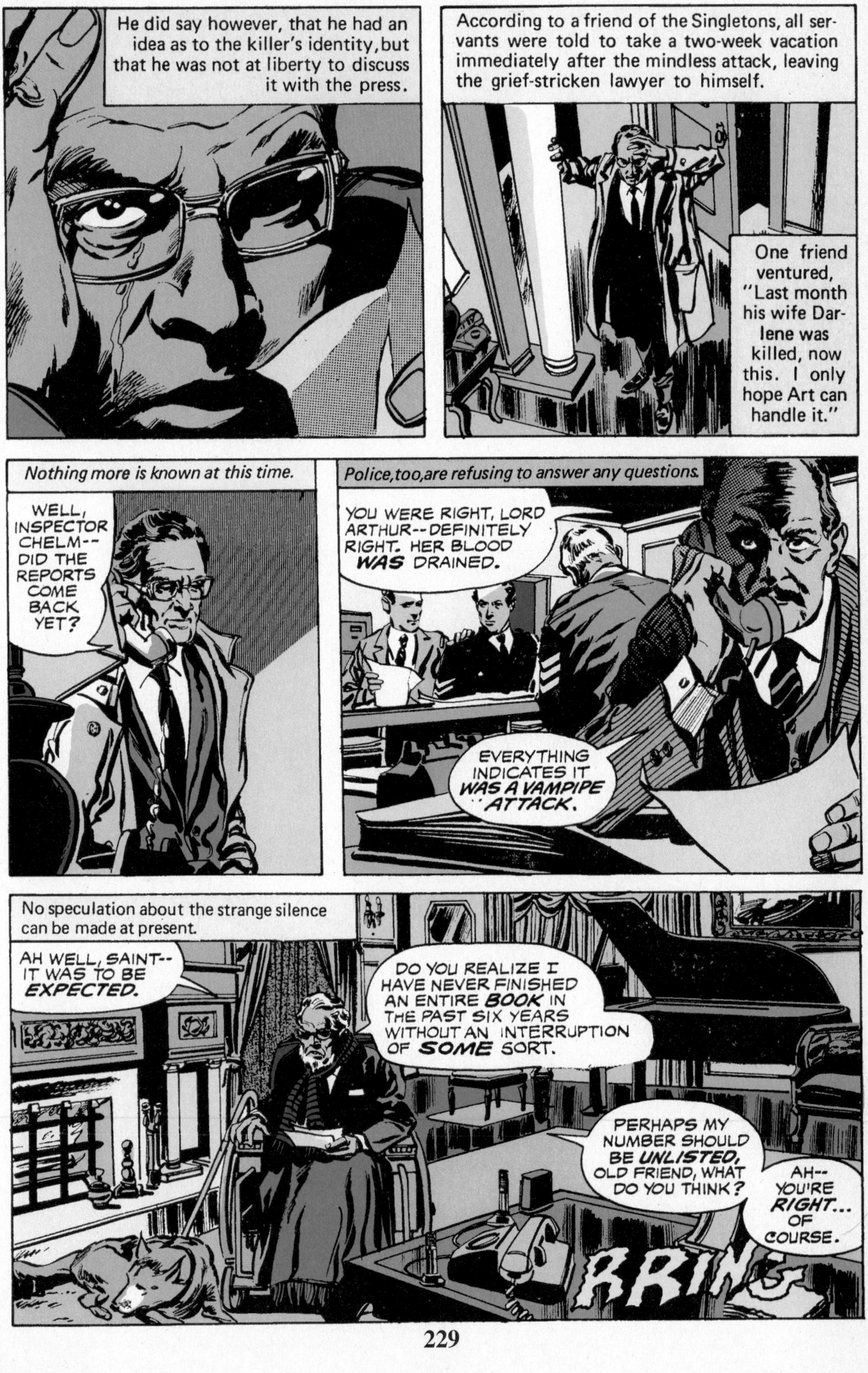
He did say however, that he had an idea as to the killer's identity, but that he was not at liberty to discuss it with the press.
According to a friend of the Singletons, all servants were told to take a two-week vacation immediately after the mindless attack, leaving the grief-stricken lawyer to himself.
One friend ventured, "Last month his wife Darlene was killed, now this. I only hope Art can handle it."
Nothing more is known at this time.
WELL, INSPECTOR CHELM-- DID THE REPORTS COME BACK YET?
Police, too, are refusing to answer any questions.
YOU WERE RIGHT, LORD ARTHUR--DEFINITELY RIGHT. HER BLOOD WAS DRAINED.
EVERYTHING INDICATES IT WAS A VAMPIPE ATTACK.
No speculation about the strange silence can be made at present.
AH WELL, SAINT-- IT WAS TO BE EXPECTED.
DO YOU REALIZE I HAVE NEVER FINISHED AN ENTIRE BOOK IN THE PAST SIX YEARS WITHOUT AN INTERRUPTION OF SOME SORT.
PERHAPS MY NUMBER SHOULD BE UNLISTED, OLD FRIEND, WHAT DO YOU THINK?
AH-- YOU'RE RIGHT... OF COURSE.
BRING

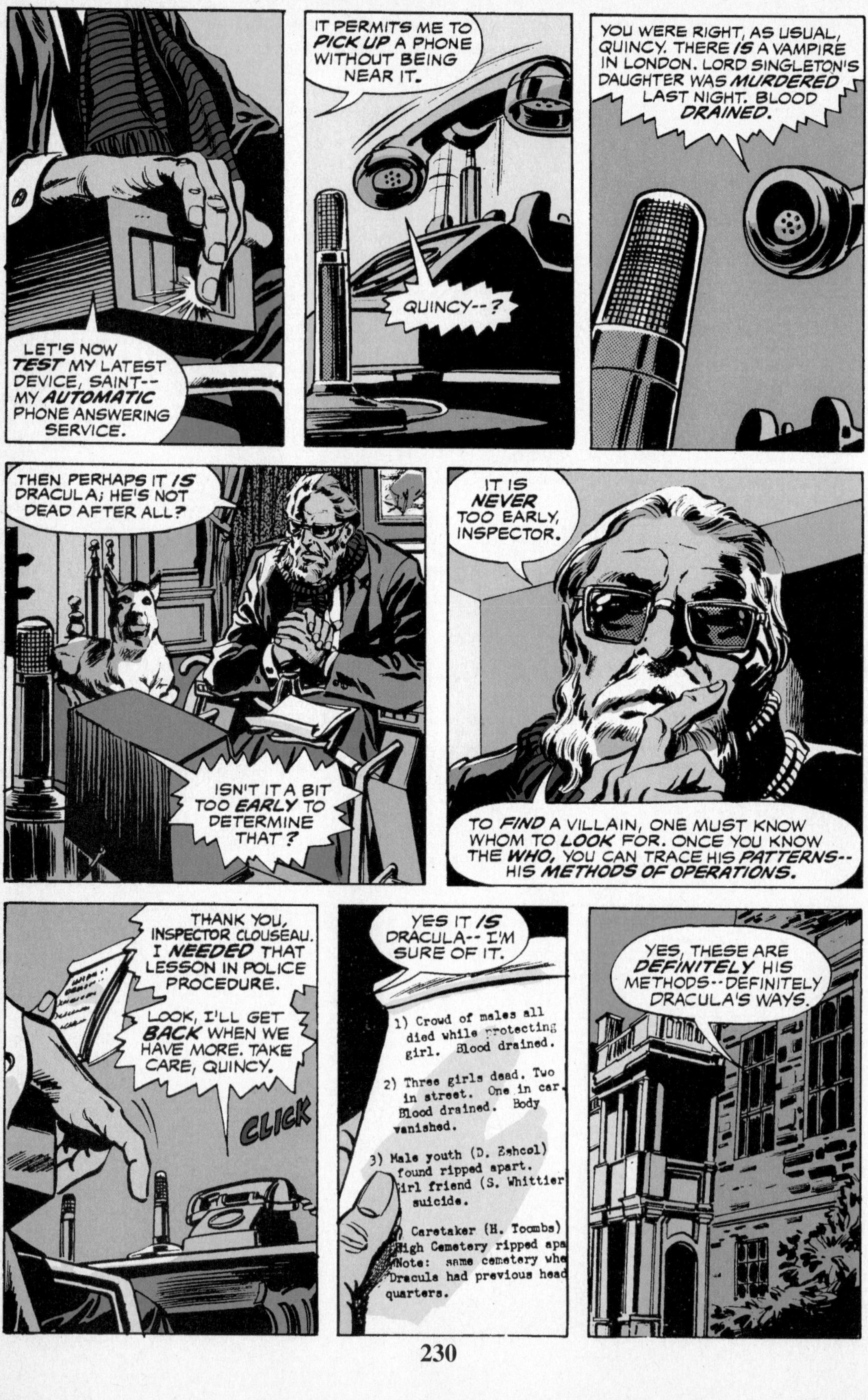
LET'S NOW TEST MY LATEST DEVICE, SAINT-- MY AUTOMATIC PHONE ANSWERING SERVICE.
IT PERMITS ME TO PICK UP A PHONE WITHOUT BEING NEAR IT.
QUINCY--?
YOU WERE RIGHT, AS USUAL, QUINCY. THERE IS A VAMPIRE IN LONDON. LORD SINGLETON'S DAUGHTER WAS MURDERED LAST NIGHT. BLOOD DRAINED.
THEN PERHAPS IT IS DRACULA; HE'S NOT DEAD AFTER ALL?
ISN'T IT A BIT TOO EARLY TO DETERMINE THAT?
IT IS NEVER TOO EARLY, INSPECTOR.
TO FIND A VILLAIN, ONE MUST KNOW WHOM TO LOOK FOR. ONCE YOU KNOW THE WHO, YOU CAN TRACE HIS PATTERNS-- HIS METHODS OF OPERATIONS.
THANK YOU, INSPECTOR CLOUSEAU. I NEEDED THAT LESSON IN POLICE PROCEDURE.
LOOK, I'LL GET BACK WHEN WE HAVE MORE. TAKE CARE, QUINCY.
CLICK
YES IT IS DRACULA-- I'M SURE OF IT.
1) Crowd of males all died while protecting girl. Blood drained.
2) Three girls dead. Two in street. One in car. Blood drained. Body vanished.
3) Male youth (D. Eshcol) found ripped apart. irl friend (S. Whittier suicide.
Caretaker (H. Toombs) igh Cemetery ripped apa Note: same cemetery whe Dracula had previous head quarters.
YES, THESE ARE DEFINITELY HIS METHODS--DEFINITELY DRACULA'S WAYS.

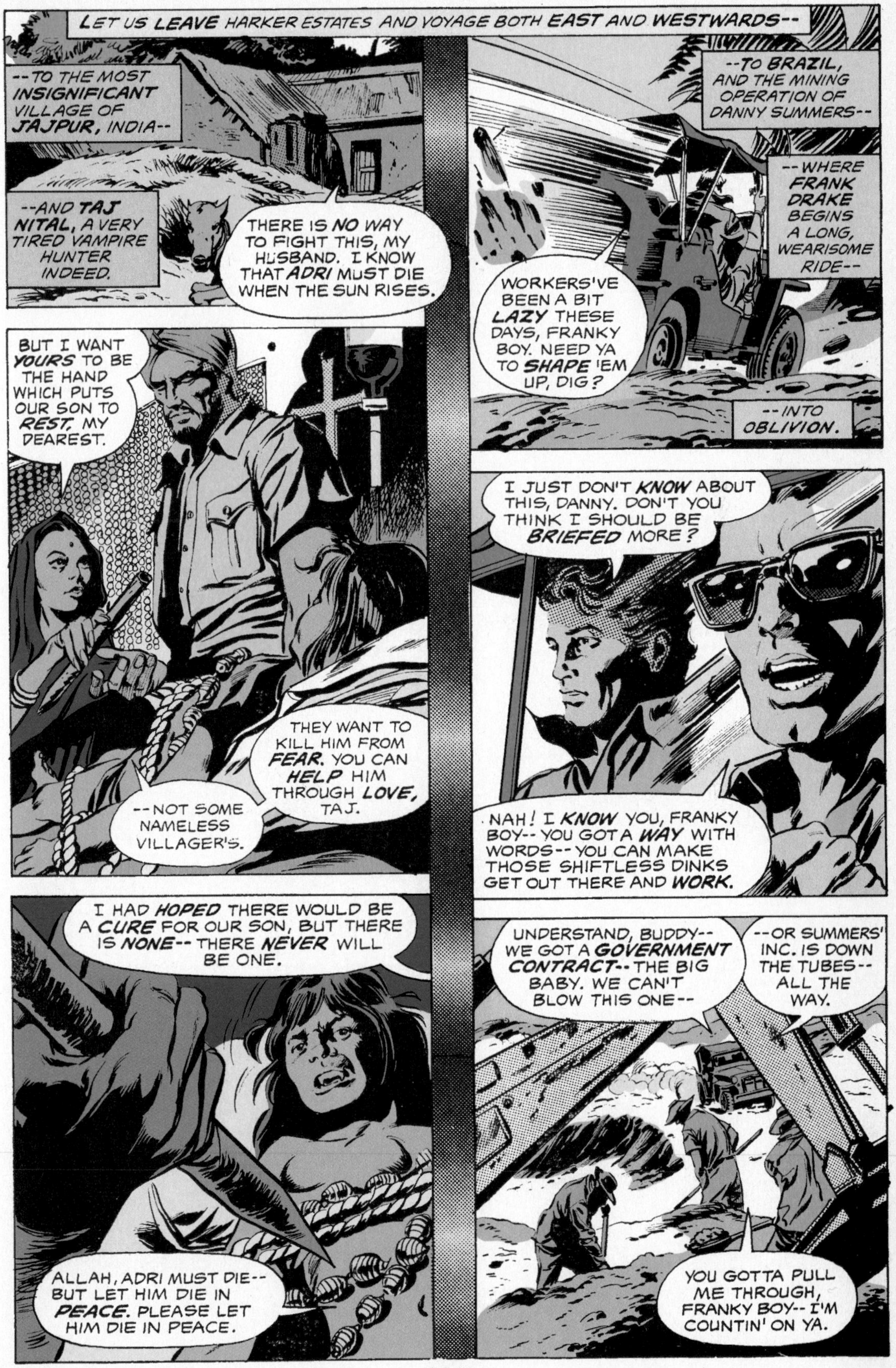
LET US LEAVE HARKER ESTATES AND VOYAGE BOTH EAST AND WESTWARDS--
--TO THE MOST INSIGNIFICANT VILLAGE OF JAJPUR, INDIA--
--AND TAJ NITAL, A VERY TIRED VAMPIRE HUNTER INDEED.
THERE IS NO WAY TO FIGHT THIS, MY HUSBAND. I KNOW THAT ADRI MUST DIE WHEN THE SUN RISES.
BUT I WANT YOURS TO BE THE HAND WHICH PUTS OUR SON TO REST, MY DEAREST.
--NOT SOME NAMELESS VILLAGER'S.
THEY WANT TO KILL HIM FROM FEAR. YOU CAN HELP HIM THROUGH LOVE, TAJ.
I HAD HOPED THERE WOULD BE A CURE FOR OUR SON, BUT THERE IS NONE-- THERE NEVER WILL BE ONE.
ALLAH, ADRI MUST DIE-- BUT LET HIM DIE IN PEACE. PLEASE LET HIM DIE IN PEACE.
--TO BRAZIL, AND THE MINING OPERATION OF DANNY SUMMERS--
--WHERE FRANK DRAKE BEGINS A LONG, WEARISOME RIDE--
WORKERS'VE BEEN A BIT LAZY THESE DAYS, FRANKY BOY. NEED YA TO SHAPE 'EM UP, DIG?
--INTO OBLIVION.
I JUST DON'T KNOW ABOUT THIS, DANNY. DON'T YOU THINK I SHOULD BE BRIEFED MORE?
NAH! I KNOW YOU, FRANKY BOY-- YOU GOT A WAY WITH WORDS-- YOU CAN MAKE THOSE SHIFTLESS DINKS GET OUT THERE AND WORK.
UNDERSTAND, BUDDY-- WE GOT A GOVERNMENT CONTRACT-- THE BIG BABY. WE CAN'T BLOW THIS ONE--
--OR SUMMERS' INC. IS DOWN THE TUBES-- ALL THE WAY.
YOU GOTTA PULL ME THROUGH, FRANKY BOY-- I'M COUNTIN' ON YA.

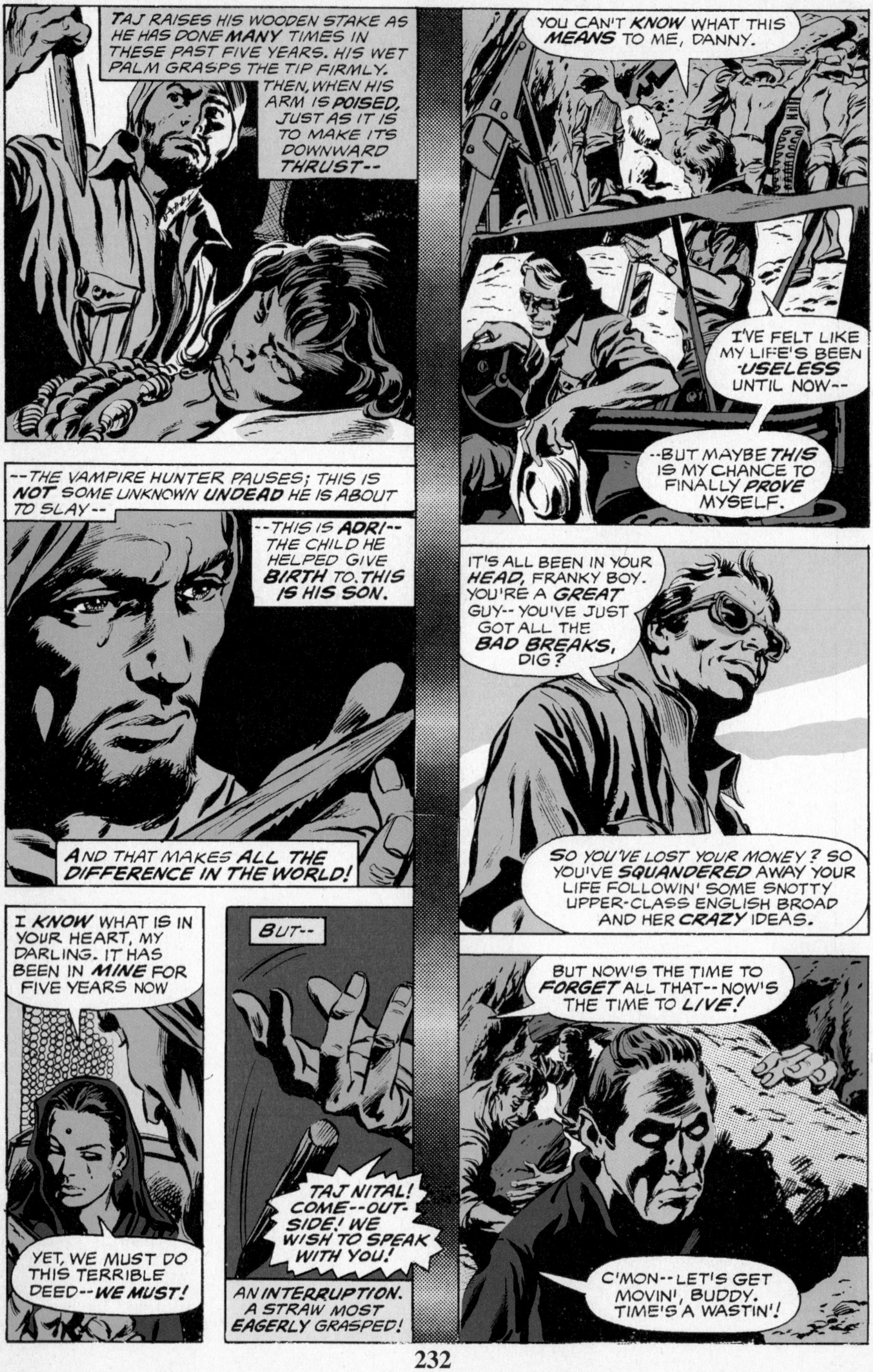
TAJ RAISES HIS WOODEN STAKE AS HE HAS DONE MANY TIMES IN THESE PAST FIVE YEARS. HIS WET PALM GRASPS THE TIP FIRMLY.
THEN, WHEN HIS ARM IS POISED, JUST AS IT IS TO MAKE ITS DOWNWARD THRUST--
--THE VAMPIRE HUNTER PAUSES; THIS IS NOT SOME UNKNOWN UNDEAD HE IS ABOUT TO SLAY--
--THIS IS ADRI-- THE CHILD HE HELPED GIVE BIRTH TO. THIS IS HIS SON.
AND THAT MAKES ALL THE DIFFERENCE IN THE WORLD!
I KNOW WHAT IS IN YOUR HEART, MY DARLING. IT HAS BEEN IN MINE FOR FIVE YEARS NOW
YET, WE MUST DO THIS TERRIBLE DEED--WE MUST!
BUT--
TAJ NITAL! COME--OUT-SIDE! WE WISH TO SPEAK WITH YOU!
AN INTERRUPTION. A STRAW MOST EAGERLY GRASPED!
YOU CAN'T KNOW WHAT THIS MEANS TO ME, DANNY.
I'VE FELT LIKE MY LIFE'S BEEN USELESS UNTIL NOW--
--BUT MAYBE THIS IS MY CHANCE TO FINALLY PROVE MYSELF.
IT'S ALL BEEN IN YOUR HEAD, FRANKY BOY. YOU'RE A GREAT GUY-- YOU'VE JUST GOT ALL THE BAD BREAKS, DIG?
SO YOU'VE LOST YOUR MONEY? SO YOU'VE SQUANDERED AWAY YOUR LIFE FOLLOWIN' SOME SNOTTY UPPER-CLASS ENGLISH BROAD AND HER CRAZY IDEAS.
BUT NOW'S THE TIME TO FORGET ALL THAT-- NOW'S THE TIME TO LIVE!
C'MON--LET'S GET MOVIN', BUDDY. TIME'S A WASTIN'!

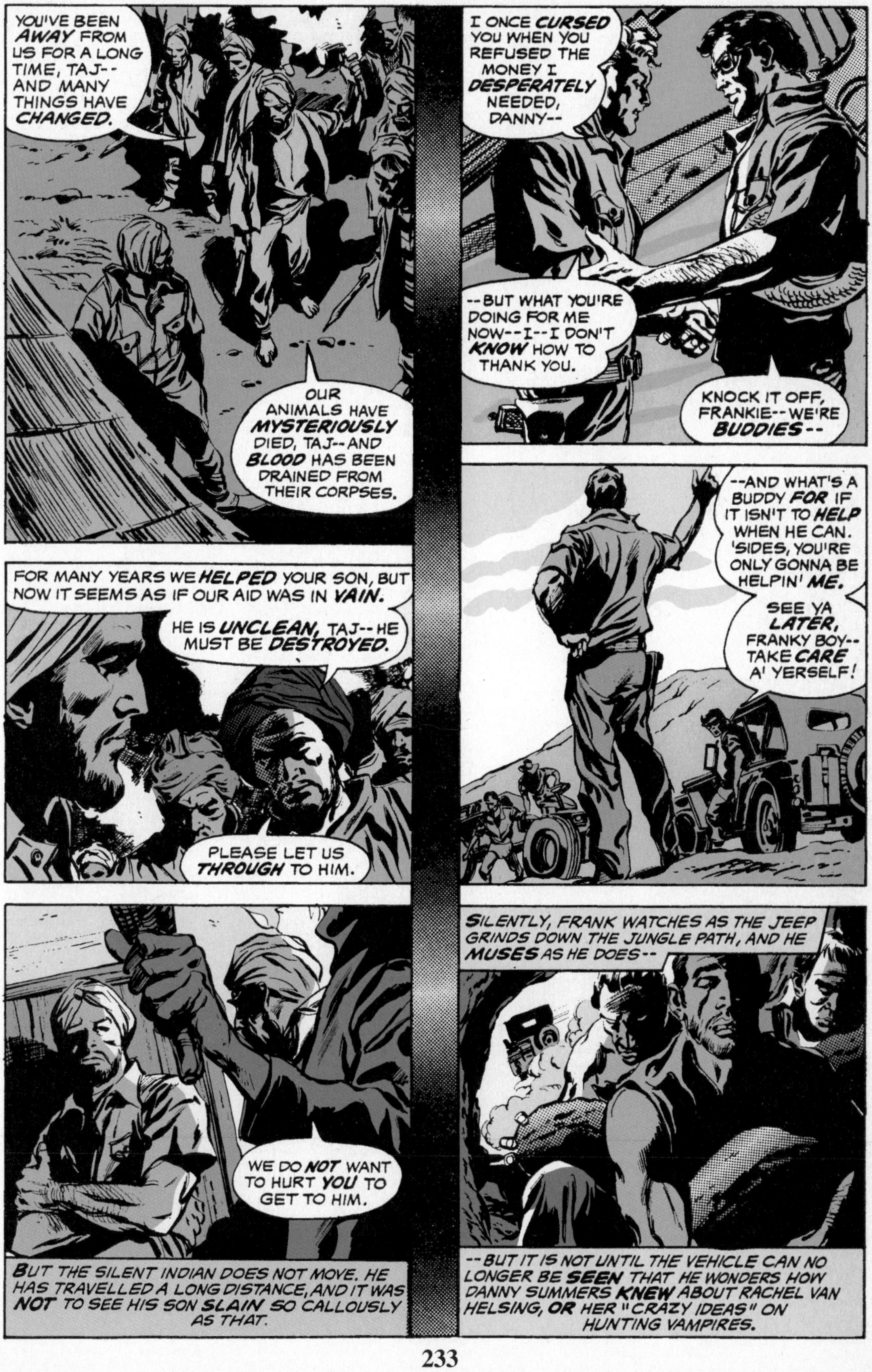
YOU'VE BEEN AWAY FROM US FOR A LONG TIME, TAJ-- AND MANY THINGS HAVE CHANGED.
OUR ANIMALS HAVE MYSTERIOUSLY DIED, TAJ--AND BLOOD HAS BEEN DRAINED FROM THEIR CORPSES.
FOR MANY YEARS WE HELPED YOUR SON, BUT NOW IT SEEMS AS IF OUR AID WAS IN VAIN.
HE IS UNCLEAN, TAJ--HE MUST BE DESTROYED.
PLEASE LET US THROUGH TO HIM.
WE DO NOT WANT TO HURT YOU TO GET TO HIM.
BUT THE SILENT INDIAN DOES NOT MOVE. HE HAS TRAVELLED A LONG DISTANCE, AND IT WAS NOT TO SEE HIS SON SLAIN SO CALLOUSLY AS THAT.
I ONCE CURSED YOU WHEN YOU REFUSED THE MONEY I DESPERATELY NEEDED, DANNY--
--BUT WHAT YOU'RE DOING FOR ME NOW--I--I DON'T KNOW HOW TO THANK YOU.
KNOCK IT OFF, FRANKIE--WE'RE BUDDIES--
--AND WHAT'S A BUDDY FOR IF IT ISN'T TO HELP WHEN HE CAN. 'SIDES, YOU'RE ONLY GONNA BE HELPIN' ME.
SEE YA LATER, FRANKY BOY-- TAKE CARE A' YERSELF!
SILENTLY, FRANK WATCHES AS THE JEEP GRINDS DOWN THE JUNGLE PATH, AND HE MUSES AS HE DOES--
--BUT IT IS NOT UNTIL THE VEHICLE CAN NO LONGER BE SEEN THAT HE WONDERS HOW DANNY SUMMERS KNEW ABOUT RACHEL VAN HELSING, OR HER "CRAZY IDEAS" ON HUNTING VAMPIRES.

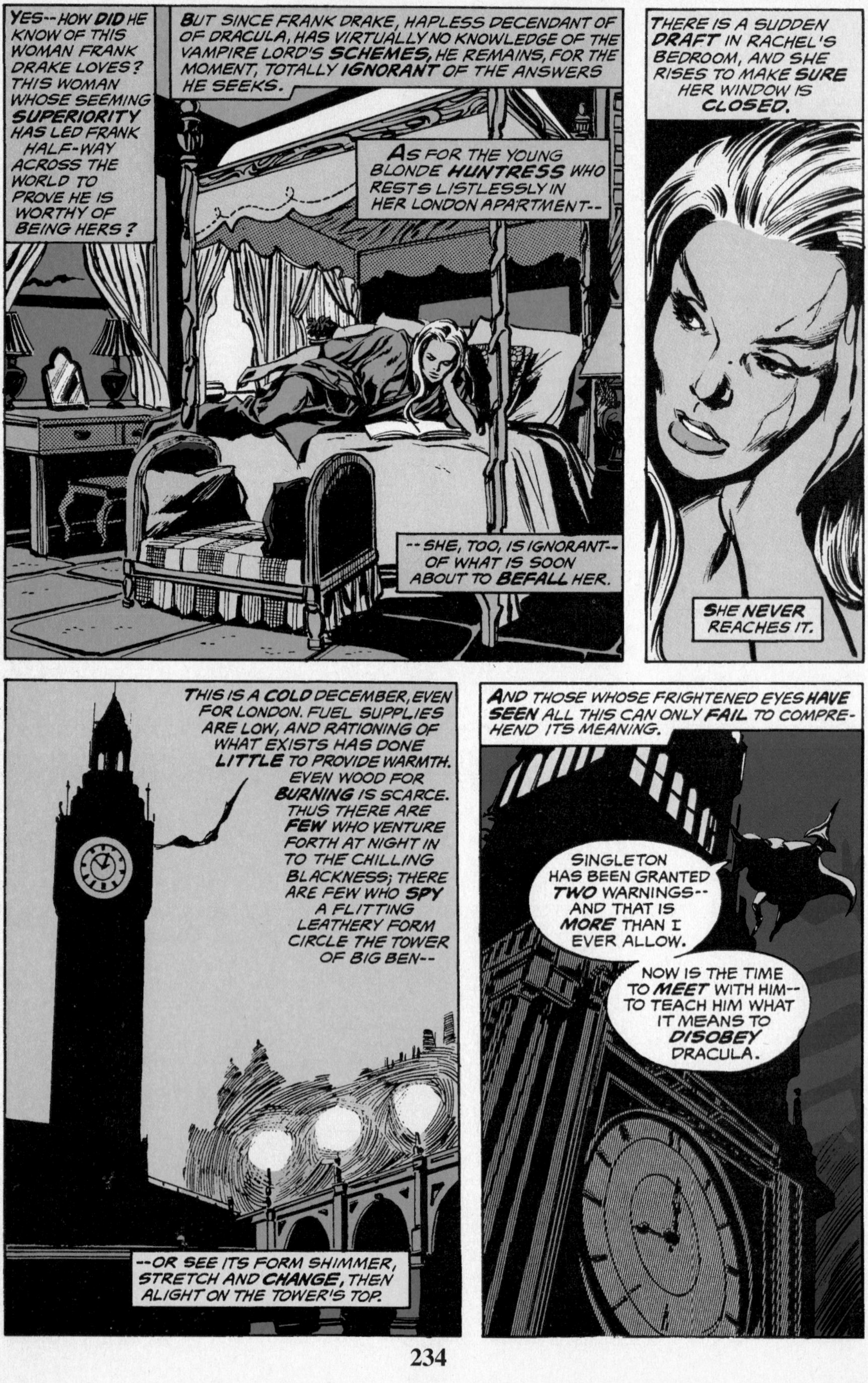
YES--HOW DID HE KNOW OF THIS WOMAN FRANK DRAKE LOVES? THIS WOMAN WHOSE SEEMING SUPERIORITY HAS LED FRANK HALF-WAY ACROSS THE WORLD TO PROVE HE IS WORTHY OF BEING HERS?
BUT SINCE FRANK DRAKE, HAPLESS DECENDANT OF OF DRACULA, HAS VIRTUALLY NO KNOWLEDGE OF THE VAMPIRE LORD'S SCHEMES, HE REMAINS, FOR THE MOMENT, TOTALLY IGNORANT OF THE ANSWERS HE SEEKS.
AS FOR THE YOUNG BLONDE HUNTRESS WHO RESTS LISTLESSLY IN HER LONDON APARTMENT--
--SHE, TOO, IS IGNORANT--OF WHAT IS SOON ABOUT TO BEFALL HER.
THERE IS A SUDDEN DRAFT IN RACHEL'S BEDROOM, AND SHE RISES TO MAKE SURE HER WINDOW IS CLOSED.
SHE NEVER REACHES IT.
THIS IS A COLD DECEMBER, EVEN FOR LONDON. FUEL SUPPLIES ARE LOW, AND RATIONING OF WHAT EXISTS HAS DONE LITTLE TO PROVIDE WARMTH. EVEN WOOD FOR BURNING IS SCARCE. THUS THERE ARE FEW WHO VENTURE FORTH AT NIGHT IN TO THE CHILLING BLACKNESS; THERE ARE FEW WHO SPY A FLITTING LEATHERY FORM CIRCLE THE TOWER OF BIG BEN--
--OR SEE ITS FORM SHIMMER, STRETCH AND CHANGE, THEN ALIGHT ON THE TOWER'S TOP.
AND THOSE WHOSE FRIGHTENED EYES HAVE SEEN ALL THIS CAN ONLY FAIL TO COMPREHEND ITS MEANING.
SINGLETON HAS BEEN GRANTED TWO WARNINGS--AND THAT IS MORE THAN I EVER ALLOW.
NOW IS THE TIME TO MEET WITH HIM--TO TEACH HIM WHAT IT MEANS TO DISOBEY DRACULA.

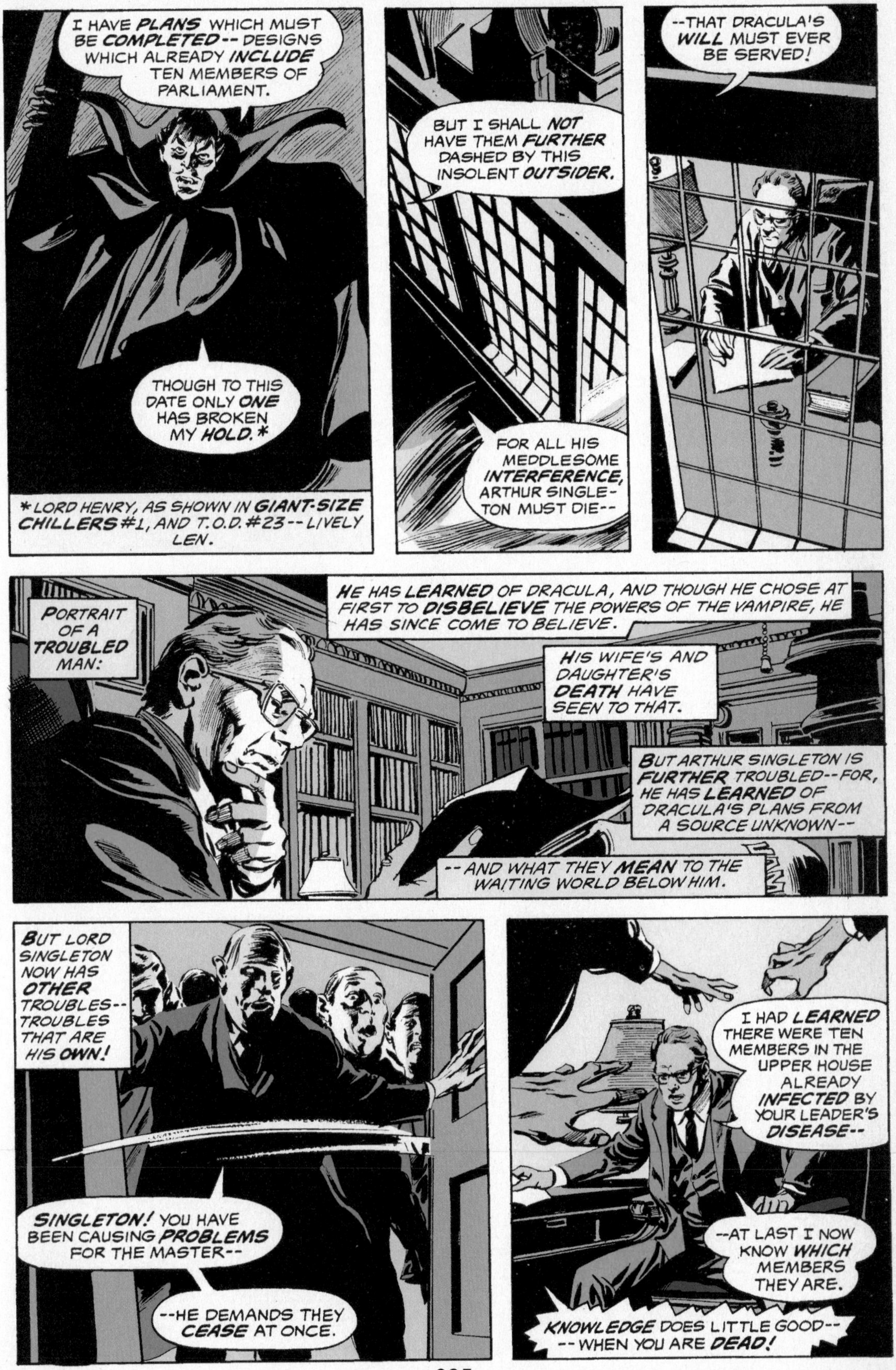
I HAVE PLANS WHICH MUST BE COMPLETED -- DESIGNS WHICH ALREADY INCLUDE TEN MEMBERS OF PARLIAMENT.
THOUGH TO THIS DATE ONLY ONE HAS BROKEN MY HOLD.*
*LORD HENRY, AS SHOWN IN GIANT-SIZE CHILLERS #1, AND T.O.D. #23 -- LIVELY LEN.
BUT I SHALL NOT HAVE THEM FURTHER DASHED BY THIS INSOLENT OUTSIDER.
FOR ALL HIS MEDDLESOME INTERFERENCE, ARTHUR SINGLETON MUST DIE--
--THAT DRACULA'S WILL MUST EVER BE SERVED!
PORTRAIT OF A TROUBLED MAN:
HE HAS LEARNED OF DRACULA, AND THOUGH HE CHOSE AT FIRST TO DISBELIEVE THE POWERS OF THE VAMPIRE, HE HAS SINCE COME TO BELIEVE.
HIS WIFE'S AND DAUGHTER'S DEATH HAVE SEEN TO THAT.
BUT ARTHUR SINGLETON IS FURTHER TROUBLED--FOR, HE HAS LEARNED OF DRACULA'S PLANS FROM A SOURCE UNKNOWN--
--AND WHAT THEY MEAN TO THE WAITING WORLD BELOW HIM.
BUT LORD SINGLETON NOW HAS OTHER TROUBLES--TROUBLES THAT ARE HIS OWN!
SINGLETON! YOU HAVE BEEN CAUSING PROBLEMS FOR THE MASTER--
--HE DEMANDS THEY CEASE AT ONCE.
I HAD LEARNED THERE WERE TEN MEMBERS IN THE UPPER HOUSE ALREADY INFECTED BY YOUR LEADER'S DISEASE--
--AT LAST I NOW KNOW WHICH MEMBERS THEY ARE.
KNOWLEDGE DOES LITTLE GOOD-- --WHEN YOU ARE DEAD!

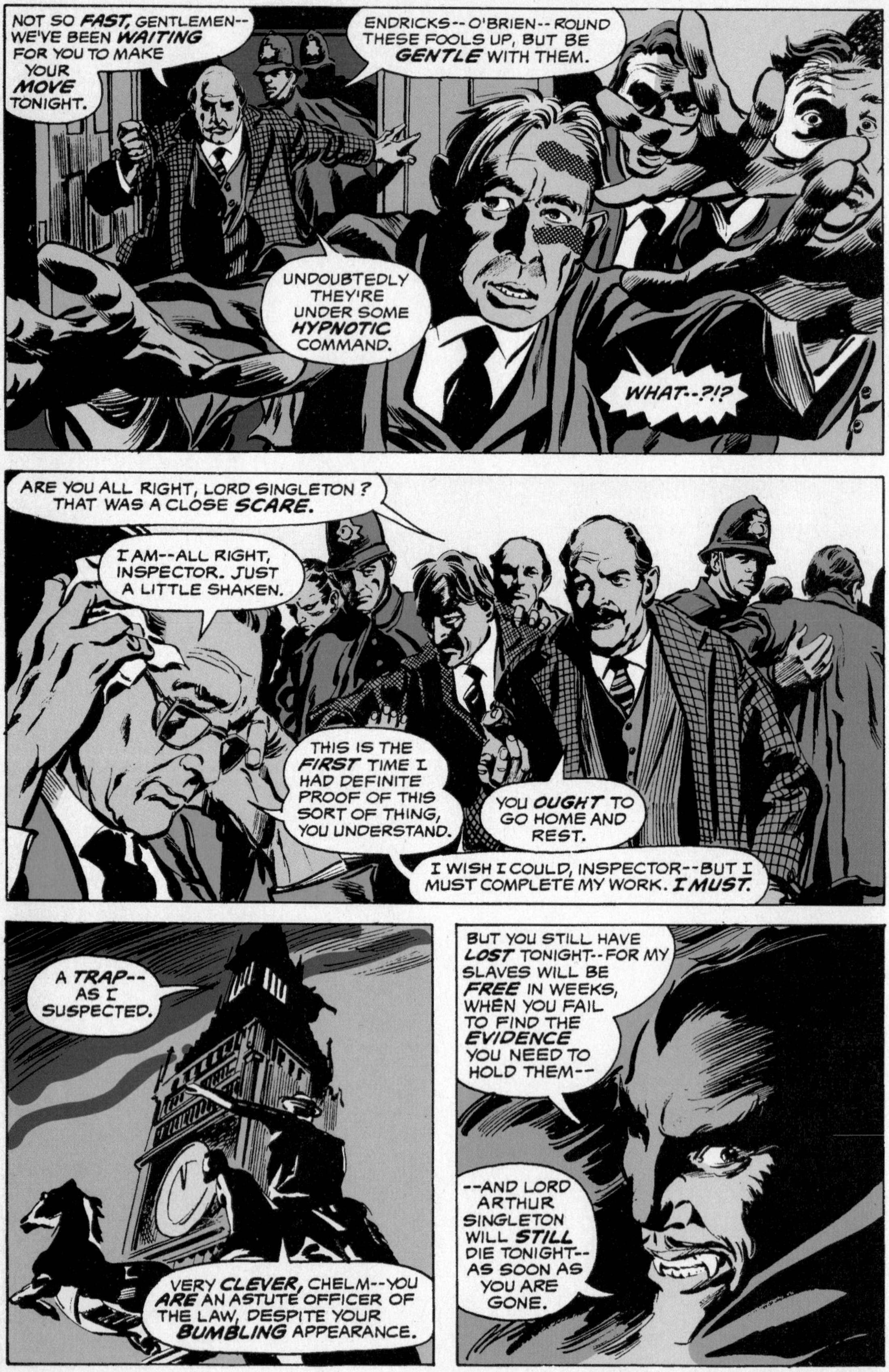
NOT SO FAST, GENTLEMEN-- WE'VE BEEN WAITING FOR YOU TO MAKE YOUR MOVE TONIGHT.
ENDRICKS-- O'BRIEN-- ROUND THESE FOOLS UP, BUT BE GENTLE WITH THEM.
UNDOUBTEDLY THEY'RE UNDER SOME HYPNOTIC COMMAND.
WHAT--?!?
ARE YOU ALL RIGHT, LORD SINGLETON ? THAT WAS A CLOSE SCARE.
I AM--ALL RIGHT, INSPECTOR. JUST A LITTLE SHAKEN.
THIS IS THE FIRST TIME I HAD DEFINITE PROOF OF THIS SORT OF THING, YOU UNDERSTAND.
YOU OUGHT TO GO HOME AND REST.
I WISH I COULD, INSPECTOR--BUT I MUST COMPLETE MY WORK. I MUST.
A TRAP-- AS I SUSPECTED.
VERY CLEVER, CHELM--YOU ARE AN ASTUTE OFFICER OF THE LAW, DESPITE YOUR BUMBLING APPEARANCE.
BUT YOU STILL HAVE LOST TONIGHT--FOR MY SLAVES WILL BE FREE IN WEEKS, WHEN YOU FAIL TO FIND THE EVIDENCE YOU NEED TO HOLD THEM--
--AND LORD ARTHUR SINGLETON WILL STILL DIE TONIGHT-- AS SOON AS YOU ARE GONE.

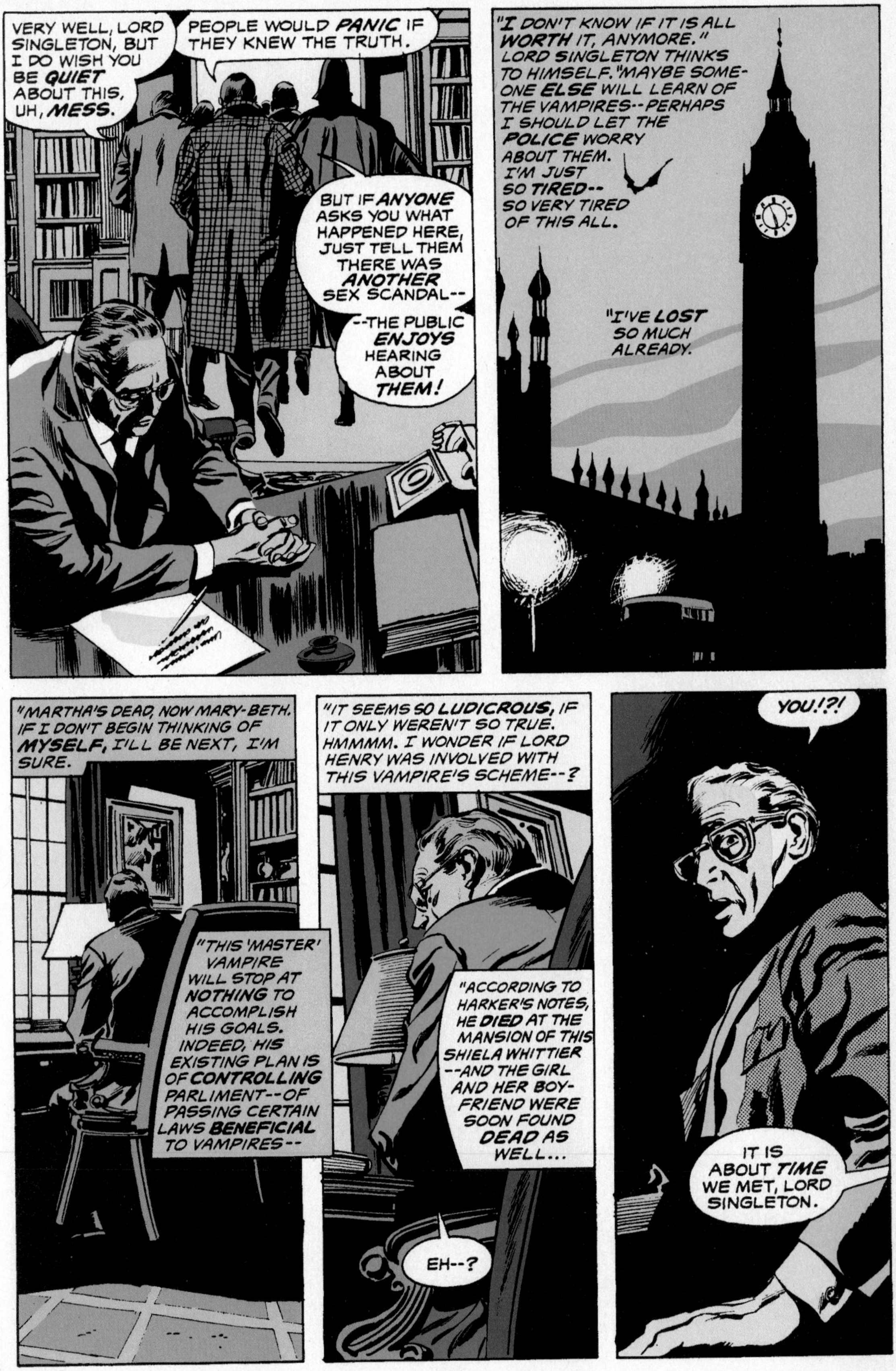
VERY WELL, LORD SINGLETON, BUT I DO WISH YOU BE QUIET ABOUT THIS, UH, MESS.
PEOPLE WOULD PANIC IF THEY KNEW THE TRUTH.
BUT IF ANYONE ASKS YOU WHAT HAPPENED HERE, JUST TELL THEM THERE WAS ANOTHER SEX SCANDAL--
--THE PUBLIC ENJOYS HEARING ABOUT THEM!
"I DON'T KNOW IF IT IS ALL WORTH IT, ANYMORE." LORD SINGLETON THINKS TO HIMSELF. "MAYBE SOMEONE ELSE WILL LEARN OF THE VAMPIRES--PERHAPS I SHOULD LET THE POLICE WORRY ABOUT THEM. I'M JUST SO TIRED-- SO VERY TIRED OF THIS ALL.
"I'VE LOST SO MUCH ALREADY.
"MARTHA'S DEAD, NOW MARY-BETH. IF I DON'T BEGIN THINKING OF MYSELF, I'LL BE NEXT, I'M SURE.
"THIS 'MASTER' VAMPIRE WILL STOP AT NOTHING TO ACCOMPLISH HIS GOALS. INDEED, HIS EXISTING PLAN IS OF CONTROLLING PARLIMENT--OF PASSING CERTAIN LAWS BENEFICIAL TO VAMPIRES--
"IT SEEMS SO LUDICROUS, IF IT ONLY WEREN'T SO TRUE. HMMMM. I WONDER IF LORD HENRY WAS INVOLVED WITH THIS VAMPIRE'S SCHEME--?
"ACCORDING TO HARKER'S NOTES, HE DIED AT THE MANSION OF THIS SHIELA WHITTIER --AND THE GIRL AND HER BOY-FRIEND WERE SOON FOUND DEAD AS WELL...
EH--?
YOU!?!
IT IS ABOUT TIME WE MET, LORD SINGLETON.

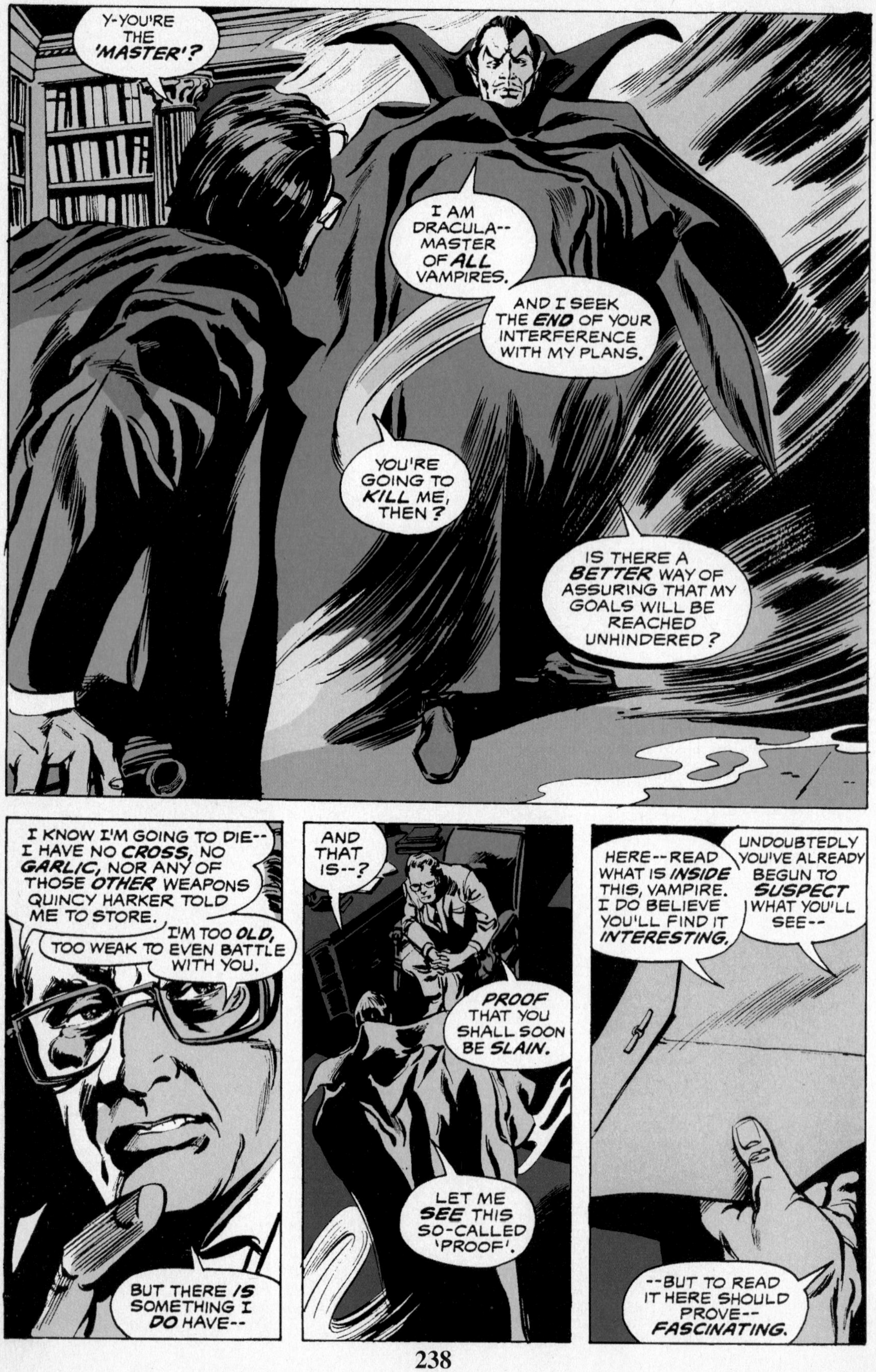

Y-YOU'RE THE 'MASTER'?
I AM DRACULA-- MASTER OF ALL VAMPIRES.
AND I SEEK THE END OF YOUR INTERFERENCE WITH MY PLANS.
YOU'RE GOING TO KILL ME, THEN?
IS THERE A BETTER WAY OF ASSURING THAT MY GOALS WILL BE REACHED UNHINDERED?
I KNOW I'M GOING TO DIE-- I HAVE NO CROSS, NO GARLIC, NOR ANY OF THOSE OTHER WEAPONS QUINCY HARKER TOLD ME TO STORE.
I'M TOO OLD, TOO WEAK TO EVEN BATTLE WITH YOU.
BUT THERE IS SOMETHING I DO HAVE--
AND THAT IS--?
PROOF THAT YOU SHALL SOON BE SLAIN.
LET ME SEE THIS SO-CALLED 'PROOF'.
HERE--READ WHAT IS INSIDE THIS, VAMPIRE. I DO BELIEVE YOU'LL FIND IT INTERESTING.
UNDOUBTEDLY YOU'VE ALREADY BEGUN TO SUSPECT WHAT YOU'LL SEE--
--BUT TO READ IT HERE SHOULD PROVE-- FASCINATING.

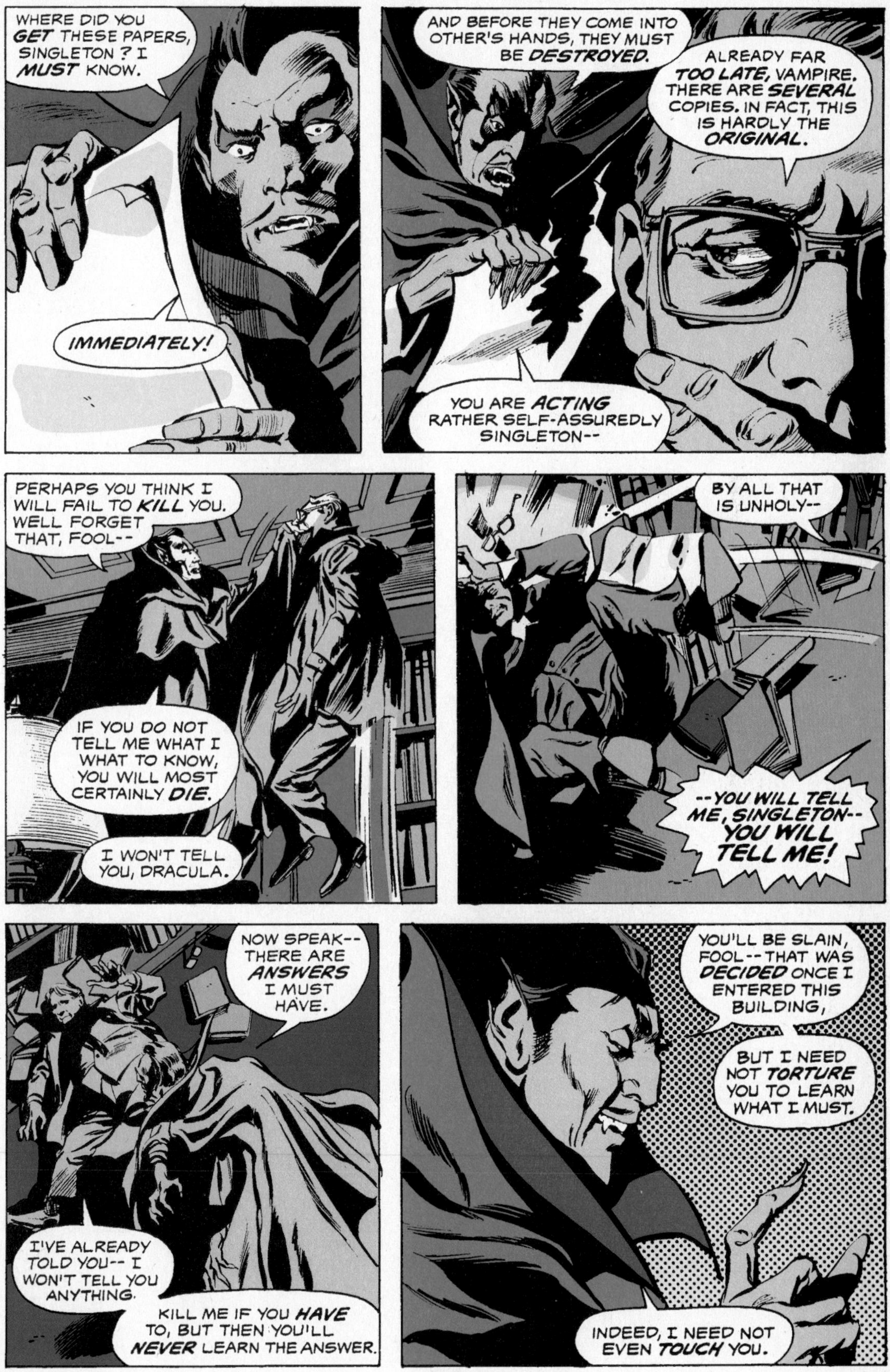
WHERE DID YOU GET THESE PAPERS, SINGLETON? I MUST KNOW.
IMMEDIATELY!
AND BEFORE THEY COME INTO OTHER'S HANDS, THEY MUST BE DESTROYED.
ALREADY FAR TOO LATE, VAMPIRE. THERE ARE SEVERAL COPIES. IN FACT, THIS IS HARDLY THE ORIGINAL.
YOU ARE ACTING RATHER SELF-ASSUREDLY SINGLETON--
PERHAPS YOU THINK I WILL FAIL TO KILL YOU. WELL FORGET THAT, FOOL--
IF YOU DO NOT TELL ME WHAT I WHAT TO KNOW, YOU WILL MOST CERTAINLY DIE.
I WON'T TELL YOU, DRACULA.
BY ALL THAT IS UNHOLY--
--YOU WILL TELL ME, SINGLETON-- YOU WILL TELL ME!
NOW SPEAK-- THERE ARE ANSWERS I MUST HAVE.
I'VE ALREADY TOLD YOU-- I WON'T TELL YOU ANYTHING.
KILL ME IF YOU HAVE TO, BUT THEN YOU'LL NEVER LEARN THE ANSWER.
YOU'LL BE SLAIN, FOOL--THAT WAS DECIDED ONCE I ENTERED THIS BUILDING,
BUT I NEED NOT TORTURE YOU TO LEARN WHAT I MUST.
INDEED, I NEED NOT EVEN TOUCH YOU.

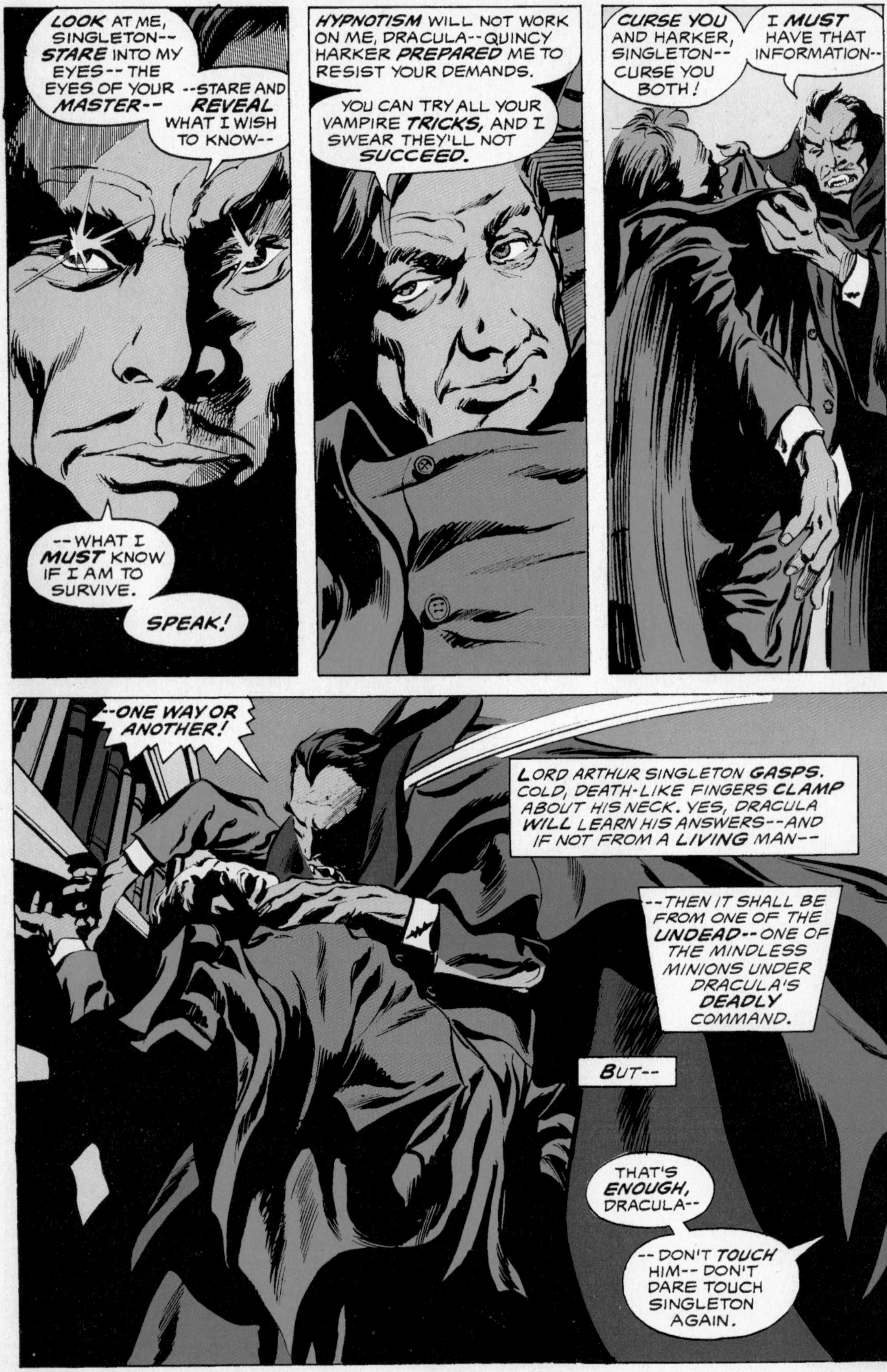
LOOK AT ME, SINGLETON-- STARE INTO MY EYES-- THE EYES OF YOUR MASTER--
--STARE AND REVEAL WHAT I WISH TO KNOW--
--WHAT I MUST KNOW IF I AM TO SURVIVE.
SPEAK!
HYPNOTISM WILL NOT WORK ON ME, DRACULA--QUINCY HARKER PREPARED ME TO RESIST YOUR DEMANDS.
YOU CAN TRY ALL YOUR VAMPIRE TRICKS, AND I SWEAR THEY'LL NOT SUCCEED.
CURSE YOU AND HARKER, SINGLETON-- CURSE YOU BOTH!
I MUST HAVE THAT INFORMATION--
--ONE WAY OR ANOTHER!
LORD ARTHUR SINGLETON GASPS. COLD, DEATH-LIKE FINGERS CLAMP ABOUT HIS NECK. YES, DRACULA WILL LEARN HIS ANSWERS--AND IF NOT FROM A LIVING MAN--
--THEN IT SHALL BE FROM ONE OF THE UNDEAD--ONE OF THE MINDLESS MINIONS UNDER DRACULA'S DEADLY COMMAND.
BUT--
THAT'S ENOUGH, DRACULA--
--DON'T TOUCH HIM--DON'T DARE TOUCH SINGLETON AGAIN.

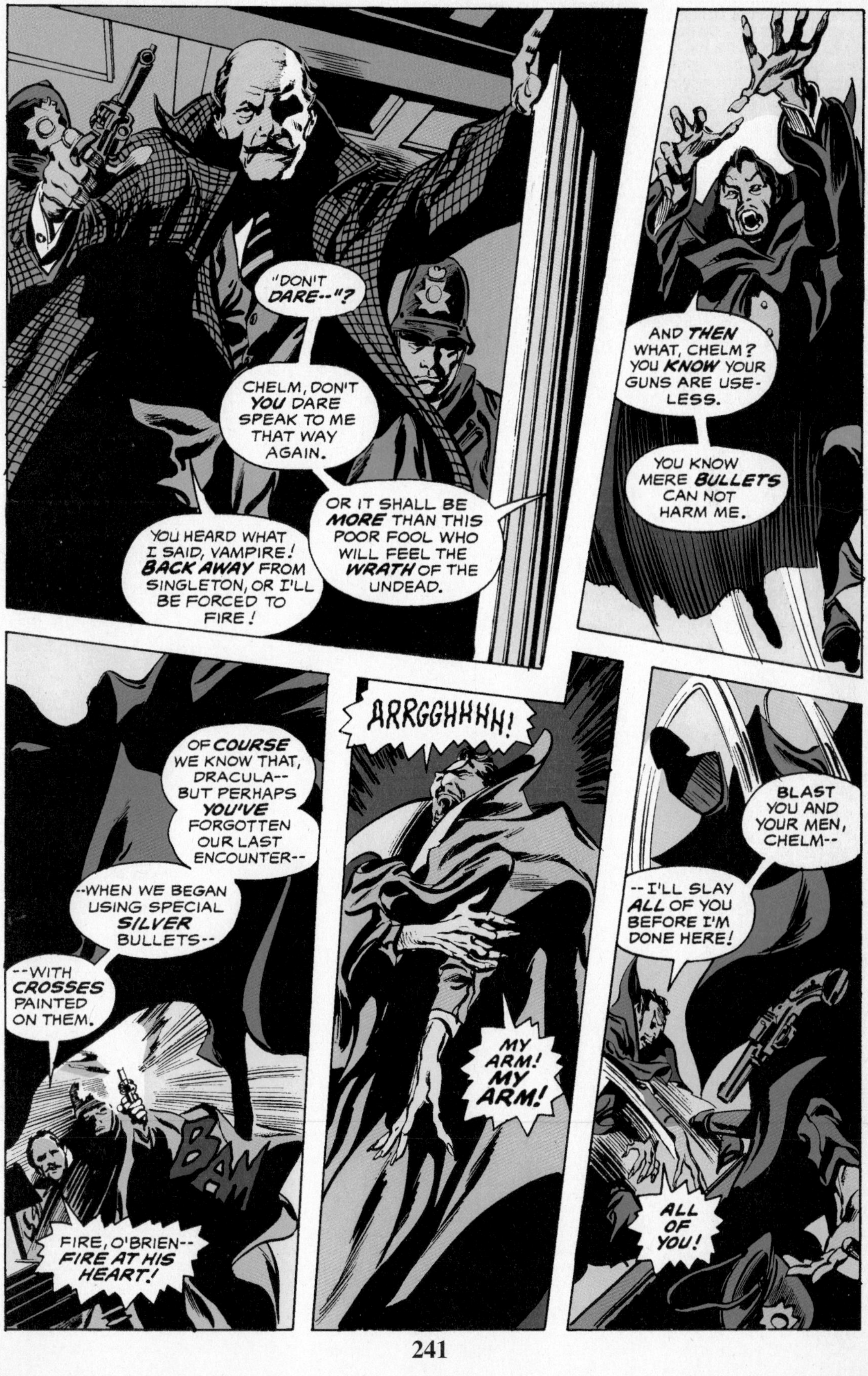
"DON'T DARE--"?
CHELM, DON'T YOU DARE SPEAK TO ME THAT WAY AGAIN.
OR IT SHALL BE MORE THAN THIS POOR FOOL WHO WILL FEEL THE WRATH OF THE UNDEAD.
YOU HEARD WHAT I SAID, VAMPIRE! BACK AWAY FROM SINGLETON, OR I'LL BE FORCED TO FIRE!
AND THEN WHAT, CHELM? YOU KNOW YOUR GUNS ARE USELESS.
YOU KNOW MERE BULLETS CAN NOT HARM ME.
OF COURSE WE KNOW THAT, DRACULA-- BUT PERHAPS YOU'VE FORGOTTEN OUR LAST ENCOUNTER--
--WHEN WE BEGAN USING SPECIAL SILVER BULLETS--
--WITH CROSSES PAINTED ON THEM.
BAM
FIRE, O'BRIEN-- FIRE AT HIS HEART!
ARRGGHHHH!
MY ARM! MY ARM!
BLAST YOU AND YOUR MEN, CHELM--
--I'LL SLAY ALL OF YOU BEFORE I'M DONE HERE!
ALL OF YOU!

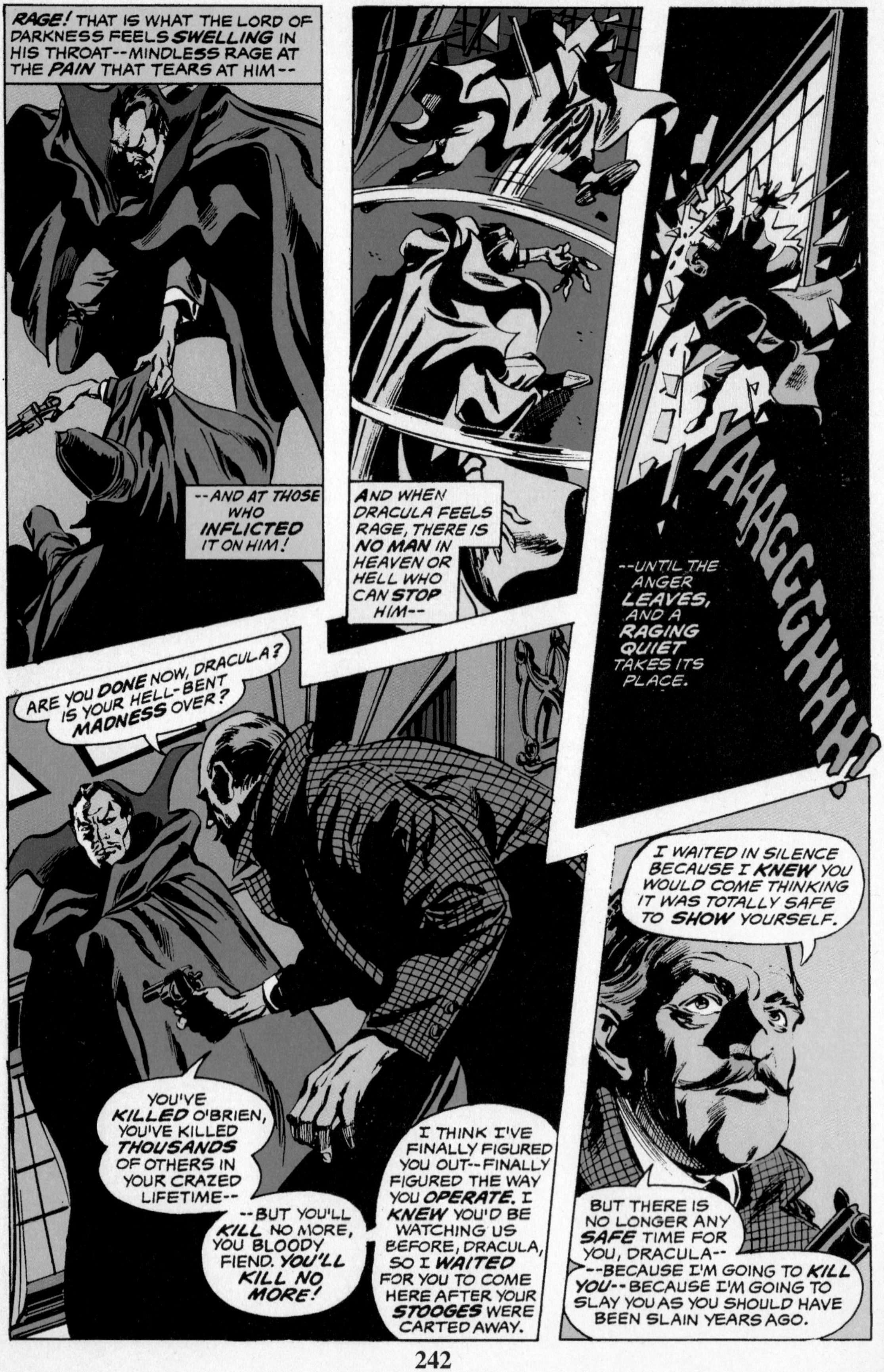
RAGE! THAT IS WHAT THE LORD OF DARKNESS FEELS SWELLING IN HIS THROAT--MINDLESS RAGE AT THE PAIN THAT TEARS AT HIM--
--AND AT THOSE WHO INFLICTED IT ON HIM!
AND WHEN DRACULA FEELS RAGE, THERE IS NO MAN IN HEAVEN OR HELL WHO CAN STOP HIM--
YAAAGGHHHH!
--UNTIL THE ANGER LEAVES, AND A RAGING QUIET TAKES ITS PLACE.
ARE YOU DONE NOW, DRACULA? IS YOUR HELL-BENT MADNESS OVER?
YOU'VE KILLED O'BRIEN, YOU'VE KILLED THOUSANDS OF OTHERS IN YOUR CRAZED LIFETIME--
--BUT YOU'LL KILL NO MORE, YOU BLOODY FIEND. YOU'LL KILL NO MORE!
I THINK I'VE FINALLY FIGURED YOU OUT--FINALLY FIGURED THE WAY YOU OPERATE. I KNEW YOU'D BE WATCHING US BEFORE, DRACULA, SO I WAITED FOR YOU TO COME HERE AFTER YOUR STOOGES WERE CARTED AWAY.
I WAITED IN SILENCE BECAUSE I KNEW YOU WOULD COME THINKING IT WAS TOTALLY SAFE TO SHOW YOURSELF.
BUT THERE IS NO LONGER ANY SAFE TIME FOR YOU, DRACULA--
--BECAUSE I'M GOING TO KILL YOU--BECAUSE I'M GOING TO SLAY YOU AS YOU SHOULD HAVE BEEN SLAIN YEARS AGO.

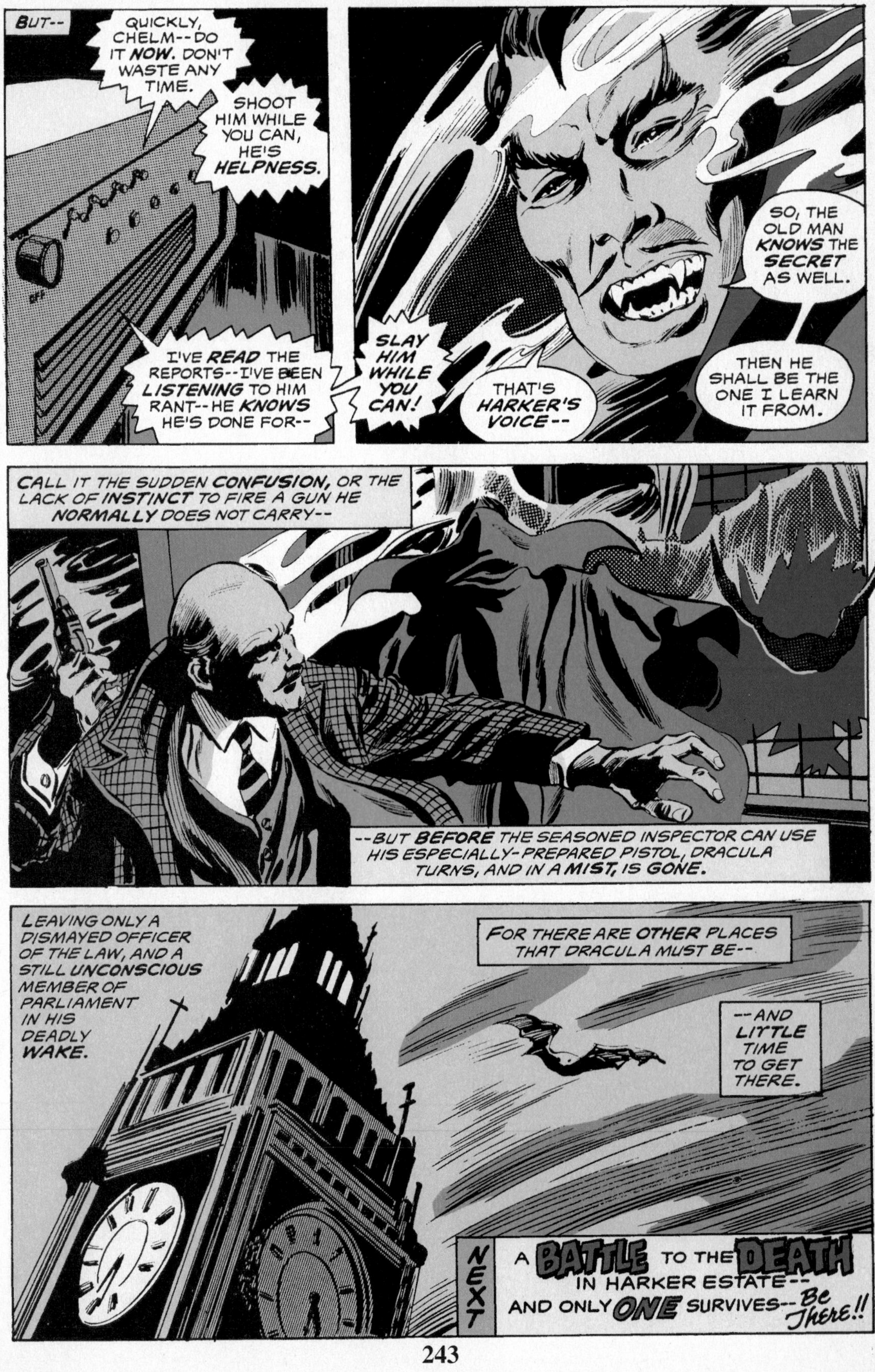

BUT--
QUICKLY, CHELM--DO IT NOW. DON'T WASTE ANY TIME.
SHOOT HIM WHILE YOU CAN, HE'S HELPNESS.
I'VE READ THE REPORTS--I'VE BEEN LISTENING TO HIM RANT--HE KNOWS HE'S DONE FOR--
SLAY HIM WHILE YOU CAN!
THAT'S HARKER'S VOICE--
SO, THE OLD MAN KNOWS THE SECRET AS WELL.
THEN HE SHALL BE THE ONE I LEARN IT FROM.
CALL IT THE SUDDEN CONFUSION, OR THE LACK OF INSTINCT TO FIRE A GUN HE NORMALLY DOES NOT CARRY--
--BUT BEFORE THE SEASONED INSPECTOR CAN USE HIS ESPECIALLY-PREPARED PISTOL, DRACULA TURNS, AND IN A MIST, IS GONE.
LEAVING ONLY A DISMAYED OFFICER OF THE LAW, AND A STILL UNCONSCIOUS MEMBER OF PARLIAMENT IN HIS DEADLY WAKE.
FOR THERE ARE OTHER PLACES THAT DRACULA MUST BE--
--AND LITTLE TIME TO GET THERE.
NEXT
A BATTLE TO THE DEATH IN HARKER ESTATE--AND ONLY ONE SURVIVES--Be There!!

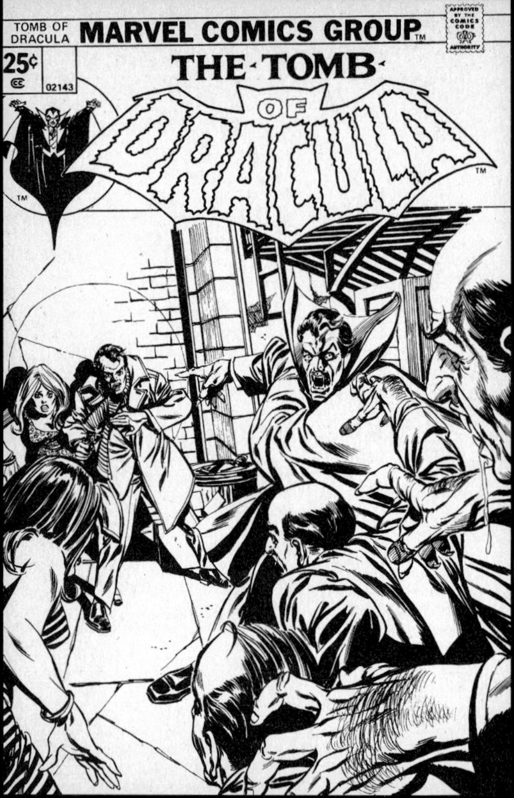
TOMB OF DRACULA
MARVEL COMICS GROUP
APPROVED BY THE COMICS CODE AUTHORITY
25¢
02143
THE TOMB OF DRACULA

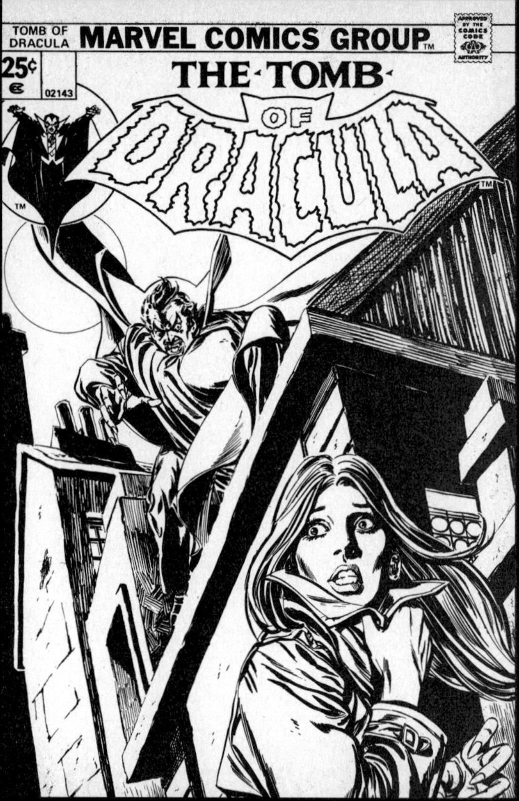
TOMB OF DRACULA
MARVEL COMICS GROUP
APPROVED BY THE COMICS CODE AUTHORITY
25¢
02143
THE TOMB OF DRACULA

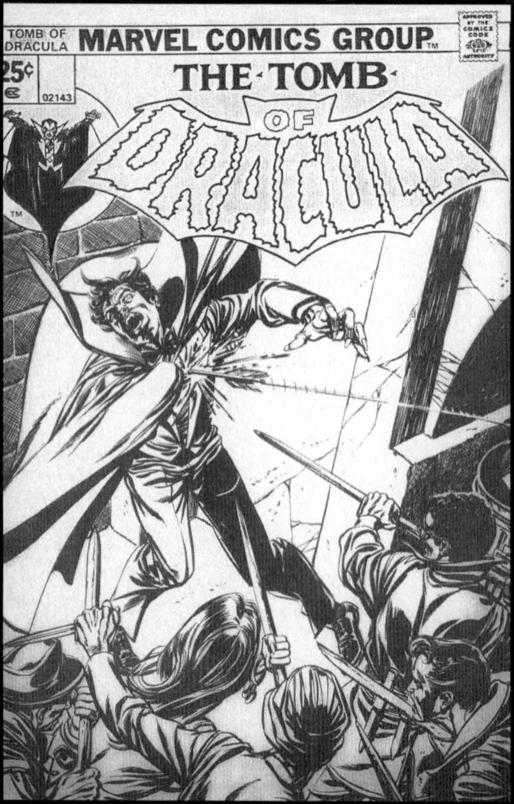
TOMB OF DRACULA
MARVEL COMICS GROUP
APPROVED BY THE COMICS CODE AUTHORITY
25¢
02143
THE TOMB OF DRACULA

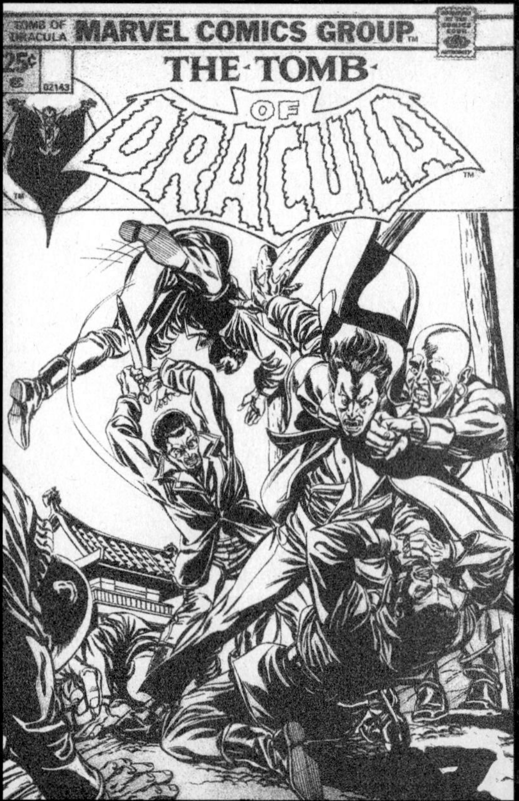
TOMB OF DRACULA
MARVEL COMICS GROUP
25¢
02143
THE TOMB OF DRACULA

The Tomb of Dracula covers before art corrections and copy placement

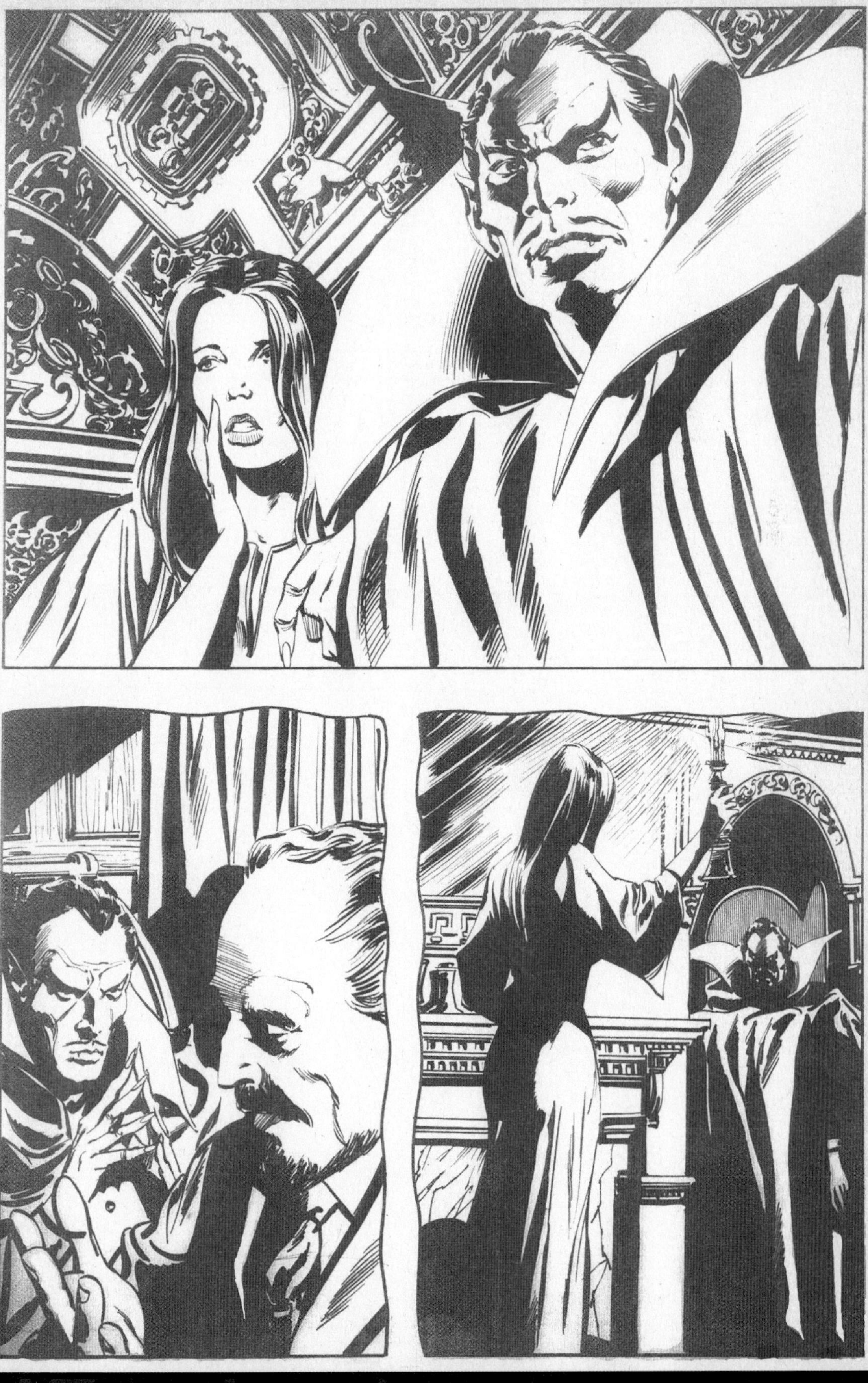

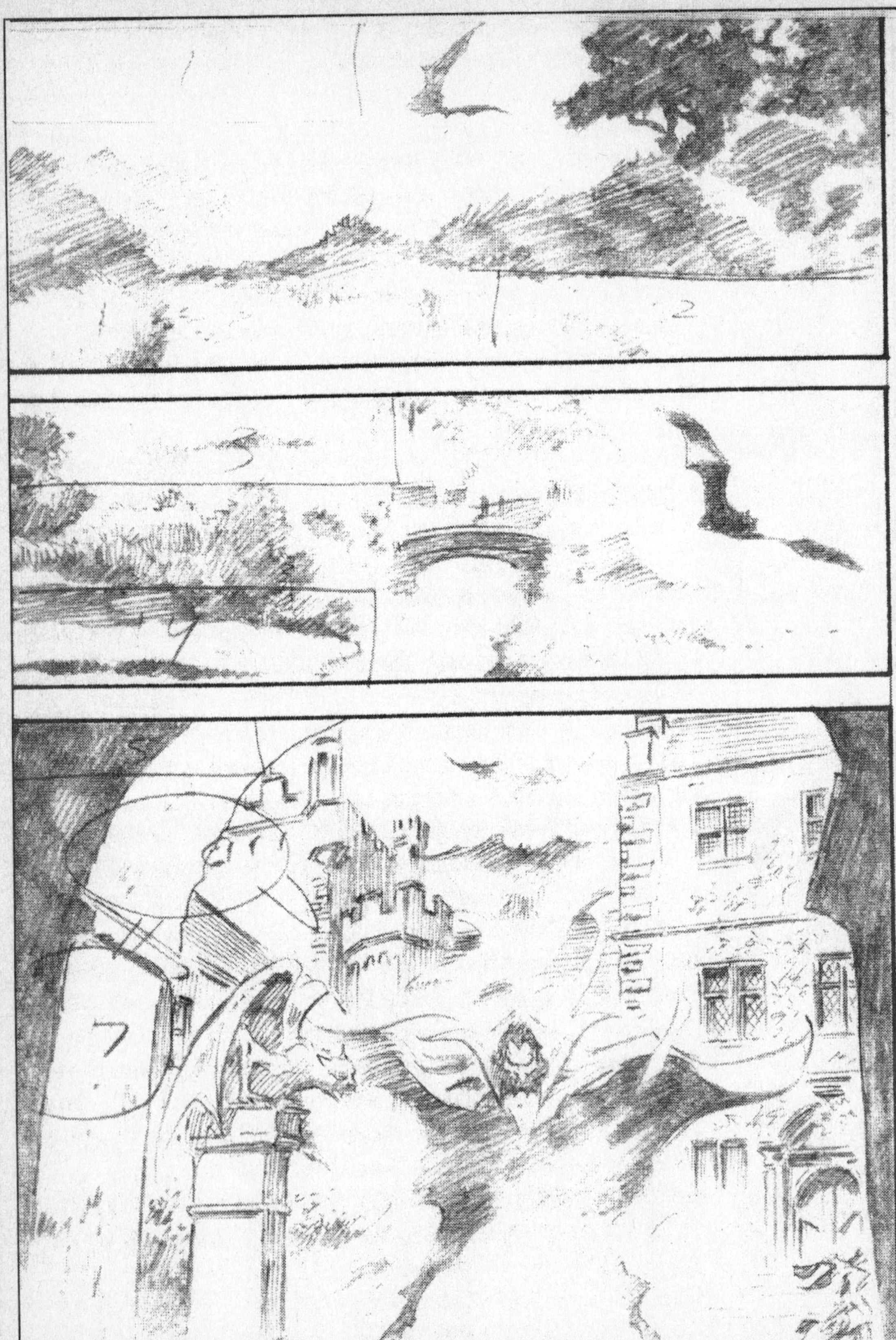

THE TOMB OF *DRACULA* #24, page 4 pencils

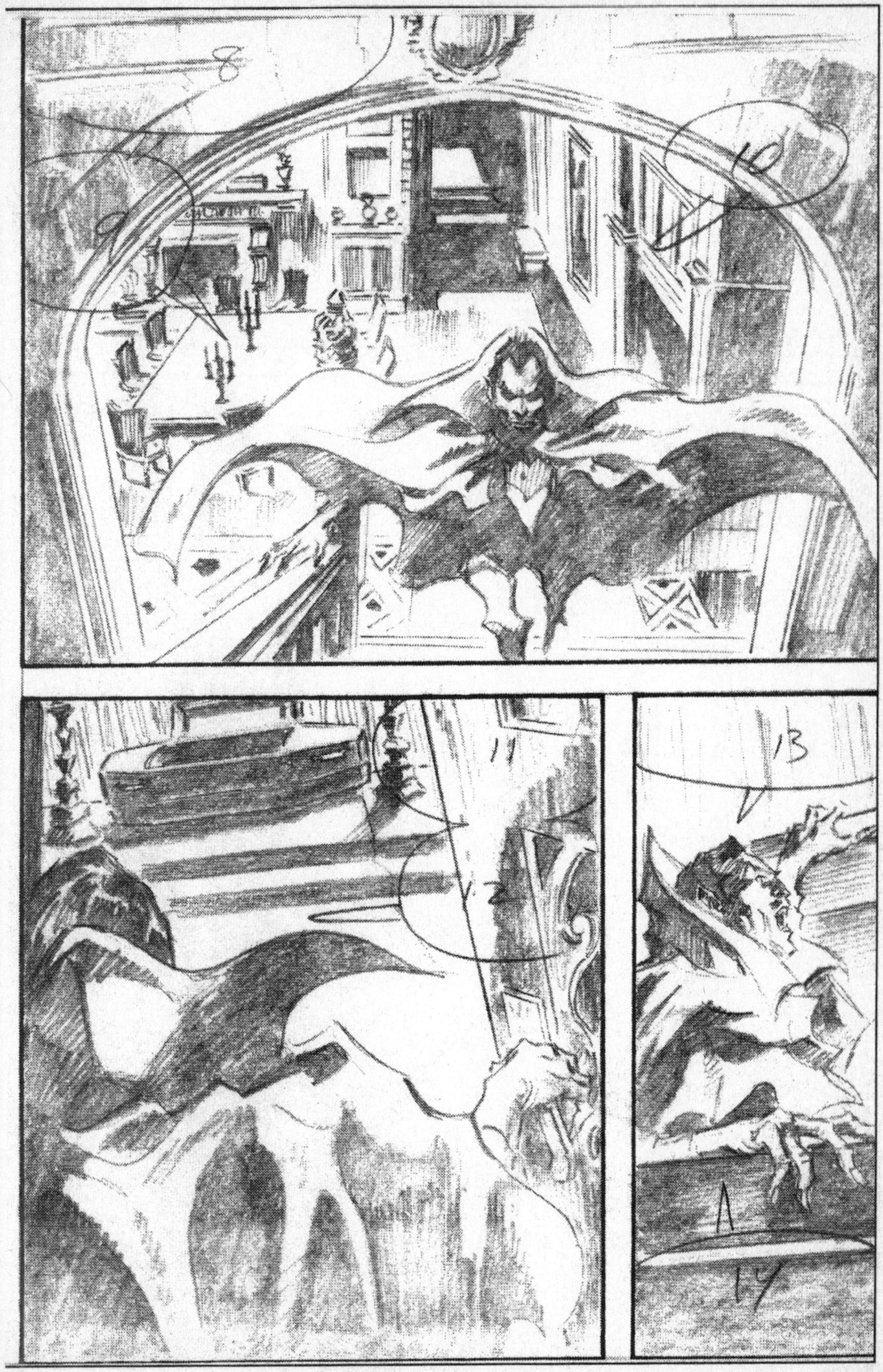

The Tomb of Dracula #24, page 5 pencils

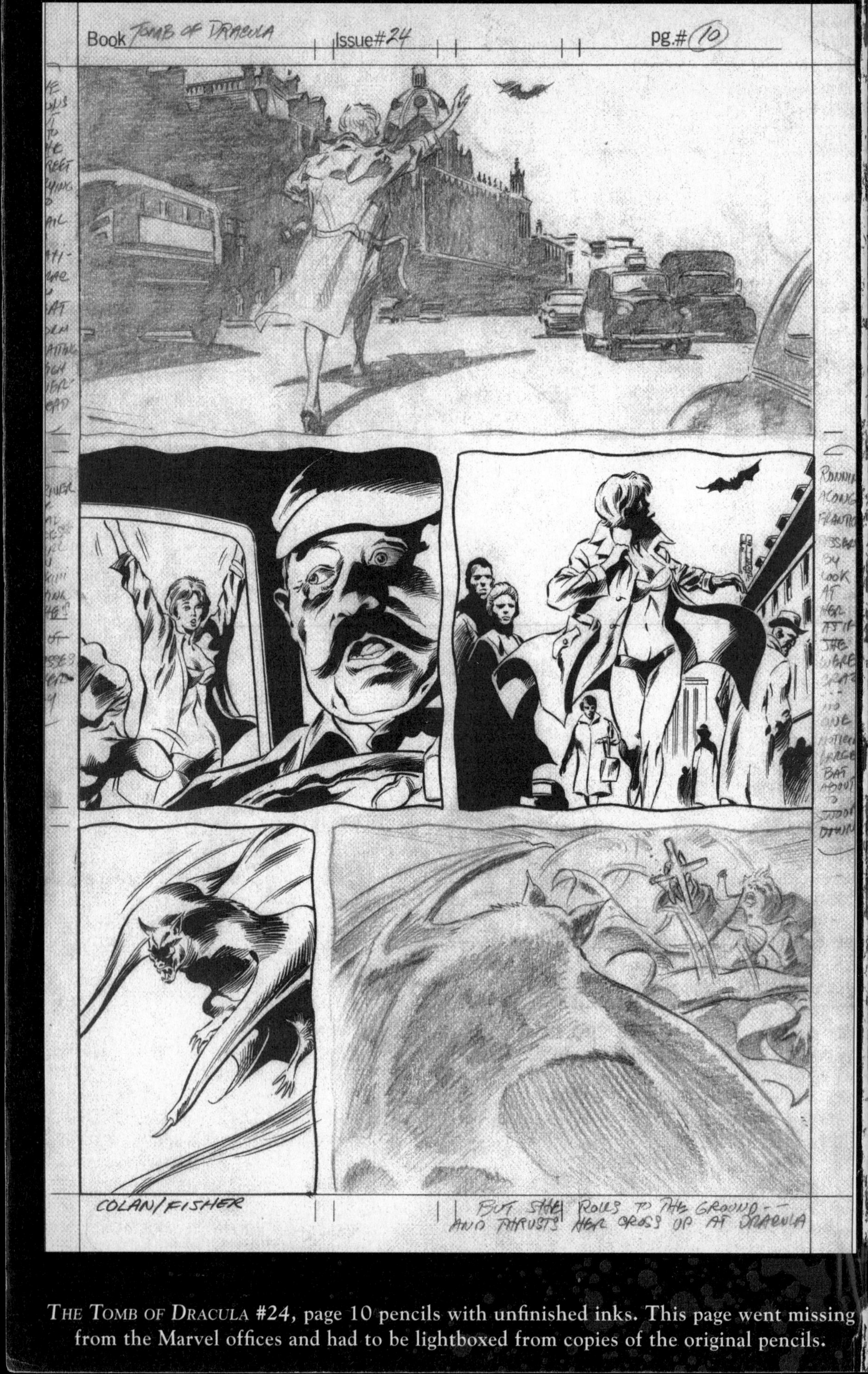
Book TOMB OF DRACULA
Issue#24
pg.# 10
COLAN/FISHER
BUT SHE ROLLS TO THE GROUND—
AND THRUSTS HER CROSS UP AT DRACULA

THE TOMB OF DRACULA #24, page 10 pencils with unfinished inks. This page went missing from the Marvel offices and had to be lightboxed from copies of the original pencils.